Justice, Crime, and Ethics

Eighth Edition

Justice, Crime, and Ethics

Eighth Edition

Michael C. Braswell

Belinda R. McCarthy

Bernard J. McCarthy

Amsterdam • Boston • Heidelberg • London
New York • Oxford • Paris • San Diego
San Francisco • Singapore • Sydney • Tokyo

Anderson Publishing is an imprint of Elsevier

ELSEVIER

Acquiring Editor: Pamela Chester
Development Editor: Ellen S. Boyne
Project Manager: Punithavathy Govindaradjane
Designer: Maria Ineŝ Cruz

Anderson Publishing is an imprint of Elsevier
225 Wyman Street, Waltham, MA 02451, USA

Notices
Knowledge and best practice in this field are constantly changing. As new research and experience broaden our understanding, changes in research methods or professional practices, may become necessary. Practitioners and researchers must always rely on their own experience and knowledge in evaluating and using any information or methods described herein. In using such information or methods they should be mindful of their own safety and the safety of others, including parties for whom they have a professional responsibility.

To the fullest extent of the law, neither the Publisher nor the authors, contributors, or editors, assume any liability for any injury and/or damage to persons or property as a matter of products liability, negligence or otherwise, or from any use or operation of any methods, products, instructions, or ideas contained in the material herein.

Library of Congress Cataloging-in-Publication Data
Justice, crime, and ethics / [edited by] Michael C. Braswell, Belinda R. McCarthy, Bernard J. McCarthy. -- Eighth edition.
    pages cm.
ISBN 978-0-323-26227-9
1. Criminal justice, Administration of--Moral and ethical aspects. I. Braswell, Michael. II. McCarthy, Bernard J., 1949- III. McCarthy, Belinda Rodgers.
    HV7419.J87 2014
    174'.9364--dc23   2014005932

British Library Cataloguing in Publication Data
A catalogue record for this book is available from the British Library

ISBN: 978-0-323-26227-9

For information on all Anderson publications
visit our website at http://store.elsevier.com

Printed and bound in the United States of America
14 15 16 17 18   10 9 8 7 6 5 4 3 2 1

Contents

ONLINE RESOURCES.. xv

A NOTE ABOUT THE EIGHTH EDITION xvii

Section 1   Introduction

CHAPTER 1   Ethics, Crime, and Justice: An Introductory Note
to Students 3
Michael C. Braswell
Three Contexts for Understanding Justice, Crime, and Ethics .. 4
Five Goals for Exploring Ethics 7
References 9

CHAPTER 2   Utilitarian and Deontological Approaches to Criminal
Justice Ethics 11
Jeffrey Gold
Normative Ethics... 12
Utilitarianism... 13
Deontological Ethics 16
    The Categorical Imperative............................... 17
Comparing Utilitarianism and Deontology 19
Justice and Duty 20
Case Study 2–1 Room at the End of the Hall 23
Notes 24
References 24

CHAPTER 3   Peacemaking, Justice, and Ethics 27
Michael C. Braswell and Jeffrey Gold
Connectedness.. 28
Caring... 34
Mindfulness.. 37
Conclusion 40
    Exercise I–1: Your Personal Philosophy 41

Case Study 3–1 To Help or Not to Help?................................42

    Exercise I–2: The Ethics of Drug Control Policy..................42

Notes 43

References 43

Section 2   Ethical Issues in Policing

CHAPTER 4   Learning Police Ethics................................. 47

Steven J. Ellwanger

Values, Value Systems, and Police Ethics...............................48

Value-Predisposition..49

    Conservatism and Conformity 49

    Noble Cause, Efficiency, and Utilitarianism.......................50

    Crime Fighting 51

Where Do Police Values Come From? 52

    Historical, Cultural, and Economic 52

    Social 52

Values-Learned Perspective: Socialization and Culturalization..54

    Choice..54

    Introduction 56

    Encounter..58

    Metamorphosis 60

The Content of Police Values 60

Moral Career 62

Police Ethics and Control, Reform, and Legitimacy.................64

Case Study 4–1 Liberty and Justice for All.............................67

References 69

CHAPTER 5   Deception in Police Interrogation................................. 73

Steven J. Ellwanger

From Brute Force to Psychological Manipulation 74

    Elimination of Brute Force..75

    Controlling Psychological Coercion 76

Reliability, Free will, and Fairness 76

    "Interview" versus "Interrogation" 78

    Role Playing 79

    Miranda Warnings..80

    Fabricated Evidence 80

    Exaggerating the Nature and Severity of the Offense.........81

    Normalization/Minimization of the Crime..........................81

    Misrepresenting Identity..82

    Use of Promises 82

The Ethics and Dilemmas of Deceptive Police Interrogation....83
Crime Control versus Due Process and Ethical Orientation....84
Reliability of Behavior Analysis...84
Conclusion 88
References 90

CHAPTER 6 Using Ethical Dilemmas in Training Police 93
Joycelyn M. Pollock and Howard E. Williams
Discretion..97
Duty..100
Honesty...102
Loyalty 103
Gratuities..105
Now That We Have Defined the Issues, What Do We Do
with Them?...106
Conclusion 109
References 110

CHAPTER 7 Police Ethics, Legal Proselytism, and the Social Order:
Paving the Path to Misconduct...................................... 113
Victor E. Kappeler, Gary W. Potter, and Edward Green
The Path to Unethical Conduct...115
Legally Permissible but Unethical Conduct............................118
Socially Situating Unethical Behavior 121
Collective Responsibility for Unethical Police Conduct.........126
Case Study 7–1 Homegrown Terrorism 128
Exercise II–1 Different Choices, Equal
Protection? 129
References 130

Section 3   Ethics and the Courts

CHAPTER 8 What Ever Happened to Atticus Finch? Lawyers as
Legal Advocates and Moral Agents............................ 133
Joycelyn M. Pollock
The Lawyer/Client Relationship..134
Guidance for Lawyers: Model Rules of Professional Conduct.137
The Prosecutor 144
Conclusion: Reconciling the Legal Advocate and Moral
Agent Views..145
Case Study 8–1 Child Rapist..146
References 147

CHAPTER 9   Ethical Challenges for Prosecutors 149
Richard R.E. Kania

Introduction 149
"The Trayvon Martin Homicide" Case 150
The 2007 Firing of Federal Prosecutors 151
The 2006 Duke Lacrosse Case 152
The 1987 Trial of Labor Secretary Raymond Donovan..........154
"The Atlanta Child Murders" Case......................................154
"The Thin Blue Line" Case 155
Ethical Problems Revealed in Prosecutorial Misconduct.......156
   Wrongful Pursuit of Personal Gain 156
   Favoritism and Bias 156
   The Abuse of Power..157
   The Denial of Due Process...157
   Deceitfulness 157
   Neglect of Duties..157
   A Flawed Personal Life..158
Unique Prosecutorial Failings 159
Discovery and the Disclosure of Evidence............................160
Plea Bargaining 160
Exercising Discretion..161
Using Unreliable "Snitches" 161
Politics, the Public, and the Media 162
Why Misconduct Persists 162
The 1947 Film *Boomerang* and True Prosecutorial
Ethics 164
Conclusion 165
Case Study 9–1 It's a Rat Race, and the Best Rat Wins.........166
References 167

CHAPTER 10 Criminal Sentencing: Goals, Practices,
and Ethics... 171
Lawrence F. Travis III

The Purpose of Criminal Punishment 172
   Deterrence 172
   Incapacitation...173
   Treatment 173
   Desert..174
   Restoration...174
Utilitarianism versus Equity 175
The Practice of Punishment 177

Contemporary Ethical Concerns in Sentencing......................179
    Honesty in Punishment 179
    Prediction in Punishment 180
    Discrimination in Sentencing 182
Conclusion 184
References 185

CHAPTER 11 Crime and Punishment: Punishment Philosophies,
and Ethical Dilemmas.................................. 187
Laurie A. Gould and Alicia H. Sitren
What is Punishment?...................................187
Punishment and Ethics...............................188
What are the Purposes of Punishment? 188
    Retribution 189
    Incapacitation 190
    Rehabilitation 191
    Deterrence 193
Unintended Consequences of Punishment...........195
Ethical Dilemmas in Punishment....................196
Conclusion 197
References 198

CHAPTER 12 To Die or Not to Die: Morality, Ethics, and the
Death Penalty.. 203
John T. Whitehead and Michael C. Braswell
The Death Penalty in Perspective: Facts about the
Death Penalty 203
Rationale for the Death Penalty 204
    Deterrence 205
    Incapacitation 207
Peacemaking Perspective.............................209
Mistakes..210
Discrimination and Racial Bias 212
Arbitrariness...214
Conditions on Death Row............................215
Jurors in Capital Cases...............................216
Religion and Capital Punishment 217
Alternatives to the Death Penalty 219
Conclusion 221
Case Study 12–1 Politics or Ethics? A Governor's
Prerogative...221
References 222

Section 4   Ethical Issues in Corrections

CHAPTER 13 Ethical Issues in Probation, Parole, and
Community Corrections 227
John T. Whitehead
Introduction 227
The Mission of Probation and Parole 228
The Effectiveness of Community Corrections 231
   The Ethics of Probation Fees 233
Acceptable Penal Content...235
Intensive Supervision Issues 236
   Officer Concerns in Intensive Supervision Programs........238
   Offender Concerns 240
Privatization...240
Supervision of Sex Offenders...243
Use of Volunteers 244
Corruption 244
Conclusion 245
Case Study 13–1 Sexual Harassment 246
Note...247
References 247

CHAPTER 14 Restorative Justice: Defining and Implementing
the Peacemaking Paradigm 251
Lana A. McDowell, Michael C. Braswell,
and John T. Whitehead
Defining Restorative Justice 253
Types of Restorative Justice Programs 256
   Family Group Conferencing 256
   Victim–Offender Reconciliation Programs 257
   Sentencing Circles..257
   Reparative Boards..258
   Victim–Offender Panels 258
Transforming Theory into Practice: Real-world
Applications of Restorative Justice 259
   Restorative Justice and Policing.......................................259
   Restorative Justice and the Courts....................................261
   Restorative Justice in the Prison Setting 264
   Restorative Justice in the Primary Educational
   Setting 266
   Restorative Justice in the College Educational Settings ..269
   Restorative Justice in the Workplace 271
   The Expansion of Restorative Justice in Cases of
   Sexual Violations 272

Restorative Justice and International Relations 273
Conclusion 274
References 274

CHAPTER 15 Keeping an Eye on the Keeper: Prison Corruption
and Its Control 277
Bernard J. McCarthy
The Role of Staff in Prison Misconduct 279
Defining Corruption in a Correctional Environment 281
Types of Prison Corruption 282
The Role of Discretion 284
Factors Associated with Corruption 286
The Role of Opportunities 286
Incentives for Corruption 288
Controlling Corruption 290
The Legal Option When Abuses Become Extreme 292
Case Study 15–1 Legacy of Corruption 294
References 296

CHAPTER 16 Ethics and Prison: Selected Issues 299
John T. Whitehead and Bradley Edwards
Introduction 299
Who Belongs in Prison 299
Disproportionate Minority Prison Populations 302
Prison Conditions: Coddling or Toughness? 303
Treatment/Rehabilitation/Programming 306
Chain Gangs 309
Safety/Security in Prison 310
Elderly Prisoners 311
Women in Prisons 312
Privatization 313
Conclusion 315
Case Study 16–1 Who's Running the Prison? 316
Note 317
References 317

Section 5 Ethical Issues in Crime Control Policy and Research

CHAPTER 17 Crime and Justice Myths 323
Egan Green
The Nature of Myths 324
Influencing Myths: Media, Politics, and Public Opinion 325

The Media and Crime Myths 325
Government, Politics, and Crime Myths 330
The General Public and Crime Myths 334
Myths about Crime 336
Myths about Criminals 338
Myths about Crime Control...340
Crime Control Policy: Where Research and Politics Collide .341
Conclusion 344
    Exercise V-1 "How Television Affects Our Perceptions
    of Crime"..345
References 345

CHAPTER 18 Juvenile Justice Ethical Issues: How Should We
Treat Juveniles?.. 349
Kimberly D. Dodson and John T. Whitehead
Juvenile Transfer to Adult Court...351
    Confinement for Juveniles...352
Juveniles Doing Juvenile Time 352
Juveniles Doing Adult Time..353
Recidivism among Juveniles Confined in Adult Jails
and Prisons 354
Sexual Victimization behind Bars..355
Suicide..356
Separate is Better: A Utilitarian Approach...........................357
Separate is Better: Applying Peacemaking...........................358
The Death Penalty and Life without Parole
for Juveniles 359
Supreme Court Decisions about the Death Penalty
and LWOP for Juveniles 360
Ethical Arguments about the Death Penalty and LWOP
for Juveniles 361
Deontological Analysis 364
Religious Ethics...366
Conclusion 368
Cases Cited...369
References 369

CHAPTER 19 Corporate Misconduct and Ethics 373
Bradley Edwards and Michael C. Braswell
Types of Corporate Misconduct...376
    Accounting Fraud..377
    Mortgage Fraud..378

Healthcare Fraud...379
Student Loan Mismanagement...............................381
Excessive Executive Compensation.......................382
Causes for Misconduct 383
Assessing Blame..385
Whistleblowers 385
The Role of Media 386
Prosecuting Corporate Crime....................................387
Deferred and Non-prosecution Agreements.............389
Corporate Misconduct: What's Next? 391
References 392

CHAPTER 20 Ethics and Criminal Justice Research.......................... 397
Belinda R. McCarthy, Robin J. King, and Michael Bush
Ethical Considerations Involving Work with Human
Participants..398
Involving People in Research without their Knowledge
or Consent 399
Coercing People to Participate...................................400
Withholding from the Participant the True Nature
of the Research...402
Deceiving the Research Participant 403
Leading the Research Participants to Commit Acts That
Diminish Their Self-respect......................................404
Guards..405
Prisoners 405
Violating the Right to Self-determination: Research
on Behavior Control and Character Change.............406
Exposing the Research Participant to Physical
or Mental Stress 407
Invading the Privacy of the Research Participant
and Maintaining Confidentiality...............................408
Withholding Benefits to Participants in Control Groups 410
Failing to Treat Research Participants Fairly and to Show
Them Consideration and Respect 414
Balancing Scientific and Ethical Concerns 415
Institutional Review Boards and Setting Ethical Standards ...415
Ethical/Political Considerations................................416
The Purity of Scientific Research..............................418
Public Policy Pronouncements and Teaching Criminal
Justice...420
Ethical Codes...420

Conclusion 423

Case Study 20–1: Research Issues 424

References 424

CHAPTER 21 Terrorism and Ethics 427

Bernard J. McCarthy

Introduction 427

The War Strategy to Combat Terrorism 429

The Use of the Military System of Justice 430

The Military Commissions/Tribunals 431

The Torture Memos 433

Harsh Interrogation and the "Torture Memos" 434

Abu Ghraib and Guantánamo Bay 436

Abu Ghraib 436

    What Has Been the End Result of Military Commissions
and the Torture Memos? 439

Using the Criminal Justice System to Handle Terrorists 439

The Question Still Persists: How Should We Respond to
Terrorism? 440

The Obama Approach 443

Closing Guantánamo 443

A Case in Point: The Times Square Bomber 446

Conclusion 447

References 448

Section 6   **Ethics and the Future**

CHAPTER 22 Criminal Justice: An Ethic for the Future 453

Michael C. Braswell and Robert C. England

The Need for Mindfulness 454

Order Keeping and Peacemaking 455

Some Suggestions for Criminal Justice 458

Law and Justice 458

    Policing 459

    Corrections 461

Justice as a Way Rather Than a Destination 463

References 464

INDEX 467

Online Resources

Thank you for selecting Anderson Publishing's *Justice, Crime, and Ethics*, Eighth Edition. To complement the learning experience, we have provided online tools to accompany this edition.

Please consult your local sales representative with any additional questions. You may also e-mail the Academic Sales Team at textbook@elsevier.com.

Qualified adopters and instructors can access valuable material for free by registering at: http://textbooks.elsevier.com/web/manuals.aspx?isbn=9780323262279.

Students and other readers can access additional resources at: http://booksite.elsevier.com/9780323262279.

A Note About the Eighth Edition

In this edition we have made changes that maintain the flow and context of previous editions. Eight chapters have undergone substantial revisions while a number of other chapters have had references updated along with minor changes. Two new chapters have been added, one on "Juvenile Justice and Ethics" and another on "Corporate Crime and Ethics." In addition, efforts have been made to include emerging issues such as the Trayvon Martin case and more recent terrorism-related events and concerns.

We continue to include a variety of case studies, exercises, links to interesting websites, and other features to stimulate critical and creative thinking and discussion about ethics, crime, and justice. Of course, all persons and names in case studies and exercises are fictional.

We continue to be grateful to our colleagues, students, and others who teach ethics for their e-mails, phone calls, and comments at conferences concerning how to make our book better. Since we teach ethics, we understand how important such conversations are. Many of the improvements in each edition are the result of their input and suggestions.

We want to thank Bradley Edwards for his help in general and work on the ancillary and other materials. We also want to thank Susan Braswell for her assistance with the revisions. We also want to offer a special thank-you to our editors, Ellen Boyne and Sara Scott. Their help and support is much appreciated.

M.B.

B.M.

B.M.

Introduction

Vision brings a new appreciation of what there is. It makes a
person see things differently rather than see different things.

Herbert Guenther

Our personal and social values shape and color the way we perceive the world
in which we live. While we are concerned with achieving personal goals and
ambitions, we also come to realize at a rather early age that the needs and
desires of others are also forces to be reckoned with. The question for us then
becomes one of reconciling the pursuit of our individual dreams within the
context of the larger community. Maintaining our individual integrity, our personal sense of right and wrong, and at the same time conforming to what is
best for the majority of persons in our society can often become a perplexing challenge. Yet we are all connected to each other in one way or another—
parents and children, inmates and correctional staff. We are even connected
to our physical environment, as evidenced in the quality of air we breathe and
water we drink. As potential criminal justice practitioners, we recognize that
our professional choices and policies will emanate from our personal beliefs
and values—from our personal philosophies. How much do we care about
trying to honestly and effectively address the pressing justice issues of the day?

Are we truly mindful of the ways we are connected to our problems? Do we have a long-term as well as short-term sense of what the costs of our proposed solutions will be?

Cultivating a greater understanding of our own philosophical perspectives can provide us with a foundation for making more informed decisions about the diverse social issues we face and the way our system of justice responds to such issues.

CHAPTER 1

Ethics, Crime, and Justice: An Introductory Note to Students

Michael C. Braswell

KEY CONCEPTS

ethics	morality	wholesight

As you approach the study of ethics, crime, and justice, it is important that you view your study as a search, journey, or exploration. This search in many ways will yield more questions than answers. It is a creative endeavor in which a number of your beliefs and assumptions will be challenged. Questions such as "Can moral or ethical behavior be illegal and legal actions be immoral?" and "Can we have a more equitable criminal justice system without addressing social problems such as poverty and discrimination?" will test the limits of your personal values and beliefs (Braswell & LaFollette, 1988). This study will also encompass a variety of disciplines that contribute to criminal justice, including law, economics, psychology, sociology, philosophy, and theology. For the purposes of our exploration we will use the terms *ethical* and *moral* interchangeably.

What is ethics? In a general sense, **ethics** is the study of right and wrong, good and evil. Who decides what is right and wrong? What one person may believe is right, another person may feel is wrong. Our beliefs and values regarding right and wrong and good and evil are shaped by our parents and friends, by the communities we are a part of, and by our own perceptions. Codes of conduct are also influenced by the law and our religious beliefs. Professional organizations involving such areas as law, medicine, and criminal justice also offer professional codes of ethics as a benchmark for people who fulfill those professional roles. This study involves all aspects of who we are—our minds, hearts, relationships with each other, and the intentions and motives for our actions regarding both our inner and outer environment. We are inclined to believe that ethical persons act in good or right ways, whereas unethical people commit evil acts and other forms of wrongdoing. Then again, it is not only a matter of a person acting "unethically"; also at issue are people who could choose to do good but instead do nothing, allowing others to do evil. So it is not simply a matter of my committing an evil or wrongful act, it is also a matter of my being an indirect accomplice to evil by silently standing by, letting evil occur when I could stand for what is right. As a result, unethical acts can occur by the commission of wrongdoing or by omission—by allowing wrongdoing to occur. Thomas Merton (as quoted in Woods, 1966), in examining a fundamental problem of omission, wrote that "moral paralysis leaves us immobile, inert, passive, tongue-tied, ready and even willing to succumb."

The study of justice and ethics, of the good and evil we do to each other, also involves a sense of community. We often hear that problems of crime and violence are the result of a breakdown in family and community values. What does our community consist of? Our community includes our family, our neighbors—even the land on which we grow food to eat and the air we breathe. Is it important that we act in ethical ways regarding our physical environment as well as with regard to people with whom we come in contact? Within our community of interdependent parts exist three contexts, or perspectives, that can help us approach a better understanding of justice, crime, and ethics.

THREE CONTEXTS FOR UNDERSTANDING JUSTICE, CRIME, AND ETHICS

A way of understanding the idea of justice in human experience is to think of it as a process that moves within three contexts or concentric circles (see Figure 1.1).

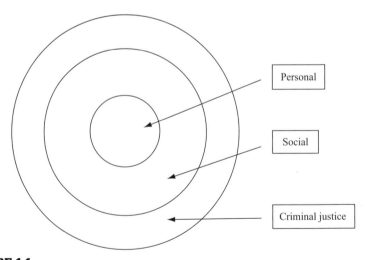

FIGURE 1.1
Three contexts for understanding justice, crime, and ethics.

The first context or innermost circle is the *personal*, which represents our individual sense of justice. This context examines right and wrong, good and evil—life experienced and lived, for better or worse, from the inside out. My life experiences come to form a set of perceptions, some easily changed and others being very resistant to change, that form my personal sense of justice—my way of looking out into the world as a safe or dangerous place, with hope or with despair.

The second circle represents the social context of *justice*. This circle includes all that is the world without—the physical environment I live in, whether rural, urban, or suburban, and the people with whom I interact through choice or necessity. I may live in a relatively just or unjust community. I may live as an oppressed member of my community, or I may act as the oppressor. During our lifetimes, perhaps on one occasion or another, and in one way or another, we will taste the experience of both.

People do not commit crimes in isolation. Crimes also require circumstances and victims. Crimes are related to social circumstances and conditions as well as being subject to the law and criminal justice system. Why did the abused wife kill her husband? In the broader social context, we might look at the abuse she suffered before she made her husband a victim of a homicide. What was her relationship to her parents and other family members? What about her neighbors? Did she have access to adequate social and support services? Could something have been done to prevent her own victimization and thus her subsequent crime?

The social context of ethics suggests that we cannot be concerned with criminals only after they have committed crimes but must also better understand the conditions and environments that encourage people to become criminals, whether such offenders physically rape their victims or economically violate them through such means as stock market fraud. We also need to remember that offenders who are incarcerated in prisons typically return to the communities from whence they came, whether they become rehabilitated or more criminalized.

The social context is not concerned merely with how we judge others as being good or evil but also how we judge ourselves in relationship to others. Buechner (1973) writes, "We are judged by the face that looks back at us from the bathroom mirror. We are judged by the faces of the people we love and by the faces and lives of our children and by our dreams. Each day finds us at the junction of many roads, and we are judged as much by the roads we have not taken as by the roads we have."

The third context we can use in our efforts to better understand justice, crime, and ethics is perhaps the most specific one; it centers on the *criminal justice* process. Too often, the criminal justice process is the only context or perspective we consider. It is important that we include both the personal and social contexts of ethics in exploring the criminal justice process. Due process, police corruption, and punishment are examples of important issues that require us to consider personal beliefs, social factors, and criminal justice consequences simultaneously. For example, I explore any new law being proposed regarding the punishment of offenders in terms of my personal beliefs. How does this proposed law square with my own value system? How do I feel about it? The proposed law also should be examined on the basis of how it will affect the social community. Is it just and fair to all parts and groups within the community? Will it contribute to the community's sense of safety and security, or is it perhaps more of a public relations or election year gimmick? Can the criminal justice process and system effectively implement the law? Are there adequate resources to finance and manage the changes that will occur in the system as a result of the proposed law?

The criminal justice context also sets legal limits for what we can do to each other. Those of us who inflict harm on others may experience legal consequences ranging from fines to imprisonment or even having to forfeit our lives. Sometimes what is legal is also what is right or good, but that is not the primary function of criminal justice. We need to remember that our justice system, due to existing laws and community attitudes, may also support tyrants or various forms of injustice and corruption on occasion, leading to suffering and oppression in our communities. Our personal and communal sense of **morality** (what is right and wrong) may often stand outside the limits of the law. In fact, some politicians often seem to confuse what is moral with what is legal. For example, although gambling may be illegal, a given community may consider it desirable and ignore the law, even demonstrating a sense of collective pride in such activities. In addition, during one period of our history, it was considered illegal for women or minorities to vote or to help people who were enslaved escape to freedom. In such cases, what was legal was immoral and what was moral was illegal. Some of us did what was right and good at great peril and personal cost during such times, even though we broke the law. Others of us remained responsible, law-abiding citizens and, by omitting to do the good we could have done, allowed others to experience unimaginable suffering and injustice.

It is important to note that the circles are more like membranes than concrete lines of demarcation. Like ocean tides, they bend and flow with each other, remaining distinct but always connected and interacting. Finally, the area beyond the third context represents the *unknown*. From our personal beliefs and values to our social relations and interaction within and outside the rule of law—all are subject to the effects of the unknown. We may call it coincidence, luck, fate, destiny, or the will of God. Whatever we call it, the outcome of our individual lives as well as the fate of our larger community includes an air of mystery, of the unexpected—sometimes welcomed and other times feared. What we can count on is that if we act as ethical people of integrity we will increase the odds that we will work and live in responsible and caring communities where the chance for justice will be greater for all who live there.

In addition to examining our study of ethics from a personal, social, and criminal justice context, it is also useful to identify several specific goals as we begin to explore issues regarding justice, crime, and ethics.

FIVE GOALS FOR EXPLORING ETHICS

The initial goal for exploring ethics is to become more aware and open to moral and ethical issues.

As we try to become more aware of ethical issues, we will discover a number of contradictions in our moral beliefs and values. We will find that there is often a difference between appearances and reality, that things are often not what they seem. What we are taught as children may be challenged by our adult experiences. As a result, some choices seem clearly to be right or wrong, whereas other events seem more ambiguous and less certain.

A part of our becoming more open includes our learning to be more aware of the full range and nature of moral and ethical issues—from telling a small lie to committing perjury, from cheating on one's income taxes to engaging in major bank fraud. This broad range of moral issues reminds us that where justice is concerned, personal values, social consequences, and criminal justice outcomes are often intertwined.

As we become more open to moral and ethical issues, it is important that we approach our second goal, which is *to begin developing critical thinking and analytical skills.*

As young children, we were often creative, as evidenced by our active imaginations. As we grew older, we learned to stand in line, follow instructions, and be seen more than heard when it came to the process of learning. In a word, we learned to become obedient. Over time, we began to lose confidence in our point of view as being anything of value. In such a context, as students, we are inclined to become more interested in asking *how* rather than *why*, in becoming more like technicians rather than philosophers. However, Albert Einstein (as quoted in Castle, 1988), in discussing science and creativity, suggested that "[t]o raise new questions, new possibilities, to regard old problems from a new angle, requires creative imagination and marks real advances in science." In other words, if we do not first ask the right questions, our solutions, no matter how well intended and efficient, simply add to our difficulties. Asking why, then, is an important aspect of developing critical thinking and analytical skills.

Asking meaningful questions requires clarity in our thinking and a sense of mindfulness as we explore moral and ethical issues. Critical thinking and analytical skills help us distinguish concepts such as justice and liberty from principles such as "the ends do not justify the means." For example, we might discuss capital punishment both as a concept and in principle. However, our critical thinking and analytical skills will allow us to go even further as we search for the truth regarding capital punishment. What are the short-term and long-term costs of such a sanction? How does it affect our criminal justice system and our society in general? What will future generations think about our decisions, laws, and policies regarding capital punishment? Although we may never be able to arrive at a perfect position on capital punishment, critical thinking and analytical skills can aid us in exploring more openly and with more integrity the various issues surrounding it. These skills encourage openness and perseverance rather than blind acceptance and obedience based on ignorance.

There will always be disagreement on such issues as capital punishment. As with any moral issue, there is a cost for the attitudes we hold and the choices we make; there is inevitably an upside and a downside, a pro and a con. As we explore such issues, critical thinking and analytical skills can help us see more clearly what the costs will be.

Becoming more open to moral and ethical issues and developing critical thinking and analytical skills will help us more fully realize our third goal: *becoming more personally responsible*. Before we can become more responsible, we must increase our ability to respond. The first two goals aid us in this endeavor. As we persevere in an open exploration and search for the truth regarding moral and ethical issues, we will feel more empowered and have more hope for the future.

A fourth goal of our ethics education is that we *understand how criminal justice is engaged in a process of coercion*. Giving tickets to drivers who exceed the speed limit and sentencing serious offenders to prison are examples of this process. In exploring the morality of coercion, we come to realize that, in large part, criminal justice is about forcing people to do things they do not want to do. Having the authority to be coercive, combined with the discretionary nature of such authority, together create the potential for corruption and abuse. Can you think of any examples where the coercive role of police, courts, or corrections could be corrupted? On a more personal level, how might parental or peer influences exercise coercion in an unethical way (Sherman, 1981, p. 181)?

The fifth goal of our exploration concerns what Palmer (1983) refers to as *developing wholesight*. It is important that we become more open to moral and ethical issues, that we develop critical thinking and analytical skills, that we increase our sense of personal responsibility, and that we understand the morality of coercion. Yet all of these abilities and skills need to be tempered by our intuitive nature. We need to explore these issues not only with our minds but also with our hearts. Our mind or intellect can often become more preoccupied with immediate problems and how to solve them. The heart asks why and looks not only to the immediate dilemma but also to the deeper level of difficulty, and it asks what the costs might be in the long run. **Wholesight** creates a vision in which our minds and hearts, our thinking and feeling, work together for the common good as we explore the ethical and moral issues that we as individuals and as members of a community face (See Box 1.1).

BOX 1.1 FIVE GOALS FOR EXPLORING ETHICS

1. Develop greater awareness of moral/ethical issues.
2. Develop critical thinking/analytical skills.
3. Become personally responsible.
4. Understand coercion in criminal justice.
5. Develop wholesight.

The following sections of this book will introduce you to some of the philosophical theories that can provide a framework for you to study and analyze ethical and moral issues in crime and justice. The police, courts, and corrections, which comprise the criminal justice system, will be explored in the light of ethical concerns. Criminal justice research and crime control policy will also be examined. Finally, a justice ethic for the future is offered for your consideration. What kind of future do you want to be a part of? What price are you willing to pay?

Discussion Questions

1. Define and discuss the term *ethics* from your own perspective.
2. Explain what ethics is using the three contexts presented in this chapter for understanding justice, crime, and ethics.
3. Explain the five goals of exploring ethics and the impact that each has on the others.

REFERENCES

Braswell, M., & LaFollette, H. (1988). Seeking justice: The advantages and disadvantages of being educated. *American Journal of Criminal Justice* (Spring), 135–147.

Buechner, F. (1973). *Wishful thinking*. New York: Harper & Row.

Castle, T. (Ed.). (1988). *The new book of Christian quotations* (p. 52). New York: Crossroads.

Palmer, P. (1983). *To know as we are known*. San Francisco: Harper & Row.

Sherman, L. W. (1981). *The study of ethics in criminology and criminal justice*. Chicago: Joint Commission on Criminology and Criminal Justice Education and Standards.

Woods, R. (Ed.). (1966). *The world treasury of religious quotations* (p. 647). New York: Garland.

CHAPTER 2

Utilitarian and Deontological Approaches to Criminal Justice Ethics

Jeffrey Gold

KEY CONCEPTS

categorical imperative	hypothetical imperative	normative ethics
consequentialism	Immanuel Kant	universalizability
deontology	Jeremy Bentham	use of force
hedonistic calculus	John Stuart Mill	utilitarian calculus
		utilitarianism

In recent years, interest in professional ethics has grown steadily. Business ethics, medical ethics, and environmental ethics are all flourishing as components in most college and university curricula. Despite this fact, until recently, "higher education programs in criminology and criminal justice have largely neglected the systematic study of ethics" (Sherman, 1981, p. 7). This is unfortunate because the ethical issues that arise in the area of criminal justice are significant and complex (Braswell, Pollock, & Braswell, 2007; Pollock, 2004; Souryal, 2010). Furthermore, even though many of the ethical issues that arise in criminal justice are common to other professions, there are other issues that are specifically tailored to criminology and criminal justice. The most significant example, as mentioned in Chapter 1, involves the **use of force** and physical coercion. Sherman points out: "Force is the essence of criminal justice …. The decisions of whether to use force, how much to use, and under what conditions are confronted by police officers, juries, judges, prison officials, probation and parole officers and others. All of them face the paradox … of using harm to prevent harm" (Sherman, 1981, p. 30). Because the use of force is central to criminal justice, this distinguishes criminal justice from other professions.

11

In addition to the issue concerning the use of force, there are other factors that seem to distinguish the moral decisions of criminal justice agents from other professionals. Sherman (1981) discusses two of them:

> First, criminal justice decisions are made on behalf of society as a whole, a collective moral judgment made in trust by a single person. That would entail a far greater responsibility than what other vocations are assigned. Second, the decisions criminal justice agents make are not just incidentally, but are primarily, moral decisions. An engineer designs a building that may or may not kill people, but the decision is primarily a physical one and only incidentally a moral one. When a police officer decides to arrest someone … when a judge decides to let that person out on a suspended sentence, the decisions are primarily moral ones. (p. 14)

As we can see, the moral issues that arise in the field of criminal justice are both distinctive and significant.

In trying to solve certain specific ethical issues, it is sometimes helpful to begin with more general, theoretical questions. When we get a handle on the more theoretical issue, we can apply that to a specific moral problem. So, with respect to criminal justice, we might begin by raising more general questions about the nature of justice. Theories of justice address broad social issues including human rights, equality, and the distribution of wealth. We might even go up one more level of generality—justice is itself a branch of an even wider sphere, that of ethics. It seems important that we view issues in criminal justice from the larger framework of ethics and morality. It would be a mistake to assume that issues in criminal justice could emerge outside the larger social and ethical context of our culture. Therefore, this chapter explores the field of ethics with the hope that such a study will provide us with a set of concepts that will shed some light on specific moral issues in the field of criminal justice. We accomplish that goal by presenting a study of two of the major philosophical theories in the field of *normative ethics*.

NORMATIVE ETHICS

Normative ethics is the study of right and wrong. A normative ethical theorist tries to discover whether there are any basic, fundamental principles of right and wrong. If such principles are discovered, they are held to be the ground or foundation of all our ethical judgments. For example, we ordinarily say lying, cheating, stealing, raping, and killing are wrong. The ethical theorist asks: Do these very different activities of lying, stealing, and killing all have something in common that makes them all wrong? If so, what is that common characteristic?

One of the most important figures in the history of Western philosophy, Socrates, was famous for seeking the universal in ethical matters.[1]

In other words, when Socrates asked, "What is Justice?" or "What is Virtue?" he was not asking for a list of actions that are just or a list of examples of virtue; rather, he was seeking the universal characteristic that all just or virtuous actions have in common.[2]

Just as all squares, no matter how large they are or what color they are, have something in common (four equal sides and four right angles), the ethical theorist wants to know if all morally right actions (whether they are cases of honesty, charity, or benevolence) also have something in common. If such a common characteristic is found, it is held to be the ground or foundation or fundamental principle of ethics. We shall now turn to our study of two standard ethical theories in an effort to locate such a foundation for ethics.

UTILITARIANISM

The most famous version of utilitarianism was developed in Great Britain in the eighteenth and nineteenth centuries by **Jeremy Bentham** (1970) and **John Stuart Mill** (1979). Utilitarianism is classified as a consequentialist ethical theory. In other words, the utilitarian holds that we judge the morality of an action in terms of the consequences or results of that action. Mill states: "All action is for the sake of some end, and rules of action, it seems natural to suppose, must take their whole character and color from the end to which they are subservient" (p. 2). The insight that motivates consequentialism is this: A moral action produces something good; an immoral action produces a bad or harmful result. Put in the simplest possible way, cheating, stealing, and murder are all wrong because they produce bad or harmful consequences, and charity and benevolence are good because they produce something beneficial. To summarize, the consequentialist holds that the morality of an action is determined by the consequences of that action—actions that are moral produce good consequences, and actions that are immoral produce bad consequences.

At this point, two questions come up: (1) What do we mean by good consequences (and bad consequences)? (2) Consequences for whom? Actions have consequences for many different people. Which people should we consider when contemplating the consequences of our actions? By giving concrete answers to these two questions, the utilitarian carves out a unique and specific version or type of consequentialist moral theory.

To explain **utilitarianism**, we shall begin with the first question: How does the utilitarian define or characterize good and bad consequences? The most famous version of utilitarianism (the one advocated by Bentham and Mill) is called *hedonistic utilitarianism*. According to Mill, the fundamental good that all humans seek is happiness. Aristotle agrees with that point, even though he is not a utilitarian. In his discussion of the highest good, Aristotle (350 BCE, pp. 15–20) says: "As far as its name is concerned, most people would agree: for both the common run of people and cultivated men call it happiness." Mill (1979) holds that "there is in reality nothing desired except happiness" (p. 37). Mill's view is that all people desire happiness, and everything else they desire is either a part of happiness or a means to happiness. Thus, the basic and fundamental good, according to hedonistic utilitarianism (hereafter called *utilitarianism*), is happiness.

According to both Bentham and Mill, happiness is identified by pleasure. Mill (1979) claims: "By happiness is intended pleasure and the absence of pain; by unhappiness, pain and the privation of pleasure" (p. 7). In his discussion of pleasure, Mill includes not only the pleasures of food, drink, and sex but also intellectual and aesthetic pleasures. In fact, Mill considers the "higher order" pleasures, that is, the intellectual, emotional, and aesthetic pleasures that nonhuman animals are not capable of experiencing, to be of a higher quality than the "lower order" pleasures that many species of animals experience. The pleasures of poetry and opera are, in Mill's view, qualitatively superior to the pleasures of drinking and playing pinball.

Consequentialism holds that the morality of an action is determined by the consequences produced by the action. For the utilitarian, the morally right action produces happiness (pleasure and the absence of pain) and the morally wrong action produces unhappiness (pain and suffering). Mill (1979) states: "The creed which accepts as the foundation of morals 'utility' or 'the greatest happiness principle' holds that actions are right in proportion as they tend to promote happiness; wrong as they tend to produce the reverse of happiness" (p. 7). Bentham (1970) states, "By the principle of utility is meant that principle which approves or disapproves of every action whatsoever, according to the tendency which it appears to have to augment or diminish the happiness of the party whose interest is in question: or, what is the same thing in other words, to promote or to oppose the happiness" (p. 2). Before we examine the theory with any more sophistication, we can already feel its intuitive appeal. Why do we think that murder, rape, cheating, and lying are immoral? Because those actions cause pain to the victims and the families of the victims. Why do we think that charity and benevolence are righteous actions? Because they produce pleasure or happiness.

Let us now move to the second question. Because utilitarianism holds that we ought to produce happiness or pleasure, whose happiness or pleasure ought we to consider? After all, the thief gets a certain amount of pleasure from a successful burglary. The utilitarian answer to this question is that we ought to consider all parties affected by the action and calculate the pain and pleasure of everyone who is influenced. After due consideration, the action that is morally correct is the one that produces the greatest good (amount of happiness) for the greatest number of people. If all the alternatives involve more pain than pleasure, the morally right action is the one that produces the least amount of pain.

For example, the thief wants money to accord himself a certain lifestyle. Stealing will bring him jewelry or other valuable items that he can trade for money that will make him feel good. However, such actions would also have another consequence: Those persons who were stolen from would become victims, with the accompanying feelings of sorrow, anger, or perhaps even fear. As a result, their pain outweighs the thief's pleasure. "The greatest good for the greatest number" creates the context for community. The proportionality of pain and pleasure must be judged in this context.

In calculating the amount of pleasure and pain produced by any action, many factors are relevant. Bentham (1970, pp. 29–32) creates a **hedonistic calculus** in which he lists those factors. I shall briefly describe some of the major elements in Bentham's calculus. First, we must consider the intensity or strength of the pleasure or pain. A minor inconvenience is much less important than a major trauma. We must also consider the duration of the pleasure or pain. For example, in the case of a rape, psychological scars may last a lifetime. Additionally, we must consider the long-term consequences of an action. Certain actions may produce short-term pleasures but in the long run may prove to be more harmful than good (e.g., alcohol and drugs). Finally, we must consider the probability or likelihood that our actions will produce the consequences we intend. For example, the prisons are full of thieves who in a personal (and not merely community) context did not make a good utilitarian choice. For instance, a certain offender commits an armed robbery to acquire money to spend on a lavish lifestyle that would make her feel good. Instead, because the offender did not consider the probability of being caught, she spends 15 years experiencing the pain of imprisonment.

Let me briefly summarize. The ethical theorist is interested in discovering the basic, fundamental principle of morality, a foundation on which all moral judgments rest. The utilitarian claims to have found such a principle and identifies it as the "greatest happiness" principle. According to utilitarianism, an action ought to be done if and only if that action maximizes the total amount of pleasure (or minimizes the total amount of pain) of all parties affected by the action.

The entire criminal justice system can be justified on utilitarian grounds. Why do we need a police force? To serve and protect. That is to say, it is in the long-term interests of a society (it produces the greatest amount of happiness for the greatest number of people) to pay police officers to protect the community from burglars, murderers, rapists, and drunk drivers. The utilitarian would argue that what we call criminal activities tend to produce much more pain than pleasure. Therefore, a criminal justice system is instituted to lower the amount of crime, thereby lowering the amount of pain produced by crime.

Despite the fact that utilitarianism can be used to justify the criminal justice system, there are certain times when we say a police officer is justified in arresting (or ticketing) a citizen, even though that arrest does not lead to the greatest good for the greatest number. For example, suppose a man is in a rush to pick up his daughter at school. He is driving on the freeway on a bright, sunny day and there is virtually no traffic. Suppose he exceeds the speed limit by 15 mph (the speed limit is 55 mph and he is driving at 70 mph). The police officer stops him and gives him a ticket for $75. One might argue that, in this case, the painful consequences of giving a ticket outweigh the pleasurable consequences. First, the driver is caused pain by having to pay the ticket. Second, by getting the ticket, the driver is late to pick up his daughter, which causes the daughter anxiety. The delay also causes inconvenience for the principal at school, who must wait with the daughter until the father arrives. What are the pleasurable consequences for giving the ticket? Who is made happier? Had the officer just given the driver a warning, the driver, the principal, and the child would all be happier. No one would be less happy. So, on utilitarian grounds, the officer should not issue a ticket in the set of circumstances just described.

The previous example leads some people to protest that the officer has a *duty* to issue the ticket, regardless of the consequences. This leads us to our next moral theory, namely, deontological ethics.

DEONTOLOGICAL ETHICS

The word *deontology* comes from two Greek roots: *deos*, meaning duty, and *logos*, meaning study. **Deontology** is therefore the study of duty. Deontologists have argued that human beings sometimes have duties to perform certain actions, regardless of the consequences. Police officers have a duty to issue traffic tickets, even when doing so does not produce the greatest good for the greatest number. Teachers have the obligation or duty to fail students who do failing work, even if failing that student produces more misery than happiness.

The most famous deontologist is **Immanuel Kant**, an eighteenth-century German philosopher. Kant believed that all consequentialist theories missed something crucial to ethics by neglecting the concept of duty. But that is not all. Kant also believed that by focusing solely on consequences, utilitarian-type theories missed something even more basic to morality, namely, a good will or the intention to do what is right. He begins his treatise on ethics as follows: "It is impossible to conceive anything at all in the world, or even out of it, which can be taken as good without qualification, except a good will" (Kant, 1964, p. 61). In other words, the key to morality is human will or intention, not consequences.

Consider the following example: Suppose John is driving down the road and sees someone on the side of the road having difficulty with a flat tire. John notices that the car is a brand-new Cadillac and the driver of the car (an elderly woman) is wearing a mink coat. John thinks to himself, "If I help this woman, she will give me a large reward." So, John stops his car and helps the woman fix her flat tire. In the second case, Mary drives down the road and sees someone on the side of the road having difficulty with a flat tire. Mary says to herself, "That woman seems to be in trouble. I think I should help her." And she does help her. Kant would argue that there is a moral difference between case one and case two, despite the fact that the consequences in the two cases are identical. In both cases, John and Mary (from a utilitarian view) did the right thing by helping the woman, thereby producing the greatest good for the greatest number. However, Kant would argue that even though John and Mary both did the right thing (Kant would say they both acted in accordance with duty), there is still a moral difference: Mary did the act because it was her duty, whereas John was motivated by self-interest. Kant would not say that John was immoral. After all, he didn't do anything wrong. In fact, he did the right thing. But because he didn't do it for the right reason, his action has no moral worth. He did the right thing for selfish reasons (which is still better than doing the wrong thing—that is to say, performing an action inconsistent with duty). Kant (1964, pp. 65–67) draws a distinction between actions that are merely in accordance with duty and actions that are taken for the sake of duty. Furthermore, he holds that only actions that are done for the sake of duty have moral worth.

Having established the importance of good will (doing an act for the right reason), Kant moves to the question: What is our duty? In other words, just as the utilitarians have a fundamental principle of morality (act so as to produce the greatest good for the greatest number), Kant argues for a different fundamental principle of morality.

The Categorical Imperative

Kant calls the fundamental principle of morality the **categorical imperative**. An imperative is a command. It tells us what we ought to do or what we should do. The categorical imperative contrasts with what Kant calls *hypothetical imperatives*. A **hypothetical imperative** is a command that begins with "if"—for example, if you want to get a good grade, you ought to study, or if you want to make a lot of money, you should work hard, or if you want to stay out of jail, you should not break the law. The categorical imperative is unhypothetical—no ifs whatsoever. Just do it! You ought to behave morally, period; not: if you want people to like you, you should behave morally; not: if you want to go to heaven, you should behave morally. It is simply "you ought to behave morally." In other words, the categorical imperative commands absolutely and unconditionally.

What is the categorical imperative? Kant gives several formulations of it. We will focus on two of those. The first formulation emphasizes a basic concept in ethics called *universalizability*. The basic idea of **universalizability** is that for my action to be morally justifiable, I must be able to will that anyone in relevantly similar circumstances act in the same way. For example, I would like to cheat on my income tax, but could I will that everyone cheats on income taxes, thereby leaving the government insufficient funds to carry out programs I support? I would like to tell a lie to extricate myself from an uncomfortable situation, but could I will that someone else lie to me to get him or herself out of a difficult situation? Kant's formulation of the categorical imperative is as follows: "Act only on that maxim [a *maxim* is a principle of action] through which you can at the same time will that it should become a universal law" (1964, p. 88).

Kant's insight is that morality involves fairness or equality—that is, a willingness to treat everyone in the same way. I am acting immorally when I make myself an exception ("I wouldn't want others behaving this way, but it is fine for me to behave this way"). Put in that way, we see a similarity to the Golden Rule, which states, "Do unto others only as you would have them do unto you."[3]

Kant's idea is that you should do only what you are willing to permit anyone else to do. The idea is that there is something inconsistent or irrational about saying that it is fine for me to lie to you, cheat you, steal from you, but it is not justified for you to do those things to me.

The next formulation of the categorical imperative focuses on the fact that human beings have intrinsic value (i.e., value in and of themselves). Because human beings have intrinsic value, they ought always to be treated with reverence and never to be treated as mere things. When I treat someone as a thing, an object, a tool, or an instrument, I am treating that person as a means to my own ends. For example, if I marry someone to get her money, I am using her as a means to my own ends. I am not treating her with dignity, respect, or reverence but as a mere thing. It is the classic case of "using someone." When I was about 10 years old, a friend and I wanted to go to a movie. My mother could drive one way, but my friend's mother was busy and couldn't drive that day. So we decided to call a neighbor (Richard). I still remember the conversation. I said, "Hi, Richard. Would you like to go to a movie with me and Kenny?" Richard responded affirmatively, saying he would enjoy that very much. I then said, "Could your mother drive one way?" Well, Richard exploded. Richard immediately recognized that we were not inviting him because we especially wanted him to come, but rather we were using him to get a ride from his mother. Unfortunately, Richard was right. That was precisely why we called him.

Kant (1964) speaks of a human being as "something whose existence has in itself an absolute value" (p. 95). He goes on to say that "man, and in general every rational being, exists as an end in himself, not merely as a means for arbitrary use by this or that will" (p. 95). On the basis of this belief, he offers the following formulation of the categorical imperative: "Act in such a way that you always treat humanity, whether in your own person or in the person of any other, never simply as a means, but always at the same time as an end" (p. 96).

Kant believed that these two seemingly different formulations of the categorical imperative really come to the same thing. Perhaps the reasoning goes as follows: What maxims or principles of action would I be willing to universalize? Only those that treated others as ends in themselves and not as things. Why? Because I myself want to be treated with reverence, respect, and dignity. And because I want to be treated as a being with intrinsic value, I can only universalize maxims that treat other people as having intrinsic value.

COMPARING UTILITARIANISM AND DEONTOLOGY

Now let us contrast deontological ethics with utilitarianism on a specific issue related to criminal justice. The issue is: What are the legitimate restraints a society should impose on police officers in the apprehension of suspected criminals? To limit this rather broad topic somewhat, let us focus on the use of techniques of deceit, including entrapment, telephone bugging, and undercover operations. In this example, I will not try to predict the answer that a utilitarian or a deontologist will give. Instead, I will simply contrast the approach or the strategy they will use in thinking about the issue.

Let's begin with utilitarianism. Utilitarianism is a consequentialist moral theory. We decide the legitimacy of deceptive tactics on the basis of the consequences of using those tactics. In particular, we must weigh the positive results against the negative results in deciding what to do. On the positive side are entrapment, bugging operations, and undercover operations work. As a result of the use of such tactics, we are able to apprehend some criminals that might otherwise go free. And, as a result of apprehending those criminals, we may deter future crime in two ways: (1) we keep known criminals behind bars where they are unable to commit further crimes, and (2) we show, by example, what happens when someone breaks the law, thereby deterring other citizens from risking incarceration.

On the negative side, we have certain individuals' right to privacy being violated by the use of deceptive tactics. The utilitarian will now weigh the positive benefits of apprehending criminals, and thereby protecting society, against the negative consequence of violating certain citizens' rights to privacy.

Kant would approach the issue from a very different reference point. As a deontologist, he would not approach this issue from the perspective of: What consequences are likely to occur? Rather than focusing on the results or ends of the behavior, he would look at the behavior itself to see if it conforms to the categorical imperative. Concentrating on the universalizability formulation of the categorical imperative, a Kantian might ask: Would I consent to having my telephone bugged if there were reason to suspect that I was guilty of a crime?

Or, if we were to attend to the second formulation of the categorical imperative, a Kantian might ask: Does the use of manipulative techniques in law enforcement constitute treating suspected criminals as mere means to our ends (by manipulating them, we are using them), or does it constitute treating them as ends in themselves (mature, responsible citizens who must answer to their behavior)?

These are difficult questions to answer. But the point of the example is not to show how a utilitarian or deontologist would solve an ethical issue in criminal justice; rather, we want to illustrate how they would approach or think about such an issue.

JUSTICE AND DUTY

Both Kant's categorical imperative and Mill's principle of greatest happiness capture some of our moral intuitions. Treating people as ends and producing the greatest amount of happiness both seem to be credible guides to the moral life. Nonetheless, both theories seem to have trouble with a certain range of cases. Utilitarianism appears to have difficulty with certain cases of injustice, and Kant's deontology seems to have no way to handle cases of conflicting duties. In this final section, we look at the weak points in both theories and propose an integrated Kantian-utilitarian ethic to handle the alleged weaknesses of both theories.[4]

According to utilitarianism, an action is moral when it produces the greatest amount of happiness for the greatest number of people. A problem arises, however, when the greatest happiness is achieved at the expense of a few. For example, if a large group were to enslave a very small group, the large group would gain certain comforts and luxuries (and the pleasure that accompanies those comforts) as a result of the servitude of the few. If we were to follow the **utilitarian calculus** strictly, the suffering (even intense suffering) of a few would be outweighed by the pleasure of a large enough majority. A thousand people's modest pleasure would outweigh the suffering of 10 others. Hence, utilitarianism would seem to endorse slavery when it produces the greatest total amount of happiness for the greatest number of people. This is obviously a problem for utilitarianism. Slavery and oppression are wrong regardless of the amount of pleasure accumulated by the oppressing class. In fact, when one person's pleasure results from the suffering of another, the pleasure seems all the more abhorrent.

The preceding case points to a weakness in utilitarianism—namely, the weakness in dealing with certain cases of injustice. Sometimes it is simply unjust to treat people in a certain way, regardless of the pleasurable consequences for others. A gang rape is wrong even if 50 people enjoy it and only one suffers. It is wrong because it is unjust. To use Kant's formulation, it is always wrong to treat anyone as a mere means to one's own ends. When we enslave, rape, and oppress, we are always treating the victim as a means to our own ends.

There are several cases related to criminal justice in which this issue comes up. However, when it comes up in these cases, it is not as simple as the slavery and gang rape cases. It is complex, subtle, and controversial. The cases I am considering involve the excessive use of force. Suppose, for example, that we want to keep order in our communities or in our prisons. Would we be justified in using excessive force on one offender as an example to the rest? If we were to beat a few citizens or prisoners severely for certain crimes, those public beatings might deter future crimes, thereby increasing the general happiness. But do we have the right to treat one offender with excessive violence to teach others a lesson? A case like this is apt to produce a lively debate, and the debate would involve utilitarian and Kantian sentiments. The utilitarian might point out that although public canings are brutal, Singapore—which uses such punishments—is virtually crime free. The Kantian would say that the beating of some citizens to protect others is too high a price. It is simply unjust to mistreat one citizen to benefit others. Our ambivalent feelings about this case show how deeply we have internalized the voices of both Kant and Mill.

We see from the preceding cases (especially the slavery case) that utilitarianism has trouble dealing with situations involving the maximization of pleasure for the majority at the expense of the minority. We also see that Kant, with his emphasis on treating people as ends in themselves, can easily handle those cases. Kant's moral theory, however, has problems of its own. In particular, although Kant talks extensively of duty, he seems to have no way to deal with cases of conflicting duties. Suppose, for example, you borrow a gun from a friend for target practice and promise to return the weapon. After you borrow the weapon, your friend becomes emotionally upset and vows to shoot someone. He then demands that you return the gun that you promised to return. He says he needs the gun back to commit a murder. On one hand, you have a duty to keep your promises and return what you owe. On the other hand, you have a duty to try to prevent a murder. Kant gives us no guidance here. Treating people as ends and not means is a nice formula, but how does it apply in this case? If you do not return the gun, aren't you treating your friend as a means? If you do return the gun, aren't you treating the potential murder victim as a means? Kant provides no obvious solution. It is precisely at this point that a utilitarian calculus might help. The utilitarian would estimate the harm done by returning the gun against the harm done by keeping the gun. Presumably, much more harm would be caused by returning the weapon.

It appears, therefore, that Kant's theory is strong where Mill's is weak, and vice versa. Kant's emphasis on justice provides a moral reason to reject slavery, even when it maximizes pleasure. The utilitarian calculus gives us a method of determining what to do in cases of conflicting duties.

Perhaps we can combine the insights of both utilitarianism and deontology and formulate a *utilitarian Kantian principle*. Cornman and Lehrer (1974) propose the following integrated principle:

> An action ought to be done in a situation if and only if (1) doing the action, (a) treats as mere means as few people as possible in the situation, and (b) treats as ends as many people as is consistent with (a), and (2) doing the action in the situation brings about as much overall happiness as is consistent with (1).

This integrated Kantian utilitarian principle avoids the problem of the many enslaving the few because such an act would violate point 1. It also avoids the problem of conflicting duties because point 2 provides a way of deciding what to do when we are faced with a conflict of duties.

Deontology and utilitarianism are two of the most significant, influential ethical theories in Western thought. Much of the moral reasoning we engage in daily is guided by utilitarian and/or deontological reflection. This is true both generally and specifically in cases involving criminal justice. The criminal justice system itself is usually justified on either utilitarian grounds (it is in the best interest of most citizens to punish criminals) or Kantian grounds (it is our duty to punish wrongdoing). The hope is that this essay will provide some tools that we can use in trying to understand and solve some of the tough ethical decisions facing our criminal justice system.

■ Learn More on the Internet

Go to www.answers.com/topic/applied-ethics for more information on a variety of social and criminal justice ethics topics. Visit www.iep.utm.edu/ethics/ for more on moral philosophy.   ■

Discussion Questions

1. Compare and contrast utilitarianism and deontology. Which of the two do you feel explains human behavior most effectively? Why?
2. Explain and discuss Kant's categorical imperative. How appropriate are his views in today's criminal justice field?
3. Think of a difficult ethical decision that someone working in the criminal justice field might face. Using one of the theories discussed in this chapter, illustrate how it might be used to improve on that situation, including the person's understanding of his or her dilemma.

CASE STUDY 2–1 ROOM AT THE END OF THE HALL

You have just showered and changed into civilian clothes. You think to yourself that, for a training officer, Sergeant Womack is all right. You have learned a lot from him during the last 6 weeks. Being a rookie police officer has gone much more smoothly than you thought it would. Finishing the last of your umpteenth cup of coffee, you can't help but overhear the sergeant and the afternoon shift dispatcher discussing several neighborhood calls complaining about a weekend fraternity party on Elm Street.

You say to the sergeant, "Sarge, I used to be a member of that fraternity when I was a criminal justice student at the university. I'd be happy to stop by on my way home and check it out. College boys can get a little out of control at times. I don't mind making a visit and getting them to quiet things down."

Sergeant Womack looks at the dispatcher and then turns to you.

"OK, Mike. Just be sure if there is any trouble, you call me pronto."

"You got it, Sarge," you respond, chuckling to yourself and remembering your wild and crazy times at the fraternity house.

Parking your truck by the street in front of the fraternity house, you can see that the situation is about what you expected. You quickly herd the people partying in the yard into the house and announce to all, pulling your badge, to hold things down since the neighbors are complaining to the police. Your voice has a firm but friendly tone to it and the partygoers, with a couple of minor exceptions expressed by several intoxicated brothers, generally comply with your request. You ask one fairly responsible-looking student in a fraternity sweatshirt where Ed, the organization's president, is, and he directs you to the last room on the right upstairs.

Entering the room, you observe seven or eight male students all watching some kind of activity in the corner of the room. Several are shouting encouragement; the rest are drinking beer and watching in silence. The observers are so enthralled with what is going on that they don't even notice your presence as you work your way through the crowd to see what is happening. You stop in your tracks. There on a bed is a male student having intercourse with a girl. Next to the bed is another male student zipping his pants up. You cannot tell what state of mind the girl is in. She seems intoxicated and confused, and perhaps even somewhat frightened. Not exactly sure what to do, you pull your badge and tell everyone to step outside the room and not leave the house. You stop Ed and two males who were obviously having sex with the girl and have them remain in the room. Ed, the fraternity president, has by this time recognized you. The girl starts

Continued...

CASE STUDY 2–1 ROOM AT THE END OF THE HALL *Continued*

to cry quietly, the two males become very nervous, and the rest of the observers quickly vanish from the room.

"Mike," begins the president, extending his hand to you, "We were just having some harmless fun."

"I'm not so sure about that, Ed," you reply, pulling out a notepad and pen and ignoring his extended hand. You direct Ed to take the two males to an adjoining room and wait for you there. You turn back to the girl, who has by now managed in some fashion to get dressed. You ask her what was going on. All she can manage between quiet sobs is that she is scared and that her name is Yvonne. You try to encourage her that everything will be all right and ask her to remain in the room while you question Ed and the other two males next door. As you leave the room, you look up and see Dr Madge Mullins, assistant dean of students, walking toward you. You know her from your days as a student.

"Mike, I got a call from a student downstairs who works in my office. What's going on here?"

You quickly explain the situation to her as you know it. You can tell from the look on her face that she is both concerned and agitated.

"Mike, you said the girl's name was Yvonne? I've dealt with her before. She doesn't have the best reputation on campus. This is a university matter and I will guarantee you that this situation will be handled in an appropriate manner. There is no need for us to further embarrass this girl or the university for that matter. You know what happens when these things get in the paper."

You carefully consider what Dean Mullins is saying. You also remember your sergeant's parting words. Do you let her take care of the situation or do you call Sergeant Womack?

Questions

1. What is Mike's duty?
2. Does the fact that the girl in this situation has a "reputation" make a difference?
3. What would be a legally responsible and morally just outcome to this particular case?

Reprinted by permission of Waveland Press, Inc., from Braswell, M., Miller, L., & Pollock, J. (2006). Case studies in criminal justice ethics. Long Grove, IL: Waveland Press, Inc. All rights reserved.

NOTES

1. In *Metaphysics* (987b1), Aristotle states: "Now Socrates was engaged in the study of ethical matters, but not at all in the study of nature as a whole, yet in ethical matters he sought the universal and was the first to fix his thought on definitions."

2. See Plato, Laches 191c, Euthyphro 5c–d, Meno 72a.

3. See Matthew 7:12; Luke 6:31.

4. I first discovered the idea of integrating Kant and Mill in Cornman, J., & Lehrer, K. (1974), *Philosophical problems and arguments: An introduction* (pp. 504–508) (2nd ed.). New York: Macmillan.

REFERENCES

Aristotle (350 BCE). Nicomachean ethics. 1095a (pp. 15-20).

Bentham, J. (1970). *The principles of morals and legislation*. Darien, CT: Hafner.

Braswell, M., Pollock, J., & Braswell, S. (2007). *Morality stories: Dilemmas in ethics, crime and justice*. Durham, NC: Carolina Academic Press.

Cornman, J., & Lehrer, K. (1974). *Philosophical problems and arguments: An introduction* (2nd ed.). New York: Macmillan.

Kant, I. (1964). *Groundwork of the metaphysics of morals* (H. J. Paton, Trans.). New York: Harper & Row.

Mill, J. S. (1979). *Utilitarianism*. Indianapolis: Hackett.

Pollock, J. (2004). *Dilemmas and decision: Ethics in crime and justice*. Belmont, CA: Wadsworth/ITP.

Sherman, L. W. (1981). *The study of ethics in criminology and criminal justice*. Chicago: Joint Commission on Criminology and Criminal Justice Education and Standards.

Souryal, S. (2010). *Ethics in criminal justice: In search of the truth* (5th ed.). Boston: Elsevier (Anderson Publishing).

CHAPTER 3

Peacemaking, Justice, and Ethics

Michael C. Braswell, Jeffrey Gold

KEY CONCEPTS

caring	connectedness	mindfulness
compassion	karma	peacemaking

The evolution of legal and social justice in America often has found itself pulled between the retribution and punishment agendas of such ancient traditions as the law of Moses, the Koran, and the rehabilitation and redemption traditions of New Testament Christianity. The tension between these traditions of retribution and rehabilitation, and punishment and reform, has been substantial.

Peacemaking as a justice and criminology perspective has been heralded in some quarters as a contemporary, "new age" phenomenon. The New Age movement itself appears to be essentially a middle-class movement that focuses on such issues as metaphysical inquiry, mind control, emotional healing, and financial well-being. While peacemaking concerns may be compatible with some of these issues, they seem more grounded in age-old traditions such as Christianity, Judaism, Islamism, Buddhism, and Hinduism. In particular, these ancient traditions emphasize the value and usefulness of suffering and service, which is often deemphasized or nonexistent in New Age movements (Bartollas & Braswell, 1993).

Peacemaking, as evolved from ancient spiritual and wisdom traditions, has included the possibility of mercy and **compassion** within the framework of justice. To put such thinking in a more personal perspective, we might consider our own experiences—times when we have been the victim and other occasions when we have been the offender. Perhaps we have never committed a crime and, hopefully, most of us have never been harmed by an offender. Yet, in our own way we have been both victim and offender. We have been betrayed by those we trusted, whether the heartbreak of a romance gone sour or the cruel gossip of a broken confidence. How did we feel when we were betrayed? What did we want from the one who hurt us? Typically, we wanted to strike back; we wanted revenge, retribution, our pound of flesh. What about the occasions when we have been the offender, when we have committed the betrayal? When our best friend found out that we were the source of the criticism or cruel gossip, what did we want? As the one who offended, what did we hope for? Did we hope for mercy and forgiveness, perhaps another chance? Can we have it both ways? Can we be for revenge and violence when we are the victim and for mercy and peace when we are the offender? Can we expect to have it both ways?

See Box 3.1 below and think about what Gandhi suggested were seven blunders that plague the world we live in. He maintained that such blunders constitute a form of passive violence that can lead to acts of violence, including crime and war.

BOX 3.1 SEVEN BLUNDERS

1. Wealth without work.
2. Pleasure without conscience.
3. Knowledge without character.
4. Commerce without morality.
5. Science without humanity.
6. Worship without sacrifice.
7. Politics without principles.

What we will try to do in this chapter is explore three themes of peacemaking: (1) connectedness, (2) care, and (3) mindfulness. It is our hope that through this exploration we will be able to better understand the possibilities of peacemaking for us as criminal justice professionals as well as on a personal level.

CONNECTEDNESS

The first and perhaps most important theme, **connectedness**, is demonstrated in the dedication to the book *Inner Corrections: Finding Peace and Peace Making*, which says, "to the keeper and the kept, the offender and the victim, the parent and the child, the teacher and the student, and the incarcerator and the liberator that is within each of us" (Lozoff & Braswell, 1989, p. iii). This simple statement suggests what Eastern philosophers such as Lao-tzu and Western philosophers such as Plato advocated ages ago—that human beings are not simply isolated individuals, but each one of us is integrally "connected" and bonded to other human beings and the environment. This environment includes not only the outer physical environment but our inner psychological and spiritual environment as well. Chief

Seattle of the Duwamish tribe, in a letter to the president of the United States, wrote the following in 1852:

> Every part of this earth is sacred to my people. Every shining pine needle, every sandy shore, every mist in the dark woods, every meadow, every humming insect .... We know the sap which courses through the trees as we know the blood that courses through our veins. We are part of the earth and it is part of us. The perfumed flowers are our sisters. The bear, the deer, the great eagle, these are our brothers. The rocky crests, the juices in the meadow, the body heat of the pony, and man, all belong to the same family ... This we know: the earth does not belong to man, man belongs to the earth. All things are connected like the blood that unites us all. Man did not weave the web of life, he is merely a strand in it. Whatever he does to the web, he does to himself.[1]

In that letter, Chief Seattle emphasizes our connection to the natural world. One can find a similar position in several different Eastern philosophies. Lozoff (1987, p. 11), articulating the position found in Yoga, states: "In Truth, we (everybody and everything in the Universe) are all connected; most of us just can't see the glue."

The idea that we just can't see the glue (that is, we can't see the connection linking ourselves to others) is the Hindu concept that we misperceive ourselves as isolated and disconnected from one another and the world. As we become more aware of how we are connected to all that we are a part of, we are encouraged to take more personal responsibility to do the best we can. Wendell Berry, a noted conservationist, writes, "A man who is willing to undertake the discipline and the difficulty of mending his own ways is worth more to the conservation movement than a hundred who are insisting merely that the government and industries mend their ways" (in Safransky, 1990, p. 51). Thomas Merton suggests that "instead of hating the people you think are war makers, hate the appetites and the disorder in your own soul, which are the causes of war" (in Safransky, 1990, p. 115). Insofar as we see ourselves as apart from nature rather than a part of nature, we end up with pollution, acid rain, destruction of forests, and the depletion of the ozone layer. As Berry and Merton indicate, an important aspect of connectedness is looking within, taking personal responsibility, and acting in a more responsible way.

In this regard, it is interesting to contrast two metaphors concerning the earth. The older metaphor of "mother earth" contrasts dramatically with the contemporary metaphor of the earth as a collection of "natural resources." A mother is someone to whom we feel connected and bound. To perceive the earth as one's mother is to see oneself as coming out of the earth. The connection could not be any more intimate. To perceive the earth as an assortment of natural resources is another matter entirely. To conceive of the earth as merely a provider of goods for our own purposes is, to borrow Kant's expression, to see the earth as merely a means of our own ends. The danger in that attitude is now obvious. Insofar as we do not consider the earth to be sacred or precious (as Chief Seattle did), but instead see it as a commodity with no intrinsic worth, we find ourselves in a world with places like Prince William Sound, Three Mile Island, Love Canal, and Chernobyl. To put such thinking in a Judeo-Christian context, does "dominion over the earth" refer to our being responsible stewards of the earth and its resources, or does it allow us to attempt to dominate the earth, exploiting its resources for profit and convenience with little or no regard for breaking environmental laws or for our children's future?

Once we accept the assumption that we are connected to everyone and everything around us, it becomes clear that our actions do not take place in a vacuum but within a complex web of interconnected people and things. Whatever I do has an impact upon those around me. My actions have consequences. This is the Hindu and Buddhist concept of **karma**. The law of karma is the law of cause and effect. All actions have effects or consequences. The law of karma is neither good nor bad. It simply is what it is.

When we integrate the notion of karma (lawful consequences) with the notion of connectedness, it becomes clear that, since we are connected to everyone around us, our actions affect those who are connected to us even when we cannot see the connections. Insofar as we have an impact on someone we are connected with, we have an impact upon ourselves. In other words, our actions ultimately come back to us. What goes around comes around. What we do to others, in one way or another, we also do to ourselves. It is the biblical idea that we reap what we sow. It is Chief Seattle's idea that "Man did not weave the web of life, he is merely a strand in it. Whatever he does to the web, he does to himself. Plant seeds of violence and reap violent fruits. Plant seeds of compassion and reap compassionate fruits." Lozoff (1987, p. 9) states: "Every thought, word, and deed is a seed we plant in the world. All our lives, we harvest the fruits of those seeds. If we plant desire, greed, fear, anger and doubt, then that's what will fill our lives. Plant love, courage, understanding, good humor, and that's what we get back. This isn't negotiable; it's a law of energy, just like gravity."

When we speak of karma, we are not talking about retribution, revenge, or punishment. Rather, we are speaking of the consequences of actions. We do not say of someone who jumps from a third-story window that his broken leg is a punishment for jumping. It is simply a consequence. Rather than thinking of karma as retribution, it is better to think of it as the principle, "You've made your bed, now you must lie in it." We must inhabit the world we create. If we pollute the world, we must live in a polluted world. If we act violently or choose to ignore violence and injustice, we must live in a violent and unjust world.

According to proponents of the idea of karma (the idea that each one of us reaps what he or she sows), no one can ever get away with one's actions. Perhaps we won't get caught by the police, but the action still has an impact on our own life. For a philosopher like Plato, the consequences are consequences for our own psyche. In Plato's *Gorgias*, Socrates compares physical health with psychological health.[2] To understand this comparison, consider the following example. I live a sedentary life, eat a diet of junk food and soda pop, smoke cigarettes, and drink alcohol excessively. This life of no exercise, poor nutrition, cigarettes, and alcohol will eventually catch up with me. After I become adjusted and acclimated to it, I may believe that I feel just fine. But from the fact that I believe that I feel fine, it does not follow that I am in an optimal state of physical health. The reason that I believe that I feel fine is precisely because I no longer even know what it is like to feel healthy. It is like a severely near-sighted boy who has never worn glasses. He will not know that his sight is not optimal; he will think the world is supposed to look the way he sees it. He will not know that there is a better way to see. Similarly, I, as the person who lives a sedentary life and eats exclusively at fast food restaurants, may not know that there is a better way to feel. But the fact that I do not know it does not stop the junk food and cigarettes from continuing to affect my physical condition. One simply cannot avoid the consequences of an unhealthy diet and lifestyle.

This is also a useful analogy for understanding suffering and violence within families. There is often a sense of disconnectedness, inconsistency, and neglect regarding relationships in unhealthy and abusive families. Over a period of years, trust becomes nonexistent, and feelings of anger and unhappiness begin to appear normal to such families. They forget how it felt to be happy and at peace (if they ever experienced such feelings). When children grow up full of pain and inconsistencies, they, along with their families, often reap a harvest of drug abuse, spousal battering, and other forms of criminality—even suicide or homicide. They did not realize things had gotten so bad. In a sense, the connections, both hidden and obvious, that animate the consequences of our actions are like a dance (and there are no spectators in the dance of life). "The flailing arms of the abusive parent and the contortions of the victim-child are locked in a dance of pain and sorrow no less significant than the dance of joy experienced by the loving elderly couple" (Braswell, 1990b, p. 87).

In *Gorgias*, Plato argues that the same is true with injustice and psychological health. One can never escape the consequences of injustice. One may escape detection by the police, one may never be brought to trial, one may never go to prison—but injustice continues to affect one's psyche, whether we know it or not. We must inhabit the unjust world that we have created. According to Plato, injustice brings strife, disharmony, and conflict. There will be strife and conflict in an unjust city. Similarly, there will be strife and conflict in an unjust individual (a lack of psychic health and wholeness). Just as the physically unhealthy man may not know he is unhealthy and the nearsighted child may not know his eyesight is poor, the unjust man may not know that he is in a state of psychic disharmony and imbalance. That is because he has become adjusted and acclimated to an unjust and violent life. He simply doesn't know what it is like to feel balanced, harmonious, and whole. Of course, consequences of poor physical or psychic health may also offer a person opportunity to learn and grow from his or her experience. For example, what does it mean when a person who ridicules and feels prejudice toward disabled persons finds himself or herself the parent of a disabled child? Some persons might suggest that such a consequence is a form of punishment. Perhaps on a deeper level, the consequence is also an opportunity—another chance for the disconnected person to see and experience the connection that his or her disabled child is lovable and an important part of the web of life. The same can be said of the harsh, uncaring critic of the drug addict, who comes to find that his own daughter or son suffers from such an affliction.

To summarize, according to what we are calling theories of connectedness, people are not isolated, disconnected beings. Rather, we are earthly beings and social beings; that is, we are creatures integrally connected to the earth and to other people on the earth. What we do has direct consequences on those to whom we are connected, whether or not we see the connection. Our actions directly affect the world in which we live. We must live in the world created by our own actions. If we act violently, cruelly, and unjustly, we will live in a world filled with violence, cruelty, and injustice. If we act compassionately and benevolently, we will live in a world that is more compassionate and benevolent.

This metaphysical view naturally leads to an ethics of nonviolence. The Sanskrit word *ahimsa*, meaning nonviolence, is a fundamental concept in Hinduism and Buddhism. Mahatma Gandhi, who advocated an ethic of nonviolence, is a contemporary representative of that idea. A Christian representative is Martin Luther King Jr. Both believed in changing the world and rectifying the injustices they saw, but both insisted on using nonviolent strategies. Martin Luther King Jr., accepting the Nobel Peace Prize, said, "The nonviolent resisters can summarize their message in the following simple terms: We will not obey unjust laws or submit to unjust practices. We will do this peacefully, openly, cheerfully, because our aim is to persuade. We adopt the means of nonviolence because our end is a community at peace with itself" (Cohen, 1971, p. 40). The idea is that violence breeds violence. You don't fight fire with fire, rather you put out fire with water. You don't end violence by violently resisting it. Perhaps that is what Jesus meant by "resist not evil" (Matthew 5:39). You don't end violence by creating more of it. If we must inhabit the world we create and we want to live in a world that is just and peaceful, we ought to act in just and peaceful ways. Richard Quinney (1993) writes, "Instead of a war on crime ("on criminals") we need to be waging peace on the economy, in the society, and within ourselves." In other words, we need to wage peace, not war.

An example of the relevance of this to criminal justice can be found in our contemporary prisons. Contemporary prisons are typically violent institutions that tend to perpetuate rather than diminish violence. According to the theories presented in this section, we must begin to treat criminals in less violent and more compassionate ways. We must stop thinking in terms of revenge, retribution, and recrimination, and begin to think in terms of reconciliation, compassion, and forgiveness. In recent years, there have been innovations and increasing numbers of alternative programs on mediation, conflict resolution, restitution, and community action. They are a part of an emerging criminology of peacemaking, a criminology that seeks to end suffering and reduce crime (Quinney, 1993). This approach to corrections is not a weak, "bleeding heart" approach. Sometimes love may have to be firm love. Still, if we choose to acknowledge our connectedness and desire to be peacemakers, we will insist on treating persons as a part of our humanity, whether they deserve such treatment or not.

The following Zen story presents this philosophy in its most radical form:

> One evening as Shichiri Kojun was reciting sutras a thief with a sharp sword entered, demanding either his money or his life. Shichiri told him: "Do not disturb me. You can find the money in that drawer." Then he resumed his recitation. A little while afterwards he stopped and called: "Don't take it all. I need some to pay taxes with tomorrow." The intruder gathered up most of the money and started to leave. "Thank a person when you receive a gift," Shichiri added. The man thanked him and made off. A few days afterwards the fellow was caught and confessed, among others, the offence against Shichiri. When Shichiri was called as a witness he said: "This man is no thief, at least as far as I am concerned. I gave him the money and he thanked me for it." After he had finished his prison term, the man went to Shichiri and became his disciple.
>
> **Reps (1919, p. 41)**

Along the same lines, Jesus teaches that if anyone sues you for your coat, let him also have your cloak (Matthew 5:40). He goes on to say: "Love your enemies, bless them that curse you, do good to them that hate you, and pray for them who despitefully use you, and persecute you" (Matthew 5:44). The radical message of these philosophies is that we should cease to repay violence with violence, whether that repayment be called "retribution" or "just deserts." Instead, we must learn to, as Paul puts it, "overcome evil with good" (Romans 12:21). Jesus also reminds us that whatever we do to the "least of those" in our society, we do to him. In terms of criminal justice, that would involve a complete reform of what we now call "corrections." See Box 3.2.

BOX 3.2 PEACEMAKING PRACTICE

Life is short
Make a difference
Perseverance more than ability is key
Keep trying

Even when you are the victim of injustice
Even when you yourself are unjust
Keep trying

Be kind to those around you
Be kind to yourself as well
And when you are not
Keep trying

And be encouraging
Especially when there is no reason to be
Seek completion not perfection
Seek truth not power

Sooner or later the truth will set you free
But not before it beats the hell out of you
Keep trying

Answers long forgotten, the question remains:
when will the peace that passes understanding come?
Not at the end of conflict but in its midst

Peace is a longshot
Justice even more so
Sometimes longshots come in
Believe that they will

From peace within to peace without
From being just to justice for all

Braswell, M. (2004). Peacemaking Boogie. Justitia, 3(1), 6.

CARING

In the previous chapter, we presented reasons in support of the utilitarian version of the fundamental rule of morality, namely, that we ought to produce the greatest good for the greatest number. We advanced Kant's arguments for what he considers to be the basic moral principle, that we ought to treat others as ends in themselves and not as mere means. We have just explored how theories of connectedness defend the moral absolute of nonviolence. Though the three theories differ from one another, all share a similarity of approach. All attempt to prove, by means of argument, justification, and reason, a specific moral rule or principle. According to Noddings (1986), proving, justifying, and arguing for rules and principles is a masculine approach to ethics. In *Caring: A Feminine Approach to Ethics and Moral Education*, she outlines an alternative. Noddings claims:

> Ethics, the philosophical study of morality, has concentrated for the most part on moral reasoning ... Even though careful philosophers have recognized the difference between "pure" or logical reason and "practical" or moral reason, ethical argumentation has frequently proceeded as if it were governed by the logical necessity characteristic of geometry. It has concentrated on the establishment of principles and that which can be logically derived from them. One might say that ethics has been discussed largely in the language of the father: in principles and propositions, in terms such as justification, fairness, justice. The mother's voice has been silent. Human caring and the memory of caring and being cared for, which I shall argue form the

foundation of ethical response, have not received attention except as outcomes of ethical behavior. One is tempted to say that ethics has so far been guided by Logos, the masculine spirit, whereas the more natural and perhaps stronger approach would be through Eros, the feminine spirit. (p. 1)

According to Noddings (1986, p. 2), the masculine approach (the approach of the father) is a detached perspective that focuses on law and principle, whereas the feminine approach (the approach of the mother) is rooted in receptivity, relatedness, and responsiveness. Noddings advocates the feminine perspective. She goes on to point out that "this does not imply that all women will accept it [the feminine perspective] or that men will reject it; indeed, there is no reason why men should not embrace it" (Noddings, 1986, p. 2).

The masculine perspective is an approach to ethics, an approach through justification and argument. The feminine perspective, on the other hand, "shall locate the very wellspring of ethical behavior in human affective response" (Noddings, 1986, p. 3). Noddings's point is that ethical **caring** is ultimately grounded in natural caring—for example, the natural caring a mother has for her child. Noddings's emphasis on natural caring leads her to the conclusion "that in truth, the moral viewpoint is prior to any notion of justification" (Noddings, 1986, p. 95). In other words, rather than viewing reason and justification as the process by which one comes to the moral perspective, Noddings indicates that the moral perspective is a natural perspective, as natural as a mother caring for her infant.

An ancient Chinese philosophy, Taoism, advocates a position that is similar to the one we find in Noddings. The two major Taoist philosophers, Lao-tzu and Chuang-tzu, suggest that not only is natural caring prior to reason, justification, and principle, it is superior to those activities. In fact, the Taoists claim that principles of ethics actually interfere with caring. Just as Nel Noddings is responding to a particular masculine tradition in Western ethics, the Taoists are responding to a particular tradition in Chinese ethics, namely, Confucianism. The Confucianists were very rule- and principle-oriented—rules for filial piety, rules for those who govern, rules for those who are governed. The Taoists responded by claiming that those rules, because of their artificiality, destroyed true, natural caring and replaced it with forced or legislated "caring."

From the Taoist perspective, the danger of advocating ethical rules and principles is that they will replace something far superior to those principles, namely, natural caring. Chuang-tzu (1964) says: "Because [the doctrine of] right and wrong appeared, the Way was injured" (p. 37).

Lao-tzu (1963) makes a similar claim. Lao-tzu doesn't make the strong claim that the doctrine of right and wrong destroyed the Way (the Tao). However, he does claim that only in unnatural states does the doctrine of right and wrong arise. In the Tao Te Ching, Lao-tzu says:

> Therefore, when Tao [the natural Way] is lost, only then does the doctrine of virtue arise.
>
> When virtue is lost, only then does the doctrine of humanity arise.
>
> When humanity is lost, only then does the doctrine of righteousness arise.
>
> When righteousness is lost, only then does the doctrine of propriety arise.
>
> Now, propriety is a superficial expression of loyalty and faithfulness, and the beginning of disorder (p. 167).

Notice how Lao-tzu concludes by discussing the superficiality of notions of propriety and how such notions are the beginning of disorder. In another section of the Tao Te Ching, Lao-tzu summarizes the preceding by saying, "When the great Tao [Natural Way] declined, the doctrine of humanity and righteousness arose" (p. 131). Lao-tzu is saying that artificial doctrines of virtue, humanity, and righteousness, doctrines that tell us how we ought to behave, arise only in unhealthy situations. Something is already terribly wrong when we tell a mother she ought to feed her child or that she has a duty to feed her child. Feeding one's child is a natural, caring response. Lao-tzu says: "When the six family relationships are not in harmony, there will be the advocacy of filial piety and deep love to children"(p. 131).

Given that we live in and are inculcated into a patriarchal society, a society of rules, principles, and laws, do the Taoists have any suggestions as to how to break free from patriarchal modes of thought, how to return to a more natural and caring way of living in the world? As you might expect, the answer to this is yes. The Taoist position can be put in the following way: Moral reasoning is the product of a mind that discriminates and draws distinctions (between right and wrong, good and bad, just and unjust). According to Taoism, these categories and distinctions are artificial and conventional, not natural. To put oneself into a more natural state, which according to the Taoist view on human nature would be a more caring state, one must undo, erase, or transcend all the conventional, artificial dualisms that have been inculcated into us. We perceive the world the way we have been taught to perceive the world. So, we must begin to unlearn the categories that have been programmed into us.

In a more contemporary vein, Myers and Chiang (1993) also compared the prevailing legalistic, masculine approach to law enforcement—which focuses on analysis, rationalization, and punishment—with the feminine perspective of nurturing, care, and treatment.

Martin (1993) examined the usefulness of incorporating transpersonal psychology into the justice and corrections process. This discipline integrates Western scientific and Eastern and Western spiritual traditions, which could open a fresh way to develop policy and treatment strategies that are more positive and growth oriented.

An ancient story involving the teacher, Ryokan, and his delinquent nephew offers another interesting, if unorthodox, approach in utilizing the ethic of care:

> Once his brother asked Ryokan to visit his house and speak to his delinquent son. Ryokan came but did not say a word of admonition to the boy. He stayed overnight and prepared to leave the next morning. As the wayward nephew was lacing up Ryokan's sandals, he felt a drop of warm water. Glancing up, he saw Ryokan looking down at him, his eyes full of tears. Ryokan then returned home, and the nephew changed for the better.
>
> **Safransky (1990, pp. 115–116)**

It goes without saying that caring is not the exclusive property of Taoism or Yoga. Mother Teresa, a recipient of the Nobel Peace Prize, encompasses this ethic of caring from a Christian perspective. She started her work as a one-woman mission in Calcutta, India, ministering to and caring for the dying. Generally speaking, in some ways we might consider the dying poor even more undesirable than incarcerated offenders. Yet Mother Teresa's Missionaries of Charity grew from a one-woman operation to a group of active missions found all over the world. When asked how she could emotionally handle constantly being around so many dying persons, she responded that when she looked into the eyes of the dying she saw "Christ in a distressing disguise."[3]

MINDFULNESS

Mother Teresa is perhaps the embodiment of the ethic of care. Internalizing such an approach requires that one develop a compassionate vision through mindfulness. The following example from one of her public addresses demonstrates such a vision in action:

> A gentleman came to our house and he told me, "There is a Hindu family with about eight children who have not eaten for a long time." So I took some rice quickly and went to their family and I could see real hunger on the small faces of these children and yet the mother had the courage to divide the rice into two and she went out. When she came back, I asked her, "Where did you go? What did you do?" And she said: "They are hungry also." "Who are they?" "The Muslim family next door with as many children." She knew that they were hungry. What

struck me most was that she knew and because she knew she gave until it hurt. I did not bring more rice that night because I wanted them to enjoy the joy of giving, of sharing. You should have seen the faces of those little ones. They just understood what their mother did. Their faces were brightened with smiles. When I came in they looked hungry, they looked so miserable. But the act of their mother taught them what true love was.

de Bertodano (1993, p. 53)

Mindfulness allows us to experience a more transcendent sense of awareness. It allows us to be fully present, aware of what is immediate, yet also at the same time to become more aware of the larger picture both in terms of needs and possibilities. Mindfulness allowed the Hindu mother not only to receive the rice from Mother Teresa with gratitude, but also allowed her to see how she was connected to the hungry Muslim family and how to have the courage to care enough to share her meager resources, thus teaching her own children one of life's greatest lessons.

Mindfulness can encourage us to move from the passion of single-minded self-interest to a growing sense of compassion that includes others and their needs. We often wring our hands about those who are victims of physical abuse and the homeless. Yet how often do we volunteer to help? (Braswell, 1990a). Mindfulness can help us, like the Hindu mother, to act on our concerns. As Wang Yang Ming states, "To know and not to do is in fact, not to know" (Lozoff & Braswell, 1989, p. 63). Developing wholesight can help us to become more mindful in turning our knowing into doing. As mentioned in Chapter 1, Palmer (1983) suggests that wholesight includes both the heart and the head in one's decision making.

A strategy or process that can help us become more mindful is meditation. Meditation is a practice through which the meditator quiets or stills the contents of the mind: the thoughts, the emotions, the desires, the inner chatter. Successful meditation culminates in the cessation of mental activity, a profound inner stillness. (See Box 3.3.)

Recall that Taoism teaches us to return to a more natural state, a state in which we are not controlled by the artificial modes of thought that have been inculcated into us by our society. The practice of meditation can teach us to control and still those modes of thought. By freeing ourselves from conventional ways of thinking, we return to a more natural state, a more connected and caring state. Some persons are concerned that emptying the mind meditatively could lead to some form of mind control. The truth of the matter is that meditation is more likely to lead to a greater sense of self-control, because most of us stay preoccupied with thoughts of things to do or

BOX 3.3 A GUIDE FOR A SIMPLE MEDITATION

1. Find a quiet, special place in which to meditate.
2. Find a time to practice meditation when the area is quiet and there are no distractions, preferably twice daily. Many persons practice meditation at the beginning of the day and at the end of the day.
3. Try to meditate for a designated period of time during each meditation experience, usually at least 10 min, and preferably 20 min.
4. Sit in a straight-backed chair, keeping the spine as straight as possible.
5. For the designated period of time, practice the following sequence:

a. Sit silently for a few moments and become *aware* of how you are breathing;
b. Gently and gradually begin to breathe more *smoothly*;
c. Now begin to breathe a little more *deeply*, gradually increasing the depth of your breathing;
d. Finally, begin to *slow* down the rate of your breathing;
e. No matter what distractions or thoughts may occur, simply acknowledge them and let them pass, then return to breathing *smoothly*, *deeply*, and *slowly* for the designated period of time.

things left undone. Busy, noisy minds often result in confused and unclear thoughts. We are less likely to be misled or do something we regret if our minds are quiet, strong, and clear.

The relevance of this approach in ethics to criminal justice can be seen in the work of Bo Lozoff, director of the Prison Ashram Project. Lozoff works with prisoners, teaching them techniques of meditation. Lozoff (1987, p. xvii) is "helping prisoners to use their cells as ashrams [places of spiritual growth], and do their time as 'prison monks' rather than convicts." In his book *We're All Doing Time*, Lozoff has a chapter on meditation in which he describes and teaches a number of meditation techniques. Much of his work in prisons involves teaching these techniques to convicts.

Lozoff (1987, p. 29) describes meditation as "sitting perfectly still—silence of body, silence of speech and silence of mind. The Buddha called this 'The Noble Silence.' It's just a matter of STOPPING." To connect this with Taoism, we might say that by achieving a state of inner silence in which we stop all the conventional modes of thinking and reasoning that have been inculcated into us, we return to a more natural state, a more caring state. And from this caring and compassionate state, we can become more mindful of how our inner and outer experiences are connected to those around us, even to our physical environment. This awareness can become a kind of awakening, encouraging us to make more informed and ethical decisions about the way we live our lives.

■ Learn More on the Internet

Go to www.academia.edu/Documents/in/Peacemaking_criminology to see articles related to peacemaking criminology. ■

CONCLUSION

If we choose to develop a greater capacity for the transformative potential of peacemaking through connectedness, care, and mindfulness, it should follow that as persons and criminal justice professionals we will act more morally and ethically (Wozniak, Braswell, Vogel, & Blevins, 2008). In addition, we are more likely to teach offenders such values from the inside out, because we will be living that way ourselves. For peacemaking to work, we have to take it personally first. We have to be grounded in the reality of where we are in terms of criminal justice problems, but at the same time peacemaking encourages us to have a vision of what we can become. Peacemaking offers us a vision of hope grounded in the reality of which we are a part. Gibbs (unpublished paper, p. 2) suggests that "the best strategy for individual peacemakers is to adopt one which emphasizes personal transformation, has a spiritual base, and avoids ideology." Mother Teresa writes, "There can be no peace in the world, including peace in the streets and peace in the home, without peace in our mind. What happens within us, happens outside us. The inner and outer are one" (de Bertodano, 1993, p. 7).

If we choose to try to become peacemakers, it does not necessarily follow that our lives will be less difficult. As Buechner (1973, p. 39) suggests in discussing the teachings of Jesus, "peace seems to have meant not the absence of struggle but the presence of love." Lozoff (1994), who along with his wife, Sita, have dedicated their lives to teaching offenders peacemaking, writes in response to an inmate's letter:

> Life is funny that way. We tend to expect a nice, easy, smooth life as a result of prayer and meditation. But more often than not, our spiritual practice seems to create more problems instead of fewer. And then we often freak out and miss the point entirely.
>
> Pain, separation, misfortune are a part of human life …. Did the martyrs of every religion avoid being tortured for their beliefs? Divine beings, saints and sages have come into this world to show us how to respond to pain, separation, misfortune, and death—not how to escape them. By their example, they have shown us the humility, patience, forgiveness, courage, compassion, and ultimate freedom which are our own divine nature. (p. 5)

Peacemaking acknowledges that while we do not control what life brings us, we do have a choice in how to respond to whatever life brings us. Through connectedness, care, and mindfulness, we can begin to change ourselves first, then others by our example, and finally our system of justice—from the inside out. See Box 3.4.

BOX 3.4 THOUGHTS ON PEACEMAKING

I have decided to stick with love. Hate is too great a burden to bear.

Martin Luther King Jr.

Love cures people—both the ones who give it and the ones who receive it.

Karl Menninger

The love we give away is the only love we keep.

Elbert Hubbard

In all conflict with evil, the method to be used is love and not force. When we use evil methods to defeat evil, it is evil that wins.

Sri Rodhakrishnan

The inner ear of each man's soul hears the voice of life, (find your work, and do it!). Only by obedience to this command can he find peace.

Frank Crane

If you do your work with complete faithfulness … you are making as genuine a contribution to the substance of the universal good as is the most brilliant worker whom the world contains.

Phillips Brooks

The vocation of every man and woman is to serve other people.

Leo Tolstoy

In real love you want the other person's good. In romantic love you want the other person.

Margaret Anderson

Once we learn to touch this peace, we will be healed and transformed. It is not a matter of fact; it is a matter of practice.

Thich Nhat Hanh

He who knows when enough is enough will always have enough.

Lao-tzu

We must be the change we wish to see in the world.

Mahatma Gandhi

Discussion Questions

1. List and discuss the three themes of peacemaking, and explain the impact they have on traditional police or corrections values.
2. In your opinion, can peacemaking, justice, and ethics ever become fully realized? Why or why not?
3. Choose one theme of peacemaking and explain why you think it would have the greater impact on justice and ethics.

Exercise I–1: Your Personal Philosophy

What is your personal/professional philosophy? The most important aspect of our personal and professional growth involves the values and beliefs that we hold dear. Now that you have covered the first three chapters, with which theories and ideas do you agree or disagree? What are your personal values and what beliefs are they based upon? How do you plan to put these values and beliefs into practice in the work environment of your chosen profession?

CASE STUDY 3–1 TO HELP OR NOT TO HELP?

To help or not to help? At 8:15 P.M., a criminal justice professor had just arrived on a flight from Albuquerque, where he had lectured the previous day at the International Academy in Roswell.

After picking up his luggage, the professor exited the airport gate and stood in line with the other passengers who were waiting for the next shuttle bus. A few minutes later, a young couple who appeared to be married arrived and elbowed their way in line, ahead of the professor and others. The professor politely called the matter to their attention, asking them to observe the social principle of "first come, first served." The couple ignored the professor's remark. When the professor repeated his request that they move to the end of the line, the husband became hostile, accusing the professor of being rude. Rather than escalate the conflict, the professor said nothing more. He and the other passengers were tired and the hour was late. When the shuttle finally arrived, everyone got on board and remained silent.

Upon reaching his car, the professor packed his luggage in the trunk and drove toward the parking lot exit. As he approached the exit, he noticed two persons flagging the passing cars for assistance to no avail. Taking a closer look at the two stranded individuals,

the professor was surprised to find that they were the same two persons who had broken into line and the man was the one who had insulted the professor 25 min earlier. Although he was tempted to continue driving, he stopped and after rolling down his window asked the couple what kind of assistance they needed. When they realized who he was, the man and woman were clearly both surprised and embarrassed. They were unable to look the professor in the eye as they explained their predicament. In response, the professor procured a jumper cable from the trunk of his car. Within 5 min he had brought their dead battery back to life. During that time, not a word was spoken. As the couple prepared to drive off, they finally looked at the professor and thanked him. The wife added, "We are sorry."

Questions

1. Would it have been just for the professor to have driven on by the stranded couple, given their previous behavior? Why or why not?
2. Evaluate this incident and the professor's response from utilitarian, deontological, and peacemaking ethical models. Which model fits best?

From a conversation with Professor Sam Souryal, Sam Houston State University.

Exercise I–2: The Ethics of Drug Control Policy

The United States continues to confront a drug crisis. While drug use in the general population seems to be declining, drug use and sales among criminals is continuing to increase. Some citizens are calling for stiffer penalties for illegal drug use, while others are calling for decriminalization, a greater emphasis on treatment, and even legalization of certain drugs, especially those associated with the management of pain. Suppose you were a staff assistant to a congressperson whose committee was investigating the ethics of drug control policy.

1. What issues would be relevant to this assessment?
2. How could a morally correct approach to drug/crime policy be developed?
3. Whose rights would have to be protected?
4. What societal benefits and deficits would you consider?
5. How could this policy be developed in a way that promoted caring and concern for all in society?

■ Learn More on the Internet

Go to www.justicestudies.org for information on an academic and professional organization dedicated to progressive activism, restorative justice and peacemaking.

See www.humankindness.org for information on a nonprofit foundation that focuses on helping prison inmates on their inner journey.

Check out www.peacemakingandcrime.blogspot.com, a website/blog dedicated to cutting-edge issues in peacemaking criminology. ■

NOTES

1. The entire letter can be found in Campbell, J. (1988). *The power of myth* (pp. 32–35). New York: Doubleday.
2. Plato, *Republic*, 351d–352a.
3. This quotation is from the documentary film, *Mother Teresa*, directed by Richard Attenborough.

REFERENCES

Bartollas, C., & Braswell, M. (1993). Correctional treatment, peacemaking, and the new age movement. *Journal of Crime & Justice, 16*, 43–59.

Braswell, M. (1990a). Peacemaking: A missing link in criminology. *The Criminologist, 15*(1), 3–5.

Braswell, M. (1990b). *Journey homeward: Stages along the way*. Chicago: Franciscan Herald Press.

Buechner, F. (1973). *Wishful thinking*. New York: Harper & Row.

Chuang-tzu. (1964). *Basic writings*. New York: Columbia University Press.

Cohen, C. (1971). *Civil disobedience*. New York: Columbia University Press.

de Bertodano, T. (Ed.). (1993). *Daily readings with Mother Teresa*. London: Fount.

Gibbs, J. Spirituality, Ideology, and Personal Transformation: Some Considerations for Peacemaking, unpublished paper.

Lao-tzu. (1963). *The way of Lao-tzu (Tao Te Ching)*. Indianapolis: Bobbs-Merrill.

Lozoff, B. (1987). *We're all doing time*. Durham: Human Kindness Foundation.

Lozoff, B. (1994). Letters. *Human Kindness Foundation Newsletter, 5*.

Lozoff, B., & Braswell, M. (1989). *Inner corrections: Finding peace and peace making*. Cincinnati: Anderson.

Martin, R. (1993). Transpersonal psychology and criminological theory: Rethinking the paradigm. *Journal of Crime & Justice, 16*, 43–59.

Myers, L., & Chiang, C. (1993). Law enforcement officer and peace officer: Reconciliation using the feminine approach. *Journal of Crime & Justice, 16*, 31–43.

Noddings, N. (1986). *Caring: A feminine approach to ethics and moral education*. Berkeley: University of California Press.

Palmer, P. (1983). *To know as we are known*. San Francisco: Harper & Row.

Quinney, R. (1993). A life of crime: Criminology and public policy and peacemaking. *Journal of Crime & Justice, 16,* 3–11.

Reps, P. (Ed.). (1919). *Zen flesh, Zen bones: A collection of Zen and pre-Zen writings.* Garden City: Doubleday.

Safransky, S. (Ed.). (1990). *Sunbeams: A book of quotations.* Berkeley: North Atlantic Books.

Wozniak, J., Braswell, M., Vogel, R., & Blevins, K. (2008). *Transformative justice.* Lanham: Lexington Books.

Ethical Issues in Policing

Man becomes great exactly in the degree in which he works for the welfare of his fellow man.

Mahatma Gandhi

Police work has been called a "morally dangerous" endeavor, and with good reason. Not only are the temptations faced by the average patrol officer much greater than those confronted in other occupations, but the nature of the work itself also requires activities that can easily cross over the line from acceptable to unethical conduct.

Police corruption is a broad area of concern. For some observers, it includes everything from the simple acceptance of a free meal from a small business owner to the receipt of kickbacks from attorneys and tow truck drivers or even police-organized theft.

Many of the problems of police corruption are linked to the tremendous amount of discretion possessed by the patrol officer. Most of us would agree that it is sometimes acceptable to use this discretion to avoid giving a ticket or making an arrest. When good judgment determines that no action is necessary or there are other means of addressing the problem, discretion is clearly being put to good use. But when these officers are influenced by offers of money, drugs, or sexual favors, the use of discretion becomes tainted and the actions corrupt.

Situations confronting police officers offer temptations of their own. The money found on a drunk, the cash and drugs found at the scene of a crime—these can tempt officers who are on their honor to report what they find. In the area of narcotics control, such temptations are always present.

There are still other dilemmas confronting the police officer who does not give in to the temptations of corruption. In many ways, crime control efforts foster an "ends justify the means" mentality. To the extent that due process guarantees are seen as somehow interfering with crime control efforts, attempts to work around these "technicalities" come to be viewed as justified. This is especially true in regard to the control of vice and narcotics activities, where proactive and deceptive methods, such as sting operations and undercover work, are routine.

In many ways, police officers must walk a fine line. Overzealousness and the use of unnecessary force are undesirable, but so is a reluctance to intervene or to back up another officer when the situation requires it. When officers use patrol time to avoid their responsibilities rather than to execute them, the professional image of the entire department suffers.

To avoid corruption, police departments must attempt to recruit and hire honorable men and women. These people must be educated and trained to deal with whatever problems they confront. There is also a need for the police organization to take steps to keep standards high. These efforts include the development of explicit policies covering a variety of potentially corrupting situations and the implementation of active internal affairs units. Perhaps more important, however, is the creation of an organizational climate that fosters candid and open public examination of police practices and a responsiveness to line officers and the dilemmas they confront.

CHAPTER 4

Learning Police Ethics

Steven J. Ellwanger

KEY CONCEPTS

apologia	militarism	values-learned
black swans	noble cause	perspective
contingencies	occupational	value-predisposition
instrumental value	predisposition	perspective
latent content	socialization model	
manifest content	terminal value	

One of the most defining characteristics of the police occupation is the potential use of coercive force to impose the will of the state, especially deadly force (Bittner, 1970). Another defining yet less well understood characteristic is ethics. Just as medicine, law, engineering, or other professions are characterized by ethics that guide individual and group behavior, policing as an occupation contains its own values and value systems that provide a basis by which individual behaviors and attitudes can be measured. In contrast to other professions, however, learning ethics in policing is not entirely the product of education, socialization, and training. In fact, learning often predates formal education and socialization efforts as a result of individual, social, and historical factors. In addition, the process of on-the-job police socialization and culturalization may both (in)advertently threaten the positive ethical ideals and values brought to the police profession by new recruits where a strong and pervasive deviant subculture passively or actively teaches unethical behaviors.

Ethics in policing bears directly on issues of reform, control, and legitimacy of law enforcement institutions in a democratic society that is presenting new challenges as a result of emerging police paradigms, changing social sentiments, and recent domestic terrorist attacks. The first step in meeting these challenges is to better understand the sources and content of police ethics so that administrators, citizens, legislatures, and the courts can more effectively control police behavior. This chapter attempts to do just this by first identifying and discussing the various frameworks for understanding the sources of police ethics, followed by the identification of several occupational ethics that run the risk of violating legal, organizational, and societal standards. The chapter then concludes with a brief discussion of the various aspects of ethical transformations and implications that police ethics hold for reform, control, and legitimacy in contemporary society.

VALUES, VALUE SYSTEMS, AND POLICE ETHICS

Policing as an occupation is argued to be characterized by a distinct subculture (Crank, 2004; Van Maanen, 1974). The term *"culture"* is often used to describe differences among beliefs, laws, morals, customs and other characteristics that set large groups apart. Sometimes there can be cultural differences among people, however, who form a single culture or group. In such an instance, this unique group within the larger social group is referred to as a *subculture*. The primary distinction between cultures and subcultures is that while sharing many of the values and beliefs of the larger culture, the subculture shares values and beliefs that set them apart from the larger culture in which they exist (Kappeler, Sluder, & Alpert, 2005).

When considering individual behavior within the subculture of policing, it is often useful to consider the values embraced and transmitted among its members. In fact, Rokeach (1973) argued that individual or group norms and behaviors can often be attributed to particular patterns of adherence to universal value orientations. A *value*, as defined by Rokeach, is "an enduring belief that a specific mode of conduct or end-state of existence is personally or socially preferable" (Rokeach, 1973, p. 5). Thus, values can be distinguished by the extent to which they prescribe a specific mode of conduct, or the extent to which they prescribe a socially preferable end-state. A value that identifies a socially preferable end-state is a **terminal value**, while a value that represents the preferred means to achieve that state is an **instrumental value** (Rokeach, 1973; Zhao, He, & Lovrich, 1998).

Values, Rokeach continued, could be arranged into a *value system*. Rokeach defined a value system as "an enduring organization of beliefs concerning preferable modes of conduct or end-states of existence along a continuum of relative importance" (Rokeach, 1973, p. 5). In addition, Rokeach contended that the total number of values of primary interest to people was relatively limited. It is these value systems that identify preferable end-states and modes of conduct that provide a basis for human decision-making by providing a socially approved standard by which one can compare their actions and decisions.

VALUE-PREDISPOSITION

There are two competing views that seek to explain the source of police ethics: learned and imported. Most students of policing are quick to point to the forging of the "police personality" resulting from the influence of Basic Training Instructors, Field Training Officers (FTO), and impersonal bureaucratic organization that shape the new recruit during their first few years. A competing—yet related—view argues for the existence of an **occupational predisposition**. Persons possessing certain traits and personality characteristics are attracted or "predisposed" to the profession of policing. In other words, policing is just one of many occupations from which individuals choose. Those with a police occupational predisposition are attracted to careers in law enforcement, while those with other personality traits and characteristics chose alternative occupations (Alpert & Dunham, 1997; Rokeach, Miller, & Snyder, 1971).

Chief among these traits and characteristics is a *value-predisposition*. This value-predisposition perspective argues that individuals bring with them an identifiable set of broader societal values into the organization. Personnel selection techniques may actively screen for these values, while the process of professionalization and/or culturalization reinforces some, and modifies and/or replaces others during the officer's career. These values ultimately find expression in officer behaviors and attitudes, or ethics. In fact, Pollock (1998) makes the distinction between morals and ethics that is useful in distinguishing between the sources that guide behaviors in both one's personal and professional life. She notes that in contrast to morals that are the sum of a person's actions in every sphere of life, ethics are behaviors that are related to an individual's profession. Police ethics are then behaviors and attitudes of police officers that find expression while acting "under the color of law." If one adopts this value-predisposition model and subscribes to this definition of ethics, several value-predispositions and their sources come to mind.

Conservatism and Conformity

One of the primary goals of police personnel systems is to identify and retain individuals who are conservative—when compared to society as a whole—and conformist. In fact, Wilson (1968) first observed that Chicago police officers tended to be unreceptive to change, while Bayley and Mendelsohn (1969) noted that the Denver police tended to be more conservative and more Republican than the community as a whole, and that age is not related to political orientation. This latter finding suggests that it is the initial selection of officers rather than their socialization that explains this tendency toward conservatism.

The literature seems to suggest that police work tends to attract local and family oriented individuals, who economically tend to be blue-collar, and are from the working class (Niederhoffer, 1967). Individuals who are attracted to police work are also inclined to espouse "old-fashioned" values. They tend to see the world in black or white while overlooking the fact that the outcomes of many decisions often involve value tradeoffs. Furthermore, these individuals generally possess military experience and come from families with a history in law enforcement (Caldero & Crank, 2011). Finally, such persons generally perceive police work to be socially significant. They view police work as having a point, weight, interest, and impact on the lives and well-being of other people (Van Maanen, 1974).

This tendency toward political and practical conservatism is reinforced and perpetuated by police personnel selection systems that place a premium on conformity to middle-class values. In fact, police selection practices, such as the use of physical agility tests, background investigations, polygraph examinations, psychological tests, and oral interviews are all tools used to screen out applicants who have not demonstrated conformity to middle-class values (Gaines & Kappeler, 2011). Many of these selection techniques often have little to do with actual police work, and more to do with assessing an applicant's "adequacy" to be a moral agent of the state. In fact, Kappeler et al. (2005) note that these techniques are designed more to determine an applicant's physical prowess, sexual orientation, gender identification, financial stability, employment history, and abstinence from drug and alcohol use, rather than to determine their ability to perform the real functions and duties associated with police work (p. 285).

Noble Cause, Efficiency, and Utilitarianism

In addition to this relative conservatism and conformity among those with an occupational predisposition toward policing, there is also a commitment to the **noble cause**. The noble cause is a moral commitment by police officers to make the world a safer place in which to live (Caldero & Crank, 2011). According to Caldero and Crank (2011), it is this moral predisposition that attracts people to the occupation of policing, while those who join but are not committed to the "noble cause" are quickly liberated from the organization (Conti & Nolan, 2005). The source of this value-predisposition can be traced to enduring societal values.

> **Noble Cause:** A moral predisposition by those seeking careers in law enforcement to make the world a safer place in which to live.

A long-standing but now debunked myth is that police neutrally and even-handedly implement the law (Bayley & Bittner, 1984; Bittner, 1970; Lipsky, 1980). The reality is that police exercise an enormous amount of discretion, and values shape behavior in the absence of objective standards by which behavior can measured. An enduring social value that is imported into the occupation is one that has historically evaluated individual and group police performance based on the crime control mandate (Manning, 1997). Society expects police to "control" crime. Unfortunately, the emphasis on the "ends" of catching criminals may often come at a cost to the institution's "duty" to protect the sanctity of the law (Pollock, 2005). In other words, police behaviors were often considered to be ethical if they achieved the desired end of getting the bad guy off the streets—even if this meant compromising individual civil liberties in the process.

The "ends justify the means" value system is reinforced by other imported American values as well. Specifically, police, like American citizens in general, tend to favor the underdog (or the victim in this instance), emphasize that no one stands above the law (Caldero & Crank, 2011), and often emphasize efficiency (for its perceived neutrality) at the cost of other values, such as effectiveness, equity, and responsiveness (Ford & Morash, 2002; Giacomazzi & McGarrell, 2002; Kettl, 1998, pp. 407–428; Manning, 1997, p. 31). Efficiency as the criterion by which police performance has traditionally been measured has been rationalized by the concept *utilitarianism*. In other words, ethical police behavior is that behavior that leads to the realization of the "greatest good for the greatest number." The greatest good for the greatest number has often come to mean under the professional paradigm of policing that efficiency (crime control) was *primus inter pares* ("first among equals") among competing values, such as equity in due process (individual rights) (Caldero & Crank, 2011; Packer, 1968) and responsiveness in police services (Cordner, 1997).

Crime Fighting

Related to efficiency in crime control is an individual's commitment to the role of "crime fighter." Several theoretical frameworks have been offered by police scholars to distinguish the various roles that police adopt in the performance of their duties (Broderick, 1977; Coates, 1972; Muir, 1977; White, 1972). Although these popular frameworks have yet to yield empirical support (Hochstedler, 1981), they are useful in organizing thoughts and comparing popular notions of various police roles. Consistent among these frameworks is the ideal of police as "crime fighters." Police do more, however, than question suspicious persons, make arrests, collect evidence, and conduct interviews. In fact, police often fulfill a "social worker" (or "human services") role, and some empirical evidence suggests that this is the role that occupies the majority of an officer's time (Frank, Brandl, & Watkins, 1997; Wilson, 1968). Police often spend more time acting as brokers who connect citizens with valuable community resources, assist stranded motorists, provide directions, resolve family and neighbor disputes, and help citizens in other important ways. Yet many new recruits come to policing with a "Dirty Harry" conception of police work, while older more experienced officers tend to emphasize this crime fighter role because it yields the greatest social rewards (Kraska & Kappeler, 1997; Manning, 1996, 1997).

WHERE DO POLICE VALUES COME FROM?

Historical, Cultural, and Economic

According to the predisposition model, ethics in police work are the product of values that are imported (or brought from the larger society) into the organization. They are enduring social values that are actively screened for during the recruitment and selection processes of police personnel systems, with conservatism and conformity being the product of individual and family life experiences. They are also the product of one's socio-economic status, and commitment to "old-fashioned" values that view reality as an objective truth with no shades of gray, while seeing efficiency as a neutral and desirable goal of individual and group actions.

The sources of individual officers' commitment to get the "bad guy" off the street not only comes from previous life and family experience, but also long-standing American values that have favored the underdog with psychological roots grounded in the idea that anyone can achieve the American Dream if they just work hard enough (Messner & Rosenfeld, 2001). Values-predisposition is also the product of the perceived legitimacy of the law resulting from a democratic process and the perceived neutrality of its application ("all are equal under the law"). The reality is, however, that even the most open and democratic processes run the risk of becoming unduly influenced by either a majority or minority group who may choose to distort the "will of the people" (Green & Shapiro, 1994; Hummel, 1994; Mastrofski, 1988; Stone, 2002). Similarly, the myth of neutral application of the law has long been debunked as institutional and extralegal factors have been shown to determine how and when the law is applied (Klockars, 1988; Mastrofski, 1988; Spears & Spohn, 1997).

Social

Popular media depictions along with societal expectations may determine not only who will be attracted to the police occupation, but also influence who will be deemed qualified for employment. The occupational predisposition perspective argues that individuals with certain traits or characteristics will be attracted to the profession. Much of this attraction is socially constructed—often inaccurately—by images of police in the media. The popular conception of police portrayed in the media is that policing is primarily about "fighting crime."

Despite the various roles played by police and the importance of the social services role in occupying an officer's time, that of crime fighter and "super-cop" are the dominant images portrayed by the media (Manning, 1996). These images misrepresent the actuality of police work, most of which is more mundane and tedious. The media also conveys images of officers with nearly "super human" abilities capable of deducing criminals and their motivations using highly complex and sophisticated forensic approaches. The reality is that in most crimes the criminal is "known" to the complainant or to the police at the time the crime initially comes to the attention of law enforcement (Reiss & Bordua, 1967, p. 43). These images not only reinforce the crime-fighter role to attract individuals with such an orientation, but have implications for the organization of police and the provision of their services.

Crime-fighter images portraying individuals possessing nearly super-human abilities attracts those persons to the profession whose view of police work is congruent with the dominant media image, while the police institution in turn reacts to the media's depictions (Manning, 1996). For example, police are now feeling increased pressure from juries, the public, and victims to quickly provide "forensic" evidence to secure a conviction where testimony would have previously sufficed as a result of popular shows such as *Crime Scene Investigation*. Shows such as these shape the public's perception of the relationship between police and the criminal justice system. In response, agencies are specializing—creating crime labs and/or specialized investigative units—and relying on reactive forms of policing (science and technology) to control crime (Ferguson, 2012; Kraska & Kappeler, 1997). Equally important is the potential impact that the media has on the police institution with respect to ensuring due process protection for citizens.

Of particular relevance are those images depicting officers using "dirty means" to achieve good ends like those popularized in *Dirty Harry* movies. Movies such as these were a response to widespread societal sentiments that the police had become "handcuffed" by the Warren Court through such landmark cases as *Mapp v. Ohio* (1961) and *Miranda v. Arizona* (1966). As a result, the media and society both influence which types of individuals will find policing to be a desirable occupation while simultaneously shaping the police agency's response to these images. The result is that agencies may feel pressure to actively recruit and screen for both those who adopt a predominately crime-fighter orientation and who view efficiency rather than ensuring due process protections as the dominant value to be pursued in police work (Caldero & Crank, 2011; Manning, 1997; Pollock, 1998).

As the occupation of policing has become more professionalized through education requirements demanding two- or four-year degrees, individuals entering law enforcement occupations are increasingly exposed to courses, such as criminal justice ethics that have the potential to transmit positive police values. Although the probability of exposure to ethics in policing is greater in some academic programs than others, curricula in most programs do not *require* such training. As a result, exposure to police ethics is most likely to occur informally—if at all—in introductory policing courses. In addition, many policing courses are taught by part-time faculty who usually work, or have worked, in law enforcement (Caldero & Crank, 2011).

Ethics taught by these instructors usually occur through real world examples, which may, on occasion, tend to reinforce the crime control model and its emphasis on efficiency at the cost of other important values, such as protecting individual rights. Because most students interested in law enforcement may already be predisposed to the moral mandate of policing (to make the world a safer place), they may not recognize this value tradeoff. Fighting crime and protecting individual rights can be a difficult balance to maintain. Should instructors be critical of the institution, students who are morally predisposed toward the noble cause may misinterpret that to mean the professor is anti-police (Caldero & Crank, 2011).

VALUES-LEARNED PERSPECTIVE: SOCIALIZATION AND CULTURALIZATION

A competing perspective to the source of police values argues that police values are not imported from society at large, but are instead learned on the job. This **values-learned perspective** argues that police values are learned through the process of socialization and culturalization within a particular police agency. Although these two frameworks are analytically distinct, in practice they are related (see Figure 4.1).

The **socialization model** of police ethics argues that norms and values are learned through the process of *professionalization*. In this regard, police are no different than other professionals such as physicians and lawyers who learn their ethics through training and practice (Alpert & Dunham, 1997; Gaines & Kappeler, 2011; Kappeler et al., 2005). The process of organizational socialization seeks to "fuse" the officer to the organization by providing them with a set of rules, perspectives, prescriptions, techniques, and tools necessary to participate in the organization (Van Maanen, 1974). In a sense, this socialization process seeks to create a "working personality" or "police personality" within the new recruit as they experience distinct occupational phases during their career: choice, introduction, encounter, and metamorphosis (see Figure 4.2).

Choice

As stated previously, although the values-learned perspective is analytically distinct from the **value-predisposition perspective**, in practice, there is much overlap and it is at this stage where most of that overlap occurs. This value-learned perspective does not deny that police work attracts individuals with certain traits and characteristics. It further elaborates, however, on the role that police personnel selection systems share with shaping an individual's

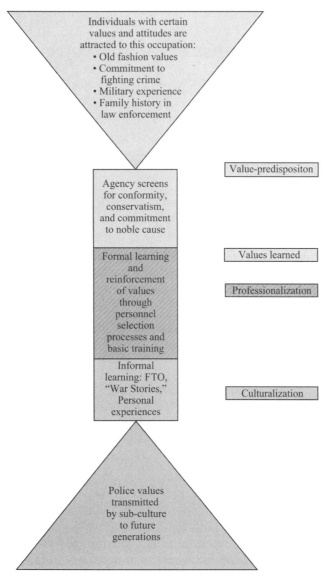

FIGURE 4.1

Analytic relationship between value-predisposition and values-learned perspectives.

value system. To a large extent, individuals choose the occupation for what the profession is perceived to offer.

Perhaps the most important virtue of the occupation for those selecting police work is the perceived "meaningfulness" of the work. In contrast to occupations that exist to generate a net profit (like a stock broker, banker, or salesperson), police work offers the promise of providing a net social benefit. Individuals

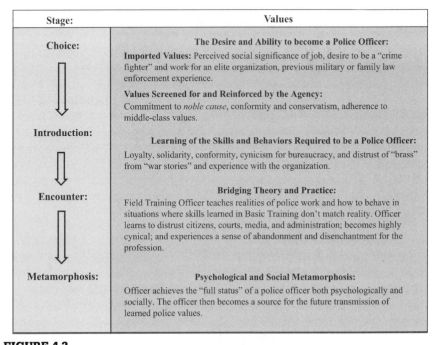

Stage:	Values
Choice:	**The Desire and Ability to become a Police Officer:** **Imported Values:** Perceived social significance of job, desire to be a "crime fighter" and work for an elite organization, previous military or family law enforcement experience. **Values Screened for and Reinforced by the Agency:** Commitment to *noble cause*, conformity and conservatism, adherence to middle-class values.
Introduction:	**Learning of the Skills and Behaviors Required to be a Police Officer:** Loyalty, solidarity, conformity, cynicism for bureaucracy, and distrust of "brass" from "war stories" and experience with the organization.
Encounter:	**Bridging Theory and Practice:** Field Training Officer teaches realities of police work and how to behave in situations where skills learned in Basic Training don't match reality. Officer learns to distrust citizens, courts, media, and administration; becomes highly cynical; and experiences a sense of abandonment and disenchantment for the profession.
Metamorphosis:	**Psychological and Social Metamorphosis:** Officer achieves the "full status" of a police officer both psychologically and socially. The officer then becomes a source for the future transmission of learned police values.

FIGURE 4.2
Occupational stages and values learned.

are often attracted to policing because they believe that the work has a positive impact on the lives and well-being of others. These characteristics of police work are also buttressed by job security and the relatively high salary with respect to the education requirements.

The value-predisposition perspective would stop here without acknowledging the role of the organization in shaping officer ethics. The values-learned perspective goes further, however, exploring and examining how the police are socialized by the profession itself to act and behave in a manner that allows them to *continue* their participation in the organization. This process of forging the "working personality" begins when an individual makes a decision to join the organization. It does so by first using a rigorous and protracted selection process. This process not only ensures a homogeneous group of individuals possessing middle-class values, but also has the effect of creating a sense among the new recruits that the organization is "elite."

Introduction

The optimism and uncritical view held by the recruit of the agency and police work soon begins to fade as the process of professionalization continues during basic training. This is where the novice officer begins to learn what police work is "really like." Aside from the technical and mechanical aspects that dominate police recruit training, such as instruction in firearms usage, driving, first aid, self-defense, and other use of force tactics, the new recruit begins to experience subtle shifts in values and attitudes during this phase of his or her career. In fact, prior to this socialization process, the recruit is said to be at his or her ethical zenith—having entered the profession with high ideals and positive values. Yet it is during basic training that the "rookie" begins to adopt negative values that are in conflict with a number of legal standards and core societal values (Conti & Nolan, 2005). The once positive view of the agency held by the new recruit is quickly challenged as they learn that the bureaucracy in which they now work is highly formal, mechanical, and often times arbitrary. The new recruit quickly learns that it is in their best interest to remain "under the radar," or become "invisible," and that group solidarity and loyalty are necessary to protect oneself from a hostile public and administration (Crank, 2004).

Informal and formal instruction during this phase also shapes the recruit's views on ethical behavior. Formally, recruits are introduced to police work through veteran officers and outside experts who provide instruction aimed at satisfying criminal and procedural minima to reduce exposure to civil liability (Buerger, 1998). Informal learning occurs primarily through the use of "war stories," and it is this type of learning that has the greatest potential to generate unethical behavior. *War stories* are narratives presented to an academy class that describe a particular incident or circumstance (Ford, 2003). These narratives are meant to provide direction to officers by giving them "guidance as to how officers should experience the world if they are to act as police officers within it." War stories often contain two sources of content: manifest and latent.

The "overt or obvious message of the story" is referred to as **manifest content**, while the **latent content** is the covert message of story-or "the message beneath the message" (Ford, 2003). Not all war stories contain latent content and some instructors inadvertently or unknowingly send a message they do not realize is being sent. The latent content of some stories may contradict the primary message of instruction. Such messages are referred to as **black swans**. For example, Buerger (1998) cites the following anonymous quotation from police trainers illustrating how war stories often contradict the primary message of instruction:

> …we're just spouting the official line on everything, all the while strongly suggesting that it was all bullshit and that we would learn the real stuff out on the street—'ya know, we can't tell you to slap the shit out of those punk gang-bangers back in the alley here, but don't worry about that, you'll learn soon enough

Although all "war stories" don't necessarily send messages that contradict social, legal, and societal standards, many still have the potential to transmit negative values and attitudes that threaten to erode positive ones. For example, in his analysis of 269 "war stories" Ford (2003) notes that the manifest and latent content of the majority of these stories contained useful messages that taught recruits street skills, while emphasizing the danger and uncertainty surrounding the occupation. There were, however, other stories that contained content ranging from ways to obtain "freebies," meet women while on duty, and to sleep and shirk duties. In addition, several of these stories contained justifications for using excessive force, such as "just hit the brakes and have the big mouth get waffled on the screen" (p. 92).

It is also during this stage that common experiences shared among police officers are learned and eventually come to serve as perceptual shorthand to identify potentially dangerous subjects. According to Skolnick (1994), police routinely encounter particular signs, such as how a person is dressed (suggesting gang affiliation), their gait (suggesting they may be carrying a weapon), their talk (lack of respect), that indicate that a person is potentially dangerous. This cluster of signs becomes a *"symbolic assailant"* that raises suspicion among police and helps them identify potentially dangerous individuals. These assailants are further refined and typically take on characteristics of marginalized segments of society and reflect populations police are directed to control (Kappeler et al., 2005; Skolnick, 1994). For example, historically, police have associated being black and male with beliefs about criminality and dangerousness, which has led to "over-policing" in the form of excessive stops (e.g., driving while black), lengthy detentions under questionable circumstances, and excessive force to achieve arrests, crime prevention, or apprehension of suspects (Jones-Brown, 2007).

Encounter

The previous stages of the police socialization process set the stage for a fundamental shift in values, rather than the fine tuning of existing ones. In fact, it is here that the popular images constructed of police by the media, the core American values, and the lofty ideals of police practice professed in basic training are transformed and replaced by distinct police subculture values. The primary mode of value transmission is through the FTO who enjoys the privilege of evaluating the rookie's job performance and ultimately making a recommendation regarding their continued employment at the end of their probationary period.

An FTO is a veteran officer who has been patrolling for several years. The FTO is the primary mechanism by which recruits learn how to perform "real" police work. In fact, the new recruit quickly learns that much of what is learned in the academy does not readily translate into practice on the street, and that the police subculture exists to protect itself from hostile and unsympathetic groups. As a result, the first thing that is often told to the new recruit by the FTO is to "forget what you learned in the academy."

This instruction by the FTO is often reinforced when many of the "war stories" told during basic training actually come to life and the new recruit discovers that there often exists a difference between the theory (as taught in basic training) and practice (as experienced on the street) of policing. For example, Van Maanen (1974) recounts one officer's experience with attempting to explain the law to a citizen regarding speeding:

> ...Keith was always telling me to be forceful, to not back down, and to never try and explain the law or what we are doing to a civilian. I didn't really know what he was talking about until I tried to tell some kid why we have laws about speeding. Well, the more I tried to tell him about traffic safety, the angrier he got. I was lucky to just get his John Hancock on the citation. When I came back to the patrol car, Keith explained to me just where I'd gone wrong. You really can't talk to those people out there, they just won't listen to reason.

Since some of the lessons learned from the recruit's basic training experiences fail to readily translate into practice, the FTO becomes the primary mechanism by which the new recruit learns which type of behavior is appropriate for different situations.

The FTO also redefines the image of police work held by the new recruit. In fact, the FTO imparts to the new recruit that much of police work is mundane and that only a few calls constitute "real police work." "Hot calls," as they are known, are those calls for service that present a threat of bodily harm to the officer or their partners. How the officer responds to those calls—demonstrating a (un)willingness to put oneself in harm's way—often become the basis by which the FTO evaluates the rookie for retention. To do so means that the rookie is not afraid to use force, protect other officers, and remain loyal (Van Maanen, 1974). Solidarity is also tested by assessing the extent that the new recruit will support or ignore behaviors that run counter to department policy (e.g., conducting personal business while on duty or accepting gratuities). Recruits unwilling to participate—or at the very least ignore—such behaviors quickly find themselves isolated within the police subculture (Caldero & Crank, 2011; Kappeler et al., 2005).

It is also during this phase that the new recruit learns that the legal system tends to be "soft" on crime. In fact, the new recruit concludes that the legal system is soft on crime when "bad guys get off on a technicality" or prosecutors decide that a case lacks merit or is better adjudicated with a plea deal. In response, new recruits are taught to manipulate and leverage the law to get the bad guy off the streets. As a result, the new recruit is encouraged to engage in several legal violations: such as to "testily" (giving false testimony), dropsy (removing drugs from a suspect during a pat-down and then discovering them in plain sight on the ground), the shake (similar to dropsy, only conducted during a vehicle stop), or stiffing in a call (calling and reporting a crime as if they were a citizen who had witnessed it) (Caldero & Crank, 2011). Finally, because the legal system is perceived to be soft and slow, the recruit learns that deterrence can only be achieved through the immediate exercise of coercion in the field. This "street justice" includes not only the legal abuses described above, but also psychological abuses, such as the use of racial epithets and intimidation, or physical abuses, such as administering the "third degree."

Metamorphosis

The final stage of the recruit's occupational career is metamorphosis. This is where the "rookie" morphs both socially and psychologically into a full-fledged officer. This transition in social status and occupational self-identity occurs at the end of the probationary period when the recruit is assigned a position free of institutional dependency and where their responsibility is more or less equalized with respect to other officers (Van Maanen, 1974). It is during this stage that the officer adopts the self-conception of "cop" that is, in part, the product of the cynicism, sense of abandonment, and ultimately disenchantment the recruit now has for the occupation as a result of the realization that police work is mundane, that the bureaucracy is impersonal and arbitrary, that the public and police administrators are often hostile and unappreciative, and that the legal system is soft, slow, and more concerned about conviction rates and managing correctional populations than helping police get the bad guys off the street.

What emerges from the socialization process is a relatively consistent set of values that are continually transmitted and reinforced among the police subculture through the process of *culturalization*. Whether or not the new recruit accepts these subcultural values is, in part, determined by the extent to which individual and organizational factors are able to counteract the influences and tendencies of a corrupt and deviant subculture. The content of values transmitted and embraced by this subculture that may contribute to unethical behavior include those governing the use of force, time, group loyalty, fringe benefits, justice, and discretion (see also Sherman, 1982).

THE CONTENT OF POLICE VALUES

Force: *Use of force should not be viewed as a last resort for controlling a situation. In fact, the use of force is necessary to achieve deterrence, convey group loyalty, and achieve some measure of justice.* Instead of being an act of last resort for controlling a situation (Fyfe, 2005; Manning, 1997), force is extolled among the police subculture for its ability to signal to the public that it is not weak, as well as conveying to other officers that he or she can be counted on should one become a victim of a violent encounter. As such, force conveys loyalty to the group while providing a measure of deterrence for those who may consider future attacks against the police. Force also acts as a crime deterrent for its immediate and concrete properties where the legal system is viewed by police to operate on the threat of punishment.

Time: *An officer can never respond too quickly to a call for "real" police services, nor can they respond too slowly to a "garbage" call. When not responding to calls for service, an officer's time is their own.* Given the complexity of police work and the difficulty in maintaining direct supervision, officers enjoy considerable latitude in defining their work. The consequence of this is that some officers relegate certain calls for service to the status of "garbage"— those that usually relate to the social work or order maintenance roles— because they do not conform to their conception of what constitutes "real" police work as depicted in the media and reinforced by their FTO and basic training instructors. Those calls for service related to the "crime fighter" role (e.g. a robbery in progress) are elevated to a much higher status because they afford the greatest opportunity for social rewards from the public, administrators, and other officers. When not responding to calls for service, an officer's time is their own and they should not be required to engage in proactive forms of policing.

Loyalty: *Don't trust anyone except your fellow officer; not the public, "brass," or the media. Group loyalty provides protection from the real dangers of police work, from a hostile and unsympathetic administration, and serves to provide emotional support for performing a difficult task.* Officers often feel socially rejected by a public that once inspired them to join the occupation. They learn that even the most seemingly innocuous events and persons may pose a problem for an officer later (e.g., a female motorist smiling and flirting with a male officer while issuing a ticket, only to later file a complaint). The officer also learns that the "brass" is more concerned about reducing their exposure to civil liability, managing the department's public image, and satisfying other organizational demands, than helping officers get the bad guys off the street. In a world filled with adversarial and unsympathetic groups, police learn that unbending loyalty is essential for the group's survival. This loyalty comes in the form of physical (use of force when necessary to protect other officers and the institution), legal (fabricating evidence, corroborating false testimony, etc.), and emotional support. Officers who do not provide unconditional loyalty quickly find themselves isolated within the police subculture.

Fringe benefits: *Police perform a difficult task, one that is dangerous and requires that they deal with society's "social garbage." Given the dangerousness of the occupation and the clientele with which they often interact, police are underpaid. The corollary is that any rewards extended for their service or in appreciation are a form of deserved and appropriate compensation.* Departments generally prohibit the acceptance of gratuities. Although citizens and merchants may wish to extend a gratuity to officers in the form of a discount or free cup of coffee as a gesture of appreciation, organizational policy generally prohibits their acceptance. The rational for such policies is that acceptance may result in the selective enforcement of the law and/or differential responses to calls for service. Despite these potential problems, gratuities are seen by officers as a form of just compensation for doing a difficult job that is otherwise woefully under compensated.

Justice: *The legal system is untrustworthy. As a result, justice is sometimes best served on the street based on personal rather than legal considerations.* Due process protections are often at odds with the crime control mandate of police. At the very least, these protections postpone and prescribe punishment in accordance with state statute. A cops' conception of justice is more personal and immediate. To them, it is the concrete exercise of coercion to control situations and individuals. Police generally resist making an arrest for misdemeanor public order offenses if another strategy can resolve the problem. If, however, a suspect is guilty of not being deferential and mutually respectful to an officer (Contempt of Cop) an arrest may be desirable for its ability to mete out immediate and concrete justice. This "distributive justice" is different than "legal justice." Distributive justice is about the officer's personal opinion that the individual deserves punishment, rather than legal standards. Many times officers are aware that arrests under such circumstances will not be carried forward by the prosecutors to achieve legal justice, so they may make an arrest based on false charges. At the very least, officers recognize that the arrest—even if charges are not formally filed by the prosecutor—is itself punishment. The social stigma associated with arrest, lost time from work, and legal expenses borne by the citizen are all forms of punishment regardless of the legal system's response (Feeley, 1992).

Discretion: *Enforcement of the law, except in the most serious instances, should not be based only on what the law says but also on individual characteristics.* Whether to enforce or not enforce the law is as much about legal considerations as it is about the characteristics of the individual suspect. Age, race, socioeconomic status, gender, relationship to the victim, and suspect demeanor are all extralegal factors that determine how and when the law is applied. The young, poor, minorities who do not share a close relationship with the victim and who are disrespectful to police, are more likely to experience full enforcement of the law than other citizens.

MORAL CAREER

Although the prevalence and strength of these questionable values are not as widespread and strong today as in the past, how officers react to these can be described as an officer's *moral career*. The moral career, as described by Sherman (1982), consists of distinct aspects that threaten to move officers from the pinnacle of positive values that drove their desire to protect persons, property, and constitutional rights in an impartial and exemplary manner, to the adoption of behaviors that are contrary to department, legal, and societal standards. The stages of an individual's moral career identified by Sherman are illustrated in Table 4.1.

The working environments experienced by officers contain a variety of factors that may encourage or discourage the adoption of unethical behaviors. Some of these **contingencies** may include things like levels of supervision and oversight experienced by officers and the type of work. Levels of supervision and type of work (e.g., patrol versus vice crime) may create opportunity and temptations to engage in certain types of unethical behavior. For example, all things being equal, those experiencing low levels of supervision or working vice crimes are more likely than others to have unethical behavior go undetected, while experiencing more opportunity and temptation to engage in misconduct (e.g., stealing).

The road to becoming a corrupt or "bent" police officer is also riddled with *moral experiences* that challenge an officer's existing morality. For example, a moral experience will likely arise when an officer witnesses another officer violate department or legal standards. Violation of these standards may run counter to values held by an ethical officer. In these instances, officers will have to make a choice as to whether they should allow or participate in such behavior, or challenge or escape them through employment termination or transfer. A moral experience often leads to the adoption of unethical behavior when it is accompanied by some rationalization.

Apologia is a situationally justified rationalization that reduces the psychological pain experienced by those who engage in behaviors that are not congruent with their ethical values and sense of responsibility. The only way then for the individual to continue the behavior is to provide a rationalization. For example, an officer may steal something from the site of a burglary and justify that behavior by convincing him or herself that "no one really gets hurt"

Table 4.1 Aspects and Environment of an Officer's Moral Career

Aspect	Experience
Contingencies	Factors experienced by the officer within his or her working environment that encourage or discourage unethical behavior.
Moral experiences	Particular experience by officers that challenge their existing morality, or allow for the interpretation of others' morality based on behavior.
Apologia	Situational justification of unethical behavior.
Stages	"Slippery slope" progression of unethical behavior.

because the item is covered by the insurance company. Other rationalizations may include convincing themselves that they deserve such rewards because of the dangerousness or nature of their work.

The final aspect of an individual's moral career, identified by Sherman (1982), concerns stages. *Stages* recognizes that the process of becoming "bent" is progressive. Unethical behavior begins on a "slippery slope." The transformation of an ethical officer to an unethical one begins with more mild and seemingly innocuous forms of behavior, such as accepting gratuities and small bribes. These actions provide the contingencies, moral experiences, and learning of situational justifications that lead to more aggressive and active forms of unethical behavior, such as stealing, testilying, extortion, and physical and legal violations, or worse, if left unchecked.

POLICE ETHICS AND CONTROL, REFORM, AND LEGITIMACY

Police misconduct is not new. It is as old as the institution itself. The learning and teaching of police ethics bears directly on issues of control, reform, and legitimacy in a democratic society. Of particular relevance is the role of emerging police paradigms, changing social sentiments, and recent domestic terrorist attacks. Police misconduct in the contemporary period is characterized more by the abuse of authority (noble cause corruption) and economic corruption than misconduct associated with using police as political instruments. This is, in large part, the product of changing social conditions and the professional era of policing, which witnessed the adoption of a crime control mandate.

Community oriented policing (COP) and problem oriented policing (POP) present issues with respect to control of the institution where the learning and teaching of police ethics are in large part the residue of informal on-the-job learning. Specifically, these emerging police paradigms require that officer discretion be increased so that they can effectively engage in proactive forms of policing to solve problems. If standard operating procedures are going to give way to discretion, then officer behaviors and attitudes are going to have to be informed by positive police values. The informal on-the-job learning, which currently exists and facilitates the transmission of negative values, presents real challenges for administrators under these emerging police paradigms.

If administrators are going to effectively manage the transition to COP and POP while controlling police misconduct, learning and teaching police ethics must rely more on formal mechanisms. Specifically, administrators may consider recruiting those who hold a more realistic view of police work, while increasing education requirements. They are also going to have to rely on teaching police ethics through "leading by example." This includes not only emphasizing and acting at the highest ethical standards, but also modifying administrative process to create incentives favoring such behaviors. For example, individual police performance has historically been evaluated on output measures that may inadvertently introduce incentives to engage in unethical behavior, such as number of arrests or crime cleared. Measures of individual performance that may enhance the likelihood of witnessing ethical behavior might include measuring citizen satisfaction with respect to an officer's provision of services. Administrators will also need to be cognizant of the role that informal messages convey in shaping officer behavior and consider formal training in ethics by Internal Affairs, or other investigative divisions.

Not only do these emerging police paradigms present challenges to police control that must be met with organizational and administrative reforms, changing social sentiments introduce some challenges with respect to the legitimacy of the institution. The importance of police services has increased in salience in recent years, as demonstrated through increasing police rolls. As with other occupations, police are viewed by society to be experts capable of solving problems. The extent to which the police are unable to fulfill this expectation is the extent to which the legitimacy of the institution will likely decline. This is particularly problematic in the era of the "war on crime" and the "war on drugs." These problems have deliberately been framed as "wars" by politicians because the metaphor implies a sense of urgency, constructs an "us versus them" mentality among the police, and implies that criminals are "foreign enemies" unworthy of the same rights as Americans because such "wars" generate political capital for (re)election, encourage deficit spending, and ultimately help to expand police power. Police administrators have often been quick to embrace these "wars" because they often increase citizen and fiscal support. Unfortunately, many of the factors related to crime are simply beyond the control of police (e.g., the economy, family, age distribution in the population, etc.), and waging an unwinnable war will likely threaten the long-term perceived legitimacy of the institution. Instead, police administrators may do better educating the public about their limits.

The war analogy also presents additional ethical dilemmas related to the learning of police ethics. To be sure, early American police forces, in part, secured their legitimacy and public support by taking care to distinguish themselves from the military in both approach and appearance. With respect to the former, early public police forces emphasized providing social services and responding to community demands. They emphasized policing by consent—rather than force—and adopted unassuming uniforms that were distinct from the military. In some instances, they were even referred to as "peace officers."

The war analogy has resulted in an increase in the militarization of America's police force, especially given an increase in domestic terrorism events in recent years. **Militarism**, as defined by Kraska (1993), is a set of beliefs and values that stress the use of force and domination as appropriate means to solve problems while glorifying the tools to accomplish this (e.g., military hardware and power, and technology). This militarism of public police neatly coincided with the freeing of resources at the end of the cold war when the military, in an effort to become more "socially relevant," began to make donations to police agencies (e.g., M16s, fatigues, armored personnel carriers, etc.) and accelerated after America's declaration of "war" on drugs (Kraska, 1999). In fact, the number of police squads modeled after military special operations units, such as the U.S. Navy Seals and U.S. Army Rangers, that served medium to large cities grew from 59% in 1982 to 89% in 1995 (Kraska & Kappeler, 1997). More importantly, police departments serving small, medium, and large jurisdictions have increasingly utilized these units "proactively" (e.g., drug and arrest warrants) rather than "reactively" (e.g., hostage situations, civil disturbances, terrorist activity, etc.) as they had been in the past. In fact, deployment of these police paramilitary units grew from an average of 13 in 1980 to 83 in 1995 (or a 583% increase) (Kraska & Kappeler, 1997), while 80–90% of these activities were proactive (Kraska, 1999).

September 11, 2001, and the more recent Boston Marathon bombings, will likely intensify the militarization of American police forces as a result of increased martial rhetoric from administrators and politicians like former President George W. Bush, who within days of the terrorist attacks stated that "every American is a soldier, and every citizen is in this fight" (Bumiller, 2001) and that "this war will not be like the war against Iraq a decade ago, with a decisive liberation of territory and a swift conclusion…Americans should not expect one battle, but a lengthy campaign, unlike any other we have seen" (Bush, September 20, 2001). Such rhetoric runs the risk of militarizing all of America into the war paradigm and encouraging police to adopt a more militant role in the detection and apprehension of potential evil doers (Brown, 2011). The increased militarization of the police, therefore, presents ethical challenges as they relate to the assimilation of military values into public police forces and ultimately the continued perceived legitimacy of the institution.

The ethical challenges related to control of the institution are also increased by this intensified militarization of American police forces. To be sure, a new type of symbolic assailant has emerged as direct result of the war on terror—individuals of Middle Eastern descent. These individuals could very easily experience an erosion of their civil liberties as police practices directed at this population (e.g., profiling, surveillance, and interrogation) challenge or violate constitutional protections provided under the Fourth and Fifth Amendments similar to that experienced by other marginalized groups (e.g., "driving while black"). In addition, militarization of America's police forces increases the risk that police will increasingly rely on aggressive and confrontational behavior

(Weber, 1999) to achieve their mandate. Thus, the militarization of the police increases the risk for unethical decision-making among officers who respond to the martial rhetoric, fear, and constant threat of harm inherent in the war on terror, or any war, for that matter (Brown, 2011).

Relatedly, militarization of American police forces runs the risk of straining police-community relationships. COP programs were created, in part, not only to increase the effectiveness of policing, but to improve strained police-community relationships. To this end, police are expected to actively involve citizens in the policing of their communities and become more responsive to their needs and demands—many of them involving public disorder (Cordner, 1997). Oliver (2004) asserts, however, that the war on terror and COP are incompatible. In fact, because the "war on terror" encourages neighborhoods to provide intelligence to police on suspicious activities and persons in the hopes of establishing an intelligence network, it might actually destroy police-community relationships as police direct resources to fighting an unseen enemy at the cost of neglecting street crime and public disorder.

Politicians and policy-makers may be charging police with impossible tasks and increasingly complex ethical challenges. It may be unlikely that these "wars" will ever come to a satisfactory end—certainly not in the short term. In an era of experts and technology, society expects that "wars" will end with clear winners and losers. The reality is that the sources of these problems span several institutions (economics, politics, education, and religion), many of which are beyond the direct control of the police. These "wars" create incentives among the police subculture and administrators to do whatever it takes to achieve what may be an unattainable mandate. Police administrators may do better in the long run by educating the public regarding their limits so that reasonable expectations may serve as a guide for evaluating present and future police officer behavior.

CASE STUDY 4–1 LIBERTY AND JUSTICE FOR ALL

You are a police officer in a large metropolitan city. For the past 8 months you worked in a middle and upper-class suburban patrol zone. Most of the people with whom you came in contact were respectable members of the community. You had good rapport with most of the community and they were generally quite cooperative with the police. Now you are being transferred to another patrol zone that is in a lower-class area near the inner city.

The first week you are in the new zone, you are assigned to work with Mike, a veteran officer who has been working this zone for almost 4 years. Mike drives you around,

pointing out informants, drunks, thieves, and places where they hang out. You immediately notice that Mike has a somewhat harsh, even punitive attitude regarding the people with whom he comes in contact on his beat.

"You have to treat these people tough; intimidation is the only way to communicate with them," Mike explains.

After 1 week in your new zone, you become aware of a great difference in police work with different types of people. You rarely made arrests in your old zone. Most problems there could be worked out by talking rationally

CASE STUDY 4–1 LIBERTY AND JUSTICE FOR ALL *Continued*

with the people with whom you came in contact. In this zone, however, you have made more arrests and have had to use more force with people. It becomes apparent to you that there are even more drunks and criminals living in the new zone than you had ever expected. People living in the slums seem to be more apathetic as well.

Mike has told you that if you need information on criminal activity, just pick somebody up and threaten to arrest them if they do not tell you what you need to know. This method works, as your new partner seems to demonstrate frequently. Mike will "plant" drugs or a gun on somebody, then threaten to arrest them if they do not give him information or become an informant for him. Mike has occasionally beat confessions out of suspects, then threatened to "get them" if they did not plead guilty to offenses.

You become aware of more violent crimes in your new zone. There are more murders, assaults, and rapes here than would happen in the middle and upper-class neighborhoods. Mike defines rape "victims" as those ones who did not get paid for their services. "Not even worth writing a report on," Mike tells you. Murder investigations are routinely handled by the investigators in this zone. The detectives seldom perform a comprehensive investigation on any offense here. In the middle and upper-class zone, all offenses were investigated thoroughly and the victims were given excellent attention by investigating officers.

You find that more police officers are assaulted in the lower-class zone than in your old zone. The people living in the lower-class zone do not appear to respect the police. It seems they only respect force.

"Don't ever turn your back on these people. And if you have to put one of these thugs down, be sure there ain't no damned video camera around," Mike advises you. Mike also advises you to have your gun ready at all times.

"Shotgun's the best, they're really scared of 'em," says Mike. You also notice that more officers in this zone

use deadly force than officers in other zones of the city. "The police shot five people here last year. And probably a few more they didn't count," Mike chuckles.

After working in the new zone for 2 months and seeing what kind of people live in this area, you find yourself agreeing more and more with Mike's attitudes and methods. You and Mike receive a radio call to back up another unit a couple of blocks away. As you pull up beside the other cruiser, you see two police officers beating up a young man in the alley.

"C'mon Mike, you want a piece of this?" shouts one of the officers. Mike takes out his slapjack and moves in with the other two officers beating the youth.

"What did he do?" you ask.

"He made the mistake of calling us names," responds one of the officers. "We're going to let this one be an example."

The young man could not be over 17 years old and appears to be badly hurt. You know the officers will leave him in the alley when they are finished beating him. Of course, there will be no arrest.

You begin to think about how you have changed. Mike always says, "fight fire with fire." Right now you are wondering who the criminals are. What should you do?

Questions

1. Explain the metamorphosis of the officer taken out of his middle-class environment. Why would there be increased conflict between citizens and police in the lower-class neighborhood? Could this increased conflict explain the behavior of the other veteran officers in this precinct?

2. From a deontological perspective, what must this new officer do to preserve his moral integrity?

3. How might an apologia be used to defend the actions of the veteran officers? Would utilitarianism allow for the battering of a minor in this case?

REFERENCES

Alpert, G. P., & Dunham, R. G. (1997). *Policing urban America* (3rd ed.). Prospect Heights: Waveland Press.

Bayley, D. H., & Bittner, E. (1984). Learning the skills of policing. *Law and Contemporary Problems, 47*, 35–59.

Bayley, D. A., & Mendelsohn, A. (1969). *Minorities and the police*. New York: Free Press.

Bittner, E. (1970). *The functions of police in modern society*. Washington: National Institute of Mental Health.

Broderick, J. J. (1977). *Police in a time of change*. Morristown: General Learning Press.

Brown, C. A. (2011). Divided loyalties: Ethical challenges for America's law enforcement in post 9/11 America. *Case Western Reserve Journal of International Law, 43*, 651–675.

Buerger, M. (1998). Police training as a Pentecost: Using tools singularly ill-suited to the purpose of reform. *Police Quarterly, 1*, 27–63.

Bumiller, E. (October 30, 2001). *A nation challenged: The President; Bush announces a crack-down on visa violators*. New York Times.

Bush, G. W. (September 20, 2001). *Address to a Joint Session of Congress and the American people*, from dhs.gov/xnews/speeches/speech_0016.shtm.

Caldero, M. A., & Crank, J. P. (2011). *Police ethics: The corruption of noble cause* (rev. 3rd ed.). Boston: Elsevier (Anderson Publishing).

Coates. R. (1972). *The dimensions of police-citizen interaction: A social psychological analysis* (unpublished Ph.D. dissertation). University of Maryland.

Conti, N., & Nolan, J. J. I. (2005). Policing the platonic cave: Ethics and efficacy in police training. *Policing & Society, 15*, 166–186.

Cordner, G. W. (1997). Community policing: Elements and effects. In R. G. Dunham, & G. P. Alpert (Eds.), *Critical issues in policing* (5th ed.) (pp. 451–468).

Crank, J. P. (2004). *Understanding police culture* (2nd ed.). Cincinnati: Anderson Publishing Co.

Feeley, M. M. (1992). *The process is the punishment: Handling cases in a lower criminal court*. New York: Russell Sage Foundation.

Ferguson, A. G. (2012). Predictive policing and reasonable suspicion. *Emory Law Journal, 62*, 259–325.

Ford, R. E. (2003). Saying one thing, meaning another: The role of parables in police training. *Police Quarterly, 6*, 84–110.

Ford, J. K., & Morash, M. (2002). Transforming police organizations. In M. Morash, & J. K. Ford (Eds.), *The move to community policing: Making change happen* (pp. 1–11). Thousand Oaks: Sage Publications.

Frank, J., Brandl, S., & Watkins, C. (1997). The content of community policing: A comparison of the daily activities of community and "beat" officers. *Policing, 20*, 716–728.

Fyfe, J. J. (2005). The split-second syndrome and other determinants of police violence. In R. G. Dunham, & G. P. Alpert (Eds.), *Critical issues in policing: Contemporary readings* (pp. 435–450). Long Grove: Waveland Press.

Gaines, L. K., & Kappeler, V. E. (2011). *Policing in America* (7th ed.). Boston: Elsevier (Anderson Publishing).

Giacomazzi, A. L., & McGarrell, E. F. (2002). Using multiple methods in community crime prevention and community-policing research. In J. K. Ford, & M. Morash (Eds.), *Transforming police organizations* (pp. 61–78). Thousand Oaks: Sage Publications.

Green, D. P., & Shapiro, I. (1994). *Pathologies of rational choice theory: A critique of applications in political science*. New Haven: Yale University Press.

Hochstedler, E. (1981). Testing types: A review and test of police types. *Journal of Criminal Justice, 9*, 451–466.

Hummel, R. P. (1994). *The bureaucratic experience: A critique of life in the modern organization* (4th ed.). New York: St. Martin's Press.

Jones-Brown, D. (2007). Forever the symbolic assailant: The more things change, the more they remain the same. *Criminology & Public Policy, 6*, 103–121.

Kappeler, V. E., Sluder, R. D., & Alpert, G. P. (2005). Breeding deviant conformity: The ideology and culture of police. In R. G. Dunham, & G. P. Alpert (Eds.), *Critical issues in policing* (5th ed.) (pp. 231–254). Long Grove: Waveland Press.

Kettl, D. F. (1998). *Public administration: The state of the field*.

Klockars, C. B. (1988). The rhetoric of community policing. In J. R. Greene, & S. D. Mastrofski (Eds.), *Community policing: Rhetoric or reality* (pp. 239–258). New York: Praeger.

Kraska, P. (Ed.). (1993). *Militarizing the drug war: A sign of the times*. New York: Garland Press.

Kraska, P. (1999). Questioning the militarization of U.S. police: Critical versus advocacy scholarship. *Policing & Society, 9*, 141–155.

Kraska, P., & Kappeler, V. E. (1997). Militarizing the American police: The rise and normalization of paramilitary units. *Social Forces, 44*, 1–18.

Lipsky, M. (1980). Street-level bureaucracy: The critical role of street-level bureaucrats. In J. M. Shafritz, & A. C. Hyde (Eds.), *Classics of public administration*. Fort Worth, TX: Harcourt Brace.

Mapp v. Ohio, 376 U.S. 643 (1961).

Manning, P. K. (1996). Policing and reflection. *Police Forum, 6*, 1–5.

Manning, P. K. (1997). *Police work* (2nd ed.). Long Grove: Waveland Press.

Mastrofski, S. D. (1988). Community policing as reform: A cautionary tale. In J. R. Greene, & S. D. Mastrofski (Eds.), *Community policing: Rhetoric or reality* (pp. 47–68). New York: Praeger.

Messner, S. F., & Rosenfeld, R. (2001). *Crime and the American dream* (3rd ed.). Belmont: Wadsworth/ Thomas Learning.

Miranda v. Arizona, 384 U.S. 436 (1966).

Muir, W. K. (1977). *Police: Streetcorner politicians*. Chicago: Chicago University Press.

Niederhoffer, A. (1967). *Behind the shield*. Garden City: Doubleday.

Oliver, W. (2004). The homeland security juggernaut: The end of the community policing era. *Crime and Justice International, 20*, 4–10.

Packer, H. (1968). *The limits of the criminal sanction*. Stanford: Stanford University Press.

Pollock, J. M. (1998). *Ethics in crime and justice: Dilemmas and decisions* (3rd ed.). New York: West/ Wadsworth.

Pollock, J. M. (2005). Ethics in law enforcement. In R. G. Dunham, & G. P. Alpert (Eds.), *Critical issues in policing* (5th ed.) (pp. 280–303). Long Grove: Waveland Press, Inc.

Reiss, A., & Bordua, D. J. (1967). Environment and organization: A perspective on police. In D. J. Bordua (Ed.), *The police: Six sociological essays*. New York: John Wiley.

Rokeach, M. (1973). *The nature of human values*. New York: The Free Press.

Rokeach, M., Miller, M. G., & Snyder, J. S. (1971). The value gap between the police and the policed. *Journal of Social Issues, 27*, 155–177.

Sherman, L. (1982). Learning police ethics. *Criminal Justice Ethics*, 10–19.

Skolnick, J. H. (1994). *Justice without trial: Law enforcement in democratic society*. New Orleans: Quid Pro Books.

Spears, J. W., & Spohn, C. (1997). The effect of evidence factors and victim characteristics on prosecutors' charging decisions in sexual assault cases. *Justice Quarterly, 14,* 501–524.

Stone, D. (2002). *Policy paradox: The art of political decision making* (2nd ed.). New York: W. W. Norton & Company, Inc.

Van Maanen, J. (1974). Working the street: A developmental view of police behavior. In H. Jacob (Ed.), *The potential for reform in criminal justice,* (Vol. 3) (pp. 83–129). Beverly Hills: Sage.

Weber, D. C. (1999). *Warrior cops: The ominous growth of paramilitarism in American police departments.* CATO Institute Briefing Papers No. 50. Washington: CATO Institute.

White, S. O. (1972). A perspective on police professionalization. *Law & Society Review, 7,* 61–85.

Wilson, J. Q. (1968). *Varieties of police behavior: The management of law and order in eight communities.* Cambridge: Harvard University Press.

Zhao, J., He, N., & Lovrich, N. P. (1998). Individual value preferences among American police officers: The Rokeach theory of human values revisited. *Policing: An International Journal of Police Strategies and Management,* 22–37.

CHAPTER 5

Deception in Police Interrogation

Steven J. Ellwanger

KEY CONCEPTS

coercion	*Miranda* warning	role playing
fabricated evidence	mirroring	slippery-slope
interrogation	misrepresenting	argument
interview	identity	

Ronald Kitchen was a 24-year-old black man living in Chicago. On January 25, 1988, he was arrested while walking home from the grocery store after purchasing cookie dough for his children. Initially, detectives charged Kitchen with theft, but they quickly changed the charge to murder. After hours of interrogation, which included being beaten with a blackjack, Kitchen confessed under extreme physical duress to the murder of two women and three children—murders that he did not commit. Kitchen believed that because there could be no physical evidence linking him to the crime, his confession could later be recanted without consequence. In fact, when asked why he falsely confessed, Kitchen stated "I gave in, hoping that the judge and jury would see that I was telling the truth" (Hartman, 2009). Unfortunately, Kitchen underestimated the power of confession evidence and was ultimately convicted and sentenced to death. In July 2010, after serving 21 years behind bars—13 of which were on death row—prosecutors dismissed charges against Kitchen after he was granted a new trial. Formal charges of torture dating back to the 1980s were filed against the Chicago police.

As Kitchen's case illustrates, in criminal law, a confession is the most damning and potent evidence a prosecutor can present during trial (Cassell & Hayman, 1996; Leo, 1996). Pressure on police to obtain confession evidence has always existed. As a result, police have implemented **interrogation** techniques designed to maximize confession rates among guilty suspects. In *Brown v. Mississippi* (1936), the U.S. Supreme Court held that confessions obtained by

73

brutality and *torture* were a violation of the due process rights guaranteed by the Fourth Amendment's protections against unreasonable searches and seizures. Prior to this landmark ruling, police relied largely on physical interrogation techniques, including beating suspects with a rubber hose until they confessed.

In response to the real or perceived hurdles introduced through this landmark case, police agencies modified interrogation practices to emphasize the psychological dimension of interrogation. To this end, interrogators would often hold suspects incommunicado from family and counsel for lengthy periods, fabricate evidence, and use other techniques to heighten anxiety and increase fatigue among suspects to secure a confession. In essence, police agencies shifted from physically coercive methods for obtaining confessions to psychological ones. The U.S. Supreme Court initially considered the issue of psychological **coercion** in 1966 with *Miranda v. Arizona*, which resulted in the now-famous *Miranda* warnings that require law enforcement officers to inform suspects of their right to remain silent (Fifth Amendment) and access to legal counsel (Sixth Amendment). The Court was very clear in stating that evidence (i.e., a confession) obtained during custodial interrogation was not admissible in court to prove guilt unless the suspect had been given his or her *Miranda* warnings and had voluntarily, knowingly, and intelligently waived those rights.

The pressure experienced by law enforcement to secure confessions did not wane with the *Miranda* ruling. Given the fact that most perpetrators do not readily admit guilt when confronted by law enforcement, police agencies have crafted deceptive interrogation techniques to secure confessions. The constitutionality of these techniques is ultimately judged by the voluntariness standard articulated by the Court in *Miranda*. Confessions not secured voluntarily, knowingly, and intelligently are deemed coercive in the eyes of the Court and are therefore inadmissible.

This chapter begins with a discussion of the case law that shapes contemporary police interrogation techniques, followed by a typology that identifies and examines deceptive—yet legal—tactics commonly utilized by interrogators to secure incriminating evidence. Finally, the ethical issues and dilemmas presented by these techniques for officers, agencies, and the broader system are considered.

FROM BRUTE FORCE TO PSYCHOLOGICAL MANIPULATION

There has always existed pressure on the prosecution to obtain confession evidence. Even today, under English common law—to which the roots of the U.S. legal system can be traced—failure to obtain a confession from the accused is seen as a serious deficiency in the prosecution's case. According to one legal scholar, "the introduction of a confession makes other aspects of the trial in court superfluous," making the confession the prosecutor's most potent and damning piece of evidence (Leo, 1996; McCormick, 1972, p. 316). In response to this pressure, police agencies adopted interrogation techniques designed to elicit confessions from guilty suspects. Initially, these techniques emphasized brute force; later they stressed psychological coercion. Subsequent judicial intervention eventually deemed both forms unconstitutional.

Despite judicial intervention, the pressure to secure confessions by the prosecution has remained. Police continue to exert pressure on suspects to obtain a confession. To this end, police agencies have adopted techniques that rely on psychological *manipulation*. Although the Supreme Court drew a bright line regarding the timing of the *Miranda* warnings, it was less clear what "specific techniques" could be considered so deceitful that they violated the voluntariness clause enumerated in *Miranda*. Thus, the constitutionality of contemporary interrogation techniques must be considered against the backdrop of existing case law.

Elimination of Brute Force

The Supreme Court first considered the issue of interrogation techniques used by states to secure confession evidence in 1936 with *Brown v. Mississippi*. Brown and two other suspected accomplices were tortured, including being beaten on their backs with a leather strap and metal buckle, for the alleged murder of a white man. The deputy sheriff told Brown and the others that the beatings would not stop until they confessed to the murder and all of the details surrounding it. One day after the confessions were secured, the trial began. With the rope marks still clearly visible on the suspects, none of those people who participated in the beating denied that it had taken place. The suspects were ultimately convicted of murder and sentenced to death. On appeal, the Supreme Court ruled that confessions obtained by brutality and torture by law enforcement officers were a violation of the due process rights guaranteed by the Fourteenth Amendment. The initial reluctance of the Court to become involved in state affairs, and its concern for the reliability of confession evidence obtained by physical coercion, is captured in its rationale:

> The State is free to regulate the procedure of its courts in accordance with its own conceptions of policy, unless it "offends some principle of justice so rooted in the traditions and conscience of our people as to be ranked fundamental." … [T]he freedom of the State in establishing its policy is the freedom of constitutional government and is limited by the requirement of due process of law. Because a State may dispense with a jury trial, it does not follow that it may substitute trial by ordeal. The rack and torture chamber may not be substituted for the witness stand.

> The state may not permit an accused to be hurried to conviction under mob domination—where the whole proceeding is but a mask—without supplying corrective process.
>
> *Brown v. Mississippi* (1936)

Controlling Psychological Coercion

The *Brown* decision had the effect of eliminating the use of brute force to secure confessions by holding that such evidence is highly unreliable and therefore inadmissible. In response, police agencies modified their interrogation practices. Interrogators began to focus on the psychological dimension of confessions. Interrogators developed standard operating procedures (SOPs) that emphasized techniques designed to increase anxiety and fatigue among suspects during questioning. These techniques first came to the attention of the Supreme Court in 1966 with *Miranda v. Arizona.*

Ernesto Miranda, who was 23 years old, poor, and had only a ninth-grade education, was accused in the kidnapping and rape of an 18-year-old girl. Miranda was subsequently arrested and identified in a police line-up by the victim. He was immediately taken to an interrogation room where he was held incommunicado for 2 h. When investigators emerged from the room, they had a fully signed confession, which had a typed paragraph at the top stating that the confession was voluntary and made without threats or promises of immunity and "with full knowledge of my legal rights, understanding any statement I make may be used against me." Miranda was subsequently sentenced to 20–30 years in prison.

On appeal, the U.S. Supreme Court held that Miranda's Fifth (right to remain silent) and Sixth (right to counsel) Amendment rights had been violated and went on to articulate the now famous *Miranda* warnings. *Miranda* was unique in two ways. First, *Miranda* signaled a willingness by the Court to become involved in the day-to-day operations of police agencies by spelling out specifically what police agencies needed to do for confession evidence to be admissible in court. The court was clear that: (1) suspects must be given their *Miranda* warnings by the police; (2) any confession evidence must be obtained after a waiver by the suspect; and (3) that waiver must be voluntary and intelligent. Second, *Miranda* was unique for what it did not do: it did not identify any specific deceitful interrogation technique that would violate the voluntariness clause beyond the use of trickery to induce a waiver of a suspect's Fifth and Sixth Amendment rights (*Miranda v. Arizona*, 1966; see also White, 1979).

RELIABILITY, FREE WILL, AND FAIRNESS

The reluctance of the Court to proscribe specific police interrogation techniques for their violation of the voluntariness clause articulated in *Miranda* has resulted in the proliferation of various forms of trickery. The constitutionality of such deceptive practices can only be judged on a case-by-case basis. Because no *per se* rules exist that prohibit specific types or categories of deception, case law has (and will continue to) define the limits and bounds of the *Miranda* protections with respect to deceptive interrogation. Of particular importance in determining these limits and bounds is the meaning of *voluntariness*. Voluntariness, as defined by the Court, is a concept "that is infused with multiple values," as Justice Harlan noted in his *Miranda* dissent (*Miranda v. Arizona*, 384 U.S. 436 (1966)). In fact, interpretations of the *Miranda* ruling—especially regarding "voluntariness"—have been guided by the values of reliability, free will, and fairness embodied in the decision.

Reliability of confession evidence was the early focus of state courts in determining voluntariness. Police interrogation techniques that would leave a defendant "willing to make any statement that the officers wanted him to make" (*Ward v. Texas*, 316 U.S. 547 (1942)) or are the result of police coercion rather than the suspect's perception of the event (*Rogers v. Richmond*, 356 U.S. 534 (1961)) are involuntary and thus unconstitutional. In addition to reliability, the Court was also concerned about the extent to which a suspect's statements were "the product of his or her *free* and rational choice." In other words, confessions could be involuntary if the techniques used were coercive, regardless of whether they produced a false confession. For example, Justice Black, speaking for the Court, found that an uninterrupted 36-h interrogation was "so inherently coercive that it was irreconcilable with the possession of mental freedom" (*Ashcraft v. Tennessee*, 322 U.S. 143 (1944)). Finally, the voluntariness standard includes a *fairness* component. The fairness component deals directly with the legitimacy of the police tactics used to secure the confession. In *Spano v. New York*, the court's primary concern was not with the potentially coercive methods but with insuring that "police obey the law while enforcing the law" (*Spano v. New York*, 360 U.S. 315 (1959)).

In the absence of any definitive guidance by the Court prohibiting specific types of interrogation techniques and the pressure experienced by police to obtain confession evidence, numerous techniques have been developed to maximize confession rates (Hess, 2010; Inbaue & Reid, 1962; Inbaue, Reid, Buckley, & Jayne, 2001). Many of these techniques are inherently deceptive because they require officers to make statements they know are untrue or to play a role that is inconsistent with their actual feelings (Box, 1999; White, 1979). In fact, Inbaue et al. (2001) openly favor "psychological tactics and techniques that may involve trickery and deceit," noting that "they are not only helpful but also frequently indispensable in order to secure incriminating information" (2001, p. xii). The authors prescribe numerous strategies designed to deliberately deceive a suspect into confessing. Deceptive techniques may be classified into eight categories initially identified by Skolnick and Leo (1992), as outlined in Box 5.1.

BOX 5.1 DECEPTIVE INTERROGATION TECHNIQUES

"Interview" versus "interrogation"
Role playing
Miranda warnings
Fabricated evidence
Exaggerating the nature and severity of the offense
Minimization/normalization of crime
Misrepresenting identity
Use of promises

"Interview" versus "Interrogation"

An **interview** can be distinguished from an interrogation by its purpose and nature. The purpose of an interview is to gather pertinent information regarding a crime. Interviews usually occur early in an investigation, when the police have little or no evidence linking a suspect to a crime, and the location is often spontaneously chosen or solely determined by convenience (i.e., taking place in an individual's home, on the street, or in a police cruiser). Questions like "Do you know who might have killed John Doe?" or "Why do you think John Doe was murdered?" are typical interview questions.

Once police have reason to believe that an individual may have been involved in a crime, the nature and purpose of the questioning will change. During interrogation, investigators are deliberately trying to elicit incriminating evidence that will be used to prosecute the suspect. Thus, interrogations are *accusatory* in nature. The location for interrogation is often chosen by design (i.e., taking place at the police station or crime scene). Questions like "Why did *you* kill John Doe?" or "Why did *you* want John Doe dead?" implicate the individual in the crime.

Miranda warnings must be given whenever there is a *custodial interrogation*. *Custodial* means that a suspect is under arrest or is deprived of his or her freedom in a significant way. *Interrogation*, again, means that the suspect is being asked questions that attempt to link him or her to the crime. One of the most popular strategies the police use is to make what is actually an interrogation appear to be an interview. This is done by questioning suspects in the field and/or frequently reminding them that they are free to leave at any time. As Skolnick and Leo (1992) have noted, this is one of the cleanest forms of deceptive interrogation techniques in that by recasting the interrogation as an interview, it becomes free of judicial control.

Role Playing

Closely associated with pretending an interrogation in an interview is the practice of interrogators assuming a nonadversarial role. The purpose of this technique is to get the suspect to forget the adversarial nature of the relationship between the interrogator and suspect or that the interrogator is attempting to elicit information that will later be used to prosecute the suspect. In **role playing**, interrogators will often assume roles that the suspect perceives to be more friendly and concerned with ensuring the welfare of the suspect rather than attempting to elicit information that will later be used to convict them.

Because masking and minimizing the perceived adversarial nature of the interrogation are often paramount to securing confessions, police manuals often advise police officers involved in role-play to dress in civilian clothes, attempt to build rapport, use flattery, and speak and behave in ways similar to suspects—a process known as **mirroring** (Hess, 2010; Inbaue et al., 2001; Kassin, 1997). The goal is to create the illusion that interrogators are friends who are interested in helping, rather than harming, the suspect. A popular and well-known role-playing technique assumed by interrogators is "good cop/bad cop," or the "Mutt and Jeff" routine. Here one interrogator ("Mutt") pretends to be extremely angry and impatient with the suspect because of his or her unwillingness to talk and confess to the crime. That interrogator paces around the interrogation room attempting to look menacing and unpredictable while making demeaning comments about the suspect. The other interrogator ("Jeff," the "good cop") tells Mutt to leave the room and "let off some steam." At this point, Jeff encourages the suspect to confide in him before Mutt returns (LaGrange, 1998).

Interrogators also routinely adopt the role of father, brother, or a religious or therapeutic counselor. Similarly to "good cop/bad cop," the success of these roles in securing a confession is largely contingent on the interrogator's ability to convey a sense of friendship, feign sympathy, and make appeals to God or religion. The constitutionality of these techniques has largely been affirmed by the courts except when they can be construed as "coercive," such as when an officer implies that God will punish suspects if they do not confess (*People v. Adams*, 143 Cal.App.3d 970 (1983)). Despite the effectiveness of these techniques and their affirmed constitutionality, legal scholars have criticized such strategies for undermining the very goal that *Miranda* was meant to achieve to make the individual more aware that he or she is engaged in an adversarial process and that the suspect is not in the presence of people who are necessarily acting in his or her interest (Kamisar, 1966). Despite this criticism, role playing is widely used and one of the most effective interrogation techniques used by police officers (Skolnick & Leo, 1992).

Miranda Warnings

The Court attempted to draw a clear line regarding when *Miranda* **warnings** must be given. Whenever a "custodial interrogation" ensues, suspects must be made aware of their Fifth Amendment right to remain silent and Sixth Amendment right to counsel. The Court did not say, however, that police had to be enthusiastic about giving the *Miranda* warnings, or that the warnings have to be read in a manner that encourages suspects to exercise their rights. As a result, *Miranda* warnings are often delivered in a manner that is intended to increase the likelihood that a waiver will be elicited. The warnings can be recited in a flat, perfunctory manner intended to imply that they are not that important and are merely a bureaucratic ritual (Skolnick & Leo, 1992). For example, one seasoned investigator would routinely interject during their reading—at the point at which suspects are informed of their right to counsel—that no person on death row got there without the help of their attorney (Hess, 2010, p. 32).

Fabricated Evidence

Police interrogators may also utilize a **fabricated evidence** ploy to induce suspects to confess. In such instances, police confront the suspect with false evidence. Leo (2008) has identified three types of false-evidence ploys: demeanor evidence, testimonial evidence, and scientific evidence. Demeanor ploys involve the fabrication of evidence gleaned from the suspect's behavior. That is, they tell the suspect that their appearance, behavior, or postures provide strong evidence of their guilt. This is, in part, the product of their training and expectations, which are shaped by training manuals that argue that guilty individuals display certain behaviors (e.g., gaze aversion, slouching posture, and/or "insufficient richness of detail" in responses) that can be observed to determine the likelihood of guilt (Inbaue et al., 2001; Jayne & Buckley, 1999). A false-evidence ploy is not the misreading of the suspect's behavior—or falsely concluding that a suspect is guilty based on the suspect's behavior. Rather, it is the fabrication of demeanor evidence that police present to the suspect in an effort to get them to confess, despite observing behaviors that actually suggest their innocence.

The most common form of false-evidence ploys utilized by police is testimonial (Leo, 2008). This technique involves police telling the suspect that they have testimony by an eyewitness, video camera, or even an accomplice that implicates the suspect in the crime. For example, police will often tell a suspect who they believed played a relatively minor role in the commission of a crime (e.g., drove the getaway car) that the suspect's accomplice is located in another interrogation room and is currently confessing to the crime and implicating the suspect. The officer then states that unless the suspect confesses his or her role, the suspect will "take the fall" for the crime. Finally, police may also fabricate scientific evidence linking the suspect to the crime. For example, police may claim that they found the individual's fingerprints at the crime scene or have found the victim's DNA in bloodstains taken from the suspect's clothing.

The Supreme Court and other courts have generally found these false-evidence ploys to be constitutional, as in *Ward v. State* (1980), which affirmed the constitutionality of providing misinformation to suspects in order to play accomplices against each other (*Ward v. State*, 408 N.E.2d 140 (1980)) and fabricating scientific evidence about nonexistent bloodstains and testimonial evidence from nonexistent eyewitnesses (*State v. Jackson*, 308 N.C. 549 (1983)). However, the courts have more recently ruled that false-evidence ploys that involve the creation of physical evidence (e.g., evidence written on official letterhead or a tape recording of a police officer portrayed as an eyewitness) are unconstitutional because their "potential for indefinite life and the facial appearance of authenticity" creates a risk for contaminating the criminal justice system (*Florida v. Cayward*, 552 So. 2d 971 (1989); *State v. Patton*, 826 A.2d 783 (2003); see also Woody & Forrest, 2009).

Exaggerating the Nature and Severity of the Offense

In an analysis of interrogation techniques, Inbaue, Reid, and Buckley (1986) proffered two broad categories that, used in combination, increase the likelihood of securing a confession (Kassin & McNall, 1991). The first technique is described as *maximization*. Here, police attempt to maximize the suspect's perceptions of the negative consequences for continuing to deny involvement in the crime. One such technique is to exaggerate the nature or severity of the offense. For example, a suspect being investigated for statutory rape may be told by the police that the accuser claims the rape was, in fact, forcible. Similarly, a suspect being accused of embezzlement may be deliberately told that the amount embezzled is substantially larger than it actually was (e.g., $1,500 instead of the actual $500). The goal is to make the individual suspect perceive that the consequences for continued deception are too great if convicted of the (exaggerated) offense—and therefore unacceptable—so as to compel him or her to confess. Lower courts have generally held that a suspect need not be informed of the *specific* nature of the charges for the police to obtain a valid waiver (*United States v. Anderson*, 533 D.C. Cir. (1976) F.2d 1210, 1212 n.3).

Normalization/Minimization of the Crime

The second of Inbaue et al.'s categories is the normalization/minimization of the crime. With this technique, police attempt to minimize the perceived consequences of admitting guilt by suggesting justifications for the suspect's behavior or trying to at least normalize it within the context of its occurrence. Minimization and normalization techniques used by police allow suspects to justify their behavior on moral or external grounds. For example, police may suggest that the battery of a prostitute is justifiable given her moral turpitude or even suggest to an alleged child molester that they understand he was only trying to show the victim love. If provided a moral justification by which behavior can be rationalized, suspects might perceive the consequences of admitting guilt as diminished (i.e., they are able to save face). Police may also provide external justifications (i.e., the behavior was drug-induced or an accident) to make the behavior appear less deliberate or even normal, given the circumstances. When maximization of the offense is combined with normalization/minimization, it serves to increase the likelihood that police will secure a confession. These tactics are generally upheld by the courts and are considered by police agencies to be one of the most effective strategies available to them (Skolnick & Leo, 1992).

Misrepresenting Identity

Police may use the tactic of **misrepresenting identity** to secure a confession. The Supreme Court's view on the constitutionality of the police misrepresenting their identity is shaped by both the norms and professional rules surrounding the particular profession or social group being assumed and the extent to which the assumed identity creates a sense of psychological compulsion. In *Leyra v. Denno* (347 U.S. 556 (1954)), the Court ruled that confession evidence obtained by a police psychiatrist acting as a physician—and who in the course of treating the defendant repeatedly assured him that he had done no wrong and would be let off—was inadmissible. In a similar vein, because of a general assumption of confidentiality, an officer pretending to be a suspect's lawyer or a priest would be impermissible. Thus, the profession or social group with which an officer identifies during questioning may, as a result of professional disclosure rules or norms (e.g., confidentiality), make confession evidence obtained inadmissible (Skolnick & Leo, 1992).

More recently, the Rehnquist court in *Illinois v. Perkins* (110 S.CT. 2394 (1990)) did uphold confession evidence obtained through the use of a "jail plant." Here, an undercover officer posed as a prison inmate and was placed in the cell of a suspected murderer named Perkins who was serving time on an unrelated drug charge. While planning a prison break, the officer asked Perkins if he had ever "done" anybody. Perkins subsequently described at length the details of a murder-for-hire he had committed. The Court ruled that the confession evidence obtained under these circumstances was admissible, because Perkins—who did not know the informant was an agent—could not have experienced any psychologically compelling reason to confess.

Use of Promises

The cajoling, trickery, and deception police use to secure confessions are often buttressed by promises to further entice suspects into confessing. The

Supreme Court has deemed certain types of promises of leniency, however, to be inherently coercive and therefore unconstitutional. Promises are considered coercive because they are meant to convince suspects that their condition will somehow be improved. That improvement is often illusory, however, because police are often only interested in securing the confession and have little interest in or control over carrying out the promises. As a result, police rely on a specific form of promise, the use of which has largely been upheld by the courts.

Because "direct" promises of leniency have been deemed by the Supreme Court to be unconstitutional since 1897 (*Bram v. United States*, 168 U.S. 532 (1897)), police have come to rely on promises that do not *guarantee* that the suspect's position will be improved but instead only *imply* such an improvement. For example, in *State v. Jackson* (1983), interrogators led the suspect to believe that if he told the truth—or confessed—the court would "view his case in a favorable light" (*State v. Jackson*, 304 S.E.2d 134 (1983)). On appeal, the North Carolina Supreme Court ruled his confession to be voluntary because there was no offer of leniency by the police. Thus, the extent to which promises are viewed constitutional in the eyes of the courts is largely determined by their directness and specificity (Ayling, 1984; Kassin, 1997; Sasaki, 1988; Skolnick & Leo, 1992; White, 1979).

THE ETHICS AND DILEMMAS OF DECEPTIVE POLICE INTERROGATION

Police experience tremendous pressure by society and prosecutors to solve crimes. Despite the common misconception that most crimes are quickly solved by some direct forensic evidence that links the suspect to the crime, most crimes are, in fact, solved by important information obtained during police questioning. Interrogation is an important part of that fact-finding process. At first glance, the use of trickery and deception in obtaining incriminating information during interrogation might seem to be without substantial criticism. In fact, one might argue that as long as the techniques police use are legal, securing a confession is the most efficient and, therefore, rational means for solving a crime.

However, the use of deception in interrogations needs to be considered from a broader perspective than its perceived utilitarian promise. In fact, a review of such techniques suggests that, despite the contention of training manuals and seasoned interrogators that liars can be distinguished from truth tellers, the promise of such claims is often overstated. Even if these claims were not overstated, the use of deception in police interrogations has potential negative effects on police conduct in other areas of their work.

CRIME CONTROL VERSUS DUE PROCESS AND ETHICAL ORIENTATION

One's view concerning the appropriateness of deceptive interrogation techniques is likely a product of fundamental assumptions that one holds about the criminal justice system. Packer's (1968) two models of the criminal justice system view the goals of the system as existing on a continuum.

At one extreme is the crime control model. Individuals who subscribe to this model believe that the primary goal of the criminal justice system is crime control, and the goal of crime control can only be maximized (thereby producing the greatest good for the greatest number of citizens) through efficiency. An efficient criminal justice system quickly identifies, apprehends, convicts, and punishes perpetrators (Packer, 1968). Existing at the other extreme of the continuum is the due process model. In contrast to the crime control model, which emphasizes efficiency and finality of the outcome, the due process model is more concerned with justice while emphasizing the process through which it is achieved. Another way of saying this is that in the due process model, the protection of the innocent is as important as the punishment of the guilty. Unfortunately, the values of "efficiency" and "justice" are often at odds with each other and exist in a zero-sum game; that is, an increase in one often comes at a cost to the other. For example, unrestrained police power increases the likelihood that individuals will be identified, prosecuted, convicted, and punished, but without sufficient safeguards it runs the risk of corrupting the process (see Caldero & Crank, 2011).

The assumptions one holds of the system—which view the central value pursued by the criminal justice system as either "efficiency" or as "justice"—will profoundly shape one's views regarding the morality of deceptive interrogation techniques. It is difficult to argue that efficiency is not an important value, because an efficient system may provide more effective public safety. Citizens, however, should recognize that one value often comes at a cost to another, and the extent to which deceptive interrogation techniques should be allowed to exist is one that will ebb and flow with political currents and the public sentiment that fuels them.

RELIABILITY OF BEHAVIOR ANALYSIS

The most popular form of interrogation practiced by police today is the *Reid Technique* (Meyer & Reppuci, 2007). The Reid Technique relies on a form of behavior analysis in which police ask suspects a series of 15 questions and assess their verbal and nonverbal responses in an attempt to determine guilt. This technique rests on the assumption that guilty suspects provide verbal and nonverbal cues that trained investigators can identify to determine deception. For example, short answers, gaze aversion, slouching, and reactive grooming of self or clothes are all considered cues of deception (Inbaue et al., 2001). According to Reid and Associates (2010), interrogators trained in this technique are 85% accurate in distinguishing guilty from innocent suspects.

The assumption that police interrogators can make accurate determinations of guilt or innocence through behavior analysis is not generally supported by existing research. It is estimated that laypeople are 54% accurate in detecting truth, whereas the trained police rate is believed to be between 45% and 60%, which may be modestly better—or even slightly worse—than random guessing (Vrij, 2001). Other studies have shown that college students have similar or higher accuracy rates than trained police officers (DePaulo & Pfeifer, 1986; Kassin & Fong, 1999; Kassin, Meissner, & Norwick, 2005), whereas other research has demonstrated that such training actually reduces police and college student abilities to detect deception (Kassin & Fong, 1999; Meissner & Kassin, 2002). Perhaps even more troubling is the finding that police who underwent training in identifying deceptive cues were more likely to make, with extreme confidence, prejudgments of guilt that were frequently in error (for a full review, see Kassin, 2008).

The consequences of inaccurate prejudgment of guilt and extreme confidence are particularly troublesome when the value of efficiency is permitted to run roughshod over justice. Caldero and Crank (2011) have argued that police do not build cases in a serial process whereby evidence is obtained prior to determination of guilt but instead make determinations of guilt more as a product of intuition and the professional socialization preceding evidence collection. An example might be when an officer determines that a particular individual or car does not belong in a particular area. Once police officers sense that a crime has been or is about be committed, they work backward to develop sufficient facts to establish "reasonable suspicion" or "probable cause." They do this to initiate a police/citizen contact or search—such as claiming that a driver failed to make a complete stop—to allow for the collection of evidence (see also Crank, 2004). In the interrogation room, officers usually begin with the presumption guilt (Gudjonsson, 1992) and then work to secure a confession. Prejudgments of guilt and overconfidence inspired by training in interrogation techniques may have the effect of blinding investigators to exculpatory evidence. Such attitudes can also lead to interrogation techniques that elicit a false confession—particularly when police are not trained with regard to the proper limits of such techniques (which they frequently are not).

Deceit and lying are encouraged by Reid and Associates, whose techniques have been utilized by generations of interrogators and are among the most widely used today (Inbaue et al., 2001; Meyer & Reppuci, 2007). However, deceit and lying are behaviors that are prohibited in other areas of police work (e.g., in supervisor/subordinate organizational relationships) and in the courts. By allowing or even encouraging behaviors that are generally condemned by society or prohibited in other areas of police work, policing runs the risk of creating a "slippery slope." The **slippery-slope argument** holds that to encourage police to lie, deceive, and fabricate evidence in the interrogation room while simultaneously believing that such behaviors may not creep into other areas of police work (e.g., falsifying police reports, warrants, and orders) may be naïve and myopic.

Police and supporters of deceptive interrogation techniques often justify them on utilitarian grounds. The constitutionality of existing and future interrogation techniques will continually be reviewed by the courts. Court decisions will on occasion remind police of the delicate balance that exists between efficiency and justice—and that sometimes police interrogation tactics violate civil liberties. Unfortunately, justifying deceitful practices in the interrogation room on the utilitarian grounds of crime control may make it easier to also apply them in other areas of police work (e.g., falsifying evidence to obtain a warrant or lying in court to secure a conviction). Unlike police interrogations, which are relatively transparent (often videotaped) and whose methods are relatively easily reviewed by the courts, lies and fabrications that find their way into other areas of police work are not as visible and subject to external review mechanisms for the protection of those who are, in fact, innocent.

A police force that lies and deceives, even if to achieve good ends, may also limit its long-term effectiveness. Police are dependent on the public to provide valuable information in solving crimes, to coproduce public safety through community involvement, and to help secure convictions from juries comprising the people they police. A police force that develops a reputation for lying and deceit—two behaviors generally not supported by the public—runs the risk of undermining the elements of confidence and trust that are necessary for effective police/citizen relationships. As a result, citizens may become less likely to furnish police with important information and/or to actively participate in the policing of their communities. In addition, police agencies that develop such a reputation are more likely to encounter juries that question the veracity of officer testimony and are more likely to acquit suspects than they otherwise would be. This is particularly true when gross miscarriages of justice resulting from false confessions obtained through deceptive interrogation techniques are revealed to the public.

A false confession is one in which an innocent person confesses to a crime he or she did not commit. Because many people assume that innocent people would not confess to crimes they did not commit, many would argue that the use of deceit to obtain confession evidence is not problematic. Although the actual rate of false confessions is unknown in the absence of an adequate method of estimation (Kassin, 1997), it is believed that the number of false confessions in the United States is between 10 and 394 per year (Cassell, 1998). See Box 5.2.

BOX 5.2 FALSE CONFESSION TYPES AND THEIR CORRESPONDING MOTIVATION

False Confession Type	Motivation or Reason
Voluntary false confession	Desire for notoriety, acceptance, recognition, or self-punishment.
Coerced-compliant false confession	Concerned with maximizing short-term gains (e.g., a drug addict confessing so they can be released to get a "fix").
Coerced-internalized false confession	Individual prone to suggestibility resulting from poor memory, high anxiety, low self-esteem, or lack of assertiveness.

Given the fact that confession evidence has a more compelling influence on jurors than eyewitness testimony (Wakefield & Underwager, 1998), it is important to understand the different types of false confessions and the motivations or reasons that give rise to each. Kassin and Wrightsman (1985) have distinguished between *voluntary false confessions, coerced-compliant false confessions*, and *coerced-internalized false confessions*. A *voluntary false confession* is one that is given in the absence of external pressure from police. The reasons suspects may give voluntary false confessions range from a desire for notoriety (as when 200 people confessed to the kidnapping of Charles Lindbergh's baby) to acceptance, recognition, or self-punishment. Another example was when a woman falsely implicated herself and a group of motorcyclists in a local murder and later claimed in a letter to police that she did so for the same reasons she used drugs and attempted suicide—for attention (Wrightsman & Kassin, 1993, pp. 87–88).

A *coerced-compliant false confession* is one in which suspects confess after intense interrogation pressure and that arises out of instrumental motivations. Here, an individual falsely confesses because he or she believes the short-term gains (e.g., being released, left alone, fed, etc.) outweigh the long-term consequences (e.g., prosecution, incarceration, loss of reputation, etc.), as was the case with Ronald Kitchen noted at the beginning of this chapter. The perceived strength of the evidence and an individual's predisposition toward compliance in social situations have both been found to be significant predictors of this type of false confession (Cassell & Hayman, 1996; Gudjonsson, 1989). Finally, *coerced-internalized false confessions* are those in which an innocent person comes to believe that he or she has, in fact, committed the crime in question.

It is difficult to understand not only how innocent individuals confess to crimes they did not commit, but also how, after being exposed to interrogation tactics that are suggestive, guilt sometimes becomes internalized by the individual. This form of false confession is particularly troublesome because here an individual's recollection of the events becomes altered and therefore unretrievable at a later date. The reasons for such internalization are not well known, but studies have shown that individuals differ with respect to their level of suggestibility during interrogation. Those people who exhibit poor memories, high levels of anxiety, low self-esteem, and lack of assertiveness are more likely to experience shifts in memory and yield to misleading questions (Gudjonsson, 1992).

Coerced-internalized false confessions are relatively rare, yet numerous cases have been documented (Ofshe & Watters, 1994; Warden & Drizin, 2009). For example, Thomas Sawyer, a golf course groundskeeper accused of raping and murdering his neighbor, was originally invited to the police station to "assist" in an investigation. After 16 h of interrogation in which police claimed they had physical evidence linking him to the crime, Sawyer was convinced by police that the reason he could not recall the event was because of an alcoholic blackout. He finally admitted to the crime and went on to state "I guess all of the evidence is in, I guess I must have done it" (Jerome, 1995, p. 30). A review by Kassin (1997) of coerced-internalized false confessions led to the conclusion that such confessions—although infrequent—occur when (1) individual memories are malleable because of youth, interpersonal trust, naïveté, suggestibility, lack of intelligence, stress, fatigue, or alcohol or other drug use; and (2) police utilize false evidence ploys that rely on seemingly irrefutable scientific evidence (e.g., DNA, hair, fingerprints, or polygraph results).

CONCLUSION

The use of deception in police interrogation has become a mainstay in police interrogation techniques. From conflating interrogations and interviews to utilizing false evidence ploys and role playing, police interrogation tactics rely on psychological manipulation to secure confession evidence. Society holds lofty expectations for police to solve crimes and to do so expediently. Because perpetrators rarely confess their involvement in criminal offenses when initially confronted by police, interrogators have adopted techniques to secure confessions that attempt to follow the "letter of the law." The meaning of the "letter of the law," however, has changed and will continue to change over time as it relates to the values embodied in the voluntariness standard articulated in *Miranda*. Changing political winds and public sentiment will undoubtedly shape future interpretations of this standard and, therefore, police practices.

The pressure experienced by police to obtain confession evidence is difficult to overstate, because this evidence is considered to be the most potent and damning type—even more so than eyewitness testimony. Deceptive interrogation is often justified on utilitarian grounds by those who believe that the primary goal of the criminal justice system (and therefore the police) is crime control. It is difficult to argue the value of eliminating deception in whole or in part if one subscribes to this view of the criminal justice system and assumes that the techniques learned and practiced by interrogators are effective in distinguishing liars from those who tell the truth. Moreover, if one assumes that lying can be confined to interrogation rooms and that innocent people do not confess, any argument for the abolition or limiting of deception in interrogation is not likely to gain traction. Unfortunately, this view is limited at best, and these assumptions are often unfounded.

Police in a democratic society must balance the need for crime control with the need for justice lest they undermine their perceived legitimacy and, ultimately, their long-term effectiveness. Empirical analyses of the most popular interrogation techniques show only a marginal improvement (or in some cases a decrease) in an individual's ability to detect deception. Police officers trained in such tactics are more likely to prejudge guilt incorrectly and experience extreme levels of confidence regarding their conclusions. The potential consequence is that intuition, socialization, and formal training in these techniques may combine in the interrogation room to blind investigators to exculpatory evidence. This may also spur cajoling, trickery, and deception to such an extent as to elicit a false confession, even if not intended. Even more worrisome is the assumption on the part of many that an innocent person will not confess. Confession evidence holds considerable sway over juries and, once presented, is difficult to discount. When false confessions lead to gross miscarriages of justice, such as in the case of Ronald Kitchen, public confidence in the institution is seriously eroded, and questions regarding the limits of police power are raised that may compromise the effectiveness of law enforcement institutions.

In a democratic society that places a high value on justice—the belief that it is better to let 10 guilty suspects go rather than wrongly convict an innocent person—it is difficult to argue for the unfettered use of deception in interrogation. The courts will ultimately define the acceptable forms and the extent to which it can be practiced. The need for efficiency will continue to exist alongside other values that are central to our conceptions of justice. It is important that we understand that many of the techniques of deception in use today fall short of their promise—while adversely affecting judgments of guilt and inspiring unfounded confidence—and that false confessions can and do occur.

■ Learn More on the Internet

For more information on police interrogation issues go to www.aclu.org and search on the term "police interrogation."   ■

Discussion Questions

1. Enumerate the different techniques police use to use interrogatory deception.
2. Explain the significance of the court case *Miranda v. Arizona*.
3. Distinguish between an interview and an interrogation. How does *Miranda* influence each?
4. Describe the "slippery slope" argument, and give an example.

REFERENCES

Ashcraft v. Tennessee, 322 U.S. 143 (1944).

Ayling, C. J. (1984). Corroborating false confessions: An empirical analysis of legal safeguards against false confessions. *Wisconsin Law Review, 4*(1121), 1191–1192.

Box, S. (1999). *Lying: Moral choice in public and private life* (2nd ed.). New York: Vintage Books.

Bram v. United States, 168 U.S. 532 (1897).

Brown v. Mississippi, 297 U.S. 278 (1936).

Caldero, M. A., & Crank, J. P. (2011). *Police ethics: The corruption of noble cause* (rev. 3rd ed.). Boston: Elsevier (Anderson Publishing).

Cassell, P. G. (1998). Protecting the innocent from false confessions and lost confessions–and from Miranda. *The Journal of Criminal Law & Criminology, 88,* 497–556.

Cassell, P. G., & Hayman, B. S. (1996). Police interrogation in the 1990s: An empirical study of the effects of Miranda. *UCLA Law Review, 43,* 1084–1124.

Crank, J. P. (2004). *Understanding police culture* (2nd ed.). Cincinnati: Anderson.

DePaulo, B. M., & Pfeifer, R. L. (1986). On-the-job experience and skill at detecting deception. *Journal of Applied Psychology, 16,* 249–267.

Florida v. Cayward, 552 So. 2d 971 (1989).

Gudjonsson, G. H. (1989). Compliance in an interrogation situation: A new scale. *Personality and Individual Differences, 10,* 535–540.

Gudjonsson, G. H. (1992). *The psychology of interrogations, confessions, and testimony.* London: Wiley.

Hartman, K. (2009). *Charges dropped against 2 men convicted of murder.* Retrieved May 5, 2010, Available from cbs2chicago.com/local/wrongful.conviction.release.2.1075800.html.

Hess, J. E. (2010). *Interviewing and interrogation for law enforcement* (2nd ed.). New Providence: LexisNexis Matthew Bender (Anderson Publishing).

Illinois v. Perkins, 110 S.CT. 2394 (1990).

Inbaue, F. E., & Reid, J. E. (1962). *Criminal interrogation and confessions.* Baltimore: Williams & Wilkins.

Inbaue, F. E., Reid, J. E., & Buckley, J. P. (1986). *Criminal interrogation and confessions* (3rd ed.). Baltimore: Williams & Wilkins.

Inbaue, F. E., Reid, J. E., Buckley, J. P., & Jayne, B. C. (2001). *Criminal interrogation and confessions* (4th ed.). Gaithersburg: Aspen.

Jayne, B. C., & Buckley, J. P. (1999). *The investigator anthology.* Chicago: Reid.

Jerome, R. (August 13, 1995). Suspect confessions. *The New York Times*.

Kamisar, Y. (1966). Dissent from the Miranda dissents: Some comments on the 'new' Fifth Amendment and the old 'Voluntariness' test. *Michigan Law Review, 59*, 594–635.

Kassin, S. M. (1997). The psychology of confession evidence. *American Psychologist, 52*, 221–233.

Kassin, S. M. (2008). Confession evidence. *Criminal Justice and Behavior, 35*, 1309–1322.

Kassin, S. M., & Fong, C. T. (1999). I'm innocent! Effects of training on judgments of truth and deception in the interrogation room. *Law and Human Behavior, 23*, 499–516.

Kassin, S. M., & McNall, J. (1991). Police interrogations and confessions: Communicating promises and threats by pragmatic implication. *Law and Human Behavior, 15*, 233–251.

Kassin, S. M., Meissner, C. A., & Norwick, R. J. (2005). 'I'd know a false confession if I saw one': A comparative study of college students and police investigators. *Law and Human Behavior, 15*, 233–351.

Kassin, S. M., & Wrightsman, L. S. (1985). Confession evidence. In S. M. Kassin, & L. S. Wrightsman (Eds.), *The psychology of evidence and trial procedure* (pp. 67–94). Beverly Hills: Sage.

LaGrange, R. L. (1998). *Policing American Society* (2nd ed.). Chicago: Nelson-Hall.

Leo, R. (1996). Inside the interrogation room. *Journal of Criminal Law and Criminology, 86*, 266–303.

Leo, R. (2008). *Police interrogation and American justice*. Cambridge: Harvard University Press.

Leyra v. Denno, 347 U.S. 556 (1954).

McCormick, C. T. (1972). *Handbook of the law of evidence* (2nd ed.). St. Paul: West.

Meissner, C. A., & Kassin, S. M. (2002). 'He's guilty!' Investigator bias in judgments of truth and deception. *Law and Human Behavior, 26*, 469–480.

Meyer, J. R., & Reppuci, N. D. (2007). Police practices and perceptions regarding juvenile interrogation and interrogative suggestibility. *Behavioral Sciences and the Law, 25*, 757–780.

Miranda v. Arizona, 384 U.S. 436 (1966).

Ofshe, R., & Watters, E. (1994). *Making monsters: False memories, psychotherapy, and sexual hysteria*. New York: Scribner.

Packer, H. (1968). *The limits of the criminal sanction*. Stanford: Stanford University Press.

People v. Adams, 143 Cal.App.3d 970 (1983).

Reid and Associates. (2010). Retrieved April 29, 2010, Available from reid.com/services/r_behavior.html.

Rogers v. Richmond, 356 U.S. 534 (1961).

Sasaki, D. W. (1988). Guarding the guardians: Police trickery and confessions. *Stanford Law Review, 40*, 1593–1616.

Skolnick, J. H., & Leo, R. (1992). The ethics of deceptive interrogation. *Criminal Justice Ethics, 2*, 3–12.

Spano v. New York, 360 U.S. 315 (1959).

State v. Jackson, 304 S.E.2d 134 (1983).

State v. Jackson, 308 N.C. 549 (1983).

State v. Patton, 826 A.2d 783 (2003).

United States v. Anderson, 533 D.C. Cir. (1976). F.2d 1210, 1212 n.3.

Vrij, A. (2001). Detecting liars. *Psychologist, 14*, 596–598.

Wakefield, H., & Underwager, R. (1998). Coerced or nonvoluntary confessions. *Behavioral Sciences and the Law, 16*, 423–440.

Ward v. State, 408 N.E.2d 140 (1980).

Ward v. Texas, 316 U.S. 547 (1942).

Warden, R., & Drizin, S. A. (Eds.). (2009). *True stories of false confessions.* Evanston: Northwestern University Press.

White, W. S. (1979). Police trickery in inducing confessions. *University of Pennsylvania Law Review, 127,* 581–629.

Woody, W. D., & Forrest, K. D. (2009). Effects of false-evidence ploys and expert testimony on jurors' verdicts, recommended sentences, and perceptions of confession evidence. *Behavioral Sciences and the Law, 27,* 333–360.

Wrightsman, L. S., & Kassin, S. M. (1993). *Confessions in the court-room.* Newbury Park: Sage.

CHAPTER 6

Using Ethical Dilemmas in Training Police[1]

Joycelyn M. Pollock, Howard E. Williams

discretion	gratuities	police ethics
duty	loyalty	utilitarianism

A police detective is investigating a case involving the disappearance under suspicious circumstances of a young woman, and investigators suspect foul play. During the investigation, the detective learns that his niece has begun dating the missing woman's ex-boyfriend, who is a "person of interest" in the case. Should the detective warn his niece that her new boyfriend is potentially involved in his ex-girlfriend's mysterious disappearance? If the boyfriend is not involved, by disclosing his suspicions will the detective damage the boyfriend's reputation? If the boyfriend is involved, will the detective jeopardize the investigation by disclosing information?

Should the detective remain silent and abide by the *Canons of Police Ethics* (1992), which require the officer to keep secret confidential information unless revelation is necessary in the performance of his duty? What if he says nothing to warn his niece and the boyfriend later harms her? What if the niece and her family then learn that the detective knew of the boyfriend's potential involvement in the disappearance of another woman and had not warned them?

Where does the detective's principle duty lie? Should the detective protect his niece, protect the investigation, protect the rights of the "person of interest," protect his family relationships, or adhere to the *Canons of Police Ethics*? How can the detective determine the proper ethical course? More importantly, how

---

[1]This chapter is based on an earlier version, "Ethical Dilemmas in Policing," by Joycelyn Pollock and Ronald Becker.

can we best prepare law enforcement officers to untangle the Gordian knot of complicated ethical dilemmas?

This chapter discusses ethics training for police officers. With the advent of video cameras and video recorders in cellular telephones, public scrutiny of police actions is greater than ever. Because of internet sharing sites, such as YouTube, Facebook, and Twitter, millions of people can view video of an officer engaged in misconduct within minutes of its happening. Clearly, it is important to prevent, or at least to reduce, the occurrence of such events, but the current emphasis on stricter personnel screening, better training, improved internal processes, and internal and external integrity units fails to fully solve the problem (Johnson & Cox, 2004).

For the police, ethical practice is not a simple matter of knowing and following a set of rules. It requires considerable exercise of discretion and split-second judgments. A long list of policy statements or a detailed rule book cannot ensure that a police officer is exercising good judgment. A framework for decision-making that fosters ethical decisions is required (Johnson & Cox, 2004).

There is a growing body of literature on the importance of teaching ethics in criminal justice curricula. The classic literature first appeared in the 1980s and early 1990s (Kleinig, 1990; Pollock, 1993, 1994; Schmalleger & McKenrick, 1991; Silvester, 1990). The new millennium witnessed a resurgence of interest in the topic (Grant, 2002; Johnson & Cox, 2004; Lord & Bjerregaard, 2003; Pollock, 2010; Wyatt-Nichol & Franks, 2009), with police ethics receiving the lion's share of attention. As interest in teaching ethics has grown, so has discussion over the most effective way to deliver the lessons. Debate has focused on the relative merits of college classroom education versus police preservice academy training, but there is increasing recognition that both forms of instruction are important.

Police ethics is particularly relevant, according to Kleinig (1990), because of the issues relevant to police, the discretionary nature of policing, the authority of the police, the fact that the police are not habitually moral, the temptations inherent in police work, and peer pressure. Moreover, in performance of their duties, the police must constantly strike a balance between legitimate but often conflicting values and rights (Marenin, 2004).

On reviewing the literature, one can readily identify the issues that have attracted the attention of researchers (although this is not an exhaustive list): gratuities, corruption, bribery, "shopping," loyalty versus whistle blowing, undercover tactics, the use of deception, discretion, sleeping on duty, sex on duty and other misfeasance, deadly force, and brutality. Because of their predominance in the literature, one might assume that these are the most problematic ethical issues in police work. However, officers often voice different perceptions. For example, undercover tactics (i.e., deception) have received a great deal of attention in the literature, but many officers never experience such issues because they are on patrol and not on assignments that require covert activity. The issues of deadly force and brutality are certainly important, but they are not day-to-day concerns for most officers because these officers are rarely involved in such situations. A National Institute of Justice study indicates that police officers use or threaten to use force in only 1.6% of face-to-face encounters with citizens, and only 55% of those encounters actually result in the police using physical force (Durose, Smith, & Langan, 2007). In a participant observation study of police/citizen encounters, Alpert and Dunham (2004) discovered that, compared to suspects' resistance, officers often used less force than the law and their departments' policies permitted.

Although most of the ethical issues discussed in the academic literature and popular press involve officer misconduct and even criminality, many ethical issues that should be covered in training do not involve misconduct at all. There are many situations in which no decision an officer makes is clearly wrong, but the officer does experience a dilemma, and training could help that officer work through the possible choices to determine the best solution to the problem.

Only recently has the topic of ethics found its place in the training curricula of law enforcement. Nearly every state now requires law enforcement recruits to receive ethics training during preservice academy training; however, in comparison to preservice academy training, ethics receives less attention in post-academy in-service instruction (Wyatt-Nichol & Franks, 2009). Post-academy education in ethics is important because it reinforces proper values and reduces the effects of exposure to inappropriate behavior within the police culture (Braswell, Miller, & Pollock, 2006; Caldero & Crank, 2011; Kratcoski, 2004).

The current emphasis on police cadet training and in-service instruction at the executive level misses a critical mass of officers who are likely to experience ethical dilemmas mid career. Supervisors in an organization, such as sergeants and lieutenants, are the most often overlooked groups for ethics instruction (Wyatt-Nichol & Franks, 2009). Department policies, which are intended to give officers direction on acceptable behavior and practices, too often create ethical dilemmas for officers. It is critical, therefore, to train everyone who is involved in creating or interpreting policy, including supervisors. Studying the dilemmas that officers confront can be the catalyst for prompting policy reforms. Additionally, ethics training can enable supervisors to better distinguish between insubordination and legitimate ethical intervention (Wyatt-Nichol & Franks, 2009).

Law enforcement agencies often view ethics instruction as a single training block, when it should be continually reinforced (Whisenand, 2009). Ethics courses can be influential, but one lone course is unlikely to develop values or to change behaviors (Lord & Bjerregaard, 2003). A study of police departments in Alabama, Kentucky, Mississippi, and Tennessee indicated that the officers involved were indifferent to their ethics training. The study's results imply that either ethics training had no impact on the officers or that the amount or quality of the training was insufficient (Lee, 2006).

Experience has taught that traditional pedagogical approaches are ineffective for developing moral reasoning skills and ethical responses among law enforcement personnel (Wyatt-Nichol & Franks, 2009). In the pedagogical approach, the teacher is the expert lecturing to the student who is expected to learn the lesson (Birzer, 2004). In their training, police officers show a preference for case studies, but they dislike role playing, breakout sessions, and small group activities (Miller, Braswell, & Whitehead, 2010; Redden, 2009).

The best way to prepare officers for policing based on democratic values is through an andragogical approach to training rather than through the traditional pedagogical approach (Marenin, 2004). In the andragogical approach, the teacher is a facilitator, guiding students through exercises that enhance the students' capacity to function as self-directed learners (Birzer, 2004). The andragogical approach is the most appropriate method to teach ethics to police recruits and police officers because it values the experience of the participants and it makes the material relevant to current and future responsibilities (Wyatt-Nichol & Franks, 2009).

Instruction limited to discussions of philosophical systems is unlikely to be effective, because officers do not find such instruction applicable to their needs and experiences. Generally, police administrators and officers prefer the case study method to learn about ethics (Van Slyke, 2007). Police officers generally find it insulting to be told that committing a crime is an ethical issue, and instructors who approach the topic that way soon lose the attention of the class participants. There is a difference between ethics and discipline. Deciding whether to participate in criminal behavior is not an ethical dilemma for police officers, and the discussion need not consume precious time during ethics training.

As an andragogical tool, one author used ethical dilemmas turned in by class participants as the foundation for course content. Ethical dilemmas are situations in which it is difficult to make a decision, either because the right course of action is unclear or the right course of action carries some negative consequences (Pollock, 2010). The instructor asked the class participants to write down a difficult ethical dilemma they had faced. This assignment took place after presentation of introductory material on ethics, morals, and value systems, but before presenting any issue-based material, so officers were not yet focused on any specific type of dilemma. It was unclear whether officers reported ethical dilemmas according to frequency, seriousness, or some other criteria. Issues that posed the most serious ethical concerns may have been those that officers least commonly faced. Officers might have identified examples of the most serious incident, the most recent incident, or the incident most frequently presented to them. This exercise, however, presented a useful way of obtaining relevant, realistic classroom material on which to base a discussion of ethics.

Content of ethical dilemmas for police officers can also be gleaned from newspapers, books on ethics, and journal articles. Delattre (2006) is a source for a number of ethical dilemmas, as is Cohen and Feldberg (1991). Both Pollock (2010) and Braswell et al. (2006) provide dilemmas for police personnel and corrections and other criminal justice professions. Pollock (1993) also discusses a number of categories of police ethics that an instructor can use to develop other dilemmas: discretion, duty, honesty, loyalty, and gratuities.

DISCRETION

Discretion is the authority to make a decision between two or more choices (Pollock, 2010). Obviously, all ethical dilemmas involve making choices. The situations categorized in this area, however, are within the purview of police discretion (e.g., whether to arrest, whether to issue a citation, how to contend with an altercation). The literature does not readily identify these dilemmas as ethical issues, but, in some situations, officers feel uncomfortable about what the law or regulations require them to do, or they are sincerely confused as to the appropriate course of action.

Typically, the law involved is relatively minor—a traffic citation, enforcing a municipal warrant, or some nonviolent misdemeanor. The reason the officers hesitate or feel that the decision presents an ethical dilemma is because of situational elements (e.g., the age or poverty of the offender or the perception that the person deserves a break). The following examples are representative of what officers report as dilemmas:

An officer receives a call regarding a business holding a shoplifter. The 75-year-old female suspect needs her medications. However, the manager of the business insists on filing charges against her. Security officers at the K-mart place a wagon call. You get there and find security has detained a 70-year-old woman for trying to steal hearing aid batteries. She is on a fixed income and unable to purchase such items. She even looks like your mother. While on patrol one day, I was dispatched to a disturbance at a gas station. On arrival, I spotted a kid I saw in the neighborhood a lot. I knew this kid lived with his grandmother and that they were barely making ends meet. I had run into problems before with the kid begging for money and washing people's windows at gas stations without being asked. The gas station attendant wanted the child arrested for trespassing because he said the child harassed the customers.

Usually in these situations, the offender is poor and/or elderly. The storekeepers insist on prosecution, leaving the officer to struggle between showing compassion and enforcing the law. The next set of dilemmas present no demanding complainant, but the officer feels torn about enforcing the law or feels that strict legality might not serve the ends of justice:

> Officer A was faced with arresting a person on a parole violation. The officer, while talking to family members, learned that the parole violator had just started a new job, which was verified by his employer. What should Officer A do? (The parole violation was for a first driving while impaired.) I arrested a lady with a baby for numerous traffic warrants. Do you take the baby to juvenile and her to jail, make arrangements for someone else to care for the baby, or just let the woman go and tell her to take care of the warrants on her own? She has no money and gave us no trouble. Riding with a partner, we stopped a person in traffic for multiple violations, no insurance, no driver's license, no ID at all, and who would face going to jail for traffic violations on Christmas Eve. Would you discourage your partner from taking him to jail?

The most frequent types of incidents that officers relate to involve women and/or families with children stopped for some sort of traffic violation. Some officers are very clear as to the criteria they use to guide their discretion, but others are less certain about the ethical role of the police in traffic enforcement.

Discussion related to traffic offenses can involve discussions of the greater good. If an officer does not want to arrest someone for traffic violations on Christmas Eve, the officer should explain what decision she would make on Erev Pesach or Ramadan. Is it the holiday itself and the officer's bias toward that religion (egoism), or is it a sincere desire not to inflict distress on the driver and his family on the eve of a religious holiday that is important to them (ethics of care)? Is it more important to be concerned for the welfare of a child than to arrest the mother who has neglected to pay or could not afford to pay for previously issued citations (utilitarianism)? Does the law always apply so that there is no excuse for the violations (ethical formalism)? The instructor can ask questions to guide the class participants through the discussion so that they can determine for themselves the proper ethical course of action.

Another category of dilemmas related to the exercise of discretion involves situations in which no law or policy is involved, but the officer is still perplexed regarding how to resolve the situation. These situations are often family disputes in which a significant problem exists prior to interaction with a police officer. Here the officer's dilemma arises from a sincere desire to do the right thing, but the officer is not sure what the right thing is. Referral sources in the community, although plentiful, are often unavailable or overused. The large number of these dilemmas submitted by the officers indicates that they perceive significant ethical issues in this area of policing. For most officers, it is not necessarily a question of doing something wrong but rather of finding the best solution to a difficult problem.

> What do you do when called to a scene to transport and find some type of housing for an elderly parent whom the family no longer wants because of mental impairment, knowing that the family, in the past, has used the parent's resources as their mainstay? Officer A received a call regarding trespassing. The officer spoke at the residence with the complainant, who wanted a female removed from his house. The female had a small child and was the complainant's ex-girlfriend, who had no family and no place to go.

Class participants very often identify this last type of dilemma as problematic. Typically boyfriends want girlfriends removed, girlfriends want boyfriends removed, parents want children removed, and husbands want wives removed, or vice versa, and the police officers called to the scene must apply the law to what is essentially a family dispute. Police officers express the frustration inherent in having to deal with what are essentially difficult interpersonal problems, such as the examples below:

> You and your partner are dispatched to a disturbance at a low-income apartment complex. The call involves a drunk husband and drunk wife calling the police for no reason. No crime has been committed. After being dispatched to the same apartment unit three or four times in one night, how should an officer resolve the situation? Arrest one or both for public intoxication inside their own residence? Unplug the phone? Continue to return every time they call? Officer A goes to a disturbance at a residence. It is his third time there. The problem is the same each time. The father gets drunk then tells his son, the son's wife, and the son's kids to leave his home. The son refuses to take his family and leave. The real problem is that the father is drunk and being unreasonable, yet the father has a legal right to tell his son's family to leave. What should you do?

Some dilemmas arise because of a personal or professional relationship between the officer and the subject. Typically, this involves stopping a speeding car and finding the driver to be another officer or responding to an altercation involving another officer or family member.

> You are on patrol, riding one man, at approximately 10:00 P.M. You and one other vehicle are stopped at a red light. The light changes and you and the other vehicle start driving. Suddenly you observe the other vehicle weaving from lane to lane. You turn on your lights and siren and after about an eight-block drive the vehicle finally pulls over. You

exit your vehicle and find that not only is the driver very intoxicated, but he is also your first cousin. What should you do? While working a side job at a nightclub, you notice a disturbance on the far side of the club. As you handle the problem, you discover that the instigator of the problem is an off-duty officer who is extremely intoxicated and refuses to follow your instructions. In addition, the other party involved, who is not an officer, is claiming that the officer assaulted him, although the other party does not know he is a police officer. Officer A is on patrol. Suddenly he spots a vehicle traveling at a high rate of speed. Officer A stops the vehicle and finds out that the person is a law enforcement officer from a different agency. Officer A observes that he is highly intoxicated. What should Officer A do?

By presenting the last two situations as dilemmas, officers indicate that they perceive special treatment given to other officers as questionable, even if they typically defend preferential treatment. Professional courtesy is an issue that always generates a great deal of debate in law enforcement groups.

Discussions arising from dilemmas concerning the use of discretion can center on which criteria the class participants consider ethical and which criteria they find have less ethical support in guiding the exercise of their discretion. For instance, the risk of future harm posed by a traffic violator is an ethical criterion in deciding whether to issue a citation, but the attractiveness of the driver definitely is not. Because full enforcement is not always an option, officers must use discretion in their decision-making. It is important for them at least to recognize the ethical issues involved in using that discretion.

As it relates to the exercise of discretion, training in ethics helps the officer in two very important ways. First, when officers are faced with difficult decisions in the field, ethics training teaches them how to consider different options and how to assess the possible consequences of choosing those options. A litany of rules and regulations cannot be comprehensive enough to do that. Second, just as it should be in a democratic society, officers are called on every day to justify their actions. Participating in discussions about ethical dilemmas better prepares officers to answer questions about their decision-making when those questions arise.

DUTY

Duty is a required behavior or action. Duty may involve situations in which the officer knows that the job requires a particular action but feels that action is either inconvenient or a waste of time. In the first situation, some of the examples of discretion we have mentioned might also apply to duty. For instance, in the case of a family altercation when a police officer responds and finds no crime has been committed, what is his or her duty? Is there a duty to try to resolve a volatile situation before it erupts into a crime? Some police officers believe that they have a duty to help the poor and homeless find shelter; other officers do not see their job as including such "social work." This is the type of discussion that inevitably brings out differences of opinion among police officers and reveals how they view their role in the community. It is, of course, also an ethical issue.

The other type of duty dilemma is more straightforward. The officer knows there is a duty to perform a certain act. A frequent situation is the temptation (and evidently widespread practice) of either driving by a minor accident scene or avoiding it because it occurs near the end of a shift. There were also dilemmas involving repetitive 911 calls and the temptation to avoid them or to respond to them halfheartedly. The following were examples:

> It is 10 minutes to off-duty time. You view an accident. Do you work the accident, even though you want to go home, or do you avoid the accident by sneaking around it? It is 10:30 P.M. and you are a late shift unit heading into the station when you notice a large traffic jam. As you near the scene, you observe that it is an accident involving two cars and a fixed object. Do you stop and respond or take the back way to the station? You get a disturbance call from the dispatcher at a certain location. You can see the location from inside a building you are in, and you see that there is no disturbance at that location. Is it necessary to leave the building to respond to the call?

Another duty dilemma issue arises concerning the risk of contracting communicable diseases. Finally, there are miscellaneous duty issues regarding using regular work hours to conduct personal business.

> You are involved in a situation in which someone is injured and is in need of cardiopulmonary resuscitation (CPR). You know the injured person is a drug addict and a criminal. Do you perform CPR or not? Whether to get "in service" after clearing a call or staying "out of service" to handle some personal business or affairs. An officer works a plainclothes assignment in a division where each squad is small and has its own supervisor. The officer's supervisor is off this day and the likelihood of being noticed leaving early is almost nonexistent. So why not cut out an hour and a half early when it will not be noticed? Your work will not go undone.

Discussion in the classroom shows participants that not all police officers view duty the same way. To move beyond a simple exchange of opinion, it is necessary to apply an ethical framework analysis that helps each officer understand that, although his or her position is legal and might be justifiable to some degree, it might have less ethical support than other positions.

HONESTY

Under the general heading of honesty, officers submit dilemmas involving self-protection or enrichment, honesty versus the need to effect an arrest, and bribery. Many participants relate dilemmas in which officers are confronted with temptations of money or other goods, typically "found" or at burglary scenes.

> Officers A and B are on the scene of a homicide involving a supposed drug dealer who is lying dead on the ground. No one is present except the officers, who then find $20,000 cash in suspect's pockets. Officer B insists that they should keep and split the money with each other. An officer is patrolling through an abandoned apartment complex when he observes in the back of the complex a stack of lumber to be used for remodeling. The officer is working on a project at home and could use a few pieces of the lumber. Nobody else is around. What should he do?

One interesting device to start the discussion is with a dilemma using a $20 bill "found" by a police officer, asking about the proper procedure, then continuing the discussion with larger amounts of money. Although officers may feel that it is a minor breach (if any at all) to keep the $20, at some point, they perceive keeping larger amounts of "found" money as unethical. The discussion then becomes whether it is the amount of money or the keeping of it that should determine the ethical nature of the response.

Another type of dilemma involves officers trying to cover up their own wrongdoing by lying or not coming forward when they commit minor acts of wrongdoing. Given the number of dilemmas reporting small "fender benders" with police cars, one might surmise that the police parking lot is an insurer's nightmare.

> An officer had an accident where there were no witnesses. Since it was an auto-fixed object, the officer was at fault, but he did not want disciplinary action. The officer was deciding whether to suggest that another car cut him off to explain how the accident occurred.

In another situation, officers must either tell the truth and lose (or risk losing) an arrest, or misrepresent facts to save the arrest. Although this is a popular topic in the literature, it is not a frequent dilemma submitted by officers.

> You stop somebody, check his pockets, and find some dope. You had no probable cause to search him, but you did anyhow because you thought he might be holding. Do you find a reason to arrest him and then put in the report that you found the dope after the arrest, so it will not be thrown out in court? Officer A sees a known crack dealer on a corner and searches him. He finds drugs, makes an arrest, and then lies about or makes up probable cause for the search in his report and in his

courtroom testimony. Nobody knows but the officer and the suspect.
The suspect did have the drug, and he is a dealer in that neighborhood.

The issue of lying about the facts of a case, called "*testilying*," is a form of "noble cause corruption" discussed by Caldero and Crank (2011). Testilying was central to the infamous Rampart scandal in the Los Angeles Police Department. A year-long investigation brought 70 Los Angeles police officers under investigation and led to the courts overturning more than 100 criminal convictions. Allegations against the officers included planting evidence, filing false reports, and perjury. The Los Angeles County District Attorney's Office prosecuted four police officers for conspiracy to obstruct or pervert justice. The city of Los Angeles faced more than 140 civil suits stemming from the Rampart scandal, the costs of which exceeded $70 million (Glover & Lait, 2005). Training can go a long way to insulate officers from the temptation to subvert legal means for short-term goals by showing what happens when an officer's lies are revealed. It is not an understatement to say that lying to save one case endangers hundreds. When officers are exposed as liars, their testimony becomes worthless.

Bribery is a reward for doing something illegal or for not performing a required duty. There are usually very few submissions from officers dealing with bribery. It might be that officers do not view bribery as a dilemma because they seldom receive opportunities, or they do not want to admit that it occurs. Officers have indicated that accepting a bribe is one of the most serious ethical violations that an officer can commit (Klockars, Ivkovich, Harver, & Haberfeld, 2000). It might be that officers understand that accepting a bribe is a criminal offense, and, as discussed previously, officers consider abstaining from committing a crime a matter of discipline, not a matter of ethics.

I was offered money for taking care of a ticket. I was also offered money for giving information about a driver's license or license plate.

In discussing honesty, the instructor must be mindful that officers will often claim that honesty and integrity are the paramount virtues in police service. Nevertheless, they will likely present several scenarios of officers being untruthful. The instructor can guide the class participants through a discussion of what happened in those instances and what could possibly have happened had the deception been discovered. Often the conversation reveals adverse consequences for everyone who knows of the lie. When the officers understand the far-reaching consequences, the lesson has more meaning.

LOYALTY

In situations or dilemmas involving **loyalty** versus whistle blowing, officers must decide what to do when faced with the wrongdoing of other police officers. The literature accurately reflects the saliency of this issue for police officers, given the frequency of this type of submission. Officers' dilemmas run the gamut, from seeing relatively minor wrongdoing (e.g., overtime abuses) to very serious violations (e.g., physical abuse of a suspect or the commission of another crime).

> You are on patrol as you roll up on a possible narcotics transaction involving a known dope dealer. You make the block to set up on the buyer, who is in a vehicle. By the time you make the block, the buyer is rolling. You go to chase down the buyer and it takes you several blocks to catch up to him. In your mind he is trying to lose you. You manage to catch up to him about a mile away. It turns out the driver is an off-duty sheriff's deputy. What do you do? An officer is dispatched as a backup unit where an alarm is going off at a large jewelry store. He insists on doing the report and listing items that were taken. A couple of days later you see him wearing items or showing off items he claims to have got [*sic*] a good deal on. These are items you saw in the store that was burglarized. What should you do?

Finally, there are dilemmas involving actions that technically are crimes and often pose risks to other officers, but they are not perceived to be as serious as buying drugs or stealing from the scene of a burglary. Several of these dilemmas involve minor traffic accidents. Because officers are disciplined for driving errors, it is always a temptation to avoid responsibility.

> You are standing in a parking lot when you notice Officer A backing his car out of his parking space. He hits the car behind him, then drives off. A few seconds later the owner of the car comes out and asks you if you saw what happened. What should you do? One day while leaving the parking lot, my partner was driving and accidentally damaged a new patrol car, which was parked next to us. We both got out of our patrol vehicle and observed the minor damage to the new vehicle. We both looked around but did not notice anyone else near. My partner told me he would report it to the sergeant at the end of the shift. However, the next day at roll call, the roll call sergeant asked if anyone knew how the new patrol car received the damage. Officer A sleeps on duty and does not run his calls. What should I (his partner) do? Officer A is an alcoholic and consumes alcohol heavily every day. Even while on duty, Officer A is intoxicated. Joe Blow, a concerned citizen who owns a liquor store in the beat, knows of Officer A's situation. He decides to call Officer B and advises him to talk to Officer A about the problem before it gets out of hand. What should Officer B do?

Because covering up for another officer is now more risky, with the possibility of individual civil liability, it might be that fewer officers are willing to draw the "blue curtain." However, it is important to discuss this topic. Research indicates that officers still feel they should cover up for other officers because the rank and file will ostracize and sanction officers who come forth with the truth. In an attitude survey, Weisburd and Greenspan (2000) discovered that 80% of police officers believe the "code of silence" was not essential for police trust and good policing, but two-thirds of the officers believed that a whistle blower would encounter sanctions.

Current research hints that the "blue curtain of secrecy" is breaking down. More officers seem to be willing to bear witness against fellow officers (Barker, 2002). However, officers are more likely to report wrongdoing of other officers if it involves acquisition of goods or money rather than excessive force or violation of departmental rules (Westmarland, 2005).

GRATUITIES

The subject of **gratuities** is hard to ignore in any law enforcement ethics class. It is represented in the policing literature and identified by laypersons as a perennial issue (Coleman, 2004; Kania, 1988, 2004; Prenzler & MacKay, 1995; Ruiz & Bono, 2004; Sewell, 2007), but even researchers disagree on the effects of certain gratuities. Critics (Coleman, 2004; Ruiz & Bono, 2004) argue against gratuities. They claim that:

1. Police officers are professionals, and professionals do not take gratuities.
2. Gratuities are incipient corruptors because people expect different treatment.
3. Gratuities are an abuse of authority and create a sense of entitlement.
4. Gratuities add up to substantial amounts of money and can constitute as much as 30% of an officer's income.
5. Gratuities can be the beginning of more serious forms of corruption.
6. Gratuities are contrary to democratic ideals because they are a type of fee-for-service for public functions.
7. Gratuities create a public perception that police are corrupt.

Kania (2004) counter-argues that:

1. Police are professionals, but other professionals accept gratuities.
2. There is nothing wrong with more frequent users of police services "paying extra" for services.
3. "No-gratuity" rules are means of playing "gotcha" that erode morale.
4. Educators and academics distort the seriousness of gratuities.

Officers themselves often feel that there is nothing wrong with gratuities. One distinction in these dilemmas is the difference between situations involving true gratuities (i.e., something given to all police as a policy) and gifts (i.e., something given to an individual in return for a specific action).

Officer A is new to his beat. Where he worked before, he would stop by a local convenience store and get something to drink and pay for it. He has learned from past experiences that people always expect something in return for free gifts. In this new beat, he stops by a store. The clerk refuses to accept payment. Officer A explains that he would prefer to pay. The clerk, now upset, accuses the officer of trying to be better than the others and will tell his supervisor, who also stops by. What does Officer A do? Officer A stopped in a store on his beat and was offered anything he wanted in the store within reason: food, cigarettes, Skoal. And the worker offered him lottery tickets, which he may or may not have taken. After several days of going to the store, the worker tells the officer he sometimes has problems and could the officer give the worker his beeper number so he can call him if he has problems. The question is, should the officer give his beeper number and feel obligated to return a call from this person because he has gotten free articles? A guy's car had broken down on the freeway. As an officer on duty, I stopped. I took him home since he only lived a short distance away in my beat. It was early in the morning, and the man was very appreciative. He wanted to buy me breakfast to show his appreciation, so he offered me five dollars.

Discussion involving the ethics of gratuities can be hampered by defensiveness on the part of police participants. It is helpful to explore regional differences and clearly discuss definitions (i.e., the difference between gratuities and gifts) and the reason that gratuities to public servants constitute a problematic issue.

Training should reinforce departmental policies. Although some departments permit certain types of gratuities, such as free drinks or meals, other departments do not. Training should also provide officers a chance to share with each other their way of dealing with gratuities. For instance, some officers will explain that they do not argue with staff in a business where they are not expected to pay, but they leave a tip equal to the cost of the meal. What often comes up in these discussions is why it is that officers may be prohibited from taking gratuities but the chief's office accepts sponsorships from restaurants or businesses for official police functions. Many see this as hypocritical and contrary to the argument that gratuities are wrong because they may lead to actual or perceived favoritism.

NOW THAT WE HAVE DEFINED THE ISSUES, WHAT DO WE DO WITH THEM?

Descriptions of dilemmas submitted by officers indicate that they view many relatively mundane issues as problematic. Decisions regarding whether to enforce a warrant or ticket, what to do in a domestic disturbance, and whether to leave early from an assignment are not as "serious" as police brutality or the use of deception in undercover work. Yet, it seems clear that if an ethics course for officers is to be relevant, it should cover these issues as well. The approach one should take in analyzing these dilemmas is up to the individual instructor. What follows is one way to utilize these dilemmas in a classroom.

Most dilemmas can be resolved in many ways, and discussions that include only two diametrically opposed positions fail to develop problem-solving skills. The instructor should ask for a variety of solutions and explore the relative merits of each, thereby helping the class participants understand the multifaceted approach to resolving ethical dilemmas. Any class of police ethics must have a philosophical basis to move it beyond a mere "bull session" of opinions. Although one may decide to simplify matters and present only one ethical framework, such as utilitarianism, and then use it to analyze ethical dilemmas, another approach may be to compare several ethical frameworks, such as utilitarianism, ethical formalism, and religion (Pollock, 2010; Williams & Arrigo, 2008).

After dilemmas are submitted, it is useful to group them together in some order so that similar dilemmas are discussed together. One benefit of this approach is that officers realize they have similar concerns. The anonymity of the method ensures that officers have the opportunity to address honestly and describe the dilemmas they feel are most prevalent and important.

The first form of analysis is to determine at what level there is disagreement. One might ask the following questions: What does the law require? What does departmental policy require? What do personal ethics require? Interestingly, there is often heated discussion regarding legal definitions and policy mandates. This is why some ethics classes become training courses in such things as domestic violence laws and victim rights legislation. There may be agreement on whether there is an applicable law but disagreement on departmental policy. There may be agreement on law and policy but not on an ethical analysis. If there is an applicable law or policy and there is still an ethical concern whether to follow such law or policy, the issue of civil disobedience and duty becomes relevant. Can an officer be ethical if he or she follows a personal code of ethics that is contrary to a departmental directive? What if the departmental directive has no support from any ethical system? These are sensitive and important issues.

If there is no applicable law or departmental policy, the discussion can quickly be directed to an ethical analysis of possible solutions. The class should incorporate a review of major ethical frameworks (e.g., utilitarianism, ethical formalism, ethics of care, egoism). Participants then can be assigned to groups and be provided an ethical framework that they must use to determine a solution that is justified by that ethical framework. Another approach is to ask the class for the best solution to the dilemma and then analyze that solution using the ethical framework. For example, one of the previous dilemmas states:

> An officer receives a call regarding a business holding a shoplifter. The 75-year-old female suspect needs her medications. However, the manager of the business insists on filing charges against her.

The first set of questions asks whether there is an applicable law. Yes, there is, and the woman obviously broke it. Is there an applicable departmental policy? Obviously, and the departmental policy would be to enforce the law, especially when there is a complainant wanting to press charges. Does this resolve the dilemma? For some officers it does. Some officers believe that their duty is to enforce the law, not mediate it. Therefore, in this situation, they merely respond to the event by enforcing the law. Other officers, however, would respond by saying there is still an ethical issue. These officers identify this situation as a dilemma. Their solution might be to try to convince the store owner to drop the charges, perhaps even going so far as to pay for the items themselves. Is this their duty? There is obviously no professional duty that dictates such action, but some believe that personal ethics require a more complete response to the situation than merely acting as an agent of the law. The ethical frameworks are then applied to the possible solutions. Ethical formalism would be concerned with duties. Ethics of care would focus on need. **Utilitarianism** would be concerned with the relative costs and benefits of arrest versus some other intervention.

Another dilemma presented previously was the following:

> Officer A is an alcoholic and consumes alcohol heavily every day. Even while on duty, Officer A is intoxicated. Joe Blow, a concerned citizen who owns a liquor store in the beat, knows of Officer A's situation. He decides to call Officer B and advises him to talk to Officer A about the problem before it gets out of hand. What should Officer B do?

The first question remains, is there an applicable law? Public intoxication laws may be applicable. There is almost certainly a violation of departmental rules. Is there an ethical issue? Yes, it is personal loyalty versus whistle blowing. The appropriate solution for any individual officer may be discussed in terms of his or her own value system. Some officers value loyalty more highly than any other virtue. Most balance loyalty against the severity of the wrongdoing. Alcohol use is considered less serious than illegal drug use. More officers would more likely take action against an officer using illegal drugs than against one abusing alcohol, despite the fact that the resultant effects on the officer might be similar. A discussion concerning this dilemma often involves the perceived unfairness of administrative responses. For example, whereas other types of professionals might be censured for alcohol problems, police officers with such problems often lose their jobs and careers. This concern can be tied to utilitarianism. What are the relative costs and benefits associated with turning the officer in, with talking to the officer, or with doing nothing? An application of ethical formalism would be concerned with the duty of the officer who knows the problem exists.

Ethics training requires officers to confront the "rightness" of certain actions that they might not honestly be able to justify. It also allows officers to hear about and discuss dilemmas they might not have confronted yet. By using an andragogical approach, officers can work through the dilemmas after being given the tools of ethical frameworks.

■ Learn More on the Internet

For more on police training and ethics issues, visit policelink.monster.com/training and search the word *"ethics."*   ■

CONCLUSION

This chapter presented the premise that the best ethics course for police officers is one that is relevant to them because it relates to their business needs and personal experiences. One way to achieve that goal is to use the officers' own dilemmas in guiding a discussion of ethics. Most ethical dilemmas fall into particular categories, such as discretion, duty, honesty, loyalty, and gratuities. The frequency of submitted examples that concern more mundane issues indicates that the literature on police ethics may have missed some important, albeit less "juicy," issues of police ethics. Such dilemmas as what to do with an elderly shoplifter, whether to enforce an outstanding warrant for a poor mother, or whether to report a minor fender bender during a shift may not constitute the plot of great cinema and television, but many police officers experience these quandaries nonetheless. The andragogical approach to teaching ethics is well suited to police cadet and police officer learning preferences, and the case study method of analysis we have presented can be utilized for various types of ethical dilemmas. Combining the andragogical approach with the case study method gives police officers the tools to identify and resolve their own ethical dilemmas.

Discussion Questions

1. If you were a police officer, what would you consider to be the five most important elements that should be included in a police code of ethics? List and describe each category.
2. Of all the categories listed in the text—discretion, duty, honesty, and loyalty—which do you think is the most important? Explain your answer. Which do you think is the least important? Explain your answer.

3. What are the dangers of accepting even minor gratuities, such as free cups of coffee, discounts, or free tickets to sporting or entertainment events? Can the acceptance of gratuities contribute to more serious problems in policing?

4. To what extent should a police department strive to minimize discretion? How can a department minimize or structure police discretion? Do officers welcome limits on their discretion? Why or why not?

REFERENCES

Alpert, G., & Dunham, R. (2004). *Understanding police use of force: Officers, suspects, and reciprocity.* New York: Cambridge University Press.

Barker, T. (2002). Ethical police behavior. In K. Lersch (Ed.), *Policing and misconduct* (pp. 1–25). Upper Saddle River: Prentice Hall.

Birzer, M. (2004). Andragogy: Student centered classrooms in criminal justice programs. *Journal of Criminal Justice Education, 15*(2), 393–411.

Braswell, M., Miller, L., & Pollock, J. (2006). *Case studies in criminal justice ethics.* Prospect Heights: Waveland Press.

Caldero, M., & Crank, J. (2011). *Police ethics: The corruption of noble cause* (rev. 3rd ed.). Boston: Elsevier (Anderson Publishing).

Cohen, H., & Feldberg, M. (1991). *Power and restraint: The moral dimension of police work.* New York: Praeger Press.

Coleman, S. (2004). When police should say 'No!' to gratuities? *Criminal Justice Ethics, 23*(1), 33–44.

Delattre, E. (2006). *Character and cops: Ethics in policing* (5th ed.). Lanham: AEI Press.

Durose, M., Smith, E., & Langan, P. (2007). *Contacts between police and the public, 2005.* Washington: U.S. Department of Justice, Bureau of Justice Statistics.

Glover, S., & Lait, M. (March 31, 2005). LAPD settling abuse scandal. *Los Angeles Times.* p. 5, Retrieved April 20, 2010, from articles.latimes.com/2005/mar/31/local/me-rampart31.

Grant, K. (2002). Ethics and law enforcement. *FBI Law Enforcement Bulletin, 71*(12), 11–14.

International Association of Chiefs of Police. (1992). *Canons of police ethics.* Arlington: author.

Johnson, T., & Cox, R. (2004). Police ethics: Organizational implications. *Public Integrity, 5*(7), 67–79.

Kania, R. (1988). Should we tell the police to say 'yes' to gratuities? *Criminal Justice Ethics, 7*(2), 37–49.

Kania, R. (2004). The ethical acceptability of gratuities: Still saying 'yes' after all these years. *Criminal Justice Ethics, 23*(1), 54–63.

Kleinig, J. (1990). Teaching and learning police ethics: Competing and complementary approaches. *Journal of Criminal Justice, 18,* 1–18.

Klockars, C., Ivkovich, S., Harver, W., & Haberfeld, M. (2000). *The measurement of police integrity.* Washington: National Institute of Justice.

Kratcoski, P. (2004). Police education and training in a global society: Guest editor's introduction. *Police Practice and Research, 5*(2), 103–105.

Lee, T. (2006). *Assessing the impact of ethical training on law enforcement personnel* (Doctoral dissertation). University of Southern Mississippi.

Lord, V., & Bjerregaard, B. (2003). Ethics courses: Their impact on the values and ethical decisions of criminal justice students. *Journal of Criminal Justice Education, 14*(2), 191–211.

Marenin, O. (2004). Police training for democracy. *Police Practice and Research, 5*(2), 107–123.

Miller, L., Braswell, M., & Whitehead, J. (2010). *Human relations and police work* (6th ed.). Prospect Heights: Waveland.

Pollock, J. (1993). Ethics and the criminal justice curriculum. *Journal of Criminal Justice Education, 4*(2), 377–391.

Pollock, J. (1994). *Ethics in crime and justice: Dilemmas and decisions* (2nd ed.). Belmont: Wadsworth.

Pollock, J. (2010). *Ethics in crime and justice: Dilemmas and decisions* (6th ed.). Belmont: Wadsworth.

Prenzler, T., & MacKay, P. (1995). Police gratuities: What the public thinks. *Criminal Justice Ethics, 14*(1), 15–25.

Redden, D. (2009). *Ethics training of law enforcement officers: The optimum means of conveyance* (Doctoral dissertation). Capella University.

Ruiz, J., & Bono, C. (2004). At what price a 'freebie'? The real cost of police gratuities. *Criminal Justice Ethics, 23*(1), 44–54.

Schmalleger, F., & McKenrick, R. (1991). *Criminal justice ethics: An annotated bibliography*. Westport, CT: Greenwood Press.

Sewell, C. (2007). Gratuities: Pay now or later. *FBI Law Enforcement Bulletin, 76*(4), 8–12.

Silvester, D. (1990). Ethics and privatization in criminal justice: Does education have a role to play? *Journal of Criminal Justice, 18*, 65–70.

Van Slyke, L. (2007). *Police ethics training: Preferred modes of teaching in higher education law enforcement* (Doctoral dissertation), University of Texas.

Weisburd, D., & Greenspan, R. (2000). *Police attitudes toward abuse of authority: Findings from a national study*. Washington: U.S. Department of Justice, National Institute of Justice.

Westmarland, L. (2005). Police ethics and integrity: Breaking the blue code of silence. *Policing and Society, 15*(2), 145–165.

Whisenand, P. (2009). *Managing police organizations* (7th ed.). Upper Saddle River: Pearson/Prentice Hall.

Williams, C., & Arrigo, B. (2008). *Ethics, crime, and criminal justice*. Upper Saddle River: Pearson.

Wyatt-Nichol, H., & Franks, G. (2009). Ethics training in law enforcement agencies. *Public Integrity, 12*(1), 39–50.

CHAPTER 7

Police Ethics, Legal Proselytism, and the Social Order: Paving the Path to Misconduct

Victor E. Kappeler, Gary W. Potter, Edward Green

KEY CONCEPTS

appeals to higher
  loyalties
collective responsibility
condemning the
  condemners

denial of injury
denial of responsibility
denial of the victim
heroic exceptionality
police use of force

techniques of
  neutralization

Crime, deviance, and unethical conduct can be found in almost every occupation and profession. Just open a newspaper, turn on the television, or listen to the radio and you will be exposed to abundant accounts of misdeeds by political leaders, government regulators, members of the clergy, people in business, and even college professors. Police are not unique in this sense, and it is safe to conclude that virtually every United States (U.S.) law enforcement agency has witnessed some form of unethical conduct, corruption, or scandal (Bracey, 1989; Kappeler, Sluder, & Alpert, 1998; Punch, 2009; Sherman, 1974). It is equally important to recognize that many police officers are honest, hardworking people, as are many doctors, stockbrokers, and college professors. Many police officers would never consider taking money in exchange for not enforcing the law or intentionally misusing their legal authority to use force. These same police officers, however, might not think twice about accepting a free cup of coffee, using deception during a criminal investigation, or even falsifying a police report to help ensure that a "dangerous" criminal is taken off the street.

If unethical conduct can be found in every profession, why should we be uniquely concerned with police ethics? The answer to this question is complex. Policing is an occupation that shares many of the characteristics of other occupations (Sherman, 1982), but it also has unique features. Like the clergy, police officers are charged with responding to people in times of need and tragedy. People often come in contact with the police during some of the most

113

difficult times in their lives. A parent who has lost a child in a car accident, a woman seeking help to escape a violent relationship, or an abused child may all find themselves coming into contact with the police. In less dramatic cases, people may seek out the police for direction, counseling, or a referral to a social service agency. People are likely to call the police for assistance regardless of whether the matter requires a traditional law enforcement response. In this sense, police, like the clergy, hold positions of public trust and are expected not to take advantage of people in their time of need. Moreover, like teachers, police officers are viewed by some (especially children) as role models. In fact, police go to great lengths to promote themselves as role models, frequently participating in school programs and often sponsoring events for children. Gaps in these early associations are filled with media and popular culture aligning the police with the "good guys" in the metaphorically ongoing war between good and evil—good being the side of law and order, and evil being represented by the threat of lawlessness and chaos. Police officers who engage in unethical conduct are surely poor role models and set negative examples for young people. Police are perhaps the most visible living symbol of government. They represent, both symbolically and literally, our systems of government and justice. The decisions made by police officers affect our perceptions of government and justice.

Society's concern with police ethics and the high standards expected of police officers cannot be solely explained based on policing's shared characteristics with other occupations. One must consider the unique occupational features of policing to fully understand the importance of police ethics. The police are vested with both powers and responsibilities that few other occupations are accorded. Unlike governmental bureaucrats, the clergy, or teachers, the police are given the power to detain and arrest people, to search and seize property, and to use force (up to and including deadly force) in carrying out legal mandates. These aspects of policing alone may require that police be held to a higher standard of behavior than other people in exchange for the enormous powers vested in them. In addition, police have the power to open the gates to the justice system and force people down a path they would not choose for themselves. A police intervention, therefore, can forcefully change the course of a life and interfere with a person's right to self-determination. These powers vest law enforcement officials with a significant amount of authority that distinguishes them from employees in other occupations.

Police in U.S. society are charged with a complex mission and are accorded extraordinary powers. Society has given this assignment with the expectation that police will fulfill their responsibilities in a fair, impartial, and ethical manner (Kappeler et al., 1998; Leo, Huberts, Maesschalck, & Jurkiewicz, 2008). This also means that the public may see the police in paradoxical roles. It is here, in this paradox, that the rules of exceptionality exist, but it is also where exceptions to the rules between ethical rights and wrongs are cultivated. The police are a governmental body whose ultimate mission is to protect the rights and liberties of citizens. This responsibility is paradoxical in two senses. First, unethical police officers represent one of the greatest threats to these same rights and liberties. In other words, police who violate the public trust by engaging in unethical behavior are one of the greatest threats to the protections extended to citizens in a free and democratic society. Unethical conduct by police officers involves a threat to the right to be free from unjust and unwarranted government restrictions and intrusions. Second, many of the coercive authorities we grant the police to accomplish their mission consist of the very behaviors from which we desire protection. Police officers are allowed to use violence to prevent violence; to protect freedom, they can take away our freedom; and they can seize property to prosecute property crimes. "Having the authority to be coercive, and the discretionary nature of such authority, creates the potential for corruption and abuse" (Braswell, 2015). In all, policing is fraught with contradiction and ethical dilemmas even before an officer pins on a badge or makes a decision.

THE PATH TO UNETHICAL CONDUCT

The path to unethical conduct does not begin with actions; rather, it begins with a way of thinking. We may not even be aware that the way we think influences our choices and actions. In a broad sense, the way we view the world, our role in it, and our relationship to it and the way we situate behavior all contribute to the choices we make and the actions we take. Many of the decisions we make are really shaped—long before we act on them—by our perception of the world around us. Do we see the world as being composed of good and evil people? Do we see ourselves as a corrective force? Is the world a dangerous and disorderly place? Are we responsible for bringing about safety and order? Do we see the world as full of predators who prey on the weak and powerless? Is our role that of the protector? Does it take exceptional and/or heroic acts to bring about law and order? The answers to these questions, of course, depend on our socialization by parents, friends, and peers; the information we are exposed to by the media, schools, and churches; and our life experiences. To some extent, the way we see the world and our relationship to it influence our decisions—even our choice of occupation. People who become police officers are no exception to these observations.

How the police think about themselves, their occupation, and the world around them sets the stage for unethical conduct. Far too many police officers see the world as a black-and-white morality play. The police often reduce their image of the world to simple snapshots. People are cast into roles as good and evil actors, predators and protectors, the forces of disorder, and the ensurers of order. People become defined by their behavior in the moment, not by their history, who they are, or where they have been. In this worldview, behaviors are decontextualized and people are dehumanized as becoming the objects of action, with all the shades of gray of social life stripped away.

Historically, the progressive movement in policing pushed toward centrally organized operations; this effort could be described by trying to eliminate political exceptionality, therein circumventing law. Much the same opportunity can be reasoned through what some have referred to as "unique opportunity for deviance" (Barker & Carter, 1994; Kappeler et al., 1998; Reiss, 1971). Within the worldview of good and evil, objects of action are either "with us or against us," decontextually aligning the cosmic order into heroes and villains. Within contemporary hero mythologies lies the reified notion of "**heroic exceptionality**" (McGowan, 2008). Although the hero mythos is as ancient as the written text, the police profession is relatively young, yet it has come to be perceived as the "thin blue line" boldly holding evil or lawlessness at bay.

Police work is also imagined in simplistic terms. The police view of the world is jaded by the perception of policing as the most critical of social functions. In this black-and-white world, police begin to believe and project for the public the image that they are the "thin blue line" that stands between anarchy and order. In this drama, police are constantly faced with danger while they attempt to ferret out evil and bring order to a chaotic world. This view of policing is reinforced by slogans and metaphors such as "brave cops on mean streets," "police on the front lines of the war on crime," and "better to be tried by 12 than carried by six." The war for social order is seen by the police as so important that it requires sweeping authority and unlimited discretion to invoke the power of law and, if necessary, the use of deadly force—after all, we are at war. A free cup of coffee, a discounted meal, a deception in court, protecting the criminal activities of a useful informant, or turning a blind eye to an intentional push or shove of some "bad guy" all seem trivial matters when you are on the front lines of a war. Likewise, using dirty or unethical means to achieve "good" ends seems a relatively minor concern. Isn't everything fair in love and war?

The vast majority of people who choose policing as a profession view themselves as moral and ethical individuals. People become police officers for an array of personal—and even noble—reasons. As Sherman (1982, p. 51) points out, "Police applicants tend to see police work as an adventure, as a chance to do work out of doors without being cooped up in an office, as a chance to do work that is important for the good of society, and not to be the 'toughest guy on the block'." This observation is accurate; in fact, young people become police officers for a variety of reasons, ranging from a desire to help and protect people and make a difference in their community to a response to their personal victimization, a desire for job security and exciting work, or just to get the "bad guys" off the streets. This does not mean, however, that these desires do not flow from a common way of seeing the world or a simplistic view of police work. Although expressed in a variety of forms, the reasons people become police officers usually flow from a black-and-white construction of the world. After all, from where do we get the notion that policing is an adventurous and exciting profession as opposed to dull and boring work? To the ex-offender seeking job skills, the patient needing surgery, or the person experiencing a life crisis, is policing really more important work than teaching, medicine, or tending souls? Is there really an endless supply of "evil" people to take off the streets and a shortage of "moral" people, or do most of us fall somewhere in the middle, like that of a masked hero? It is not that the people who go into policing are predisposed to unethical behavior; it is that they are predisposed to missing all the gray aspects of social life.

As good and moral people, police and those desirous of becoming police officers are compelled to believe in the goodness of maintaining order, the nobility of the occupation, and the fundamental fairness of the law and existing social order. To maintain their self-perception, the police are compelled to view disorder, lawbreaking, and lack of respect for police authority as enemies of a civilized society. "They are thus committed ('because it is right') to maintain their collective face as protectorates of the right and respectable against the wrong and the not-so-respectable. ... Thus, the moral mandate felt by the police to be their just right as the societal level is translated and transformed into occupational and personal terms" (Van Maanen, 1978, p. 227). For many people, policing is not just what they do; it becomes who they are. Much like the heroes of contemporary myths—for example, Frank Miller's aging Batman in the comic book classic, *The Return of the Dark Knight*—when crime becomes too much for the police to handle, they take it personally (1986). Law, authority, order, and the profession become extensions of their moral selves. Challenges to any of these are seen as a personal assault on police officers' morality, integrity, and sense of self.

If law, authority, and order are seen as fostering inequity or injustice, the police self-perception would be tainted and the "goodness" of the profession would be questioned by the public and the police themselves. Police could see themselves no longer as partners in justice and protectors of the good but rather as partners in repression—a role most police neither seek nor would be willing to recognize. A black-and-white view of the goodness of order and law can, in fact, blind police to unethical conduct. Enforcing "slave codes" becomes a means of maintaining order, not a way of supporting a criminal system of agricultural production. Carrying out the legal edicts of an immoral regime, such as that of the Nazis, is viewed as supporting social transformation of a society under the rule of law, not as participation in a holocaust. Arresting labor union agitators and civil rights organizers is seen as an action enhancing the rule of law as a mechanism of social change, not as the use of brutal force to maintain exploitation and discrimination. It is out of this historically defining era of "pure evil" that characters such as Superman and Batman were born. The characters were the embodiment of heroic exceptionality in a period in which moral supremacy gave exception to and warranted even a superhero capable of fantastic feats of heroic exceptionality (Vollum & Adkinson, 2003).

Police who begin to question the goodness of the profession, the equity of law, or the criticality of maintaining the existing social order often flee the occupation for other careers, leaving behind those who have the strongest belief in this black-and-white world of morality. Most certainly, unethical or even corrupt police officers do not get up in the morning, look into the mirror, and say to themselves, "I'm really going to be bad or unethical today." The police construction of the world, the occupation role, and the law itself provide more than ample legitimization for departing from ethical expectations.

LEGALLY PERMISSIBLE BUT UNETHICAL CONDUCT

Almost every criminal justice student has heard a professor remark that law, morality, and ethics are very different things. The law is neither a system of ethics nor a moral orientation; it is a set of formal statements of authority that may or may not be in keeping with ethical principles or moral beliefs. The law may represent little more than the brutal use of state force to maintain injustice. Jim Crow and segregation laws in the South, laws allowing for the detention of immigrants, and laws suppressing the right of political protest and free speech are often little more than the state's bald attempts to maintain power. The law may represent little more than the canonization of economic power, allowing corporate criminals to kill and maim with impunity while criminalizing only the actions of the poor. The law may be ambiguous, badly written, and poorly constructed. The law may be little more than a fraud, such as the Racketeer Influenced Corrupt Organizations Act passed by the Nixon administration, ostensibly to control organized crime. The Racketeer Influenced Corrupt Organization Act was used not once by that administration against the mob, but it was used repeatedly to attack groups opposing the administration's policies in Vietnam. The law may be inherently discriminatory, such as present laws heavily penalizing the use of crack cocaine by the poor but providing far lesser penalties for the use of cocaine hydrochloride by the affluent. The importance of this distinction, however, often vanishes when students leave the academic community and enter the world of policing. The transformation from student to police officer involves extensive indoctrination. This process begins with formal training police receive at the academy.

Although many police academies provide new recruits with 4 or 5 h of ethics training, this exposure pales compared with the legal training given. During hundreds of hours of legal training, recruits are exposed to a very rigid way of looking at human behavior and what constitutes right and wrong. Recruits are asked to memorize and parrot back to their trainers the elements of literally hundreds of criminal statutes. Rarely are discussions of the ambiguity of the law, the gray areas of human behavior, or the distinctions between ethics and law ever held in these settings. The law is presented as an unquestionable system of rights and wrongs. In the world of police training, the law is not something to be challenged; it is to be mastered as the foundation for moral action. During this experience, recruits slowly internalize a simple value system: What is legal is good and what is illegal is bad. People, behavior, and the police role are once again cast into simplistic distinctions between right and wrong.

The formality, precision, and seemingly unambiguous nature of the law are seductive to young scholars and recruits struggling to find their moral place in the world. Recruits learn formal statements of authority that support their black-and-white picture of the world. People become defined by their legal behavior, and the difference between good and bad is often as simple as the elements of a crime. The law is comfortingly seductive to people looking to make sense of all the evil, chaos, and disorder they see around them every day. Recruits also learn that they have a special place in this system of legal authority and that their actions will be judged not by the ethical nature of the choices they make but rather by the extent to which their actions fall within legal bounds. What is good, what is right, and what is ethical become intertwined with what is legally permissible.

The special legal privileges accorded the police provide unprecedented opportunities to engage in legally legitimated conduct that can be ethically questionable. Police, for example, are granted the authority to use force to accomplish their legal objectives. They are legally justified to use force under certain circumstances. The justification and legal authority to use deadly force may, however, mask an unethical use of force. Police have been known to contrive situations that would allow them to use deadly force when lesser means, or no force at all, could be used to accomplish the same legal objective. Sensational cases such as the Federal Bureau of Investigation storming of the Branch Davidians' home in Waco, Texas, and the sniper execution of two members of the Weaver family at Ruby Ridge, Idaho, come to mind. In both cases, constitutional rights were set aside by members occupying the highest levels of federal government. The legal construction of **police use of force** neither requires police officers to seek out alternatives to the use of force nor recognizes the officer's motives for using force as a factor in determining whether a use of force is legally reasonable. Likewise, the government sets aside its own legal rules when it becomes politically convenient to do so. In this sense, an unethical use of force can be perfectly legal and considered a "just" or even "righteous" use of force.

The use of the law in narcotics investigations provides a similar example. The activities of one drug dealer may be deemed sufficiently reprehensible to allow police to pursue him or her with vigor, often protecting other drug dealers who provide information or facilitate arrests in the process. In this case, the police make a legal decision to grant a crime-committing license to some violators in order to "get" others. Police frequently construct informant relationships with fences to get information on specific thefts or on the flow of money through the criminal underworld. Here, again, some people are permitted to violate the law, inviting heroic exceptionality, to enhance enforcement of the law.

Not long after graduating from the police academy, officers learn that the law is not merely a statement of authority that restricts behaviors, but that it can be used to make progress in the war against crime. The law is often written and can be interpreted in ways that give the police sufficient latitude to engage in unethical conduct in their pursuit of their crime control objective. Richard Ericson (1981, p. 91) has noted in this respect that "substantive laws are written broadly enough, and with sufficient ambiguity, that they can be applied across a range of circumstances. Causing a disturbance, a breach of the peace, obstructing police, and many others serve as a pretext for making the arrest." Because of the ambiguity in criminal law and the police situational interpretation of these legal mandates, the law itself contributes to unethical conduct. Ericson's discussion of the legal discretion available to police illustrates how the police can use the law as a tool that facilitates achievement of enforcement objectives rather than as a guide to how those objectives are to be achieved. The structure of the law itself allows for an ends-over-means justification of police misconduct. The mass appeal to a new extremist hero could be viewed in the successful Fox network TV show *24*, specifically in the character Jack Bauer emerging within the perpetual threat into which terrorism has evolved.

In short, manipulation and the situational application of the law to achieve enforcement objectives are often seen as acceptable (or even masterful) police work rather than unethical conduct. For example, identical legal infractions—such as two traffic violations—can result in different outcomes, depending not on the violation but on the motives of the police. First, police can merely release the citizen with no more than a verbal warning—there is no legal mandate that the police enforce all minor infractions of the law. Second, the police employ the force of law by issuing a citation or summons for the violation. Third, if police feel that the citizen fits the "mold" or "profile" of one in need of state control, the person may be arrested. Fourth, the police may arrest the person for the sole purpose of searching his or her vehicle for criminal evidence. Because the law does not recognize the motives of the officer and considers only the initial violation, the officer has acted in a legally permissible fashion. Racism, sexism, retribution, and a desire to skirt the Fourth Amendment are all washed away with the "good arrest." Examples of unethical but legally permissible police behavior abound. They can range from stacking or jacking up charges against citizens for purposes of coercion to contriving situations that allow officers to use deadly force (Kappeler et al., 1998).

SOCIALLY SITUATING UNETHICAL BEHAVIOR

Living and working in the world of policing provides officers with the ability to rationalize, excuse, and justify unethical behavior while maintaining a moral self-image. The police occupation provides its members with a handy conceptual toolbox that allows officers to engage in unethical behavior without suffering the cognitive dissonance and social stigma normally associated with wrongdoing. Police are, in essence, prepared to act unethically because of their worldview, the way police work is legally and perceptually framed, and the manner in which their actions are socially situated.

Although the police may view themselves as moral agents in a dangerous world full of evil people, they must first frame the use of force as a viable response to people and as an effective means of crime control before it can become a course of action. Whether this perceptual frame is expressed or experienced intuitively or learned as legal doctrine, it prepares police to use force. A perceptual frame begins to take shape and become a reality when an "event" unfolds, falls within the pre-established frame, and is incorporated into an actor's collective experience. Our perceptual frames are reinforced and strengthened as events meet our expectations. Events become factors that help interpret future events and courses of action. As Harold Garfinkel (1967, p. 113) instructs, "It consists of the possibility that the person defines retrospectively the decisions that have been made … in order to give their decisions some order…'officialness'," or justification.

Sykes and Matza's (1957) theory on the **techniques of neutralization** used by juveniles to explain their delinquency is particularly instructive for understanding how police officers draw on preconstructed frames of reference to excuse, justify, and rationalize a variety of unethical behaviors. Sykes and Matza theorized that delinquents use techniques of neutralization that allow them to maintain a positive self-image even though they have engaged in wrongdoing. These techniques included denial of responsibility, denial of injury, denial of the victim, condemnation of condemners, and appeals to higher loyalties.

Denial of responsibility prepares police for unethical conduct and provides a justification after the commission of an unethical act. Denial of responsibility is the belief that the potential or real injury caused by conduct is "due to forces outside the individual and beyond his control…" (Sykes & Matza, 1957, p. 667). Police rationalize their conduct by viewing themselves as little more than "billiard balls on a pool table" rebounding from external influences. Police see themselves as being buffeted back and forth between administrative policies and political decisions made at headquarters by administrators who no longer understand the "reality of the streets," by citizen calls and complaints identifying specific criminal actions to be investigated and acted on, and by a pervasive panorama of criminality that they see and feel all around them. They are following orders, serving the public, or making their own choices about who is worse among an endless sea of the bad and the law breaking. Political pressures may have them arresting drunk drivers 1 week, prostitutes the next, and crack dealers the next. They are simply responding to pressures beyond their control and to the actions of a seemingly endless number of miscreants who could have chosen not to behave criminally. From this frame of reference, police officers view their actions as predetermined by criminals, events, and situations that they cannot influence or control.

The training police receive in the use-of-force continuum is a good example of how police officers are socialized into viewing themselves as passive actors who are merely responding to the provocative behaviors of citizens. In this training, police are instructed that their use of force is always a response to a citizen's behavior—whether verbal or physical. Police are instructed that when a citizen takes an aggressive action, the officer is to respond to that action with a higher level of force than that of the citizen. No allowance is made for the ambiguity of the situation or the law, for the ability of the citizen to understand or respond, or for the simple human emotions that the citizen may feel. At each stage of action, the police officer moves up the continuum until the citizen's action is halted. This construction of police use of force assumes that police are merely responding to citizens' behaviors and that police action, verbalization, and demeanor have no contribution to the citizens' behavior. Accordingly, police officers are not responsible for their contribution to the situation or their forced response. Defiant citizens are viewed from this frame as provocateurs in need of police control. When police use violence or an unethical application of law, they are merely responding to the provocation of citizens, situations, and events over which they have little or no control and for which they are not responsible, regardless of their own contributions to the situation or their departure from ethical principles.

Denial of responsibility provides police with an after-the-fact justification for their abuse of authority. Police who engage in brutal assaults on citizens often allege that they were forced into it because there was no alternative course of action or that it was expedient—the citizen or situation "forced their hand." Waco and Ruby Ridge are two classic examples of the police being "forced" into violence when simply waiting might have resulted in different outcomes. These forced choices, however, are constructed by the manner in which police work and the use of force have been constructed. For the police, "never back down," "no duty to retreat," and "no legal obligation to seek out alternatives to the use of force" construct their thinking. By offering these excuses, police can violate ethics while maintaining an ethical self-image. Police can make the legal choice to enforce the requirements of a minor municipal ordinance, such as those governing parades and demonstrations, vigorously and violently while ignoring the overarching reasons for that demonstration. While ignoring segregation and racism, police in Birmingham, Alabama, can turn dogs and fire hoses on peaceful demonstrators whose only crime is not having a permit. While ignoring the immorality of an undeclared war, police in Chicago can riot against antiwar demonstrators who have no permit to be in a park after dark. Police can enforce loitering laws against prostitutes while never questioning the social and economic arrangements of a sexist and patriarchal society that makes prostitution a viable alternative for many women. "By learning to view himself as more acted upon than acting," an officer "prepares the way for deviance from the dominant normative system without the necessity of a frontal assault on the norms themselves" (Sykes & Matza, 1957, p. 667). Police are able to sidestep their ethical violations by shifting responsibility to victims and invoking their legal authority and training as the basis for self-evaluation.

Denial of injury is a technique of neutralization that provides police with a host of justifications for their unethical acts. Because many police breaches of ethics do not involve the direct physical injury of a citizen or seem of little consequence to police, they are free to pursue them. From this frame, "wrongfulness may turn on the question of whether anyone has clearly been hurt by his deviance, and this matter is open to a variety of interpretations" (Sykes & Matza, 1957, p. 667). Denial of injury occurs when police steal evidence from suspects, when they violate civil rights to make arrests or get convictions, and when they abuse their authority to establish or maintain their personal sense of order. Planting evidence on a suspected drug dealer, committing perjury to justify an illegal search, and harassing prostitutes are all seen to have no deleterious impacts either to the individual or to the rule of law. Changing reports and rehearsing testimony to iron out contradictions and in the end change the facts are all acceptable procedures in prosecuting a war on crime. The police can employ this technique to maintain that the suspect should not have had contraband in the first place, the citizen was a criminal deserving of something less than the full protection of civil rights, or the juvenile had to be "moved along" to prevent crime and ensure order.

For police, the theft of property from a suspect can be socially situated as "confiscation." The padding of overtime records can be viewed as "just compensation" for someone on the front lines of the war on crime. Perjury is just "embellishing" the facts or recalling previously forgotten information to convict someone who is "guilty anyway" and needs to be taken off the street.

Denial of the victim is not the assertion that victims do not exist but rather a characterization of victims and victimization in an attempt to justify unethical behavior. Sykes and Matza explain that "the moral indignation of self and others may be neutralized by an insistence that the injury is not wrong in light of the circumstances. The injury, it may be claimed, is really not an injury; rather, it is a form of retaliation or punishment" (Sykes & Matza, 1957, p. 668). This technique of neutralization provides police with viable targets for victimization by characterizing certain individuals and situations so that police misconduct is seemingly justified, given the imputed character of the target and the interpretation of the circumstances. Socially situating people into good and evil, dangerous and friendly, deserving and not so deserving allows those people to become acceptable victims. For example, consider a situation in which a traffic violator decides to run from the police. The offender and situation can be viewed in several different ways. The officer can perceive the situation as consisting of a relatively minor violation of the law—someone has committed a traffic offense and has overreacted by selecting a very poor course of action. Alternatively, the officer may define the citizen as a dangerous fleeing felon who has taken a drastic and hazardous course of action. Depending on perception and definition, the citizen may be seen as deserving a little more of the full force of law. In these situations, police are prone to exact a pound of flesh. In other words, police reason away their use of force as the justifiable punishment of people deserving of such treatment. In essence, the officer "moves himself into the position of an avenger and the victim is transformed into a wrongdoer. ... To deny the existence of the victim, then by transforming him into a person deserving injury ..." is to recognize "appropriate and inappropriate targets" for victimization (Sykes & Matza, 1957, p. 668). Denial of the victim also invokes a kind of legitimated prejudice for police. The poor, young, minority-group drug dealer is seen as being less worthy than the drunk-driving middle class executive. No consideration is made for the family of the drug dealer. No consideration of who will pay the rent, who will buy the family food, or who will provide for the children is necessitated by the law. However, the impact of an arrest on the social status of the middle class drunk driver often allows for a greater and more humane exercise of discretion. It is all legal; it is all justified in the black-and-white world of order maintenance. This pattern repeats itself often in policing. The middle class housewife victimized by a confidence game is more deserving of protection than the prostitute raped by her john. The middle class juvenile is more likely to "get help" and straighten out his or her life than the impoverished teen who must be arrested and detained to protect society.

Police often invoke what Sykes and Matza (1957, p. 668) have characterized as the technique of **condemning the condemners**. This technique involves a reaction to the detection of unethical conduct and a response to those who either allege or sanction it. By employing this technique, the police officer "shifts the focus of attention from his own deviant acts to the motives and behaviors of those who disapprove of his violation. His condemners, he may claim are hypocrites, deviants in disguise, or impelled by personal spite" (Sykes & Matza, 1957, p. 668). Police condemn the edicts of external examiners when they conflict with their frames of reference by imputing motive on those justice personnel who attempt to curtail police autonomy, authority, and wrongdoing. As opposed to heroic exceptionality, the exclusionary rule is used by lawyers who are just out to "make a buck." Those who developed this rule did so just to provide a "loophole" for criminals and make it more difficult for the police to make progress in the crime war. Criminal charges brought by the police against citizens are reduced in plea-bargaining arrangements because judges and prosecutors are "soft on crime." The goodness of the legal code remains, but the actors and the legal process have become corrupted. A second form this technique takes is a condemnation of those people who bring charges of misconduct against the police. Citizens who bring complaints against the police are merely "hostile" toward law enforcement, "resentful" for being ticketed or arrested, or merely "money-grubbing" individuals out to make a "quick buck" by filing a lawsuit against the police. Certainly, evil people would have no problem with making these unfounded claims. A third use of this technique is to condemn those people who pass judgment on police conduct. When police officers are convicted of crimes or held liable in civil proceedings, the condemners of police are often characterized as unable to understand the "realities" of police work or the "dangerousness" of criminals. To the police, these people are merely "armchair quarterbacks" who use 20/20 hindsight to pass judgment on actions they do not understand.

As with the other techniques of neutralization, condemning the condemners serves to prepare the police for exploits by predetermining that the legal rules of police conduct, those who may allege misconduct, and those who may be called on to sanction misconduct are themselves unjust, corrupt, deviant, or ignorant. Through condemnation, police sever the link between their potential courses of action and the negative stigma of unethical conduct. Police reject the exclusionary rule before its application, thus freeing themselves to collect evidence in an illegal manner; they reject citizens' allegations of police wrongdoing by attributing them to resentment and hostility; and they reject challenges to their authority and autonomy by condemning those who pass judgment on them. Police can therefore deviate with a steadfast belief that they are righteous in their actions, even if such actions involve "bending," "sidestepping," or "twisting" ethics.

Police **appeals to higher loyalties** are perhaps the most powerful technique of neutralization used by police. More than any other, this technique allows police to break the bonds of ethical behavior. In Sykes and Matza's (1957, p. 669) words, "internal and external social controls may be neutralized by sacrificing the demands of the larger society for the demands of the smaller social group ..." Applied to police, this means that officers may be forced to choose between the sanctions that are associated with violating or adhering to one or another set of values. For example, a police officer who sees her partner brutalize a citizen may be called on to give testimony. The officer is forced to make a decision between committing perjury (so as not to implicate her partner) and adhering to the police code of secrecy that prohibits "giving up" another cop. The officer can testify either that she saw nothing or that the partner did not engage in brutality, in so doing escaping the sanction of peers but running the risk of being charged with perjury. One might suspect that this is a wrenching decision. The officer must protect her partner but do so in a manner that preserves a law-abiding and conformist self-image. Quite the contrary, though, this decision is often relatively easy. Protecting a fellow officer is expected and even considered noble rather than criminal. The officer who commits perjury to protect a fellow officer has demonstrated loyalty and solidarity to the group by placing himself or herself in harm's way. After all, who is more deserving of protection, the police officer on the frontlines of the crime war or the criminal? As Sykes and Matza (1957, p. 669) note, "the most important point is that deviation from certain norms may occur not because the norms are rejected but because other norms, held to be more pressing or involving a higher loyalty, are accorded precedence."

COLLECTIVE RESPONSIBILITY FOR UNETHICAL POLICE CONDUCT

It is not just the police whose black-and-white view of the world makes this ethical quagmire inevitable. There is **collective responsibility** for unethical police conduct. The entertainment media contribute with their fictional views of good and evil. There is little ambiguity in police dramas on television. The police are always seen as good, effective, and successful. They must overcome the legal protections provided to citizens, and they must circumvent bureaucratic and administrative controls. The inherent "badness" of the suspect is not mitigated by social concerns or economic circumstances. Television criminals rarely have low IQs that make it impossible for them to understand the law. Television criminals rarely act out of fear, anger, or desperation; instead, they plan and connive to achieve their ends. The news media are not much better. The view of police under siege, the view of police being outgunned and overwhelmed, the view of police as holding back a tide of criminality—all are standard news magazine fare. Politicians also contribute to this worldview. All politicians are anti-crime, pro-police, law-and-order activists. The poor, who bear the brunt of the criminal laws passed by politicians, neither vote in sufficient numbers nor make sufficiently attractive political contributions to gain any consideration in the criminalization process.

Crime becomes a societal passion play, but a very disturbing one when viewed closely. As we watch this black-and-white world portrayed on television and in the newspapers, nagging questions emerge—questions that are all but ignored by the legal orientation of policing. For example, is it really a war on crime we are fighting or is it a war on troublesome and unsettling people? How many mentally ill individuals denied care by this society have become criminal problems? How do we explain the fact that 15 percent of all illegal drug users in this society are black, whereas 45 percent of all those arrested for drugs and portrayed on the television news as drug dealers are black? Is it law that we are enforcing or is it a system of legalized apartheid? And how do we judge the police who enforce those laws in either an ethical or unethical manner? Do we judge them on the basis of narrow legal definitions that protect injustice and promote unethical conduct or on the basis of the social consequences of their actions?

■ Learn More on the Internet

For more on police ethics, misconduct and abuse, visit www.aclu.org and search on the term *police abuse*.   ■

Discussion Questions

1. In preparing for criminal trial, police are frequently interviewed and rehearsed by prosecutors. Words, phrases, and recollections that might lead to troublesome cross-examination are excised, and other terminologies more favorable to the prosecution are substituted. Potential police witnesses are warned about inconsistencies and incongruities in their testimony and reports. In the end, the actual content of the officer's sworn testimony may be substantially changed from his or her original recollection. Is this practice legal? Is this ethical? When does the rehearsal and preparation of a witness so substantially change the way an incident is portrayed that it becomes perjury?

2. It is common practice in narcotics units to cultivate informants, usually drug dealers or drug users. Information these informants provide to the police may result in the arrest of other dealers or users. Virtual immunity is often granted to those who cooperate with the police. Where are the ethical lines to be drawn in this arrangement?

3. *Street justice* is a term frequently employed by the police to justify the use of physical force against suspects. Street justice is seen as a symbol, a warning, a caution to others that both enhances social control and in some instances protects the police from potential acts of violence. Frequently, these beatings are "legal" in the sense that a narrow legal justification may exist for the incident. Is being legal a sufficient justification? Are such beatings ethical?

4. Should police in slave-holding states have enforced slave codes that required them to track down and return runaway slaves? Should police in Nazi Germany have enforced laws displacing and confiscating the property of Jews? Should police enforce laws they know to be unjust and immoral just because they are the law?

5. Do all police officers, regardless of their worldview, have an ethical obligation to report the corruption, brutality, and misconduct of other police officers? If a police officer does not report such illegal conduct, is there any real difference between that officer and other criminals?

CASE STUDY 7–1 HOMEGROWN TERRORISM

From Braswell, Miller, and Pollock (2006). Reprinted with permission.

"I don't know why you're hassling us. It's his kind that flew that plane into the World Trade Center and killed real Americans! Who knows what he and his friends were planning to do next?" the 16-year-old boy protests.

"Yeah, my Daddy says they won't rest until all Americans are dead, and besides, they worship the devil!" his 15-year-old sidekick adds.

You look at your patrol partner, Mary Bivins, before responding to the two youths you have just arrested for assault and vandalism. After a deep breath, you return your gaze directly to the youths.

"You two brave patriots beat up a seventy-five-year-old American citizen and tried to burn his house down. Mr Hafiz and his wife have lived in this neighborhood for the last twenty years. In fact, one of his sons is a police officer over in the twelfth precinct, and he has another son who works as a fireman up in Albany. You two boys are in a whole lot of trouble."

Mrs Unger, the 15-year-old's mother, brings coffee into the living room where the two boys, their parents, and the two police officers are sitting.

"How is Mr Hafiz?" she inquires.

Officer Bivins's response is to the point. "He has a concussion and two broken ribs—"

Mr Evans, the 16-year-old's father, interrupts Officer Bivins impatiently: "C'mon, officers! They were just being rambunctious teenagers who got carried away. I'll make sure they apologize to the Hafiz family, and we and the Ungers will see that their house is repaired.

Who knows where kids get the crazy ideas they have these days? They didn't mean no serious harm."

Putting the coffee cup down, you look at the Evans and Unger families.

"I can't say what your sons' intentions were or where they got the idea to do what they did. The fact is, they committed a serious assault and caused extensive property damage. Officer Bivins and I will have to take them to the juvenile detention center. You can try to arrange to have them released to your custody tomorrow until the court hearing."

You and your partner ride in silence on the way back from the detention center. Finally Mary speaks: "I can't believe those parents, especially Mr Evans."

"Yeah," you respond, "I'm not so sure they shouldn't have been arrested as well."

Questions

1. What are the ways that parents can instill, even if unintentionally, racial, ethnic, or religious prejudice in their children?

2. Is it difficult to maintain an unbiased perspective and sense of balance when acts of terrorism result in the loss of innocent lives? Should the police and/or the courts take this into consideration under circumstances like the one outlined in the case study?

3. How can schools, police, and other social and government institutions educate and help prevent such acts against people of different ethnic or racial backgrounds?

4. What would be a just outcome to this case?

Exercise II–1 Different Choices, Equal Protection?

"You folks need to settle your differences and get along," Sergeant Waddell mumbles as he leaves the apartment with you trailing behind him. The sergeant, a 30-year veteran, switches on the ignition of the cruiser and continues, half-talking to you and half-talking to himself.

"I don't know what the world's coming to! Two men living together like that. It just ain't natural. It's tough enough dealing with the Saturday night husband-and-wife drunks without having to try and calm down the likes of them. They like to call themselves gay, but from the looks of that smaller one, it don't look like he was having too gay of a time! Looked like the bigger feller whipped up on him. Besides, with him being thin like that, I wouldn't be surprised if he didn't have AIDS. I'll tell you one thing. I was glad to get out of there. Who knows what kind of germs were in their apartment?" Lighting a cigarette, he turns to you. "I bet they didn't teach you how to deal with those kinds of people in college." You pause before you respond, not wanting to offend the sergeant, who is also your training officer. "We were taught that it would be difficult and challenging when dealing with the homosexual community, because of AIDS and our own biases and prejudices, as well as a lot of myths that are going around."

"Myths, my ass," Sergeant Waddell interrupts. "That AIDS disease will kill you stone-cold dead. I don't trust the government. You can't tell me you can't catch that stuff from mosquitos either. Who knows how you can catch it? All I know is I want to wash my hands."

"Well, I would agree that there are a lot of questions," you reply. "But our professors always reminded us that every citizen was entitled to equal opportunity under the law, regardless of their sexual preferences. I was taught that I was to treat them professionally, just as in any domestic disturbance. It seems to me that we should have done something besides just telling them to quiet down and get along with each other. I mean, we should have arrested the big guy just like we would have done if it was a spousal abuse case."

Turning into McDonalds, the sergeant turns once more to you, "Simpson, you're a good kid and I believe you will make a fine officer. But you need to remember that the classroom is one thing and the real world is another. I don't hate those kinds of people, but they made their own bed and now they'll have to lie in it. I don't know what else we could have done. They weren't married and, even if they were, I don't believe it's legal in this state. We couldn't take the little guy to a spousal abuse shelter, they'd laugh their asses off at us. And I don't think that domestic violence law covers people like that anyway. Why don't you go order us a couple of black coffees to go while I wash my hands?"

Waiting for the coffee, you reflect on Waddell's words. He is a respected veteran police officer and you understand his uneasiness. You felt it, too. You also remember the look of fear and helplessness on the face of the battered guy, Eddie, who called the police. One part of you wanted to go back and check on him and do something, even if it meant arresting the other guy for domestic violence. Another part of you wanted to stay on Sergeant Waddell's good side. After all, he is your training officer. What are you going to do?

Questions

1. What police ethics might this new recruit be torn between? Explain.
2. How might a department with stricter objectives or codes of conduct have influenced the behavior of the officers? Explain.
3. Address this case from the three ethical models of utilitarianism, deontology, and peacemaking. Which perspective do you feel would be most helpful in this instance? Why?
4. Research the local laws of your area and report back to the class. Are homosexual relationships covered by the local laws in your area? How might this information affect the officers' behavior?

REFERENCES

Barker, T., & Carter, D. L. (Eds.). (1994). *Police deviance* (3rd ed.) Cincinnati: Anderson.

Bracey, D. H. (1989). Police corruption. In W. G. Bailey (Ed.), *The encyclopedia of police science*. New York: Garland.

Braswell, M. (2015). *Ethics, crime, and justice: An introductory note to students.* (Chapter 1), (this volume).

Braswell, M., Miller, L., & Pollock, J. (2006). *Case studies in criminal justice ethics.* Long Grove: Waveland Press.

Ericson, R. V. (1981). Rules for police deviance. In C. Shearing (Ed.), *Organizational police deviance 83–110.* Toronto: Butterworths.

Garfinkel, H. (1967). *Studies in ethnomethodology.* Englewood Cliffs: Prentice Hall.

Kappeler, V. E., Sluder, R. D., & Alpert, G. P. (1998). *Forces of deviance: Understanding the dark side of the force* (2nd ed.). Prospect Heights: Waveland.

Leo, W., Huberts, J. C., Maesschalck, J., & Jurkiewicz, C. L. (2008). *Ethics and integrity of governance: Perspectives across frontiers.* New York: Edward Elgar.

McGowan, T. (2008). *The exceptional darkness of 'The Dark Knight'. Jump cut: A review of contemporary media.* Retrieved from ejumpcut.org/currentissue/darkKnightKant/index.html.

Miller, F. (1986). *Batman: The dark knight returns.* New York: DC Comics.

Punch, M. (2009). *Police corruption: Deviance, accountability and reform in policing.* Portland: Willan.

Reiss, A. J. (1971). *The police and the public.* New Haven: Yale University Press.

Sherman, L. W. (1974). *Police corruption: A sociological perspective.* Garden City: Anchor.

Sherman, L. W. (1982). Learning police ethics. *Criminal Justice Ethics, 1*(1), 10–19.

Sykes, G. M., & Matza, D. (1957). Techniques of neutralization. *American Sociological Review, 22,* 664–670.

Van Maanen, J. (1978). The asshole. In P. K. Manning, & J. Van Maanen (Eds.), *Policing: A view from the street.* Santa Monica: Goodyear.

Vollum, S., & Adkinson, C. D. (2003). The portrayal of crime and justice in the comic book Super-hero Mythos. *Journal of Criminal Justice and Popular Culture, 10*(2), 96–108.

Ethics and the Courts

A man can only do what he can do. But if he does that each day, he
can sleep at night and do it again the next day.

Albert Schweitzer

It has been argued that although our criminal justice system is not perfect,
it does yield a kind of "rough justice." No one is guilty of exactly the crime
for which they are convicted, and no one receives exactly the penalty they
deserve, but the majority of people do receive a disposition that approximates
justice.

This view is probably accurate, but it is also somewhat troubling. Though it
is an eminently pragmatic approach, one may question the extent to which
justice can be "approximated." One can also question the process by which
this approximation is achieved. When defense attorneys and prosecutors
struggle against each other in the adversarial process, is truth the likely outcome or just a lucky possibility? Is the process any more agreeable when
there is little real argument, just a negotiation over charge and sentence
recommendation?

This is hardly the process one would design to find the right punishment to fit
the crime or the criminal. But in whose hands should such decisions be placed?

The legislature can attempt to ensure greater consistency through determinate sentencing, but such efforts often result in higher penalties than judicial discretion would yield. And in this period of prison overcrowding, what is the correct use of incarceration? One is forced to juxtapose a moral obligation to minimize prison costs that serve to shortchange state health, education, and welfare programs against an equally important obligation to protect the community from crime.

The decisions that defense attorneys, prosecutors, judges, and legislators must make are difficult ones, requiring a balancing of sound ethical judgments with the pragmatic realities of their positions. To assist their students in dealing with these problems, law schools provide instruction in professional ethics. This is normally achieved by requiring students to complete a course that addresses the practicing attorney's obligations to the client, to the bar, and to the court. Questions have been raised, however, about the utility of requiring a single isolated ethics course, as opposed to integrating a concern for ethics into the general curriculum. Although the former provides more intense and focused study, the latter encourages the incorporation of ethical concerns into every aspect of law. This incorporation may be a more effective means of instilling high standards, because many ethical dilemmas seem to be a direct result of the conflicting obligations inherent in the practice of law.

What Ever Happened to Atticus Finch? Lawyers as Legal Advocates and Moral Agents

Joycelyn M. Pollock

KEY CONCEPTS

active role	ethics of rights	moral agent
client-centered/	guru/godfather role	moral dialogues
friend role	hired-gun role	passive role
ethics of care	legal advocate	

Atticus Finch, the character created by Harper Lee for the book and movie *To Kill a Mockingbird*, was the epitome of the "gentleman" lawyer: courteous, honest, brave, and intelligent. He was a consummate professional, but more than that, he was an admirable man. In the plot of the story, he was a comfortable, respected attorney in a small Southern town who agreed to defend a black man accused of raping a white woman. In a time of lynchings, this decision exposed him and his family to ostracism and danger, yet at all times he maintained a professional courtesy, even toward those whose actions were condemning an innocent man to die. In contrast to this ideal of an attorney, there is the stereotype of the "ambulance chaser" lawyer who, like a parasite, exploits and profits from others' misfortune. The criminal defense attorney is often perceived as unscrupulous and uncaring, stopping at nothing to "get his client off." So, where is Atticus? Of course, it helped that he defended an innocent client; real-world attorneys are not always so lucky.

One of the reasons for the public's disdain for lawyers is found in the role they play vis-à-vis their clients: Are attorneys in an amoral **"hired-gun role"** or are they professionals who balance their clients' interests against respect for the law and some objective standard of justice? This concept of the lawyer as a **legal advocate** (with no individual contribution of morality) versus a **moral** agent (whereby the lawyer imposes a personal view of morality into his or her activities for the client) has been discussed and debated vigorously in the literature.

THE LAWYER/CLIENT RELATIONSHIP

Cohen (1991) presented the argument that only an attorney acting as a moral agent had the capacity to be moral. A legal advocate, one who pursued his or her clients' wishes even if they were immoral, could not possibly be considered good because he or she might be doing bad acts. He suggested some principles (see Box 8.1) that attorneys had to follow to be considered moral.

BOX 8.1 PRINCIPLES FOR ATTORNEYS AS MORAL AGENTS

1. Treat others as ends in themselves and not as mere means to winning cases.
2. Treat clients and other professional relations who are relatively similar in a similar fashion.
3. Do not deliberately engage in behavior that is apt to deceive the court as to the truth.
4. Be willing, if necessary, to make reasonable personal sacrifices—of time, money, popularity, and so on—for what you justifiably believe to be a morally good cause.
5. Do not give money to, or accept money from, clients for wrongful purposes or in wrongful amounts.
6. Avoid harming others in the process of representing your client.
7. Be loyal to your client and do not betray his confidence.
8. Make your own moral decisions to the best of your ability and act consistently on them.

Cohen (1991, pp. 135–136).

Cohen's position that attorneys should be moral agents and decide independently what is right and wrong has been attacked vociferously. For instance, Memory and Rose (2002) argue that a lawyer can be effective and morally good by subscribing to the American Bar Association (ABA) Model Rules of Professional Conduct. They argue, basically, that a lawyer who follows the Model Rules can be a zealous advocate for his or her client but still never do wrong because the Model Rules prohibit illegal and unethical behaviors, such as lying. They especially do not agree with Cohen's idea that lawyers should apply their own definitions of morality in any case where they are being paid to pursue the client's interest. Morality is "subjective," they argue, and therefore it would only result in a loss of trust in attorneys and damage to the client relationship if attorneys were to pursue their own definitions of justice rather than the clients' definitions.

Cohen (2002), in a rebuttal, continues to argue his case, proposing that legal advocates become used to imposing injury on others and that they do so without feelings of guilt. He argues that the Model Rules do not prohibit all acts that could be defined as unethical and immoral. For instance, they do not prohibit a situation whereby an attorney would maintain silence in an instance that results in third parties being financially harmed. Although Cohen wrote his article before the Enron, WorldCom, and Adelphia corporate debacles, these examples certainly seem to be cases in point because attorneys were involved when corporate officers misled shareholders about the financial holdings of the companies (Rhode & Paton, 2002). As Powell (2003, p. 316) pointed out:

> ... how could it be ... that with over a thousand lawyers at Arthur Andersen, over 300 lawyers at Enron, and, minimally, another dozen or so lawyers at Vinson and Elkins, the only person willing to blow the whistle was a senior vice president with a business degree?

Actually, the two sides seem to agree that the most egregious acts of attorneys who pursue their clients' interests, regardless of truth, justice, or who gets hurt, would be unacceptable for either the moral agent (because these actions offend some larger definition of morality) or the legal advocate (because they violate the Model Rules). However, there are still a number of issues and situations that fall between the two sides. For instance, if a defense attorney had a weak case and the only available tactic was to challenge the credibility of the prosecution's witness, should the attorney expose the witness (who is telling the truth and the defense attorney knows it) with evidence of past misdeeds and current failings of character, and, in general, attack his or her character? What if such treatment ruined the witness's reputation, health, or relationship with a loved one? The legal advocate would have no problem with such behavior; he or she must pursue the client's interest in creating reasonable doubt for the jury. What about the moral agent? If the moral agent refused to attack an honest prosecution witness, what good would he or she be to the guilty defendant who has no other means of obtaining an acquittal? What does a defense attorney owe to his or her client?

Wishman (1981) describes a case in which he challenged a rape victim's account of an alleged brutal rape and sodomy. He was able to convince the jury that she was lying and, months later, was confronted with her anger.

> ... as all criminal lawyers know, to be effective in court I had to act forcefully, even brutally, at times. I had been trained in law school to regard the "cross" as an art form. In the course of my career I had frequently discredited witnesses. My defense of myself had always been that there was nothing personal in what I was doing. This woman was obviously unwilling to dismiss my behavior as merely an aspect of my professional responsibility; instead of an effective counsel, she saw me simply as a "motherfucker."
>
> **Wishman (1981, pp. 6–7)**

The literature in jurisprudence is filled with articles seeking to clarify or instruct in the attorney/client relationship. Condlin (2003, pp. 220–221, notes omitted) explains the ethical dilemma of attorneys who find themselves forced to decide how to act when pursuing the client's interests:

> Lawyers can find themselves in situations, therefore, in which they have social and moral obligations to behave in one way, and legal and professional obligations to behave in another. When norms collide in this fashion, when what a client asks is legal but also unfair or destructive of societal interests generally, lawyers face a difficult question. Should they be moral or legal, social or self-interested, communitarian or individualistic, or as some put it, persons or lawyers?

Granfield and Koenig (2003, p. 513) observe that law school ethics classes do not help lawyers answer such questions: "... the codes do not tell lawyers how to reconcile conflict between their personal sense of ethics and the rules...." In their survey of 40 Harvard graduates, they found that many experienced deep personal conflict in representing clients whose tactics or positions with which they disagreed. However, they tended to resolve such conflict by adapting a "role-based morality." In effect, their definition of good became a judgment of their technical competence—they exchanged being good persons with being good lawyers. Those who could not make that adaptation left the field.

Condlin (2003) describes the role of lawyers as falling into one of the following categories: the hired-gun role (most similar to our preceding legal-advocate description), the **guru/godfather role** (in which the lawyer tells the client what should be done), and what some call the **client-centered/friend role** (in which, it is assumed, the client can be persuaded not to engage in unethical or immoral practices). Condlin (2003) is critical of those who propose the last category, arguing that, in the end, if the client insists on immoral actions, the attorney either tells the client "no" (guru/godfather) or does the client's bidding (legal advocate).

Although some writers (e.g., Simon, 1993, 1998) argue that the attorney—even the criminal defense attorney—should balance client interest against social justice, others argue that zealous advocacy is not only desirable but also honorable (Freedman, 2002). Many advocates for the "client first and foremost" position use a famous quote from Lord Brougham that describes the client/attorney role: "... by the sacred duty which he owes his client, knows, in the discharge of that office but one person in the world—that client and no other ..." Cited in Markovits (2003, p. 213)

Smith (2003) points out that the whole argument against zealous advocacy presumes that allowing perjury, browbeating victims, and other "aggressive tactics" are rampant. The more typical situation, Smith argues, is that criminal defendants get barely more than a "warm body sitting next to them" and, in fact, "Actually a warm body might be benign compared to some of the dangerous, dim-witted defenders that roam the criminal courts" (2003, p. 91).

He presents the case that the more typical attorney barely meets the definition of competent and comes nowhere near zealous in his or her defense of clients' interests.

It should also be noted that not all subscribe to the idea that the lawyer is always seeking the client's best interest. Scheingold (1984, p. 155), for example, argues:

> … the practice of defense law is all too often a "confidence game" in which the lawyers are "double agents" who give the appearance of assiduous defense of their clients but whose real loyalty is to the criminal courts.

In this view, lawyers on the two sides of the bar have more in common with each other than with the client (or victim), so they really are advocates in name only. Defense attorneys and prosecutors share some vision of what is fair, and the system operates to enforce this vision, regardless of impositions from the outside or drama displayed for the client's benefit. (For a discussion of this model and others, see Pollock, 2004.)

GUIDANCE FOR LAWYERS: MODEL RULES OF PROFESSIONAL CONDUCT

All attorneys are guided by the ABA and the bar association of their own state. The ABA has created and continues to update the Model Rules of Professional Conduct. The most recent revisions were proposed in 2000 and passed in 2002. The Rules cover the client–lawyer relationship, maintaining the integrity of the profession, courtroom behavior, conflicts of interest, use of the media, and relationships with opposing attorneys, among other areas. A standing committee on ethical responsibility, which provides formal and informal written opinions, enforces the Rules. Each state bar association enforces its own rules by sanctions that range from a private censure to disbarment.

Although we have been discussing zealous defense and the extent to which lawyers should ignore their personal ethics to do their client's bidding, it should be noted that the most common complaint lodged with state bar associations is incompetence or negligence. Most clients who are unhappy with their attorneys are unhappy because of real or perceived neglect—that is, the attorney does not return their calls, the attorney missed a legal deadline, and so on. Very few complaints result in serious sanctions taken against attorneys (Pollock, 2004).

So, what do the Rules dictate regarding the relationship between an attorney and client? First, the Rules demand that the lawyer "shall abide by a client's decisions concerning the objectives of representation .... [and] shall consult with the client as to the means by which they are to be pursued"

(ABA, 2002, Rule 1.2). Barker and Cosentino (2003) point out that the revisions to this rule attempted to clarify the authority of the client and attorney in the relationship. The old rule distinguished between the objectives of the case (with greater authority given to the client) and the means or strategies used (with greater authority given to the attorney). The new rule encourages the client's participation in all decision making, but the use of the term *consult* may be interpreted to mean that the client does not have absolute authority over decisions regarding means or strategies. Mather (2003) argues that the Model Rules are still "vague, contradictory, and ambiguous" with regard to the appropriate power differential in the attorney–client relationships.

This issue becomes extremely relevant in criminal defense cases when clients insist on courses of action that attorneys feel are self-destructive or not helpful to the defense. Barker and Cosentino (2003) discuss, for instance, cases in which the defendant does not want attorneys to pursue insanity pleas or does want to present defenses that clearly have no basis in fact. They also note that the revision takes away any disciplinary sanctions for attorneys who decide to go against clients' wishes unless the action also violates other laws. This may, they argue, encourage attorneys to act on their conscience when a client desires to do something morally repugnant. They conclude, however, that the revised rule continues to leave much ambiguity in who has control over decision making—the client or the attorney.

Mather (2003) finds that an attorney's inclination to let the client take the lead in making decisions about objectives and tactics depends on the type of client. Studies indicated that public defenders were much more likely to believe in an attorney-led relationship, partially because of a belief that the client was too "unsophisticated" or ignorant to make good decisions. Corporate attorneys, however, were more "client-centered" and more likely to do the client's bidding, regardless of what they personally thought. This was because corporate executives could simply take their business elsewhere and the attorney would lose money. According to Mather (2003, p. 1081):

> The client-sensitive or agent role in representation could become the role of the lackey in situations of unequal power between client and lawyer. As a result, the broader public interest, including the requirements of law, may suffer.

Rule 1.2 also cautions that the lawyer "shall not counsel a client to engage, or assist a client, in conduct that the lawyer knows is criminal or fraudulent …" Thus, a lawyer cannot knowingly participate in ongoing criminal or fraudulent activity. One assumes that when a corporate attorney is involved in activities that later are exposed as fraudulent, it is because there is more "wiggle room" in interpreting corporate acts—and more incentive for attorneys to decide that the actions are not "strictly illegal," even though they may later be defined to be.

The attorney–client privilege refers to the client's right to not have the attorney be called to offer testimony about information obtained during the course of representing the client. The Model Rules have enlarged this privilege to prohibit any form of divulging information that is injurious to the client's interests, except for a few exceptions. Rule 1.6 states that lawyers "may not reveal information relating to the representation of a client unless the client gives informed consent" (ABA, 2002, Rule 1.6).

The exceptions to this rule include an exception to prevent "reasonably certain death or substantial bodily harm" or to "prevent … a crime or fraud that is reasonably certain to result in substantial injury to the financial interests or property of another and in furtherance of which the client has used or is using the lawyer's services." Seemingly, the last exception is simply a restatement of Rule 1.2, which prohibits the lawyer from participating in an ongoing crime or fraud but does not allow an attorney to come forward if the attorney simply knows of the fraud but his or her services are not being used in furtherance of the activity.

This rule has been substantially revised from earlier versions. For instance, in the 1983 version of the Rules, the exception was only the prevention of a crime that involved death or substantial bodily harm. In this earlier rule, financial injury, less than substantial physical injury, or the wrongful conviction of another could not justify disclosure (Vogelstein, 2003).

Martyn (2003) discusses both utilitarian and deontological rationales for the attorney–client privilege. Arguably, for instance, the rule is necessary for clients to be open with attorneys and share information that they must have to conduct an effective defense in criminal law and to further the client's interests in civil law. The deontological rationale is that it is the duty of the attorney to pursue the client's interests above all others. Martyn (2003) gives an example of an attorney who was consulted by a man seeking to sue an apartment manager for wrongful termination. During the course of that conversation, the man told the attorney that he was going to burn down the apartment building. The attorney informed the police, and they caught the man in the act after he had already spread an accelerant. The moral agent attorney could have done nothing else, but some questioned this attorney's actions because he could not have been "reasonably certain" that the man was going to commit arson and he was not involved in furthering the crime.

One much-discussed case involved two lawyers who knew the location of the bodies of two teenagers who had been killed and buried by their client. Instead of divulging this information, they kept their client's confidence and used the location to bargain for a reduced sentence (for a discussion, see Pollock, 2004). Certainly a legal advocate would have kept quiet, but what would a moral agent have done? A similar case occurred more recently in Texas when an attorney was compelled by the Texas courts to produce a map drawn by a client that showed the location of a child she had murdered. The court decided that the abandonment of the privilege was necessary because although the client had said that the child was dead, in another interview she had said that the child was still alive, so the location was necessary to prevent a future crime (if the child had still been alive). Because the attorney had to be compelled to produce the map through legal means, can we assume that she knew the child was already dead? A moral agent would have never kept such information to herself, but what about a legal advocate?

Blakleyn (2003) discusses a different sort of confidentiality issue. He asks whether attorneys, as officers of the court, owe a general duty to the public in cases that are sealed but in which, arguably, the public interest dictates divulging information from the case to a wider audience. His examples included sealed settlements with clergy members who were sued for sexually molesting children. The sealed settlements prohibited any of the parties from breaking the confidentiality clause of the contracts, but in some cases, especially when the same clergymen engaged in similar behavior over time, it is clear that the public's interest would have been served by knowing.

The case involving a young child and the late pop star Michael Jackson is also a good example of how sealed settlements may not be in the public interest. Several years before the charges imposed in this case, a family leveled similar allegations against Jackson but settled the case out of court for an undisclosed sum of money. The family and child refused to cooperate with prosecutors in that case. Then, allegedly, another child was sexually molested. Did the attorneys in the prior case have some responsibility for this latter incident, given the fact that they did not divulge information to prosecutors that might have helped prevent future crimes? Would a moral agent attorney have found some way not only to protect the public but also to get a settlement for his or her client? What responsibility does a judge have in this situation? After all, a judge must agree to the confidentiality clause in any settlement agreement.

Vogelstein (2003) presents a description of psychologist Carol Gilligan's "ethics of care" in juxtaposition to the "ethics of rights" approach of the legal system and the ethical principles for lawyers. The **"ethics of care"** centers on morality as tied to relationship and the understanding of connectedness; the **"ethics of rights"** is rule based and emphasizes legality. Vogelstein applies this reasoning to the specific issue of when attorneys should divulge confidential information to third parties. She argues that the rule contributes to the negative stereotype of attorneys:

> By orchestrating a legal system where "zealous advocacy" for one individual trumps virtually any concern for and responsibility to the collective body, the confidentiality rule contributes significantly to the marred perception of the legal profession currently shared by the American populous.
>
> **Vogelstein (2003, p. 159)**

Vogelstein (2003) points out that the current rule has protected more third parties than the earlier versions of the rule but that it still ignores other types of harm—specifically, commission of a crime or fraud that results in substantial harm but is not furthered by the lawyer's services, wrongful incarceration or execution of another, and substantial emotional injury.

She further points out that to ensure that lawyers do protect the interests of third parties, the rule to disclose should not be a permission to do so, but rather should be mandatory. She argues that lawyers have an inclination to protect their clients—for pecuniary reasons if for no other. Therefore, the ABA should use forceful persuasion via the rules to make sure attorneys act as moral agents following an "ethics of care" toward third parties and the public at large.

Rule 2.1 seems to offer support for the proposition that the lawyer is a moral agent by proposing that the lawyer "shall exercise independent professional judgment and render candid advice." Furthermore, the rule goes on to state that "a lawyer may refer not only to law but to other considerations such as moral, economic, social, and political factors …" (ABA, 2002, Rule 2.1). Dinnerstein, Ellman, Gunning, and Shalleck (2004) explain that attorneys rarely engage in **moral dialogues** with their clients, but they explain how one might go about such a discussion. They also observe that attorneys may approach giving moral advice in an oblique way or couch their argument in practical rather than moral terms. The authors discuss elements of whether to engage in moral arguments, including such things as the seriousness of the issue (see Box 8.2).

BOX 8.2 MORAL DIALOGUES WITH CLIENTS: SUGGESTIONS FOR LAWYERS

1. *The moral stakes of the issue.* The more serious the issue, the more reason there is to engage in a discussion about a course of action.
2. *The debatability of an issue.* If it is in a gray area, there may be more reason to allow client latitude in decision making.
3. *The client's capacity to make a moral decision.* Some clients may not have the intellectual capacity to reasonably make decisions.
4. *The presence of shared values.* When the attorney is very different from the client there may be more room for disagreement.
5. *The nature of a legal relationship.* A simple exercise in contract writing may not create the same need for moral discussions as a criminal defense or custody battle.
6. *The lawyer's objectivity or self-interest.* The attorney needs to be sure that his or her moral advice isn't influenced by self-interest.

Dinnerstein et al. (2004).

Rule 3.1 mandates that lawyers "shall not bring or defend a proceeding, or assert or controvert an issue therein, unless there is a basis in law and fact …" (ABA, 2002, Rule 3.1). However, in this rule there is a special exception or allowance for criminal defense attorneys, who are allowed to defend their clients in a way to "require that every element of the case be established." Therefore, even if the attorney knows the client is guilty, the attorney's ethical responsibility is to defend the case in a way that challenges every assertion by the prosecution.

This rule defines why defense attorneys must ethically question prosecution witnesses, even if they know they are telling the truth. They must challenge technicalities and question physical evidence. Their role is to test the evidentiary weight of the prosecution's case and to offer up any evidence that might create reasonable doubt. If they do not, then, arguably, they have failed to live up to their role. This rule, along with much commentary in the literature, sets the criminal defense attorney apart from the corporate attorney. The distinction, however, does not solve the moral quandaries of some defense attorneys when they "do what they are supposed to do," such as imply that a rape victim is lying.

The most obvious dilemma for attorneys representing guilty defendants is the situation in which the defendant wants to commit perjury or have someone commit perjury to help the case. The Rules state that a lawyer shall not knowingly "make a false statement of fact or law to a tribunal" or "offer evidence that the lawyer knows to be false" (ABA, 2002, Rule 3.3). Although this seems to resolve the matter, criminal cases merit special rules. Rule 3.3 goes on to say that "[a] lawyer may refuse to offer evidence, other than the testimony of a defendant in a criminal matter, that the lawyer reasonably believes is false."

In the comments section to this rule, it becomes clear that an attorney must "know" the testimony is false before he or she can ethically refuse to offer it in trial. If the attorney merely "reasonably believes" the testimony is false, then it must be offered. Thus, if a defendant tells an attorney that he was home alone when the crime was committed, but then when the case is not going well and the client offers a girlfriend who wants to testify that the client was with her the day of the crime, what should the attorney do? The attorney believed that the client was telling the truth the first time, but does the attorney know the truth? Do the rules require the attorney to use the testimony of the girlfriend? What if the defendant originally confessed to the crime but then wanted to take the stand and testify that he did not do it? The attorney tells him that he cannot assist in perjury, so the client claims he was lying in his confession. Does the attorney know which is the truth? How would an attorney truly know what is the truth or not versus a reasonable belief, anyway?

Pellicotti (1990) describes what an attorney does after his or her client commits perjury. The **passive role** is to ignore the perjured testimony during summation or any arguments. The **active role** is to disclose the perjury to the court. However, as stated before, the rules state that the attorney must *know*, not simply reasonably believe, that the client has committed perjury. The culture of the defense bar includes the idea that all defendants lie: "I was surprised, at first, that a client would lie to his own lawyer, but after a while I got used to it" (Wishman, 1981, p. 37). Thus the rationale of many defense attorneys is that they do not know anything. They ask not whether the person did the crime, but rather what they need to know to defend the case.

The proscriptions regarding the attorney's direct use of deception are stringent. In a much publicized case in Colorado in 2002, an assistant district attorney was helping police negotiate with a murderer to surrender. While talking to a police negotiator over the telephone, the murderer had already confessed to brutally killing three women and raping and terrorizing a fourth. He insisted that he would not surrender until he spoke with a public defender. The assistant district attorney pretended to be a public defender and assured him that he would not be harmed if he turned himself in. The attorney did not solicit additional inculpatory information or offer legal advice. However, he was brought up on disciplinary charges for violating the Colorado Bar Association's Rule 8.4, which prohibited attorneys from engaging in conduct that involved "dishonesty, fraud, deceit or misrepresentation." On appeal, the Colorado Supreme Court affirmed the suspension (Cross, 2003; see *In re Paulter*, 47 P.3d 1175 (Col. 2002)). Was this attorney acting as a moral agent? Should he have been disciplined?

Those who defended the action of this lawyer argued that he was trying to save lives because the murderer might not have surrendered and would have murdered again. It was important to his supporters that he did acquire no inculpatory evidence; the sole motivation for his deception seemed to be public safety. Those who agreed with the finding that he deserved discipline pointed out that he had other options open to him; that is, he could have gotten a real public defender to talk him into surrendering. According to this argument, whenever there are alternative options to violating a rule, attorneys should take them.

Finally, Rule 3.4 covers actions taken by the attorney in pursuing his or her client's interests. An attorney cannot "unlawfully obstruct … access to evidence or unlawfully alter, destroy or conceal a document or other material having potential evidentiary value," nor can an attorney "falsify evidence" or counsel another to do so. Furthermore, an attorney cannot assert "personal knowledge of facts in issue" or "state a personal opinion as to the justness of a cause, the credibility of a witness … or the guilt or innocence of an accused." Does this mean that the attorney cannot, in closing arguments, profess to the jury that the defendant is innocent if the attorney knows him to be guilty? But then again, how would the lawyer know for sure? This rule illustrates that, although an attorney must ethically conduct a zealous advocacy, there is a line to be drawn as to what the difference is between ethical zeal and over-the-line aggressive lawyering. The line is difficult to see, to be sure, and there is vigorous debate as to where it is. Some argue that zealous defense is the only ethical approach; others, as stated previously, argue that the lawyer should moderate the client's interests with larger issues of social justice.

Etienne (2003) points out that the federal courts impose a sanction against clients whose lawyers take the aggressive lawyering approach. In this study, it was found that the federal sentencing guidelines allow judges to impose longer sentences on defendants who show no remorse. Increasingly, judges appear to use longer sentences to punish clients whose lawyers employ "zealous defense" strategies:

> Zealous advocacy is recast as a question of strategy to be balanced against other strategic considerations rather than as a requirement of ethical and professional representation.
>
> **Etienne (2003)**

It seems, therefore, that what one attorney would see as ethical advocacy another sees as inappropriate "strategy" that deserves sanctions. Ironically, though, when that other person is also a judge, it is the client who is often punished, not the attorney.

THE PROSECUTOR

Most of the discussion thus far has involved defense attorneys or corporate attorneys, but the same issues apply to prosecutors. Defense attorneys are supposed to be advocates for the defendant; prosecutors are supposed to be advocates for justice. Even so, many prosecutors have committed actions that violate the ethical rules in their zeal to win. They become, in effect, legal advocates, but instead of pursuing justice, they are merely pursuing convictions. Wishman (1981, pp. 52–53) writes: "Some prosecutors lied out of personal ambition, some out of a zeal to protect society, but most lied because they had gotten caught up in the competition to win."

Gershman (1991) describes cases in which prosecutors engaged in false promises, fraud, and threats during plea bargaining. Other studies have found that prosecutors ignore, suppress, and even conceal exculpatory evidence as well as misrepresent evidence to the jury (Hessick, 2002). For instance, cases are cited in which prosecutors misrepresented animal blood as human blood in arguments to the jury; hid the fact that the victim had a gun, to undercut the defendant's self-defense plea; and concealed evidence that showed that the chief witness (not the defendant) was the killer (Armstrong & Possley, 1999).

Gershman (2003) also writes of prosecutors who willfully misuse forensic evidence in a number of ways, including suppressing test results that do not match the theory of the case, using the testimony of forensic experts who are incompetent or biased, rejecting expert reports that are exculpatory, and overstating the findings of forensic experts in summary argument. Obviously, prosecutors who engage in such behavior are not moral agents, nor are they legal advocates—they are violating the law. Unfortunately, sanctions for such behavior are rare (Armstrong & Possley, 1999).

There is a growing perception that prosecutorial misconduct has gotten out of hand, and there has even been a legislative proposal to create an agency that would investigate allegations of such misconduct (Hessick, 2002). Because that task is already supposed to be done by the Department of Justice, the creation of a special agency is unlikely to happen, but it does indicate that some believe that legal advocate prosecutors have forgotten that their client is the public at large—and the public's interests are not served by securing convictions at all costs.

■ Learn More on the Internet

Go to www.abanow.org and search the term *legal ethics* for more information.   ■

CONCLUSION: RECONCILING THE LEGAL ADVOCATE AND MORAL AGENT VIEWS

There are literally volumes of literature on the ethics of attorneys and, especially, whether they should be pure legal advocates for their clients or whether they should abide by and enforce some external moral principles. The dilemma has no easy answer. This may be why the ABA Model Rules have not provided one. Should murderers have attorneys who use "aggressive lawyering" to obtain a dismissal? Should corporations have attorneys that help them thwart judgments that are just and moral? Should attorneys engage in practices that they would not do for themselves but are insisted on by their clients? In the end, attorneys and their clients must decide for themselves what they feel is the right thing to do. A strong personal ethical or moral code can help everyone make those decisions for themselves.

Discussion Questions

1. Describe the moral agent and legal advocate roles of attorneys. Give examples of how these two groups might make different decisions in criminal or civil cases.
2. What is the source for the definition of right or wrong behavior for attorneys?
3. Explain the difference between the ethical obligations of a defense attorney and the ethical obligations of a prosecutor. Explain how these different roles may affect their responsibilities in a criminal trial.
4. What is attorney–client privilege? What justifications are used for its existence?
5. What are the criteria used to decide whether to engage in a "moral dialogue" with a client?

CASE STUDY 8–1 CHILD RAPIST

You are an assistant district attorney in a small circuit court region. The region consists of three counties, with an average population of 80,000 people per county. The community you serve is primarily composed of middle class people with middle class values. Having come from a large city, you were particularly impressed with the small-town atmosphere and easy way of life.

The district attorney general hired you straight out of law school 2 years ago. You felt that a job with the DA's office would be an excellent opportunity to gain needed experience and develop a reputation as a good lawyer. Your ambition is to enter the political arena and perhaps run for state representative in a couple of years. You have stressed a "law and order" image to accomplish your career ambitions.

As you prepare to look over the court docket for tomorrow's cases, your secretary advises you that Sheriff's Investigator John Wainwright is waiting to see you. "John, come in," you greet him. "I was going to call you about our burglary case tomorrow. You didn't have to come over here in person today."

"Thanks, Bill, but I need to talk with you about another matter. You know, we arrested a young man by the name of Fred Granger a couple of days ago for rape, and I wanted to fill you in on some details," the investigator begins.

"Yes, I was at the arraignment, remember?" you jokingly respond. Fred Granger is a 22-year-old white male who works in a nearby factory. He has a high school education and no prior felony arrests or convictions, but he does have a previous conviction for driving under the influence (DUI) 2 years ago and one for possession of marijuana 3 years ago. He has been charged with the rape of a 13-year-old girl under state code 37-1-2702:

> Any adult who carnally knows a child under the age of fourteen by sexual intercourse shall be guilty of the capital offense of rape.

The punishment for same shall be not less than 10 years nor more than 30 years in the state penitentiary without parole. It shall be no defense that the child consented to the act or that the defendant was ignorant of the age of the child. The punishment for this offense is no different than for the crime of forcible rape in your state. Fred

Granger was arrested on a complaint from the parents of a 13-year-old girl named Debbie. It seems Fred picked Debbie up for a date, took her out to the lake, and had sexual intercourse with her. It was a clear violation of the law and an apparently easy conviction since Fred admitted to arresting officers that he had sex with Debbie.

"So, what information do you have for me, John?" you ask.

"We've obtained statements from everyone involved. This is basically what went down: Fred knew Debbie's sister, Nina, who is 20 years old. Fred and Nina had gone out on a couple of dates in the past and have had intercourse. It seems Nina and her younger sister, Debbie, have the reputation of being 'easy'. Anyway, Fred called Nina for a date and Nina wasn't at home. Debbie answered the phone and started flirting with Fred. Fred asked Debbie if she wanted to go with him to the lake and Debbie agreed. Debbie apparently wore a very revealing bathing suit and 'came on' to Fred. They had intercourse and Fred dropped Debbie back home. Debbie's parents inquired about her activities for the day and Debbie told them everything, even about the sex. That's when we got the call. Fred states that he thought Debbie was over 18 and that Debbie consented to having sex with him. Debbie supports this story. Both of them were drinking beer at the lake," the investigator continued.

"Yes, well, I see. But it's no defense for Fred to be ignorant of her actual age and no defense for him that Debbie consented. He probably got her drunk anyway. The law is clear on this matter," you advise.

"Yes, I know. But this Debbie has a reputation of being very promiscuous. She is very open about the fact that she consented. She now says she's in love with Fred. Needless to say, her parents aren't very happy about her attitude, but they seem to have very little control over her or her sister. In addition, anyone can look at Debbie and make a mistake about her age." The investigator pulls out and shows you a recent photograph of Debbie.

The photograph surprises you. You had not previously seen the victim but from the photography Debbie looks well over 20 years old.

"Hey, she does look 20," you respond. "She certainly would have fooled me."

CASE STUDY 8–1 CHILD RAPIST *Continued*

"Yeah. Anyone could have made that mistake," the investigator replies.

Looking over the statements that the investigator brought, you begin to feel uneasy about the case. In the legal sense, Fred is a criminal. He violated the state law. He has no legal defense. The girl is under 14, which means she cannot testify that she consented. The fact that she has had intercourse before cannot be used as a defense for Fred. It seems to be an open-and-shut case. Fred is looking at 10–30 years with no chance of parole. Even if he got the minimum 10 years, it is still a stiff punishment for ignorance. You decide to call on the district attorney general for advice.

"Yes, Bill," the DA says after you explain the situation. "I see why you are concerned. It seems to me you have three options here. One, you could *nolle prosequi* the case (a formal entry on the record by the prosecuting attorney that he will not prosecute the case further). Two, you could reduce charges through a plea bargain agreement. Or, three, you could prosecute to the fullest extent of the law. It's basically a choice between legal ethics and personal ethics. Legal ethics would dictate that you prosecute to the fullest. A crime by statutes has been committed and you are sworn to uphold the law. In that sense, it would not

be legally ethical for you to *nolle prosequi* or plea bargain when you have such a strong case. And, if you did, it might affect your political career. The news media and the public would not take your letting a 'child rapist' off without comment. However, your personal ethics dictate that this Fred fellow is not a typical criminal. He's guilty of stupidity, maybe. But apparently when you look at Debbie, you can see why. If you prosecuted the case, the jury might see Debbie the way Fred saw her and acquit him. But that is a big chance to take. Juries are unpredictable and you can't bring up the fact that she 'looks' of age. I don't know, Bill. It's your decision. I'll back you on whatever you decide."

Questions

1. Examine this case in terms of the moral agent and the legal agent. Compare and contrast the two in terms of the decision that the prosecuting attorney must make.

2. Develop a position in regard to what you would do if you were the prosecuting attorney. Explain your reasoning. What do you think would be the most likely outcome of this case?

REFERENCES

American Bar Association. (2002). *Model Rules of Professional Conduct*. Retrieved from abanet.org/cpr/mrpc.

Armstrong, K., & Possley, M. (1999). "Break rules, be promoted" series: Trial and error, how prosecutors sacrifice just to win. Five in a five-part series. *Chicago Tribune*, 1.

Barker, J., & Cosentino, M. (2003). Who's in charge here? The Ethics 2000 approach to resolving lawyer-client conflicts. *Georgetown Journal of Legal Ethics, 16*, 505–520.

Blakleyn, A. (2003). To squeal or not to squeal: Ethical obligations of officers of the court in possession of information of public interest. *Cumberland Law Review, 34*, 65–93.

Braswell, M., Fletcher, T., & Miller, L. S. (2006). *Human relations and corrections* (5th ed.). Long Grove: Waveland Press.

Cohen, E. (1991). Pure legal advocates and moral agents: Two concepts of a lawyer in an adversary system. In M. Braswell, B. R. McCarthy, & B. J. McCarthy (Eds.), *Justice, crime, and ethics* (4th ed.) (pp. 125–157). Cincinnati: Anderson.

Cohen, E. (2002). Pure legal advocates and moral agents revisited: A reply to Memory and Rose. *Criminal Justice Ethics, 21*(1), 39–55.

Condlin, R. (2003). What's love got to do with it? It's not like they're your friends for Christ's sake: The complicated relationship between lawyer and client. *University of Nebraska Law Review, 82*, 211–311.

Cross, R. (2003). Ethical deception by prosecutors. *Fordham University Law Journal, 31*, 215–234.

Dinnerstein, R., Ellman, S., Gunning, I., & Shalleck, A. (2004). Connection, capacity, and morality in lawyer-client relationships. *Clinical Law Review, 10*, 755–805.

Etienne, M. (2003). Remorse, responsibility, and regulating advocacy: Making defendants pay for the sins of their lawyers. *New York University Law Review, 78*, 2103–2174.

Freedman, M. (2002). How lawyers act in the interests of justice. *Fordham Law Review*, 1717–1727.

Gershman, B. (1991). Why prosecutors misbehave. *Criminal Law Bulletin, 22*(2), 131–143.

Gershman, B. (2003). The use and misuse of forensic evidence. *Oklahoma City University Law Review, 28*, 17–41.

Granfield, R., & Koenig, T. (2003). It's hard to be a human being and a lawyer: Young attorneys and the confrontation with ethical ambiguity in legal practice. *West Virginia Law Review, 105*, 495–524.

Hessick, C. (2002). Prosecutorial subornation of perjury: Is the fair justice agency the solution we have been looking for? *South Dakota Law Review, 47*, 255–280.

Markovits, D. (2003). Legal ethics from the lawyer's point of view. *Yale Journal of Law and the Humanities, 15*, 209–245.

Martyn, S. (2003). In defense of client-lawyer confidentiality. *University of Nebraska Law Review, 81*, 1320–1350.

Mather, L. (2003). Ethics symposium: What do clients want? What do lawyers do? *Emory Law Journal, 52*, 1065–1088.

Memory, J., & Rose, C. (2002). The attorney as moral agent: A critique of Cohen. *Criminal Justice Ethics, 21*(1), 28–39.

Pellicotti, J. (1990). Ethics and the criminal defense: A client's desire to testify untruthfully. In F. Schmalleger (Ed.), *Ethics and criminal justice* (pp. 67–78). Bristol: Wyndam Hall Press.

Pollock, J. (2004). *Ethics in crime and justice: Dilemmas and decisions*. Belmont: Wadsworth.

Powell, B. (2003). Integrity in the practice of law: The limits of integrity or why cabinets have locks. *Fordham Law Review, 72*, 311–332.

Rhode, D., & Paton, P. (2002). Lawyers, ethics, and Enron. *Stanford Journal of Law, Business and Finance, 9*.

Scheingold, S. (1984). *The politics of law and order*. New York: Longman.

Simon, W. (1993). The ethics of criminal defense. *Michigan Law Review, 91*, 1703–1743.

Simon, W. (1998). *The practice of justice: A theory of lawyer's ethics*. Cambridge: Harvard University Press.

Smith, A. (2003). Promoting justice through inter-disciplinary teaching, practice, and scholarship: The difference in criminal defense and the difference it makes. *Washington University Journal of Law and Policy, 11*, 83–140.

Vogelstein, R. (2003). Confidentiality vs. care: Re-evaluating the duty to self, client, and others. *Georgetown Law Journal, 92*, 153–171.

Wishman, S. (1981). *Confessions of a criminal lawyer*. New York: Penguin Books.

CHAPTER 9

Ethical Challenges for Prosecutors

Richard R.E. Kania

INTRODUCTION

The office of the prosecutor is invested with great power over the lives of those suspected of crimes. While the police make the arrest, it is the prosecutor who decides if a case goes to trial, what charges will be filed, and what evidence and witnesses will be presented in court. The prosecutor also has some control over when a case comes up for trial, and can negotiate guilty pleas in exchange for reduced charges or reduced penalties. With these powers come great responsibilities to pursue justice and fairness, and with these the ethical challenges these responsibilities invite.

In the federal system and in a few states, prosecutors are appointees (Bureau of Justice Statistics, 2001), but in most states local prosecutors and state attorneys general are elected officials (Ellis, 2012). Because they need to run for elective office, prosecutors are highly visible political figures in most jurisdictions. They often will run for reelection by advertising their favorable conviction rates (Bresler, 1996), ideally 100%. Even appointed prosecutors are political appointees and should be seen as beholden to the elected political figures who appoint them. Therefore, we may assume that they, too, are highly political, but we also expect them to be politically neutral in selecting cases for trial and in conducting themselves in trial courtrooms.

Most prosecutors effectively maintain this balance and uphold high standards of ethics. The complaints against prosecutors are relatively rare. Yet, when a prosecutor is accused of behaving unethically, it can become a major scandal, drawing media attention and discrediting the American criminal justice system. A few select cases from the past help illustrate where and how ethical problems have intruded upon the generally honorable reputation of America's prosecutors.

Recent events in the United States have brought numerous criticism of prosecutors to the attention of the public, notably the 2012–2013 "Trayvon Martin Shooting Case," the 2007 "Federal Prosecutors Firings Case," involving the dismissal of several federal prosecutors by the Bush administration, and the 2006 "Duke Lacrosse Case." Some earlier cases also are noteworthy: *"The Thin Blue Line* Case," the "Atlanta Child Murders Case," and the "Labor Secretary Raymond Donovan Case," which involved the repeated prosecutions of former U.S. Labor Secretary Raymond J. Donovan. There are also many thousands of exemplary cases of prosecutors behaving ethically, even at some risk to their own careers. One famous example of this is described in the *"Boomerang* Case," named after a 1947 film by that name. From these tangible examples, we can identify and discuss in some depth the ethical obligations and challenges of our prosecutors as well as their occasional ethical failings and their likely causes.

"THE TRAYVON MARTIN HOMICIDE" CASE

The confrontation between George Zimmerman and Trayvon Martin in 2012 left Zimmerman bruised and bleeding, and Martin dead. Initially the local Sanford police and prosecutor declined to arrest and prosecute Zimmerman for the homicide, accepting his account of the events, which described the shooting as self-defense. But political outrage and lobbying by civil rights leaders and political leaders, extending from local officials to the Florida governor's mansion and the White House, created pressure on the State of Florida to bring the case to trial (Morgenstern, 2013; McLaughlin, 2013), and a special prosecutor was named by the state, Angela Corey.

Legal luminary Alan Dershowitz was highly critical of prosecutor Corey for seriously overcharging Zimmerman soon after the original charges were filed (Wilson, 2012). Both Corey and some of her defenders disagreed with the criticism (Broward, 2012). One issue then raised was that the filing deliberately excluded information about Zimmerman and his injuries, which should have been included.

After the acquittal of Zimmerman in July 2013, the prosecutor was again criticized for bringing the case to trial at all, and by others for overcharging Zimmerman, in the belief that a lesser manslaughter charge might have produced a conviction.

There is no doubt that political pressures were brought to bear to bring Zimmerman to trial after the local police and prosecutor felt that no crime had been committed (McLaughlin, 2013). The politicalization of the case was not covert and may not have been unethical, but is ethically troubling. Within days of the acquittal there were calls for a federal civil rights indictment, again giving evidence to the political pressures still being brought to bear on the case. How much political pressure in a controversial case is acceptable? Influential people have a right to express their opinions, pro and con. At what point is an ethical line crossed?

The police chief in Sanford was fired over his handling of the case (McLaughlin, 2013). There also was a revelation that one of the state's investigators had been dismissed for releasing information to the defense and the public that portrayed Martin in a highly negative light (Hennessy-Fiske, 2013). The attempt by the prosecution team to suppress that information, if true, would violate legal norms calling for full discovery, and represent a form of deception on the part of the prosecution team. Regardless of the feelings that one may have about the guilt or innocence of George Zimmerman, if information was withheld from the defense team, the prosecution was behaving unethically.

THE 2007 FIRING OF FEDERAL PROSECUTORS

In 2007, then-Attorney General of the United States Alberto Gonzales, came under considerable criticism for dismissing seven federal prosecutors. Gonzales initially explained their dismissal as based on unspecified "performance" matters, implying that their work was sub-par. Later revelations showed that the firings were at least somewhat political, because the Bush administration sought to appoint in their place prosecutors perceived as being more supportive of the Bush Administration agenda.

Federal prosecutors are political appointees of the president, and dismissing them for political purposes is a normal practice. However, Bush Administration critics raised the suspicion that the dismissed attorneys were singled out by Attorney General Gonzales to punish them for investigating Republican office holders and not investigating Democrat office holders. Countercharges that the dismissed prosecutors were lax in pursuing immigration cases or other Bush administration priorities were raised. Whatever the truth of the charges and countercharges, the case raised several important points bearing on ethical issues.

Federal prosecutors are political appointees and serve at the pleasure of the President. However, once appointed and confirmed, they swear an oath that makes it clear that their first obligation is to the Constitution and to its requirements of due process of law. Their loyalty to the administration appointing them is secondary. Attorney General Gonzales's prepared remarks before the Senate Judiciary Oversight Committee are in total agreement with the ethical principal involved (Gonzales, 2007):

> U.S. Attorneys serve at the pleasure of the President. There is nothing improper in making a change for poor management, policy differences, or questionable judgment, or simply to have another qualified individual serve. I think we agree on that.
>
> I think we also agree on what would be improper. It would be improper to remove a U.S. Attorney to interfere with or influence a particular prosecution for partisan political gain.
>
> I did not do that. I would never do that.
>
> Nor do I believe that anyone else in the Department advocated the removal of a U.S. Attorney for such a purpose.

THE 2006 DUKE LACROSSE CASE

In 2006, an elected prosecutor in North Carolina, Michael B. Nifong, brought a rape case before a county grand jury and charged three Duke University students from the lacrosse team with felonies, based on an allegation brought by a young African-American woman, Crystal Magnum. Magnum had been hired as an exotic dancer for a party the young men attended. Responding to media attention to the case and aware that he was facing reelection later in the year, the prosecutor made multiple media presentations condemning the suspects and alleging he had evidence that subsequently was shown never to have existed.

In the months that followed, the original rape allegations were dropped. Then, the case was transferred from county to state jurisdiction, and eventually, in April 2007, the Attorney General of North Carolina, Roy Cooper, dropped all of the charges. The controversial case did not end with the dismissal of the case. Nifong was criticized extensively in the media, and an ethics investigation was initiated against him (Wilson & Barstow, 2007).

Nifong found himself under a North Carolina State Bar ethics investigation. The Bar complaint referred to participating in "prejudicial" actions and "conduct involving dishonesty, fraud, deceit, or misrepresentation" (Associated Press, 2007). Charges against him appearing in the press included assertions that he pursued the case for personal gain, using his office to promote his personal aim of reelection, and thus harboring and advancing excessive ambition (Setrakian & Francescani, 2007). Others were critical of him for showing a class **bias** against the Duke University students, whom some described as being children of privilege, an expression of class discrimination.

Issues of race also were involved, because the suspects were Euro-American and the complainant was African-American. Several highly vocal leaders in the minority community and some Duke University faculty were publicly sympathetic to the alleged victim and the prosecutor wanted their support for the upcoming election. The **abuse of power** also was alleged, because defenders of the students were critical of what they saw as unjustified arrests and prosecutions.

The prosecutor also was accused of hiding key facts about DNA evidence, violating requirements for "discovery" that would have helped exonerate the students, an expression of **deceitfulness**. His behaviors were counter to the ABA Standard 3-3.11 on full disclosure of "information which tends to negate the guilt of the accused" (Cassidy, 2005, p. 164) and established case law (*Brady v. Maryland*, 1963) about suppression of evidence (Kania & Dial, 2008, p. 166). In June 2007, Nifong resigned from office and was disbarred by the state (Wilson, 2007) (Box 9.1).

BOX 9.1 EXTRACT FROM AMERICAN BAR ASSOCIATION STANDARD 3-3.11

A prosecutor should not intentionally fail to make timely disclosure to the defense ... the existence of all evidence or information which tends to negate the guilt of the accused ...

A prosecutor should not intentionally avoid pursuit of evidence because ... it will damage the prosecution's case ...

The **denial of due process** also was asserted in the Duke Lacrosse Case. In failing to disclose the information he had that would have helped clear the lacrosse players, Nifong behaved counter to the standards for pretrial due process established long before in *Mooney v. Holohan* (1935), which ruled that nondisclosure of key facts to the defense is a violation of due process (Kania & Dial, 2008, p. 167), a failure to provide "discovery" to the defense. Speaking before the media, Nifong used inflammatory statements about the accused students and thus was in violation of ABA Rule 3.6, which states that a lawyer will not disseminate information to the public on a case that could have "substantial likelihood of materially prejudicing a proceeding" (Cassidy, 2005, p. 117). His next major due-process failure was in continuing the prosecution when the evidence to support it evaporated (Kania & Dial, 2008, p. 167). This prosecutor also was criticized for **neglect of duties** when it was revealed that he had not reviewed key evidence in person and never had interviewed the complaining witness, opening him to a potential complaint of nonfeasance in office.

THE 1987 TRIAL OF LABOR SECRETARY RAYMOND DONOVAN

Raymond J. Donovan was the U.S. Secretary of Labor in the administration of President Ronald Reagan from 1981 to 1985. A Bronx County, New York prosecutor, Mario Marola, indicted Donovan on several complaints having to do with construction contracts Donovan had negotiated before his appointment as Labor Secretary. In May 1987, Donovan, a Republican, and all other defendants were acquitted of all charges. Donovan addressed the press asking rhetorically, "Which office do I go to get my reputation back?" Both during the trial and soon after the jury made its decision, the prosecutor, a Democrat, was widely criticized. Allegations were made that Marola pursued the case for purely political reasons. His defenders argued that he was politically independent, and disputed the complaints of bias that originated with Donovan's defense attorneys as part of their defense strategy (Raab, 1987).

The same charges also had been investigated by the Federal Bureau of Investigation and a special federal prosecutor appointed in December 1981, but the charges were not substantiated in their initial investigations (*Time*, 1982). Soon after the acquittals, another Bronx prosecutor initiated an investigation into jury tampering in the case. Once again the federal investigation did not substantiate the complaint, and the federal prosecutor in New York then, Rudolph "Rudy" Giuliani, did not pursue the case. He was, however, criticized for not doing so (*The New York Times*, 1988).

The back-and-forth claims of political motivation in the decisions to prosecute or not prosecute make the tragedy of Raymond Donovan a strong example of the problems of bringing charges against political figures. Donovan has the dubious claim to fame that he was the only federal cabinet secretary indicted while in office. His ultimate acquittal cannot erase that or undo the damage done to his reputation and political career. Were the indictments against him "purely political," or did they have legal merit? It is a question still much debated among scholars of that case and that period. If the indictments were brought primarily or exclusively for political ends, then Marola acted unethically and exemplified a form of *political bias*.

"THE ATLANTA CHILD MURDERS" CASE

Between 1979 and 1981 there were 28 murders of young people reported in the greater Atlanta area. Suspicion fell upon Wayne Williams, a young adult black male. He was subsequently tried and convicted of two of those murders. The prosecution could not link Williams directly to the deaths of the other 26 victims. Moreover, not all of the homicide victims were children, and the two men Williams was convicted of killing were both adults. The prosecutor was unwilling to supply all of the investigative reports on those cases not being brought to trial to the defense. Yet, the media linked Williams to all of the cases, and much of the public seemed satisfied that his conviction closed the case.

The decision not to prosecute on the remaining cases was an exercise of prosecutorial discretion, but the failure to make it clear to the public that Wayne Williams was not tried and convicted of those other murders allows the shadow of suspicion to hang over Williams to this day. The prosecutor did imply that Williams was guilty of at least five additional child murders in his argumentation.

As James Baldwin wrote, "How, then, does it happen—legally—that a man charged with *two* murders can be tried for twenty-eight?" (1985, p. 12). Although Baldwin was being rhetorical, the image given to the public was that Williams was responsible for all or most of the murders, and that his arrest ended the serial murders of Atlanta children.

Joseph Drolet, the prosecutor in the case, has stood by Williams's convictions, saying that when Williams was arrested, "the murders stopped, and there has been nothing since" (RoyalPurple209, 2005). The suspicion that Williams committed all or most of the murders, introduced by the prosecutor at trial and subsequently maintained, may be valid, but under our system of laws, Williams remains innocent of those other murders until a trial court says otherwise.

"*THE THIN BLUE LINE*" CASE

The award-winning documentary film, *The Thin Blue Line*, told the story of the killing of a police officer and the subsequent arrest, trial, and conviction of Randall Dale Adams for the murder. The case was based largely upon the testimony of David Ray Harris, a likely accessory to the crime and possibly the actual shooter. At least, that is the implicit message of the Errol Morris film. The prosecutor in the case agreed to a pretrial deal with David Ray Harris, a juvenile at the time of the 1976 crime, in which he agreed to testify against Adams to escape prosecution for the murder (Lankford, 2001). Certainly, turning one suspect against another is a time-tested method of securing a conviction, but the possibility that the actual murderer might be set free by one's perjured testimony against another is a frightening prospect.

The film retells the crime from several perspectives and is a useful vehicle for illustrating the concept of "reasonable doubt." A truly open-minded viewer would be severely challenged to decide which of the two unsavory men really was the killer of police officer Robert Wood. That is precisely the point that makes the case especially important as an example of questionable prosecutorial ethics. Should the prosecutor in the case not have been equally open-minded and willing to consider both options—that Harris did the shooting and then pinned the crime on Adams, and that Adams committed the crime alone, as Harris claimed? *Washington Post* film critic Desson Howe took from the film a vision of "shady backroom deals, unreliable testimony and court-room players" (Howe, 1988).

ETHICAL PROBLEMS REVEALED IN PROSECUTORIAL MISCONDUCT

There are seven recurring ethical failings common to criminal justice professions. These seven ethical failures tarnish the reputations of all public servants, not just prosecutors (Kania & Dial, 2008, p. 169; see Box 9.2).

BOX 9.2 SEVEN RECURRING ETHICAL PROBLEMS IN CRIMINAL JUSTICE

1. Wrongful Pursuit of Personal Gain
2. Favoritism and Bias
3. Abuse of Power
4. Denial of Due Process
5. Deceitfulness
6. Neglect of Duties
7. Flawed Personal Life

Wrongful Pursuit of Personal Gain

One should not use public service for **personal gain**, meaning personal enrichment, profit, pleasure, or benefits that are not specifically authorized by law, the work contract, or work rules. Included in this category are prohibitions against:

- taking bribes and extorting payoffs
- accepting gratuities and unauthorized benefits
- receiving excessive compensation and benefits
- using the office to promote personal aims
- harboring and advancing excessive ambition

Favoritism and Bias

It can be unethical to use one's office to aid those whom we like (i.e., **favoritism**) and (in the negation) to interfere with those whom we dislike. These biases often arise from divided and mixed loyalties, placing one's obligation to the public interest below that of oneself (egoism), family (paternalism or nepotism), friends, personal associates, coworkers and peers (peer bias), a political party (patronage or ideological bias), or church and spiritual faith (theological bias). Included in this category are rules against:

- political and ideological patronage and bias
- racial, ethnic, and religious bias (favorable and unfavorable)
- nepotism and other family favoritism
- overt and covert discrimination (racial, ethnic, sexual, political, etc.)

The Abuse of Power

When public officials use their offices to place their values, desires, needs, or preferences above those of the public they serve and over the rules and laws they must uphold, they risk abusing their power. These actions need not involve personal material gain. These violations include such activities as:

- acting in an authoritarian, coercive, and harassing manner
- arranging or condoning unjustified arrests
- denying opportunities for reasonable bail
- denying suspects their liberty by arranging lengthy pre-detention.

The Denial of Due Process

There are requirements for procedural correctness in dealing with all administrative matters within the justice system. All public servants are required to follow the policies set out for them, and not invent personal solutions to the situations they encounter. Citizens have the right to expect that their cases will be dealt with fairly and in accordance with the rules for such cases. Failures include:

- ignoring civil rights and constitutional protections
- not following agency rules and procedures
- failing to comply with internal bureaucratic rules
- ignoring regulatory and statutory guarantees

Deceitfulness

We expect that our public officials will be honest and forthright with the public on matters involving their work. Thus, there are rules against:

- overt lying, duplicity, "loop-holing," and evasions
- covering up misdeeds
- unwarranted secrecy in the conduct of the public business
- fraud, trickery, and hypocrisy

Neglect of Duties

All public-service occupations and positions have duties and obligations that must be fulfilled. A public figure who does not fulfill these duties is violating a specific social contract, counter to the deontological mandate that one must do one's duty. Such failures may even lead to violating laws against:

- malfeasance
- nonfeasance
- misfeasance
- disobeying lawful orders
- abusing discretion
- failing to comply with regulations and standing orders

A Flawed Personal Life

These are the prohibitions against personal activities outside the workplace that serve to bring discredit upon the public servant and the servant's agency or profession. These include private violations of the criminal law and moral violations that are not necessarily illegal but are generally frowned upon by the public. We would be suspicious of the integrity of a prosecutor who was a member of the Ku Klux Klan, who harassed coworkers sexually, who willfully evaded paying taxes, or openly expressed prejudicial opinions. Thus, we condemn public officials who engage in:

- criminal wrongdoing
- financial improprieties and tax evasion
- sexual misconduct, deviance, or unconventionality
- civil illegality (tax, regulatory, and civil law violations)
- questionable associations and membership in controversial organizations
- private prejudicial expressions and actions (Box 9.3)

BOX 9.3 NEGLECT OF ONE'S DUTIES

Both the law and ethical standards obligate public office holders to be faithful to their lawful duties. Three common failures are:

Nonfeasance—the failure to perform one's duty by oversight or omission, usually inadvertent (willful nonfeasance is typically considered malfeasance).

Misfeasance—the wrongful performance of one's duties, usually in the form of making mistakes, not following procedures correctly, or other unintentional blunders.

Malfeasance—the intentional performance of an official act or use of one's official powers to achieve an end that is circumstantially illegal, harmful, and/or unjustified.

Actual ethical failures frequently overlap two or more of these categories. In the Duke Lacrosse Case, Nifong has been criticized for six of the seven common failings, omitting only the standard against leading a flawed personal life. Moreover, the cases also reveal ethical failings that are unique to the role of the prosecutor.

UNIQUE PROSECUTORIAL FAILINGS

There are a number of recurring ethical challenges that are distinctly associated with the mission and duties of the office of public prosecutor.

Prosecutors are attorneys first, and as such are obligated to conform to the ethical codes of the legal profession. Both prosecutors and defense attorneys are "moral agents" in the theory of the law. According to Cohen (1991, pp. 123–161) they should be just, truthful, morally courageous, morally respectable, benevolent, trustworthy, and morally autonomous. Because of their special status, prosecutors have additional and somewhat different ethical requirements (Kania & Dial, 2008, p. 173).

A public prosecutor may be said to have responsibility to a client, just as a defense attorney does, but the prosecutor's client is the public at large, which includes even the person under suspicion or indictment. Gershman (2005) refers to this ethical standard as a "duty to neutrality."

There is no duty for a prosecutor to maintain client confidentiality, as exists for defense counsel. Indeed, the prosecutor has a legal obligation to aid in the "discovery" process. The counterpart to zealousness of defense could become overzealousness in prosecution. The prosecutor is charged with the duty to be zealous in "pursuit of the truth," even if that defeats the prosecution.

Prosecutors must comply with specific rules for their offices, the Rules of Professional Conduct of their state bar associations, the laws of their states, their state constitutions, and the Constitution of the United States (Kania & Dial, 2008, p. 173). The American Bar Association has prepared model standards for the prosecution function (Cassidy, 2005, pp. 150–169) covering many details of their prosecutorial roles.

Both prosecutors and defense attorneys may engage in "judge shopping," which some criticize as unethical conduct. Both often will engage in some degree of "coaching" and rehearsing witnesses, another practice criticized by some (and objected to by most at its extremes). Both also can be faulted for the misuse of expert witnesses (the so-called "hired guns" and "dueling experts").

Certain legal processes also are under the control of a prosecutor, including:

- plea bargaining (Heumann, 1978, pp. 92–126)
- the exercise of prosecutorial discretion, merging and dropping charges
- selective prosecution
- *nolle prosequi* (Latin for "to be unwilling to pursue") decisions
- deals and promises made to secure testimony

DISCOVERY AND THE DISCLOSURE OF EVIDENCE

A prosecutor has an obligation to reveal the evidence acquired for trial and to name the witnesses who may be called to testify. This is the process of **discovery**. Some unethical prosecutors have failed to disclose what evidence they have, especially when it may serve to undermine their own cases (Nocera, 2012). Others engage in providing defense counsels an "avalanche of paper" within which critical exculpatory evidence may be found, but only after an exhaustive search of all of the material. Some prosecutors fail to submit evidence from parallel investigations that produced no alternative suspects. A National Institute of Justice study found that the withholding of evidence by prosecutors was a significant factor in erroneous convictions prosecutorial (Gould et al., 2012).

For example, as noted earlier, the Atlanta Child Murders Case involved the investigation of the murders of 28 persons between 1979 and 1981, but only two of those murder cases were brought to trial in 1982. The defense team wanted to know about those other 26 parallel investigations, too. The prosecution was reluctant to share those files, because they were still open investigations and, in the prosecution's opinion, had no bearing on the two cases coming to trial. Is it evidence if it is not to be used at trial? This is a moral question as much as it is a legal one. If such evidence can be used by the defense to create doubt in the minds of jurors, then perhaps it also should be revealed.

PLEA BARGAINING

Plea bargaining is an essential tool in criminal justice in which the accused accepts a reduction in the charge or reduced punishment in exchange for pleading guilty at the arraignment or trial. It speeds up the criminal prosecution of cases. It is an efficient means to see that the guilty willingly acknowledge their wrongdoing and accept their punishment. A prosecutor can make an offer to the defense attorney or the accused directly, or can entertain an offer made by the defense attorney or the accused. When there is little doubt about the commission of a crime and near certainty about who was responsible, the offer or acceptance of a plea bargain is legitimate and ethical.

But when the prosecutor knows he or she has a weak case, or there is genuine doubt about the guilt of the accused, ethical red flags should be raised. Trading off efficiency for a wrongful conviction is not ethical. Often persons held in pretrial detention for lengthy periods of time will accept plea bargains for "time served" rather than risk an even longer term of incarceration after a conviction. Again, this is efficient and ethical if the person in custody freely admits to his or her guilt, but allowing long delays in bringing a case to trial is either nonfeasance or malfeasance by a prosecutor and should never be used to coerce an accused person into accepting a plea deal.

EXERCISING DISCRETION

Prosecutors have great latitude in exercising discretion. This, too, is an essential tool of the criminal justice system. Discretion is necessary for a number of reasons, among which the most important of these are that (1) there are not enough prosecutors and trial courts to hear every known violation of law, (2) not all violations of the law are of true significance to warrant prosecution, and (3) often those victimized by a criminal act are unwilling to support the prosecution of the offender. A prosecutor has to make a judgment on the quality of the evidence in a case and also with regard to the believability and veracity of the witnesses available to testify.

The prosecutor also has a duty to select cases that are worthy of prosecution. This "selective prosecution" can be ethical and efficient. Not every violation of the law or even every law justifies the same degree of attention before the courts. Some laws can and should be ignored because they have become obsolete as social customs have changed. Some cases can be referred to pretrial programs or dealt with by other means of alternative dispute resolution.

When a case is very weak, a prosecutor has a duty to terminate the prosecution, or *nolle prosequi* the case. This decision can lead to an actual dismissal of the charges, or to a postponement until better evidence of guilt can be acquired. Both actions are ethical when based on evidentiary grounds. However, the appellate courts have questioned the use of *nolle prosequi* "with leave," in which the prosecutor uses the action to extend jurisdiction over a case indefinitely, extending the statute of limitations (*Klopfer v. North Carolina*, 1967). In *Klopfer*, the Supreme Court held that an indefinite prolonging of court jurisdiction over a case deprives the accused of the constitutional right to speedy trial to which one was entitled under the Sixth Amendment (Kania & Dial, 2008, p. 175).

Discretion also is employed when a prosecutor consolidates or merges charges, or reduces charges from those initially filed. Often the police and magistrates may "overcharge" or "pile on" counts at the time of arrest. The prosecutor has an ethical obligation to select and present to the grand jury, the preliminary hearing, and the arraignment only those charges most relevant to the case.

Discretion, like plea bargaining, can be abused. Favoritism can intrude wherein guilty parties with strong cases against them can avoid trial, or serious charges can be replaced with trivial complaints. Similarly, the denial of plea bargains and the refusal to exercise leniency in the implementation of discretion can be an expressions of bias and prejudice.

USING UNRELIABLE "SNITCHES"

Another area of great concern is the use of "snitches" who have been offered special consideration by prosecutors (Broder, 2004). This was the essential problem in *The Thin Blue Line* Case. In securing the testimony of David Ray Harris, the prosecutor willfully overlooked his involvement in the crime and his prior criminal offenses (including motor vehicle theft). In the trial of Labor Secretary Raymond Donovan some of the testimony supposedly linking him to bribes and organized crime figures came from "snitches" under investigation for their own organized crime connections and activities.

To make a case against a suspect, the police and the prosecutor may have to rely upon unsavory potential witnesses, but they have a moral obligation to avoid suborning perjury and should seek independent confirmation of evidence derived from suspicious sources. Moreover, when favors or deals are offered to witnesses, these must be made known to the defense so that they can question the motivation of the witness before the judge and jury.

POLITICS, THE PUBLIC, AND THE MEDIA

Political, community, and media influences contribute to potential misconduct. Prosecutors are political figures. In many states, they run for elective office. In the federal service and other states, they are appointed, but even appointees must be politically aware, as the "Firing of Federal Prosecutors" Case shows. Highly vocal and influential voices in the community cannot be totally ignored, but catering to their wishes irresponsibly, as in the Duke Lacrosse Case, can result in unethical and unjust prosecutorial actions. The attention of the news media to a case will tempt a prosecutor to "grandstand" and play to media attention, again as appeared to happen in the Duke Lacrosse Case. Clearly, politics were involved in the Labor Secretary Raymond Donovan Case, but one can take sides as to which side was more politically motivated. Donovan's defense team clearly played to the media and were reasonably successful in creating an image of DA Mario Marola as being politically motivated and vindictive. Similar opinions have arisen regarding the efforts of special prosecutor Kenneth Starr to bring indictments against then-President William Jefferson Clinton (*Christian Century*, 1998), and, more recently, about the Trayvon Martin shooting case.

WHY MISCONDUCT PERSISTS

A certain amount of prosecutorial misconduct can be attributed to error, poor investigative support, unreliable sources and witnesses, and similar weaknesses that exist in the criminal justice system. Prosecutors are human, and they will make mistakes. Some of the ethical lapses attributed to Mike Nifong in the Duke Lacrosse Case may be nothing more than mistakes. It seems that he wanted to believe in the account of the complaining witness, and was blind to the many flaws in her account.

The main motivation, however, for prosecutors to take a blind eye to such flaws in the cases brought before them may well be the desire to win. In the American criminal justice system, the trial is an adversarial process—a contest between a defense attorney and a prosecutor. The DA has taken a side, and with good moral purposes wants that side to be victorious.

"DAs want the perfect case, one that's utterly impossible to mess up. They want the hundred-percent certifiable DBW, the Dead Bang Winner," writes Gary Delsohn (2003, p. 137), but they rarely get handed a perfect investigation or perfect witnesses. So they must work with what is available, and that is often flawed. They must take corrective action to strengthen and win their cases.

But the desire to win can go too far, and prosecutors can lose sight of their real objective—justice—in the process. Even a truly guilty person brought to trial retains fundamental rights and should be afforded all the protections of the criminal justice system, including those under the control of the prosecutor. Both exculpatory and damning evidence needs to be made available to the defense in the process of discovery. Nifong was justly criticized for holding back the evidence from DNA testing that lent support to the statements of the Duke lacrosse players (Box 9.4).

BOX 9.4 GERSHMAN'S VIEW OF "WHY PROSECUTORS MISBEHAVE"

1. Prosecutors will inject inadmissible evidence to influence juries and therefore win their cases, especially if they are presenting weak cases.
2. They know that strong opening statement, even if very inaccurate, will leave a lasting impression on the jury in their favor.
3. They know that strong closing argument, even if inaccurately representing the case just presented, will influence the jury.
4. Their "prestige" and "glamour" as official spokespersons for the government and the people and as "the good guys" in the trial will be employed to influence the jury in their favor.
5. Their unethical conduct "works" because it helps them win cases.
6. Even when their improprieties in the courtroom are exposed and appealed, the appellate process often finds their misconduct is protected under the "harmless error rule" of the courts.
7. Typically prosecutors are not held personally liable for their acts and generally are immune from civil suits even when malice can be shown.

Gershman, B. L. (1991). "Why Prosecutors Misbehave."

Bennett Gershman sought answers to "why prosecutors misbehave" and "why misconduct occurs," and found answers in legal procedures and practices (Gershman, 1991, 2002). He observed that prosecutors perceive themselves as "the good guys of the legal system" (Gershman, 1991, p. 167), but face pressures to achieve objectives beyond their capacities, producing stress and lending temptation to take short cuts around proper due process. Side-stepping proper due process can provide a major advantage in the trial process, handing the prosecutor an "easy win" in an otherwise tough environment. Misconduct "works," according to Gershman's terse commentary (Gershman, 1991, p. 164). Ideally the prosecutor should not endeavor just to "win the case" but has a moral obligation to reveal the truth and to achieve justice (Gershman, 1991, p. 163). The use of tainted, misleading, prejudicial, and totally inadmissible information as evidence is legally impermissible and clearly unethical, yet it does occur with unacceptable frequency. For some prosecutors, like some football coaches, "Winning isn't everything; it's the only thing!"

When a prosecutor does misbehave, the consequences can be severe. Nifong in the Duke Lacrosse Case was disbarred. An assistant DA in New York City was compelled to resign and later had his license to practice law suspended after he concealed the existence of a potential witness whose testimony could help the defense and falsely representing the interpretation of forensic ballistics evidence (Sapien, 2005a,b). When a prosecutor is exposed for being unethical, it often is the defense attorney who initiates the investigation. Judges also have a role in addressing prosecutorial misconduct (Engelberg, 2013).

However, the consequences for those brought to trial are far more severe. A wrongful conviction often follows from prosecutorial misconduct. Of the 250 wrongful convictions reported by Garrett (2011), a great many are the direct result of prosecutorial misconduct, often occurring in conjunction with faulty police work or defective forensic testimony.

THE 1947 FILM *BOOMERANG* AND TRUE PROSECUTORIAL ETHICS

The exemplary conduct of the prosecutor in the *Boomerang* Case, featured in the 1947 film of that name, exemplifies a local prosecutor whose duty to truth leads him to undermine the very case he brought to the court. Under major political pressure to identify, arrest, and bring an indictment against the suspect in the murder of a popular priest, the police and the prosecutor identified the likely murderer. The circumstantial evidence and eyewitness testimony draws the metaphorical noose around his neck well ahead of the real one that he will face if convicted. This film tells the real story of a murder case prosecuted in the years immediately after World War I, although the film is set in the post-World War II era. The actual events upon which the film was based occurred in the 1920s, and the suspected killer was a World War I veteran rather than a World War II South Pacific hero. Names and locations were changed, and identifying real persons and places in the story cannot be done easily. Therefore, the story is not a docudrama but a piece of film fiction loosely based on a factual case. More important, though, is that the dramatic moment—when the DA methodically destroys his own case by challenging his own witnesses and identifying the flaws in the forensic evidence—is very closely based on what happened in the actual preliminary hearing. The film shows that the charges against the accused are dismissed and he goes free. Some of the film dialogue is exactly what was transcribed from that original preliminary hearing. The DA in the film is drawn from the real-life figure Homer S. Cummings. Taking his ethical duties seriously, even at the cost of losing a high-visibility case, Cummings risked his future as a district attorney and as a reform politician. His heroic reversal of role did not harm his reputation in the long term. Cummings was to become a highly respected national political figure and went on to serve as the U.S. Attorney General from 1933 to 1939 under President Franklin Delano Roosevelt. He was both morally courageous and benevolent, those elements to which Elliot Cohen speaks as requirements for being a moral agent of the law (Cohen, 1991, pp. 125–126).

■ Learn More on the Internet

For more on ethical issues involving prosecutors go to: www.abanow.org/ and search "prosecutorial ethics."   ■

CONCLUSION

The prosecutor has an obligation to serve justice first and secure convictions second. The temptation to win at all costs, play up to the media, and advance one's career in the process will often tempt a prosecutor to succumb to ethical lapses.

In common with other actors in the criminal justice system, prosecutors occasionally will violate the seven ethical problem areas facing all those who take on responsibilities in the name of justice: (1) the wrongful pursuit of personal gain, (2) favoritism and bias, (3) the abuse of power, (4) the denial of due process, (5) deceitfulness, (6) the neglect of duties, and (7) a flawed personal life.

In addition, prosecutors have special and unique obligations in fulfillment of their duties. Their powers of discretion allow them great latitude in deciding what cases to present to grand juries and submit to trial and which to *nolle prosequi* or to dismiss outright. They have the final say on who will testify for the state, and can enter into deals with witnesses in exchange for their testimony. They can recommend plea bargains to those under indictment and can accept plea offers from their attorneys. In each of these activities there are opportunities for abuse and ethical misconduct.

Fortunately, there are relatively few known cases of serious ethical lapses on the part of our prosecutors. Every day, thousands of cases are sent to grand jury, heard in preliminary hearings, dismissed, *nolle prosequi*, plea bargained, and sent to trial without ethical problems. But the exceptions do exist, and these must be avoided in the pursuit of justice.

Discussion Questions

1. Name the seven common failures of ethics encountered in criminal justice, and give an example of each type potentially involving misconduct by a prosecutor.
2. Distinguish among nonfeasance, misfeasance, and malfeasance in office, identifying which requires an intention to do wrong.
3. Explain the term *nolle prosequi*, and give an example when a prosecutor should, in an ethical sense, *nolle prosequi* a criminal case.
4. Explain the concept of "discovery" and why our system of justice imposes an obligation on a prosecutor to reveal all of his evidence to the defense before trial.
5. Explain how "the desire to win" can lead a prosecutor to pursue a case that should be dropped.
6. Plea bargaining is a crucial tool in the efficient conduct of criminal prosecutions, but it is a tool of the prosecutor that easily can be abused. Under what ethical circumstances would a plea bargain be in the best interests of justice?
7. Discuss Bennett Gershman's seven reasons for why prosecutors will misbehave and the circumstances in which such misconduct often will occur.

CASE STUDY 9–1 IT'S A RAT RACE, AND THE BEST RAT WINS

You have been a prosecutor for less than a year. Most of the other prosecutors in the office are generous with their advice, and you have learned a lot in the year since you graduated from law school. One of the senior prosecutors—Joey Ralston—is a jokester around the office but is considered one of the best litigators in the office. He is funny, fearless, and the source of some outrageous office pranks. For instance, one night he nailed the door shut to another DA's office so when the poor guy came in the next morning, he unlocked the door and pulled and pulled on it, without success, much to the amusement of everyone watching. He had to call maintenance to get the nails removed, which made him late for court, and the judge threatened him with contempt because his excuse sounded so implausible. Although Joey denied it, it was fairly common knowledge that he was the culprit.

He was equally unpredictable in his trial tactics. Others have told you that Joey would "push the envelope" to get evidence in or to get a jury to buy into his theory of the case. One time he reenacted the crime by having the medical examiner-witness show how the victim

was decapitated, using the courtroom dummy. The head flew across the room and rolled right in front of the jury. Needless to say the defense attorney was extremely perturbed by the demonstration. Another time, he offered a confused defendant a "double or nothing" deal. He asked the defendant if he wanted to gamble—if the verdict came back guilty he'd get twice the time as what was being offered now. The defendant was seriously contemplating the wager until his attorney told him that the prosecutor could not bet on sentencing.

Today, you watched him in trial. He was by turns condescending, intimidating, and sympathetic, depending on the witness. In the closing he argued passionately that "If the victim's blood is on his clothing, it is because the defendant put it there," waving a dirty, torn tee-shirt stained with blood, for emphasis. The victim was a homeless man who was found stabbed to death. The defendant was another homeless man who was found with the victim's possessions. It looked like a slam-dunk case, especially with the jury gazing in rapt attention as the bloody tee-shirt was

CASE STUDY 9–1 IT'S A RAT RACE, AND THE BEST RAT WINS
Continued

waved in front of them. You could see their eyes going back and forth, following the gruesome display.

Later, you are talking with Joey back in his office about the case, and looking through the file. It appears there is not much direct evidence to link the defendant to the killing. There were no witnesses and the victim's blood was not found on him. You wonder how that could be.

"If the victim bled so much, you'd think some of it would have ended up on the defendant," you muse to yourself as you scan the documents in the file.

"The victim didn't bleed much at all, the doc says. It was a deep puncture in the back and he bled out into the ground," Joey answered you, even though you had not directly asked the question.

"Well, how'd the blood get on the front?" At this point you stopped talking because you were reading a blood analysis report from the crime lab that appeared to say that the blood found on the tee-shirt was not the victim's. In fact, it wasn't even human blood. You look up at Joey, who has an expression of smugness mixed with a little guilt and with a look that says, "So what?"

He explains that the tee-shirt was found in the victim's possession but that he wasn't wearing it when he was found. It appeared likely that the blood was from his dog that had been hit by a car earlier in the day.

"But you told the jury the blood was the victim's!" You are shocked that he would lie to the jury like that.

"No I didn't," he explained. "I said that if there was the victim's blood on the tee-shirt, it was because the defendant did it. I didn't say there was the victim's blood there, did I? Hey, it's a rat race, you know—you gotta do what you need to do to hit the finish line. Don't you think that the other side does the same sort of stuff?"

You know that he has misled the jury and violated the spirit, if not the letter, of the law. On the other hand, it was not a crucial piece of evidence. The presence or absence of blood on the tee-shirt was not exculpatory or inculpatory evidence. At most, it created an emotional response in the jury that might have affected their decision making. Still, you wondered if the judge knew that the tee-shirt did not have the defendant's blood on it, since the evidence brought out in trial simply established that the tee-shirt was the defendant's. You know that the defense attorney is a young kid, fresh out of law school, who is even more naive than you. You wonder what, if anything, you should do about Joey's little stunt.

Questions:

1. Where is the line between "zealous prosecution" and a subversion of the due process system?
2. Do you think there is an ethical duty to inform the judge of what you know? What about the defense attorney?
3. Do you think that the state bar would sanction Joey for such behavior?

REFERENCES

Associated Press (December 28, 2007). *N.C. Bar files ethics charges against Duke Lacrosse Prosecutor.* Associated Press.

Baldwin, J. (1985). *The evidence of things not seen.* New York: Holt, Rinehart and Winston.

Brady v. Maryland, 373 U.S. 83 (1963).

Bresler, K. (1996). "I never lost a trial": When prosecutors keep score of criminal convictions. 9 *Georgetown Journal of Legal Ethics, 18,* 537–541.

Broder, J. M. (February 3, 2004). Citing thin evidence, judge voids a 1980 murder verdict. *New York Times.* Retrieved at nytimes.com/2004/02/03/national/03RELE.html?ex=1076816405&ei=1&en=ed4575f4fd41d10a.

Broward, C. (2012). Angela Corey takes on well-known legal commentator, Harvard Professor Alan Dershowitz. *Jacksonville Times-Union On-Line.* Posted: June 7, 2012. Retrieved at jacksonville.com/news/crime/2012-06-07/story/angela-corey-takes-well-known-legal-commentator-harvard-professor-alan#ixzz1xDH6Ib4z.

Bureau of Justice Statistics (BJS). (2001). Prosecutors in state courts, 2001. *Bureau of Justice Statistics Bulletin, July 1, 2002* . Washington: US Department of Justice.

Cassidy, R. M. (2005). *Prosecutorial ethics.* St. Paul: Thompson-West.

Christian Century (October 7, 1998). Appalling behavior—criticism of both Bill Clinton and Kenneth Starr for immoral behavior and confusing sexual behavior with political responsibility—Editorial. *Christian Century.* Retrieved at findarticles.com/p/articles/mi_m1058/is_n26_v115/ai_21236092.

Cohen, E. D. (1991). Pure legal advocates and moral agents: Two concepts of a lawyer in an adversary system. In M. Braswell, B. McCarthy, & B. McCarthy (Eds.), *Justice, crime, and ethics* (4th ed.) (pp. 125–157). Cincinnati: Anderson.

Delsohn, G. (2003). *The prosecutors.* New York: Penguin.

Ellis, M. J. (April 2012). The origins of the elected prosecutor. *Yale Law Journal, 121*(6), 1518.

Engelberg, S. (2013). *A simple fix: Should New York compel judges to report problem prosecutors?* ProPublica. Retrieved at propublica.org/article/a-simple-fix-should-new-york-compel-judges-to-report-problem-prosecutors. Retrieved April 10, 2013.

Garrett, B. L. (2011). *Convicting the innocent: Where criminal prosecutions go wrong.* Cambridge: Harvard University Press.

Gershman, B. L. (1991). Why prosecutors misbehave. *Criminal Law Bulletin, 22*(2), 131–143.

Gershman, B. L. (2002). *Prosecutorial misconduct* (2nd ed.). St. Paul: West.

Gershman, B. L. (2005). *Prosecutorial ethics and victims' rights: The prosecutor's duty of neutrality.* Pace Law Faculty Publications. Paper 122. Retrieved at digitalcommons.pace.edu/lawfaculty/122.

Gonzales, A. R. (April 19, 2007). *Prepared remarks of Attorney General Alberto R. Gonzales at the Senate Judiciary Oversight Hearing,* Washington, DC. Retrieved at *127.0.0.1:4664/cache?event_id=57416&schema_id=6&q=Alberto+Gonzales +statement+to+hearing&s=vWKhS2gzaEgjpGK-opxy-iyxCSmA.*

Gould, J. B., Carrnao, J., Leo, R., & Young, J. (2012). *Predicting erroneous convictions: A social science approach to miscarriages of justice.* National Institute of Justice, Office of Justice Programs, United States Department of Justice.

Hennessy-Fiske, M. (Saturday, July 13, 2013). *Florida staffer fired over evidence in Zimmerman case.* Los Angeles Times. Retrieved at *latimes.com/news/nation/nationnow/la-na-nn-zimmerman-evidence-firing-20130713,0, 4147108.story.* Retrieved July 15, 2013.

Heumann, M. (1978). *Plea bargaining: The experiences of prosecutors, judges, and defense attorneys.* Chicago: University of Chicago Press.

Howe, D. (September 2, 1988). *The thin blue line.* film review The Washington Post. Retrieved at *washingtonpost.com/wp-srv/style/longterm/movies/videos/thethin bluelinenrhowe_a0b1bb.htm.*

Kania, R. R. E., & Dial, A. (2008). Prosecutor misconduct (Chapter 8). In M. Braswell, B. McCarthy, & B. McCarthy (Eds.), *Justice, crime, and ethics* (6th ed.) (pp. 165–182). Newark: LexisNexis Matthew Bender (Anderson Publishing).

Klopfer v. North Carolina, 386 U.S. 213 (1967).

Lankford, R. D., Jr. (2001). *The Thin Blue Line,* film review for *Documentary Films.Net.* Found at: documentaryfilms.net/Reviews/ThinBlueLine/.

McLaughlin, E. C. (July 11, 2013). *Ex-Sanford police chief: Zimmerman probe 'taken away from us.* CNN. Retrieved at cnn.com/2013/07/10/justice/sanford-bill-lee-exclusive. Retrieved September 6, 2013.

Mooney v. Holohan, 294 U.S. 103 (1935).

Morgenstern, M. (July 12, 2013). Geraldo Rivera blames Al Sharpton for Zimmerman case: 'Brought because of political pressure, race politics. *The Blaze*. Retrieved at theblaze.com/stories/2013/07/12/geraldo-rivera-blames-al-sharpton-for-zimmerman-case-brought-because-of-political-pressure-race-politics/. Retrieved September 6, 2013.

Nocera, J. (November 12, 2012). *A Texas prosecutor faces justice*. The New York Times. Retrieved at nytimes.com/2012/11/13/opinion/nocera-a-texas-prosecutor-faces-justice.html?_r=0. Retrieved November 14, 2012.

Raab, S. (May 28, 1987). *Merola defends handling of 2 big cases*. The New York Times. Retrieved at: *query.nytimes.com/gst/fullpage.html?res=9B0DE3D6133 DF93BA15756C0A961948260&n=Top%-2fReference%2fTimes%20Topics%2fOrganizations%2fN%2fNew%20York%20City%20Transit.*

RoyalPurple209 (2005). *Atlanta child killings investigation reopened, Crimeshots© True Crime Forums,* Retrieved at crimeshots.com/forums/showthread.php?t=904. Retrieved July 19, 2013.

Sapien, J. (2005a). *Lasting damage: A rogue prosecutor's final case*. ProPublica. Retrieved at propublica.org/article/lasting-damage-a-rogue-prosecutors-final-case. Retrieved April 10, 2013.

Sapien, J. (2005b). *Who polices prosecutors who abuse their authority? Usually nobody*. ProPublica. Retrieved at propublica.org/article/who-polices-prosecutors-who-abuse-their-authority-usually-nobody. Retrieved April 10, 2013.

Setrakian, L., & Francescani, C. (June 16, 2007). *Former Duke prosecutor Nifong disbarred*. ABC News. Retrieved at abcnews.go.com/Video/playerIndex?id=3286420.

The New York Times (September 30, 1988). *Bronx inquiry into tampering with jury in Donovan's trial*. The New York Times. Retrieved at query.nytimes.com/gst/fullpage.html?res=940DE3D8173F-F933A0575AC0A96E948260.

Time. (May 10, 1982). *Less than full disclosure*. Time. Retrieved at *time. com/time/magazine/article/0, 9171, 925360,00.html.*

Wilson, D. (June 17, 2007). *Prosecutor in Duke case disbarred by ethics panel*. The New York Times.

Wilson, G. (April 25, 2012). *Dershowitz: Prosecutor in Trayvon Martin case overreached with murder charge*, Retrieved at Foxnews.com/Us/2012/04/25/Dershowitz-Trayvon-Prosecutor-Overreached-With-Murder-Charge/?Test=Latestnews.

Wilson, D., & Barstow, D. (April 12, 2007). *All charges dropped in Duke case*. The New York Times.

CHAPTER 10

Criminal Sentencing: Goals, Practices, and Ethics

Lawrence F. Travis III

KEY CONCEPTS

desert	false negative	restoration
deterrence	false positive	truth in sentencing
disparities in criminal punishments	incapacitation	utilitarian rationale
	paradox of retribution	

Sentencing is the decision of what to do with the person convicted of a criminal offense. Traditionally, our society has responded to criminality by imposing a punishment on the criminal. von Hirsch defined criminal punishment as "the infliction by the state of consequences normally considered unpleasant, on a person in response to his having been convicted of a crime" (1976, p. 34). For our purposes, then, criminal punishment is the purposeful infliction of pain on a person as a result of a criminal conviction.

There is an element of reflex in punishment. When we are harmed by someone or something, we tend to strike back in reaction. Mackie (1982) traced the origins of criminal punishments to such reflex responses. Criminal punishment is, at least partly, a return of harm for harm, or wrong for wrong. Yet there is an old saying that "two wrongs don't make a right." Others, like Garland (1990), argue that punishment, whatever its origins, is also a product of social structure and cultural values. Whom we punish, when we punish, and how we punish are determined by the role of punishment in society. Furthermore, punishment itself affects social values in a number of important ways. These include defining what is improper behavior, building a sense of togetherness among the law abiding, and supporting our beliefs about the nature of humankind and society.

If ethics is the study of morality and what is right or wrong, it is likely that no aspect of the criminal justice process is more amenable to ethical examination than sentencing. By committing a crime, the offender has wronged society. By punishing that offender, society arguably "wrongs" the offender. The purpose of this chapter is to examine the question: How can punishment be justified? Following that, we will briefly explore three ethical issues that remain, even if punishment itself is accepted.

Although we do not normally apply the saying about "two wrongs not making a right" to the question of criminal punishment, it seems apropos. How can we justify the purposeful infliction of pain, even on those convicted of crimes? What factors make punishment right and whether we should punish are inter-related questions. The answers to these questions depend on how we define the word *punishment*.

THE PURPOSE OF CRIMINAL PUNISHMENT

Should we punish? This question is so basic that it is often unasked and unanswered. Yet when, whom, and how we punish are contingent on why we punish. We tend to believe that criminals should be punished. The wrong they do by committing crimes demands a punitive response. We often disagree, however, on why crime requires punishment. Traditionally, four reasons for punishment have been advanced: deterrence, incapacitation, treatment, and desert. More recently a fifth justification has emerged: restoration.

Deterrence

Deterrence supports punishment as an example of what awaits lawbreakers. This example is expected to convince would-be offenders to avoid criminal behavior. Deterrence is based on a conception of human beings as rational and guided by a pleasure principle. That is, humans do things that please them and avoid things that hurt them. They weigh the likely consequences of their behavior and choose activities accordingly (Paternoster, 1987).

For a punishment to deter, it must meet two conditions. First, the penalty must be severe enough that the pain of the punishment exceeds the benefit of the crime. For example, a $50 fine for theft of $100 would not deter because the crime results in a "net gain" of $50. Second, the penalty must be imposed. If the criminal is unlikely to be caught and/or punished, the threat of the penalty is not likely to be "real." The lower the chance of punishment, the greater the chance of crime.

Deterrence works on two levels. *General deterrence* applies when the offender is punished so that others will be afraid to commit crimes. The purpose of the punishment is to deter the general public from crime. *Specific deterrence* occurs when the penalty is designed to convince the particular offender not to commit another crime in the future.

As a justification for punishment, deterrence emphasizes the needs of the collective over those of the individual. The purpose of punishment is to control future crime. A deterrence rationale would allow the imposition of a severe penalty for a minor offense if that penalty would prevent a large enough number of future offenses. For example, a $10,000 fine for a $10 theft could be justified under deterrence if it would prevent at least 1,000 such thefts. Research to date does not indicate that we are very effective at deterrence (Lippke, 2002; Paternoster, 1987; Sherman et al., 1997).

Incapacitation

Like deterrence, **incapacitation** is a justification for criminal punishment based on the promise of reducing future crime. In contrast to deterrence, however, incapacitation supports penalties that prevent offenders from having the chance to commit new crimes. Deterrence seeks to convince offenders that crime will not pay; incapacitation seeks to limit the offender's ability to commit a new crime.

One reason to incarcerate a convicted offender is that, at least while in prison, that person is not able to harm society by committing more crimes. The primary problem with incapacitation as a justification for punishment is our inability to predict accurately who is likely to commit future crimes (Visher, 1987). Research to date seems to indicate that incapacitative penalties entail a significant increase in prison population (Greenwood, 1982; Van Dine, Conrad, & Dinitz, 1979). To be sure that dangerous offenders are "locked up," we must also incarcerate relatively large numbers of nondangerous offenders (Sherman et al., 1997).

Treatment

A third justification for punishment is to allow for the *treatment* or rehabilitation of criminal offenders. This philosophy assumes that crime is caused by a variety of factors, such as poverty, discrimination, or individual pathology. Punishments are designed to change the offender's need or desire to commit crime. Like deterrence and incapacitation, the ultimate goal of treatment is a reduction in future crime. Unlike the other two rationales, however, treatment emphasizes the individual offender (Cullen & Gilbert, 2013).

Studies of the effects of treatment suggest that most currently available programs are not very effective (Bailey, 1966; Martinson, 1974; Sherman et al., 1997). Efforts to treat criminal offenders continue, and many programs show promise of effectiveness with some types of offenders (Gendreau, Little, & Coggin, 1995; Gendreau & Ross, 1987; Van Voorhis, 1987). As with the prediction problems of incapacitation, treatment attempts are limited by our ability to design and implement effective programs matched to suitable types of offenders (Latessa, 2004).

Desert

Another rationale for criminal punishment is **desert**, also sometimes called *retribution*. This justification for punishment is the only one of the four that is backward looking. Unlike deterrence, incapacitation, or treatment, a desert rationale does not seek to reduce future crime. Rather, desert is based on the idea that the offender deserves to be punished as a result of committing a crime.

As a justification for punishment, desert places limits on both who may be punished and the degree to which someone may be punished. Desert requires that penalties be imposed only on those who have committed a crime. Furthermore, a desert rationale requires that the punishment be commensurate with (proportional to) the severity of the crime. In these ways, desert may be considered to emphasize the interests of the individual offender over those of the collective (i.e., society).

Restoration

Beginning around the 1970s in the United States, some observers came to question the effects of formal criminal justice processing on both offenders and victims. By the 1990s, victim's rights had emerged as an important force in criminal justice, and the idea of restoring victims from the harms of crime was established. Braithwaite (1989) published an influential book in which he argued that informal sanctioning by people close to the offender was a more powerful force for offender reform and victim satisfaction than the formal punishments of the justice process. In short order, *restorative justice* emerged.

O'Hear (2005) described the basic model of restorative justice. It includes face-to-face meetings between the victim and the offender, who develop a consensus about how to resolve the problem or repair the harm caused by the criminal offense. This solution typically involves a public acknowledgment of wrongdoing, some kind of reparations (restitution, community service, etc.), and perhaps some traditional penal sanctions. Most often, restorative justice replaces sanctions, such as imprisonment. The state of Vermont has operated a reparative probation program for several years that seeks to accomplish restorative justice aims, in part through using community representatives in determining punishments (Karp & Drakulich, 2004).

Restorative justice punishments reflect an attempt to balance the needs and interests of victims, communities, and offenders. The imposition of pain on the offender for having broken the law is not a priority. Some evaluations of these programs show promise for reduced recidivism and increased victim satisfaction, even with violent offenses (Sherman & Strang, 2007, pp. 1–94). Still, restorative justice has not been widely used with serious offenses and offenders and may not be suitable for the most serious crimes (Karp & Drakulich, 2004).

Restorative justice sentencing raises many issues. Non-law-trained people, who are not justice system officials, make sentencing decisions. The offender typically must plead guilty before the reparative sentencing discussions can begin. The entire process "privatizes" the offense, removing the punitive role and goals of government. Sentences are based on the unique circumstances of each offense and offender so that consistency in sentencing, defined as similar sentences for similar crimes, is lost (O'Hear, 2005). Restorative sentencing represents a revolutionary shift in the purposes and practices of criminal sentencing.

UTILITARIANISM VERSUS EQUITY

These five rationales and their varying emphases on the individual or collective interests in punishment highlight the ethical dilemma identified by Packer (1966). The core issue involves the role of social utility in punishment. *Utility* means the benefit, or the "good," expected to result from punishment. Those who support punishment for the good emphasize a **utilitarian rationale**. In contrast, those who support punishment regardless of effects, based on a notion that crime deserves punishment, emphasize equity or fairness.

In brief, we can say that deterrence, incapacitation, restoration, and treatment are utilitarian purposes of punishment. Desert is nonutilitarian. Only the desert principle supports the imposition of punishment regardless of effects. The other rationales depend on some good resulting from that penalty.

If someone is convicted of a crime, should they be punished? If no one else will know that the crime went unpunished and the offender will not commit another crime in the future, there is no reason to punish under a deterrence rationale. No one will be deterred by the penalty. Similarly, given that the offender will not commit a new crime, there is no need to incapacitate or treat the offender. Thus, most utilitarian purposes cannot support the imposition of a penalty in this case. **Restoration** supports "punishment" as a means to restore the victim and the community to their former state—whatever the conditions were before the crime. This restoration is also expected to be beneficial for the offender and contribute to a positive change in the offender.

Yet most of us will be uncomfortable with allowing a criminal to escape punishment—the imposition of an unpleasant or painful consequence for the law-breaking behavior. At base, most of us support a desert rationale for punishment. Someone breaking the law has "earned" a punishment. Because those who do not commit a crime are not rewarded for law-abiding behavior, those who violate the law should be punished. This seems only fair, or equitable.

Mackie (1982) referred to this as the "**paradox of retribution**." By this he meant that it is not possible to explain or develop a desert rationale within a reasonable system of moral thought, yet it is also not possible to eliminate desert from our moral thinking. Retribution does not make sense. Desert suggests that wrongful acts should be punished but offers no reason for punishment. Mackie resolves the paradox by saying that punishment is essentially a reflex based on emotions. We react to things and people who hurt us by hurting them in return.

Given this emotional need to harm those who harm us, we will punish criminals without regard for possible beneficial effects of punishment. As punishment became institutionalized in society, jurists and philosophers developed more rational justifications for punishment based on utilitarian notions (Garland, 1990). These notions may explain particular punishments and the selection of specific offenders for punishment, but they do not explain why we punish. It is likely that we punish because punishment seems "right." Just as good deeds should be rewarded, bad ones should be punished. People should receive rewards and punishments for their good and bad behavior. This conception of reward and punishment as earned is the core of the concept of equity.

If Mackie's assessment is correct, it means that we will punish criminals routinely, without regard to the effects of punishment. Nonetheless, we would like the two wrongs of crime and punishment to make some sort of right—to produce some good. We are not satisfied with a system of penalties that merely reacts to behavior. We want to influence the future. Thus, most criminal sentences involve a mix of equity and utilitarian justifications.

It is these utilitarian purposes of punishment that raise the ethical dilemma of sentencing as a balance between the needs of the collective and those of the individual. During the 1970s, retribution or desert experienced a renaissance (Cullen & Gilbert, 2013). This renaissance defined retribution as a limiting factor in punishment (Fogel, 1975; Frankel, 1972; von Hirsch, 1976; Twentieth Century Fund, 1976).

The resurgence of desert was directed at fairness in criminal punishments (Kramer, 2009). Proponents of desert-based sentencing were concerned with what they perceived as unfair **disparities in criminal punishments**. Under the laws of most states, it was possible for offenders convicted of the same offense to receive widely different penalties. One person convicted of burglary might be placed in prison, while another might receive probation. Reliance on a desert rationale would narrow this range of penalties, ensuring that similar offenders convicted of similar crimes would experience similar penalties.

Desert would lead to more equitable punishment. Supporters of desert believed that it was unjust to punish similar people differently, because each had "earned" the same penalty. It was also wrong to impose a very harsh penalty on someone in order to deter others or to prevent a possible future offense by the person. Desert required that the offender be guilty of the offense for which punishment was imposed and that the offense, not the offender, was the subject of punishment.

Restorative sentences raise problems of equity because the outcome of sentencing is the product of a negotiation between the offender and the victim. Furthermore, the outcome is often a group product involving the input of several community representatives. The point of restorative justice is to individualize and "personalize" punishments to achieve both reparation for harm and offender empathy for the victim.

At the level of fairness to the individual offender, general deterrence and collective incapacitation (Visher, 1987)—by which everyone convicted of the same offense receives the same sentence in hopes of reducing general levels of future crime—are less troublesome than individual predictions. If everyone convicted of an offense receives a similar punishment, whether for incapacitative or general deterrent purposes, individual fairness in terms of equivalent penalties is achieved. If these penalties are excessive in comparison to the seriousness of crime (all burglars receive a term of life imprisonment, for example) although the sentences are equal, they are not equitable. The harm of the punishment exceeds the harm of the crime.

Equity in terms of retribution is both an explanation of punishment and a limit on punishment. We will punish criminals because they have earned a penalty. We can punish only guilty criminals and only in proportion to the seriousness of their crime. Von Hirsch and Hanrahan (1979) proposed a "modified just deserts" sentencing rationale that includes these two dimensions of equity. They argued that desert justifies the imposition of a penalty and sets the outer limits of the punishment. Within these limits, however, utilitarian considerations could be used to allow different penalties to be imposed on offenders convicted of the same offense. Thus, burglary may deserve imprisonment of between 1 and 3 years. The sentencing judge would be able to impose a 3-year term for incapacitation or treatment or deterrence but would not be allowed to impose more than the upper limit. So, too, the judge could impose a 1-year term for the burglary but not a term less than 1 year, because burglary deserves at least that level of punishment.

THE PRACTICE OF PUNISHMENT

Punishment is established firmly in our culture and our history. It seems safe to say that we will continue to punish criminals in the future, just as we have punished them in the past. The core dilemma in punishment is trying to achieve a balance between considerations of equity, which are at the base of punishment, and desires for utility that can be realized through punishment. Over time and across different types of offenders and offenses, this balance shifts.

At any time, the practice of punishment reflects the current balance between concern for the interests of the individual, as expressed in terms of equity, and concerns for the needs of society, expressed in terms of utility. The ethical question remains constant, however. That question is: Under what circumstances is the state justified in applying how much punishment to individuals?

Is there ever a time when it would be all right to impose the death penalty on someone convicted of theft? Should prison crowding (and the expense of prisons) justify reducing the prison term of a violent offender? As these questions illustrate, sentencing involves the fundamental issue of individual interests versus societal needs. The ethical problem exists in our attempts to determine the "right" balance of the two.

The power to punish primarily rests with the legislature. The legislature defines crimes and punishments. Most often, criminal laws grant some authority over punishment to both judges and the executive branch. The "sentencing structure" of a jurisdiction defines the distribution of punishment authority. There are two basic structures: indeterminate sentencing and determinate sentencing. In each, the legislature defines the absolute limits of punishment (maximum and minimum penalties). In indeterminate systems, some power is left to a paroling authority so that when a prison term is imposed, the exact length of the sentence is unknown. The judge might order a prison term of 5–10 years. The actual length of term remains unknown until the parole authority orders release. In determinate systems, the sentencing judge imposes an exact penalty—say, imprisonment for 6 years.

Although sentencing is much more complex in practice, determinate sentences are best for retribution, general deterrence, and collective incapacitation. Indeterminate sentences are best for rehabilitation, specific deterrence, and individual incapacitation. That is, determinate sentences tend to support punishments aimed at social utility, whereas indeterminate punishments are better suited to individual interests.

In the past 3 to 4 decades in the United States, sentencing structures have moved toward more determinate punishments (Koons-Witt, 2009). This reform sought to reduce variation in punishment applied to similar crimes and offenders. It also supported what has been called the *penal harm* movement (Clear, 1994). The sentencing reform embraces the increased use of incarceration and more restrictive and punitive community supervision practices. Specific sentencing laws proliferated, including mandatory minimum sentences and enhanced penalties for repeat offenders (e.g., "three strikes" laws). The balance between social needs and individual interests shifts over time and results in sentencing changes.

The restorative justice model emerged partly as a reaction to increased punishment severity. Widespread reliance on incarceration as the primary punishment for crime clearly hurts offenders. Incarceration also hurts communities by increasing costs for the handling of criminal offenders and by removing community members. To make matters worse, incarceration of offenders rarely completely satisfies victims and often prevents offenders from being able to pay restitution or otherwise make reparations.

CONTEMPORARY ETHICAL CONCERNS IN SENTENCING

Beyond the questions of whether and how we should punish (purposes), there are several important ethical considerations in contemporary sentencing. Even if our current system of criminal punishment achieves an acceptable balance between concern for individual interests and social needs, it still contains some ethical dilemmas. Among the most important considerations are those dealing with honesty in the sentencing of criminals, the role of prediction in the allocation of criminal penalties, and the problem of discriminatory punishment.

Honesty in Punishment

People released from state prisons in 2006 served less than 50% of the prison terms imposed by the judge (Bureau of Justice Statistics, 2010). Of those receiving their first release from state prison on a violent offense conviction in 2006, the average offender had served less than two-thirds of the original prison term. Ten years earlier, violent offenders were serving less than half of their terms in prison. The sentences announced in court are often quite different from the penalties served by convicted offenders. There is growing pressure for criminal justice officials to be more honest about sentencing practices. Federal legislation includes incentives to promote "**truth in sentencing**." A goal of the "truth in sentencing" movement is to ensure that violent offenders serve at least 85% of the prison terms they receive from the court.

Several current practices lead to the mistruths in sentencing. Most states award or allow inmates to earn "good time." Good time is a reduction in the length of sentence given for good behavior in the institution. It is common for such reductions to be in the one-third to one-half range so that a sentence of 9 years, if all good time is applied, becomes a term of 4 and one-half to 6 years. Discretionary release on parole also affects time served. An inmate sentenced to 10 years might be paroled after serving only 3 years. Even most offenders who receive life sentences are expected to be released at some point (Beck & Greenfeld, 1995, p. 2).

Critics of this "dishonesty" in sentencing contend that current practices are wrong. Early release of offenders undermines the deterrent effect of the law and fails to provide adequate protection to the public (incapacitation). In addition to these negative effects on potential utilitarian benefits of punishment, critics also make the point that it is wrong to mislead the public. When citizens learn that offenders are not being punished as they had expected, critics contend, they lose respect for the law and question the integrity of the criminal justice system.

The question of honesty in sentencing is complicated. Assuming that truth in sentencing is desirable, how can we achieve such honesty? One solution is to simply keep offenders incarcerated longer. The problem, of course, is that in doing so we must increase the harm of the punishment relative to past practice, and we must somehow find ways to pay for the increased prison population. Another solution is to lower court-imposed sentences to terms that are closer to what prisoners typically serve. This solution faces the political problem of appearing to lessen the seriousness with which we view crime and the perception that criminal justice agents have become "soft on crime." A third, and perhaps most common solution, is to combine the two by increasing the time served by violent offenders while reducing sentences for nonviolent offenders. As with any compromise, this third solution has the strengths and weaknesses of the first two. It is not clear that the compromise solves the dilemma of dishonesty in sentencing.

Perhaps as important, the compromise position, which we seem to have adopted, aggravates the differences between responses to types of crimes. Although the proportion of prison sentences served by violent offenders before release increased, those convicted of other crimes may have served even less of their prison sentences. Drug offenders served about one-third of their sentence in prison, and property offenders served only 40.8% of their maximum term. Adding to these differences in proportion of prison sentences actually served is the fact that offenders charged with nonviolent crimes are eligible for diversion programs and restorative justice sentencing, whereas violent offenders are often excluded. Here, again, we try to balance social utility—protection from the most dangerous offenses and offenders—with individual interests in similar treatment for criminal behavior.

One of the pressing issues in sentencing today is finding a way to achieve truth in sentencing. Whatever strategy is selected, we must be aware of the implications of changes in punishment for the balance between individual interests and social needs. If we opt to compromise, we must reexamine the distribution of punishments. What crimes ought to receive more punishment than they currently do, and which crimes should receive less? If we change the distribution of punishment, what other effect might this have on fairness in punishment?

Prediction in Punishment

A second contemporary (and continuing) ethical issue in sentencing concerns the role of prediction in the assignment of criminal penalties. Clear and O'Leary (1983, pp. 35–38) recognized the central role of prediction in all aspects of criminal justice. Society expects its criminal justice apparatus to protect it from crime, and part of this protection involves the identification of risk and taking steps to minimize the chance of future crimes. The assignment of criminal penalties involves the prediction of future criminality and an assessment of the likely harm of that future crime. Indeed, one reason to increase terms for violent offenders and decrease the punishment of nonviolent offenders is because violent crimes are more damaging and, thus, justice system agents have a greater interest in preventing violent crimes.

In any attempt to predict "dangerousness" among a population of offenders, two types of error are possible. An offender who does not pose a risk of future crime may be erroneously predicted to be dangerous. This type of error is called a **false positive** because the offender was falsely (erroneously) predicted to be positive for danger. Conversely, an offender who actually poses a danger of future crime may be erroneously predicted to be "safe." This type of error is called a **false negative** because the offender was falsely (erroneously) predicted to be negative for danger.

False positives are subjected to greater levels of punishment than they need or deserve based on their actual dangerousness (Burrell, 2006). Because these offenders are predicted to be dangerous, we will incapacitate them or subject them to more severe sanctions to ensure specific deterrence or treatment. It may be that because we expect them to be dangerous, we watch them more carefully and, thus, we doom them to failure (Auerhahn, 2006). False negatives are punished less than they need or deserve based on their actual dangerousness. Because they are predicted to be safe, we return them to society quickly and allow them to commit additional crimes.

If we accept prediction as an appropriate consideration in sentencing, the use of differential sanctions is ethically justifiable based on the need to protect society. Yet, it remains wrong to subject a nondangerous offender to more severe punishment. Similarly, it is wrong not to more severely punish an offender who is actually dangerous. Both false positives and false negatives are treated unfairly, and both errors place increased burdens on society.

We currently do not have total accuracy in our predictions, so we make both kinds of errors. In practice, false positives occur about seven times for every true positive. Furthermore, we correctly predict only about half of the truly dangerous offenders, so our false negative rate is roughly equal to our true negative rate (Wenk, Robison, & Smith, 1972). That is, we make many mistakes.

Beyond the limits to predictive accuracy for an entire population of offenders, there is increasing debate about the appropriateness of our predictive devices for specific subgroups (Morash, 2009; Taylor & Blanchette, 2009). Do the same factors that predict the behavior of men also predict what women will do?

Are risk assessment instruments suitable for use with both whites and racial/ethnic minorities? Do our predictions work to unfairly punish or otherwise disadvantage specific groups of offenders? Given our inaccuracy, do we create injustice?

An alternative solution to this dilemma is to impose harsher penalties on all offenders, as though they were all dangerous. This would lead to "fair" punishment in that everyone would receive a similar penalty, but it is a very expensive policy. In addition, critics argue that such a policy is unethical because it subjects all offenders to more severe punishment when most do not deserve it.

Even if we could achieve complete accuracy in our predictions of future crime, the ethical question remains: Should we punish people for crimes they have not yet committed? If I knew you were going to break the speed limit next week, should I collect a fine from you today? If I do, what should I do next week when I catch you speeding? That is, by sentencing based on a prediction, have we allowed the offender to "prepay" for crime, so that when the crime actually occurs there is no punishment after the crime? Must we wait for someone to actually commit an offense before we punish? Suppose we predict that someone will commit a murder. If we incarcerate that person now, he or she does not have the chance to commit the murder, and so the crime never occurs. Because the crime never occurred, do we have a right to imprison the predicted offender?

Concern about repeat offenders and career criminals raises the issue of prediction. Recent attention to "three strikes and you're out" laws illustrates the point. These laws impose long prison sentences on people convicted of their third felony offense. The logic behind such laws is that three-time losers are dangerous and need to be incapacitated. Many states have passed or are considering such laws. The ethical issues around prediction in sentencing are complicated and do not disappear, even if we manage to achieve completely accurate predictions. We must still determine the balance between individual interests and community needs. Does the community's need for safety outweigh the individual's interest in liberty if we predict that the individual will eventually commit a crime? Under what circumstances might the community's needs be more important? Under what circumstances is the individual's interest in liberty most important?

Discrimination in Sentencing

The purpose of prediction is to discriminate between those offenders who require more punishment and those who can be safely given less punishment. A related ethical concern is how the predictive system achieves this discrimination. It is possible that errors in prediction are not random but that they result in differential punishment for some people as opposed to others. The data concerning the characteristics of people who receive severe sanctions indicate that sentencing decisions are disproportionate. Men, minority group members, young adults, and the poor are more likely to receive harsh sentences than are women, older adults, whites, and the more affluent (Petersilia, 1983; Visher, 1983). The third ethical issue in contemporary sentencing concerns discrimination in the assignment of criminal penalties.

Klein, Turner, and Petersilia (1988) reported that criminal sentences in California were based more on the seriousness of the offense, prior criminal record of the offender, and justice process variables than on race. The fact remains, however, that the ethically acceptable factors that predict future crime and explain sentence severity—prior record, criminal justice history, and offense seriousness—appear to be related to sex, race, age, and social class. The conclusion that these factors are more determinative of punishment than race or sex does not necessarily mean that sentencing decisions do not discriminate.

The problem of the relationships between race, sex, socioeconomic status, age, and the factors that explain sentences are complex. Race, for example, may be related to unemployment because of societal discrimination. In turn, unemployment may be related to involvement in crime and criminal justice processing decisions (bail, probation, and parole supervision, and the like), which in turn are related to future criminality. Punishments based on the likelihood of future criminality as predicted from prior record or criminal justice history will reflect the effects of race, sex, and social class. However, because the sentencing decision relies only on prior criminal record and criminal justice history, the effect of race, sex, and class may be hidden from those making the punishment decision.

A related issue concerns definitions of offense seriousness. The "war on drugs" provides an excellent example. Under federal sentencing rules, offenses involving crack cocaine were treated more severely than those involving powder cocaine. Racial differences in the use of these drugs (blacks were more likely to use crack, whites more likely to use powder cocaine) resulted in disproportionate sentencing of cocaine offenders as black offenders more often received prison terms and received longer terms than white offenders. So, too, an emphasis on certain types of drug offense, such as street sales versus possession, produces racial differences in punishment (Barnes & Kingsnorth, 1996).

There is growing evidence that discrimination in sentencing can be controlled through guidelines or other decision-making aids (Wooldredge, 2009). There is also evidence that the problem of discrimination in sentencing was not as serious as many believed (Engen, 2009). The problem of discrimination in sentencing may be less serious in practice than in perception, but the perception of widespread discrimination persists, especially among members of minority groups. Beyond perceptions, the real potential for discrimination continues.

The ethical problem here is akin to that faced by automobile insurance underwriters. Punishments based on predictions of future crime treat some individual offenders unfairly, just as does blanket assignment of certain groups of drivers to "high-risk" classes for insurance. Treatment of different kinds of criminal behavior as more serious is like assigning different insurance rates based on the type of automobile driven, not the skill of the driver. At what point, if ever, does this unfair treatment of individual offenders (or drivers) render the assignment process unethical? Is crack cocaine use more serious than powder cocaine use? If it is, how concerned should we be over racial differences in preference for types of drugs? When, if ever, is discrimination ethically acceptable?

■ Learn More on the Internet

For more on sentencing and court issues, go to bjs.ojp.usdoj.gov.   ■

CONCLUSION

An example of the ethics of criminal sentencing raises many questions but provides few answers. The answers are judgment calls that depend on the individual doing the judging. A central determinant of how one may resolve these ethical issues is the resolution of the conflict between utility and equity. If the interests of the individual predominate, one is likely to support a desert (or possibly treatment) justification for punishment and oppose most predictive efforts. Similarly, one is likely to opt for truth in sentencing by reducing sentences imposed to more closely match time currently served and to oppose prediction in sentencing and be very cautious about potential discrimination resulting from law and practices. However, if one emphasizes utility, it is likely that he or she will support prediction, solve the truth-in-sentencing problem by increasing penalties (at least for more serious offenses), and be less concerned about potential discriminatory effects of laws and practices.

This difference in perspective is reflected in how one views errors of prediction. If false positive errors are more troubling than false negative errors, there is a greater concern for equity than utility. If false negative errors are more troublesome, it evidences a greater concern for public safety. Those who emphasize community protection are usually willing to accept false positive errors, arguing that it is not unjust to punish them more severely than their actual risk would warrant.

Each of us may very well answer the questions about sentencing differently. In essence, these are all ethical questions that require us to think about what is right or wrong with sentencing and criminal punishment. The ethics of sentencing can be stated as a question of justice. We need to determine what are just punishments and how sentences can be imposed justly. As von Hirsch states, "While people will disagree about what justice requires, our assumption of the primacy of justice is vital because it alters the terms of the debate. One cannot, on this assumption, defend any scheme for dealing with convicted criminals solely by pointing to its usefulness in controlling crime: one is compelled to inquire whether that scheme is a just one and why" (1976, p. 5).

Discussion Questions

1. Should criminal punishments be based on predictions of crime? If so, what types of errors would we expect to make with such predictors?
2. Why do sentencing decisions discriminate against certain groups, and what should be done to minimize discrimination?
3. Compare and contrast the four traditional purposes of criminal punishment, and explain some advantages and disadvantages that may be found in each case.
4. What is "restorative justice," and how does it compare to traditional justifications for criminal sentencing?
5. What, if anything, prevents us from being honest about our criminal penalties?

REFERENCES

Auerhahn, K. (2006). Conceptual and methodological issues in the prediction of dangerous behavior. *Criminology & Public Policy, 5*(4), 771–778.

Bailey, W. (1966). Correctional outcome: An evaluation of 100 reports. *Journal of Criminal Law, Criminology & Police Science, 57*, 153–160.

Barnes, C., & Kingsnorth, R. (1996). Race, drug, and criminal sentencing: Hidden effects of the criminal law. *Journal of Criminal Justice, 24*(1), 39–55.

Beck, A., & Greenfeld, L. (1995). *Violent offenders in state prison: Sentences and time served.* Washington, DC: Bureau of Justice Statistics.

Braithwaite, J. (1989). *Crime, shame, and reintegration.* New York: Cambridge University Press.

Bureau of Justice Statistics (2010). *First release from prison: Sentence length, time served, and percent of sentence served in prison, by offense—2006*, National Corrections Reporting Program. bjs.ojp. usdoj.gov. Accessed 01.06.10.

Burrell, W. (2006). Violence risk screening: Editorial introduction. *Criminology & Public Policy, 5*(4), 737–742.

Clear, T. (1994). *Harm in American penology: Offenders, victims, and their communities.* Albany: State University of New York Press.

Clear, T., & O'Leary, V. (1983). *Controlling the offender in the community.* Lexington: Lexington Books.

Cullen, F. T., & Gilbert, K. E. (2013). *Reaffirming rehabilitation* (2nd ed.). Boston: Elsevier (Anderson Publishing).

Engen, R. (2009). Policy essay: Assessing determinate and presumptive sentencing—making research relevant. *Criminology & Public Policy, 8*(2), 323–336.

Fogel, D. (1975). *"We are the living proof…" The justice model for corrections* (2nd ed.). Cincinnati: Anderson.

Frankel, M. (1972). *Criminal sentences: Law without order.* New York: Hill & Wang.

Garland, D. (1990). *Punishment and modern society.* Chicago: University of Chicago Press.

Gendreau, P., Little, T., & Coggin, C. (1995). *A meta-analysis of the predictors of adult offender recidivism: What works!* St. John. Canada: University of New Brunswick.

Gendreau, P., & Ross, R. (1987). Revivification of rehabilitation: Evidence from the 1980s. *Justice Quarterly, 4*(3), 349–407.

Greenwood, P. (1982). *Selective incapacitation.* Santa Monica: RAND.

von Hirsch, A. (1976). *Doing justice.* New York: Hill & Wang.

von Hirsch, A., & Hanrahan, K. (1979). *The question of parole*. Cambridge: Ballinger.

Karp, D., & Drakulich, K. (2004). Minor crime in a quaint setting: Practices, outcomes, and limits of vermont reparative probation boards. *Criminology & Public Policy, 3*(4), 655–686.

Klein, S., Turner, S., & Petersilia, J. (1988). *Racial equity in sentencing*. Santa Monica: RAND.

Koons-Witt, B. (2009). Equal justice versus individual justice: Discretion and the current state of sentencing guidelines. *Criminology & Public Policy, 8*(2), 279–284.

Kramer, J. H. (2009). Policy essay: Mandatory sentencing guidelines: The framing of justice. *Criminology & Public Policy, 8*(2), 313–322.

Latessa, E. J. (2004). The challenge of change: Correctional programs and evidence-based practices. *Criminology & Public Policy, 3*(4), 547–560.

Lippke, R. L. (2002). Crime reduction and the length of prison sentences. *Law and Policy, 24*, 17–35.

Mackie, J. (1982). Morality and the retributive emotions. *Criminal Justice Ethics, 1*(1), 3–10.

Martinson, R. (1974). What works? *The Public Interest* (Spring), 22.

Morash, M. (2009). Gender and risk assessment: Editorial introduction. *Criminology & Public Policy, 8*(1), 173–182.

O'Hear, M. (2005). Is restorative justice compatible with sentencing uniformity? *Marquette Law Review, 89*, 305–325.

Packer, H. (1966). *The limits of the criminal sanction*. Stanford: Stanford University Press.

Paternoster, R. (1987). The deterrent effect of the perceived certainty and severity of punishment: A review of the evidence and issues. *Justice Quarterly, 4*(2), 173–217.

Petersilia, J. (1983). *Racial disparities in the criminal justice system*. Santa Monica: RAND.

Sherman, L., Gottfredson, D., MacKenzie, D., Eck, J., Reuter, P., & Bushway, S. (1997). *Preventing crime: What works, what doesn't, what's promising*. Washington: National Institute of Justice.

Sherman, L., & Strang, H. (2007). *Restorative justice: The evidence*. London: The Smith Institute.

Taylor, K., & Blanchette, K. (2009). Policy essay: The women are not wrong: It is the approach that is debatable. *Criminology & Public Policy, 8*(1), 221–229.

Twentieth Century Fund Task Force on Criminal Sentencing. (1976). *Fair and certain punishment*. New York: McGraw-Hill.

Van Dine, S., Conrad, J., & Dinitz, S. (1979). The incapacitation of the chronic thus. *Journal of Criminal Law & Criminology, 65*, 535.

Van Voorhis, P. (1987). Correctional effectiveness: The high cost of ignoring success. *Federal Probation, 51*(1), 56–62.

Visher, C. (1983). Gender, police arrest decisions and notions of chivalry. *Criminology, 21*(1), 5–28.

Visher, C. (1987). Incapacitation and crime control: Does a 'Lock 'em Up' strategy reduce crime? *Justice Quarterly, 4*(4), 513–543.

Wenk, E., Robison, J., & Smith, G. (1972). Can violence be predicted? *Crime & Delinquency, 18*(3), 393–402.

Wooldredge, J. (2009). Short- versus long-term effects of Ohio's switch to more structured sentencing on extralegal disparities in prison sentences in an urban court. *Criminology & Public Policy, 8*(2), 285–312.

CHAPTER 11

Crime and Punishment: Punishment Philosophies, and Ethical Dilemmas

Laurie A. Gould, Alicia H. Sitren

KEY CONCEPTS

deterrence	incapacitation	rehabilitation
general deterrence	punishment	retribution
hedonistic calculus	proportionality	specific deterrence

WHAT IS PUNISHMENT?

The punishment of offenders is a central feature of our criminal justice system and highlights the coercive nature of criminal justice. This topic is of great concern to researchers, government officials, correctional employees, and the general public. These stakeholders have varying opinions pertaining to the proper use and justification of punishment. However, before a critical examination can take place, it is necessary to define punishment.

There are many possible definitions for the term **punishment**. For example, Hudson (2002) notes that we often speak of a punishing work schedule or the punishment of children by their parents, but these examples fail to provide a useful working definition for the punishment of law violators. Von Hirsch (1976) provides one possible definition of punishment: "Punishment means the infliction by the state of consequences normally considered unpleasant, on a person in response to his having been convicted of a crime" (p. 35). In addition, proportionality between the sanction and the offense is an essential ingredient of the punishment process in the United States. **Proportionality** requires that the severity of the sentence be dependent on the seriousness of the crime (von Hirsch, 1976). For example, a person who commits a petty theft should receive a sanction commensurate with the offense (i.e., a short jail term or probation) rather than the death penalty or a very long prison term.

PUNISHMENT AND ETHICS

There are three major frameworks that address the purpose and ethics of punishment: utilitarianism, deontology, and peacemaking. Utilitarianism views the purpose of punishment in terms of the end result. For Bentham, punishment should be utilized to maximize the total pleasure or minimize the total pain of all parties affected by the crime (Gold, 2015). Deontology, which is associated with the work of Immanuel Kant, differs from utilitarianism in that the focus of actions is on the intent and not the consequences (Gold, 2015). For Kant, punishment by a court can never be inflicted simply as a means to promote good for the criminal or society. Instead, punishment must always be inflicted because the offender has committed a crime (Kant, 1996).

Peacemaking as a justice perspective seeks to incorporate three elements into the criminal justice system—connectedness to each other, caring as the primary element in corrections, and mindfulness of the needs of others (Braswell & Gold, 2015; Lanier & Henry, 1998). The peacemaking perspective argues that our correctional system should change its response to crime away from one of violence through the use of death and prison. Instead it should move, whenever possible, to deescalate violence through the use of meditation, mediation, spiritual growth (Braswell, Fuller, & Lozoff, 2001), dispute resolution, and forms of conciliation (Lanier & Henry, 1998).

WHAT ARE THE PURPOSES OF PUNISHMENT?

The philosophical punishment literature addresses the rationale behind punishment by posing questions of justification. Typical questions raised by philosophical debates include: Why do we punish? How much do we punish? What kinds of punishment should we utilize? Possible answers to these questions include: because offenders deserve to be punished, to protect society from dangerous people, to stop offenders from committing future crimes, and to discourage other people from committing the same criminal act (Hudson, 2002). Specifically, the philosophies of retribution, incapacitation, rehabilitation, and deterrence outline these answers (Clear, 1994; Duff, 1986; von Hirsch, 1976; Murphy, 1995; Montague, 1995).

Typically, one or more of these penal philosophies has dominated throughout the past 2 centuries. In the past few decades, the application of punishment has been marked by a move away from rehabilitative efforts and toward more punitive, incapacitative efforts (Feeley & Simon, 1992; Pratt, 2000). Currently, it seems that punishment "in its very conception is now acknowledged to be an inherently retributive practice" (Bedau, 2003, p. 1). The following discussion provides an overview of the major justifications for punishment and highlights some important ethical dilemmas and questions currently affecting punishment.

Retribution

One possible reason to punish wrongdoers is for the simple reason that they deserve it; this perspective is known as **retribution**. Retribution was often dismissed by criminologists as little more than revenge, and it was not afforded the status of penal theory until the 1980s (Hudson, 2002). When we think of retribution, we often think of *lex talionis*—an eye for an eye, a tooth for a tooth, a life for a life (Wesley, 2003). However, contemporary retribution is far different from this view. Although revenge is still fundamental in contemporary retribution, the focus now is on proportionality between the criminal act and the punishment. Retribution is manifested in contemporary punishment through the use of determinate sentences.

Until the 1970s, the primary sentencing rationale, to a large extent, went unchallenged—the punishment should fit the criminal, not the crime (Juarez, 1976). A typical indeterminate sentence would include a minimum and a maximum term of punishment, with the actual time served being determined by the progress of the offender. Offenders who could demonstrate successful progress toward rehabilitation could be released from supervision by parole authorities (MacKenzie, 2001). Parole was a privilege to be earned only by those offenders who displayed that they were rehabilitated and had ties to the community (Petersilia, 2001).

Great disparity resulted from indeterminate sentences, such that a property offender could end up serving a longer prison sentence than a violent offender. These concerns, coupled with prison riots, prompted the introduction of sentencing reforms by way of determinant sentences (Hudson, 2002). Liberal critics of indeterminate sentences pointed to the gross abuses suffered by inmates, whereas more conservative opponents of rehabilitation argued that offenders were being treated far too softy. Determinate sentencing schemes were lauded by both liberals and conservatives, but for very different reasons. For the left, determinate sentences offered a way to curb judicial discretion and the disparities that occurred as a result; for the right, it offered a way to "get tough" with offenders (Hudson, 2002).

The resulting sentencing guidelines offered harsh penalties for severe offenders and penalties that were more lenient for lesser offenders. Many states replaced indeterminate sentences with determinate sentences, which clearly identify fixed penalties for crimes. Under this type of sentence, offenders receive a fixed term of punishment, which is determined by guidelines

(MacKenzie, 2001; Petersilia, 2001). Once offenders complete their term of punishment, they are automatically released from prison, thus eliminating parole boards (MacKenzie, 2001; Petersilia, 2001). Determinate sentencing does allow the consideration of certain circumstances of the crime to act as either aggravating or mitigating factors, so there is some individualization of justice. In general, the guidelines offer a range of possible sanctions for each type of offense—for example, a crime might carry a penalty of 3–5 years, with less serious offenders receiving sanctions at the low end of the spectrum.

With regard to actual administration of punishment, retributivists argue that punishment serves as a means of restoring balance between the offender and society. It is argued that the commission of the criminal act has allowed the offender to seize an unfair advantage over law-abiding people—theft of property, excitement, or the release of tension (Hudson, 2002). Punishment, it is argued, is necessary to remove this unfair advantage.

Despite the focus on fairness and proportionality, retribution still has some problems. Because retribution stresses impartiality and fairness above all else, the system becomes depersonalized (Wesley, 2003). Retribution forces the justice system to ignore potentially relevant facts (such as whether the offender was raised in abusive foster homes) in the pursuit of justice. In short, retributive justice leaves little room for the consideration of human needs and focuses on just deserts (Wesley, 2003).

A discussion of retribution would not be complete without introducing the ultimate sanction—death. Capital punishment is often justified primarily in terms of retribution and demands that murderers should suffer in approximately the same way that the victim suffered (Finkelstein, 2002). The retributive argument for the death penalty typically centers on what Byron (2000) calls the "their shoes gambit," that is, if you had a loved one who was murdered, what type of justice would you demand? According to Byron, the gambit goes something like this: "People who are opposed to capital punishment imagine themselves in circumstances in which they would be strongly motivated to demand justice. This demand focuses on retribution, or punishing the guilty as much as they deserve … [This gambit] heightens the aggrieved person's demand for retribution, in particular on the person's sense that nothing short of the death of the perpetrator could approach a just retribution for the crime" (p. 308).

Although this argument may be important, Byron (2000) argues that vengeance has no place in public policy and should not serve as a justification for the death penalty in the absence of other salient functions of punishment, such as deterrence and rehabilitation (see also Chapter 12).

Incapacitation

If we hold that neither deterrence nor rehabilitation is effective, another option is simply to incapacitate offenders in jails and prisons. Supporters might point to the value of maintaining custody and control over offenders; critics may suggest that **incapacitation** is little more than warehousing offenders, making it more likely that they will be unable to succeed in any world outside prison. Many attempts have been made by the state to get "hard-core" repeat offenders off the streets. Incapacitation through incarceration or the death penalty is one way to ensure that chronic offenders curtail their criminal activity, but it is certainly not without problems—most notably prediction.

How do we predict chronic offenders? Several studies have attempted to isolate the characteristics of chronic offenders in an effort to predict the likelihood of chronic offending (see, e.g., West & Farrington, 1973). Such studies have been unable to predict with high levels of accuracy whether someone would reoffend. Several ethical dilemmas present themselves when we consider false positives—those individuals who were predicted to offend but ultimately would not. Because there is really no way to demonstrate these false positives, it remains a theoretical dilemma.

In an attempt to incapacitate repeat violent offenders, some form of "three strikes and you're out" laws were implemented by 23 states in 1993 (Dickey & Hollenhorst, 1999). For the most part, three-strikes laws had minimal impact in most states. However, California's wide scope of three-strikes law provisions affected many of the state's systems (i.e., political, educational, criminal justice, human services, and budgetary systems; Meehan, 2000). Cost implementations alone were substantial (Dickey & Hollenhorst, 1999), with increases being seen in almost every area of offender processing. Preconviction jail time, case processing, trials, and prison-building costs have all increased dramatically since the passage of the three-strikes legislation. Because three-strikes laws entail longer prison sentences in addition to reducing good time credits, such laws contribute to prison crowding as well as the long-term costs of incarceration for geriatric inmates.

Additional problems stem from the application of the three-strikes laws. In California, for example, prosecutors are able to exercise their wide discretion in the charging decisions of offenders. In some cases, offenders who commit third-strike-eligible offenses are charged with a misdemeanor instead of a felony. In other cases, relatively minor infractions are charged as felonies, leading to a disproportionately severe punishment (see Box 11.1). Wide sentencing disparity has resulted so that an offender could receive an 8-month sentence in one county and a 25-to-life sentence in another county for the same crime (Dickey & Hollenhorst, 1999).

Rehabilitation

Since the development of the prison, punishment in the modern era has been characterized by a belief that the problem of crime can be solved through the identification and treatment of the root causes of crime (i.e., rehabilitation). **Rehabilitation**, which has dominated penal strategies for nearly a century and

BOX 11.1 SEVERE PUNISHMENTS

Gary Ewing received a prison term of 25 years to life for stealing golf clubs from a country club in Los Angeles. The prosecutor in the case had the option of charging Ewing with a misdemeanor but decided to charge him with a felony. Had Ewing been charged with a misdemeanor, he likely would have received a short term in jail and possibly a fine.

In a similar case, Leandro Andrade was sentenced to 25 years to life for stealing nine children's videotapes,

including *Snow White, Cinderella,* and *Free Willy 2.* The estimated value of these tapes was $153.54.

The crime reduction capabilities of three-strikes laws are tenuous at best. Thus far, research findings have not been able to illustrate a link between three-strikes laws and the reduction and/or prevention of crime (Meehan, 2000). Some have noted that increased preventive efforts, such as education and social programs, may be more effective than incapacitative strategies at reducing crime rates in the long run (Dickey & Hollenhorst, 1999).

a half (von Hirsch, 1976; MacKenzie, 2001), characterizes the offenders as being sick and in need of treatment. According to this alternative philosophy, the criminal is in need of treatment, reeducation, or reformation (von Hirsch, 1976). In an effort to "treat" the criminal, rehabilitative strategies have relied on a multitude of different medical and education models (von Hirsch, 1976). In the 1970s, U.S. Attorney General Ramsey Clark issued a call for rehabilitation programs to address both the addiction problems suffered by inmates and the need for vocational training (Clark, 1970).

For some, rehabilitation is often seen as the opposite of punishment. Such a view would be in error in that rehabilitation is in a very real sense a form of crime control—one that attempts to change the offender so that he or she is less likely to reoffend. Thus, a primary goal of rehabilitation is to reduce recidivism (von Hirsch, 1976). Cullen and Gilbert (1982, 2013), in their classic work, reaffirmed the rehabilitative ideal in the face of the conservative "nothing works" (Martinson, 1974) onslaught, which fueled the get-tough punishment revival. Cullen and Wright (1996) offer a convincing argument for the measured and responsible use of evolving rehabilitative strategies. They suggest that, with regard to the state's response to offenders, neither liberal "doing for" treatment programs nor conservative "doing to" punishment strategies will offer significant opportunities for offenders to learn and take responsibility for the crimes they committed and, just as important, for assisting in shaping the law-abiding citizens they need to become.

A variety of treatment programs have been implemented, such as intensive supervision on the streets, rehabilitative boot camps, well-equipped vocational training programs, the use of probation, behavioral control techniques, and "community-based" programs, such as intensive counseling and group therapy. The efficacy of these treatment programs has been monitored by testing the effects of recidivism. Findings from empirical research on these programs have been inconclusive, with some studies indicating a significant reduction in the recidivism of program participants versus nonparticipants and others not finding a significant difference (Alschuler, 2003; Kempinen & Kurlychek, 2003; Petersilia, 1998; Petersilia & Turner, 1990).

Some rehabilitation programs appear to be effective for some types of offenders. Contemporary movements that complement more traditional rehabilitation and social support models include family therapy, restorative justice, and peacemaking initiatives. For example, McCord, Tremblay, Vitaro, and Desmarais-Gervais (1994) found that a 2-year treatment program that focused on family management and social skills resulted in higher school achievement and less antisocial behavior among delinquent boys. Similarly, Gordon, Graves, and Arbuthnot (1995) found that delinquents who received family therapy had a lower rate of adult offenses compared to delinquents who received only probation service.

Deterrence

Deterrence is a forward-looking punishment philosophy. Because it is recognized that we cannot change the past, forward-looking philosophies, such as deterrence, hold that the best society can do is prevent wrongs from being committed in the future (Wesley, 2003). Deterrence as a penal strategy generally refers to discouraging reoffending or offending by law-abiding citizens through the threat and fear of the potential punishment (Hudson, 2002, p. 19).

Deterrence is generally divided into two major categories: general and specific. **General deterrence** seeks to use the offender as an example to the rest of society. Through the use of general deterrence strategies (increasing the fear and certainty of punishment), it is hoped that the general public will be prevented from engaging in criminal acts. Some examples of general deterrence strategies include increasing police activity in certain areas, the use of special police task forces to target specific crimes, such as narcotics, and the death penalty (Siegel, 2003). **Specific deterrence** seeks to influence the future behavior of a particular offender. Specifically, strategies are implemented to prevent the offender from engaging in future criminal acts. For example, the drunk driver who pays a substantial fine and serves some time in jail should, at least in theory, find the punishment unpleasant enough to refrain from driving drunk in the future (Siegel, 2003).

The philosophy of deterrence was introduced by Cesare Beccaria and later articulated by Jeremy Bentham. For both classical contemporary deterrence theorists, the criminal is viewed as a rational actor who has free will. Theoretically, an individual's choice can be deterred by the anticipation of punishment if he or she does engage in the criminal act (Hudson, 2002). Essentially, the criminal actor is viewed as a rational actor who weighs the costs and benefits of the criminal act prior to its commission. Bentham termed this calculation the **hedonistic calculus**, and it is based on the idea that people seek pleasure over pain. Thus, if the pain derived from the punishment of the criminal act outweighs the pleasure derived from that act, the rational actor will choose not to engage in crime.

Contemporary deterrence theorists hold that three elements are essential in the deterrence of criminal activity: the likelihood of arrest, the likelihood of conviction, and the severity of punishment (Mendes, 2004). In theory, a government can reduce the crime rate if the likelihood of arrest and conviction is increased and the severity of punishment is increased (Mendes, 2004).

Although deterrence theory has several merits, it is not without its problems. For example, there is considerable difficulty in determining what (if anything) will deter individuals from committing crimes. Deterrence assumes that an individual makes a rational decision to commit a crime, and that simply is not the case in all circumstances. In some cases, an individual is unable to weigh the costs and benefits associated with a criminal event. This is particularly true in the case of crimes that occur in the heat of the moment.

There is great debate in the literature regarding the importance of severity and certainty in the ability to deter crime. Some theorists posit that the severity of punishment has little deterrent effect (Decker & Kohfeld, 1990; Eide, 1994; Witte, 1983). Others suggest that the certainty of punishment is more important than the severity of punishment (Becker, 1968; Ehrlich, 1973). Still others believe that certainty and severity are equally important in the deterrence of crime (Antunes & Hunt, 1973; Chambliss, 1966; Gibbs, 1968; Grasmick & Bryjak, 1980; Gray & Martin, 1969; Logan, 1972; Mendes & McDonald, 2001; Tittle, 1969).

Other difficulties arise when we examine the use of various sanctions as a deterrent. For example, it is believed by some that the use of the death penalty serves as a deterrent for would-be murderers (Reitan, 1993). Critics of the deterrence argument point to a brutalization effect of the death penalty, whereby murder rates actually increase after an execution (Cochran & Chamlin, 2000). An examination of brutalization and deterrence by Cochran and Chamlin (2000) revealed only a slight deterrent effect of the death penalty and an increase in the level of nonstranger, argument-based murders. Recent crime statistics reveal that of the estimated murders in the United States, 43.6% were reported in the South, 21.1% were reported in the Midwest, 21.0% were reported in the West, and 14.2% were reported in the Northeast (Federal Bureau of Investigation, 2013). The South also has the highest execution rate in the United States, with almost 82% of all executions taking place in southern states (Death Penalty Information Center, 2013). Overall, the majority of research studies have failed to find support for the link between capital punishment and murder, especially when other penalties, such as life without parole, are available (Bailey & Peterson, 1997; Radelet & Borg, 2000).

UNINTENDED CONSEQUENCES OF PUNISHMENT

Determinate sentencing strategies and retributive punishments have contributed to the unprecedented increases in the inmate population in the past few decades. Recent statistics indicate that there are approximately 1.5 million adults confined in U.S. state and federal prisons (Carson & Golinelli, 2013). This high level of incarceration has prompted the concern of system officials about overcrowding and has led many state departments of correction to search for cost-saving alternatives. Full-scale privatization is one solution used by many states and the federal government as a way to save resources. Unfortunately, privatization leaves many questions unanswered and has some serious ethical implications.

Overcrowding in prisons and jails has severe impacts on the correctional system, most notably in the conditions of confinement. Overcrowding in the correctional system has arguably contributed to the decline of physical, social, and operational conditions inside prison facilities (Tartaro, 2002). Often, offenders are doubled up in cells meant for one, jam-packed into dormitories, basements, corridors, converted hospital facilities, tents, trailers, and warehouses (Allen, Simonsen, & Latessa, 2004).

Even though the Supreme Court has ruled that "double bunking" does not violate the Eighth Amendment (see, e.g., *Bell v. Wolfish*, 441 U.S. 520, 1979; *Rhodes v. Chapman*, 452 U.S. 337, 1981), overcrowding in correctional facilities does cause some problems. For example, overcrowding impedes correctional officers' abilities to classify and separate inmates according to treatment, safety, and security needs (Tartaro, 2002). Additional problems stem from the frequency of medical problems in overcrowded facilities (Allen et al., 2004). State prison inmates suffer from a variety of diseases, including tuberculosis, sexually transmitted diseases, hepatitis, and HIV/AIDS (see Box 11.2). Because mass screening programs are currently not in place in most correctional facilities, the data regarding inmates with sexually transmitted

---

BOX 11.2 ETHICAL QUESTIONS

Issue	Ethical Question
Privatization	Who should punish: the state or private correctional firms?
Death penalty	What types of punishments should we utilize, and how severe should they be?
Special populations	Should we punish all offenders the same way?

diseases (STDs) are incomplete. However, anecdotal evidence and results from behavioral studies indicate that inmates likely suffer from STDs at disproportionately high rates (Hammett, Harmon, & Maruschak, 1999). STDs and other infectious diseases can be exacerbated in overcrowded conditions (Allen et al., 2004).

ETHICAL DILEMMAS IN PUNISHMENT

There are a variety of current ethical dilemmas in punishment, including the use of full-scale privatization, the punishment of special populations (such as the mentally ill and juveniles), and the death penalty. Each of these issues raises important questions about the institution of punishment.

Privatization of correctional facilities requires that we ask: Who should punish? There are a variety of important issues relating to the privatization of prisons; the ethical questions provoke interesting and meaningful debate. Should corrections be a money-making enterprise? Should governments delegate coercive authority to private entities? These represent just some of the ethical questions and concerns about private correctional facilities.

Although privatization can take any number of forms, full-scale privatization of corrections typically refers to those institutions that are privately owned and operated by a corporation (Pratt & Maahs, 1999). Essentially, a private company is contracted by the state to administer correctional services. People who are vehemently opposed to full-scale privatization believe that "the state is the sole source of legitimate force and that allowing private organizations to wield the coercive power of the state (particularly in the incarceration and punishment of prisoners) undermines the legitimacy of government" (Vardalis & Becker, 2000, p. 136).

The use of the death penalty also poses some ethical problems and requires that we ask: What types of punishments should we utilize? For some, death, as the ultimate punishment reserved for those persons who are found guilty of committing the most heinous crimes, is just. For others, the death penalty represents an inhumane punishment that violates the Eighth Amendment provision barring the use of cruel and unusual punishments. This thinking, coupled with other pressing concerns, such as the execution of innocent people, arbitrary application of the punishment, and the execution of juveniles, has led death penalty opponents to argue that capital punishment presents too many ethical problems and should be stricken from the range of available punishments.

The punishment of special populations, such as the mentally ill and juvenile offenders, presents another range of ethical dilemmas. Mentally ill offenders make up approximately 16% of prison and jail inmates (Lunney & Brown, 2002) and pose a variety of unique demands on correctional systems. An ethical issue arises when one is faced with the quality of life for severely mentally ill inmates (Faust, 2003). Such inmates are more likely to be victimized or beaten and more likely to commit suicide compared to those who are not sick (Faust, 2003). Scholars argue that jails are no place for the mentally ill because they lack adequate resources for treatment services (Faust, 2003; Hodulik, 2001; Pawel; 2001).

Treating juvenile offenders as adults is a key ethical concern (Gaarder & Belknap, 2002; Redding, 1999; Roberts, 2004). According to Gaarder and Belknap (2002), there has been a nationwide effort to treat juvenile delinquents as adults, mainly with the get-tough movement. However, many scholars tend to agree that sentencing should be different for juvenile offenders (Gaarder & Belknap, 2002; Roberts, 2004) because the offenders lack the mental development necessary to form intent. Redding (1999) examined the consequences of treating juveniles as adults and found that "criminal prosecution and/or imprisonment retards rather than enhances community protection and diminishes rather than enhances juvenile offenders' accountability and their development of competencies" (p. 97).

CONCLUSION

In sum, penal strategies have increasingly moved away from rehabilitation in recent years. Although rehabilitation is still espoused by system officials, it is no longer the primary goal of correctional authorities. In place of rehabilitation, correctional policies are increasingly using retributive and incapacitative strategies. The overall crime rate has witnessed moderate decreases in the past few years (Federal Bureau of Investigation, 2013), possibly because of the implementation of such strategies as well as a variety of other factors. However, incapacitative strategies have had the unintended consequence of overcrowding our nation's prison facilities and thus increasing the number of violent and health-related consequences. Only time will tell if we can implement a penal policy that balances the need for rehabilitation with the need for public safety.

■ Learn More on the Internet

For more on crime and punishment, visit plato.stanford.edu/entries/legal-punishment/.   ■

Discussion Questions

1. Compare and contrast punishing for retribution with punishing for deterrence. Discuss the unintended consequences of each.
2. Describe the ideologies for both prevention and treatment. What are their key assumptions about criminality? How does each claim to reduce criminal behavior.

3. What are some of the challenges that special populations face in prison? Examine the ethical implications of incarcerating the mentally ill and juvenile offenders.
4. Compare and contrast contemporary retribution with retribution as revenge. Do you think that revenge has a place in contemporary punishment? Explain your answer.
5. What are the policy implications of retribution, incapacitation, and rehabilitation?
6. Describe the three ethical frameworks for punishment: utilitarianism, deontology, and peacemaking. Which one do you think should serve as the ethical framework for punishment today? Why?

REFERENCES

Allen, H. E., Simonsen, C. E., & Latessa, E. J. (2004). *Corrections in America* (10th ed.). Upper Saddle River: Prentice Hall.

Alschuler, A. (2003). The changing purposes of criminal punishment: A retrospective on the past century and thoughts about the next. *The University of Chicago Law Review, 70*(1), 1–22.

Antunes, G., & Hunt, A. L. (1973). The deterrent impact of criminal sanctions: Some implications for criminal justice policy. *Journal of Urban Law, 51*(2), 145–161.

Bailey, W., & Peterson, R. (1997). Murder, capital punishment, and deterrence: A review of the literature. In H. Bedau (Ed.), *The death penalty in America: Current controversies*. New York: Oxford University Press.

Becker, G. S. (1968). Crime and punishment: An economic approach. *Journal of Political Economy, 78*, 169–217.

Bedau, H. (2003). Punishment. In E. N. Zalta (Ed.), *The Stanford encyclopedia of philosophy*. Retrieved from plato.stanford.edu/archives/sum2003/entries/punishment/.

Bell v. Wolfish, 441 U.S. 520 (1979).

Braswell, M., Fuller, J., & Lozoff, B. (2001). *Corrections, peacemaking and restorative justice*. Cincinnati: Anderson.

Braswell, M., & Gold, J. (2015). *Peacemaking, justice, and ethics*, Chapter 3, this volume.

Byron, M. (2000). Why my opinion shouldn't count: Revenge, retribution, and the death penalty debate. *Journal of Social Philosophy, 31*(3), 307–316.

Carson, E. A., & Golinelli, D. (2013). *Bulletin: Prisoners in 2012: Trends in admissions and releases, 1991–2012*. Washington: U.S. Department of Justice, Bureau of Justice Statistics.

Chambliss, W. (1966). The deterrent influence of punishment. *Crime & Delinquency, 12*, 70–75.

Clark, R. (1970). *Crime in America: Observations on its nature, causes, prevention, and control*. New York: Simon & Schuster.

Clear, T. (1994). *Harm in American penology: Offenders, victims & their communities*. Albany: State University of New York Press.

Cochran, J., & Chamlin, M. (2000). Deterrence and brutalization: The dual effects of executions. *Justice Quarterly, 17*(4), 685–706.

Cullen, F. T., & Gilbert, K. E. (1982). *Reaffirming rehabilitation*. Cincinnati: Anderson.

Cullen, F. T., & Gilbert, K. E. (2013). *Reaffirming rehabilitation* (2nd ed.). Boston: Elsevier (Anderson Publishing).

Cullen, F. T., & Wright, J. P. (1996). Two futures for American corrections. In B. Maguire, & P. F. Radosh (Eds.), *The past, present and future of American criminal justice*. Dix Hills: General Hall.

Death Penalty Information Center (2013). *Number of executions by state and region since 1976.* Retrieved from www.deathpenaltyinfo.org/number-executions-state-and-region-1976.

Decker, S., & Kohfeld, C. W. (1990). Certainty, severity, and the probability of crime: A logistic analysis. *Policy Studies Journal, 19*(1), 2–21.

Dickey, W. J., & Hollenhorst, P. (1999). Three-strikes laws: Five years later. *Corrections Management Quarterly, 3*(3), 1–18.

Duff, R. A. (1986). *Trials and punishments.* Cambridge: Cambridge University Press.

Ehrlich, I. (1973). Participation in illegitimate activities: A theoretical and empirical investigation. *Journal of Political Economy, 81*(3), 521–565.

Eide, E. (1994). *Economics of crime: Deterrence and the rational offender.* Amsterdam: North Holland.

Faust, T. N. (2003). Shift the responsibility of untreated mental illness out of the criminal justice system. *Corrections Today, 65*(2), 6–8.

Federal Bureau of Investigation (2013). *Uniform crime reports.* Retrieved from www.fbi.gov/about-us/cjis/ucr/crime-in-the-u.s/2012/crime-in-the-u.s.-2012/.

Feeley, M., & Simon, J. (1992). The new penology: Notes on the emerging strategy of corrections and its implications. *Criminology, 30*(4), 449–474.

Finkelstein, C. (2002). Death and retribution. *Criminal Justice Ethics, 21*(2), 12–22.

Gaarder, E., & Belknap, J. (2002). Tenuous borders: Girls transferred to adult court. *Criminology, 40*(3), 481–518.

Gibbs, J. P. (1968). Crime, punishment, and deterrence. *Southwestern Social Science Quarterly, 48*(4), 515–530.

Gold, J. (2015). *Utilitarian and deontological approaches to criminal justice ethics,* Chapter 2, this volume.

Gordon, D. A., Graves, K., & Arbuthnot, J. (1995). The effect of functional family therapy for delinquents on adult criminal behavior. *Criminal Justice and Behavior, 22*(1), 60–73.

Grasmick, H. G., & Bryjak, G. J. (1980). The deterrent effect of perceived severity of punishment. *Social Forces, 59*(2), 471–491.

Gray, L. N., & Martin, J. D. (1969). Punishment and deterrence: Another analysis of Gibbs' data. *Social Science Quarterly, 50*(September), 389–395.

Hammett, T., Harmon, P., & Maruschak, L. (1999). *1996–1997 update: HIV/AIDS, STDs, and TB in correctional facilities issues and practices.* Washington, DC: U.S. Department of Justice, National Institute of Justice, NCJ 176344.

von Hirsch, A. (1976). *Doing justice: The choice of punishments.* New York: Hill and Wang.

Hodulik, J. (2001). The drug court model as a response to 'broken windows': Criminal justice for the homeless mentally ill. *Journal of Criminal Law and Criminology, 91*(4), 1073–1101.

Hudson, B. (2002). *Understanding justice: An introduction to ideas, perspectives, and controversies in modern penal theory* (2nd ed.). Philadelphia: Open University Press.

Juarez, G. (1976). Modifying the indeterminate sentence: The changing emphasis in criminal punishment. *California Law Review, 64*(2), 405–418.

Kant, I. (1996). *The metaphysics of morals.* (M. Gregor, Trans. and Ed.). Cambridge: Cambridge University Press.

Kempinen, C., & Kurlychek, M. (2003). An outcome evaluation of Pennsylvania's Boot Camp: Does rehabilitative programming within a disciplinary setting reduce recidivism? *Crime & Delinquency, 49*(4), 581–602.

Lanier, M., & Henry, S. (1998). *Essential criminology*. Boulder: Westview Press.

Logan, C. H. (September 1972). General deterrent effects of imprisonment. *Social Forces, 51*, 64–73.

Lunney, L., & Brown, R. (2002). Action speaks louder than words: Addressing the mentally ill in jails. *Sheriff, 54*(6), 18–21.

MacKenzie, D. (2001). Corrections and sentencing in the 21st century: Evidence based corrections and sentencing. *Prison Journal, 81*(3), 29–312.

Martinson, R. (1974). What works. *The Public Interest* (Spring).

McCord, J., Tremblay, R., Vitaro, F., & Desmarais-Gervais, L. (1994). Boys' disruptive behavior, school adjustment, and delinquency: The Montreal prevention experiment. *International Journal of Behavioral Development, 17*(4), 739–752.

Meehan, K. E. (2000). California's three-strikes law: The first six years. *Corrections Management Quarterly, 4*(4), 22–34.

Mendes, S. (2004). Certainty, severity, and their relative deterrent effects: Questioning the implications of the role of risk in criminal deterrence policy. *The Policy Studies Journal, 32*(1), 59–74.

Mendes, S. M., & McDonald, M. D. (2001). Putting severity of punishment back in the deterrence package. *Policy Studies Journal, 29*(4), 588–610.

Montague, P. (1995). *Punishment as societal defense*. Lanham: Rowman & Littlefield.

Murphy, J. (1995). *Punishment and rehabilitation*. Belmont: Wadsworth.

Pawel, M. A. (2001). Imprisoning the mentally ill: Does it matter? *Criminal Justice Ethics, 20*(1), 2–4.

Petersilia, J. (1998). A decade of experimenting with intermediate sanctions: What have we learned? *Federal Probation, 62*, 3–10.

Petersilia, J. (2001). Prisoner reentry: Public safety and reintegration challenges. *Prison Journal, 81*(3), 360–375.

Petersilia, J., & Turner, S. (1990). Comparing intensive and regular supervision for high-risk probationers: Early results from an experiment in California. *Crime & Delinquency, 36*(1), 87–111.

Pratt, J. (2000). The return of the wheelbarrow men: Or, the arrival of postmodern penalty? *British Journal of Criminology, 40*, 127–145.

Pratt, T., & Maahs, J. (1999). Are private prisons more cost-effective than public prisons? A meta-analysis of evaluation research studies. *Crime & Delinquency, 45*, 358–372.

Radelet, M., & Borg, M. (2000). The changing nature of death penalty debates. *Annual Review of Sociology, 26*, 43–62.

Redding, R. E. (1999). Examining legal issues: Juvenile offenders in criminal court and adult prison. *Corrections Today, 61*(2), 92–101.

Reitan, E. (1993). Why the deterrence argument for capital punishment fails. *Criminal Justice Ethics, 12*(1), 26–34.

Rhodes v. Chapman, 452 U.S. 337 (1981).

Roberts, J. V. (2004). Harmonizing the sentencing of young and adult offenders: A comparison of the Youth Criminal Justice Act and part XXIII of the Criminal Code. *Canadian Journal of Criminology and Criminal Justice, 46*(3), 301–327.

Siegel, L. (2003). *Criminology* (8th ed.). Belmont: Wadsworth/Thomson Learning.

Tartaro, C. (2002). The impact of density of jail violence. *Journal of Criminal Justice, 3*(6), 499–510.

Tittle, C. R. (1969). Crime rates and legal sanctions. *Social Problems, 16*(4), 409–423.

Vardalis, J., & Becker, F. (2000). Legislative opinions concerning the private operation of state prisons: The case of Florida. *Criminal Justice Policy Review, 11*(2), 136–149.

Wesley, C. (2003). *The practice of punishment: Towards a theory of restorative justice.* New York: Taylor & Francis.

West, D., & Farrington, D. (1973). *Who becomes delinquent?* New York: Crane, Russak & Co.

Witte, A. D. (1983). Economic theories. In S. H. Kalish (Ed.), *Encyclopedia of crime and justice* (Vol. 1). New York: Free Press.

CHAPTER 12

To Die or Not to Die: Morality, Ethics, and the Death Penalty

John T. Whitehead, Michael C. Braswell

KEY CONCEPTS

arbitrariness	deterrence	incapacitation
death penalty	discrimination	life without parole (LWOP)

The **death penalty** fascinates us: its merits are debated, producers make movies about the death penalty (*Dead Man Walking*, *The Life of David Gale*, *The Green Mile*), and politicians use it as a sign that they are serious about the crime issue. The fascination with the ultimate sanction persists even though most murderers do not receive the death penalty, and of those who are sentenced to be executed, many get off death row in other ways, such as through court appeals.

In this chapter, we focus on the ethics of the death penalty. First, to put the death penalty in perspective we present some basic information. Then we outline how the three ethical theories—deontology, utilitarianism, and peacemaking—approach the issue of the ethics of the death penalty. Finally, we consider the specific issues concerning the debate on the ethics of the death penalty.

THE DEATH PENALTY IN PERSPECTIVE: FACTS ABOUT THE DEATH PENALTY

The latest available information indicates that nine states executed 43 inmates in 2012 and that 3,082 persons were on death row at year-end 2010 (Snell, 2013). California led the nation with 731 offenders on death row, followed by Florida (412), Texas (298), and Pennsylvania (198) (Death Penalty Information Center, 2013). Of prisoners under sentence of death at year-end, 55% were white and 42% were black. The 387 Hispanic inmates under sentence of death accounted for 14% of inmates with a known ethnicity. Death row prisoners were overwhelmingly (98%) male (Snell, 2013).

RATIONALE FOR THE DEATH PENALTY

There are two basic questions regarding the death penalty. The first addresses whether we should even have a death penalty. This question is essentially philosophical in nature. Such a question is often argued in terms of religious values and beliefs. For example, one can find both support and opposition for the death penalty among various Christian denominations, often based on scriptural passages from the Old and New Testaments. This aspect is discussed in more detail later in this chapter. The second question is judicial in nature. Does the criminal justice system process and prosecute capital cases justly and equitably? Are the laws, procedures, and decisions about such cases administered fairly and consistently, or does discrimination occur against any group? Issues such as race, gender, and economic bias are often debated and discussed in attempting to answer this question.

Concerning the philosophical question, some argue that if an individual takes the life of another person, that individual should have to forfeit his or her own life, whereas others might contend that two wrongs don't make a right—that the state also commits murder when it executes a convicted murderer. People who support this line of thinking maintain that advanced or evolved societies do not include the death penalty as a punishment option. Individuals who do support the death penalty counter by suggesting that the ultimate crime requires the ultimate penalty. Proponents of the death penalty might place their argument in a deontological frame of reference: It is society's duty to punish the most serious crime with the most severe penalty.

The late Ernest van den Haag perhaps put it most eloquently: "Can any crime be horrible enough to forfeit the life of the criminal? Can death ever be a deserved punishment. … I am confident that the following excerpt may help answer this question." van den Haag went on to describe a gruesome murder in which two men tortured and sexually abused a female victim, including pouring salt into her wounds before strangling her. Afterward, they broke her neck and arms so that they could fit her body into a trunk, and then dumped her body in a dumpster (for more details, see van den Haag, 2003, pp. 235–237). van den Haag thinks the answer is simple: "A murder as horrendous as this deserves the death penalty—even cries out for the penalty of death." In fact, van den Haag is in favor of the death penalty for all murders that so qualify according to the laws and jury decisions in the death penalty states.

Capital punishment opponents counter that a severe penalty is appropriate for the crime of murder, but this penalty does not have to include the taking of a human life. Opponents argue that severe punishments, such as life without parole (LWOP), life with the possibility of parole, or a lengthy prison sentence short of life are serious enough penalties to serve as commensurate punishment for the crime of murder. Additionally, opponents argue that sentences short of capital punishment have the advantage that if any error is made in determining either guilt or sentence, the error can be corrected, to some extent, if the offender is serving a life sentence or a lengthy prison term. If the offender has been executed, however, any mistake that is discovered years after the conviction and sentencing cannot be corrected. So, in a deontological framework, opponents could argue that LWOP, life, or a lengthy prison term can both satisfy the societal duty to demand a severe penalty for a severe offense and satisfy any societal duty to rectify mistakes to the fullest extent possible. (Mistakes are a separate topic that follows.)

Utilitarians go further than simply offering a philosophical justification that capital punishment offers a severe penalty for a severe offense. Utilitarians argue that the death penalty has additional positive consequences that justify or demand its use, such as deterrence and incapacitation. Here, we discuss each of these issues in turn.

Deterrence

One such additional consequence, according to utilitarians, is **deterrence**. Utilitarians who favor capital punishment argue that capital punishment is a general deterrent: It is so severe a penalty that it deters or frightens individuals who might be contemplating committing a murder out of committing one. Capital punishment proponents usually argue from personal experience or common sense. They argue that most of us can recall experiences in which we were tempted to do something wrong, such as shoplift or speed down the highway, but saw a police officer or thought of being caught and decided not to steal or speed. Proponents also offer some empirical evidence: studies by Ehrlich and by Cochran and Chamlin claim that capital punishment has a deterrent effect (e.g., Cochran & Chamlin, 2000).

Capital punishment opponents argue that there are several problems with the deterrence argument. First, relying on our own experiences or common sense about deterrence is misleading. Most of us are law abiding; we are good citizens who have been appropriately socialized. Many of the people who murder may not be so law abiding and, thus, may not think about possible penalties. Second, many murders are committed on the spur of the moment or when the offender is in an unstable emotional state that does not readily allow for a calm assessment of the possible penalty. Many homicides occur in argument situations in which the offender is agitated. Others occur in robbery situations in which both the offender and the victim are under considerable stress. In both situations and others, the perpetrators are not thinking rationally about the penalty for murder or other tragic consequences that are likely to result from their actions. Instead, a robber is often quite nervous and might well interpret a normal fear response by a store clerk (e.g., a twitch) as a sign that the clerk is going to reach for a gun or alarm button and could end up fatally shooting him or her.

Social scientists have conducted some research on the death penalty and on other penalties that shed some light on how much deterrent impact the death penalty has or might have. One of the first studies on the deterrent impact of the death penalty was conducted by Thorsten Sellin. What he did was to compare homicide rates in contiguous states that did have or did not have the death penalty. He chose Ohio, Indiana, and Michigan. These three states are Midwestern states that share similar climates and economies. All three have both manufacturing (auto, steel, and related industries) and agriculture (such as soybeans). All three are a mix of urban, suburban, and rural areas. There are also cultural, political, and social similarities among the three. Comparing homicide rates across these three states over decades, Sellin concluded that there is no discernible impact of the death penalty. States that have the death penalty do not have lower homicide rates than states without the death penalty (Sellin, 1980).

Peterson and Bailey conducted a review of studies on the deterrent impact of capital punishment. After looking at many different types of research studies, they concluded: "In short, the empirical evidence does not support the belief that capital punishment was an effective deterrent for murder in years past. Nor is there any indication that returning to our past execution practices would have any deterrent impact on the current homicide problem" (Peterson & Bailey, 2003, p. 277).

Other studies of deterrence also show negligible impact. For example, in the late 1970s, Scared Straight programs surfaced as a popular way to supposedly prevent delinquency. Scared Straight was the name of a program in New Jersey in which prison inmates gave prison tours to predelinquents or delinquents and then literally tried to scare the youths out of committing any further crime. The inmates yelled at the kids and informed them of all the horrible events that could befall them if they wound up in prison, such as physical and sexual assaults and even being killed in prison and carried out in a body bag. Although the documentary that promoted the program claimed tremendous success, systematic scientific research studies on the effectiveness of Scared Straight-type programs indicate that there is no significant difference between youths who experience such a program and youths who do not (Lundman, 1993).

To be fair, some studies do show some deterrent effects for some punishments. Granted, many of us fear penalties enough to avoid crime. A point to be considered, however, is that opponents to the death penalty are not arguing for no penalties for murder. Rather, they are advocates for either LWOP, life with the possibility of parole, or lengthy prison sentences for murderers. What is at issue is this: What is the true effect of the death penalty? This means that proponents for the death penalty need to demonstrate that the ultimate penalty has more impact than a penalty such as LWOP, which to date has not occurred.

Some proponents of the death penalty argue that a serious problem in looking at the deterrent impact of the death penalty is that it is not imposed in such a way that it can be a deterrent. Deterrence theory maintains that for any punishment or sanction to be an effective deterrent, the penalty in question must be severe, certain, and quick. The death penalty is clearly severe, but it is not always certain or quick. Concerning certainty, although most murderers are caught, not all are convicted and not all receive the death penalty. In fact, even those who receive the sentence of death do not necessarily get executed. Between 1977 and 2011, 7,958 people were sentenced to death, but 46% received other dispositions instead. They had their sentences or convictions overturned, received commutations, or died a natural death before they could be executed (Snell, 2013). Quickness is also problematic. The average stay on death row is about 10 years. Death penalty proponents argue that such lack of certainty and lack of speed in imposing the death penalty detract from its effectiveness. They argue that improvements in certainty and quickness could result in findings that deterrence works. A more recent discussion of the research on deterrence, however, disagrees that improvements will result in new findings of effectiveness (Peterson & Bailey, 2003).

One problem with increasing the speed at which death row offenders proceed to execution is that a major reason for the lengthy time on death row is to allow time for appeals. States usually have a mandatory appeal of the case. Then offenders often pursue discretionary appeals in an effort to save their lives. Liebman and his colleagues have shown that many of the appeals show reversible error. They studied more than 4,500 appeals from 1973 to 1995 and found the overall rate of prejudicial error to be 68%. "In other words, courts found serious, reversible error in nearly seven of every 10 of the thousands of capital sentences that were fully reviewed during the period" (Liebman, Fagan, & West, 2000). Death penalty opponents argue that if states were to shorten the time between sentencing and execution, it would cut short the time for appeals. This would reduce the number of errors that are found. So it would become more likely for states to execute individuals who either did not commit the murder or deserved a conviction and sentence for a noncapital offense, such as manslaughter that does not involve the death penalty. The issue ends up being one of efficiency versus effectiveness, shortening the appeal process versus guarding against error when execution is the penalty to be rendered.

Incapacitation

Death penalty proponents are right about one thing: the death penalty is perfect **incapacitation**. Executing an offender prevents him or her from ever killing again. Therefore, in a way, the death penalty does satisfy the utilitarian goal of incapacitation.

Opponents cannot deny the incapacitative impact of the death penalty, but they can argue that other penalties can also achieve very high degrees of incapacitation. LWOP, for example, will ensure that a murderer cannot commit another homicide on the street. He or she may kill a fellow prisoner or a prison guard, but they will not kill another person on the outside. Moreover, the number of killings in prison is quite small. For example, Bedau noted in 1997 that approximately one prisoner per state is murdered in prison every year, and about 20 prison staff members are killed every 5 years (Bedau, 1997, p. 177). Any loss of life is tragic, but, unfortunately, these statistics are incomplete and dated. These statistics also do not tell us if convicted murderers were in fact the perpetrators of these in-prison crimes.

There is also substantial evidence that if society punished murderers with 10–20 years of imprisonment and then released them on parole, the released murderers would have very low recidivism (new crime) rates. Parole statistics consistently show that murderers make good parolees. Paroled murderers have the lowest crime rates of all parolees. One of the best pieces of evidence about the safety of parole for murderers comes from the *Furman* cases. *Furman* was a Supreme Court case that ruled the death penalty, as then practiced, unconstitutional. As a result, death row inmates in affected states were switched to parole-eligible status and were in fact later (after serving years of their sentences) paroled. The so-called *Furman* parolees performed quite well in the community. In one study of 188 murderers who were released on parole and served an average time of 5.3 years on parole, only one committed a new murder. Twenty (10.6% of those released) committed a new felony (Marquart & Sorensen, 1997).

Why do paroled murderers do so well on parole? There are several reasons for the success. One is that parole boards are more careful in deciding whether a murderer gets parole than in deciding, for example, whether a car thief gets parole. If the parole board makes a mistake about a car thief, the damage is just one more stolen car. If they make a mistake about a murderer, there is the possibility that another murder will take place. Parole board members are concerned about avoiding such serious mistakes. A second reason is that even if the parole board releases a murderer, they usually make him or her serve quite a few years (10 or more) in prison before release. Those years allow maturation to occur; the parolee is often not the impulsive and immature person who entered prison. Simple aging also occurs; the released murderer is not as young, energetic, and angry as he or she once was.

As stated previously, the death penalty achieves perfect incapacitation: no executed killer can kill again in society. However, LWOP also prevents killers from killing again on the street. Parole statistics, especially the *Furman* cases, indicate that even parole for murder is not necessarily a costly choice in terms of outcomes. Very few paroled murderers kill again, but a minority (about 10%) do indeed commit a new felony. So, if society wants perfect incapacitation, the death penalty delivers perfection in one specific dimension. If society is willing to tolerate some error (e.g., some new crimes but very few murders), then parole is available as an option.

PEACEMAKING PERSPECTIVE

As noted in Chapter 3, the peacemaking perspective focuses on caring, connectedness, and mindfulness. Peacemakers oppose the death penalty because they think that it does not promote caring, connectedness, and mindfulness, whereas other penalties do.

A living example of peacemaking and the death penalty is Jarvis Masters. Masters is a death row inmate in California. His time on death row has been an opportunity for him to examine his life and turn from crime and violence to Buddhism and promoting peace. By becoming a Buddhist, he has come to realize that we are all connected so that what each one of us does indeed affects others and oneself as well. In his book *Finding Freedom* (1997), Masters gives two dramatic examples of connectedness and caring.

One Fourth of July, two guards who normally worked another cellblock were assigned to death row. They were anticipating a holiday barbecue that evening, so they were in a hurry to get through the day. Consequently, they practically threw the food at the inmates that day and ignored simple requests for silverware or toilet paper. Their disdain for inmates was causing rage to rise in the prisoners. Masters saw what was happening and felt he should do something to calm the prisoners. He decided that if the inmates stuffed their toilets with towels and flooded the cellblock, the flood would be a way for the inmates to respond to the guards in a controlled way. It would be an expression of prisoner anger, and it would make the guards late for their barbecue that evening because they would have to clean up the cellblock before they could leave work. More important, this minor expression of prisoner anger would prevent the inmates' anger from building up to a point at which inmates might attack a guard.

Another incident involved the guards putting a new prisoner into the yard in such a way that they were basically setting him up for an attack. Apparently, the new prisoner was homosexual and was dressed in some fashion to draw attention to his sexual orientation. At the time, says Masters, there was considerable hatred for homosexuals in San Quentin Prison. Masters saw the guards let this new prisoner onto the yard and, shortly thereafter, saw an inmate coming toward the new prisoner with a shiv (prison weapon). Masters intervened; he simply went up to the new prisoner and asked him for a cigarette. Seeing

Masters stopped the inmate from attacking the new prisoner. Afterward, Masters wondered why he had risked his own life for someone he really didn't know. He asked himself if he was the only Buddhist there.

The example of Jarvis Masters shows that offenders can change in prison and have a positive effect on other prisoners. Although Masters did receive a death sentence, his time on death row allowed him to question his former lifestyle and change to a lifestyle of genuine spirituality. If he had been executed sooner, he would not have had the chance to change. Nor would he have had the chance to do some of the positive things he has done in prison, such as the two examples just noted. Parenthetically, a death penalty proponent might argue that the inmate on death row did not give his or her victim a chance to mature or experience such personal transformation.

Peacemaking criminologists might also be concerned about the effects of death row on the family members of the death row inmates. One mother of a death row inmate notes that a detective magazine came out with an article depicting her son's "killing spree." She was so distraught that she tried to buy every copy so that her friends and neighbors would not see the story (Lezin, 1999). A few years later, a brother noted his painful experiences when friends would talk about criminals and say that "they ought to hang the bastard" (Lezin, 1999, p. 18).

Sending offenders to death row seems to foster seeing these criminals as outside the human family and permitting the rest of us to depict them as less than human. Unfortunately, parents, spouses, or siblings of the offender have to listen to and live with such depictions. The relative knows the offender as a flawed human, with good and bad traits, but the media and careless citizens may describe a relative on death row as a cold-blooded killer, a monster, an animal, and so on. It is painful to see and hear someone you love depicted in such extreme terms.

MISTAKES

Determining who is eligible for the death penalty is far from an error-free process. Juries and judges make mistakes in determining guilt and determining sentences. Mistakes about guilt result in an innocent person being placed on death row and experiencing the stress of anticipating an execution that he or she does not deserve. Mistakes about the penalty—the sentencing phase—mean that a person who perhaps deserves a lengthy prison sentence is instead anticipating death/execution and spends his or her time trying to appeal an incorrect sentence.

A major source of the mistakes in the death penalty decision-making process is the quality of defense representation that many offenders get. Many offenders are poor and cannot attract the best defense attorney available. Moreover, many states are willing or able to spend only a limited amount of money on indigent offender defense representation. Liebman and his associates found that defense lawyers "who didn't even look for—and demonstrably missed—important evidence that the defendant was innocent or did not deserve to die" was one of the most common errors causing a majority of the reversals at the state post-conviction stage (Liebman et al., 2000, p. ii).

In one case in Georgia, the state paid for an assigned defense attorney who was actually a talented lawyer. The problem was that he was a skilled divorce attorney who had never worked a death penalty case. To make things worse, the attorney thought that just because he had done the judge a favor before the case, the judge would return the favor in the totally unrelated death penalty case (Lezin, 1999). Some states, such as New York, do provide competitive pay to attorneys assigned to death penalty cases so that they can put forth an adequate defense. However, many other states provide very modest compensation, so it is often difficult, if not impossible, to attract qualified individuals to work death penalty cases.

Studies have shown that in the "death belt" (nine southern states that use the death penalty frequently), more than 10% of the attorneys who have represented indigent capital defendants have been disbarred, suspended, or disciplined at rates significantly higher than average, even in those states. In fact, most of the attorneys in the death belt had not handled a capital case before, and the death belt states did not have training programs for these attorneys (Mello & Perkins, 2003, p. 369).

The result is that many death penalty defendants do not get adequate (much less superior) representation. Less than adequate representation means that some unknown number of death row defendants receive the death penalty improperly. Adequate defense counsel would mean at least a lesser sentence, if not exoneration.

Apart from what O.J. Simpson, Kobe Bryant, or Michael Jackson actually did or did not do concerning their alleged criminal actions, it is clear that these celebrities were able to hire the best defense attorneys. Many of the people who wind up on death row quite simply could not afford that level of defense representation. If they could afford such high-quality attorneys, they would probably not end up on death row. The question, then, is whether it is ethical for wealth or the lack of it to have such impact on who is sentenced to capital punishment. One could argue that the prosecution may be at a disadvantage if the person who is tried for first-degree murder is very wealthy, but the prosecuting attorney and state have a substantial advantage if the defendant is poor.

Opponents of the death penalty argue that mistakes stemming from factors, such as inaccurate eyewitness testimony and inadequate defense representation, occur too frequently and are reason enough to abolish the death penalty. As noted, the Liebman et al. (2000) study of appeals found the rate of prejudicial error to be 68%. Abolitionists maintain that an error rate this high is simply unacceptable.

The proponent response to the issue of mistakes in the administration of capital punishment is that mistakes happen in all walks of life. Ernest van den Haag still supports the death penalty, arguing that all human institutions are flawed. For example, he has argued that driving to school or work is a very accident-prone activity. Every time we get in our cars and drive somewhere, we are taking our lives in our hands. We trade off the danger of driving for the convenience of driving to work or classes. Even ambulances, notes van den Haag, kill some innocent pedestrians, but they save more innocent people than they kill (van den Haag, 2003, p. 241). In sum, he thinks that the death penalty is justified, despite mistakes, as long as it deters and the mistakes are few.

As noted, the deterrent impact of the death penalty is not as certain as van den Haag contends. Most social scientists conclude that the deterrent impact is either unknown or nonexistent. Moreover, the frequency of mistakes appears to be much more prevalent than few. Former Governor George Ryan of Illinois was so concerned about mistakes that he put in place a temporary moratorium on executions. (For a look at the personal impact of mistakes, see Box 12.1.)

BOX 12.1 THE PERSONAL IMPACT OF MISTAKES

One of the authors of this chapter likes to have his classes consider that because human beings aren't perfect, neither is our system of justice absolutely perfect. Given that reality, is it acceptable to you that there are some mistakes about who gets the death penalty (for instance, one innocent is executed for every 10,000 who are deserving of death)? After the students raise their hands in support of this statement, he says, "Okay, now keep your hands raised if you can live with such a mistake about the death penalty if it is your brother, your son, your spouse, or yourself who is the innocent victim of the mistake." Without exception, hands drop one by one.

What about you? Are mistakes in determining who goes to death row all right with you? Are they still acceptable if you or a loved one is the one experiencing the mistake? Are you so much in favor of the death penalty that you can still support it, even if it means you or a loved one will be wrongfully executed?

DISCRIMINATION AND RACIAL BIAS

As noted at the beginning of this chapter, death row is disproportionately populated by blacks. Although African Americans make up only about 12% of the U.S. population, they constitute about 42% of the prisoners on death row (Snell, 2013).

The first ethical concern is whether **discrimination** in fact occurs. The high percentage of African Americans on death row does not in itself prove discrimination. If blacks commit about 42% of the capital murders (the homicides that deserve capital punishment), then they should make up about 42% of the prisoners on death row.

A review of research on discrimination in the administration of the death penalty led to several conclusions. First, the race of the defendant is not a significant factor in the prosecutor's charging decision. Second, the data "document race-of-victim disparities reflecting more punitive treatment of white-victim cases among similarly aggravated cases, regardless of the race of the defendant" (Baldus & Woodworth, 2003, p. 241). These disparities seem to stem more from the prosecutor's charging decision than from judge or jury decisions. Third, "in several jurisdictions for which data are available, cases involving black defendants and white victims are treated more punitively than cases with all other defendant/victim racial combinations" (Baldus & Woodworth, 2003, p. 241). Fourth, a few studies do show negative impact on black defendants or on defendants who killed white victims; these disparate impacts "arise from disproportionately punitive charging practices in counties with either particularly large numbers of black-defendant cases or particularly large numbers of white-victim cases on their capital case dockets" (Baldus & Woodworth, 2003, p. 242).

The Capital Jury Project has discovered some interesting findings about how jurors make their decisions. Project researchers have found that the number of white men or even the presence of one black juror on a jury can make a significant difference in the decisions made by juries. Specifically, the Capital Jury Project found a "white male dominance" effect in black defendant/white victim cases. That is, the jury voted for the death sentence in only 30% of the cases when the jury had fewer than five white male jurors, but the jury voted for death in 71% of the cases when there were at least five white male jurors on the jury. The researchers also found a "black male presence" effect: "Having a black male on the jury reduced the probability of a death sentence from 71.9 percent to 37.5 percent in the B/W [black defendant/white victim] cases, and from 66.7 percent to 42.9 percent in the B/B [black defendant/black victim] cases" (Bowers & Foglia, 2003, p. 77).

Discussions regarding the actual extent of discrimination in the death penalty are important and need to continue. It is imperative to eliminate discrimination. It is also important to end any appearance of discrimination. The high percentage of African Americans who receive the death penalty implies to many observers that there is discrimination. Even if careful investigation shows that discrimination is not occurring and that prosecutors and juries are perfectly unbiased in their decisions, many individuals interpret the high percentage of blacks on death row as apparent evidence of discrimination. Discrimination or the appearance of discrimination can influence minority members to have negative attitudes toward police, judges, and others in the criminal justice system. Such negative attitudes can affect the administration of justice.

ARBITRARINESS

Closely related to the issue of discrimination is the issue of **arbitrariness**, that is, the arbitrary selection of individuals for the death penalty. Although approximately 14,000 to 15,000 murders are committed each year in the United States, very few cases result in the death penalty. Ideally, those cases should be the most deserving of the death penalty. Practically, however, that is simply not the case. As noted, race appears to play some factor in the selection of cases for the death penalty. For one thing, black defendant/white victim cases are more likely to result in the death penalty than black defendant/black victim cases. Even apart from any instances of racial impact, other factors, such as location, judge, prosecutor, and case notoriety, can play a role in determining whether one murderer gets capital punishment, while another gets a life sentence or even less.

The deontologist would be quick to argue that arbitrariness should play no role in such a critical decision. The principle of the categorical imperative calls for not making exceptions but treating similar situated individuals in similar fashion. Given the demonstrated arbitrariness in the death penalty, a deontologist could oppose the death penalty for this reason alone.

Arbitrariness is hard to eliminate. The federal courts now use a guidelines system that is meant to reduce arbitrariness in all criminal sentencing. Problems persist. For one thing, the Federal Sentencing Guidelines allow for reductions based on offenders providing information on other criminals. Therefore, offenders who either have no information to give or refuse to give information receive no reductions. One first offender, for example, refused to implicate her own mother and was given a 10-year sentence, while an offender caught with 20,000 kilos of cocaine served only 4 years in prison because he "cooperated," that is, gave information on other dealers (Schlosser, 2003, p. 61). Another effort to reduce arbitrariness is proportionality review. This means that courts review death penalty cases in the jurisdiction (usually one state) to attempt to ensure that only the most horrible murders get the death penalty and that all homicides less serious than the least serious death penalty case get a sentence less severe than the death penalty. The basic problem is that such a proportionality review is difficult to do (Mandery, 2003). Measuring severity is not as simple as measuring blood pressure, especially in light of the fact that "the fundamental equality of each survivor's loss creates an inevitable emotional momentum to expand the categories for death penalty eligibility" (Turow, 2003, p. 47).

Abolishing the death penalty will not eliminate arbitrariness. Some murderers will get LWOP, some life with the possibility of parole, some shorter prison sentences, and some even probation. However, abolishing the death penalty could end the arbitrariness of some murderers being executed and others receiving much less severe penalties.

CONDITIONS ON DEATH ROW

Because more than 3,100 prisoners are currently on death row (Death Penalty Information Center, 2013), it is important to consider death row conditions. What are death row prisoners experiencing as they wait for execution?

There are two main types of death row: unreformed and reformed (Johnson, 1998). Unreformed death row involves a great deal of isolation. Prisoners are kept in solitary cells and are released from their cells only for short periods of exercise or showers. Such prisoners spend a considerable amount of time reading or watching television.

Reformed death row, however, allows prisoners to spend much more time out of their cells for work and recreation. Prisoners might work at jobs, such as making clothes or entering computer data. Both work and recreation allow

BOX 12.2 DONALD CABANA: A FORMER EXECUTIONER SPEAKS OUT ON DEATH ROW

Former warden Donald Cabana came to have doubts about working in corrections after executing some prisoners that he became quite close to, but he had no doubts about not wanting to supervise any more executions. "Of one thing I was certain, whatever the future might hold, I had privately concluded that I would not supervise another execution" (Cabana, 1996, p. 191).

Several factors had caused Cabana to change. One factor was executing a man that Cabana knew had changed dramatically during his years on Mississippi's death row. "I was absolutely convinced that Connie Ray Evans would never kill again, and that he would present no threat to other inmates if his sentence were commuted to life. … Evans had arrived on death row a streetwise drug abuser, bitter and scornfully contemptuous of authority. He had changed, and I personally had watched the change, especially over the past three years." Cabana pleaded for a commutation from the governor, imploring the governor that "Isn't that [change] what prisons are supposed to be about?" (Cabana, 1996, p. 179). The

governor, however, refused to commute the sentence to life, and Cabana had to carry out Evans's execution.

If you are preparing for a career in criminal justice and you go to work in a capital punishment state, you too might secure a position like Don Cabana's. He wound up having to supervise executions. You could end up arresting and investigating capital case defendants, prosecuting capital cases, defending capital defendants, guarding death row inmates, or, like Cabana, actually supervising executions. What do you think about actually being involved in executions or death row or capital cases? Would it bother you to be involved in any stage of the process? Now that about 80% of the states have capital punishment, a considerable percentage of criminal justice workers may become involved in the process to some extent.

Many people think that a reformed death row represents considerable improvement over an unreformed death row because the inmate on a reformed death row is out of his or her cell more often and has more opportunities to work and engage in recreation or socializing with other inmates.

Continued...

BOX 12.2 DONALD CABANA: A FORMER EXECUTIONER SPEAKS OUT ON DEATH ROW *Continued*

Robert Johnson, a strong opponent of capital punishment, is not so positive about reformed death row environments. Johnson argues that even a reformed death row does not help a prisoner get ready for his or her own death. In fact, Johnson thinks that there will never be a death row environment that truly prepares an inmate for death. Such a death row would be too painful, says Johnson, for both inmates and guards:

> Officials would be unable to ignore the hurt and loss they, as persons, would inflict on their prisoners, whom they would know to be frill human beings. The prisoners, too, no longer dulled to their own feelings, might well suffer greatly. Executions would be traumatic events, the virtual antithesis of their current bureaucratic reality.
>
> **Johnson (1998, p. 215)**

Aside from Johnson, most inmates and guards as well as most critics would probably endorse the reformed death row over the unreformed one. With more opportunities for work and recreation, the reformed death row seems to be the best that prisons can offer for those condemned to death by the courts.

for more socializing with other prisoners. One death row resident in Texas spent much of his time painting pictures, including pictures of Jesus and of how he imagined the execution room to look (*Frontline: The Execution*) (Box 12.2).

JURORS IN CAPITAL CASES

Something relatively new in the debate on capital punishment is the examination of juror behavior in capital cases. The Capital Jury Project in particular has brought forth considerable information on how jurors go about making the decision to vote for or against capital punishment. Unfortunately, much of this information is quite disturbing.

First, many jurors make the decision in favor of the death penalty too soon. Specifically, 30% of jurors in capital cases make the decision at the guilt stage, prior to the penalty stage. This means that 3 out of 10 capital jurors decide on the sentence before they have a chance to hear the evidence about sentencing (Bowers, Fleury-Steiner, & Antonio, 2003).

Second, many jurors hold inaccurate beliefs about how many years a prisoner would have to serve in prison if he received a prison sentence instead of the death penalty. For example, in both Alabama and California, the mandatory minimum sentence that a prisoner would have to serve would be LWOP. However, jurors thought the mandatory minimum sentences in those two states were 15 and 17 years, respectively. Therefore, jurors thought prisoners would be out in a decade and a half, whereas the statutes stipulated LWOP. Such erroneous beliefs about alternative prison terms can easily influence jurors to vote for the death penalty to prevent perceived heinous murderers from being released from prison.

Third, capital jurors are often confused about mitigating factors, which are a critical part of the decision to impose the death penalty. Many jurors mistakenly think that mitigating factors must be proven beyond a reasonable doubt or that all jurors must agree that a factor is a mitigator (Bowers et al., 2003).

Finally, as we noted previously, the Capital Jury Project has thrown new light on the issue of the impact of race on the capital punishment decision. If there is no black juror on the jury, compared to the presence of at least one black male juror, a death sentence is twice as likely. In trials with no black juror, death sentences resulted 71.9% of the time versus 37.5% of the cases that had at least one black male juror (Bowers et al., 2003). It appears that the presence of at least one black male juror can convince the other jurors to consider the evidence more deliberately.

RELIGION AND CAPITAL PUNISHMENT

Many people use religion to justify their views on the death penalty. This is not the place for a thorough theological debate on the death penalty, but because the death penalty debate often includes religious arguments, we think it important to note some of the Judeo-Christian-based religious arguments surrounding capital punishment.

Sister Helen Prejean is a powerful example of someone who sees the message of Christ and Christianity as condemning the death penalty. While she was a nun working with the poor in New Orleans, a friend asked her to become a spiritual advisor for a death row inmate. That led to being a spiritual advisor for additional inmates and a book and movie entitled *Dead Man Walking* (Prejean, 1994). In the book, she outlines her opposition to the death penalty. For example, she once asked a warden the following question:

> Do you really believe that Jesus, who taught us not to return hate for hate and evil for evil and whose dying words were, 'Father, forgive them,' would participate in these executions? Would Jesus pull the switch?
>
> **Prejean (1994, p. 122)**

Yet many Christians apparently do not see a contradiction between Sister Prejean's merciful Jesus and a perceived duty to execute. Many Christians point to Paul's *Letter to the Romans* (13.4) as proof that God endorses the death penalty when used appropriately (see, e.g., the June 2000 Southern Baptist Convention Resolution on Capital Punishment (www.sbc.net/resolutions/)) (supporting "the fair and equitable use of capital punishment by civil magistrates as a legitimate form of punishment for those guilty of murder or treasonous acts that result in death").

Some see the story of Jesus and the woman caught in adultery as another indicator of Jesus' stance against the death penalty. In this incident, the religious leaders brought to Jesus a woman allegedly caught in the act of adultery. The typical penalty was capital punishment, but Jesus told the questioners that "he who is without sin should cast the first stone." Ashamed, they all walked away (John 8:1–11). Many see this as evidence of Jesus' rejection of the death penalty.

One scholar disagrees. H. Wayne House argues that, in this incident, Jesus is really concerned about the other party, the man who also committed adultery. House argues that, under Mosaic Law, both parties to adultery should be charged. Furthermore, the witnesses are guilty of a capital crime by charging only the woman. House argues that here Jesus is taking the procedural issues very seriously and thus is not condemning capital punishment but calling for correct process (House, 1997).

In their official statement on the death penalty, U.S. Catholic bishops urged fellow Christians "to remember the teaching of Jesus who called us to be reconciled with those who have injured us" (Matthew 5:43–45) and to pray for forgiveness for our sins "as we forgive those who have sinned against us" (Matthew 6:12) (U.S. Catholic Bishops' Statement on Capital Punishment, 1980, p. 7).

Although Biblical scholars and theologians can argue about these and other passages, Sister Prejean's comment that it seems incongruous that the Jesus who preaches love and forgiveness (e.g., "Love your neighbor as yourself"; "Forgive seven times seventy") would favor capital punishment seems logical. Furthermore, societal conditions have changed considerably since the time of Jesus. Lengthy prison terms were not the norm (nor a viable alternative to capital punishment) 2000 years ago, when Jesus walked the earth, but they are quite possible today.

Several Christian churches have issued formal statements against capital punishment based on their interpretation of the teachings of Jesus. For example, both the Roman Catholic Church and the Presbyterian Church have issued formal statements opposing the death penalty (U.S. Catholic Bishops' Statement on Capital Punishment, 1980; Presbyterian Moratorium on Capital Punishment). However, as noted, the Southern Baptist Convention has issued a statement in favor of the death penalty.

Theologian George Boyd has an interesting opinion about the death penalty. He opposes the death penalty because he thinks that a convicted murderer might think that his or her debt to society can be paid by accepting the death penalty. Boyd does not want any murderer to be able to feel that way: "Murderers should never be allowed the comfort of the illusion that they can 'pay' for their crime" (Boyd, 1988, p. 163).

In conclusion, churches and theologians are not in agreement over the death penalty. Some religious people, such as Sister Helen Prejean, are very active in trying to abolish the death penalty. Others, however, such as the Southern Baptist Convention, endorse capital punishment. It is somewhat perplexing that followers of the same religious leader, Jesus Christ, sincerely maintain dramatically different positions on such a fundamental issue as the death penalty. Perhaps this controversy indicates that believers must struggle with such basic issues and try to come up with a workable solution.

ALTERNATIVES TO THE DEATH PENALTY

If states were to abolish the death penalty, the most likely current alternative would be a sentence of life without any possibility of parole. In recent years, this option has been mentioned most frequently as an alternative punishment. A 2006 Gallup Poll examining American opinion about the death penalty found that when given a choice between the sentencing options of **LWOP** and the death penalty, only 47% of respondents chose capital punishment. Forty-eight percent favored life without parole for those convicted of murder. The poll also revealed that overall support for the death penalty remained low at 65%, down significantly from 1994 when 80% supported capital punishment (Death Penalty Information Center, 2006).

Some utilitarians question LWOP in terms of costs. Assuming that it costs approximately $20,000 to keep an offender in prison for 1 year and assuming about 50 years of incarceration for a typical murderer, LWOP could easily cost the state about $1 million per inmate. That is a considerable expense. It is not uncommon to hear citizens question the expenditure of so much money on someone who has taken a human life ("Why should I as a taxpayer have to pay to keep a murderer alive?").

Opponents of the death penalty contend that it is, in fact, more expensive to execute a murderer sentenced to capital punishment. This statement at first seems difficult to believe, but capital cases take extra time and money, states mandate at least one court appeal, defendants usually pursue additional discretionary appeals, and death rows can be expensive if the inmates are not working. When all the costs of capital punishment are added up it can cost the state from $2.5 to $5 million to execute one individual (Bohm, 2012, p. 188).

To be fair, if capital punishment was abolished and LWOP was the most serious penalty, it is likely that murderers would pursue many appeals of that sentence as well. It also seems reasonable, though, that trials and other costs of LWOP sentences would never come to equal the time and expense of capital punishment verdicts.

Many murderers would probably accept LWOP sentences instead of capital punishment. Most seem to want to stay alive even if it means endless years in prison. However, it is important to note that not every murderer would agree. One murderer on death row, for example, was very clear in insisting that he was not desirous of spending the rest of his natural life on death row. In his words, he did not want to be "locked in Hell for all of eternity" (Arriens, 1997, p. 82).

The other alternative to the death penalty is a life sentence with the possibility of parole. This option is not very popular at present. Most of the research focuses on either the death penalty or LWOP. A major reason seems to be public sentiment; the public wants murderers either executed or locked up permanently.

An argument in favor of the possibility of parole for murderers is the fact that some murderers succeed quite favorably on parole. The ABC television channel did a fascinating documentary about 20 years ago that followed the lives of 40 death row inmates in California. A state appeals court overturned the death penalty in California, and the death row prisoners (108 of them at the time) became eligible for parole. Over the years, the parole board paroled 40 inmates.

BOX 12.3 SCOTT TUROW'S COMMENTS ON THE DEATH PENALTY

Scott Turow, the author of such best-selling novels as *Presumed Innocent* and *Reversible Errors*, was a prosecutor who served on a governor's commission in Illinois looking into the death penalty in that state.

On one hand, he notes that he himself would be willing to inject the fatal poison if the murderer were a killer such as John Wayne Gacy, who tortured and killed 33 young men. Along these lines, he and the other members of the commission voted to limit capital punishment to five criteria: multiple murders, murder of a police officer or firefighter, a killing in prison, a murder impeding the criminal justice system, or a murder with torture.

On the other hand, Turow is painfully aware that "[n]ow and then, we will execute someone who is innocent ..." (Turow, 2003, p. 47). Thus, when the commission came to a final vote on whether Illinois should have the death penalty or not, Turow reports, "I voted no" (Turow, 2003, p. 47).

Thirty-four of the individuals "succeeded"—got jobs, married, raised kids, and even did such things as speaking to high school students to try to encourage them to live positive lives and stay out of crime. Some failed, however; one committed a new murder and one committed a horrible rape.

Although the current climate is not favorable for the option of life with the possibility of parole, evidence that some parole murderers do so well in terms of jobs, relationships, and parenting raises the issue that perhaps this should be an option for some. (See Box 12.3 for Scott Turow's comments on the death penalty.)

CONCLUSION

In this chapter, we tried to present some of the ethical questions about the death penalty. This chapter is not meant to provide complete coverage of the topic. For further coverage, see Bohm (2012) or Costanzo (1997).

Utilitarians would consider the consequences of the death penalty, such as deterrence, incapacitation, mistakes, and discrimination. Deontologists would consider the duty to punish and whether the death penalty is the deserved penalty for murder or whether other penalties, such as life without parole, can be a sufficient punishment for the crime of murder. The peacemaking perspective focuses on the core principles of caring, connectedness, and mindfulness as they pertain to the death penalty. As we have noted, many people also bring religious arguments into the debate.

What each person must do is examine the reasons for his or her current position on the death penalty and ask if those reasons seem sufficient. If they do not, the individual should investigate further and come to a new position that is in line with the information that is currently available about the death penalty and its administration.

■ Learn More on the Internet

For more information on the death penalty, go to www.deathpenalty-info.org.   ■

CASE STUDY 12–1 POLITICS OR ETHICS? A GOVERNOR'S PREROGATIVE

"Joe, get in here. It looks like trouble with that DA down in Blackshear County."

The governor's middle-aged chief of staff sat down on the leather chair facing the governor's desk, a fax in his hand.

"It looks pretty bad, Governor. Boscoe's the DA down there. It looks like a major political screw-up, not to mention a legal nightmare."

Roy Maden, the governor of his great state, drummed his fingers impatiently on his desktop. "And of course,

Boscoe just happens to be one of the most vocal and high-profile Republicans in our fine state. That will be just dandy with me running for election next year. The Democrats will have a field day."

Joe shifted in his chair as he looked solemnly at his friend of many years.

"No question about Boscoe's political ambition. He has a perfect batting average with capital cases. He's sent 'em all to death row. Fact is, he's sent a little over four times as many to the row as any other DA in the state. Most

Continued

CASE STUDY 12–1 POLITICS OR ETHICS? A GOVERNOR'S PREROGATIVE *Continued*

of the folks around here feel like he's setting himself up for a run at governor after you finish your next term."

"Well, 'the best laid plans of mice and men'... Boscoe the Bozo wasn't counting that group of law students and their professor taking a closer look at his cases."

Governor Maden rubbed his forehead as he stared out his office window.

"Joe, what's the bottom line?"

"According to the legal and forensics experts I've talked to, there's pretty solid buzz that at least a quarter of his cases are bogus and there are questions about a number of others. Missing DNA that's supposed to be on file, withholding evidence from defense attorneys, and even worse, the names of two detectives keep popping up in the most suspicious cases."

The governor's eyes widened. "You don't mean ...?"

"Yes, sir, it looks like a criminal conspiracy could be involved."

Roy Maden could feel a headache coming on.

"Give it to me straight, Joe. What are my options?"

Joe stroked his chin and considered the choices at hand before speaking.

"You could stall the investigation until after you are reelected, then go after Boscoe. The downside is that two of the inmates on death row are out of appeals and are scheduled to be executed before the election. I've checked their rap sheets, and they both have a long list of assaults. Some of our folks say that the world would be better off without them."

The governor looked intently at his trusted friend.

"What do you say, Joe?"

Questions

1. Discuss the various choices the governor could make from utilitarian, deontological, and peacemaking perspectives.
2. What would be the most moral and ethical course of action the governor could take? What would be the probable consequences for the governor, the district attorney, and death row inmates?

Discussion Questions

1. How serious an ethical issue is the problem of mistakes relating to the death penalty? Is the death penalty ethical if there is only one mistake a year? One every 5 years? Is perfection necessary? Why or why not?
2. Discuss the relative merits and problems of a sentence of life without parole versus the death penalty. Which seems more ethical? What are the problems of each?
3. Would death penalty opponents really be satisfied if life without parole became the most serious penalty? If the death penalty were abolished, would death penalty opponents then try to abolish life without parole, claiming it to be too harsh?
4. Discuss religious arguments for and against the death penalty. What do you think religion suggests we should do about the death penalty?

REFERENCES

Arriens, J. (Ed.). (1997). *Welcome to hell: Letters and writings from death row*. Boston: Northeastern University Press.

Baldus, D. C., & Woodworth, G. (2003). Race discrimination in the administration of the death penalty: An overview of the empirical evidence with special emphasis on the post-1990 research. *Criminal Law Bulletin, 39,* 194–226.

Bedau, H. A. (1997). Prison homicides, recidivist murder, and life imprisonment. In H. A. Bedau (Ed.), *The death penalty in America* (pp. 176–182). New York: Oxford University Press.

Bohm, R. M. (2012). *Deathquest: An introduction to the theory and practice of capital punishment in the United States* (4th ed.). Boston: Elsevier (Anderson Publishing).

Bowers, W. J., Fleury-Steiner, B. D., & Antonio, M. E. (2003). The capital sentencing decision: Guided discretion, reasoned moral judgment, or legal fiction. In J. R. Acker, R. M. Bohm, & C. S. Lanier (Eds.), *America's experiment with capital punishment: Reflections on the past, present, and future of the ultimate penal sanction* (pp. 413–467). Durham: Carolina Academic Press.

Bowers, W. J., & Foglia, W. D. (2003). Still singularly agonizing: Law's failure to purge arbitrariness from capital sentencing. *Criminal Law Bulletin, 39,* 51–86.

Boyd, G. N. (February 17, 1988). *Capital punishment: Deserved and wrong.* Christian Century pp. 162–165.

Cabana, D. A. (1996). *Death at midnight: The confession of an executioner.* Boston: Northeastern University Press.

Chamlin, M. B., & Cochran, J. K. (2000). Deterrence and brutalization: The dual effects of executions. *Justice Quarterly, 17,* 685–706.

Costanzo, M. (1997). *Just revenge: Costs and consequences of the death penalty.* New York: St. Martin's Press.

Death Penalty Information Center (2006). *New Gallup Poll reveals growing number of Americans favors life without parole.* Retrieved at www.deathpenaltyinfo.org/node/1738.

Death Penalty Information Center (2013). *Death row inmates by state.* Retrieved at www.deathpenaltyinfo.org/death-row-inmates-state-and-size-death-row-year.

van den Haag, E. (2003). Justice, deterrence and the death penalty. In J. R. Acker, R. M. Bohm, & C. S. Lanier (Eds.), *America's experiment with capital punishment: Reflections on the past, present, and future of the ultimate penal sanction* (pp. 223–249). Durham: Carolina Academic Press.

House, H. W. (1997). The new testament and moral arguments for capital punishment. In H. A. Bedau (Ed.), *The death penalty in America: Current controversies* (pp. 415–428). New York: Oxford University Press.

Johnson, R. (1998). *Death work: A study of the modern execution process.* Belmont: West/Wadsworth.

Lezin, K. (1999). *Finding life on death row: Profiles of six inmates.* Boston: Northeastern University Press.

Liebman, J. S., Fagan, J., & West, V. (2000). *A broken system: Error rates in capital cases.* Retrieved at www.law.Columbia.edu/instructionalservices/liebman.

Lundman, R. J. (1993). *Prevention and control of juvenile delinquency* (2nd ed.). New York: Oxford University Press.

Mandery, E. J. (2003). The principles of proportionality review. *Criminal Law Bulletin, 39,* 157–193.

Marquart, J. W., & Sorensen, J. R. (1997). *Correctional contexts: Contemporary and classic readings.* Los Angeles: Roxbury.

Masters, J. J. (1997). *Finding freedom: Writings from death row.* Junction City: Padma.

Mello, M., & Perkins, P. J. (2003). Closing the circle: The illusion of lawyers for people litigating for their lives at the Fin de Siècle. In J. R. Acker, R. M. Bohm, & C. S. Lanier (Eds.), *America's experiment with capital punishment: Reflections on the past, present, and future of the ultimate penal sanction* (pp. 347–384). Durham: Carolina Academic Press.

Peterson, R. D., & Bailey, W. C. (2003). Is capital punishment an effective deterrent for murder? An examination of social science research. In J. R. Acker, R. M. Bohm, & C. S. Lanier (Eds.), *America's experiment with capital punishment: Reflections on the past, present, and future of the ultimate penal sanction* (pp. 251–282). Durham: Carolina Academic Press.

Prejean, H. (1994). *Dead man walking: An eyewitness account of the death penalty in the United States.* New York: Vintage Books.

Schlosser, E. (2003). *Reefer madness: Sex, drugs, and cheap labor in the American Black Market.* Boston: Houghton Mifflin.

Sellin, T. (1980). *The penalty of death.* Beverly Hills: Sage.

Snell, T. L. (2013). *Capital punishment, 2011—Statistical tables.* Washington, DC: U.S. Department of Justice. Retrieved at www.bjs.gov/content/pub/pdf/cp11st.pdf.

Turow, S. (January 6, 2003). *To kill or not to kill: Coming to terms with capital punishment.* The New Yorker (pp. 40–47).

United States Conference of Catholic Bishops (1980). *Statement on capital punishment.* Available at www.usccb.org/sdwp/national/criminal/death/uscc80.shtml.

Ethical Issues in Corrections

What lies behind us and what lies before us are tiny matters compared to what lies within us.

Ralph Waldo Emerson

Can offenders be corrected by encouraging them to behave more ethically? By teaching them how to recognize and analyze moral dilemmas? While few would argue that this practice alone will dissuade many people from crime, it is equally clear that an ability to assess the harmfulness of one's acts and to anticipate consequences may be prerequisites to moral and law-abiding conduct. Given that ability, one can then specify the skills and contexts likely to encourage ethical conduct.

Correctional staffs inside and outside institutional boundaries also need to know how to assess moral dilemmas and how to behave in an ethical fashion. Too often, situational factors work against this objective. Many correctional institutions are plagued by high staff turnover, which means that a high percentage of guards are rookies. These individuals must confront a population of offenders housed in crowded circumstances, inmates whose chief objective is to do their time with as little discomfort as possible. Prison inmates are generally quite interested in paying off guards to improve their living circumstances, to turn a blind eye to various institutional infractions, and/or to bring illicit substances or weapons into the institution. Because these inmates may know as much about running the institution as some of the guards, it is often very easy for correctional officers to become dependent on inmates for assistance in doing their jobs, only to find that inmates expect something in return.

Probation and parole officers face different but related problems. The "burned-out" probation or parole officer may be as reluctant to supervise his or her clients as the "burned-out" police officer is to answer calls. Or misuse of authority might mean that a probationer or parolee is harassed by his or her supervisor. Discrimination results when the conditions of release are enforced differently against certain offenders.

The ultimate power of the probation or parole officer is the ability to initiate revocation proceedings that can send the offender to prison. The challenge is to use this authority in the same manner as the ethical police officer employs his or her coercive power—with an understanding of humanity but with a willingness to intervene for the greater good.

While probation and parole officers have worked hard to establish themselves as professionals, correctional officers have had greater difficulty in this regard, largely because the positions often require little education and offer very low pay. For many persons, working as a correctional officer is only an interim job.

The Federal Bureau of Prisons offers a notable exception to this pattern. There, the correctional officer's position is viewed as the entry point on a career ladder. This practice, employed in conjunction with the conscientious screening of new employees and the use of a management scheme that serves to discourage corruption, works to make the federal prison system an environment more likely to promote high ethical standards.

CHAPTER 13

Ethical Issues in Probation, Parole, and Community Corrections

John T. Whitehead

INTRODUCTION

Probation and parole are critical parts of corrections. In 2011 (the latest figures available), more than 3.9 million adults were on probation, and more than 860,000 adults were on parole. High percentages of both probationers and parolees were on supervision for drug offenses (approximately 25% of probationers and 33% of parolees) (Maruschak & Parks, 2012).

It is no accident that more movies and television shows are made about police officers than about probation and parole officers. Because probation and parole are not as dramatic as policing, the ethical issues in probation, parole, and other types of community correctional programs are somewhat more ordinary. Probation and parole officers simply do not have the opportunities to become involved in dramatic matters, such as the drug busts and corruption, involving some police officers in large cities.

This does not mean that there are no ethical issues in probation and parole. It just means that the issues are usually less dramatic and more subtle. This chapter will discuss some of the problems that can arise in probation and parole work, including ethical issues concerning intensive supervision, electronic monitoring, and house arrest.

Before delving into the ethical issues in community corrections, it may be helpful to state some assumptions. In this chapter, it is assumed that there are certain values to guide ethical choices, such as truth, honesty, fairness, hard work, and consideration for others. For this discussion, it does not matter whether these values are considered moral absolutes or simply mutually agreed upon conventions. Whatever their sources, the following discussion assumes such values exist and that most individuals subscribe to them. For example, it is assumed that it is ethical for probation and parole employees to put in a full day's work for a full day's pay. Employees who do less are considered to be acting unethically.

THE MISSION OF PROBATION AND PAROLE

The major ethical issue in probation and parole is the definition of the mission of community supervision. This refers to deciding on the purpose or objective of supervision. Traditionally, the mission of probation and parole supervision has been described as some combination of assistance and control, treatment and security, or service and surveillance (Skeem & Manchak, 2008; Studt, 1973). In other words, officers are supposed to provide services to offenders while also monitoring them so that the community is protected from new crimes.

In the last few years, a number of voices have been calling for corrections to revert back to a very punishment-oriented philosophy. It is not unusual to hear calls for Spartan prisons with few or no amenities for prisoners. Critics have voiced their opposition to television (both cable and regular broadcast programing), weight-lifting equipment, and athletics as needless frills that prisoners, by virtue of their crimes, simply do not deserve. Extremists call for the reinstatement of chain gangs, while slightly less strident souls simply suggest hard labor for all prisoners to keep them busy and to punish them for their transgressions.

The community corrections corollary to this would be stringent supervision: frequent reporting, curfews, work or community service requirements, fines, supervision fees, and drug testing. These measures would make probation and parole as punitive as possible. The mission would be punishment, pure and simple. The role of the officer would be to make sure that the punishment is being delivered.

Just as prison extremists urge the return of chain gangs, probation-parole extremists urge several harsh changes for community supervision offenders. One is the wearing of an insignia to mark one's status as an offender. Offenders would wear shirts or vests or license plates proclaiming their status as an offender (e.g., "drunk driver," "shoplifter," etc.) to the world as they shop at the mall or drive down the street. Society would mark offenders with a "scarlet letter": "D" for drunk driver or "S" for shoplifter, just as puritan New England branded the Hester Prynnes of its day for adultery. (This issue will be considered further in a later section concerning acceptable penal content.)

The new penology (Feeley & Simon, 1992) takes a less strident stance and argues that probation and parole should be efficient monitors of the conditions of supervision. If an offender fails to follow the conditions of supervision, then the officer should be swift to report the failure to the court or the parole board. Sufficiently serious or frequent violations would land the offender in prison. Ironically, failure becomes success in this model. Whereas old-fashioned officers who aimed for the rehabilitation of offenders would consider recidivism (new crimes) a failure of supervision, new penology officers would consider a new crime a success as long as it is noted and used to get the offender back into prison. Here, the officer claims that one is doing one's job because signs of continuing criminal tendencies are used to get the offender off the street. The objective is to classify offenders into various categories of risk and to place them into the proper risk-management response. There is no pretense of trying to rehabilitate or cure the offender.

The most recent variation on rethinking the mission of probation emphasizes deterrence and treatment but with modifications. First, programs in Hawaii (HOPE) and Delaware (DYT–Decide Your Time) emphasize the certainty and swiftness aspects of deterrence rather than severe punishments (O'Connell, Visher, Martin, Parker, & Brent, 2011). Second, these programs offer treatment options but only make treatment compulsory for those who fail. Some of the key components are clear rules, strict monitoring of compliance, including frequent drug testing, and graduated sanctions for rule breaking, especially positive drug tests. Preliminary research has shown that HOPE probationers did better in drug testing and revocations of probation than regular probationers (Hawken & Kleiman, 2009). The federal government has funded replications of HOPE in other states.

One of the most hopeful philosophies of probation and parole is the restorative justice model. This model of criminal justice is concerned with reparation to the victim and involvement of the victim in the criminal justice process, remorse and accountability for offenders, and peace and justice for the community (McDowell & Whitehead, 2009). This model argues that neither punishment nor treatment alone is effective in changing offenders or restoring the victim or the community to its precrime state. Instead, the model focuses on reparation, restitution, dialogue, and negotiation in order to restore the victim and the community to its precrime state. The model involves both a micro dimension (offender reparation and restitution to the victim[s]) and a macro dimension (a community responsibility for crime control and the need for order and safety in the community).

One ethical issue underlying these reconceptualizations of the mission of probation and parole is the question of what society owes the offender. The easy answer is that society owes the offender nothing. The criminal has broken the law, and he or she must pay his or her debt to society. This view is congruent with classical or neoclassical theories of criminal behavior that emphasize free will and accountability (for more discussion, see, for example, Miller, Schreck, & Tewksbury, 2008). Offenders are seen as choosing crime and as responsible for their actions. The only questions are the determination of the debt the offender must pay to society and the control of the offender so new crimes are prevented. Thus, the focus is on retribution, deterrence, and incapacitation. There is little or no emphasis on assistance to the offender.

Positivist theories of crime, on the other hand, contend that crime is not so simple. Biological, psychological, and sociological factors explain criminal behavior (Miller, Schreck, & Tewksbury, 2008). Human behavior reflects all sorts of influences, ranging from genetic makeup to parental upbringing to the availability of educational and job opportunities. Positivist perspectives imply that society has a responsibility to assist the offender because societal factors have contributed to the criminal behavior. Thus, there is a direct link between positivist perspectives and programs to assist offenders in prison and in the community. Furthermore, research on correctional treatment indicates that programs not only are logical implications of positivism but that they in fact are effective in reducing recidivism (Lipsey & Cullen, 2007).

The peacemaking perspective outlined in an earlier chapter in this book suggests that all of us have a responsibility to the offender. The principles of caring and connectedness imply that we cannot just ignore offenders—that our common humanity is the basis for remembering that offenders are like us and want and deserve humane treatment and assistance.

The ethical question is this: Can society embrace a neoclassical perspective—assume offenders are totally free and responsible—and simply ignore any consideration of assistance to offenders? Or does society have some obligation to help offenders to some degree?

Research suggests an answer to this question. The ideal probation program appears to be a balance of punishment and treatment. The punishment side includes monitoring of probation conditions, taking action if the probationer violates the conditions, and also enforcing such punitive conditions as paying court costs, fines, and restitution. The treatment side involves recognizing that the probation officer has a critical role in helping to motivate the offender to change and in monitoring the offender's progress. One approach is to set up a behavioral contract with the probationer so that the offender earns points for treatment attendance and other positive activities. A leading proponent of

BOX 13.1 VOTING RIGHTS FOR PROBATIONERS/PAROLEES

In 2001, Connecticut passed a law restoring the voting rights of convicted felons on probation. As a result, about 36,000 felons on probation were given back the right to vote.

The original intent of laws limiting voting rights was to punish criminals. Efforts such as the Connecticut law arose out of several concerns. One concern was the disproportionate racial impact of laws denying voting rights to felons. For example, in Connecticut, it was estimated that about 20% of the state's adult black male population could not vote because they were in prison or on probation or parole. Another concern was that such laws are unfair.

One reason is that these citizens had other responsibilities of citizens, such as paying taxes, so denying them the right to vote was taxation without representation. What do you think? Are states such as Connecticut correct to now allow felons on probation to vote? Or, for at least some period of time, is it fair to deny voting privileges to felons as a collateral punishment for their crimes?

For details on the law change in Connecticut, see McMiller (2008). "The Campaign to Restore the Voting Rights of People Convicted of a Felony and Sentenced to Probation in Connecticut." *American Behavioral Scientist, 51*, pp. 645–658.

---

this model, Faye Taxman, argues that the objectives should be realistic, such as lowering overall recidivism from a current average of 45% to a significantly lower average of 35% (Taxman, 2008).

An evaluation of a probation program in Maryland that used the new model of probation showed promising results. Probationers were given risk assessments, probation officers used motivational interviewing techniques, and offenders were given three goals a month, including participation in treatment services. Only 30% of the new probationers were arrested during 2 years versus 42% of the control group (Taxman, 2008).

So the best current answer seems to be a reasonable blend of punishment and treatment, not a strident call for overly harsh models of probation and parole. This seems to make the most sense ethically and in light of the research evidence.

(For a related discussion of allowing probationers to vote, see Box 13.1.)

THE EFFECTIVENESS OF COMMUNITY CORRECTIONS

Both probation and parole have had questions raised about their **effectiveness**. Although probation is often effective, a disturbing study of felons on probation found that 65% were rearrested within 40 months of being placed on probation (Petersilia, Turner, Kahan, & Peterson, 1985). Subsequent research has indicated that this particular study indicated an unusually high rate. Studies of felony probation in both Missouri and Kentucky showed new arrest rates at just slightly over 20%, and a study in New Jersey showed an arrest rate of 36% for approximately 3 years under supervision (Whitehead, 1991). Another positive note about probation is that 66% of probationers who exited probation in 2011 were either discharged early or completed their term (Maruschak & Parks, 2012).

The Urban Institute did a major study of parole effectiveness in 2005. Their primary conclusion was that parole does not really work. Approximately 60% of offenders either released directly from prison or released to parole supervision were rearrested within 2 years of release. Concerning parole exits, more than half (52%) of parolees who exited parole in 2011 were either discharged early or completed their sentence (Maruschak & Parks, 2012). A recent report by the Pew Center reports that 45% of inmates released in 1999 and 43% of inmates released in 2004 were reincarcerated either for a new crime or for a violation of parole within 3 years (Pew Center on the States, 2011).

A smaller study in New Jersey found a slight advantage for parolees in recidivism. Specifically, 60% of parolees were rearrested up to 4 years after release, compared to 70% of prisoners released directly from prison (Schlager & Robbins, 2008).

A documentary on parole suggests several critical issues affecting parole success rates. The documentary *A Hard Straight* (2004) looks at four California parolees as they leave prison and enter parole. One parolee has no place to live. He asks his parole officer to help him find a place to live but the officer offers no help at all. In a short period of time, this parolee absconds and then winds up back in prison. A second parolee is seen drinking a glass of wine on the train from prison back to her hometown even though we later learn that drinking was a significant problem for her before her prison sentence. Apparently, prison did little or nothing to help her with her substance abuse problems.

The ethical issue is the responsibility of society to help offenders both in prison and during the reentry process. If we as a society are releasing people from prison and they have no place to live, or if they still have a drinking problem, recidivism rates of 60% or 70% are not surprising. If a person goes into prison without a high school diploma, with no job skills, with a drinking or other drug problem, and comes out of prison with no job or no place to live, is there any reason to expect success?

A deontological approach to this issue is this question: What duty does society have to help offenders? A corresponding question for the offender is this: What is the duty of the offender to try to take advantage of programs in prison or on parole? The utilitarian perspective is the consequences of maintaining probation, prison, and parole systems that seem set up for failure rather than success. If high percentages of probationers and released offenders are committing new crimes on probation or after release, society is experiencing the costs of those new crimes and the costs of sending people back to prison instead of seeing probationers and parolees occupying responsible positions in the economy, their families, and their neighborhoods. Such costs do not appear to represent the greatest good for the greatest number.

There are two dimensions to the ethics of probation and parole supervision. One dimension is the agency or institutional dimension. Both probation and parole agencies need to have effective programs in place. They both need to have educational, job training and job placement, substance abuse, and other programs available for offenders.

The second dimension is the individual dimension. Each officer has a duty to work effectively with his or her probationers/parolees to help them take advantage of the programs that are available. In the documentary noted above, one parole officer was very concerned about her parolee and was trying to get her to see that her drinking was a significant problem, a problem directly related to criminal activity in her case. However, the parole officer who was explaining the conditions of parole supervision to the new parolee who had no place to live seemed uncaring. Granted, he noted that the parole agency no longer had a program for linking parolees to places to reside. However, he seemed burned out and appeared to offer no assistance at all. One would hope that a parole officer would be aware of shelters or halfway houses and could at least tell such a parolee that Shelter X or Place Y could take the offender in for a few nights while the offender and the officer together tried to figure out a plan.

Both the agency and the officer need to be working to help probationers and parolees with problems, such as education, substance abuse, job training, and overall adjustment. If either the agency or the officer neglects his or her responsibilities, recidivism is more likely to result.

The Ethics of Probation Fees

Offender fees in probation appear to be on the increase. There are two types of fees: program fees and service fees. Program fees are supervision fees charged to all probationers to pay for the cost of supervision. Service fees are charged for the receipt of specific services, such as drug treatment programs or anger management programs. Only the probationers who are ordered or referred to such service programs pay these service fees.

Probationers or parolees may pay up to $100 a month in supervision fees and a recent article noted that at least 28 states were charging supervision fees and that fees might generate more than one-half of an agency's operating budget (Teague, 2011).

Some states (e.g., Georgia and Tennessee) have turned over supervision of misdemeanant probationers to private companies that charge fees and possibly get a percentage of the fines and court costs they collect.

A major ethical concern is the ability of probation and parole clients to pay fees, fines, and court costs. A study in Washington State showed how quickly such costs can mount. That study showed that a random sample of 500 offenders had been assessed an average of $11,471 by the courts (Beckett & Harris, 2011). As offenders have difficulty finding employment, and especially finding employment that pays well, fees, fines, and court costs can easily become insurmountable.

One consequence of this has been labeled "**back-end net-widening.**" What this means is that probationers are initially (on the front end) diverted from prison: they are placed on probation instead of being sent to prison. But perhaps 1 year into probation, they might be brought up on a violation for failing to pay supervision fees, fines, or court costs. If the violation results in the revocation of their probation, they could be sent to prison. Hence, the term "*back-end* net-widening." Offenders who initially were considered suitable for a sentence in the community, now (on the back end, so to speak) are being sent to prison.

Another concern is to what extent such fee-based probation becomes focused on collecting fees, fines, and court costs. Given the lucrative nature of collecting such fees (Teague, 2011), some probation agencies might easily divert their energies to whatever enhances financial coffers instead of what probationers need.

To put a human face on this, consider a probationer who works a minimum-wage job and has to pay even $45 a month for a supervision fee (the fee in one state a few years ago). Add to that court costs, fines, restitution, and so on, of perhaps $100 a month. It would take 6.2 h to earn the $45 supervision fee and 13.9 h to earn the $100 monthly costs. So the probationer would be handing over 3 days' pay to pay for all these fees and costs. Given fixed costs such as rent and gasoline for one's car, it is easy to see that fees and other costs can easily become overly burdensome. It is not inconceivable that an offender could even be tempted to turn to crime to pay his or her fees. Or a probationer might be forced to get a second job even if that second job interferes with how much time the offender can spend with children or a spouse.

So the ethical issue is whether it is ethical to charge such fees and, if so, how much would be excessive? A utilitarian perspective might argue that if fees are leading to a significant proportion of probation violation revocations and returns to prison, then those negative financial consequences are so detrimental as to place the practice in question. Some have concluded that excessive fees are setting up probationers to fail. The costs are so burdensome and the probationers are so financially strapped that it is inevitable that they will fall behind in payments. Then the probation department will bring them up on revocation charges and they will be found to be in violation of probation. By the way, this is very similar to payday loan companies that lend money to financially strapped individuals and set them up for constant re-borrowing at high interest rates (see Brook, 2009).

ACCEPTABLE PENAL CONTENT

In the discussion of the **mission of probation and parole**, it was noted that extremists argue that some offenders should wear shirts or bumper stickers marking them as drunk drivers, shoplifters, or whatever crime the person has been convicted of. In a thought-provoking piece, von Hirsch (1990) notes the ethical concern that any such innovations not insult or demean offenders but satisfy the standard of **acceptable penal content**[1]:

> "Acceptable penal content, then, is the idea that a sanction should be devised so that its intended penal deprivations are those that can be administered in a manner that is clearly consistent with the offender's dignity. If the penal deprivation includes a given imposition, X, then one must ask whether that can be undergone by offenders in a reasonably self-possessed fashion. Unless one is confident that it can, it should not be a part of the sanction."
>
> **von Hirsch, 1990, p. 167**

Thus, von Hirsch is opposed to shirts or bumper stickers for offenders that make drunk drivers advertise their offense because there "is no way a person can, with dignity, go about in public with a sign admitting himself or herself to be a moral pariah" (1990, p. 168). Similarly, he would be opposed to chain gangs because it is not possible to undergo such a measure with any sense of dignity.

Proponents of identifying labels for offenders would argue that they enhance the punishment value of community corrections. Such marks make probation or parole tougher rather than a lenient "slap on the wrist." Supporters would also argue that there may be deterrent value in the measures. It is embarrassing to wear such markings, and this could serve to deter others from drunk driving or whatever offense results in the added penalty.

von Hirsch also relates the concept of acceptable penal content to home visits. Traditionally, probation and parole officers have made unannounced home visits to check on offenders and to offer assistance and counseling. von Hirsch approves of such visits

> "only as a mechanism to help enforce another sanction that does meet our suggested standard of acceptable penal content. ... It is not plausible to assert that, without any other need for it, the punishment for a given type of crime should be that state agents will periodically snoop into one's home."
>
> **von Hirsch, 1990, p. 169**

INTENSIVE SUPERVISION ISSUES

For the last decade or more, reformers have advocated intensive supervision as a way to improve regular probation and parole supervision. Giving officers smaller caseloads so that they can provide closer supervision—more frequent contacts—has been supported for both crime control and rehabilitation goals. Intensive supervision raises some ethical concerns.

The major concern about intensive supervision can be labeled a "truth in advertising" issue. Intensive supervision has been promoted as the cure for the failure of traditional probation to decrease the recidivism of felony offenders. The major problem with this claim is that it is simply not true. A major evaluation of several intensive supervision programs concluded that there were no differences between intensive and routine supervision programs (Petersilia, Peterson, & Turner, 1992). Many offenders do benefit from the programs, but intensive supervision is not a panacea or cure-all for the ills of ordinary probation. However, research indicates that treatment-oriented intensive supervision—rather than supervision with no treatment dimensions—is effective at reducing recidivism and reducing costs (Barnoski, 2009; see also, Petersilia, 1997). Second, the programs divert some offenders from prison, but not as many as had been anticipated. Many of the offenders placed into intensive supervision programs would have gone into regular probation if the intensive programs were not available. One study estimated that only one-half of the offenders placed into the program studied would have gone to prison if the program had not been available to judges (Whitehead, Miller, & Myers, 1995). Third, ironically, intensive supervision programs can and do operate to increase prison populations. The more intensive monitoring involved in these programs (e.g., urinalysis testing) can lead to the detection of illegal drug use or other offenses, which can result in violations. Therefore, offenders on intensive supervision face a higher risk of being detected for behaviors that will send them to prison than do offenders on regular supervision (see Clear & Braga, 1995). Fourth, although intensive supervision can be less expensive than prison, it is more expensive than ordinary supervision.

The ethical issue is whether to continue to promote intensive supervision as a means to reduce recidivism and to reduce prison populations when, in fact, intensive supervision fails to achieve the dramatic results many had promised. Probably the most honest summary statement about intensive supervision is that it can serve as a probation enhancement. It can make probation tougher than it used to be. This, however, is a much less dramatic claim than was originally made. One wonders if such a reduced claim will be enough to keep intensive supervision popular.

Another concern is that both punitive and risk-control conditions of intensive supervision "are applied across-the-board without much attention to the individual circumstances of the case" (Clear & Hardyman, 1990, p. 54). For example, every intensive supervision offender may be subject to urinalysis checks for drug use even though many have never shown any indication of drug use. This can create a problem of discovering that an offender is adjusting positively on supervision except for recreational marijuana use. The dilemma, then, is how to react to the drug violation. A violation and incarceration would be an ironic twist to the stated intent of many programs to divert offenders from prison. A likely scenario is that "the probation officer is forced to play a type of game—warning the offender and noting the violation but trying to avoid action unless something else happens in the case" (Clear & Hardyman, 1990, p. 54). Such game-playing is hardly new (see McCleary, 1978; for example), but it cannot be avoided in face of the fiscal fact that the "resources simply do not exist to carry out all the threats made in the ISPs [intensive supervision programs] ..." (Clear & Hardyman, 1990, p. 54).

Another ethical concern is the contention that electronic monitoring is an insidious invasion of the privacy of the home—a principle enshrined in the Fourth Amendment. Corbett and Marx (1991, p. 409) argue that electronic monitoring destroys the privacy of the home:

> "Figuratively, prisons have been dismantled, and each individual cell has been reassembled in private homes. Once homes start to serve as modular prisons and bedrooms as cells, what will become of our cherished notion of "home"? If privacy is obliterated legally in prison and if EM [electronic monitoring] provides the functional equivalent of prison at home, privacy rights for home confinees and family members are potentially jeopardized."

Such concern for any alleged violation of privacy is certainly less of a problem when it comes to sex offenders, a group of offenders who are quite likely to get house arrest with electronic monitoring. Most citizens would argue that sex offenders merit such monitoring in light of the seriousness of their crimes. Parenthetically, one company alone (BI Incorporated) had about 55,000 offenders wearing an anklet tracking device a few years ago (Wood, 2010).

In short, there are some serious problems surrounding intensive supervision, house arrest, and electronic monitoring. To expect that recent interventions are correctional cure-alls is to invite unnecessary disillusionment.

(For the related issue of probation officers carrying guns, see Box 13.2.)

BOX 13.2 ARMED PROBATION OFFICERS

It appears that more and more probation officers are carrying firearms. For example, most federal judicial districts (85 of 94) permit federal probation officers to carry firearms. Increased carrying of guns appears to be related to fears of probationers who are perceived as increasingly violent and involved in drugs (Teague, 2011).

Some agencies carry guns and have done so for years. For example, New York State Parole has authorized guns for officers for decades. This policy is related to the power of New York parole officers to arrest parole violators. In New York State, probation officers by law are permitted to carry a gun, but it is left up to each county to decide if the officer in that county probation agency can or cannot carry a gun while on duty. For information on which probation/parole agencies authorized weapon carrying and which have arrest powers, go to the website of the American Probation and Parole Association.

One ethical concern about gun carrying is whether a probationer might interpret gun carrying as in conflict with the rehabilitative mission of probation. Most clients who go to a counselor or a social worker do not imagine that he or she will be carrying a gun. So a logical question is whether a probationer who sees his or her probation officer wearing a holster will then want to confide in a gun-toting law enforcement representative? For example, might an offender who is having difficulty with her substance abuse problem fear talking about this with a probation officer who has his suit jacket off and holster and gun in plain view on his side? Or would this offender fear discussing her substance abuse problem even with a non-armed officer because all officers are system officials and hence probationers are suspicious about opening up to all officers, guns or no guns?

Many officers see the issue as one of officer safety. One officer said:

> "I'm simply amazed that there is still a debate whether probation officers should be armed or not. Are you kidding me?? Last time I checked, EVERY PERSON I COME IN CONTACT WITH IS A CONVICTED FELON. I'm not a gun-ho, cowboy officer either…" (Long, 2005; cited in Teague, 2011).

Parenthetically, the author of this chapter was a probation officer in a department that did not allow officers to carry guns. On the one hand, I felt unsafe only in a few situations over a period of 7 years. If a situation seemed dangerous, a home visit did not have to be made that day. An officer could just drive away. On the other hand, some probationers lived in public housing projects that at least seemed dangerous. Some officers carried guns in such infrequent situations despite the director's edict against carrying a firearm.

Officer Concerns in Intensive Supervision Programs

A frequently ignored consideration in the development of intensive programs is what impact such programs will have on the line personnel. Several scenarios are foreseeable. One is popular acceptance by workers. Given the greater role clarity inherent in contemporary intensive supervision programs, compared to the role ambiguity and role conflict frequently found in traditional probation, positive worker attitudes are a distinct possibility. Another possible scenario, however, is initial euphoria followed by more negative attitudes. Given the expectations of line officers to monitor offenders 24 h a day, 7 days a week, officers may temporarily experience the special aura of an exciting innovation only to sink into a depression occasioned by unrealistic expectations. Who wants to be on call all hours of the night every day of the week?

Because of the fiscal constraints on state and local government, it is very possible that officers in intensive supervision programs will be called on to perform such Herculean tasks without the resources for backups and relief. Physicians can join group practice arrangements to find some relief from never-ending demands, but the officers in these new programs will not have that luxury. There are too many state and local governments experiencing financial exigency to warrant optimism about the resources that will be allocated to correctional programs.

Another possible reaction of line officers is that officers assigned regular probation caseloads may resent the special status and pay of intensive supervision officers. Regular officers may become envious about the reduced caseloads of intensive officers, especially if officers with regular caseloads suspect that the intensive supervision officers' caseloads show little or no difference in risk levels compared to the regular probationers (Clear & Hardyman, 1990).

Evaluations of intensive supervision in Georgia, Illinois, and New Jersey have reported positive reactions of line personnel (Tonry, 1990). One partial inquiry into the effects of home confinement on a nonrepresentative sample of federal probation officers showed that the officers did not report widespread negative impacts even though overtime was routine (Beck, Klein-Saffran, & Wooten, 1990). These findings suggest that negative effects on workers are not a necessary by-product of recent innovations. More research needs to be conducted, however, before firm conclusions are drawn, especially in light of the fact that corrections employment has proven to be conducive to stress and burnout (Whitehead, 1989; Williamson, 1990).

A more specific problem that intermediate punishments may pose for correctional workers is role conflict: "a tension between his control function and his casework function, having to be both a policeman and a social worker" (Morris & Tonry, 1990, p. 183). The enforcement of the conditions of intermediate punishments, such as urinalysis checks for drug use, necessarily places the officer in the role of an enforcer because there "is no way in which effective, regular, but unpredictable urine testing ... can be made other than as a police-type function" (Morris & Tonry, 1990, p. 185).

One way to resolve this is through team supervision of offenders placed on intermediate punishments. With this approach, one team member emphasizes the enforcement of the conditions of the sanction and the other provides assistance. Another possible resolution is closer cooperation with local police (Morris & Tonry, 1990). In the State of Washington, however, it was found that many probation officers in police-probation partnerships tended to over-identify with the law enforcement role, contrary to the hopes of those who began the program (Murphy & Lutze, 2009). Whatever approach is attempted, however, the basic conflict needs to be addressed.

Offender Concerns

Another concern is the reaction of offenders to community supervision programs. Although many assume that offenders would automatically prefer intensive supervision, house arrest, or electronic monitoring to prison, research in Oregon found that one-quarter of the offenders there chose prison over intensive supervision (Petersilia, 1990). Byrne (1990, p. 23) interprets this finding to mean that "some offenders would rather interrupt their lifestyle (via incarceration) than deal with attempts to change it (via compliance with probation conditions)." Another study found some offenders opting for prison over community supervision in order to avoid financial conditions such as restitution orders (Jones, 1996). Cynics or conservatives may wonder who really cares what offenders think, but probation officers know from experience that the attitude of the offender affects, at the very least, the quality of the supervision experience for officers.

From another perspective, there is concern that class bias may affect decisions regarding which offenders are selected for these programs. Some offenders may not have a private residence and thus would be ineligible for house arrest. Some offenders may not be able to afford the supervision fees associated with either intensive supervision or house arrest, especially if those fees are high enough to offset the costs of expensive electronic monitoring equipment. Consequently, "there may well be a tendency to apply house arrest and electronic monitoring to the more privileged and to deny it to the indigent" (Morris & Tonry, 1990, pp. 217–218). In effect, this could lead to a dual system of sanctions: incarceration for the poor and alternatives for the wealthy.

PRIVATIZATION

Another ethical issue is **privatization**: whether states should privatize probation and parole services or continue to keep them public. (This topic is also considered in the chapter on ethical issues and prison.) Privatization of probation appears to be growing. About 10 states now use private probation agencies to supervise misdemeanant probationers. Private agencies are also providing specific classes or group counseling, such as anger management, alcohol and other drug assessments, domestic violence programs, job training, and others, to probationers under traditional public agency supervision (Alarid & Schloss, 2009).

Proponents of privatization argue that there are several benefits of turning over various governmental services to private corporations. One alleged benefit is the reduction of operating costs. Proponents claim that private enterprise can do things more efficiently and less expensively than the government. Government operation is equated with waste and inefficiency. Some of this is attributed to the civil service system, which guarantees job tenure except in extreme circumstances when jobs are abolished. Civil service workers are not under the same pressures as workers in private industry, who must consistently show a profit.

Opponents of privatization argue that government agencies can be efficient and effective. According to this perspective, government offices can adopt efficiency- and effectiveness-enhancing strategies just as do privately run agencies.

Perhaps the main argument against privatization is whether it is appropriate for the government to turn over functions as basic as the correctional supervision of offenders to private businesses. Many question whether the symbolic task of punishing offenders should be handed over to workers who wear uniforms that say "Brand X Corrections" rather than the "State of ____" (American Bar Association, 1986). The most dramatic example of this would be for "Brand X Corrections" to carry out capital punishment. Should the state surrender the symbolism of the state executing an offender? Less dramatically, is it right for the state to contract out prison operations that involve the deprivation of liberty and serious disciplinary measures, such as solitary confinement? Set against this context, is it ethical to allow a private company to operate a probation or parole operation that involves the very important decision of whether to allow an offender to remain in the community or be revoked for a violation and sent to prison? Or does the deprivation of liberty involve a basic right that ought not to be relinquished by the government?

Another concern with regard to privatization is whether the profit motive can debase corrections. For example, would private probation or parole agencies be under pressure to keep clients under supervision beyond an appropriate release time so as to keep caseloads and reimbursements high? Would private agencies try to pay their employees fair salaries, or would profit pressures work to minimize salaries and benefits for officers? Would private agencies try to cut services for offenders (e.g., counseling, drug treatment) to a minimum?

In the nineteenth century, the profit motive did operate to cause significant problems in many state prison systems. In one juvenile system, for example, boys were leased out to private contractors for their labor. Hardworking boys would be kept under supervision longer than necessary because the contractor did not want to lose their productivity (Pisciotta, 1982).

A survey of prosecutors and defense attorneys showed that high percentages of both groups (79% of prosecutors and 69% of defense attorneys) endorsed the use of private agency service providers. Both prosecutors and defense attorneys, however, did have concerns about private agencies. More than 50% of prosecutors and more than 40% of defense attorneys expressed concern over the staff qualifications of private agencies, and about half of prosecutors and two-thirds of attorneys expressed concerns over the costs charged to probationers going to private service providers (Alarid & Schloss, 2009).

This last issue of costs merits emphasis. A documentary on plea bargaining in Texas ("Frontline: The Plea") showed a probation system (apparently public) that emphasized probation officers collecting court costs and supervision fees from probationers who were working minimum-wage jobs, or jobs paying just slightly above the minimum-wage. Granted, taxpayers have a right to argue that criminals should pay at least some portion of court and supervision costs. On the other hand, as noted in the earlier section on probation fees, a number of probation systems, public and private, are setting probationers up to fail. If the court orders a probationer to pay $1000 or more in court costs and even a modest supervision fee of $20 a week, paying those costs off can be impossible if the offender is also trying to support himself or herself and children. So the probationer gets behind, the probation officer files a violation of probation charge, and the judge revokes probation for failure to pay. It is a contemporary version of debtors' prisons; society winds up incarcerating probationers who cannot afford costs and fees.

It could be argued that private agencies might be under even greater pressure than public agencies to emphasize fee collection. Given the need for private agencies to show cost advantages over public agencies, it is easy to imagine a private agency that would consider it a priority to collect fees and court costs in order to show a positive bottom line.

One response to such problems is spelling out a private agency's responsibilities to offenders in a carefully devised contract and then monitoring the implementation of the contract. If state inspectors enforce the contract conditions, then problems can be prevented or quickly resolved. If a private agency does not resolve any problems, they are in violation of the contract and the agency can be dropped. Opponents of privatization argue that there is a problem with this argument. If the state wants to end a contract, there may not be another service provider willing and able to step in and take over the contracted service. At the very least, it would take some time for another company to be ready to provide the needed service.

Still another problem with privatization is that private agencies can be overly selective of the clients (offenders) they want to manage. Private agencies in corrections and in areas such as welfare (for example, training public assistance clients to become job-ready) have been criticized for picking the most capable clients (Rosin, 1997). The criticism is that these individuals may have been able to succeed on probation or in getting off of public assistance with little or no help. Statistics showing them to be success stories are thereby misleading. Private agencies have selected the individuals most likely to succeed and ignored the individuals most in need of intervention, leaving the state to deal with the more difficult cases.

In summary, proponents of privatization argue that private agencies can provide needed services, such as probation and parole supervision, more effectively and efficiently than the government has done in the past. Opponents argue that government agencies can themselves become more effective and efficient, and that there can be serious problems with privatization. They question whether it is right to allow the state to give away the highly symbolic function of depriving citizens of their freedom and supervising the deprivation of liberty.

SUPERVISION OF SEX OFFENDERS

Some community supervision programs for sex offenders have done quite well in preventing recidivism. For example, a life-time probation program in Arizona showed sexual recidivism of only 1.5% per year, and a Canadian intensive supervision parole program had a recidivism rate of less than 4% for a 3-year period. A Vermont program found overall new crime recidivism of 19% and new sex crime recidivism of 7% over a 5-year period (Stalans, 2004). Additional research has shown that what is needed is a containment approach that includes careful probation or parole supervision, the use of polygraph tests and field searches of offenders' homes, cognitive-behavioral treatment, and sharing of communication between probation officers and treatment providers. Research has also indicated that some offenders are more amenable to treatment and supervision than others (Stalans, 2004).

Sex offenders face additional problems on probation and parole. Many parolees have been returned to prison because they were unable to find suitable housing. In addition, parole rules, such as house arrest and electronic monitoring, can make it difficult for parolees to find a job or to work at a job that is not a 9-to-5 job (Burchfield & Mingus, 2008).

The number of sex offenders on parole may be decreasing in the next few years. The Supreme Court has just ruled that sex offenders who complete their prison sentence can be given a civil commitment if they are considered too dangerous to be released (U.S. v. Comstock, 2010). This decision raises important ethical issues. Is it ethical to keep someone locked up who has served the prison sentence that was handed down in court? How far can society go in trying to prevent crime, even if the crime is as abhorrent as a sex crime?

Given the fears of many citizens concerning sex crimes and sex offenders, it is very possible that this Supreme Court decision will open the door for the continuing confinement of many sex offenders who would otherwise have received parole.

USE OF VOLUNTEERS

Several ethical issues arise in the use of volunteers in probation and parole. The basic issue is whether it is responsible to use volunteers in the first place. If volunteers are sought merely to save a government agency from hiring needed probation or parole officers, some people (e.g., officers and their unions) would argue that this represents an unethical use of volunteers, and that offenders, officers, and society are being shortchanged. According to this argument, when volunteers are employed, offenders do not receive the professional supervision and assistance they need; officers (actually would-be officers) are denied jobs because volunteers are being used instead of hiring additional officers; and, finally, society does not get the effective supervision it desires.

On the other hand, if volunteers are being used for tasks that officers cannot and should not be doing, then there is a valid use for volunteers. An example of this type of volunteer activity is the establishment of a one-to-one relationship with the offender. Here the volunteer acts as a "big brother/big sister" or friend in relation to the offender. Officers do not have the time to establish such personal relationships with offenders, nor would it be proper for officers to do so, given their authority over offenders. Because such one-to-one relationships are the most frequent volunteer assignments (Shields, Chapman, & Wingard, 1983), it appears that many volunteers are being used properly.

The critical issue is whether volunteers are doing what additional officers would be doing or whether they are making unique contributions to the department. A complicating issue is the fiscal fact that many probation and parole departments must proceed with reduced funding. Los Angeles County Probation, for example, lost approximately one-third of its staff because of voter-approved cost-cutting. As a result, caseloads doubled. One part of the department's response to this crisis was to use more than 1000 volunteers to provide a number of services (Nidorf, 1996). Ideally, a sufficient number of paid officers should be budgeted for every department in the country. Realistically, many government bodies are facing financial limitations and are not funding the number of officer positions that are needed. In such circumstances, volunteers may allow a department to provide services it otherwise could not provide.

CORRUPTION

Like police officers and prison guards, probation and parole officers can become involved in **corruption**. They can take money from clients improperly or they can sexually harass clients. It appears that such problems have not been as widespread in community corrections as in policing, but such problems do sometimes occur.

In some cases, the problem is easy to resolve. An officer in one agency was pocketing the fine and restitution money he was collecting from offenders. The agency discovered the problem and changed its collection system from having the individual officer collect such monies to having a cashier's office do so. Under the new system, offenders would go to the cashier's office to make payments and get a written receipt, and officers and supervisors would receive a printout each week detailing payments and outstanding balances. The new system removed any possibility of individual officers pilfering payments. Similarly, one way to prevent probation and parole officers from sexually exploiting clients, which has been a significant problem for male guards in women's prisons (Rathbone, 2006), is to have sex-segregated caseloads, that is, women supervise women probationers/parolees and male officers supervise only male probationers/parolees. Finding a solution to corruption, however, is not always so direct. Managers must be vigilant to detect corruption, yet they must also foster a sense of trust among their employees.

CONCLUSION

Although the problems of community corrections may not be as dramatic as those involved in policing, this chapter has shown that ethical problems do arise. One of the principle ethical issues is the question of the purpose or mission of probation, parole, and other types of community corrections. Many are calling for punitive approaches to the supervision of offenders. Others, such as those in the peacemaking school, remind us that religious strands in the American tradition teach us to respect the humanity of offenders even when it appears that such offenders have done horrible deeds and seem to no longer merit humane treatment. This very basic conflict of ideas is prominent in probation and parole—and it affects other issues, such as privatization and corruption. As the new century unfolds, it will be important to watch how states and counties decide to answer such questions about the supervision of offenders in the community.

■ Learn More on the Internet

For more on probation issues go to www.uscourts.gov/ and search "Federal Probation Journal." ■

Discussion Questions

1. What do you think is the mission of community corrections? Give reasons for your choice.
2. Discuss the privatization of correctional services. What are some of the arguments for and against privatization?
3. An ethical issue, when considering the job of the probation/parole officer, is the question of what, if anything, society owes the offender. Can society embrace

a classical or neoclassical perspective, assume offenders are totally free and responsible, and simply ignore any consideration of assistance to offenders? Or does society have some obligation to help offenders to some degree? How does the author feel about this issue? What is your opinion? Explain.

4. What do you think of the Supreme Court decision allowing for civil commitment of sex offenders even past the expiration of their prison sentence? Does the protection of society justify such an extreme measure?

CASE STUDY 13–1 SEXUAL HARASSMENT

What a mess! You let out a deep sigh as you hang up the telephone. Sitting at your desk staring out the window, you listen to the rain and try to slowly collect your thoughts.

Maria Diaz has just called you in tears. Three years ago, she was part of your caseload. This time around she is assigned to Ned, your office supervisor. Where Maria was originally assigned to you for case supervision, she had been convicted of drug possession and prostitution. You remember her well: an attractive 16-year-old Latina with a 1-year-old daughter, a drug addiction, a police record, and very little education.

You worked with her for 2 years and watched her gradually dig her way out of the hole in which she had found herself and build a life with some hope. She earned a General Educational Development degree, and, with help and support of a caring grandmother, she learned how to become a mother herself. When she finished her term of probation, she found a job in an upscale department store selling cosmetics and women's fashions. You felt her chances to make it were excelled. She seemed to have improved her sense of self-esteem and had dreams of one day owning and operating her own fashion boutique.

Apparently, something has happened in the year after her release from probation that could jeopardize Maria's success. Relapses happen. You have been in the business for 15 years and it still disappoints you when someone doesn't make it. What makes Maria's current situation even more frustrating is that it involves Ned, your supervisor.

Ned is white, 46 years old, and divorced. Maria has just tearfully informed you that Ned has grown increasingly aggressive over the last 3 months, trying to force her into a sexual relationship with him. Apparently, he is offering her unsupervised probation in exchange for sexual favors and threatening her with revocation if she refuses his

advances. You recall Maria's words, "He told me that since I once was a prostitute, it shouldn't be a big deal. He even offered me money if I was good enough." You get a sick feeling in your stomach when you recall what she said.

You have heard rumors about Ned. This probably isn't the first time he has done something like this. You have never seen any proof of the rumors, so you never accepted them as being true. Besides, Ned has always been good to you. Now you find yourself feeling angry and foolish. This time you are going to have to act. You gave Maria all the reassurance you could and promised to get back to her.

You have to respond to this problem, but how? You consider calling Tom Johnson, the regional supervisor, but are uncertain about this course of action because he and Ned are good friends. In fact, they play golf together every week. You also realize that getting caught in the middle of this problem can harm your own career. After all, you do have a wife and children. Besides, Maria hasn't exactly been a model of virtue in the past. She has brought a lot of this trouble on herself. Still, it isn't right for Ned to abuse his power over a client. He's white, she's Hispanic and a woman, and you are caught in the middle of a very uncomfortable situation.

Questions

1. While sexual harassment is both illegal and unethical, how is Ned using his position to intimidate the probationer in question?
2. What can you do about this situation?
3. What are some safeguards that might diminish the potential for such problems?

NOTE

1. Much of the material in this section on acceptable penal content and the following section on intensive supervision issues is a revision of an earlier analysis of community corrections written for a chapter in a different book (Whitehead, 1992).

REFERENCES

A Hard Straight (2004). By Goro Toshimo. New Day Films.

Alarid, L. F., & Schloss, C. S. (2009). Attorney views on the use of private agencies for probation supervision and treatment. *International Journal of Offender Therapy and Comparative Criminology*, *53*, 278–291.

American Bar Association (1986). *Section of criminal justice, report to the house of delegates.* Chicago: American Bar Association.

Barnoski, R. (2009). *Providing evidence-based programs with fidelity in Washington State Juvenile Courts: Cost analysis.* Olympia: Washington State Institute for Public Policy. Available at www.wsipp.wa.gov/.

Beck, J. L., Klein-Saffran, J., & Wooten, H. B. (1990). Home confinement and the use of electronic monitoring with federal parolees. *Federal Probation, 54*(4), 22–31.

Beckett, K., & Harris, A. (2011). On cash and conviction: Monetary sanctions as misguided policy. *Criminology & Public Policy, 10*(3), 509–537.

Brook, D. (April 2009). Usury country: Welcome to the birthplace of payday lending. *Harper's*, 41–48.

Burchfield, K. B., & Mingus, W. (2008). Not in my neighborhood: Assessing registered sex offenders' experiences with local social capital and social control. *Criminal Justice and Behavior, 35*, 356–374.

Byrne, J. M. (1990). The future of intensive probation supervision and the new intermediate sanctions. *Crime & Delinquency, 36*, 6–41.

Clear, T. R., & Braga, A. A. (1995). Community corrections. In J. Q. Wilson, & J. Petersilia (Eds.), *Crime* (pp. 421–444). San Francisco: Institute for Contemporary Studies.

Clear, T. R., & Hardyman, P. L. (1990). The new intensive supervision movement. *Crime & Delinquency, 36*, 42–60.

Corbett, R., & Marx, G. T. (1991). No soul in the new machine: Technofallacies in the electronic monitoring movement. *Justice Quarterly, 8*, 399–414.

Feeley, M., & Simon, J. (1992). The new penology: Notes on the emerging strategy of corrections and its implications. *Criminology, 30*, 449–474.

Hawken, A. & Kleiman, M. (2009). *Managing drug involved probationers with swift and certain sanctions: Evaluating Hawaii's HOPE. Report submitted to the National Institute of Justice on December 2, 2009.*

Jones, M. (1996). Voluntary revocations and the "Elect-to-Serve" option in North Carolina probation. *Crime & Delinquency, 42*, 36–49.

Lipsey, M. W., & Cullen, F. T. (2007). The effectiveness of correctional rehabilitation: A review of systematic reviews. *Annual Review of Law and Social Science, 3*, 299–320.

Maruschak, L. M., & Parks, E. (2012). *Probation and parole in the United States, 2011. Bureau of Justice Statistics Bulletin.* Washington: U.S. Department of Justice.

McCleary, R. (1978). *Dangerous men: The sociology of parole.* Beverly Hills: Sage.

McDowell, L. A., & Whitehead, J. T. (2009). Varieties of restorative justice: Therapeutic interventions in context. In D. Polizzi, & M. Braswell (Eds.), *Transforming corrections: Humanistic approaches to corrections and offender treatment.* Durham: Carolina Academic Press.

McMiller, D. L. (2008). The campaign to restore the voting rights of people convicted of a felony and sentenced to probation in Connecticut. *American Behavioral Scientist, 51,* 645–658.

Miller, J. M., Schreck, C. J., & Tewksbury, R. (2008). *Criminological theory: A brief introduction* (2nd ed.). Boston: Pearson/Allyn & Bacon.

Morris, N., & Tonry, M. (1990). *Between prison and probation: Intermediate punishments in a rational sentencing system.* New York: Oxford University.

Murphy, D., & Lutze, F. (2009). Police-probation partnerships: Professional Identity and the sharing of coercive power. *Journal of Criminal Justice, 37,* 65–76.

Nidorf, B. J. (1996). Surviving in a 'Lock Them Up' era. *Federal Probation, 60*(1), 4–10.

O'Connell, D., Visher, C. A., Martin, S., Parker, L., & Brent, J. (2011). Decide your time: Testing deterrence theory's certainty and celerity effects on substance-using probationers. *Journal of Criminal Justice, 39,* 261–267.

Petersilia, J. (1990). Conditions that permit intensive supervision programs to survive. *Crime & Delinquency, 36,* 126–145.

Petersilia, J. (1997). Probation in the United States. In M. Tonry (Ed.), *Crime and justice: A review of research* (Vol. 22) (pp. 149–200). Chicago: University of Chicago Press.

Petersilia, J., Peterson, J., & Turner, S. (1992). *Intensive probation and parole: Research findings and policy implications.* Santa Monica, CA: RAND.

Petersilia, J., Turner, S., Kahan, J., & Peterson, J. (1985). *Granting felons probation: Public risks and alternatives.* Santa Monica: RAND.

Pew Center on the States. (2011). *State of recidivism: The revolving door of America's prisons.* Washington: The Pew Charitable Trusts.

Pisciotta, A. W. (1982). Saving the children: The promise and practice of Parens Patriae, 1838–1898. *Crime & Delinquency, 28,* 410–425.

Rathbone, C. (2006). *A world apart: Women, prison, and life behind bars.* New York: Random House Trade Paperbacks.

Rosin, H. (1997). About face: The appearance of welfare success. *New Republic, 217*(August, 4), 16–19.

Schlager, M. D., & Robbins, K. (2008). Does parole work?—Reframing the discussion of the impact of postprison supervision on offender outcome. *The Prison Journal, 88,* 234–251.

Shields, P. M., Chapman, C. W., & Wingard, D. R. (1983). Using volunteers in adult probation. *Federal Probation, 46*(2), 57–64.

Skeem, J. L., & Manchak, S. (2008). Back to the future: From Klockars' model of effective supervision to evidence-based practice in probation. *Journal of Offender Rehabilitation, 47,* 220–247.

Stalans, L. J. (2004). Adult sex offenders on community supervision: A review of recent assessment strategies and treatment. *Criminal Justice and Behavior, 31,* 564–608.

Studt, E. (1973). *Surveillance and service in parole: A report of the parole action study.* Washington: National Institute of Corrections.

Taxman, F. S. (2008). No illusions: Offender and organizational change in Maryland's proactive community supervision efforts. *Criminology & Public Policy, 7,* 275–302.

Teague, M. (2011). Probation in America: Armed, private and unaffordable. *Probation Journal, 58,* 317–332.

Tonry, M. (1990). Stated and latent functions of ISP. *Crime & Delinquency, 36,* 174–191.

U.S. v. Comstock et al., (2010). Slip Opinion No. 08–1224.

von Hirsch, A. (1990). The ethics of community-based sanctions. *Crime & Delinquency, 36,* 162–173.

Whitehead, J. T. (1989). *Burnout in probation and corrections.* New York: Praeger.

Whitehead, J. T. (1992). Control and the use of technology in community supervision. In P. J. Benekos, & A. V. Merlo (Eds.), *Corrections: Dilemmas and Directions* (pp. 155–172). Cincinnati: Anderson.

Whitehead, J. T., Miller, L. S., & Myers, L. B. (1995). The diversionary effectiveness of intensive supervision and community corrections programs. In J. O. Smykla, & W. L. Selke (Eds.), *Intermediate sanctions: Sentencing in the 1990s* (pp. 135–151). Cincinnati: Anderson.

Whitehead, J. T. (1991). The effectiveness of felony probation: Results from an eastern state. *Justice Quarterly, 8*, 525–543.

Williamson, H. E. (1990). *The corrections profession*. Newbury Park: Sage.

Wood, G. (September 2010). Prison without walls. *The Atlantic*. Available at: www.theatlantic.com/magazine/archive/2010/09/prison-without-walls/308195/.

CHAPTER 14

Restorative Justice: Defining and Implementing the Peacemaking Paradigm

Lana A. McDowell, Michael C. Braswell, John T. Whitehead

KEY CONCEPTS

family group conferences	restorative justice	victim-offender reconciliation
peacemaking	sentencing circles	programs
reparative boards	victim-offender panels	

In Chapter 1, the three contexts for understanding justice, crime, and ethics are discussed. The personal context is described as what constitutes one's inner definition and idea of justice. Individuals who possess a personal sense of **peacemaking** have the ability to join together to create a greater social context that can encourage peacemaking. Looking through the lens of the social context, an individual may understand why some criminals may be more predisposed than other offenders to make criminal choices because of the social environment created within a given community and society. As a greater number of individuals believe in peacemaking in a personal context of justice, a greater number of persons will also understand and practice peacemaking in the social or community context. This leads to the conception of relating to offenders not as isolated, disconnected persons who commit crimes, but rather as members of the community who have made poor choices and moved away from the core social values. The collaboration of individuals who subscribe to a personal peacemaking context moves communities to create new methods and approaches such as restorative justice to intervene with offenders.

When individuals embrace personal and social peacemaking, practices are more likely to evolve within the criminal justice context to accommodate such perspectives. Some of the programs developed from peacemaking perspectives that fall under the umbrella of restorative justice have included victim–offender panels (Braswell, Fuller, & Lozoff, 2001), family group conferencing

(Hackler, 2004), victim–offender reconciliation programs (Lovell, Helfgott, & Lawrence, 2002), reparative boards (Dzur & Wertheimer, 2002), and sentencing circles (Keeva & Newell, 2004). With such approaches, the offender and punishment are no longer considered the sole responsibility of the court system. Community members have a degree of responsibility as well. The justice system utilizing restorative justice techniques and the peacemaking perspective in the criminal justice process can be viewed as a form of community justice.

Restorative justice is different from the traditional view of justice. As mentioned previously, the traditional view is more reactive, relies heavily on law enforcement, specifies punishments, and is highly connected to retributive philosophies of justice. The traditional view of justice is reactive in that offenders do not typically come into contact with the criminal justice system until after a crime has been committed and often have little or no contact with the victim(s). Restorative justice and peacemaking criminology take a more proactive approach to crime by helping the offender more fully understand and take responsibility for the personal harm he or she has caused others. Such an approach can at least increase the odds that the offender will more seriously consider the effects and consequences of his or her future actions.

One inevitable aspect of life is conflict. Acknowledgment of this truth leads to the consideration of how individuals resolve instances of conflict. Do individuals talk with the other person they feel harmed by or who they harmed? Do individuals truly listen to other people's perspectives? Do individuals avoid the perceived wrongdoer or do they make small talk, but refrain from dealing with the epicenter of the conflict? Conflict occurs in interpersonal relationships between family members and friends as well as between individuals who are not intertwined in personal relationships, such as when an individual harms another as defined through criminal codes. Conflict may also occur in workplace and educational settings and between governmental entities and those who are governed. On a larger scale, conflict may also exist between different countries. Examining justice in different situations requires numerous considerations and may be defined in many ways. One method of resolving conflict includes the practice of restorative justice.

It is understandable why people often question the meaning of the term restorative justice. There are a number of reasons. First, restorative justice seems to unfold as an ever-evolving process that appears in many forms. The utilization of restorative justice can be within police organizations, court systems, correctional entities, primary education, higher education, families, business organizations, international relations, and in many other unique settings. The restorative process dynamic may be constructed differently based on the setting, the individuals involved, and the harms produced from a given conflict situation.

Restorative justice may also be misunderstood because the application of the concept is not yet an integral part of the traditional American criminal justice system. When restorative justice is utilized, the definition of the term is shaped by the elements of a given process. For example, teaching a young child how to resolve conflict effectively through circle processes will differ from teaching individuals imprisoned for life sentences about the concept. Restorative justice acknowledges that the involved parties are at different developmental stages, have experienced different life circumstances, and have different perceptions of a given situation. For this reason, no one particular conceptualization of the term surfaces as a concrete meaning of restorative justice.

Another reason the restorative justice concept may be difficult to fully grasp is due to the traditional verbiage and jargon used in the system of justice. Few individuals will question the definition of terms such as guilt, innocence, punishment, and justice. It follows that when an individual commits an action, the behavior is deserving of some form of punishment or the individual did not act illegally. The outcome of the process that determines guilt or innocence ultimately leads to justice. In such a framework, all of the terms are generally understood by members of society. However, adding additional aspects such as reparation, inclusion, and amends to the concept of a just response may leave individuals questioning the true meaning of such terms as well as how they may contribute to obtaining justice in a given instance.

One simple reason why restorative justice may not be completely understood is because the implementation of such processes under the umbrella term "restorative justice" began to take shape only during the 1990s. Hackler (2004) explains: "Rather than being a true innovation, restorative justice may actually have been the predominant form of justice as societies evolved" (p. 345). In other words, restorative justice practices may not be an innovative idea, but rather a journey back to past techniques relating to justice. More than two decades since the creation of the term, the meaning of restorative justice is still evolving, which suggests the concept is fluid in nature. Furthermore, researchers question if the concept is a theory, a practice, or a combination of both. An evolving debate exists regarding whether restorative justice primarily operates within the current system or if restorative justice occurs on the outskirts of traditional justice processes. So how do we define restorative justice? How does one practice restorative justice? How do we know if restorative justice is occurring?

DEFINING RESTORATIVE JUSTICE

Restorative justice can be defined through a circular process dynamic (Figure 14.1) by including a number of the values found within restorative programs (Box 14.1). The elements of this process include the following: acknowledgment that crime

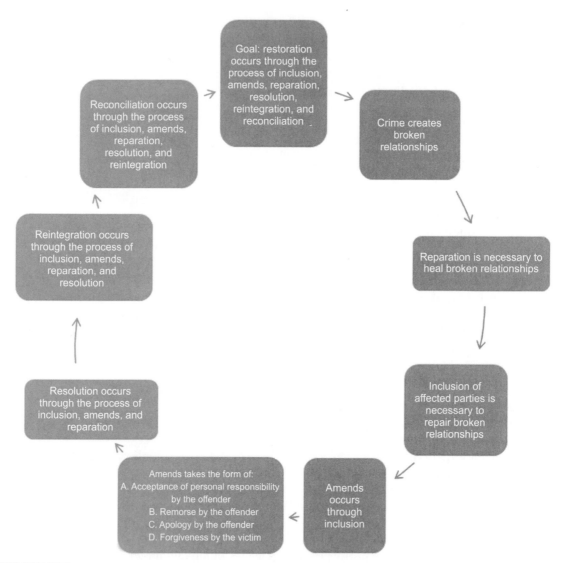

FIGURE 14.1

A definition of restorative justice. (For color version of this figure, the reader is referred to the online version of this book.)

creates broken relationships, reparation, inclusion, amends (personal responsibility, remorse, apology, forgiveness), resolution, reintegration, reconciliation, and lastly restoration and/or transformation (McDowell, 2012, p. 24).

An example of how the restorative justice value process occurs may be explained as follows. Two children are playing with a ball and a third child joins the group and attempts to obtain the ball. The two children who were initially playing

BOX 14.1 TYPES OF RESTORATIVE JUSTICE PROGRAMS

Family Group Conferences

The offender, victim, family members, supporters of each primary party, community members, other necessary parties, and a restorative facilitator meet to discuss the wrongdoing and create a plan regarding the most appropriate method for restoration or transformation.

Victim–Offender Reconciliation Programs

The victim and offender meet face to face with a mediator/facilitator present to discuss the transgression at hand. A resolution plan may or may not be developed based on the dynamics of the conflict.

Sentencing Circles

The victim, offender, community members, and criminal justice officials each have the ability to speak and jointly create a solution regarding the outcome of the criminal action through a circle process.

Reparative Boards

Includes a series of public meetings organized and implemented by community members regarding steps an offender shall take to restore the harm done to the victim(s) and the community.

Victim–Offender Boards

Victims are provided the opportunity to speak with a group of offenders who have committed a crime the victim has experienced without being required to meet their personal assailant.

with the ball may become upset because they perceive a sense of harm. This harm may result in less than positive feelings about the child who offended them. The conflict has created a rift in the relationship structure of the three children; hence a *broken relationship* has developed. Therefore, some form of reparation among the three children seems necessary. The manifestation of *reparation* occurs in many forms and is specifically defined within the context of a given situation. Because the removal of the toy by a child in our example occurred, the individuals involved in the conflict need to come together in order to determine the appropriate response to repair the relationship. *Inclusion* is necessary; however, inclusion must also be a voluntary decision by each affected party.

An element of reparation encompasses making *amends* for the perceived wrongdoing. In our example, amends may occur if the child who took the toy acknowledges that they committed the action and accepts *personal responsibility* for doing so, shows genuine *remorse* for his/her action, or provides an authentic *apology* for his/her action. Once the child who is perceived as the offending party accepts personal responsibility, shows remorse, and/or provides an apology, the two children who felt harmed by the action have the option to forgive the child who attempted to take the ball. The children may decide that *forgiveness* is a good option in the situation or they may not. If the children do forgive the perceived offender, the group can move forward to create a *resolution*. The children may decide that simply the apology and forgiveness are a sufficient resolution. The children may also decide that they should all play with the ball together and/or take turns playing with the ball. Once the three kids have formulated an acceptable resolution for all parties, *reintegration* may begin to occur. In this example, reintegration may appear as the children playing together with the ball. At the heart of reintegration is the feeling of being a member of the group in which one was previously an outsider.

Through reintegration, the *reconciliation* process may begin to occur. During this stage, all of the children involved feel that the conflict has been discussed, amends have been exhibited, a resolution has been made, reintegration is occurring, and, therefore, the children can move past the conflict. Because the children acknowledged the conflict created broken relationships and therefore reparation as well as amends was needed, this led to a resolution that resulted in the ability to reintegrate and reconcile differences, allowing *restoration* and/ or transformation to occur.

In the example, the children may perceive that the relationships have been restored to the previous state or the children may learn new aspects about one another during the circle process which led to a transformation of their relationships. For instance, the child who took the ball may have perceived that the other children did not like him or her. In such a case, the goal of such a process may not be to restore the relationships to the previous state but rather to transform the relationships into more positive future relational experiences for all of the children.

While every conflict may not come full circle, Zehr (2002) explains that restorative processes may be viewed on a continuum including "fully restorative, mostly restorative, partially restorative, potentially restorative, or pseudo/ non-restorative" in nature (p. 55). Common types of restorative justice processes are outlined below for further clarification.

TYPES OF RESTORATIVE JUSTICE PROGRAMS

There are a variety of restorative justice programs utilized around the world. Restorative practices include **family group conferences, victim-offender reconciliation programs, sentencing circles, reparative boards,** and **victim-offender panels** (see Box 14.1).

Family Group Conferencing

Conferencing is "the coming together of those affected in a systematic and thoughtful process for the purpose of restoring harmony, reintegration, and healing" (Hackler, 2004, p. 346). During such processes, "the family members receive significantly more information than usual from the state about their case, including the actions of the social worker, the official concern about the abuse or neglect, and any other pertinent facts about resources and constraints that could affect decision-making"(Adams & Chandler, 2004, pp. 97–98).

While there is still a legal aspect to these procedures, the sole focus is not on punishment but rather repairing the harm done in an effective manner. Burford and Adams (2004) suggest that "in restorative justice, the family group conference brings together extended family members with professionals and others involved in the situation who can provide information to assist the family in developing a plan to keep all its members safe" (p. 19). Procedures utilized in Canada with juveniles provide an example of family group conferencing. In this type of conference, a young offender and the person harmed by the offense are brought together along with their families and friends, and other key persons affected by the harm (Hackler, 2004). In this conference process, the victim and family members of the victim are invited to attend. This is important because often the family members of the victim have incurred discomfort on some level due to the actions of the offender.

Victim–Offender Reconciliation Programs

Victim–offender reconciliation programs are said to "bring victims and offenders together with a trained mediator" in an attempt to resolve an offense as either an "alternative to court proceedings" or "after conviction as a condition of probation" (Hackler, 2004, p. 250). The utilization of a mediator provides a neutral viewpoint in a stressful and conflicted situation. Mediators have the ability to lead the encounter between victims and offenders while keeping a watchful eye on the anticipated results. An example of a victim–offender reconciliation program is located at the Washington State Reformatory Prison. This program "provides offenders and victims with opportunities to restore victim-offender relationships, to educate offenders about the experiences of victims, and to facilitate a healing process among interested community members" (Lovell et al., 2002, p. 261). One victim indicates that the program is accomplishing the goal at hand, while another victim suggests he would "like the guy who murdered (his) son to admit guilt and take responsibility..." (Lovell et al., 2002, p. 264). Victim–offender reconciliation programs provide a level of accountability from the offender and require the victim to be courageous in their quest for justice by personally interacting with the person who committed the crime against them.

Sentencing Circles

In Canada, an example of sentencing circles provides aboriginal sentencing circles for juveniles. Community members, including the offender, victim, supporters, court officials, and the judge or a respected elder, may oversee the proceeding (Hackler, 2004). Each participant has the ability to speak during the process in order to reach consensus regarding sentencing or other consequences (Hackler, 2004). Aboriginal sentencing circles are viewed as equivalent to a normal court proceeding. However, community involvement and the unique role of the criminal justice professionals within this setting are what separates such circles from more traditional court proceedings.

Reparative Boards

Reparative boards typically are "public meetings" that take place in such settings as libraries and community centers (Dzur & Wertheimer, 2002). An interesting aspect of reparative boards is that members of a board do not view any crime to be victimless. For this purpose, when a victim is unknown, "the offender may be asked to perform restitution or write a letter of apology" (Dzur & Wertheimer, 2002, p. 10). This suggests that reparative boards hope to help offenders understand that even if no one individual is harmed, society still bears the burden of the crime in many different ways. If a victim is known, he or she may also take part in the process. In order for offenders to learn different ways of behaving, reparative boards create "classes tailored to the offense or general tasks like writing an essay on the importance of law and the social consequences of offenses such as the one that was committed" (Dzur & Wertheimer, 2002, p. 10).

With reparative boards, the offender is required to attend a series of meetings. After a given specified time, there is a closure meeting where offenders who have successfully completed their tasks are congratulated and acknowledged. The board can remand offenders back to court if they fail to complete their tasks (Dzur & Wertheimer, 2002). In the traditional justice system, offenders are less likely to consider the reasoning behind their arrest, conviction, and incarceration. By encouraging offenders to gain a better understanding of themselves and the effects of their actions, personal transformation is more likely to occur.

An example of reparative boards is located within the Yukon and Northwest Territories of Canada. This program involves a panel of individuals who are required to oversee the process. Panel members' responsibilities include making sure the agreement is proportionate and fair. Panel members must be certain the agreement provides a balance between welfare and justice. The panel members are also required to make sure the agreement has reparative value instead of only being punishment-oriented (Mackay, 2003). Reparative boards require a social web and network that support and offer to aid in the reintegration of the offender back into society.

Victim–Offender Panels

Victim–offender panels allow victims to address offenders who have committed the same type of crimes the victims have experienced (Braswell et al., 2001). Victim–offender panels have been effective with some "victims of drunk drivers and with victims of burglary" (Braswell et al., 2001, p. 149). It may be better for some victims to discuss their experience with individuals who have committed the same crime the victim has experienced rather than talking face-to-face with the particular offender who harmed them.

TRANSFORMING THEORY INTO PRACTICE: REAL-WORLD APPLICATIONS OF RESTORATIVE JUSTICE

While the term restorative justice is difficult to conceptualize because of the vast array of embedded values and process dynamics, a number of programs have developed worldwide that may be conceived as restorative in nature. Such programs include the utilization of restorative justice within police organizations, court systems, prison systems, primary educational settings, college educational settings, workplace settings, sexual violations, and international relations.

Restorative Justice and Policing

While a substantial amount of literature focuses on perceptions of police officers with regard to restorative concepts, a number of restorative programs have been applied within police organizations. For instance, the Bethlehem police in Pennsylvania implemented a diversionary program for juveniles in which adolescents who fit the program criteria are randomly selected for the process (McCold, 2003). In order for an individual to be accepted into the program, the primary offender is required to accept personal responsibility. After that, the program coordinator notified the primary victim in the case to explain the process and to gauge the inclusion interest level of the participant. If both parties agree to the conditions of the process, the case is forwarded to an officer who acts as a facilitator. Additional support persons are recruited for the offender and victim. If either of the primary parties decide to opt out of the restorative process of justice, the case is returned to the traditional justice system for processing. Results of the program indicate that "participants overwhelmingly said they were satisfied with how their cases were handled…, they perceived the process as fair…, they would choose to do the conference again…, and they would recommend conferences to others" (McCold, 2003, p. 384).

In Canada, a referral system has been created to divert young offenders to the Community Youth Justice program otherwise known as *Circles* (Abramson, 2003). This program evolved out of the Canadian Youth Criminal Justice Act, which focuses on crime prevention, rehabilitation, and reintegration of youth into society. Circles attempt to provide young wrongdoers fair, prompt, and meaningful consequences within the boundaries of proportionate accountability (Chatterjee & Elliott, 2003). It is explained that in many cases, a police officer is the initial responder to conflict and/or criminal situations; therefore, the Act implies officers should consider the additional option of "referrals (with consent of the young person) to community programs or agencies that address the root causes of the offense" (Chatterjee & Elliott, 2003, p. 354).

Within the Circles program, the police do not act as facilitators as in the Bethlehem processes. Instead, trained volunteer facilitators are responsible for preparing involved parties for a conference as well as leading the facilitation of the circle. While some restorative justice processes may note conditions for inclusion, the Circles program does not require such restrictions. The volunteer facilitators make contact with the parties, conduct the necessary preparation for circle inclusion, and facilitate the conference. Through the Circles process, a resolution is agreed upon and the included parties attempt to achieve the conditions of the agreement. If the resolution is not carried out in a timely manner, an additional conference is scheduled. If the offending party is unwilling to complete the agreement, the case is sent back to the police, the initial referral point. Abramson (2003) found that members of the referral organization, the Port City Police Department, were less apprehensive about referring individuals who had committed perceived minor offenses than more serious offenses. This finding may be connected to the perception that harm and justice are based on a continuum. As harm increases, it may be perceived that traditional forms of justice are more appropriate. Such beliefs may also be connected to a lack of extensive knowledge of restorative justice goals, values, processes, and research.

Upon obtaining greater knowledge of restorative justice, two police departments in Northern Ireland implemented a diversion program for young offenders through the development of *restorative cautions* in which a police officer acts as the facilitator (O'Mahony & Doak, 2004). Because of the nature of some offensive actions, a primary victim may not always be identifiable; therefore, restorative caution conferences do not always include an actual victim's perspective, but may include surrogate victims. O'Mahony and Doak (2004) found police officers involved in the process "believed (restorative caution conferences are) a fairer and more human and emotional process" and suggested "a belief that it avoids the tendency to write young people off" (p. 494).

It has also been suggested that restorative justice values may be found within probationary practices. Gregory (2011) interviewed probation officers in Europe to gain a better understanding of how restorative justice is exhibited through their roles as officers. One respondent contended there is a level of importance of restorative values within the probation officer role stating, "being a good listener, being empathetic, and knowing something about change and emotions" are important qualities of a probation officer (Gregory, 2011, p. 68). The author explains that probation officers who are "skilled in care" may not be utilizing their full skill set when more punitive philosophies become the more prominent goal of probationary services (Gregory, 2011, p. 72).

It can be inferred from the previous studies that restorative justice within policing may become manifest in different ways. Themes include an openness to such processes with youthful offenders by police officers as well as an openness to embed a restorative option within police procedures by administration.

Restorative Justice and the Courts

One example of restorative justice within the court system is located within the juvenile justice system of Washington State. In 1999, victim–offender mediation became a viable option within the state's court system (Wood, 2013). During the mediation sessions, individuals who have been harmed are given the opportunity to explain their feelings and the perpetrator is provided the chance to respond. Afterward, an agreement plan is developed if necessary, which includes the perceptions of the participating stakeholders. In 2001, an additional component was added to the victim–offender mediation program that allowed a juvenile the ability to complete community service that is more specific to a given delinquent action. An example includes the request from one affected party who explained he "owned a house that (had) been vandalized by two young people. After explaining that it was his elderly parents who lived in the house, and that they had been shaken by the event, he asked the offender to complete his community service at a retirement home or similar facility" (Wood, 2013, p. 12). In 2003 the court also implemented a victim impact program that does not require victims "…to agree to mediation to be able to suggest or ask for specific outcomes related to community service and restitution…" (Wood, 2013, p. 13). While the addition of restorative processes began as a diversionary practice for individuals who would most likely receive probation for their actions, the victim impact program was expanded in 2005 to include felony cases. This addition allows a restorative court manager to contact victims of felony cases more swiftly. In 2000, fewer than 100 mediation cases occurred. However, approximately 1,150 cases were processed by 2005, which indicates the effectiveness of such processes (Wood, 2013).

In one area of Hawaii, restorative justice appears in the form of alternative dispute resolutions (Keanini, 2011). The Pono Kaulike restorative program began to process cases in 2003 and offers three different types of restorative processes (Walker & Hayashi, 2007).The first program entails a restorative conference in which the affected party, the perpetrator, and supporters engage in a circle process in order to create an agreement plan. The second program is known as restorative dialogues and includes the affected party, the perpetrator, and respective inner circle family and friends. The primary goal in this type of process is the ability for the perpetrator to exhibit genuine remorse. The third program is called a restorative session and differs from the two previously noted processes because only one party, the affected party and/or the perpetrator, is involved. This type of program occurs when one party is reluctant to participate in the restorative process. During the restorative session, the participating party and his or her supporters create a plan usually focused on self-improvement, be it either offender or victim centered (Walker & Hayashi, 2007). Through practice, facilitators and organizers found that individuals who are harmed or who have harmed loved ones are most appropriate for such processes. Furthermore, the types of cases that have been processed through the Hawaii Pono Kaulike program include "disorderly conduct, harassment, assault, terroristic threatening, negligent vehicular homicide, criminal property damage, and animal nuisance..." (Walker & Hayashi, 2007, p. 23). The importance of joint responsibility is noted by one participant as well as the ability for involved parties to implement plans to improve themselves through restorative processes. In this case, a woman who was assaulted by her nephew explained the following:

> Being able to apologize to (her) nephew was the most useful thing about the conference. When her nephew was arrested, she was also intoxicated and felt partly responsible for their fighting and his arrest. Both she and (the) nephew agreed to attend substance abuse treatment programs in their Restorative Conference Agreement.
>
> **Walker and Hayashi (2007, p. 24)**

A juvenile arbitration program has been implemented in Aiken County, South Carolina. One goal of the program is to assist first-time delinquent perpetrators. Hazen (2012) explained that the program centered on restorative values and that approximately one-third of juveniles who enter the system take part in the juvenile arbitration program. Hazen (2012) reported that the arbitration program cost the state "...$1.95 daily..." for each individual, while "probation supervision averaged $3.29 daily per juvenile and intensive probation... cost $7.10 daily" per individual. If a juvenile is incarcerated or requires placement, the average cost per day " was $300..." (p. 116). A total of 82 juveniles completed the diversion program. A simple tabulation of the numbers reveals that if each juvenile were required to be housed within the state system rather than diverted, the cost to the tax payers would have been more than two million dollars for a 90 day period. If the 82 juveniles were all placed on intensive supervision for three months, the approximate cost to the state would have been roughly $52,000 while traditional probation would have cost approximately $24,000 (Hazen, 2012). However, because the 82 juveniles were diverted from traditional avenues into the restorative program, the total cost over 90 days equaled "...$14,391 for all 82" juveniles (Hazen, 2012, p. 116). Therefore, Hazen (2012) explains that the diversion program "...operates at 59% lower costs than traditional probation, offering an effective method of reducing the financial cost of juvenile justice to the legal system" (Hazen, 2012, p. 116). While Hazen's findings are impressive, it is also possible to wonder if the juvenile offenders who became involved in the new arbitration/restorative justice program may have received a warning or a quick counseling session if the program were not in operation. While the new program could be a meaningful and effective diversion option, it could also possibly be an example of "net-widening," where juveniles with relatively minor delinquent offenses are sent to a new program because it is available. While restorative justice programs make sense on a number of ethical, treatment, and economic levels, it is important to keep a clear eye regarding evaluating such programs.

Fulkerson (2009) contends the evolution of drug courts within the United States is restorative in nature. The author states that drug treatment courts were "not the product of academic research and reflection, but resulted from experimentation by practitioners who recognized the failures of the existing model" (Fulkerson, 2009, p. 264). The author discusses the importance of considering the causes of drug addiction, the individualized treatment plans for individuals based on each person's circumstances, reparation to affected parties as well as the inclusion of family members and supporters. Fulkerson (2009) also discussed how the roles of the traditional courtroom work group shift within drug court settings, including that it is more likely that the judge "accept(s) the disease model of addiction," the prosecutor "accept(s) the rehabilitative and therapeutic approach of (drug treatment courts)," and that defense attorneys emphasize the importance of truthfulness of the offender in terms of recidivism activities with the courtroom work group rather than deflecting criminal transgressions (p. 255). The author also emphasizes that drug treatment courts infuse both traditional and restorative methods. Fulkerson (2009) implies that the purpose of such courts is "to interrupt the recurring pattern of addiction and criminal behavior, restore the person to a life without drugs and crime, help the addict accept responsibility for her(his) actions, restore drug addicts to their families, make society safer, and repair the harm caused by drug addiction" (p. 264). It can be inferred that while drug treatment courts were not designed specifically as restorative practices, the noted elements are restorative in nature.

Restorative justice values can also be seen within international courts. For instance, "...the Extraordinary Chambers in the Courts of Cambodia (ECCC), established under the agreement of the Government of Cambodia and the United Nations (UN) in 2003, was conceptualized as the most appropriate institutional response" to previous harms such as genocide within Cambodia (Jasini & Phan, 2011, p. 380). Within this court, victims were afforded an opportunity to be included in the justice process. Adding the element of victim participation will hopefully increase the perception of justice for victims of international atrocities by providing the opportunity for such individuals to have a voice in conflict situations. Jasini and Phan (2011) contend that victim participation within international court systems has stemmed from the "...International Criminal Court (ICC), which became the first international criminal tribunal to endorse active victim participation in an unprecedented expansion of victims' right at the international level" (Jasini & Phan, 2011, p. 394).

Restorative justice values are exhibited through greater involvement of victims locally and globally. As suggested by the previous examples, restorative processes not only allow for acceptance of personal responsibility and address the needs of offenders, but can also assist in reducing budgetary cost with court systems.

Restorative Justice in the Prison Setting

Dhami, Mantle, and Fox (2009) examine the need for greater consideration of restorative justice in the traditional correctional system because such an initiative could result in an increase in prisons' efforts to reduce crime by utilizing such alternative strategies. The authors believe that current restorative correctional programs include offender behavior programs, victim awareness programs, community service work, victim-offender mediation, and prisons that operate through a more complete restorative philosophy (Dhami et al., 2009). Instead of simply focusing on recidivism rates as defining program effectiveness, the authors suggest that possible outcomes of such processes include "…learning responsibility, listening and communication skills, prosocial skills, changing attitudes and beliefs, developing a sense of civic responsibility, forgiveness, reconciliation, destigmatization, empowerment, increased positive emotions such as respect, hope, and empathy, and reduced negative emotions…" as well as other attributes (p. 441).

One example of how restorative justice ideals are becoming more embedded within the prison environment is occurring in San Francisco, California. Administrators have developed an understanding that effective reintegration of members of subpopulations within correctional institutions is important. One such group includes incarcerated US military veterans. In recognition of this group, the San Francisco Sheriff's Department developed a program called the *Community of Veterans Engaged in Restoration (COVER)* (Schwartz & Levitas, 2011).

> In developing COVER, SFSD (San Francisco Sheriff's Department) leadership recognized that, as a society, we train military personnel to fight and even kill, but we do not provide the much-needed support for them to return home in a safe and healthy way, which will enable them to thrive in civilian life. The very conditioning that enables them to serve and protect our country often results in difficulty re-socializing upon return from deployment. Drug use, domestic violence, and mental health issues become the pathways that lead many veterans into the criminal justice system.
>
> **Schwartz and Levitas (2011, p. 55)**

The program includes housing veterans together while in the prison setting. The communal group dynamic allows the members of the dormitory access to a therapeutic design that includes lessons geared toward the reformulation of ideals and actions. It is suggested that "the program combines case management with a five-day per week structured program rooted in the classic restorative justice model of offender accountability, victim restoration, and community restoration" (Schwartz & Levitas, 2011, p. 56).

Restorative justice circles are also utilized with inmates in Green Bay, Wisconsin. The circle process includes a "broken ball" as a symbolic tool within the practice. This program encourages individuals to speak "one at a time, moving around the circle, the speaker holding two pieces of glass that, together, form a large ball" (Keeva & Newell, 2004, p. 73). The symbolism of the ball helps all persons involved in the circle to provide their undivided attention to the speaker. "Like them, it is broken, and no matter how hard they try to rebuild their lives they are still filled with cracks" (Keeva & Newell, 2004, p. 73). Such symbolism produces an understanding of the troubles possessed by each person involved in the group and aids in their sense of connectedness and the importance of caring.

Oftentimes, the "victim" concept is perceived as limited to individuals primarily harmed by a criminal offense. However, restorative justice initiatives may also be helpful in healing harms felt by those closest to the perpetrator in a given criminal situation. One example is the Haikahi Restorative Circles in Hawaii. Within the circles, incarcerated individuals are provided the opportunity to apply for circle processes with others he or she identifies as potential circle members. Walker (2010) explains the perpetrator defines personal goals and supporters assist the individual with achievement of their aspirations. While the circles focus on the needs of the offender, the process also allows family members the opportunity to vocalize their needs and attempts to rebuild relationships between multiple parties may occur. Within these circles, "each loved one in the group describes how the incarcerated person has affected them and what she or he could possibly do to repair the harm" (Walker, 2010, p. 88). Additionally, the circle process allows for a dialogue regarding the needs of family members who are not present for the circle as well as victims that are not a part of the traditional family unit. A priority of the Circle interview is to encourage the incarcerated person's hopefulness and understanding that they have some control over their future (Walker, 2010).

In Canada, restorative-based initiatives have made it possible for the introduction of restorative programing such as *Stride Circles*. Such circles provide "weekly recreation and leisure activities that involve community volunteers and federally sentenced women participating together" that focus on "the crisis of leaving the institution, friendship as a site for resistance and empowerment-in-community" (Fortune, Thompson, Pedlar, & Yuen, 2010, pp. 24–25). It is suggested that justice may occur through the formulation of relationships of community members and female offenders who are facing the transition back into society. One unique aspect of Stride Circles is that relationships formulate in the institution yet extend beyond the prison environment upon release back into society. The rationale for this program lies in the need for reintegration. One participant of Stride Circles articulates the following: "…they were my lifeline… because where else would I have been able to turn, I didn't have nobody there, you know I would have just walked out and into my old life because I wouldn't have had anything on that side to hold me" (Fortune et al., 2010, p. 30).

Just as with policing, restorative justice has also been implemented in juvenile correctional populations. Two examples entail the inclusion of juvenile offenders within restorative justice classes on university campuses (Holsinger & Crowther, 2005; Vigorita, 2002). One finding of a study conducted by Vigorita (2002) suggests that both traditional college students and juvenile offenders within the course perceived methods of rehabilitation to be of greater significance than punitive measures. In a study conducted by Holsinger and Crowther (2005), the researchers found that participants did not believe that multiple needs of involved parties are addressed within the current justice system. Furthermore, one participant stated, "When you do something it affects your family and the community, I realized what I did was wrong" (Holsinger & Crowther, 2005, p. 335). One important finding suggests that through restorative justice education, members of the course gained a greater acknowledgment of the commonalities among the participants rather than differences (Holsinger & Crowther, 2005; Vigorita, 2002). One college student in the study conducted by Vigorita (2002) stated, "I realized that the only difference between him (juvenile) and some of my other friends is that he got caught" (p. 421). Such insights may reduce the tendency to place labels on individuals that could influence future deviant or law-abiding actions.

Researchers have indicated that restorative justice in the prison setting begins on a grassroots level; however, programs have difficulty growing and remaining within the correctional setting unless prison administrators see the value of such processes and provide the necessary tools and expenditures necessary for effective program development (Dhami et al., 2009).

Restorative Justice in the Primary Educational Setting

While restorative justice was first introduced as an alternative to the traditional criminal justice system, expansion has occurred within educational settings. One example is occurring at a prep school in New York City, Humanities Preparatory Academy. Hantzopoulos (2013) explains that "grounded in the school's core values of respect for humanity, diversity, truth, and the intellect, and commitment to democracy, peace, and justice, Prep endeavors to provide a transformative schooling experience for those who come through its doors" (p. 8). The school utilizes restorative justice through a practice called *Fairness* in which committee members are selected based on a given case of conflict and members consider the goals of the educational setting during Fairness meetings.

Hantzopoulos (2013) explains actions brought before the committee include "cutting classes, unfair grading policies, and missing homework, …disrespectful and hurtful speech, vandalism, and silencing other community members" and further suggests that "the committee seeks out appropriate consequences for those infractions, rather than simply (handing) out prescribed punishments" (p. 8). The purpose of the program is to address actions that do not fall in line with the values of the setting as well as to restore and reintegrate students who have committed such actions back into the educational community.

Qualitative interviews with participants demonstrated the importance of including restorative-based programs within school settings. For example, one student recommended his friend for the Fairness program for "not respecting the intellect" due to his friend's continued school absence (Hantzopoulos, 2013, p. 9). The Fairness program resulted in a plan to assist the student in completing missed assignments, increased advising, and reintegration within the community. Research focused on participants' perceptions suggests that the majority of students perceive the following:

> The school creates a humane environment in which a culture of respect, tolerance, and democracy flourishes, crystallized in structures like Fairness. Many students feel the Fairness Committee positively contributes to a safe environment and helps them grow personally. They also view it as a fundamental mechanism to build community and forge stronger relationships among student peers and teachers. As a result, many students, including those who had previously felt marginalized from schooling, find refuge and acceptance at this school and are able to succeed and thrive academically.
>
> **Hantzopoulos (2013, p. 7)**

While such educational attributes seem honorable, the author suggests that discomfort may occur for students once they have transitioned to the college educational experience. For instance, one alumna student found herself "frustrated with the way that the administration at her college, a predominantly white liberal arts college, dealt with issues of race and gender;" furthermore, the student suggested traditional practices did not consider the harm to the overall community when values were negated (Hantzopoulos, 2013, p. 9). The author explains restorative practices should not be made mandatory within a given school; however, the inevitable core values of an educational setting should serve as a basis for consideration of the implementation of restorative practices (Hantzopoulos, 2013).

Restorative justice values are also found within alternative schools such as the Montgomery County Youth Center in Pennsylvania. The school includes various aspects of restorative justice within the mission statement such as the promotion of "…the value of individual accountability for choices, decisions, actions and their consequences…" and the importance of "…meet(ing) the individual learning needs of each student..." (Devore & Gentilcore, 1999, p. 97). The alternative school intertwines aspects of restorative justice within the disciplinary process by explaining to students that committing an undesirable action does not equate to being a "bad" human being. Additionally, restorative justice has been utilized within such settings to create the ability for important dialogues to occur. For example, a circle occurred that included a teacher, a campus supervisor, and a student. The circle developed because of a homophobic statement made by the student. The teacher suggested in a pre-circle meeting that "he (the student) and I were close and I truly care for him. Why did he do this?" (Gold, 2011, p. 42). Through the circle process the student was able to provide what was perceived to be a sincere apology for his actions; however, the teacher had a difficult time providing forgiveness to the student during the circle process. This is an important point.

Forgiveness occurs at different points in time for different people in different situations. There is no specific time frame in which one should be ready to forgive. It is individualistic in nature. The teacher did suggest during the resolution round that she would like for the student to address the issue when he heard others make similar homophobic comments as part of the agreement plan. The ability for teachers and students to come together to resolve conflict in an effective manner is essential to teaching children how to resolve conflict in general. If the student was only punished through a traditional method such as suspension, the student would not have had the ability to hear how his action personally affected his teacher. Furthermore, upon returning to school, the break in the teacher/student relationship would not be on the path to genuine restoration or transformation. This is one benefit of communicating through restorative processes.

Another example of restorative justice within the educational setting comes from an infraction centered on high school students who were hazing incoming freshmen into their social circle (DeWitt & DeWitt, 2012). Officials of the school gathered together in order to create an action plan that would help curb future acts of hazing. This plan included a restorative component where the students would meet with a facilitator to discuss the actions. While this example further explains how restorative justice may be applied to multiple types of events, the manner in which the school administrators initiated a dialogue process is less than desirable from a restorative outlook. In this case, if the students did not agree to the restorative plan, they would be suspended from school and would not be allowed to attend major high school events. Further, if the students did not complete the process, the case would be referred to the criminal justice system for consideration of charges. The plan constructed by the administration also required the students to be involved in a number of educational sessions for other students geared toward explaining how hazing is handled by the school administrators (DeWitt & DeWitt, 2012). In order for this process to be truly restorative, the administration and the students should have voluntarily come together in order to determine an action plan. Because the students were not involved in the process, the idea of justice in this case was more coercive. Taking the voluntary nature out of the process essentially violates an important restorative justice tenet.

It appears the implementation of restorative justice within school settings may reduce negative labeling of students and aid in rebuilding relationships within school communities. The previous examples also imply that a well-rounded educational experience not only focuses on learning academic lessons but also assists students in personal growth and relationship building skills.

Restorative Justice in the College Educational Settings

Restorative programs and education are also expanding to university settings. Smith-Cunnien and Parilla (2001) explain that incorporating aspects of restorative justice into the curriculum for criminal justice students is important because of "its influence on criminal justice policy and practice." In addition, the authors argue the importance of creating an elective course that may be voluntarily selected by students which focuses on restorative justice concepts and application of restorative processes.

One example of the implementation of elective courses focused on restorative values and application has been implemented by the primary author of this chapter. Within an introduction to restorative justice course, students are exposed to the values embedded within such processes and students participate in role-playing types of restorative justice processes noted previously within the chapter. Furthermore, students have also been provided the opportunity to select an additional elective course that focuses on applying restorative values within a given setting decided on by the students of the course. Through the application course, students have had the opportunity to provide restorative workshops to students who resided in a particular residential hall on campus. One of the goals of the housing program was to assist students in learning how to approach conflict situations and how to utilize the dialogue communication method during conflicts. The students within the application course also decided to focus their attention on providing an informative session about restorative justice to the university public safety officers. One benefit of providing restorative justice education and application within the criminal justice curriculum is that it provides interested students an ability to become a more active member of their university community. Second, when participants are open to the process, community members may often begin to further explore restorative practices during their personal time and gain a greater sense of community.

Restorative justice is also beginning to be incorporated into college student judicial processes. The Skidmore Integrity Board in Vermont is one such example (Karp & Conrad, 2005). The rationale for including a restorative component within the options of the university judicial process centers on the following idea:

> Colleges cannot effectively respond to student disciplinary problems… through apprehension and removal. The continual student population turnover guarantees that individual-level solutions cannot resolve community-level problems. Instead, solutions must continuously strive to socialize students to be community members, able to consider the consequences of their behavior on the welfare of the community.
> **Karp and Conrad (2005, p. 316)**

The goals of traditional student judicial processes differ from restorative-based judicial processes. While traditional methods usually primarily focus on the guilt or innocence of a student regarding an action, restorative processes tend to move beyond this determination and focus on reparation and reintegration on the involved parties. The two processes may also differ in that in the traditional approach, possible general sanctions are prepared without consideration of a given action or the individual's circumstances who committed the action (Karp & Conrad, 2005). Restorative judicial processes are more focused on making such considerations and constructing a sanction that includes the harms, needs, and causes of a particular action.

Kara and MacAlister (2010) argue that "the overreliance on suspensions and expulsions are elements of a retributive framework that often produce more adverse effects than the ones initially intended. Furthermore, the use of sanctions employed in many colleges and universities is not always in compliance with institutional values and goals" (p. 446). The authors believe it is important to consider restorative processes when academic dishonesty occurs rather than traditional judicial sanctions.

When international students cheat or plagiarize, the researchers contend restorative justice processes are significant because the root causes of the issue must be considered (Kara & MacAlister, 2010). Is the problem rooted in admission standards for international students? Is the problem rooted in a lack of resources for non-English speaking students? Do the academic dishonesty policies take into consideration aspects that may affect international students? Kara and MacAlister (2010) contend one possible answer to curtailing the number of students who find themselves before a traditional student judicial board for academic dishonesty entails that "each department should consider designating an individual faculty member to become a trained facilitator who would be available to be called into the circle by other faculty in that department who are faced with academic misconduct matters" (p. 449). The authors further state the following:

> For restorative justice to be effective in theory and practice, institutional values and goals need to coincide with individual

values and goals. As a culture that adheres to the ideas of respect, tolerance and understanding, campus communities need to foster and cultivate an environment where this can exist. With individual growth and development comes institutional growth and development, where a unified approach that demonstrates honesty, integrity and responsibility become mutually reinforcing.

Kara and MacAlister (2010, p. 452)

In order for such innovations to occur, in most cases, "amendments to university disciplinary policies are necessary to permit the alternative approach envisioned…" (Kara & MacAlister, 2010, p. 449). While intertwining restorative justice values within campus policies and procedures may seem like a difficult task, the benefits of teaching students the importance of care, communication, and consideration of relationships can aid in sculpting a more attentive, responsible citizen who considers the needs of others in addition to their own needs. This educational component can assist in building stronger communities where conflict may be viewed as an opportunity to address important issues.

Restorative Justice in the Workplace

Goodstein and Butterfield (2010) bring to light the importance of considering the integration of restorative justice within the workplace setting. The authors contend that "paying particular attention to perceptions of workplace justice, restoring personal integrity, and the repair of interpersonal trust" should be considered during ethical issues within the business environment (Goodstein & Butterfield, 2010, p. 458). They suggest that when business managers utilize restorative techniques, greater relational bonds within the workplace will occur. Goodstein and Butterfield (2010) state:

> …the manager-as-disciplinarian focuses on punishment and deterrence whereas the manager-as-repairer focuses on restorative justice and moral repair… although both roles place an emphasis on vicarious learning, they differ dramatically in what managers teach observers about how offenders will be treated. In the retributive approach, observers learn that offenders will be disciplined in a manner consistent with the offense. In the restorative justice approach, observers learn that offenders will be restored and reintegrated into the community. (p. 473)

The benefit of such an implemented philosophy in the workplace is that "managers who adopt this approach and emphasize the rebuilding of damaged relationships can provide employees and other stakeholders with a supportive climate that fosters a sense of justice, trust, and hope" (Goodstein & Butterfield, 2010, p. 473). In situations that are non-criminal in nature, a restorative approach is helpful in assisting stakeholders through a healing process. The authors also point out the importance of awareness of variables within a given organizational entity that may allow for reparation and restoration among parties. Goodstein and Aquino (2010) further explain that "the values of an organization, as reflected in its mission statement and organizational culture may be of particular importance in identifying restorative practice potential" (p. 627).

The Expansion of Restorative Justice in Cases of Sexual Violations

McGlynn, Westmarland, and Godden (2012) provide a case study of one affected individual's restorative journey. The individual was sexually assaulted during her adolescent years by a juvenile family member in England. In order for a restorative conference to occur, the authors explain the importance of the affected party to perceive herself as ready to discuss the incidents as well as the importance that meeting the aggressor was completely her decision. After a rape crisis counselor and the victim met weekly for three months, the conference occurred. The victim stated "in retrospect… it was more important to have my say and have him listen than for him to go prison" (McGlynn et al., 2012, p. 228). Effectiveness of sexual violence restorative conferences is said to hinge on "…intensive, survivor-focused support and detailed preparation by someone experienced in this area of work" as well as consideration of "the stage of recovery of the victim-survivor" (McGlynn et al., 2012, p. 229). This point implies that implementation of such restorative processes should not be offense specific but rather individual stakeholder specific. The authors conclude the following with regards to utilizing restorative justice in instances of sexual violence:

> Restorative justice in cases of sexual violence has a role to play in meeting some of the needs and expectations of some victim-survivors, by giving them a voice by which to tell of their harm, by granting a measure of control over the treatment of their complaint, by helping to ensure that their experience is honoured, treated seriously and with respect, such that they gain some measure of justice. This approach must not pit restorative justice against conventional criminal justice in some sort of mirror of the adversarial process itself. Each process has its role; each has limitations.
>
> **McGlynn et al. (2012, p. 239)**

McNevin (2010) explains how restorative justice may be infused within incest-based family therapy processes and provides a case study of a young woman who suggested that her brother had been sexually abusing her for an extended period of time. McNevin (2010) notes how the family therapy process may assist the affected party in moving toward the ability and desire to see her brother again. Likewise, elements of restorative justice are exhibited within the family therapy process through statements of personal responsibility by the brother. The author further explains how the family therapy process mirrors that of a restorative pre-circle preparation phase. Three different therapists work with different parties, including the young woman, the brother, as well as the mother and an additional sister. The goal of incorporating a restorative process within this particular family therapy session was to allow the brother to acknowledge genuine personal responsibility, provide an apology, show remorse, and agree to refrain from such behaviors. For the overall family, the addition of restorative justice to the therapy process may allow each member to verbalize his or her personal experiences, which may lead to stronger relationship ties in the future among the family members (McNevin, 2010).

Restorative Justice and International Relations

While restorative justice may be applied with individual cases, the process dynamic may also be used to address international conflicts as well as post-conflict situations. Nikolic-Ristanovic (2008) indicates that "...possible innovative and restorative ways of dealing with (global) cycles of violence produced by international involvement in local conflicts as well as by terrorism and the war against it" should be provided serious consideration (p. 102). The author contends there is a problem with the "just war theory," which he describes as "...help(ing) one side involved in the local conflict, selected (by the aggressor) as the just or good side, to prevail against the unjust or bad side" (Nikolic-Ristanovic, 2008, p. 102). The author argues that taking such a position creates additional victimization among the members of a given community because "existing international mechanisms are not very suitable for dealing with interconnected international and local conflicts in terms of overcoming denial and fostering the acknowledgment of atrocities and sufferings of people from both powerful and powerless states" (Nikolic-Ristanovic, 2008, p. 111).

Reddy (2008) suggests that restorative justice theory "...has the capacity to provide values, principles and alternatives to the way responses to large-scale violence and civil armed conflict are formulated" (p. 128). One noted example occurred within a sector of Papua New Guinea, Bougainville. Restorative practices occurred in this region following a war that spanned approximately a decade. During this time period "disputes over land and environment related to the Australian-owned Panguna copper mine became the impetus for a rebellion that reignited in many people a longstanding urge for independence from PNG (Papua New Guinea)..." (Reddy, 2008, pp. 118–119). Following the war, a peace operation took place over a six year period. The stakeholders included military personnel, local citizens, as well as citizens from Australia, Fiji, New Zealand, and Vanuatu (Reddy, 2008). In order for reconciliation ceremonies to occur, a negotiation had to be made that included parties prior to the conference process. Within the ceremony, members of the circle were provided with the opportunity to "*Tarout*," which means "unrestrained emotional outpourings are allowed – even encouraged" (Reddy, 2008, p. 123). After this portion of the process was complete, personal responsibility and perceptions of the incident were provided, which were followed by apologies. Next, reparation was provided through "gifts and compensation… to the survivors or the victim's relatives" (Reddy, 2008, p. 123). Obviously, in cases of death, it is difficult to repair the harm; therefore, reconciliation on some level may be the goal. In such instances, examples such as "returning the bones of a victim who has been killed occurs, and there have been occasions where former militia fighters have rebuilt buildings they destroyed" (Reddy, 2008, p. 124). Lastly, a closing to the process occurs through individuals partaking in food and/or song and dance. One important aspect within the process noted above is that once forgiveness is provided, the parties move forward from the instance.

Restorative justice is often exhibited globally through Truth and Reconciliation Commissions. Examples include the Sierra Leone Truth and Reconciliation Commission (Park, 2010), the Ghana National Reconciliation Commission (Ameh, 2006), and the Truth and Reconciliation Commission of South Africa (Danaher, 2010). While the specifics of a particular commission may differ, a general goal of such processes is to provide an arena for discussion regarding perceived harms that occur during wars, due to human rights violations or violent episodes.

CONCLUSION

The values of restorative justice that appear in various restorative processes are derived from the peacemaking paradigm and are essential to a moral life and ethical policies and practice. The tenets of peacemaking criminology include care, connectedness, and mindfulness and are the foundation of restorative practices. As a global society, a consideration regarding how justice is defined is also important. What will happen to members of the current and future generations if individual and societal conflicts are not resolved in a moral and just manner? The values underlying restorative practices may often be perceived as unachievable, yet the ideas embedded within restorative justice and peacemaking criminology seem to flow from a deeper, more humane level of understanding—an understanding that victims and offenders alike are human beings who have a capacity for remorse, forgiveness, and restoration—transformation.

REFERENCES

Abramson, A. M. (2003). Sustainable relationships and competing values: Restorative justice initiatives and the police — a case study. *Police Practice and Research, 4*(4), 391–398.

Adams, P., & Chandler, S. M. (2004). Responsive regulation in child welfare: Systemic challenging to mainstreaming the family group conference. *Journal of Sociology & Social Welfare, 31*(1), 93–116.

Ameh, R. K. (2006). Uncovering truth: Ghana's National Reconciliation Commission excavation of past human rights abuses. *Contemporary Justice Review, 9*(4), 345–368.

Braswell, M. C., Fuller, J., & Lozoff, B. (2001). *Corrections, peacemaking, and restorative justice: Transforming individuals and institutions.* Cincinnati: Anderson Publishing.

Burford, G., & Adams, P. (2004). Restorative justice, responsive regulation and social work. *Journal of Sociology & Social Welfare, 31*(1), 7–26.

Chatterjee, J., & Elliott, L. (2003). Restorative policing in Canada: The Royal Canadian mounted police, community justice forums, and the youth criminal justice act. *Police Practice and Research, 4*(4), 347–359.

Danaher, W. J., Jr. (2010). Music that will bring back the dead? Resurrection, reconciliation, and restorative justice in post-apartheid South Africa. *Journal of Religious Ethics, 38*(1), 115–141.

Devore, D., & Gentilcore, K. (1999). Balanced and restorative justice and educational programming for youth at-risk. *The Clearing House, 73*(2), 96–100.

DeWitt, D. M., & DeWitt, L. J. (2012). A case of high school hazing: Applying restorative justice to promote organizational learning. *National Association of Secondary School Principals: NASSP Bulletin, 96*(3), 228–242.

Dhami, M. K., Mantle, G., & Fox, D. (2009). Restorative justice in prison. *Contemporary Justice Review, 12*(4), 433–448.

Dzur, A. W., & Wertheimer, A. (2002). Forgiveness and public deliberation: The practice of restorative justice. *Criminal Justice Ethics, 21*(1), 3–20.

Fortune, D., Thompson, J., Pedlar, A., & Yuen, F. (2010). Social justice and women leaving prison: Beyond punishment and exclusion. *Contemporary Justice Review, 13*(1), 19–33.

Fulkerson, A. (2009). The drug treatment court as a form of restorative justice. *Contemporary Justice Review, 12*(3), 253–267.

Gold, S. (2011). Restorative justice in alternative education. *Encounter: Education for Meaning and Social Justice, 24*(1), 41–44.

Goodstein, J., & Aquino, K. (2010). And restorative justice for all: Redemption, forgiveness, and reintegration in organizations. *Journal of Organizational Behavior, 31*(1), 624–628.

Goodstein, J., & Butterfield, K. D. (2010). Extending the horizon of business ethics: Restorative justice and the aftermath of unethical behavior. *Business Ethics Quarterly, 20*(3), 453–480.

Gregory, M. J. (2011). Practical wisdom and the ethnic of care in probation practice. *European Journal of Probation, 3*(3), 60–77.

Hackler, J. (2004). Conferencing in the youth criminal justice act of Canada: Policy developments in British Columbia. *Canadian Journal of Criminology & Criminal Justice, 46*(3), 343–366.

Hantzopoulos, M. (2013). The fairness committee: Restorative justice in a small urban public high school. *The Prevention Researcher, 20*(1), 7–10.

Hazen, N. (2012). An exploratory view of the juvenile arbitration program of Aiken County, South Carolina. *International Social Science Review, 87*(3/4), 102–126.

Holsinger, K., & Crowther, A. (2005). College course participation for incarcerated youth: Bringing restorative justice to life. *Journal of Criminal Justice Education, 16*(2), 328–339.

Jasini, R., & Phan, V. (2011). Victim participation at the extraordinary chambers in the courts of Cambodia: Are retributive and restorative principles enhancing the prospect for justice? *Cambridge Review of International Affairs, 24*(3), 379–401.

Kara, F., & MacAlister, D. (2010). Responding to academic dishonesty in universities: A restorative justice approach. *Contemporary Justice Review, 13*(4), 443–453.

Karp, D., & Conrad, S. (2005). Restorative justice and college student misconduct. *Public Organization Review: A Global Journal, 5*(1), 315–333.

Keanini, L. (2011). ADP in Hawai'i courts: The role of restorative justice mediators. *Asian-Pacific Law & Policy Journal, 12*(2), 174–185.

Keeva, S., & Newell, T. (2004). Facing the victims. *ABA Journal, 90*(1), 71–73.

Lovell, M. L., Helfgott, J. B., & Lawrence, C. (2002). Narrative accounts from the citizens, victims, and offenders restoring justice program. *Contemporary Justice Review, 5*(3), 261–273.

Mackay, R. E. (2003). Restorative justice and the children's hearings: A proposal. *European Journal of Crime, Criminal Law & Criminal Justice, 11*(1), 1–17.

McCold, P. (2003). An experiment in police-based restorative justice: The Bethlehem (PA) project. *Police Practice and Research, 4*(4), 379–390.

McDowell, L. A. (2012). *Criminal justice students' perceptions of restorative justice: A study of demographic variables and restorative justice values* (Doctoral dissertation). Retrieved from search. proquest.com.logon.lynx.lib.usm.edu/docview/1277441795?accountid=13946.

McGlynn, C., Westmarland, N., & Godden, N. (2012). 'I just wanted him to hear me': Sexual violence and the possibilities of restorative justice. *Journal of Law and Society, 39*(2), 213–240.

McNevin, E. (2010). Applied restorative justice as a complement to systemic family therapy: Theory and practice implications for families experiencing intra-familial adolescent sibling incest. *The Australian and New Zealand Journal of Family Therapy, 31*(1), 60–72.

Nikolic-Ristanovic, V. (2008). Local conflicts and international interventions: Victimisation of civilians and possibilities for restorative global responses. *Contemporary Justice Review, 11*(2), 101–115.

O'Mahony, D., & Doak, J. (2004). Restorative justice – Is more better? The experience of police-led restorative cautioning pilots in northern Ireland. *The Howard Journal, 43*(5), 484–505.

Park, A. S. J. (2010). Community-based restorative transitional justice in Sierra Leone. *Contemporary Justice Review, 13*(1), 95–119.

Reddy, P. (2008). Reconciliation in Bougainville: Civil war, peacekeeping and restorative justice. *Contemporary Justice Review, 11*(2), 117–130.

Schwartz, S., & Levitas, L. (2011). Restorative justice for veterans: The San Francisco Sheriff's Department's Community of Veterans Engaged in Restoration (COVER). *Washington University Journal of Law & Policy, 36*(47), 47–63.

Smith-Cunnien, S. L., & Parilla, P. F. (2001). Restorative justice in the criminal justice curriculum. *Journal of Criminal Justice Education, 12*(2), 385–403.

Vigorita, M. S. (2002). Planning and implementing a criminal justice course with university students and youthful offenders. *Journal of Criminal Justice Education, 13*(2), 403–432.

Walker, L. (2010). Huikahi restorative circles: Group process for self-directed reentry planning and family healing. *European Journal of Probation, 2*(2), 76–95.

Walker, L., & Hayashi, L. A. (2007). Pono Kaulike: A Hawaii criminal court provides restorative justice practices for healing relationships. *Federal Probation, 71*(3), 18–24.

Wood, W. R. (2013). Victims as stakeholders: Research from a juvenile court on the changing roles of victims in restorative justice. *Western Criminology Review, 14*(1), 6–24.

Zehr, H. (2002). *The little book of restorative justice*. Intercourse: Good Books.

CHAPTER 15

Keeping an Eye on the Keeper: Prison Corruption and Its Control[1]

Bernard J. McCarthy

In Chapter 1 of this volume, Michael Braswell states, "Ethics is the study of right and wrong, good and evil." This chapter focuses on a troublesome and damaging problem in the administration of justice involving conduct that is both wrong and evil in U.S. prison systems. It involves a personal choice by employees to engage in behavior that is clearly wrong and damaging.

Corrupt practices within the criminal justice system undermine and neutralize the administration of justice as well as destroy public confidence in the system. Corruption serves to negate the goals and processes of corrections and breeds disrespect for the process and the aims of justice. The purposes of punishment are also undermined.

The prison system is one of the most visible and symbolic aspects of the coercive nature of criminal justice, yet at the same time it is one that is most closed to the public. As Supreme Court Justice Kennedy (2003) stated to the American

[1]Adapted from McCarthy, B. J. Keeping an eye on the keeper: prison corruption and its control. *The Prison Journal, 64*(2), 113–125.

Bar Association, "Even those of us who have specific professional responsibilities for the criminal justice system can be neglectful when it comes to the subject of corrections. The focus of the legal profession, perhaps even the obsessive focus, has been on the process for determining guilt or innocence. When someone has been judged guilty and the appellate and collateral review process has ended, the legal profession seems to lose all interest. When the prisoner is taken way, our attention turns to the next case. When the door is locked against the prisoner, we do not think about what is behind it." This chapter takes a glimpse at what goes on behind the door—and exposes the student to a little-known area of ethical misconduct.

With the exception of the imposition of death, the deprivation of liberty is the most serious action society takes against an offender. The prison represents society's ultimate penalty. By being sent to prison, offenders are involuntarily removed from the community through a legal process and placed in a confinement facility where their liberties are circumscribed. In the United States, prison systems are a huge and expensive enterprise. The 50 states, the federal government, and the District of Columbia all operate prisons. More than 1.6 million people are confined in prisons, with terms ranging in length of time from 1 year to life without parole. An additional 786,000 inmates are confined in jails throughout the United States. In addition, based on the threat that individuals pose to society and the crimes committed, inmates are confined in conditions that severely restrict their freedom, and they are deprived of goods, services, and liberties from which nonincarcerated citizens are free to choose. More recently, prisons in the United States have become more punitive in their outlook and operating philosophy, and conditions of confinement have become more severe. *Harsh Justice*, a book by Yale law professor James Q. Whitman, makes the controversial suggestion that the goals of the U.S. prison system have shifted from rehabilitation to purposes that degrade and demean prisoners.

In this chapter, the problem of **corruption** and its control is examined as one form of ethical misconduct in state correctional systems. Historically, staff misconduct in the form of prison corruption has been a persistent and pervasive feature of corrections, periodically erupting in the form of scandals that are usually brought to our attention by the press. No prison system is immune from this problem; in recent years, major prison scandals have been reported in Alabama, California, Delaware, Florida, Hawaii, Illinois, Michigan, New York, Pennsylvania, Tennessee, and Texas. Political payoffs, organized crime, large-scale street gangs, and the general avarice of people who have been hired to work in prisons have contributed or played a role in a number of these scandals. Other than media reports and the occasional state investigation, little is known about the problem. Prison systems are not open to the public, and much of what goes on inside is hidden from public view. In fact, Supreme Court Justice William Kennedy, in a speech to the American Bar Association, described the prison as "the hidden world of punishment; [and] we would be startled by what we see" if we were to look.

Periodically, the prison becomes exposed to the general public when extreme abuses make their way to the public eye, as in the case of the charges of torture and sexual abuse occurring in the military prison in Abu Ghraib. Military police officers working in a U.S. Defense Department confinement facility used digital cameras to record their abuses of inmates, and these photographs were disseminated worldwide on the Internet. Philip Zimbardo, a social psychologist and architect of the Stanford Prison Experiment, described these actions as an example of the Lucifer Effect. The Lucifer Effect describes the process of transformation by which good people are working at jobs that transform them into evil people.

■ Learn More on the Internet

For more details on Zimbardo's Lucifer Effect concept, see www.luciferef-fect.com.   ■

THE ROLE OF STAFF IN PRISON MISCONDUCT

One of the most critical elements in any correctional system is the quality of the staff hired to work in prisons. The critical role played by employees in the correctional enterprise has long been noted by correctional practitioners and prison reformers:

> [It] is obvious, too, that the best security which society can have, that suitable punishments will be inflicted in a suitable manner, must arise from the character of the men to whom the government of the prison is entrusted.
>
> **(Boston Prison Discipline Society, 1972, p. 18)**

In 1870, the Reverend James Woodworth, Secretary of the California Prison Commission, stated:

> Until [prison guard reform] is accomplished, nothing is accomplished. When this work is done, everything will be done, for all the details of a reformed prison discipline are wrapped up in this supreme effort, as oak is in the acorn.
>
> **Fogel, 1979, p. 69**

Jessica Mitford (1973) maintained that the mental health and stability of the keepers may be more important in understanding prisons than the mental health and character of the kept.

Generally, in the area of public service, the integrity of government workers has been viewed as a significant factor in the effective and efficient operation of government. The most visible forms of corruption occur in the front end of the criminal justice system and involve the police. In criminal justice, a voluminous literature exists on police corruption, yet this subject represents one of the least-understood areas in corrections. This chapter shifts the focus to prisons and the types of corrupt practices occurring behind their walls (both figuratively and literally). Here, we examine the forms, functions, and impact of corrupt practices on the correctional process.

Corrupt practices in prisons range from simple acts of theft and pilferage to large-scale criminal conspiracies (e.g., drug trafficking, counterfeiting rings, sale of paroles). These forms of correctional malpractice may be directed at inmates and their families, other employees, the state, and the general community.

The impact of such practices cannot be underestimated. They are destructive and dangerous. In terms of their impact on the criminal justice system, corrupt practices undermine and erode respect for the justice system by both offenders and the general public and lead to the selective nullification of the punishment and the "**pains of imprisonment**" (i.e., the correctional process for certain offenders). For example, offenders may be able to arrange the purchase of paroles and pardons, arrange for confinement in a less secure setting, or drastically improve their standard of living in custody. Corrupt practices may also lead to a breakdown in the control structure of the organization and to the demoralization of correctional workers. It also dramatically increases the threat to their safety when drugs, cell phones, or weapons are smuggled into prison. The existence of corrupt practices also undermines the impact of correctional programs designed to change offenders. For example, the importation of drugs into a prison may completely undo the efforts of maintaining a drug-free facility.

The pernicious effects of employee misconduct were pointed out by Massachusetts Public Safety Director Ed Flynn when commenting on the unjust treatment suffered by a prison inmate that led to his death. Flynn said, "If nothing else, inmates must leave our custody with a belief that there is a moral order in the world...If they leave our care and control believing that rules and regulations do not mean what they say they mean, that rules and regulations can be applied arbitrarily or capriciously for personal interest then we fail society. We fail them and we will unleash people more dangerous than when they went in" (Belluck, 2004).

As one might expect, the incentives and opportunities for corrupt behavior for employees engaged in low-visibility discretionary actions in prison systems are many. From the offenders' perspective, they have everything to gain to persuade staff to make decisions that benefit them personally (i.e., the so-called "pains of imprisonment" may be neutralized or their release from custody secured) and very little to lose. Some inmates seek to exploit any weaknesses they may find in the system, including those of the staff. From the employees' perspective, corrupt practices represent a lucrative, albeit illicit, way to supplement one's income (and, in some systems, usually without significant risk). In one investigation nicknamed Operation Bad Fellas, U.S. Bureau of Prison correctional officers were charged with smuggling heroin, marijuana, steroids, Italian food, vodka, wine, vitamins, clothing, and electronic equipment into a federal correctional facility in New York City. Bribes received by staff ranged from $100 to $1,000 per delivery (Suro, 1997).

In examining staff corruption within a prison system, three basic questions are raised: First, what is corruption, and what forms does it take in a prison setting? Second, what factors appear to be associated with it? Third, what steps should be taken to control the problem?

DEFINING CORRUPTION IN A CORRECTIONAL ENVIRONMENT

In the correctional literature, the concept of corruption has been used frequently, usually referring to a general adulteration of the formal goals of the correctional process (Rothman, 1971; Sykes, 1956, 1958). The literature on corruption, particularly police corruption, provides a much narrower definition, which aids researchers interested in studying the more specific problem (see Kleinig, 1996). For the purposes of this chapter, corruption is defined as the intentional violation of organizational norms (i.e., laws, rules, and regulations) by public employees for personal material gain.

This definition was formulated on the basis of a review of the corruption literature—particularly the literature on police corruption—and guides our discussion of the issue. As one might expect, varying definitions and corresponding approaches to the study of corruption exist (Heidenheimer, 1970). In the research on police corruption, most studies appear to use what has been referred to as a public office-centered definition of corruption (Simpson, 1978). The public office-centered definition views corruption as essentially a violation of organizational norms by a public employee for personal gain (Heidenheimer, 1970). Examples of this approach may be found in the writings of Sherman (1974), Meyer (1976), Goldstein (1977), Barker (1977), and Kleinig (1996), and the approach has been adopted in this chapter. Corruption occurs when a public servant (prison employee) violates organizational rules and regulations for his or her own personal material gain.

In operationalizing this definition of corruption for research purposes, certain conditions must be satisfied before an act can be defined as corrupt. First, the action must involve individuals who function as employees. Second, the offense must be in violation of the formal rules of the organization. Third, the offense must involve an employee receiving some personal material gain (something of value) for the misuse of one's office. These conditions are used to distinguish corrupt behavior clearly from other forms of staff misconduct, such as excessive use of force. A standard definition of corruption, consistent with the general literature, is critical in building an information base regarding corrupt practices in corrections and for comparative purposes with the larger criminal justice system.

TYPES OF PRISON CORRUPTION

In contrast to the literature on police corruption, very little is known regarding the types of corrupt practices experienced by correctional agencies, especially prisons. Court cases, media accounts, and inmate and staff surveys could be conducted, but they would provide an incomplete view of the issue. Another approach is to examine the internal affairs records of a state correctional agency (see McCarthy, 1981). From an administrative point of view, this approach examines the types of misconduct that are reported and acted on within a system.

An internal affairs unit has the responsibility for investigating all allegations of misconduct by staff or inmates. The cases during a specific time period were reviewed first to identify those that fit the preceding definition of corruption and, second, to identify and analyze the range and types of corrupt practices experienced by this agency. Admittedly, this information source provides a limited view of the problem because it is based on official statistics. However, as researchers in the field of police corruption have suggested, the records of the internal affairs unit represent one of the best available sources of information for examining this topic (Meyer, 1976; Sherman, 1979).

A content analysis of the case files identified several types of corrupt conduct: theft, trafficking in contraband, embezzlement, misuse of authority, and a residual or miscellaneous category.

Theft generally involved accounts of items reported as stolen from inmates during frisks and cell searches (drugs, money, jewelry), visitors who were being processed for visiting, and staff members. This form of misconduct was generally committed by low-level staff (e.g., correctional officers) and was opportunistic in nature.

Trafficking in contraband involved staff members conspiring with inmates and civilians to smuggle contraband (illicit drugs, alcohol, money, steroids, food, and weapons) into correctional facilities for money, drugs, or services (usually of a sexual nature). The organization of this activity varied considerably. Some were large-scale conspiracies involving street gangs or organized crime officials on both the inside and the outside. Others were individuals acting on their own. As part of their sentence, inmates are deprived of access to many things that are accorded to free-world citizens. The items smuggled into prisons range from items such as food, makeup, and cigarettes to much more serious items such as drugs, guns, bullets, and explosive devices. In recent years, dozens of staff and inmates across the country have been arrested for smuggling in cell phones to inmates. These phones have been used to continue outside criminal activities (organized crime), intimidate witnesses, and engage in criminal activities such as drug smuggling. According to one report, in Philadelphia, guards were indicted for smuggling drugs, cigarettes, and cell phones. One guard made up to $10,000 for bringing in cigarettes and a phone before being caught (Butterfield, 2004).

Acts of embezzlement were defined as systematically converting state property for one's own use. This offense was differentiated from theft. Theft tended to occur in single events that were opportunistic in nature. Embezzlement involved employees, sometimes with the help of inmates, systematically stealing money or materials from state accounts (inmate canteens or employee credit unions), state property, and warehouses.

Misuse of authority is a general category involving the intentional misuse of discretion for personal material gain. This form of corruption consisted of three basic offenses directed against inmates: the acceptance of gratuities from inmates for special consideration in obtaining legitimate prison privileges (e.g., payoffs to receive choice cells or job assignments); the acceptance of gratuities for special consideration in obtaining or protecting illicit prison activities (e.g., allowing illegal drug sales or gambling); and the mistreatment or extortion of inmates by staff for personal material gain (e.g., threatening to punish or otherwise harm an inmate if a payment is not forthcoming).

An additional form of misuse of authority is the taking of bribes by correctional administrators to award contracts to private vendors for services needed by the correctional system. As the privatization movement continues to grow in corrections, we can expect more reports of this form of misconduct as some companies vie for an unfair advantage. The use of an open bidding process for contracts helps minimize this problem.

Another form of misuse of authority that is getting attention in the media is sexual misconduct involving staff and inmates, staff against staff, and staff and offender family members/friends. A National Institute of Corrections (2000) study found that roughly one-half of the agencies in the Department of Corrections have been involved in litigation related to sexual misconduct. At least 22 state correctional agencies were facing class action or damage suits as a result of sexual misconduct by staff. One major reason for this upswing in allegations and charges is the use of cross-gender assignments in prisons, that is, male officers assigned to supervise females and female officers assigned to supervise male offenders. Several studies have concluded that this is a major problem in corrections (see, e.g., Buell, Layman, McCampbell, & Smith, 2003).

Staff sexual misconduct with other employees usually involves a supervisory relationship and exploits the imbalance in power. Sexual exploitation of family members and friends of inmates occurs when a staff member either accepts an offer of sexual favors and/or takes advantage of the power relationship he or she has over the inmate and the inmate's family by extorting sexual services.

THE ROLE OF DISCRETION

All forms of corruption involve the misuse of discretion by public employees. The role played by discretion in corrections is significant. By law, correctional officials are provided with a broad mandate to develop and administer correctional agencies. This broad authority extends to devising rules, regulations, and procedures designed to control and otherwise handle offenders under custody. Corruption occurs when officials misuse this discretionary power for personal material gain.

At a general level, three forms of discretionary misconduct can be identified: misfeasance, malfeasance, and nonfeasance. For the purpose of understanding the relationship between corrupt practices and the misuse of authority, the different forms of corruption have been sorted into the three categories of discretionary misconduct (see Table 15.1).

Table 15.1 Pattern of Corruption by Type of Decision

Corrupt Acts by Discretionary Decisions	Officials Involved Misfeasance
Provide preferential treatment and special privileges	Line staff
Selective application of rewards and punishments	Line staff
Forms of legitimate release	Administrators
Misappropriation of resources	Administrators
Malfeasance trafficking (cell phones, drugs, alcohol, weapons, and money)	Line staff
Extortion/exploitation	Line staff
Protection rackets	Line staff
Embezzlement/theft	Line staff & Administrators
Criminal conspiracies	Line staff
Facilitation of escapes	Line staff
Nonfeasance failure to enforce regulations	Line staff
Coverups	Administrators & Line staff

Misfeasance refers to the improper performance of some act that an official may lawfully do (Black's Law Dictionary, 2004). Offenses in corrections that fall into this category include the acceptance of gratuities for special privileges or preferential treatment (e.g., assignment to honor blocks, access to phone calls), the selective application of formal rewards and punishments to inmates for a fee, the sale of paroles or other forms of release, and the misuse or misappropriation of state resources for one's own personal gain. All these acts involve an employee misusing the lawful authority vested in his or her office for personal gain.

Corrupt practices falling into the category of misfeasance are directed at improving the living conditions of inmates and, as a result, they reduce the deprivations associated with imprisonment. The misuse of lawful authority appears to be in an area in which line staff have the greatest opportunities to maximize their personal gain (especially in supplementing their income through the commission of illicit acts), because the nature of their work permits them the greatest influence over routine prisoner conditions. These acts are also considered low-visibility ones with little oversight at the lowest levels.

Malfeasance refers to misconduct or wrongdoing by a public official or employee (Black's Law Dictionary, 2004), as opposed to the improper use of legitimate power or authority. Corrupt practices that fall into this category involve primarily criminal acts and include theft; embezzlement; trafficking in contraband; extortion; exploitation of inmates or their families for money, goods, and services; protection rackets; assisting escapes (as opposed to arranging paroles or sentence communications); running prostitution rings; and engaging in criminal conspiracies with inmates for such purposes as forgery, drug sales, and counterfeiting.

Acts of malfeasance appear to represent more aggressive and serious acts by staff to supplement their incomes. This type of offense is similar to the grass eater/meat eater distinction found in studies of police corruption (Knapp Commission, 1973). Meat eaters are viewed as aggressively exploiting every possible situation for personal gain. Grass eaters, however, take whatever comes their way. For instance, a meat eater might sell drugs in prison, whereas a grass eater might respond to an inmate's request for drugs. This type of behavior is destructive to the correctional environment and in a very real way poses a danger to inmates and staff.

The last category is **nonfeasance**. Nonfeasance refers to the failure to act according to one's responsibilities or the omission of an act that an official ought to perform (Black's Law Dictionary, 2004). McKorkle (1970) has suggested that nonfeasance is more responsible for corrupting correctional officers than malfeasance. Two types of corrupt practices appear to be involved in this type of decision: (1) selectively ignoring inmate violations of institutional rules, such as permitting inmates to engage in sexual activities with visitors or looking the other way when marijuana or other drugs are smuggled into the facility by visitors in return for payment; and (2) the failure to report or stop other employees involved in misconduct. This second practice might typically consist of a low-level employee not informing on a fellow officer or superior because of an implied or direct promise of personal gain, such as promotion, transfer, or time off or reduced duties. In other cases, an administrator may fail to stop staff misconduct for fear of public scandal and possible loss of position.

As Braswell aptly points out in the introductory chapter to this book, "Our beliefs and values regarding right and wrong are shaped by many forces ... being unethical is not simply committing an evil or wrong act (commission), it is also a matter of being an indirect accomplice to evil by silently standing by when evil occurs (omission)." In prisons, this might occur when misconduct is committed and you know about it and do not do anything about it. For instance, the revelations of torture in the U.S. prisons in Iraq were brought forward by individuals who were working there and bore witness to the actions of their fellow soldiers. The conduct is wrong and involves both action and witness: commission and omission.

FACTORS ASSOCIATED WITH CORRUPTION

Research has shown that certain factors are associated with varying levels of corruption in an agency. In a U.S. Department of Justice study on municipal corruption (1978), two factors were identified as having a major influence on the level and degree of corruption experienced by a particular governmental agency. These factors were (1) the opportunities for corruption and (2) the incentives within the workplace to make use of those opportunities (Gardiner & Lyman, 1978). In the following section, these two factors are examined within the context of a prison environment.

A third driving force identified by other studies of public corruption was the influence of politics (Gardiner, 1970; Sherman, 1978). Sherman suggests that a leading explanation for police corruption was the capture of the department by the political environment. Prison systems come under the executive branch of government, and their leaders are political appointees. As such, corrections is not immune from the power of politics. Correctional programs at the state and local levels are influenced by the political process, particularly in terms of the appointment of administrative staff and the allocation of resources.

THE ROLE OF OPPORTUNITIES

Three external forces influence prison systems and directly affect the incentives and opportunities for corruption. One is the continuing trend to incarcerate criminals. This has led to unprecedented levels of crowding in state and federal prison systems. Second, career criminals are receiving longer sentences as the public sentiment toward punishment continues to harden (e.g., "three strikes and you're out" laws), and these long-term offenders are making up a larger percentage of the inmate population. A third is that citizen attitudes toward the treatment of prisoners have led to a toughening of programs directed at prison inmates (e.g., chain gangs, the introduction of tobacco-free prisons, and the elimination of amenities such as college-level educational programs and recreation). These forces increase the deprivations associated with imprisonment and provide extra incentive to inmates to attempt to mitigate or neutralize the pains of imprisonment.

The opportunities for corruption arise from the tremendous amounts of discretionary authority allocated by the legislature to correctional officials. As Costikyan has noted, "Corruption is always where the discretionary power resides" (1974). In the prison, employees—particularly low-level ones (e.g., correction officers, counselors, and other line workers)—are responsible for monitoring and controlling virtually all inmate behavior. These officials constantly make low-visibility discretionary decisions that reward positive behavior and penalize negative behavior. These decisions directly affect the day-to-day living conditions experienced by inmates in custody.

In a prison environment, staff members—armed with a limited arsenal of formal rewards and punishments—are given the task of controlling a reluctant, resistant, and sometimes hostile inmate population. Special privileges in the form of extra television time, phone calls, job assignments, cell changes, conjugal visits, transfers, and furloughs may be used to reward positive behavior. Punishments in the form of withdrawal of privileges, transfers, or various forms of deprivation (from restriction of calls to solitary confinement and loss of good time) are used to control inmates.

The way that staff members apply these rewards and punishments has both short-term and long-term consequences for inmates and their experiences in the correctional system. Accordingly, when one considers the conditions of confinement, one recognizes the many incentives and pressures for inmates to attempt to corrupt staff as one means of improving their living conditions or for staff to exploit their power. Individuals sentenced to prison are subjected to various levels of deprivations, commonly referred to as "pains of imprisonment," that affect both the physical and psychological states of the individuals. Sykes defined these pains of imprisonment as the deprivation of liberty, goods and services, heterosexual relations, autonomy, and security (Sykes, 1958). In dealing with these "pains" associated with confinement, inmates make various adaptations to their immediate environment to help soften its psychological and physical impact. One of the techniques they use is the corruption of correctional employees as a means of neutralizing or improving their conditions of confinement (e.g., through the smuggling of drugs, food, radios, or money, or the purchase of privileges).

In her journalistic study of an inmate incarcerated in a maximum-security prison, Sheehan made the following comment regarding the motivation of inmates in prison: "Most men in the prison are in prison precisely because they were not willing to go without on the street. They are no more willing to go without in prison, so they hustle to afford what they cannot afford to buy." (1978, p. 9) Hustling usually brings the inmates and/or confederates into situations in which they need the cooperation of a staff member, to overlook an infraction, perform a favor, or smuggle in some item. As such, the incentives or pressures for inmates to influence the reward-and-punishment structure through corruption are enormous. Gardiner and Lyman underscore this point when they state: "Corruption can only occur when officials have an opportunity to exercise their authority in ways which would lead others to want to pay for favorable treatment" (1978, p. 141). When it comes to the prison, nowhere in society are deprivations found that exceed the harsh conditions of confinement found in the deep end of confinement facilities.

INCENTIVES FOR CORRUPTION

There are many incentives for employees to take advantage of the power associated with their position in an institutional setting. They range from structural and organizational characteristics of prison management to individual factors (e.g., honesty of staff, the financial needs of employees).

A major incentive for corrupt practices results from defects in the prison organization's control structure. The prison, which is essentially a coercive organization, formally bases its control on the use of coercive power (Etzioni, 1964, p. 59). However, correctional employees, particularly line staff, find that there are limits to the degree of compliance achieved through the use of coercive power (Cloward, 1960; Sykes, 1958). To do the job successfully, coercive power must be supplemented with informal exchange relations with inmates. These informal control practices are utilized by staff for control purposes and are responsible for the smooth functioning of the institution and for maintaining an uneasy peace (Cloward, 1960; Irwin, 1980; Sykes, 1958). As Sykes pointed out more than 40 years ago:

> "The custodians (guards) … are under strong pressure to compromise with their captives for it is a paradox that they can insure their dominance only by allowing it to be corrupted. Only by tolerating violations of minor rules and regulations can the guard secure compliance in the major areas of the custodial regime."
>
> (1956, p. 158)

According to Sykes, three factors are responsible for undermining the formal control structure of the prison: (1) friendships with inmates, (2) reciprocal relationships, and (3) defaults. Each of these factors develops at the line-staff level as a function of long-term and close working associations between guards and inmates in a close setting. Irwin (1980), in a contemporary update, cited corrupt favoritism as a significant factor in the day-to-day management of the prison.

Corruption through friendship evolves from the close contact that prisoners and guards share in their daily interactions. In many cases, they get to know one another as individuals, and friendships may develop. These friendships may, in turn, affect how staff members use their authority. **Corruption through reciprocity** occurs as an indirect consequence of the exchange relations that develop between inmates and staff: "You do something for me, I'll do something for you." **Corruption through default** occurs when staff members (e.g., cellblock officers) begin to rely on inmates to assist them with their duties, such as report writing and cell checks. In time, the employee depends on the inmates for their assistance in satisfactorily performing his or her duties.

Cloward (1960) also pointed out how defects in the prison organization's control apparatus lead staff members to develop informal means of control through the development of various accommodations between the keepers and the kept. **Material accommodations** occur when staff provide certain inmates with access to forbidden goods and services or contraband in return for their cooperation. Cloward provides an example of this when he quotes an inmate explaining how he makes home brew:

> You go to make arrangements with the mess sergeant. He gets the ingredients and when we're in business … it's one of those you do this for me and I'll do this for you sort of thing… The sergeant has to feed 1,500 men. It don't look good if he goofs. He wants the job done right. Now we're the ones who do the work, the cooking and all of that. So the sergeant, he says, okay you can make a little drink. But see to it that you get that food on the lines or the deal's off.
>
> **1960, p. 7**

Power accommodations occur when selected inmates are provided with access to restricted information, such as the date and time of an impending shakedown (search of cells) or access to key correctional personnel. Frequently, these take the form of reciprocal relationships in which valuable information is exchanged by both staff and inmates. Inmates inform on one another, and staff in turn may disclose administration plans regarding such activities as the time and place of cell searches.

Status accommodations result when staff provide special deference to certain inmates. According to Cloward:

The right guy … seems to be left alone (by staff) in spite of conspicuous deviance from official values, and this mark of untouchability results in high status among his peers.

1960, p. 40

The cumulative effect of these accommodations may predispose certain correctional employees to take advantage of their situation and attempt to materially benefit from their working relationships with inmates, staff, and contractors.

Another factor that complicates matters is the type and quality of people recruited and hired to work in correctional facilities. Frequently, the quality of the workforce is uneven and sometimes substandard because of low pay and poor working conditions. These individuals are placed in situations in which they are given considerable discretionary authority (without much training in its use) in a setting in which the visibility of their actions is quite low. When this situation occurs, the probability of corrupt practices increases. Another factor that provides an incentive for corruption is the impact of politics. If the selection and promotion of employees are influenced by politics, employee decisions may benefit the political party in power.

CONTROLLING CORRUPTION

First, it must be recognized that corruption is a regular feature of government processes. The problem of corruption will always be hovering in the background and can probably never be eradicated; however, certain steps may be taken to reduce and control the problem (Gardiner, 1970, p. 93). In this section, we examine several strategies that a correctional administrator may adopt to address the problem of corruption within a correctional agency.

A first step in dealing with the problem of corruption is to develop and enforce a strict, zero-tolerance policy on corruption, and implement and communicate a strong and forceful anticorruption policy. This policy should define specifically what the agency means by corruption as well as specify the penalties associated with such practices (see Ward & McCormack, 1979, for an example of developing an anti-corruption policy for police departments). Once this policy has been formulated, it needs to be disseminated to all workers. Training should also be provided to employees regarding the nature, causes, impact, and consequences of corrupt practices. This training should be integrated into both preservice and in-service training modules. Without enforcement, these policies will have no impact. For deterrence to work, these policies must be enforced. Employees charged with corruption should be investigated and prosecuted if warranted—not merely asked to resign.

Second, the correctional agency should develop a proactive mechanism to detect and investigate corrupt practices. This includes the establishment of an internal affairs unit and processes that encourage employees, inmates, and civilians to report allegations of staff misconduct. Many states use a whistleblower hotline to deal with governmental misconduct, and this can be extended to prison systems. In addition, the use of routine and special audit procedures on a random basis will ensure the proper expenditure of funds. In one state, state-level investigators randomly target prisons and conduct interdiction investigations to search for contraband. Inmates, staff, and civilians are subject to searches and drug testing, including a drug-detection system known as IONSCAN. In 1 year, these searches resulted in the seizure of a large quantity of drugs (powder cocaine, crack cocaine, and marijuana) and weapons, including 13 firearms and 280 rounds of ammunition in one state system (Florida Department of Corrections, 1997). Drug testing of employees and the screening of correctional employees as they enter and leave institutions should also be considered.

Third, correctional administrators should attempt to improve management of material practices in the prison. This internal reform is directed at improving the control of the organization. In prior studies of corruption where it was shown that leadership and control of persons were weak, the potential for corruption increased (Gardiner, 1970). Management must take affirmative steps toward reducing the opportunities for corruption. One step in this direction is to structure the use of discretion and make the visibility of low-level decision makers more public and subject to review. Guidelines for the use of discretionary rewards and punishments should be public. For example, specific criteria and a review process should be established to review cell changes, job assignments, and transfers or temporary releases. In addition, the disciplinary process should be opened up to review. These decisions should be periodically reviewed by supervisors to ensure the accountability of decision makers. An example of the misuse and abuse of the disciplinary process occurred a few years ago in the state of Massachusetts, where John Geoghan, a defrocked priest convicted of molesting dozens of children, was falsely accused of disciplinary infractions by guards so that he would be transferred to a more punitive and restrictive setting. Geoghan was later killed by an inmate in a supposedly more secure but more punitive correctional facility. Internal reform should also include screening of employees to improve their overall quality.

Another management enhancement practice is to upgrade employee selection procedures to include psychological testing and formal preservice training designed to screen out questionable employees. In addition, simple police checks of an individual's background should be expanded to include in-depth background investigations of prospective employees. Some states are finding that members of street gangs are applying for jobs as correctional officers to assist in the expansion of the gang's power inside prisons. Routine investigations have also found that individuals with felony convictions and even escapees have been hired as correctional employees. Another step entails improving the working conditions of employees so that the quality of correctional worker is raised. Employees making just barely above the minimum wage might be attracted to supplement their incomes through illicit behavior. Improving wage scales, enlarging job responsibilities, and broadening employee participation in decision making, as well as increasing efforts toward professionalism, will all help address the issue of staff commitment to the mission of the agency.

A fourth and final recommendation addresses the political environment of prisons. Prisons are located in the executive branch of government, and top administrators serve at the pleasure of the state governor or the President. Correctional administrators have little control over political and community attitudes toward prisons and prisoners, but they should take steps to insulate their employees from external pressure placed on them to act in a way that benefits some constituent or campaign donor who seeks to intervene on behalf of an inmate. By requiring merit selection and promotion of employees, a correctional administrator reduces the impact of political interference in the operation of the agency.

THE LEGAL OPTION WHEN ABUSES BECOME EXTREME

The Eighth Amendment of the U.S. Constitution prohibits cruel and unusual punishment. The study of corruption usually involves an examination of so-called "bad apples" within a system. Sometimes the level of misconduct rises to a system level and it becomes a matter of not only bad apples but also a bad barrel. The violations and abuses become pervasive in a prison or system. This is what occurred in the state of Michigan, where there was widespread sexual abuse of female prisoners by male correctional officers. In a consent decree with the U.S. Department of Justice, the state of Michigan agreed to remove male officers from female prisons because of high levels of sexual abuse. Legal action was subsequently taken within the state court system as well, and 10 female inmates were awarded $15 million in damages (USA Today, February 1, 2008).

When abuses rise to this level, federal protections are available for inmates under custody of the state. The U.S. Constitution's Eighth Amendment prohibits the infliction of cruel and unusual practices. Within the context of the Eighth Amendment, legislative action has followed with the passage of the **Civil Rights of Institutionalized Persons Act of 1980 (CRIPA)** (U.S. Statutes *42 U.S.C. § 1997*).

This act authorizes the Civil Rights Division of the U.S. Department of Justice to investigate complaints. This unit has broad authority to investigate constitutional violations that occur in institutions, including jails and prisons, and covers protections from abuse by staff.

■ Learn More on the Internet

Information on the complaints the U.S. Department of Justice receives, and actions taken, can be found at www.justice.gov/crt/split/cripa.php. ■

Another source of protection of inmates comes from the Prison Rape Elimination Act (PREA) of 2003. This federal law focuses specifically on the sexual assault of prisoners. The act was designed to reduce or eliminate sexual assaults and rape in custodial settings. The act called for national standards and reporting requirements both to document the dimensions of the problem and to come up with solutions (including national standards designed to address the issue). The National Prison Rape Elimination Commission produces reports on the problem. In addition, the U.S. Bureau of Justice Statistics has been assigned the responsibility of carrying out a survey each calendar year as well as an analysis of the incidence and effects of prison rape on a nationwide basis.

In sum, controlling corruption requires correctional administrators' commitment to provide leadership in setting high standards of ethical conduct, communicating and upholding standards of ethical behavior, and holding people accountable for their actions. This includes improving and upgrading the general correctional environment (particularly the working conditions for staff) to protect employees from political pressures and to replace a tendency toward complacency with a concern for accountability. Kathleen Hawk Sawyer, the retired director of the Federal Bureau of Prisons, summed up the problem by stating that dealing with staff "sexual misconduct has been the single most frustrating issue" she encountered during her years as director of the U.S. Federal Bureau of Prisons. Dealing with staff misconduct is not a simple or easy thing to respond to:

> [T]here are many pieces to dealing with the issue of sexual misconduct. There is the investigative piece, the personnel piece, training, and also the inmate management piece. It's not only about the investigation and nailing someone to wall then getting rid of them. It is a whole system response that will produce positive outcomes. Otherwise, you're missing the mark. Your strategy has to be very integrated and cross-system oriented to have any positive impact at all (U.S. Department of Justice, 2005). Opportunities for corruption must be identified and addressed, and the risks taken by people predisposed to misconduct must be increased. It is doubtful that corrupt practices can be eliminated, but they can be reduced and controlled. It is important to keep in mind the words of Supreme Court Justice Kennedy when he addressed the American Bar Association:

> We have a greater responsibility, as a profession, and as a people, we should know what happens after the prisoner is taken away. To be

sure the prisoner has violated the social contract; to be sure he must be punished to vindicate the law, to acknowledge the suffering of the victim, and to deter future crimes. Still, the prisoner is a person; he or she is part of the family of humankind. It is no defense if our current prison system is more the product of neglect than of purpose. Out of sight, out of mind is an unacceptable excuse for a prison system that incarcerates over 2 million human beings in the United States.

To upgrade and improve the prison in a democracy, we must make sure that the prison is opened to the public and its workings exposed to citizens. The light of day shined on prison practices will ensure that our expectations for ethical conduct will be met.

Discussion Questions

1. What kinds of motivation might a correctional officer have for engaging in corruption? Are some forms of corruption worse than others? Explain.
2. If you were an inmate serving time in a punitive prison, would you attempt to curry favor with staff to obtain extra privileges? Would you pay for those privileges?
3. Is corruption an unavoidable result of discretion? Discuss your response in detail.
4. Working in corrections can be morally challenging for employees. What does this mean? What are some of the temptations that might exist?
5. Should the goals of the prison system include degrading and demeaning prisoners?
6. What implications would this have for staff working in prison?
7. You have been serving as a prison commissioner for several months without any political pressure placed on you. During a friendly conversation with the governor's chief of staff, the Chief mentioned that a former political ally doing time for bribery would like to be transferred to a minimum-custody classification facility close to his family's hometown. The Chief said he would really appreciate your assistance

CASE STUDY 15–1 LEGACY OF CORRUPTION

You are a young woman, born and reared in a rural area in the South. Your family was above average in relation to the income of the working-class families in your town. Your father, a farmer, worked hard and saved his money. As a result, he was able to provide you, your brother, two sisters, and your mother with a life of dignity and a sense of belonging-belonging to family, to town, and to country.

There was dignity, but no extras. Work was hard and income uncertain. Thriftiness was no mere virtue; it was

a necessity. Your parents imbued you with the "American dream"—that hard work and education would make your life easier and more productive than theirs had been. By education, your parents meant high school and possibly some vocational training. After high school, you and one of your best friends decided to join the Air Force, enlisting for the full four years. You were assigned to a base in the North where you were able to learn a profession. Since your Air Force job was in personnel, you planned to seek work in a similar field when you were finally discharged.

CASE STUDY 15–1 LEGACY OF CORRUPTION *Continued*

When you returned to Smallberg and your family, you were ready to seek a career and a life of your own. Smallberg was home to you and you wanted to settle there, but there were no personnel jobs available. You felt that you would like to do something meaningful with your life. You wanted a job that would give you both security and a sense of accomplishment. You even considered reenlistment. Then you saw an advertisement:

> Correctional Officers needed at State Prison. Civil service position, fringe benefits, career opportunity. High school diploma required. Beginning salary $24,000. Apply at personnel office, main prison.

You couldn't believe your eyes! 24,000 dollars a year! Who could live on that? But after several more weeks in a fruitless job search, you decided to apply for a position. You could live at home for awhile and at least the work would be meaningful.

Six weeks later you completed your basic correctional officers' training and with your fellow trainees you signed your oath of office as provided for in Section 26 of the state code:

> I do solemnly swear or affirm that I will faithfully and diligently perform all the duties required of me as an officer of the Department of Corrections and will observe and execute the laws, rules, and regulations passed and prescribed for the government thereof so far as the same concerns or pertains to my employment; that I will not ill treat or abuse any convict under my care, nor act contrary to the laws, rules and regulations prescribed by legal authority, so help me God.

During the 3 years since you took the job at the state prison, you have observed worsening conditions. You have been promoted twice, but your annual gross pay is still only $26,500. The inmate population has increased 40%, while there has only been a 10% increase in correctional officer positions. To make matters worse, the political and public mood has become increasingly negative. The education and recreation specialist positions have been eliminated, and three of the eight counselor positions have been frozen. No educational programs, little if any organized recreation, more inmates, and fewer correctional officers have resulted in dismal working conditions.

Now, to increase your sense of frustration, you have learned that your captain and several other of your fellow officers are taking bribes from inmates in exchange for choice assignments. You mentioned to the captain that word has reached you with regard to the purchased assignments. Instead of being embarrassed or evasive, the captain tells you, "These scumbags would sell their mothers for a dime and they deserve whatever happens to them." He then offers to assign you to the unit in charge of housing so that you can "get in on the action." There are even reports that several of the female officers are earning extra income by having sex with some of the better-connected inmates. Since you yourself have been propositioned twice during the last month, you have little doubt that the rumors are true.

Conflicting needs flood your consciousness. The last officer to complain about this particular captain was summarily dismissed and threatened with prosecution for possession of contraband that he claimed he was not even aware of. The captain's father is also a former warder of this prison, and his brother is the present business manager of the institution.

Needless to say, the situation has created a major crisis in your life. Your decision will be crucial because of its lasting implications for you. You value your personal integrity and you believe in the intrinsic value of your profession, yet you could use more money. In addition, there is the pragmatic necessity of your employment and your hope for advancement within the system—what there is left of it. You live in a beautiful, if depressed, economic area where few decent jobs exist. What should you do?

Questions

1. In this case, should the correctional officer contact the prison superintendent or someone at the state level?
2. What kind of oversight or programs could effectively address corruption among corrections officers?

in this matter. As an aside, he mentioned that your performance review was coming up. How should you respond?

8. What forms of sexual misconduct by staff might take place in a maximum-security prison?

REFERENCES

Barker, T. (1977). Social definitions of police corruption. *Criminal Justice Review, 1*(Fall), 101–110.

Belluck, P. (February 4, 2004). *Inquiry lists prison system errors in case of slain priest.* The New York Times. A16.

Boston Prison Discipline Society (1826–1854) (1972). *Reprint of 1st–9th annual report: An introductory report.* Montclair: Patterson-Smith.

Buell, M., Layman, E., McCampbell, S., & Smith, B. (2003). Addressing sexual misconduct in community corrections. *Perspectives: The Journal of the American Probation and Parole Association, 2*(27), 26–37.

Butterfield, F. (June 21, 2004). *Inmates use smuggled cellphones to maintain a foot on the outside.* The New York Times. 1, 18.

Cloward, R. (1960). *Theoretical studies in social organization of the prison.* New York: Social Science Research Council.

Costikyan, E. N. (1974). The locus of corruption. In J. A. Gardiner & D. J. Olsen (Eds.), *Theft of the city: Readings on corruption in urban America.* Bloomington: Indiana University Press.

Etzioni, A. (1964). *Modern organizations.* Englewood Cliffs: Prentice Hall.

Florida Department of Corrections, (1997). *Office of the inspector general annual report.*

Fogel, D. (1979). *"We are the living proof": The justice model for corrections.* Cincinnati: Anderson.

Gardiner, J. A. (1970). *The politics of corruption.* New York: The Russell Sage Foundation.

Gardiner, J. A., & Lyman, T. R. (1978). *Decisions for sale, corruption and reform in land use and building regulations.* New York: Praeger.

Garner, B. A. (Ed.), (2004). *Black's law dictionary* (8th ed.). St. Paul: West.

Goldstein, H. (1977). *Policing in a free society.* Cambridge: Ballinger.

Heidenheimer, A. (1970). *Political corruption: Readings in comparative analysis.* New York: Holt, Rinehart & Winston.

Irwin, I. (1980). *Prisons in turmoil.* Boston: Little, Brown.

Kennedy, A. M. (August 9, 2003). In *An address to the American Bar Association annual meeting.* Associate Justice, Supreme Court of the United States.

Kleinig, I. (1996). *The ethics of policing.* New York: Cambridge University Press.

Knapp, W. (1973). *Knapp commission on police corruption.* New York: Brazilier.

McCarthy. B. J. (1981). Exploratory study in corruption in corrections (Ph.D. dissertation). The Florida State University.

McKorkle, L. (1970). Guard-inmate relationships. In Johnston, et al. (Ed.), *The sociology of punishment and control.* New York: John Wiley and Sons.

Meyer, J. D. (1976). Definitional and etiological issues in police corruption: An assessment and synthesis of competing perspectives. *Journal of Police Science and Police Administration, 4,* 46–55.

Braswell, M., Miller, L., & Pollock, J. (2010). *Case studies in criminal justice ethics* (6th ed.). Long Grove: Waveland.

Mitford, I. (1973). Kind and usual punishment. In S. T. Reid (Ed.), *The correctional system*. New York: Holt, Rinehart & Winston. (1981).

National Institute of Corrections. (2000). *Sexual misconduct in prisons: Law, remedies, and incidence*. U.S. Department of Justice.

Rothman, D. (1971). *The discovery of the asylum: Social order in the New Republic*. Boston: Little, Brown.

Sherman, L. (1974). *Police corruption: A sociological perspective*. New York: Anchor Books.

Sherman, L. (1978). *Scandal and reform, controlling police corruption*. Berkeley: University of California Press.

Sherman, L. (1979). Obtaining access to police internal affairs files. *Criminal Law Bulletin, 15* (September–October), 449–461.

Simpson, A. (1978). *The literature of police corruption*. New York: John Jay Press.

Suro, R. (1997). *Officials wonder if bribery arrests at federal prison are isolated or trend*. The Washington Post. June 1, 1977, A08.

Sykes, G. (1956). The corruption of authority and rehabilitation. *Social Forces, 34*, 157–162.

Sykes, G. (1958). *The society of captives: A study of a maximum security prison*. Princeton, NJ: Princeton University Press.

U.S, Department of Justice, Office of the Inspector General, April 2005). *Deterring staff sexual abuse of federal inmates*.

USA Today, February 1, 2008). *Jury awards 15.4 million in damages*.

Ward, R., & McCormack, R. (1979). *An anti-corruption manual for administrators in law enforcement*. New York: John Jay Press.

CHAPTER 16

Ethics and Prison: Selected Issues

John T. Whitehead, Bradley Edwards

INTRODUCTION

Prisons are a source of fascination for many of us. Although prisons are intended to repel us, they seem to be a source of mysterious interest. Moviemakers have capitalized on this interest with countless movies set in real or fictitious prisons, especially traditional "Big House" prisons such as Sing Sing or Walla Walla. Another testimony to the uncanny attractiveness of prisons is the conversion of Alcatraz, the former disciplinary prison of the federal prison system, to a museum where tourists can walk around and even be locked in a cell for a few minutes of imaginary incarceration.

This chapter will examine some of the ethical issues about prison. It will discuss prison composition, discrimination, prison conditions, treatment, victimization, elderly offenders, women in prison, and privatization. Guard corruption will not be considered because McCarthy discussed that issue in Chapter 15.

WHO BELONGS IN PRISON

A basic ethical question about prison is: Who belongs there? What kinds of offenders deserve to be sentenced to prison? A number of critics contend that many of the people sent to prison do not need to be there. According to these critics, these prisoners are neither violent nor career criminals, and most citizens do not really want such people incarcerated. Irwin and Austin

(1997, pp. 58–59), for example, cite 1992 prison admission statistics that show that only 27% of prison admittees that year were admitted to prison for a violent crime conviction. This is especially evident in the federal prison system, where less than 9% of inmates sentenced in 2007 were convicted of violent crimes, and 53% of prison admittees were drug offenders (West & Sabol, 2009).

Conservatives, on the other hand, applaud the growth in the prison population. DiIulio, for example, argues that average citizens want prisons to be used and that prison incapacitates and saves money: "'prison pays' for most prisoners: it costs society about twice as much to let a prisoner roam the streets in search of fresh victims as it does to keep him locked up for a year" (DiIulio, 1995, p. 41). DiIulio (1994) also argues that greater use of incarcerative sentences will reduce crime in our nation's crime-ridden neighborhoods.

A complete analysis of this issue is beyond the scope of this chapter,[1] but some consideration is necessary. First, critics of increased incarceration fail to mention several crucial points about prison/prisoner statistics. For example, critics often fail to note that approximately 15% of the offenders admitted to prison each year are admitted for burglary (Maguire & Pastore, 1996, p. 567). Although prison critics conventionally label burglary as a "property" crime, many citizens regard this crime as a much more serious crime than other property crimes, such as shoplifting. Burglary involves trespass into one's personal space (one's "castle" or home), and it also involves a very real potential for violence. Either the burglar or the victim may have a weapon at hand and resort to using it. A qualitative indicator of the seriousness with which some people regard burglary is the criminal law allowance of deadly force against burglary in at least one state (see, e.g., Alabama Code, 13A-3-23). Another connection of burglary to violent crime is that many burglars are looking for guns (Wright & Decker, 1994, p. 144). Clearly, there is some probability that these guns will be fenced or otherwise transferred to other criminals directly engaged in violent crime. Second, many of the "nonviolent" offenders admitted to prison in any year were repeat offenders and/or offenders who had been under community supervision of some sort. In 1991, for example, 45.9% of all state prisoners were either probation or parole violators at the time of their admission to prison (Cohen, 1995). In 1992, parole violators represented 29% of prison admissions (Maguire & Pastore, 1996, p. 567). Thus, it is misleading to argue that only 27% of new admissions to prison are violent, when another 15% are burglars and another 29% are repeat offenders (parole violators).

In addition, in giving admission statistics, critics may overlook composition statistics. For example, in 2010, more than one-half (53%) of the prisoners in state prisons were in prison for a violent crime (Carson & Sabol, 2012).

Another 10% were in prison for burglary. Thus, approximately six out of 10 prisoners were in prison for either burglary or a violent crime.

Moreover, drug offenders may be more threatening than Irwin and Austin consider them to be. One investigation found that many crack cocaine users were involved in both crack dealing and other crime. Inciardi, Horowitz, and Pottieger (1993) studied serious delinquents in Miami at the start of the crack epidemic in the mid-1980s. They found that more than one-half of the crack users in their sample were dealers and 18% were "dealers plus" (i.e. they also manufactured, smuggled, or wholesaled the drug). More importantly, these dealers were far from innocent, recreational purveyors: "Degree of crack-market participation was also related to earlier and greater general crime involvement, including violent crime" (emphasis in the original) (Inciardi et al., 1993, p. 178). Further, a number of studies "have shown that lethal violence is used commonly by drug traffickers in the pursuit of their economic interests" (Brownstein, Spunt, Crimmins, & Langley, 1995, p. 475).

On the other hand, prison proponents also omit or fail to emphasize some important points about **prison composition**. For example, the contention that the average citizen wants criminals incarcerated (see, for example, DiIulio, 1995) is only partially correct. There is substantial agreement in the literature that the public is not as punitive as surmised but rather still wants rehabilitation and will opt for nonincarcerative sentences for many offenders. For example, in 2003, 72% of a national sample agreed that the criminal justice system "should try to rehabilitate criminals, not just punish them" (*Sourcebook of Criminal Justice Statistics*, 2010). Similarly, in 2006, 65% of Americans stated that more money and effort should go to attacking social problems, while only 31% favored more spending on law enforcement to lower the crime rate (*Sourcebook of Criminal Justice Statistics*, 2010). Research in California found that citizens did indeed initially express a preference for prison for 25 hypothetical cases varying from petty theft to rape. After being informed of costs and alternatives to incarceration, however, these same citizens wanted only 27% of the hypothetical offenders to be incarcerated (DiMascio, 1995). Research in Ohio showed that on a global measure of support, 88% of the sample favored a "three strikes and you're out" law. On more specific measures, however, only 17% of the respondents favored life sentences; most favored sentences of five to 15 years in prison. Thus, it is safe to say that "underneath more punitive global attitudes, in specific situations, the American public tends to be less punitive and to favor a more diversified response to crime than simply locking up offenders …" (Applegate, Cullen, Turner, & Sundt, 1996, p. 519).

Similarly, the matter of incapacitation is much more complex than many prison proponents portray. Spelman (1994) found that collective incapacitation is at best a "gamble" that "may pay off" (p. 289) and that the effect of selective incapacitation is at best—and under ideal conditions—only 4–8% (p. 289). This led Spelman to caution that "the crime problem can never be substantially reduced through incapacitation alone" (1994, p. 312). Instead, criminal justice policies that deter and rehabilitate individual offenders; broader-based policies aimed at ameliorating continuing social problems such as chronic poverty and unemployment, teenage pregnancy and child abuse, and the like; and entirely different approaches aimed at reducing the number of criminal opportunities rather than just the number of criminals, all deserve continued attention (Spelman, 1994, p. 312).

In summary, the debate about who should go to prison is often clouded by partisan positions that fail to consider some important pieces of information. Critics of prison tend to overemphasize the use of prison for nonviolent offenders. Proponents oversell the alleged benefits of prison and ignore polling research that indicates the public's willingness to use nonincarcerative options. Hopefully, a peacemaking approach mindful of as much clarity as possible will help resolve the debate.

■ Learn More on the Internet

Go to www.loc.gov for images of prisons and prisoners throughout American history.   ■

DISPROPORTIONATE MINORITY PRISON POPULATIONS

A more specific concern in the larger question of prison composition is the disproportionate number of African Americans, especially black males, behind bars. In 2010, African Americans made up 13.6% of the general population, but 38% of state and federal prison populations (Carson & Sabol, 2012; Rastogi, Johnson, Hoeffel, & Drewery, 2011). Disturbingly, black men are between five and seven times more likely to be behind bars than white men of the same age group (Carson & Sabol, 2012). Although the black imprisonment rate is decreasing (Sabol, West, & Cooper, 2009), **disproportionate minority representation** is still a concern.

The overrepresentation of African Americans in prisons is nothing new. This group made up 30% of the prison population in 1940, more than 40% in 1980 (Walker, Spohn, & DeLone, 1996), 46% in 1985, and 49% in 1990 (Mumola & Beck, 1997). However, one aspect of the problem that is new is the increased number of African Americans incarcerated for drug offenses (Mumola & Beck, 1997). Several observers argue that police "target minority communities—where drug dealing is more visible and where it is thus easier for the police to make arrests—and tend to give less attention to drug activities in other neighborhoods" (Walker et al., 1996, p. 209).

A few cautions are in order. Drug offenders may be more threatening than some of the critics of the incarceration of drug offenders consider them to be. As noted in the previous section, drug use may also mean involvement in drug dealing, criminal activity, and violence (including lethal violence) (Brownstein et al., 1995; Inciardi et al., 1993).

These observations are not meant to justify discriminatory policing and/or sentencing of African-American drug offenders. They are simply offered to show that there is some reason for society to be concerned about drug offending, no matter which racial or ethnic group is involved.

It would seem that the ethical course of action is to pursue a drug policy that treats all races the same. It would also seem that any drug policy should not discriminate or give the appearance of discrimination. At the very least, our nation's drug policy has failed on the latter account. A number of observers have judged the drug war to violate the appearance of impartial handling. Steps need to be taken to correct that appearance. If the famous O.J. Simpson murder trial said anything, it is that how the criminal justice system treats African Americans is clearly under scrutiny, and even the perception of bias can have harmful consequences. Continuing the recent drug policy runs the risk of alienating still further minority members who are already substantially alienated.

Space limitations do not allow for a complete discussion of whether discrimination leads to disproportionate minority representation in prison, or if disproportionate criminal involvement accounts for the overrepresentation. Whatever the sources of disproportionate minority prison populations, the issue needs to be addressed.

PRISON CONDITIONS: CODDLING OR TOUGHNESS?

Another fundamental ethical issue concerning prisons is the question of **prison conditions**, or what kind of prison environment society should provide for prisoners. A number of voices are calling for tough, spartan-like prisons with no "frills" such as television, recreational facilities, or athletic equipment. More traditional voices think that prison intrinsically involves a number of pains or deprivations and that we do not need to make it much tougher than it is. To these people, what looks like a frill may in fact be justified for one or more logical reasons.

One example of critics who argue for spartan prisons is van den Haag (1975). He argues that prisoners should work many hours each day for the purpose of punishment and that such hard labor should be sufficient to tire them out. At night they would be so exhausted that they would just rest before bed. This type of prison would serve retributive, incapacitative, and deterrent objectives. It would be tough punishment for crime, it would keep offenders off the streets and away from opportunities to commit crime, and it would serve to frighten potential offenders from committing crime because persons considering crime would not want to be sentenced to a hard-labor prison.

Bidinotto (1997) has criticized our nation's prisons for coddling prisoners. In an article originally published in Reader's Digest, he alleged that hard labor was out of fashion. In style, he said, were electronic exercise equipment, horse-shoe pits, bocce, conjugal visits (even at such supposedly spartan prisons as Attica Prison in New York), and opera appreciation classes.

More extreme critics argue for even tougher prisons. In addition to removing any frills or amenities from traditional prisons, these individuals contend that prison should be made as tough as possible. Possible changes would be very limited diets and the introduction of chain gangs. Chain gangs would add humiliation to prison labor. Prisoners would be chained to each other and forced to work outside prison walls so that the public could see them at work. In this scenario, scorn would return to the criminal justice system. (See the separate section below on chain gangs.) Perhaps the most well-known advocate of this position is Maricopa County (Arizona) Sheriff Joe Arpaio, who the media named "America's toughest sheriff." Arpaio proudly notes that the cost of an inmate's food is approximately 60 cents per day, and inmates are fed only twice daily (Griffin, 2001).

More traditional voices note that prison already contains numerous painful features that are sufficient punishment for offenders. These inherent pains of prison are harsh enough to make prison punitive and also serve as a deterrent to potential offenders. Sykes (1958), for example, noted more than 50 years ago that prison involves a number of pains or deprivations. These are deprivation of freedom, autonomy, possessions, security, and heterosexual contact. Deprivation of freedom or liberty is self-explanatory; inmates lose their freedom to come and go as they please. Deprivation of autonomy refers to the removal of choices; inmates are told what to do and when to do it by virtue of a schedule that governs every minute of the day. Unlike free citizens, inmates have no choices about when to get up in the morning, when to go to meals, what to eat, what to wear, when to watch television, and when the lights go out. The prison dictates the decisions that those of us in the community take for granted each day and treats the inmate like a child who is incapable of making autonomous decisions. Likewise, with possessions, the administration allows only minimal possessions such as a picture or poster or two and no distinguishing clothing. In a society that exalts material possessions as signs of status, accomplishment, and individuality, the prison restricts possessions to the minimum and thereby depersonalizes each inmate. Security is far from a given in prison. Inmate assaults are a real possibility, especially for the weak. Even the strong have to fear attacks from groups of inmates who can overpower any one individual (more on this below). Finally, deprivation of heterosexual contact is the norm in most prisons. Very few prisons allow conjugal visitation, and a prisoner must be married to participate.

Guenther (1978) has noted some additional deprivations or pains. The subjective experience of time in prison can be very painful. For example, weekends are periods of "hard time" because the inmate does not have to go to a job that helps him or her pass the time during the week. Through the holiday season, inmates see holiday shows and advertisements that remind them that they are missing contact with loved ones at a special time of the year. Even letters from home can be painful because sometimes the letter writer expresses anger or hurt at the offender for the things the offender did to the writer. Children, for example, may express anger at their father for abandoning them and not being with them to do simple things like take them fishing. Visits can be occasions for other inmates to offer taunts. Other inmates may tease the inmate who receives a visit from his or her spouse, reminding the offender that the spouse is free and might be seeing other people behind the offender's back. Or a visit from a spouse may cause the inmate "to question how 'the government' can deny him sexual access to his spouse" (Guenther, 1978, p. 602). At the very least, visitors have to be searched, and they see the offender in prison clothing that reminds both the visitor and the offender that he or she is a lawbreaker who has been arrested and convicted.

Traditionalists argue that these inherent pains of prison are sufficient suffering. Additional torments such as removing exercise equipment or televisions and radios are unwarranted. Traditionalists also argue that amenities can serve to keep inmates occupied and thereby help prevent restlessness, attacks on other inmates, attacks on guards, and, ultimately, prison riots.

Conrad (1982, p. 313) frames the question aptly: "What do the undeserving deserve?" His answer is worthy of consideration. He argues that they deserve "safety, lawfulness, industriousness, and hope" (Conrad, 1982, p. 328). Safety and lawfulness are self-explanatory; unfortunately, they are often lacking in our prisons. Inmates often fear that they will be victimized in some way while behind bars. By industriousness Conrad does not mean mere busywork but that "everyone puts in a full day of work at jobs that are worth doing and paid accordingly" (p. 328). Hope is the most important consideration: "… where everyone has some reason to hope for better things to come—or could have such a reason if he or she were willing to look for it—the prison will not only be safer, but it will also be a place in which its staff can take some pride" (Conrad, 1982, p. 328).

Sometimes the debate over prison conditions can make it sound like prisoners are living in expensive luxury resorts in which every whim is satisfied, but "[i]f our prisons are such resorts, simply open the gates and see how many run out … and how many walk in" (Taylor, 1997, p. 92).

TREATMENT/REHABILITATION/PROGRAMMING

Related to the issue of the appropriate conditions for prisoners is the issue of whether **treatment** opportunities should be provided for prisoners. Although rehabilitation was once routinely provided, many voices question providing anything other than punishment to inmates.

There is no question that most prisoners are in need of various types of assistance. Many prisoners are high-school dropouts, do not have employable skills, had alcohol or other drug problems prior to entering prison, and may suffer from psychological difficulties such as lack of self-esteem.

An argument for providing services to offenders is that such services may help reduce recidivism when the inmate is released. Employment, for example, has been shown to be a clear correlate of success on parole (Pritchard, 1979). Similarly, studies of correctional rehabilitation have demonstrated that offenders who received treatment for various problems recidivated less (were less likely to reoffend) than offenders who did not receive appropriate treatment (Lipsey & Cullen, 2007). Such empirical evidence for the efficacy of treatment (see, also, Lee et al., 2012) suggests that the ethically correct course of action is to provide treatment opportunities.

In spite of its effectiveness, some still argue that treatment is not appropriate for prisoners. One argument is the principle of least eligibility, which maintains that prisoners do not deserve anything better than what is given to the least eligible in our society. Because many people cannot afford college or vocational training or psychological counseling, a strict adherent of this principle might argue that prisoners should not benefit from any such treatments. To do so would give them something better than that had by a significant minority of the free population.

One response to this is that the deprived status of the neediest in American society is not sufficient justification for depriving inmates. The answer is to address both problems. Law-abiding citizens deserve the opportunity to attend college or learn a vocational trade. Prisoners too should have such opportunities, which will hopefully help prevent any return to crime. Years ago, the Vienna Correctional Center in Illinois attempted to solve the problem by opening up a number of prison programs to any interested citizens from the community. That way, the area residents did not feel that the inmates were benefiting from programs that were not available to them (Silberman, 1978).

Another argument against services for inmates is that the prison environment is highly likely to sabotage such efforts. Drawing on the prison research of Sykes (1958), the mental hospital research of Goffman (1961), and other research, some argue that so much suspicion, distrust, and animosity arise between inmates and prison staff that it is impossible to offer meaningful treatment options in the prison environment. In Goffman's terms, inmates are so involved in seeking secondary adjustments that mitigate the intended punishments of prison that they would not benefit from treatment programs. In Sykes's terms, inmates are so busy trying to soften the pains of prison by such strategies as making home-brewed alcoholic beverages, achieving status by boisterousness or physical prowess, or prowling for sexual conquests that any treatment efforts would fall on deaf ears. The counter argument is that prison officials have often failed to implement rehabilitation programs as needed. Instead, wardens and guards put custody concerns over treatment concerns in terms of both dollars and emphasis. Thus, prison staff get what they want: custody rather than rehabilitation.

An important reminder in any debate over providing treatment is that most offenders will be released back into society. If society makes no effort to educate or train offenders for gainful employment after release, the offenders will not have a legal means of support and may well resort to crime. Releasing offenders without any improvement of their condition seems highly unlikely to improve their chances for success. Some states, such as Florida, and the federal prison system have invested heavily in **faith-based programming** for prisoners. Four concerns stand out.

First, a major concern is whether faith-based programming is effective. This usually translates into whether or not faith-based program graduates recidivate less than other prisoners. The evidence regarding the effectiveness of faith-based programs is quite mixed. To date, most studies have found no impact of faith-based programming on recidivism (Aos, Miller, & Drake, 2006). One study, however, found that lower proportions of inmates in faith-based programming in federal prisons committed serious misconduct than non-faith-based prisoners. For some reason, there was no difference in less serious acts of misconduct (Camp, Daggett, Kwon, & Klein-Saffran, 2008).

Measuring recidivism is a utilitarian concern: a search for positive consequences. One religious writer argues that this utilitarian perspective is misguided when it comes to faith-based programs. He argues that faith-based programming is justified as a means of seeking religious redemption or conversion for the inmate. He thinks religious outcomes are not necessarily measurable—that you cannot measure grace or redemption, or that it may take years for the process to take effect. This writer thinks we should offer such programs to prisoners based on religious principles, not out of a concern to reduce criminal activity (Hewitt, 2006).

A second concern is that any research that attempts to measure the effectiveness of a faith-based program needs to attend to the fact that inmates who volunteer for faith-based programming might very well be more motivated inmates. In other words, they may be the inmates most motivated to change, and so therefore self-motivation might be the true cause of any positive results. It is critical to measure the motivation levels of inmates going into such programs as well as that of the comparison inmates in other programs or undergoing no programming (Camp, Klein-Saffran, Kwon, Daggett, & Joseph, 2006).

A third concern is over-reliance on religious volunteers and possible neglect of prisoners who do not volunteer for faith-based programming. Many faith-based programs rely on church groups or religiously motivated individuals to volunteer for work in faith-based programs. For example, a faith-based program may emphasize the role of mentors (Duwe & King, 2012). While it is commendable that religiously motivated individuals step forward to work as mentors with prisoners or parolees or probationers, it might be easy for a prison to neglect the needs of offenders who are not in faith-based programs. Or it may be more difficult to ensure that such offenders still have similar opportunities as offenders in faith-based programs in which churches are volunteering and perhaps also contributing to monetarily. From the perspective of deontology, one could argue that the state has a duty to provide programming for all prisoners. The state cannot simply pass off this duty to churches or religious individual volunteers. The state still must provide effective treatment opportunities to offenders who do not sign up for faith-based programming.

A fourth concern is that faith-based programs should not be proselytizing, that is, trying to convert prisoners. Some faith-based programs simply want the offender to commit to change and involve commonly shared values such as respect for others, honesty, and caring. But some programs emphasize doctrinal requirements such as teaching that there is no salvation outside that particular church. Volokh (2011) argues that such explicit religious components might put a particular church-based program in opposition to First Amendment doctrine about separation of church and state. Volokh thinks that perhaps a way around First Amendment issues is for a state to follow a voucher system. Each inmate, for example, would have a certain dollar amount of vouchers to pay for certain services. If the inmate wished, he could choose a religious program; if not, he could choose a non-church based program.

The history of American corrections is linked historically to religion and faith. The very term "penitentiary" refers to the religious experience of doing penance for one's sins. While most advocates of faith-based programming do not advocate an explicit return to such a specific religious focus, many do think that religious programming has much to offer. As Whitehead and Braswell (2000) have argued, a significant part of any positive life is a sense of meaning and purpose.

It is imperative to help offenders deal with substance abuse issues and obtain adequate education and job training. However, a critical component of any human life is a sense of meaning and purpose in what one does and how one goes about every day of one's life. Faith-based programs are directly positioned to address the question of meaning and purpose in life. So,

> ...perhaps the Quakers had it right. The spiritual dimension of life is critical....If probation is ever to achieve the hopes of its founder John Augustus, it must somehow address the spiritual needs of offenders. Ignoring the spiritual dimension of life is ignoring its most important element.
>
> **Whitehead and Braswell (2000, p. 229)**

CHAIN GANGS

Chain gangs were reintroduced in Alabama in 1995, but the move was followed by court challenges. Governor Fob James justified their use as a way to save money and to make incarceration tougher. He argued that a prison guard can supervise only 20 unchained men on a road crew but the number doubles to 40 prisoners if the men are shackled. Concerning toughness, he argued that some men were declining parole because they thought incarceration was easier (Morris, 1997). An argument can also be made that chain gangs are constitutional because the Thirteenth Amendment to the US Constitution prohibits involuntary servitude "except as punishment for crime." The only current chain gangs are in the Maricopa County jail in Arizona, where Sheriff Joe Arpaio (mentioned in previous section) operates voluntary boot camps as a step to return from disciplinary lockdown (Griffin, 2001).

A major argument against chain gangs is that they are discriminatory or, at best, give the appearance of discrimination. Observers have noted that 70–90% of the Alabama chain gang prisoners were black (Corsentino, 1997). For African Americans, chain gangs are a reminder of the Reconstruction Era in the South when racism was still rampant. After the Civil War, the South needed to rebuild railroads and roads, and prison labor was leased out to contractors to engage in such direly needed projects. Many of the prisoners were blacks, as the South used its criminal justice systems as a way to get around the legal abolition of slavery. As in slavery, the offenders were classified as "full hands" or "half hands," tacit recognition that slavery had simply taken another form (McKelvey, 1997). A constitutional question is whether the use of chain gangs violates the cruel and unusual punishment prohibition of the Eighth Amendment.

Another argument against reintroducing chain gangs is von Hirsch's (1990) principle of acceptable penal content. What he means is that sanctions are only acceptable if the offender can endure them and still maintain his or her human dignity. Von Hirsch, who argues that punishments such as bumper stickers on the cars of drunk drivers proclaiming their DUI (driving under the influence of alcohol) status are too demeaning, would oppose chain gangs because they are intrinsically humiliating and do not allow the offender the necessary minimum condition of human dignity.

Finally, it is important to consider what emotions might be generated in offenders by the use of measures like chain gangs, especially after release. Do we want offenders living next to us who have been humiliated and scorned? Or do we want offenders who feel that prison was a painful but appropriate punishment for the wrongs they committed?

SAFETY/SECURITY IN PRISON

As noted, Sykes (1958) listed deprivation of security as one of the pains that prisoners suffer. There is some controversy about how much lack of security prisoners should undergo. A number of studies have detailed the **victimization** that many prisoners have had to face. For example, Wolff, Blitz, Shi, Siegel, and Bachman (2007) found 21% of an inmate sample had been a victim of physical violence in the previous six-month period. Wachtler (1997), former Chief Judge of the New York Court of Appeals, reported being stabbed in a federal facility. Therefore, it appears that although federal facilities are supposed to be relatively safe and secure, even a prominent white-collar criminal has a considerable risk of being attacked in prison. Sexual violence is also of concern, although difficult to measure accurately. Official statistics show that 4% of prison inmates and 3.2% of jail inmates report being the victim of sexual violence, but these numbers likely underrepresent the extent of sexual victimization (Beck, Berzofsky, Caspar, & Krebs, 2013).

More generally, Bowker (1980) provides a thorough (but now-dated) catalog of the various types of victimization that prisoners suffer. Irwin and Austin have argued that prison produces harmful effects on offenders: "The disturbing truth is that growing numbers of prisoners are leaving our prisons socially crippled and profoundly alienated" (1997, p. 82). They are also concerned that the increasing use of maximum-security confinement compounds the harmful effects of prison so that contemporary prison systems are "spewing out such damaged human material" (Irwin & Austin, 1997, p. 106). Indeed, a survey of prisoners revealed disciplinary practices, including beatings that were characterized as capricious and brutal (Hamm, Coupez, Hoze, & Weinstein, 1994).

Several studies, however, have painted a less negative picture. A study of coping in New York prisons concluded that "most prisoners serve fairly trouble-free terms" and that their overall experience in prison is "no more overwhelming to them than other constraining situations they have encountered in their lives" (Toch, Adams, & Grant, 1989, p. 254). A longitudinal study of the incarceration experience in Canada led Zamble and Porporino to compare a prison sentence to a "deep freeze" after which the offenders are unchanged: "As they had done on the outside, most of the inmates in this study followed a path of least resistance, and they focused on the fine line of present time passing" (Zamble & Porporino,1988, p. 150). A 1990 review of prison studies failed "to show any sort of profound detrimental effects" (Bonta & Gendreau, 1994, p. 57).

In summary, a number of studies have shown that victimization is problematic in at least some prisons or for some prisoners in many prisons. Other studies have shown that a number of prisons are relatively secure and safe and that a considerable number of offenders come out unscathed. The ethical mandate is to make all prisons safe and lawful. Even the undeserving deserve this minimal guarantee (Conrad, 1982).

ELDERLY PRISONERS

With longer sentences, mandatory sentences, and "three strikes and you're out" laws, state prison systems and the federal prison system can expect an increase in the number of **elderly offenders**. In fact, in 2012, the number of federal and state inmates age 55 and older was 124,900, and some experts project the number to exceed 400,000 by 2030 (American Civil Liberties Union, 2012). Because age 50 is considered the true age that should define elderly prisoners, that projection is very conservative. This increase raises some ethical issues.

A basic question concerns the release of elderly prisoners once they are no longer a danger to others. In other words, given some of the changes in sentencing in the last 10 years, it is reasonable to expect that prison officials will see increasing numbers of prisoners in their sixties, seventies, or eighties. As prisoners become elderly in prison, it is clear that many of them will be little or no danger to society. A prisoner who has Alzheimer's disease or arthritis or heart disease is hardly at risk of engaging in burglary, armed robbery, or murder. At some point, age reduces the risk of further criminal behavior to zero or close to zero.

If there is little incapacitative or rehabilitative value in keeping such prisoners locked up, should we release them? Or does the goal of retribution dictate that they stay in prison for as long as their original sentence dictated? If a prisoner gets to the point at which he or she does not even understand where he or she is (for example, due to a disease like Alzheimer's), does it make any retributive sense to keep the prisoner confined? Doesn't the concept of punishment require that the prisoner understand what is being done to him or her?

Conversely, society may want to release elderly offenders to save money. As prisoners age, it is logical to expect that their health care expenses will rise. They generally will need increasing medical care. As a result, it now costs more than $68,000 per year to house an older offender, compared to $34,000 per year for a younger offender (American Civil Liberties Union, 2012). A statistical analysis of costs estimates that releasing elderly offenders would save states $66,000 per prisoner per year, even taking into account costs states would incur by releasing such offenders (American Civil Liberties Union, 2012). Should society keep these offenders in prison so that they can receive the medical attention they need, or should society release them to save money? Parenthetically, a system of national health care could eliminate this dilemma by removing any incentive to release them.

WOMEN IN PRISONS

Women make up a small but significant proportion of the United States prison population. At year's end 2011, there were 103,852 female prisoners in state and federal institutions, constituting 6.7% of the total prison population (Carson & Sabol, 2012).

Although prison conditions are not as violent for women as for men, there are some problems that are unique to women's prisons. Because women constitute a much smaller proportion of any state's prison population, there are usually fewer prisons for women and also fewer opportunities for education and training. Part of this is related to stereotyped conceptions of the appropriate role for women in society. Traditional notions of appropriate roles have played a part in providing programs to train women to become cosmetologists or cooks instead of auto mechanics or television repair workers. Traditional notions of appropriate female behavior have also led to prison disciplinary practices that can be more dictatorial than those found in men's prisons. Beliefs that women should be "prim and proper" have influenced many officials to enforce rules against arguing and talking back to guards more stringently in women's prisons than in men's prisons. Thus, while women's prisons may look more pleasant than men's prisons, the appearance of a softer regime may in fact belie an institution that oppresses by intruding into more dimensions of behavior than occurs in the typical male prison.

Perhaps the fundamental ethical question is that suggested by Durham (1994): Would it be right to treat women exactly like men when such a shift in orientation might very well take away some of the benefits—such as single rooms rather than cells—that have benefited many women prisoners? Equal treatment would mean some positive changes, such as increased opportunities for vocational training, but would the overall results be beneficial for women, or would equal treatment actually mean generally worse conditions for women?

PRIVATIZATION

Another ethical issue is whether states should privatize prisons or continue to keep them public. As noted in Chapter 13 on ethical issues in probation and parole, proponents of **privatization** argue that there are several benefits for turning over prisons to private corporations. One alleged benefit is budgetary savings. Proponents claim that private enterprise can do things more efficiently and less expensively than the government. Government operation is equated with waste and inefficiency. Some of this is attributed to the civil service system that guarantees job tenure except in extreme circumstances when jobs are abolished. Civil service workers are not under the same pressures as workers in private industry who must constantly show a profit. Competition forces private industry to be effective, efficient, and accountable (Logan, 1990).

Opponents of privatization argue that government agencies can be efficient and effective. Government offices can adopt strategies that enhance efficiency and effectiveness just as can privately run agencies.

A number of states have turned over some of their prisons to private corporations. Several evaluations of private prisons, jails, and juvenile facilities have been conducted. In most of these studies, a private prison and a public prison from the same state are compared in terms of costs and inmate and/or staff satisfaction. One reviewer of a number of such studies concluded that the results are very inconclusive (Perrone & Pratt, 2003). The reviewer went on to note that while some studies have shown a small cost savings in private prisons, many of these studies did not account for important factors such as the number of inmates, the age of facility, and the security level of the facility. Perrone and Pratt thus agree with the conclusion of the General Accounting Office study that private prisons have not yet been proven superior.

Perhaps the main argument against privatization is whether it is appropriate for the government to turn over functions as basic as correctional supervision of offenders to private businesses. Many question whether the symbolic task of punishing offenders can be handed over to workers who wear uniforms that say "Acme Corrections Company" rather than the "State Department of Corrections" (American Bar Association, 1986). The most dramatic example of this would be for "Brand X Corrections" to carry out capital punishment. Should the state surrender the symbolism of the state executing an offender? Less dramatically, is it right for the state to allow private companies to impose deprivation of liberty and serious disciplinary measures such as solitary confinement? Or does incarceration involve a basic right that ought not to be relinquished by the government? Going further, is it right to bring the profit motive into this area? One answer is that it is wrong to do so; "it can be found morally troubling that corporations will try to make a profit on the punishment of people (which is a deliberate cause of suffering by representatives of society)" (Shichor, 1995, p. 258).

Another concern regarding privatization is whether the profit motive can debase corrections. For example, would private prisons be under pressure to keep clients incarcerated beyond an appropriate release time so as to keep prison populations and reimbursements high? Would these companies begin to lobby for lengthier sentences and fewer release opportunities? Would private prisons try to pay guards fair salaries or would profit pressures work to minimize salaries and benefits for officers? Would private agencies try to cut services for inmates (counseling, drug treatment) to a minimum?

In the nineteenth century, the profit motive did operate to cause significant problems in many state prison systems. In one juvenile system, for example, boys were leased out to private contractors for their labor. Hard-working boys would be kept under supervision longer than necessary because the contractor did not want to lose their productivity (Pisciotta, 1982). Evidence has also substantiated some of the other concerns, showing that the private sector offers both a lower starting salary, less potential for salary advancement, and larger inmate-to-staff ratios than public prisons (Blackely, 2005).

A response to such problems is spelling out a private agency's responsibilities to offenders in a carefully devised contract and then monitoring the implementation of the contract. If state inspectors enforce the contract conditions, then problems can be prevented or quickly resolved. If a private agency does not resolve any problems, it is in violation of the contract and the agency can be dropped. Opponents of privatization contend that there is a problem with this argument. If the state wants to end a contract, there may not be another service provider willing and able to step in and take over the contracted service. At the very least, it would take some time for another company to be ready to do so.

Still another problem with privatization is that private agencies can be overly selective of the clients (offenders) they want to manage. Private agencies in corrections and in areas such as welfare have been criticized for picking the most capable clients (Rosin, 1997). The criticism is that these individuals may have been able to succeed on probation or in getting off of public assistance with little or no help. Statistics showing them to be success stories are thereby misleading. The private agency selected the individuals most likely to succeed and ignored the individuals most in need of intervention. The state is left to deal with these more difficult cases.

Proponents of privatization argue that contracting of services can make spending on correctional services more visible. When the government operates its own prisons, the prisons "have been ignored by the public and given … 'hands-off' treatment by the courts" (Logan, 1990, p. 256). Because there has been some criticism of contracting, there would be a number of eyes scrutinizing the privately run prisons.

In summary, proponents of prison privatization argue that private agencies can provide needed services more effectively and more efficiently than the government has done in the past. Opponents argue that government agencies can become more effective and efficient. Opponents also contend that there can be serious problems with privatization and question whether it is right to allow the state to give away the highly symbolic function of depriving citizens of their freedom and supervising that deprivation of liberty.

CONCLUSION

This chapter has examined a number of ethical issues pertaining to prisons. Probably the most basic question is Conrad's: What do the undeserving deserve? One's choice of answer to this question permeates most of the other issues raised in this chapter. At this moment in our nation's history, it appears that many answer that prisoners deserve little or nothing. Because they treated their victims with no compassion, they deserve no compassion in return.

The three theories that form the framework for this book, however, suggest that the current answer to Conrad's question may not be the ethical answer. Kant's categorical imperative urges us to treat others as subjects. Utilitarianism urges us to consider the consequences of our actions, including the consequences of treating inmates very harshly for years and then simply releasing them back onto the streets. The peacemaking perspective reminds us that we are all connected, including offender, victim, and public, and that caring is a basic ethical principle. It seems that all three ethical theories suggest that while punishment is appropriate, we cannot lose sight of the humanity of offenders even when they have appeared to lose sight of their own humanity and the humanity of others.

The challenge for the next century is to try to punish offenders in ways that are fitting and to remain mindful of the need to treat offenders with dignity. The Quakers and others tried to do this 200 years ago. It is not an easy task.

Discussion Questions

1. What do you think the "undeserving deserve"? Describe an ethical prison. What would it look like? How would prisoners live? What would be their daily regimen? If you were a state commissioner of corrections and could design your own prison system, what would it be like? Could you sell your ideal system to the governor and to the public?
2. Is there any place for chain gangs or other harsh measures in an ethical prison? Why or why not?
3. A 51-year-old prisoner has 10 years remaining on his sentence. He is neither terminal nor incapacitated but his health is starting to deteriorate. Risk analysis puts him at extremely low likelihood of committing a new crime if released from

prison. Releasing him would save the state more than $60,000 a year, that is, more than $600,000 over 10 years (a very conservative estimate of savings). Should the state keep him in prison to achieve retribution and deterrence OR should the state release him to save $600,000 that could be put to other uses?

4. Should women prisoners be treated exactly like male prisoners? Would equal treatment be advantageous for female prisoners? Discuss.

5. Is it desirable for a state to contract out its prison operations to a private correctional company? What are the ethical considerations in doing so?

CASE STUDY 16–1 WHO'S RUNNING THE PRISON?

You came to the state correctional system with good credentials. You feel that your background—as an ex-military officer with 15 years' experience in high-level correctional management positions and a recently completed master's degree in criminal justice—qualifies you for almost any correctional-related position. You have a practical, no-nonsense attitude and feel quite comfortable in being appointed superintendent of the state penitentiary, which had been suffering from incompetent leadership and political intrigue.

The facility was in the state's most isolated corner, and the inmates there were either considered to have little potential for rehabilitation or were serving such long-term sentences that rehabilitation was of little immediate interest. In accepting the job as superintendent, you stated that your top priorities were to upgrade conditions in the prison, especially the physical plant, and to improve the quality of the correctional officer staff. Recently the two problems have become entwined in an unexpected way.

You had only been on the job for one week when the county commissioner for the district in which your institution is located came to see you. The commissioner, as you soon learned, was a political power in the county and could make conditions miserable for you if he wanted. It seems that his son-in-law needed a job, and he wanted you to find a place for him on your staff. One word led to another, and before you knew it you responded by stating, "Hell no! I won't hire anybody unless they are qualified."

The county commissioner left angrily, and a day later Senator Nester called. Senator Nester was on the state corrections committee and represented the district in which

your institution was located. At the time he called you did not know that he was also on the appropriations committee. You learned later that if someone wanted a management job at the institution, he had to call Senator Nester in order to be hired. Senator Nester stated in his call to you that he just wanted to "get acquainted" and give you a little friendly advice. First, he indicated that you should make a serious effort to get along with all the local officials, and second, he recommended that you hire the county commissioner's son-in-law. You told the senator that you would look at the son-in-law's application when he submitted it, and if he was qualified, you would give him serious consideration, but beyond that you could make no promises.

Your review of the son-in-law's hastily submitted application revealed that he had a high school diploma, had been a police officer on a local force, and had held several other unrelated jobs, all of rather short duration. In short, he might be qualified for an entry-level correctional officer slot. However, his work record was spotty and the reason for his departure from the police department was unclear. Although no one was talking openly about it, there were some allegations circulating from certain members of the department of police brutality involving the son-in-law. Since you did not want an unqualified and questionable political hack in your organization, you placed his application in "file 13."

After a week Senator Nester's office called "on behalf of a constituent" and inquired about the son-in-law's application. Your personnel officer told the senator's office that a letter had been sent to the applicant thanking him for his application, but informing him that applications were competitive and, unfortunately, he had not been selected.

CASE STUDY 16–1 WHO'S RUNNING THE PRISON? *Continued*

Later in the day Senator Nester called back in person; he was enraged. "Why wasn't I informed of your decision? I've done a hell of a lot for this correctional system and have a right to expect the courtesy of a reply. I never had this problem before." Nester was clearly threatening when he said, "You may find that these upcoming hearings will question your practices in dealing with the legislature, and I'll have some questions about your personnel policies, too." You finally told Senator Nester that you were running the institution, and until you were replaced you would continue to hire people based on merit.

Two months later at budget hearings in the legislature, you found out Senator Nester was a man of his word. Because of his influence, a new car for the prison superintendent was stricken, slots for 18 new correctional officers were also stricken, and to make matters worse, the committee voted to nullify the badly needed pay raises that had been budgeted for all the prison employees.

The senator's message has come through to you loud and clear. You realize that the two of you will have to reach some sort of working agreement, unless you can marshal enough support from other more friendly legislators, which at present does not seem likely. How should you approach Senator Nester? How can you maintain your standards and at the same time appease him? Should you give and take a little, should you look for a new job, or should you do both? You are not a quitter; you would prefer to work with Senator Nester, but you keep asking yourself how.

Questions

1. What are some ways a powerful senator can corrupt a correctional facility located in his district?
2. Is there anything the prison superintendent can do to remedy the situation?

From Braswell, M., Miller, L., & Pollock, J. Case studies in criminal justice ethics. Long Grove, IL: Waveland Press; 2006. Reprinted with permission.

NOTE

1. For a more thorough analysis of the issue of prison composition, see Irwin and Austin (1997) and Braswell and Whitehead (1997). This section of the chapter relies heavily on the latter source.

REFERENCES

Alabama Code, 13A-3-23.

American Bar Association (1986). *Section of criminal justice, report to the House of Delegates.* Chicago: American Bar Association.

American Civil Liberties Union (ACLU) (2012). *At America's expense: The mass incarceration of the elderly.* New York: American Civil Liberties Union.

Aos, S., Miller, M., & Drake, E. (2006). *Evidence-based adult corrections programs: What works and what does not.* Olympia, WA: Washington State Institute for Public Policy.

Applegate, B. K., Cullen, F. T., Turner, M. G., & Sundt, J. L. (1996). Assessing public support for three-strikes-and-you're out laws: Global versus specific attitudes. *Crime & Delinquency, 42,* 517–534.

Beck, A. J., Berzofsky, M., Caspar, R., & Krebs, C. (2013). *Sexual victimization in prisons and jails reported by inmates, 2011–2012.* Washington: U.S. Department of Justice.

Bidinotto, R. J. (1997). Prisons should not coddle inmates. In C. P. Cozic (Ed.), *America's prisons: Opposing viewpoints* (pp. 85–92). San Diego: Greenhaven Press.

Blackely, C. (2005). *America's prisons: The movement toward profit and privatization*. Boca Raton: Brown Walker Press.

Bonta, J., & Gendreau, P. (1994). Reexamining the cruel and unusual punishment of prison life. In M. C. Braswell, R. H. Montgomery, & L. X. Lombardo (Eds.), *Prison violence in America* (2nd ed.) (pp. 39–68). Cincinnati: Anderson.

Bowker, L. H. (1980). *Prison victimization*. New York: Elsevier.

Braswell, M., & Whitehead, J. (1997). The middle way: The debate about prisons. In *Paper presented at the 1997 annual meeting of the Southern Criminal Justice Association*. Richmond, VA.

Brownstein, H. H., Spunt, B. J., Crimmins, S. M., & Langley, S. C. (1995). Women who kill in drug market situations. *Justice Quarterly, 12*, 473–498.

Camp, S. D., Daggett, D. M., Kwon, O., & Klein-Saffran, J. (2008). The effect of faith program participation on prison misconduct: The life connections program. *Journal of Criminal Justice, 36*, 389–395.

Camp, S. D., Klein-Saffran, J., Kwon, O., Daggett, D. M., & Joseph, V. (2006). An exploration into participation in a faith-based prison program. *Criminology & Public Policy, 5*, 529–550.

Carson, E., & Sabol, W. (2012). *Prisoners in 2011*. Bureau of Justice Statistics. Washington: Government Printing Office.

Cohen, R. L. (1995). *Probation and parole violators in state prison, 1991*. Washington: U.S. Department of Justice.

Conrad, J. P. (1982). What do the undeserving deserve? In R. Johnson, & H. Toch (Eds.), *The pains of imprisonment* (pp. 313–330). Beverly Hills: Sage.

Corsentino, M. (1997). Inmate chain gangs are an improper form of punishment. In C. P. Cozic (Ed.), *America's prisons: Opposing viewpoints* (pp. 120–127). San Diego: Greenhaven Press.

DiIulio, J. J., Jr. (1994). The question of black crime. *The Public Interest, 117*, 3–32.

DiIulio, J. J., Jr. (1995). White lies about black crime. *The Public Interest, 118*, 30–44.

DiMascio, W. M. (1995). *Seeking justice: Crime and punishment in America*. New York: Edna McConnell Clark Foundation.

Durham, A. M. (1994). *Crisis and reform: Current issues in American punishment*. Boston: Little, Brown.

Duwe, G., & King, M. (2012). Can faith-based correctional programs work? An outcome evaluation of the inner change Freedom initiative in Minnesota. *International Journal of Offender Therapy and Comparative Criminology, 57*, 813–841.

Goffman, E. (1961). *Asylums: Essays on the social situation of mental patients and other inmates*. Garden City: Anchor Books.

Griffin, M. (2001). *The use of force by detention officers*. New York: LFB Scholarly.

Guenther, A. (1978). The impact of confinement. In N. Johnston, & L. D. Savitz (Eds.), *Justice and corrections* (pp. 596–603). New York: John Wiley & Sons.

Hamm, M. S., Coupez, T., Hoze, F. E., & Weinstein, C. (1994). The myth of humane imprisonment: A critical analysis of severe discipline in U.S. maximum security prisons, 1945–1990. In M. C. Braswell, R. H. Montgomery, & L. X. Lombardo (Eds.), *Prison violence in America* (2nd ed.) (pp. 167–200). Cincinnati: Anderson.

Hewitt, J. D. (2006). Having faith in faith-based prison programs. *Criminology and Public Policy, 5*, 551–558.

Inciardi, J. A., Horowitz, R., & Pottieger, A. E. (1993). *Street kids, street drugs, street crime: An examination of drug use and serious delinquency in Miami*. Belmont: Wadsworth.

Irwin, J., & Austin, J. (1997). *It's about time: America's imprisonment binge* (2nd ed.). Belmont: Wadsworth.

Lee, S., Aos, S., Drake, E., Pennucci, A., Miller, M., & Anderson, L. (2012). *Return on investment: Evidence-based options to improve statewide outcomes, April 2012.* Olympia: Washington State Institute for Public Policy.

Lipsey, M., & Cullen, F. (2007). The effectiveness of correctional rehabilitation: A review of systematic reviews. *Annual Review of Law and Social Sciences, 3,* 297–320.

Logan, C. H. (1990). *Private prisons: Cons and pros.* New York: Oxford.

Maguire, K., & Pastore, A. L. (Eds.), (1996). *Sourcebook of criminal justice statistics 1995.* Washington: U.S. Department of Justice.

McKelvey, B. (1997). American prisons: A study in American social history prior to 1915. In J. W. Marquart, & J. R. Sorenson (Eds.), *Correctional contexts: Contemporary and classical readings* (pp. 84–94). Los Angeles: Roxbury.

Morris, R. L. (1997). Inmate chain gangs are a proper form of punishment. In C. P. Cozic (Ed.), *America's prisons: Opposing viewpoints* (pp. 111–119). San Diego: Greenhaven Press.

Mumola, C. J., & Beck, A. J. (1997). *Prisoners in 1996.* Bureau of Justice Statistics Bulletin. Washington: U.S. Department of Justice.

Perrone, D., & Pratt, T. (2003). Comparing the quality of confinement and cost effectiveness of public versus private prisons: What we know, why we do not know more, and where to go from here. *Prison Journal, 83*(3), 301–321.

Pisciotta, A. W. (1982). Saving the children: The promise and practice of *Parens Patriae*, 1838–98. *Crime & Delinquency, 28,* 410–425.

Pritchard, D. A. (1979). Stable predictors of recidivism: A summary. *Criminology, 17,* 15–21.

Rastogi, S., Johnson, T., Hoeffel, E., & Drewery, M. (2011). *The Black population: 2010,* 2010 Census Briefs. Retrieved at www.census.gov/prod/cen2010/briefs/c2010br-06.pdf.

Rosin, H. (August 4, 1997). About face: The appearance of welfare success. *New Republic, 217,* 16–19.

Sabol, W. J., West, H. C., & Cooper, M. (2009). *Prisoners in 2008.* Washington: U.S. Department of Justice.

Shichor, D. (1995). *Punishment for profit: Private prisons/public concerns.* Thousand Oaks: Sage.

Silberman, C. E. (1978). *Criminal violence, criminal justice.* New York: Random House.

Sourcebook of criminal justice statistics (2010). Available online at www.albany.edu/sourcebook.

Spelman, W. (1994). *Criminal incapacitation.* New York: Plenum Press.

Sykes, G. M. (1958). *The society of captives: A study of a maximum security prison.* Princeton: Princeton University Press.

Taylor, J. M. (1997). Prisons do not coddle inmates. In C. P. Cozic (Ed.), *America's prisons: Opposing viewpoints* (pp. 85–92). San Diego: Greenhaven Press.

Toch, H., Adams, K., & Grant, J. D. (1989). *Coping: Maladaptation in prisons.* New Brunswick: Transaction.

van den Haag, E. (1975). *Punishing criminals: Concerning a very old and painful question.* New York: Basic Books.

Volokh, A. (2011). Do faith-based prisons work? *Alabama Law Review, 63,* 43–95.

von Hirsch, A. (1990). The ethics of community-based sanctions. *Crime & Delinquency, 36,* 162–173.

Wachtler, S. (1997). *After the madness: A judge's own prison memoir.* New York: Random House.

Walker, S., Spohn, C., & DeLone, M. (1996). *The color of justice: Race, ethnicity, and crime in America.* Belmont: Wadsworth.

West, H. C., & Sabol, W. L. (2009). *Prisoners in 2007.* Washington: U.S. Department of Justice.

Whitehead, J. T., & Braswell, M. C. (2000). The future of probation: Reintroducing the spiritual dimension into correctional practice. *Criminal Justice Review, 25,* 207–233.

Wolff, N., Blitz, C., Shi, J., Siegel, J., & Bachman, R. (2007). Physical violence inside prisons: Rates of victimization. *Criminal Justice and Behavior, 34*(5), 588–599.

Wright, R. T., & Decker, S. (1994). *Burglars on the job.* Boston: Northeastern University Press.

Zamble, E., & Porporino, F. J. (1988). *Coping, behavior, and adaptation in prison inmates.* New York: Springer-Verlag.

Ethical Issues in Crime Control Policy and Research

Justice and power must be brought together, so that whatever is
just may be powerful, and whatever is powerful may be just.

Blaise Pascal

How should we approach problems related to crime control? We are spending increasing sums of money in areas of law enforcement and corrections,
and we have continued to pass new legislation with an eye toward developing
more effective crime control policies. Still, violent crime continues to increase.
In addition, we have to contend with public perceptions regarding crime and
the justice system's response that are largely shaped by the media. Newspaper
headlines, television programs, and films each try to attract readers or viewers.
How much is fact and how much is fiction? Whether founded entirely on fact
or not, our citizens' fear of crime is certainly real to them.

An increasing awareness of the scope and nature of corporate crime challenges the
abilities and resources of our justice system on additional fronts. Our traditional
approach to controlling crime seems more comfortable when addressing familiar

criminal behavior in such areas as burglary, robbery, and assault. The "bad guys" are typically more clearly defined. This is not always the case with much of corporate crime. Problems involving consumer safety, pollution, and other related issues often involve business executives who are considered upstanding members of their communities; and with the rapid development of the computer, such crimes are increasingly difficult to track down. In some ways it seems that our traditional approach to administering justice is simply not adequate to resolve the more sophisticated problems of much of the corporate world. Still, the demands of culture can encourage and stimulate us to develop new ways of thinking about crime and, as a result, more innovative responses to crime-related problems.

There are also a variety of ethical concerns surrounding criminal justice research. The scientific life provides no barrier to unethical conduct. The problem of employing unethical means to an otherwise desirable end is ever present in the research setting, where scientists are sometimes tempted to sacrifice the well-being of their subjects for the sake of scientific knowledge. Subjects can easily come to be viewed as the means to an end when the products of scientific research are equated with the utilitarian's "greater good."

In the name of scientific research, subjects may experience invasions of privacy, unknowing participation in simulated research experiments, and physical and emotional stress. In experimental research designs, which systematically withhold an intervention from one group while exposing another, research subjects may be denied participation in programs offering medical, educational, or psychological treatment.

Although the nature of the research task poses many ethical dilemmas, additional problems involve the political context of the research. No one wants to hear bad news about a popular new law enforcement or correctional program, least of all the people who administer the program. Researchers can find themselves in very difficult circumstances when results indicate that the program is not achieving its goals. Is the correct response to redo the results until a more palatable outcome is achieved, or to report findings honestly? How is this decision affected when the people administering the program are the same ones paying the researcher's salary?

Researchers should police themselves, using standards of professional ethics and censure to provide appropriate guidance. It must be recognized, however, that there are significant pressures against the objective exercise of such standards. Competition for research funds is considerable—few universities or research centers are interested in forfeiting research funds on ethical grounds, and few scholars are interested in creating any more obstacles to their research efforts than necessary. It is therefore very important to establish a climate of high ethical standards in the graduate schools that produce researchers and in the organizations ultimately responsible for conducting research.

Crime and Justice Myths

Egan Green

Walter Snyder waited in prison for more than seven and a half years for justice. He had been convicted of a rape that nearly seven years after his trial the prosecutor's office even agreed he could not have committed. Due to a legal technicality, the Virginia court system's rules prevented his release through court procedures; it was up to Virginia's governor to grant Snyder clemency. Nevertheless, Governor Wilder refused to do so, out of concern for appearing soft on crime. It was important to the governor that his actions and policies reflect the public's "get tough" mood toward crime (Scheck, Neufield, & Dwyer, 2003).

Public opinion influences criminal justice policies throughout the United States. While this is a reflection of democracy in action, the premises for the policies are often based on myths about crime in society. All policies shape citizens' lives, but criminal justice policies have to meet a higher ethical threshold than many other policies. Policies that may typically be considered immoral, such as restricting freedoms or causing harm to someone, have an aura of legitimacy when associated with enforcing a law. If the policies are created out of information that is inaccurate, people suffer wrongfully regardless of the intentions of the policies that legitimate them. Whether the sanction is a simple fine or a state-sponsored execution, the resulting suffering caused by a policy is supported by the power of the state. In some cases, wrongfully convicted people and citizens who might not have been criminals pay the price for the influence myths have on policies that turn out to be biased or unjust. Baer and

Chambliss (1997) note that fear of crime based on inaccurate information also causes harm to all of society. The concern is therefore how crime myths, whether accidental manifestations of stereotypes or intentionally created propaganda, affect the policy-making process.

THE NATURE OF MYTHS

Myths have historically served a number of purposes, including perpetuating a culture's ideals and protecting valued behaviors from outsider influence. They may be read or heard as stories of events or characters, but whatever the mode, they transmit values and accepted codes of behavior. Kappeler and Potter (2005, p. 2) state, "While myths seem to *explain* events, they more often *instruct* us on how to integrate an event into our belief systems and world views."

> "The great enemy of truth is very often not the lie—deliberate, contrived, and dishonest—but the myth, persistent, persuasive, and unrealistic. Too often we hold fast to the clichés of our forebears. We subject all facts to a prefabricated set of interpretations. We enjoy comfort of opinion without the discomfort of thought."
>
> *John F. Kennedy*

It is the mythmaker's values that are integrated into the events that are presented as facts. Nimmo and Combs (1980) define a myth as a "... socially constructed re-presentation of perceived realities that people accept as permanent, fixed knowledge of reality while forgetting (if they were ever aware of it) its tentative, imaginative, created, and perhaps fictional qualities" (p. 16).

Because myths are passed to consumers who are typically in agreement with the expressed values, their authenticity is seldom questioned. Kappeler and Potter (2005) note, myths are unverifiable and unscientific. Yet when people accept myths as fact it is because they agree with the beliefs about proper behavior, so they are not likely to conduct an exhaustive search for supporting facts and evidence. Myths are a unifying force for similar people and consequently create animosity toward outsiders who do not share the expressed value system. The outsiders' beliefs and actions are depicted as threatening and eventually destructive. To prevent such a disaster, people who accept the myth see the importance of protecting their way of life from the outsiders. The "us versus them" mentality evolves from such thinking supporting Pfuhl's (as cited in Hawley, 1989, p. 135) point that myths are used to "justify (1) the proposed moral environment, (2) the distribution of authority, (3) the proposed disposition of the deviant, and the superiority of the nondeviant."

Ryan (1976) refers to the outsiders as "different ones" who have a number of inferior qualities. Myths allow differences in groups of people to be qualitative differentiations that dehumanize the group that is painted as inferior by the myth. The differences may be based on a class of characteristics or a single characteristic that is magnified to raise concern. In terms of crime myths, the threatening or uncivilized characteristics and behavior of the group of outsiders mandate a need for control. This will not only protect the status quo for the socially powerful, but will also keep in check the outsiders. Laws provide the needed controls. Kappeler and Potter (2005, p. 147) state:

> Myths of crime and criminal justice, for the most part, revolve around two central themes. First, there is a criminal act or behavior. That behavior is seized upon by the media, law enforcement bureaucracies, and politicians as a way to attract public attention and to win support for policy issues related to crime… The second recurring theme in myths of crime and criminal justice is a massive law enforcement response to the behavior in question.

American society has come to depend on laws as a way of confronting societal concerns. Therefore, myths may raise an often fictional need for creating the criminals, yet they may also arouse belief in a need for more controls on existing criminals. Either way, people labeled as criminals become the "them" in our society. Once society becomes indifferent to the needs and treatment of the myths' villains, unfair treatment is likely to follow. Society may become so enamored by the myth and the initial reaction to it that the result is often overlooked. In the end, human beings pay the price for society's reaction to crime myths, just as Walter Snyder paid the price for the myth of a criminal justice system that is soft on crime.

INFLUENCING MYTHS: MEDIA, POLITICS, AND PUBLIC OPINION

Like all myths, crime myth origins are often hard to pinpoint. Folklorists have noted the persistence of a *Friend of a Friend* (FOAF) who assists in passing helpful information to others based on his or her experiences (Nicolini, 1989). Folklorists have noted that these apparently fictional people are often referred to by people spreading urban legends as evidence of their authenticity. This FOAF can never be located, so the origin of the tale can never be verified. This is true to some degree with crime myths. However, it is evident that due to the power of crime myths, the influence of powerful forces such as the media, politicians, and the government as well as public perception aids in their dissemination and sustainability.

THE MEDIA AND CRIME MYTHS

The growth of media in the late twentieth century and early twenty-first century has been unprecedented and changed the way television news has been reported. Fox, Van Sickel, and Steiger (2007) note that television news reporting seemed to enter an era of tabloid reporting as early as 1991. The problem has only grown worse since then. Britto and Dabney (2010, p. 199) state, "…a tradition of investigative journalism has largely been replaced by a cavalier brand of journalism, driven by market forces and aimed at attracting viewers by tapping into their emotional response to current events." This trend has also contributed to the spread of crime myths in a number of ways. There are more television channels than in earlier decades. They require programming that will lure viewers away from other networks. Crime and policing programs often serve that end. News networks are under tremendous pressure to report an event before the competition. Crime events are often used to lure viewers with the most graphic and violent news available. The seriousness of these crimes makes them more newsworthy than lesser crimes, but they are therefore reported out of proportion to their actual occurrence. This leads to the public impression that serious crime occurs more frequently than it does. Pollak and Kubrin (2007, p. 59) refer to this as the *law of opposites*, stating, "(T)he characteristics of crime, criminals and victims represented in the media are in most respects the polar opposite of the pattern suggested by official crime statistics."

Crime is covered more frequently in local newspapers and local broadcast news programs than national news programs (Yanich, 2005). While crime is a newsworthy event, the frequency of the reporting and presentation of the stories often present unique cases as normal societal interaction and typical of criminal justice practitioners' work. This is not entirely coincidental (Bennett, 1996). Yanich (2005) notes the manner in which local television news broadcasts shape the importance of news events by how, when, and from where they are reported. For example, criminal acts are more likely than other news to lead the broadcast. The old adage "if it bleeds it leads" is true. Furthermore, Yanich (2005) notes that a series of crimes are often reported in a montage that clumps them together and in doing so creates an impression of crime occurring frequently.

Research also reveals a tendency among local news programs in large television markets to treat juvenile crime differently than adult crime. Juvenile crime is more likely to receive coverage that depicts it as occurring more often than it proportionally occurs. The combination of how and when juvenile crime stories are covered creates an illusion of greater juvenile crime than actually occurs (Pollak & Kubrin, 2007; Yanich, 2005). Yanich (2005, p. 130) states, "The Kids Crime stories perpetuated the notion that juveniles live in a violent and dangerous world. However, that is only true for a very small percentage of juveniles and, for that matter, adults." Additionally, news sources often make connections between youthful offenders and other crimes that are not the focus of a particular story (Pollak & Kubrin, 2007). This has the effect of leading news consumers to believe that the reported event is a case study of the offender's other crimes as well as leading them to believe that juvenile crime is random and irrational.

While national news media outlets can influence perceptions, Weitzer and Kubrin (2004) conclude that local television news has a greater impact on fear of crime among some portions of their sample than national news programs, radio news, Internet news sources, and daily newspapers. They also point out that this finding corroborates earlier research (Chiricos, Eschholz & Gertz, 1997) about the impact of local television news. Weitzer and Kubrin (2004) explain why local television news would be expected to have a greater impact on citizens' fear of crime.

> Local television is literally "close to home" for viewers, whereas national television news tend to be far removed from viewers' everyday lives… and compared to newspapers and radio, local television news broadcasts are often televised live from crime scenes and presented in a graphic, sensational, or disturbing manner (p. 503).

In support of the "close to home" notion, Dowler (2004a) compared crime stories on broadcast news in Canada with those in the United States and concluded that national stories were more likely to be shown on local Canadian news than on local news programs in the United States. Nonetheless, local news broadcasts for both countries showed stories that supported popular or mythical views of crime and justice. They also made efforts to keep station owners and advertisers from becoming disgruntled about their broadcasts.

Other researchers have found evidence to support the notion that local television news is a source of information about, and therefore understanding of, criminal justice interactions. Waid-Lindberg, Dobbs, and Shelley (2011) found that more frequent exposure to local television news led to more punitive attitudes toward criminals. Yanich (2004) noted discrepancies in how local television news channels report urban and suburban crime, which created an impression that crime was more prevalent in low-crime areas. Romer, Jamieson, and Aday (2003) concluded that local television seemed to be related to increased fear of crime among residents of Philadelphia. Dowler (2004b) found local newscasts distorted images of criminal defendants by race through predictors such as firearm usage, length of the story, and showing handcuffs. Klein and Naccarto (2003) also found support for the local news programs' practice of disproportionately representing racial minorities as criminal and suggest that the motive for this practice may be as simple as financial gain. It is important to note that these researchers were conducting their research during times when crime rates were actually falling. Yet fear of crime stayed high (Yanich, 2004). It therefore appears that local television news programming and editing perpetuates myths of crime, thereby creating greater public anxiety about it even when it is a declining problem (Yanich, 2004, p. 537).

Local television news seems to play a different role in influencing crime myths than other news sources. Research on the role of newspapers has generally failed to find support for a strong influence regarding fear of crime (Chiricos, Eschholz, & Gertz, 1997; O'Keefe & Reid-Nash, 1987; Weitzer & Kubrin, 2004). This may be because newspaper readers have control over the news to which they are exposed. They may simply decide not to read a specific story. Perhaps it is because newspapers are less visual media. Yet ideas of crime and criminals that lead to myths are different from fear of crime. For example, Cobbina (2008) found that print media coverage of crack and methamphetamine users often referenced crack cocaine users as African-Americans and associated them with violent crime. Stories about methamphetamine use by whites depicted the users as poor white people and portrayed the drug issue as a public health problem. Moreover, when whites were depicted in crack cocaine stories, they were portrayed as victims of the drug rather than as criminals. Newspaper crime coverage is more likely to focus on infrequent crimes involving sex and or violence (Chadee & Ditton, 2005). While this practice may be attributable to the importance of reporting serious crime, the failure to report other less serious offenses still distorts readers' understanding of crime.

Local sources are not alone in their responsibility for the dissemination of crime myths. Network news may also influence the public's perception of crime as being a greater problem than it is. The Center for Media and Public Affairs (July–August, 2000) reported that crime was the most common topic on the three major American television networks during the 1990s. The *Tyndall Reports* (ADT Research, 1994) found that the three networks' news programs more than doubled their broadcast minutes of crime stories from 1991 to 1994, even though crime rates were simultaneously declining. This is important because Lowry, Nio, and Leitner (2003) found that news story lengths accounted for fear of crime better than the number of crime stories that networks broadcast. They also concluded that network crime news reporting better explained public concern of crime than the actual crime rates during the early 1990s.

Major news networks also use the political talk show format to discuss criminal justice issues. Britto and Dabney (2010) found that these shows do not take an objective approach to criminal justice issues; rather the hosts or guests are often advocating a position. Conservative guests were given more time to provide their viewpoints, but only 15% of the guests from the sampled episodes actually relied on research evidence to augment their arguments. Additionally, male offending (minority males in particular) was exaggerated compared to actual crime rates. Further, the crime events discussed on these shows tend to focus on crimes with white female victims.

The myths perpetuated about crime through news outlets also extend to crime victims. Pollak and Kubrin (2007) concluded that news outlets commonly discuss juvenile victims of crime as lacking blame in their victimization and emphasize positive characteristics. This is often accomplished by interviewing a crime victim's relatives and friends who describe the victim's aspirations or positive attributes of the victim's personality. Pollak and Kubrin (2007) also found that newspaper stories and televised news stories provide more details about victim injuries in juvenile crime stories than in adult crime stories. Britto and Dabney (2010) point out that white female crime victimization is reported on political talk shows at a rate that is 250% greater than the victimization data provide. In analyzing television news depictions of crime victims, Bjornstrom, Kaufman, Peterson, and Slater (2010) found that television news stories about crime involving female victims were more likely to report the victim's race if she was white than if she was black or Hispanic. Stories involving minority female victimization often excluded the victim's race. Further, they also concluded that when crime victims' races were reported, the race of white victims was more likely to be reported than that of other races for all types of crime regardless of gender.

Popular media sources such as movies and television programs also present distorted images of crime as well as police, courts, and corrections work. Some media sources blur the line between popular media and news media by showing atypical depictions of illegal criminal justice events as standard practice. Entertainment shows that are formatted in such a way that they resemble actual news events have also distorted reality. These programs provide "infotainment" by blending drama with reality. The result is a group of viewers who view these programs with mixed content as partially informative and partly entertaining (Surette & Otto, 2002). Eschholz (1998) refers to programs such as *Hard Copy* as providers of false news. She concludes that they influence fear of crime among white males and African Americans. The same was true for reality shows like *COPS*. She also notes that fictional television shows such as crime dramas produced more fear of crime than nonfictional shows. However, the differences between these types of shows are not always clear. Eschholz, Mallard, and Flynn (2004) found fictional crime programs often embellish story lines from factual events that were reported in the news. These shows perpetuate crime myths by showing stories with close similarities to actual events but offer a distorted picture of the races of offenders and criminal justice officials. For example, regarding crime dramas, African-American criminals were nearly twice as likely to be shown wearing handcuffs than white criminals, and African Americans were nearly five times more likely to be portrayed as an offender than a victim. This is in contrast to official crime rates. Eschholz, Mallard and Flynn (2004) conclude that prime-time television programming distorts true crime figures while sensationalizing solutions to crime in the United States. They discuss the effect of these kinds of media misrepresentations.

> The combination of the crime control model and the criminal typification of minorities... may reinforce that perception that minorities pose a "social threat" to the white majority... and that the only way to deal with this threat is by giving the police more power and punitive policies... (p. 174).

Rader and Rhineberger-Dunn (2010) found that white female victimization is also exaggerated in a number of popular television shows. Additionally, these shows often depict victim-offender relationships as nonacquaintances. Further, when offenders and victims are acquainted in television dramas, victims are more negatively characterized.

Public perception of crime is likely to be shaped by all of these types of media influences. This means the public may be more likely to believe stereotypes of a failing criminal justice system that is hampered by the defendant protections as well as media-fed images of typical offenders, crime fighters, and victims. Such images often do not agree with actual crime facts. Of course, even the government and politicians contribute to crime myths.

■ Learn More on the Internet

For more on how the mass media influence perceptions on crime and justice, go to: law.jrank.org/pages/1582/Mass-Media-Crime.html. ■

GOVERNMENT, POLITICS, AND CRIME MYTHS

While society should be able to rely on the government and official crime facts and statistics to correct the course of crime myths, the unfortunate truth is that they are too often contributors to such images. Criminal justice enforcement agencies are in the difficult quandary of needing to fail in order to demonstrate their need for additional budgetary resources, yet they must also demonstrate some level of success to ward off accusations of incompetence. This creates a criminal justice system that Reiman (2007) has theorized is designed to fail.

Politicians often play on public fear of crime as a problem to be addressed. During the 1988 Presidential campaign, Democratic candidate and Massachusetts governor Michael Dukakis presented an image of being soft on crime as a result of two major events. First, during a debate with Republican incumbent George H.W. Bush, Dukakis stated that he would not support the death penalty for a criminal who hypothetically raped and killed his wife. Second, the Bush campaign, using data collected suggesting the public saw Dukakis as soft on crime, began airing television commercials telling the story of a convicted murderer named Willie Horton who had been released on a furlough program in Massachusetts while Dukakis was governor. Horton had committed a multiple rape and robbery and never returned from his furlough. This appearance of "coddling criminals" went against the societal belief in crime control policies and helped Bush defeat Dukakis in the general election.

The message was clear to all politicians. In order to be elected, candidates understood they must not appear soft on crime. The public's fear of crime was an easy issue to address with answers such as greater enforcement and more severe punishment. Moreover, rising crime rates can work for either politician in a campaign if framed in the right manner. For example, a politician in office can refer to high crime rates as evidence of a social problem that requires more funding and cooperation on crime control policies. The incumbent can then note the need to keep him or her in office so progress is not stymied. A politician running for the same office can use the same high crime rates as evidence that the incumbent is not adequately handling the crime problem. Either way, crime appears out of control to the public and raises concerns while both incumbent and candidate vie for public support of their interpretation concerning rising crime rates.

Governments are expected to address crime issues. This means they have a virtual monopoly on crime information such as how often police respond to calls, what types of offenses occur most often, where they occur, as well as by whom and against whom they are committed. The public depends on them as *information keepers*. The data to verify or dispute crime myths often lie with the criminal justice agencies. Because of this control, the government is "… one of the most powerful mythmakers in the criminal production enterprise" (Kappeler & Potter, 2005, p. 10). The government influences other mythmakers, such as news media, through information released in press conferences (Herman & Chomsky, 1988), public service announcements, and edited government research reports (Kappeler & Potter, 2005). Due to the access and control of information pertaining to crime, the government releases that information which serves its interest. This puts government officials at an advantage as more reliable sources than other sources who do not have access to the information needed for news stories (Welch, Fenwick, & Roberts, 1998).

The government influences which actions are considered the most nefarious through funding of research and law enforcement initiatives. For example, the federal government makes grants available to researchers who propose projects that the government deems worthy of funding. With competitive grants, the information brokers determine which research proposals will receive requested funds. When the government has prioritized crime policies, the concern becomes whether researchers exploring other worthy crime proposals will fail to receive funding because their ideas are not in accord with the government's priority. For example, during the 1980s the federal government's main crime priority focused on using criminal justice resources to confront illicit drug use and trafficking. Researchers seeking funding for other criminal justice issues were less likely to receive funding for their projects, hence the government's control of funding dictates which crime problems are most widely publicized and understood (Potter & Kappeler, 2005).

During the 1930s, the Bureau of Narcotics implemented a publicity campaign to garner public support for controlling marijuana. To do this, the Bureau collected a series of crimes and dangerous acts committed by marijuana users. Kappeler and Potter (2005) state:

> These stories included the murder of a Florida family and their pet dog by a wayward son who had taken one toke of marijuana. Newspapers printed this story and others like it. The war on drugs had begun. The myth of the "dope fiend" was born out of the minds of law enforcement officials (p. 12).

This type of governmental propaganda eventually contributed to the creation of several drug control laws.

Government reports about crime are often so politicized that they present a blurred view of criminal justice. They can be politicized for political purposes. Crime rates in Indianapolis over the course of 30 years have been found to be manipulated up or down depending on the political needs of the time (Selke & Pepinsky, 1984). Sherman (1998) reported that during the 1980s the Federal Bureau of Investigation (FBI) stopped including two southern states' crime reports in aggregate national numbers because of faulty and unreliable reporting. By the late 1990s major metropolitan areas in the United States were caught reporting false crime numbers to the FBI (Kappeler & Potter, 2005).

The federal government is also responsible for making faulty claims about crime rates to protect political interests. For example, the cover of the 1992 Uniform Crime Reports (UCR) shows a line chart with a line rising as though it is representative of crime. However, actual examination reveals that most major crime rates had declined for that year (Baer & Chambliss, 1997). In addition, only the most serious crime in a series of crimes is reported by the UCR, which shows the overall crime rate lower than it actually is while raising the reported violent crime rate. The National Crime Victimization Survey results have at times been reported in such a way that summarized attempted but unsuccessful crimes, or crimes without any harm felt by the victim, as being violent crimes (Baer & Chambliss, 1997).

To achieve the goal of creating a need for larger law enforcement budgets while still appearing successful, crime rates have been manipulated to present some problems as being solved while new ones are rising. For example, official violent crime rates were declining in the 1990s. The government presented this as evidence of crime policy success while referring to the growing threat of violence from strangers. This makes crime seem more random and frightening. Yet the rates of stranger violence were shown as rising due to their classification as unsolved murders (Baer & Chambliss, 1997). This new threat was released to news outlets claiming a newly discovered "trend." News organizations accepted the grim outlook from the information brokers in the government and quickly publicized it. This myth was designed to keep the public concerned and maintain public support for increasing budgets and furthering crime control policies.

The government also perpetuates myths about who is and is not a criminal through its prosecutorial efforts. The cases of Edward Snowden (see Box 17.1) and Jeff Olson serve as examples. In 2012, Olson wrote messages with water-soluble chalk on the sidewalks outside of Bank of America bank branches in

BOX 17.1 WHISTLEBLOWERS AND GOVERNMENT SPYING: VIRTUOUS MYTHS OR FLAWED REALITIES

The conflict against terrorism has led to greater concerns in society about governmental intrusion into our lives. Edward Snowden and Bradley Manning serve as examples of whistleblowers of controversial government actions. Snowden had worked for a government contractor before he revealed the scope of a secret program that allowed the government to collect phone and Internet records of American citizens, even within the boundaries of the United States. (Greenwald, 2013; Greenwald & Ackerman, 2013). The leak revealed the scope of National Security Agency's (NSA) warrantless spying on American citizens as well as international entities including ally governments. The actions included having private companies provide the government with records detailing phone calls as well as e-mail exchanges. The federal government charged Edward Snowden with violating the 1917 Espionage Act (Finn & Horowitz, 2013) despite the fact that he had fled the country. The example is similar to the case of Bradley Manning, an army private who in 2010 leaked nearly 700,000 secret military and diplomatic documents to the Internet website Wikileaks. The army charged him with violating the Espionage Act. His court martial resulted in convictions for 17 of 22 counts with which he was charged (Pilkington, 2013).

While being charged as criminals, each of these whistleblowers does not appear to fit the profile of most criminals; their actions may be more altruistic. Both appear to have been motivated by their concerns over the extent of unmitigated government actions and government intrusion into citizens' lives. Manning stated that he had released the information he leaked to inform the public about the extent of domestic spying and "spark debate about foreign policy" (Bradley Manning Chronology, 2013). Likewise, Snowden claimed to have leaked information to the press because of his concerns about the lack of public knowledge about the extent of government intrusion.

The leaks caused government officials to defend the spying programs but also revealed that the government had been untruthful about domestic spying in inquiries prior to the leaks (Shane & Weisman, 2013). In defending the practice, a number of government officials stated that these practices had diverted multiple terrorist attacks. Officials also point out the reliance on secrecy for their programs to successfully detect and prevent terrorism. However, this means that the public is expected to trust the judgment of government officials. This gives government officials a unique ability as mythmaker: they can create myths about crime or terrorism with limited oversight. Furthermore, the government's ability to charge Snowden and Manning with crimes gives it the ability to label them as criminals despite claims that they were altruistic whistleblowers.

Opponents of the government's spying program, including some members of Congress, claim that the collection of everyone's phone and Internet records is unconstitutional or an unintended power resulting from anti-terrorism laws. The Fourth Amendment prohibits unreasonable searches. If a person's records are being searched without a reason particular to that individual, the search lacks reason. Moreover, internal audits conducted by the NSA revealed that the agency had violated rules or court orders thousands of times in the years since it was given expanded powers, suggesting the limitations placed on the agency are ineffective (Gellman, 2013). Others are less concerned about the spying, believing it is for the greater good. However, Snowden's revelation of NSA spying led to increased concern about governmental intrusion (Bump, 2013). The question becomes whether the partial social acceptance of the practice is the result of the governmental claim that it is impeding terrorism. The government's responsibility to protect the public gives it the unique ability among mythmakers to tell the public to trust officials to do what is in the public's interest without providing verification of their claimed threats and to label those who question this power as criminals.

San Diego (Associated Press [AP], 2013). The messages were fairly innocuous; he wrote "No thanks, big banks" and similar messages. Despite using the type of chalk that children use when writing on sidewalks, the San Diego city attorney's office filed vandalism charges against Olson that could have resulted in a maximum penalty of 13 years in jail and fines totaling $13,000. The city attorney's office stated, "Graffiti remains vandalism in the state of California" (AP, 2013; para. 9). Mr Olson attempted to justify the act as a constitutionally protected right to freedom of speech; however, the judge rejected the claim. But this is hardly the type of criminal that concerns society. In fact, San Diego's mayor said the case was "stupid" and a "nonsense prosecution" (AP, 2013; para. 5 & 6). Nevertheless, the prosecution plodded to trial with the charges.

A successful prosecution of this case would have resulted in a criminal record for Olson. The government's ability to prosecute people has the impact of labeling them as criminals, which can impact defendants' future employment prospects. Yet, society does not view these types of acts as worthy of prosecution. Moreover, crimes that bank employees committed causing the 2008 economic turmoil have never been prosecuted. The result of these types of practices is that white-collar criminals do not wear the label of being a criminal. In the Olson case, the government refused to acknowledge Olson's messages as freedom of speech and attempted to convict him. In this case, the jury gave an acquittal; however, too often the general public contributes to the mythology of crime.

THE GENERAL PUBLIC AND CRIME MYTHS

Nimmo and Combs (1980) point out that one of the functions of myths is to provide "social glue" (p. 13) for society. Myths obviously assist in building a consensus in society about the regulation of behaviors. As pointed out earlier, forces such as the government, politicians, and the media spread crime myths to society. Too often, the public is willing to believe an unsubstantiated myth if it fits the public perception of reality but requires absolute proof to believe information that does not meet with their desires or perceptions. In this way, the general public often puts up little resistance to the influence of damaging myths. Myths provide convenient guides for the "us versus them" dichotomy. The unconscious desire for easy labeling of bad or evil people reinforces the fantasy of a clear-cut enemy. Nimmo and Combs (1980, p. 12) state, "... individuals have dreams, whereas whole societies have myths."

Buying into and perpetuating crime myths are easier behaviors than confronting the more complicated issues of achieving society-wide justice. Bohm (2002, pp. 292–293) notes the different ways the general public contributes to crime myths as:

1. Overgeneralizing personal experiences
2. Relying on inaccurate communication

3. Relying on atypical information
4. A lack of consciousness

Bohm (2002) notes that members of society often generalize their own experiences with crime or the criminal justice system as typical of everyday functioning of crime processing. Any perceived injustice buttresses the believed dysfunctions of the criminal justice system that may already be in place as a result of the other mythmakers. In terms of inaccurate communication, Bohm states, "Some people embellish crime experiences and thus distort their own conceptions or the conception of those to whom they communicate" (2002, p. 293). Because crimes are often emotional experiences, emotion bleeds into the discussion of experiences about crime. This means that the communication of the experiences may include bitter or resentful feelings.

People who have not had many direct dealings with crime and its consequences are often left to rely on the communications of those acquaintances who have. They will then generalize the communicators' experiences as examples of criminal justice at work without realizing how atypical that experience may have been. Additionally, the public often passively accepts media depictions of crime and criminals that are untrue or highly publicized court cases that are uncharacteristic of actual crime. Having had limited experience with criminal justice situations, the distorted picture of criminal justice issues seems like reality to much of the public.

Finally, Bohm (2002) refers to a lack of consciousness as the general public's failure to recognize, understand, or even know about many types of crime. When we are not aware of our victimization to corporate or environmental crime, we cannot conceptualize crime in those terms. We focus on street-level crimes such as robbery and drug dealing instead of the dangers resulting from pollution, for example. In this way, we perpetuate the myth of criminals being unpleasant people instead of corporate leaders.

In extending Bohm's (2002) point, it is worth noting that this lack of consciousness can also be broadened to a lack of involvement in the criminal justice system and community outreach programs. Because we are often busy with our own lives, we seldom focus much attention on events in the criminal justice system until we are forced to be involved or drawn into its functioning by high-profile crimes. This makes us more susceptible to mythmaker influences. The same is true when we fail to be involved in community outreach programs for at-risk youths, drug addicts, or convicts who are reintegrating into society. This lack of effort means that these groups will feel less accepted in society. Not getting to know at-risk youths through a community mentoring program keeps them depersonalized. Myths about classes and types of people are therefore allowed to flourish. Furthermore, we often fail to reach out to individuals different from us who may be troubled or seek acceptance. When those individuals lash out in violent ways, such as the shootings on the Virginia Tech campus in April 2007 or the Columbine shootings, society is bewildered. Yet these people are often lumped into the category of violent predatory criminals when early warning signs were apparent and more personal relationships and interventions may have prevented their violent acts. By refusing to assist stereotypical or potential criminals, society implicitly refuses to do away with myths about criminals.

MYTHS ABOUT CRIME

We are socialized to believe that laws mark the boundaries of right and wrong behavior. This message implies that there is an objective difference between good and evil and that those committing crime are on the immoral side. Crime myths feed this message and therefore perpetuate it. A deeper understanding helps us see that legal and illegal labels are often not related to ethical behavior. Drug suppliers and providers in the United States serve as an example.

Since the "war on drugs" was initiated, Americans have been socialized to believe that marijuana is dangerous and should therefore be prohibited by the government. Yet, the first laws prohibiting the cultivation, selling, and possession of marijuana were not created until the twentieth century, and then primarily as a means of controlling immigrants who were coming into the United States (Yaroschuk, 2000). Time now has eroded the impact of dangerous marijuana myth evidenced by the marijuana legalization movement: as of 2013, 17 states had lowered the criminal penalties to fines for possessions of small amounts of marijuana, two had legalized it for recreational use (Knowles, 2013), and 20 states as well as the District of Columbia were allowing marijuana to be used for medicinal purposes (Wisniewski, 2013). Nevertheless, the government created and continues to enforce, to a limited degree, laws prohibiting marijuana. The idea of marijuana's dangerousness seems to be a myth in transition, with the notion of its dangerousness remaining steadfast in some segments of society.

Meanwhile, prescription drugs are socially accepted and legal, though controlled, due to their legitimate medical purposes. A close examination of pharmaceutical company influence on Food and Drug Administration (FDA) approval of prescription drugs indicates unethical influences on government agencies. For example, pharmaceutical companies present research on drugs for which they are seeking approval, but the research is selected so that only benefits are demonstrated and dangerous side effects are often concealed (Cohen, 2001). These unethical practices provide the pharmaceutical companies with huge profits but also contribute to more than 100,000 deaths annually in the United States as a result of preventable side effects and overdoses. The legal response to these drug problems is to first apply warning labels to the prescription drugs and only pull the drugs from the market if problems persist. The marketing practices of pharmaceutical companies have also come under criticism for contributing to growing drug problems. For example, Tunnell (2005) notes legal cases brought against the manufacturer of a powerful pre-scription pain killer by officials in three states. These officials contend that the pharmaceutical company placed profit ahead of health concerns and that these practices are evident in the drug's marketing, its promotion, and its distribution practices. Yet, despite these and other questionable practices by pharmaceutical companies, none of these prescription deaths show up in murder statistics.

Also excluded from murder statistics are accident deaths attributable to mining companies ignoring safety considerations, as well as cancer deaths stemming from environmental pollution. Our socialization says that these kinds of issues are complex accidents that should not be called crime, yet the perpetrators' behaviors are virtually identical to the criminal equivalent. Illegal drug dealers who sell drugs to an individual who overdoses and dies are charged with some form of homicide, depending on the legal circumstances. If an individual poisons another person slowly until the victim dies of a disease, the criminal law treats it as a homicide. On the other hand, though, when corporations carry out the same behavior, it is labeled as an unfortunate accident. Falsified safety reports that eventually lead to worker deaths are reported as accidents instead of crimes despite the premeditated actions that led to the deaths. Behaviors carried out by entities with the social and political power to label their actions as "legal" trump similar behaviors by those criminals without power.

The socialized belief that the law is an unbiased regulator of right and wrong largely comes from the consensus view of society. This explanation of the law states that actions are criminalized because much of society deems the actions as so bad that the social code is canonized. While there is substantial evidence to support this view with regard to crimes such as murder and rape, our social-ization process limits the use of those labels. Lawmakers, mythmakers, and law enforcement personnel all demonstrate a bias against street crime while more often overlooking corporate misconduct.

As is evident from the discussion of the news' depiction of crime, street crime grabs headlines in part because of the public's fear of crime. This public leads to the public consensus to implement policies that focus on limiting this street crime. In turn, there is a difference in law enforcement between street crime and corporate crime. For example, the Federal Bureau of Investigation employs nearly 14,000 special agents and more than 22,000 support personnel (Federal Bureau of Investigation (FBI), n.d.(a)), but the Mine Safety Health Adminis-tration employs less than 1100 enforcement personnel (Mine Health Safety Administration, 2013). This is not to suggest that enforcement of street crime should be discontinued but that crime myths resulting from the actions we call criminal lead to a lack of uniform law enforcement for actions that are just as dangerous as street crime.

Beyond applying the term "criminal" to behaviors, there are myths about crime itself that concern the public the most. The myth that is perhaps the most persistent is that crime in the United States is rising, particularly violent crime. While crime rates in the United States are higher than other industrialized nations (Kappeler & Potter, 2005; Messner & Rosenfeld, 2013; Reiman, 2007), official crime data indicate that crime rates have had fluctuations but overall reported violent crime as well as property crime incidents and rates were lower in 2010 than 1991 (FBI, n.d.(b)). Victimization data also demonstrated a lower likelihood of crime victimization in 2011 than in the early 1990s (Truman & Planty, 2012, p. 20). Official crime rates indicate that violent crime occurs much less frequently than property crime (FBI, n.d.(b)).

One of the tragedies of the differential labeling and enforcement of crime is that the law, which is supposed to arbitrate justice, on occasion actually serves to further injustice. People who have contributed to the deaths of others do not bear the scarlet letter proclaiming them criminals, while people who have committed more harmless offenses are often lumped into the social category of criminals.

MYTHS ABOUT CRIMINALS

Who are our criminals? An understanding of law creation and enforcement indicates that society has some firmly held ideas about who the law should control. The people who frighten most of society feel the brunt of law creation movements and law enforcement crackdowns. These myths may be the most comfortable set of crime myths for the public to accept because it serves directly to create the "us versus them" societal dichotomy. Yet, as we have seen, this fear is often the result of myths. The people who are most often given the title "criminal" meet a small number of criteria. Typical criminals are presented through the media as predatory males. They are either teenagers or hardened convicts, and sometimes they are both.

After increases in juvenile crime during the late 1980s and early 1990s, predictions of "juvenile superpredators" started making their way into media and political discussions (Annin, 1996; Bennett, DiIulio, & Walters, 1996; Zoglin, 1996). The prognostications were based on media portrayals of youths who were more likely to join gangs and use firearms in violent crimes more often than previous generations of adolescents. It was suggested that the members of this new wave of criminals were unable to inhibit violent impulses. Furthermore, they were said to have little fear of arrest or incarceration (Bennett et al., 1996).

This myth was quickly disseminated to the public. Politicians began writing legislative mandates to increase the punitiveness of juvenile court processing.

Protections from the long-lasting consequences of adult conviction and incarceration that the juvenile court system had originally provided were targeted. Juvenile protections were dismantled through sentencing changes and the removal of confidentiality protections for juvenile offenses. Juvenile transfers to adult court became more common with the intent of incarcerating juveniles for longer terms (Kappeler & Potter, 2005). Kappeler and Potter (2005, p. 219) note, "[John Ashcroft] sponsored crime bills that made the receipt of federal financial support dependent on a state's willingness to try juveniles aged 14 and older as adults and removed restrictions that required juveniles to be separated from adults in jails." These measures led to an increased rate of juvenile incarceration.

While all these efforts were being implemented to more effectively control the juvenile superpredator crime wave, an interesting thing never happened—the crime wave. A report by the Office of Juvenile Justice and Delinquency Prevention (1999) shows that juvenile violent crime rose slightly in the early 1990s, but came back to typical levels and even dropped by the late 1990s. The report also concludes that the rise in serious juvenile crime in the early 1990s was comparable to a similar trend that had occurred with previous generations of juveniles. Zimring (1998) examined the rates of juvenile crime in the 1980 and 1990s and concluded that the apparent rise in juvenile violence was more a result of police reporting practices than an actual increase in crime. He further explains that predicting future crime among youth populations is unscientific. Nevertheless, the initial dissemination of the juvenile superpredator myths led to radical policy changes that have drastically altered the life course of many juvenile offenders. They paid the price for the myth.

Bohm (2002) examines another crime myth about society's criminals. He points out that the belief of stranger violent victimization has been a persistent concern. Crime statistics do not lend validity to this belief. Violent crime committed by strangers is not as common as violence between family members and acquaintances (Harrell, 2012, p. 19). Nevertheless, the fear of being attacked by a stranger, and the media portrayals that reinforce this fear, serve to further distort society's image of criminals. These ideas lead to policies regulating how the assumed criminals should be handled by the criminal justice system. Such beliefs have historically led to greater efforts at controlling crime through tougher sentences on crime and more enforcement efforts. These attempts to control crime also bring their own flaws.

■ Learn More on the Internet

For information about school shooting myths, go to: www.msnbc.com/id/15111438. ■

MYTHS ABOUT CRIME CONTROL

Society often accepts and even embraces a number of myths about controlling crime. Garland (2002) states:

> ...mandatory sentences, victims' rights, community notification laws, private policing, "law and order" politics and an emphatic belief that "prison works," have become commonplace points in the crime control landscape and cause no one any surprise, even if they still cause dismay and discomfort in certain circles (p. 1).

Above the jungle of myths discussed to this point is the canopy that covers them all: the myth that crime can be controlled or even brought to a halt. This is the manifest goal of many criminal justice policies. Much of this mind-set results from the influences of the previously discussed mythmakers. When crime myths are presented for public consumption, they are often accompanied by the implicit message that new policies or strategies *can* control the crime. This is to be expected because our criminal justice system is largely based on early criminological explanations that revolved around deterrence. For example, Cesare Beccaria's classic work *On Crimes and Punishment* (as cited in Cullen & Agnew, 2011) pointed out shortcomings in criminal justice practices in Europe prior to the Era of Enlightenment. In recommending changes, Beccaria focused largely on deterring crime by setting punishments to be slightly more harsh than the benefit derived from committing the crime. His ideas were revolutionary at the time. They influenced the French and American Revolutions and criminal justice policies that are still used. Once they were instituted, they became commonplace in societal expectations of controlling crime.

Crime control policies continue to revolve around the idea of *deterrence*. The rational choice explanation fathered by Beccaria assumes that potential criminals will be deterred from committing crime if the likelihood of being caught is too high, or if the punishment for the offense is severe enough to outweigh the gain from committing the crime. These ideas have been accepted to a large extent by society and are often used to explain crime. If people are still committing crimes, it is assumed that they need to spend more time in prison to decide to reform their ways. Society responds to concerns about crime with new laws, greater law enforcement, or more punitive penalties. A casual understanding of crime rates and the public's fear of crime makes it clear that controlling crime through such measures is a myth.

Because crime persists despite new and revised policies, the public often assumes that crime is out of control because the criminal justice system is too lenient to create an adequate level of deterrence. Kappeler and Potter (2005) state:

> The choice of words in describing legislation as "get tough" is a direct response to the belief – and myth—that courts are too lenient with

offenders. Politicians, most police officers, and many vocal citizens allege that criminals escape the severe punishments they deserve. If judges would impose tougher sentences, then we could deter some violent crimes and incapacitate those who choose to ignore the laws (p. 313).

Research shows that the United States is already implementing some of the most severe sanctions for crime in the world (Kappeler & Potter, 2005). In terms of incarceration rates, the United States locks up far more offenders than Western nations such as Sweden, France, Germany, the Netherlands, Denmark, Wales, and England (Messner & Rosenfeld, 2013; Kappeler & Potter, 2005). Even nations that are more socially and economically similar to the United States have lower incarceration rates: the United States puts more than six times as many citizens in prison than Canada and Australia (Kappeler & Potter, 2005). Confinement in American jails occurs at a higher rate than in other industrialized countries, as does being sentenced to supervised probation. In addition, imposition of life and death sentences is higher in the United States than in comparable nations. The fact that the punitive sentences have been on a trajectory of becoming more severe and more frequent only harshens the American criminal justice system's punitiveness.

All of these strict sanctions are explained by van Zyl Smit (2002) as resulting partly from the death penalty. In examining sentences for a variety of criminal justice systems, van Zyl Smit concluded that maximum punishments set the bar of acceptable punishments for lower sentences. Nations employing capital punishment as a sentence demonstrate higher punishments for lesser offenses than nations with lower maximum sentences. It seems evident that myths about controlling crime have an impact on the policy-making process.

CRIME CONTROL POLICY: WHERE RESEARCH AND POLITICS COLLIDE

With myths about criminals and crime in place, and a society susceptible to their placement, the public is looking for solutions. As noted earlier, politicians are included among crime mythmakers and disseminators. They do this partly to create concern about previous policies, but also to build support for their proposed solutions to crime. Because our society uses law as the tool to achieve justice, a new policy or policy revision typically involves some form of deterrent or crime control theme. This is in accordance with the tendency for crime myths to point to a need to control a particular group of people.

Policies often implement *get tough measures* such as putting more police on the streets or lengthier sentences. Yet, as Reiman (2007) notes, the implementation of these types of measures has resulted in more public concern about crime over the course of several years. The myths have accomplished their latent purpose to a large degree: they have unified much of society against criminals and labeled the deviants as the threat to the accepted norms of behavior.

Research on the policies created in response to the myths demonstrates that efforts to control crime often cause more problems than the laws foresee. One only need look at the war on drugs to see such failure. American society has used laws to grapple with drug issues for decades, so defining the start of the "war on drugs" is a debatable topic. It is now clear that crime control policies aimed at curbing illicit drug distribution and use in the United States have slowly been increasing, with particularly focused crime control efforts increasing in the 1960s and again in the 1980s. As more crime control policies have been implemented to address the drug problem, conventional reason dictates that the problems must be declining, yet research suggests otherwise.

Federal monies spent on the drug war increased more than 25-fold from 1969 to 1982, and then grew to more than 11 times the 1982 budget by 2002 to 19 billion dollars (Kappeler & Potter, 2005, p. 176). The fact that it would remain a policy priority for so long indicates the failure of these crime control efforts. Much of the focus of these expenditures addressed reducing drug supplies at their sources (domestically and abroad) and crime control enforcement efforts on the streets. During the times when these policies have been enforced, drug manufacturing and distribution have increased. When illicit drug production is decreased in one area of the world, another area simply increases production to meet the demand (Kappeler & Potter, 2005; Nadelmann, 2003). Illicit drug prices have fallen during the time when policies aimed at reducing their availability have been enforced (Reiman, 2007). This indicates that supply is up in spite of the reduction efforts. Street-level law enforcement attacking drug use has also shown negligible effect on drug availability while dramatically increasing the numbers of offenders incarcerated for nonviolent drug offenses.

Blumstein's (as cited in Reiman, 2007) research points to the likelihood that crime control policies focusing on illicit drugs may actually contribute to more violent crime. He found that older drug dealers incarcerated during the 1980s and 1990s were simply replaced by juveniles. Blumstein concluded that these less mature drug dealers were more likely to use violence to settle disputes in the crack cocaine market.

Three-strikes laws demonstrate another example of how crime control policies may actually increase crime problems. Johnson and Saint-Germain (2005) examined the impact of California's three-strikes law on law enforcement officers. While their findings did not show greater dangers to police statewide, they did find a greater risk of arrestees resisting arrest and assaulting officers in Los Angeles. Knowing the incarceration that awaited them apparently contributed to their decision to exert more effort in attempting to avoid apprehension. They also found a significant increase in a five-year period after the law's implementation of police officer victimizations resulting in an offender's second and third strike. In examining the impact of three-strikes laws across 24 states, Marvell and Moody (2001) concluded that the legislation increased homicide rates because criminals were more likely to kill victims and witnesses to their crimes to reduce the likelihood of being convicted for their third offense. In examining the effect of three-strikes laws across the 188 largest cities across the United States, Kovandzic, Sloan, and Vieraitis (2004) concluded that three-strikes laws were not effective in impacting crime rates or recidivism. They also noted a number of social and financial costs of implementing get tough policies on crime.

If crime control policies such as three-strikes laws were effective in deterring crime, previously convicted offenders would be deterred from any further violations. Yet Reiman (2007) notes, "We know that more than 70 percent of the inmates in the nation's prisons or jails are not there for the first time" (p. 32). In fact, increasing the number of citizens incarcerated may actually create a culture of prestige associated with having done time. The stigma of being an inmate is being replaced by street credibility and greater respect from peers who have not been imprisoned.

What is evident from these societal crime control experiments is that there have been huge financial and social costs. The financial price has been documented above. The social costs refer to a number of costs, including the vacuum created in communities with higher rates of incarceration. Many of the get-tough policies have taken greater tolls on minority neighborhoods than other areas. Therefore these neighborhoods lose a large portion of their male population as a result of these policies. Reiman (2007) states:

> [B]ecause so much of the recent increase in imprisonment has been of inner-city black men who were involved in families and who had at least part-time employment at the time of their arrest and incarceration, social scientists are beginning to study the ways in which imprisonment is undermining the family and other community institutions depriving children of male role models, and depriving women of potential husbands and support. Several criminologists have found limited evidence suggesting that massive imprisonment may weaken inner-city institutions of informal social control and thus lead to more crime in the long run. (pp. 33–34)

Increased crime control policies resulting from myths also contribute to social problems such as corruption among criminal justice officials and a greater number of wrongful convictions. Sagarin, Huff, and Rattner (2003) estimate that there may be more than 10,000 wrongful convictions in the United States annually. Many of these miscarriages of justice result from pressures on criminal justice personnel to win convictions. While arrest and conviction rates may be used to placate the public's fear of crime, innocent people lose freedoms and suffer the consequences of inappropriate policies in action.

CONCLUSION

Media outlets, politicians, and the government all contribute to the public's perception of crime. These perceptions include the societal label of what behaviors are called "crime" and who bears the title "criminal." Myths about crime end up harming all of society. Research indicates that viewers of news programs are more likely to blame crime on minorities than whites (Dixon, 2006), to overestimate juvenile violent crime (Goibel, Freeman, & Procopio, 2006), and to support harsher punishments for those convicted of crimes (Trautman, 2004). Obviously, the public feels more fear of crime when fed a stream of images showing the threat coming from particular segments of society. Yet, the wrongly convicted and harmless offenders who have to serve severe sentences pay the highest price.

The intent of myths is partly to bond a social group against outsiders. Once the mythmakers have the capability to write laws that reflect their biases, outsiders are more vulnerable. The resulting irony is that a system that is based on the beliefs of protecting people can often do the opposite. It is easy to see why wrongly convicted people like Walter Snyder might view the term "justice" as the biggest myth of all.

Discussion Questions

1. Describe the persistence of the "Friend of a Friend" concept discussed in the chapter.
2. The authors contend that local television news contributes more to crime myth creation than the national news. Explain this phenomenon.
3. How are crime myths a type of "social glue" for society?
4. What has the "war on drugs" done to perpetuate crime myths? How has the "war on terrorism" changed how society labels criminals?
5. Juvenile crime is an often exploited topic in the media. What do the authors offer as an explanation for this?
6. How are crime control policies negatively affected by crime myths?

Exercise V-1 "How Television Affects Our Perceptions of Crime"

Watch your local television news, paying particular attention to the crime stories. Take note of when and how often during the telecast the crime stories are reported in comparison to noncrime stories. Keep notes on the following:

- Write down the race of the defendants whose pictures are broadcast. Do you see any trends regarding the characteristics of defendants whose images are broadcast?
- Note the words used to describe crime and/or criminals in the broadcast. Is the language exaggerated, deceptive, biased, or misleading, based upon what you learned in this chapter?
- In your notes, keep up with the stories that are reported from remote locations. How much time has passed since the crime has been committed? Why is the journalist reporting the story from outside the studio? Does the reporter have something substantive to say, or do you think he or she is at the remote location primarily for dramatic effect?

Discuss with your classmates how you feel your findings might influence public perceptions of crime and whether such reporting perpetuates crime myths. You might consider repeating this exercise for several evenings while your classmates do the same, reviewing different channels and networks, and then comparing your results.

REFERENCES

ADT Research (1994) Country and city. *Tyndall Report, 65,* 5.

Annin, P. (January 22, 1996). Superpredators' arrive. *Newsweek, 127,* 57.

Associated Press (July 2, 2013). *13 years in jail for a little sidewalk chalk?* USA Today. Retrieved on July 17, 2013, from www.usatoday.com/story/news/nation/2013/07/02/san-diego-sidewalk-chalk/2482201/.

Baer, J., & Chambliss, W. J. (1997). Generating fear: The politics of crime reporting. *Crime, Law and Social Change, 27,* 87–107.

Bennet, W. L. (1996). *News: The politics of illusion* (3rd ed.). White Plains: Longman.

Bennett, W., DiIulio, J., & Walters, J. (1996). *Body count: Moral poverty and how to win America's war against crime and drugs.* New York: Simon & Schuster.

Bjornstrom, E. E. S., Kaufman, R. L., Peterson, R. D., & Slater, M. D. (2010). Race and ethnic representations of lawbreakers and victims in crime news: A national study of television coverage. *Social Problems, 57,* 269–293.

Bohm, R. M. (2002). Crime, criminals, and crime control policy myths. In M. C. Braswell, B. R. McCarthy, & B. J. McCarthy (Eds.), *Justice, crime & ethics* (4th ed.). Cincinnati: Anderson.

Bradley Manning Chronology. (2013). *New York Times,* Retrieved on July 17, 2013 from topics.nytimes.com/top/reference/timestopics/people/m/bradley_e_manning/index.html.

Britto, S., & Dabney, D. A. (2010). "Fair and balanced?" Justice issues on political talk shows. *American Journal of Criminal Justice, 35,* 198–218.

Bump, P. (July 10, 2013). *Poll reveals dramatic shift in American worries about privacy intrusions*. The Atlantic Wire. Retrieved on August 1, 2013 from www.theatlanticwire.com/politics/2013/07/poll-reveals-dramatic-shift-american-worries-about-privacy-intrusions/67016/.

Center of Media and Public Affairs. (July-August, 2000). The media at the millennium: The network's top topics, trends, and joke targets of the 1990s. *Media Monitor, 14*, 1–6.

Chadee, D., & Ditton, J. (2005). Fear of crime and the media: Assessing the lack of relationship. *Crime, Media, Culture, 3*, 322–332.

Chiricos, T., Eschholz, S., & Gertz, M. (1997). Crime, news, and fear of crime. *Social Problems, 44*, 342–357.

Cobbina, J. E. (2008). Race and class differences in print media portrayals of crack cocaine and methamphetamine. *Journal of Criminal Justice and Popular Culture, 15*, 145–167.

Cohen, J. S. (2001). *Overdose: The case against the drug companies*. New York: Jeremy P. Tarcher/Putnam.

Cullen, F. T., & Agnew, R. (2011). *Criminological theory: Past to present* (4th ed.). New York: Oxford University Press.

Dixon, T. (2006). Schemas as average conceptions: Skin tone, television news exposure, and culpability judgments. *Journal of Mass Communication Quarterly, 83*, 131–154.

Dowler, K. (2004a). Comparing American and Canadian local television crime stories: A content analysis. *Canadian Journal of Criminology and Criminal Justice, 46*, 573–596.

Dowler, K. (2004b). Dual realities? Criminality, victimization, and the presentation of race on local television news. *Journal of Crime & Justice, 27*, 79–99.

Eschholz, S., Mallard, M., & Flynn, S. (2004). Images of prime-time justice: A content analysis of NYPD blue and law and order. *Journal of Criminal Justice and Popular Culture, 10*, 161–180.

Eschholz, S. L. (1998). "Television and fear of crime: The effect of context on audience perceptions." Unpublished doctoral dissertation, The Florida State University.

Federal Bureau of Investigation. (n.d. (a)). *About us—Quick facts*. Retrieved on August 1, 2013, from www.fbi.gov/about-us/quickfacts.

Federal Bureau of Investigation. (n.d. (b)). *Table 1: Crime in the United States by volume and rate per 100,000 inhabitants, 1991–2010*. Retrieved on August 1, 2013 from www.fbi.gov/about-us/cjis/ucr/2010/crime-in-the-u.s.-2010/tables/10tbl01.xls.

Finn, P., & Horowitz, S. (June 21, 2013). *U.S. charges Snowden with espionage*. The Washington Post. Retrieved on July 21from articles.washingtonpost.com/2013-06-21/world/40116763_1_hong-kong-nsa-justice-department.

Fox, R., Van Sickel, R., & Steiger, T. (2007). *Tabloid justice: Criminal justice in the age of media frenzy* (2nd ed.). Boulder: Lynne Reinner.

Garland, D. (2002). *The culture of control: Crime and social order in contemporary society*. Chicago: University of Chicago Press.

Gellman, B. (August 15, 2013). *NSO broke privacy rules thousands of times per year, audit finds*. The Washington Post. Retrieved on August 16, 2013 from www.washingtonpost.com/world/national-security/nsa-broke-privacy-rules-thousands-of-times-per-year-audit-finds/2013/08/15/3310e554-05ca-11e3-a07f-49ddc7417125_story.html?hpid=z1.

Goibel, R., Freeman, C., & Procopia, S. (2006). The impact of television viewing on perceptions of juvenile crime. *Journal of Broadcast Electronic Media, 50*, 119–139.

Greenwald, G. (June 5, 2013). *NSA collecting phone records of millions of Verizon customers daily*. The Guardian. Retrieved on July 19, 2013 from www.theguardian.com/world/2013/jun/06/nsa-phone-records-verizon-court-order.

Greenwald, G., & Ackerman, S. (June 27, 2013). *NSA collected US mail records in bulk for more than two years under Obama*. The Guardian. Retrieved on July 27, 2013 from www.theguardian.com/world/2013/jun/27/nsa-data-mining-authorised-obama.

Harrell, E. (2012). *Violent victimization committed by strangers, 1993–2010*. NCJ 239424: Bureau of Justice Statistics.

Hawley, F. (1989). Cockfight in the cotton: A moral crusade in microcosm. *Contemporary Crises, 13*, 129–144.

Herman, E. S., & Chomsky, N. (1988). *Manufacturing consent: The political economy of the mass media*. New York: Pantheon Books.

Johnson, J. L., & Saint-Germain, M. A. (2005). Officer down: Implications of three-strikes for public safety. *Criminal Justice Policy Review, 16*, 443–460.

Lowry, D. T., Nio, T. C. J., & Leitner, D. W. (2003). Setting the public fear agenda: A longitudinal analysis of network television crime reporting, public perceptions of crime, and FBI crime statistics. *Journal of Communication, 53*, 61–73.

Kappeler, V. E., & Potter, G. W. (2005). *The mythology of crime and criminal justice* (4th ed.). Long View: Waveland Press.

Klein, R. D., & Naccarato, S. (2003). Broadcast news portrayal of minorities: Accuracy in reporting. *American Behavioral Scientist, 46*, 1611–1616.

Knowles, D. (June 6, 2013). *Vermont becomes 17th state to decriminalize marijuana, making possession of less than an ounce of pot punishable by fine*. New York Daily News. Retrieved on August 2, 2013 from www.nydailynews.com/news/national/vermont-decriminalizies-possession-small-amounts-pot-article-1.1365354.

Kovandic, T. V., Sloan, J. J., & Vieritis, L. M. (2004). 'Striking Out' as crime reduction policy: The impact of 'Three Strikes' laws on crime rates in U.S. cities. *Justice Quarterly, 21*, 207–239.

Marvell, T. B., & Moody, C. E. (2001). The lethal effects of three-strikes laws. *Journal of Legal Studies, 30*, 89–106.

Messner, S. F., & Rosenfeld, R. (2013). *Crime and the American dream* (5th ed.). Belmont: Wadsworth.

Mine Safety and Health Administration. (2013). *(FTE levels)* Unpublished raw data.

Nadelmann, E. (2003). Addicted to failure. *Foreign Policy, 137*(July/August), 94–95.

Nicolini, M. B. (1989). Is there a FOAF in your future? urban folk legends in room 112. *The English Journal, 78*, 81–84.

Nimmo, D., & Combs, J. E. (1980). *Subliminal politics: Myths and mythmakers in America*. Englewood Cliffs: Prentice Hall.

O'Keefe, G., & Reid-Nash, K. (1987). Crime news and the real-world blues: The effects of the media on social reality. *Communication Research, 42*, 109–142.

Pilkington, E. (July 30, 2013). *Bradley Manning verdict: Cleared of 'aiding the enemy' but guilty of other charges*. The Guardian. Retrieved on August 2, 2013 from www.theguardian.com/world/2013/jul/30/bradley-manning-wikileaks-judge-verdict.

Pollak, J. M., & Kubrin, C. E. (2007). Crime in the news: How crimes, offenders and victims are portrayed in the media. *Journal of Criminal Justice and Popular Culture, 14*, 59–83.

Potter, G. W., & Kappeler, V. E. (2005). Research ethics and Research Funding: A case study of easy virtue. In M. C. Braswell, B. R. McCarthy, & B. J. McCarthy (Eds.), *Justice, crime, & ethics* (5th ed.) (pp. 395–414). Newark: LexisNexis Matthew Bender.

Rader, N. E., & Rhineberer-Dunn, G. M. (2010). A typology of victim characterization in television crime dramas. *Journal of Criminal Justice and Popular Culture, 17*, 231–263.

Reiman, J. (2007). *The rich get richer and the poor get prison: Ideology, class, and criminal justice* (8th ed.). Boston: Allyn & Bacon.

Romer, D., Jamieson, K. H., & Aday, S. (2003). Television news and the cultivation of fear of crime. *Journal of Communication, 53*, 88–104.

Ryan, W. (1976). *Blaming the victim*. New York: Vintage Books.

Sagarin, E., Huff, C. R., & Rattner, A. (2003). *Convicted but innocent: Wrongful conviction and public policy*. Thousand Oaks: Sage.

Scheck, B., Neufield, P., & Dwyer, J. (2003). *Actual innocence*. New York: New American Library.

Selke, W., & Pepinsky, H. (1984). The politics of police reporting in Indianapolis, 1948–1978. In W. Chambliss (Ed.), *Criminal law in action*. New York: John Wiley.

Shane, S., & Weisman, J. (June 11, 2013). *Earlier denials put intelligence chief in awkward Position*. New York Times. Retrieved on July 19, 2013 from www.nytimes.com/2013/06/12/us/nsa-dis-closures-put-awkward-light-on-official-statements.html?pagewanted=all&_r=0.

Sherman, L. (December 3, 1998). Needed: Better ways to count crooks. *The Wall Street Journal*, A22.

Surette, R., & Otto, C. (2002). A test of a crime and justice infotainment measure. *Journal of Criminal Justice, 30*, 443–453.

Trautman, T. (2004). Concerns about crime and local television news. *Communication Research Reports, 21*, 310–315.

Truman, J. L., & Planty, M. (2012). *Criminal victimization, 2011. Bureau of justice statistics*, NCJ #239437.

Tunnell, K. D. (2005). The oxycontin epidemic and crime panic in Kentucky. *Contemporary Drug Problems, 32*, 225–259.

van Zyl Smit, D. (2002). *Taking life imprisonment seriously in National and International Law*. Norwell, MA: Kluwer Law International.

Waid-Lindberg, C. A., Dobbs, R. R., & Shelley, T. O. (2011). Blame the media? The influence of primary news source, frequency of usage, and perceived media credibility on punitive attitudes. *Western Criminology Review, 12*, 41–59.

Weitzer, R., & Kubrin, C. E. (2004). Breaking news: How local TV news and real-world conditions affect fear of crime. *Justice Quarterly, 21*, 497–520.

Welch, M., Fenwick, M., & Roberts, M. (1998). State managers, intellectuals, and the media: A content analysis of ideology in experts' quotes in feature newspaper articles on crime. In G. W. Potter, & V. E. Kappeler (Eds.), *Constructing Crime: Perspectives on making news and social problems*. Prospect Heights: Waveland Press.

Wisniewski, M. (August 1, 2013). *Illinois governor signs law allowing medical marijuana*. Reuters News Service. Retrieved on August 2, 2013 from www.reuters.com/article/2013/08/01/us-usa-mari-juana-illinois-idUSBRE97018920130801.

Yanich, D. (2004). Crime creep: Urban and suburban crime on TV news. *Journal of Urban Affairs, 26*, 535–563.

Yanich, D. (2005). Kids, crime, and local television news. *Crime & Delinquency, 51*, 103–132.

Yaroschuk, T. (2000). *Hooked: Illegal drugs and how they got that way*. Motion picture, A&E Television Networks.

Zimring, F. E. (1998). *American youth violence*. New York: Oxford University Press.

Zoglin, R. (January 15, 1996). Now for the bad news: A teenage time bomb. *Time, 147*, 52–53.

CHAPTER 18

Juvenile Justice Ethical Issues: How Should We Treat Juveniles?

Kimberly D. Dodson, John T. Whitehead

KEY CONCEPTS

deontologist	juvenile transfer	*Miller v. Alabama*
Graham v. Florida	life without parole	*Roper v. Simmons*
habilitation	(LWOP)	superpredator myth

The underlying philosophy of the juvenile justice system is the belief that young offenders are developmentally different from adult criminals. Thus, a separate justice system is preferable for juveniles who commit delinquent or criminal acts because they lack the emotional and/or psychological ability to fully appreciate the consequences of their actions, not only for themselves but others as well. Because juvenile offenders are developmentally immature many consider them to be less culpable or deserving of blame than adult offenders (Campaign for Youth Justice, 2011; Grisso & Schwartz, 2000) and this seems to hold true historically (Blackstone, 1759). In addition, studies show that the public largely favors the differential treatment of juvenile and adult offenders (Cauffman & Steinberg, 2012; Clarke, 2005; Scott, Reppucci, Antonishak, & DeGennaro, 2006).

Studies also show there is a considerable amount of public support for rehabilitation rather than punishment for younger offenders in comparison to older offenders (Clarke, 2005). The public is inclined to believe that juveniles are more amenable to change, and, as a result, they are more likely to benefit from rehabilitation. In a recent *Frontline* interview, Bridgett Jones, former supervisor of the juvenile division of the Santa Clara Public Defender's Office, summed up the importance of rehabilitation for youthful offenders:

> ...the community understands, or should understand, that the younger a person is, the more likely it is that they can change. And the best way

I've heard it put is from a victim in a very serious case, in a shooting case where this person had been maimed for life. He indicated he... would rather meet up with this person ten years down the road as a graduate from a college versus a graduate from a penal institution. Because he had the wherewithal to understand that this person was eventually going to get back out and be in our community. They don't go away. They come back. And the younger they are, the more likely it is that they are going to come back into our community. So I guess as a community we have to decide [who] is it we're willing to get back in the long run.

Frontline (2013, para. 7)

Not everyone supports a separate system of justice for juveniles. Critics believe that it is a mistake to perpetuate a system in which juvenile offenders are viewed as less culpable than adult offenders. In fact, some argue that abolishing delinquency should be the first step in dismantling or significantly reducing the need for the juvenile system. For example, Jeffery Butts, a senior research associate of the Urban Institute, objects to the use of delinquency because, in his opinion, it implies that young offenders are not entirely responsible for their behavior, which presupposes they should be handled differently than adult criminals (Butts, 2000, para. 3). Like many others, he believes that juveniles who commit serious crimes should have their cases handled in criminal court or that criminal courts should have juvenile divisions. He reasons that if juveniles are violating criminal codes then, just like adults, they should be processed through criminal court.

Butts (2000) also offers evidence that this change is not so radical when one considers that juvenile courts are essentially masquerading as criminal courts. For instance, he claims juvenile courts no longer live up to or embrace their rehabilitative beginnings and have morphed into pseudo-criminal courts that are more interested in meting out retribution. Juvenile court judges, he argues, render their decisions based almost exclusively on the severity of the offense rather than the unique circumstances of each juvenile offender. Others concur with Butts and suggest that juvenile courts are merely "scaled-down, second-class criminal courts" and that retributive practices are commonplace (Feld, 1998, p. 68). In other words, the original intent of a separate system for juveniles is so unrecognizable that the promise of rehabilitation has been all but abandoned.

The question remains—is a separate justice system for juveniles more desirable than processing them through the adult criminal courts? To this question, we answer a resounding "yes!" In the sections that follow, we will discuss why the juvenile justice system should remain in place. To achieve this goal, we will explore the downside of applying adult criminal justice practices and policies to juvenile offenders. We also will explore whether rehabilitation or retribution is the appropriate goal for juvenile offenders. Finally, we also will present an ethical analysis supporting our claim that a separate system for juveniles is better than processing them through the adult criminal justice system.

JUVENILE TRANSFER TO ADULT COURT

"Transfer," "waiver," or "remand" refers to the decision to try juveniles in adult criminal courts. The implementation and use of **juvenile transfer** is largely the result of an increased fear of juvenile offenders starting in the 1990s. Analysts fanned the flames by insisting that we were witnessing a swing toward a generation of "superpredators" (DiIulio, 1995a) who should be regarded as a "new breed" of cold-blooded killers (DiIulio, 1995b, p. 23). They added additional fuel to the fire when they predicted that there would be a "new" wave of unprecedented juvenile violence between 1995 and 2010 (DiIulio, 1995a, 1996; Wilson, 1995). Practitioners heeded these dire predictions and began implementing punitive policies across the United States. Juvenile transfer is one of the most obvious outgrowths of DiIulio's (1995a) predictions.

Unfortunately, these punitive policies rested on three faulty assumptions: (1) the proportion of juveniles engaging in serious and violent offending was growing at an alarming rate; (2) juvenile offenders were getting younger and younger; and (3) juveniles were committing more crime (Howell, Feld, & Mears, 2012). Of course, none of these assumptions were correct and "superpredators" never materialized. However, the damage has been done. The **superpredator myth** has been cited as the greatest contributing factor to the adoption of policies in which juveniles were to be treated as adults (Snyder, 1998; Snyder & Sickmund, 2000).

Today, every state in the United States has some mechanism to try juvenile offenders as adults. Some suggest that the use of juvenile transfers not only erodes the rehabilitative intent of the juvenile justice system (Bakken, 2007), it has little or no impact on juvenile offending (Jensen & Metsger, 1994; Lee & McCrary, 2005; Singer & McDowall, 1988). Individuals often support juvenile transfer because they believe it is a specific and/or general deterrent. Specific deterrence focuses on preventing future offending by a specific individual through punishment. General deterrence focuses on preventing offending of the general public by making an example of a specific offender. Many people may be surprised to learn that juvenile transfer is neither a specific deterrent (Jensen & Metsger, 1994) nor a general deterrent (Singer & McDowall, 1988; Steiner & Wright, 2006). To make things worse, some studies actually show that transferred juveniles are more likely to recidivate than non-transferred juveniles. For example, Steiner and Wright (2006) examined the effects of juvenile transfer laws in 14 states between 1975 and 2000. They found that in 13 of the 14 states, juvenile crime remained constant or increased after the enactment of transfer laws (see also Risler, Sweatman, & Nackerud, 1998). Put differently, treating juvenile offenders as adults has not yielded the reduction in crime that we might expect.

■ Learn More on the Internet

For both statistical reports and research reports on issues in juvenile justice, go to the website of the Office of Juvenile Justice and Delinquency Prevention (OJJDP): www.ojjdp.gov.   ■

Confinement for Juveniles

Incarceration is the number one strategy we use to punish juvenile offenders in the United States. The majority of young offenders serve their time in juvenile jails or prisons. However, a smaller percentage of juveniles are housed in adult jails and prisons. We will discuss the issues and concerns posed in each of these settings.

JUVENILES DOING JUVENILE TIME

Correctional facilities vary widely in their delivery of inmate rehabilitation programs. Jails, because of their transient populations, tend to offer fewer programs than prisons. However, nationally more jails are offering programs than in the past and there seems to be a greater emphasis on implementing evidenced-based policies (Whitehead, Dodson, & Edwards, 2013). Evidence-based practices refer to implementing programs and policies that have been shown empirically to reduce crime. Some of the programs that "work" to reduce recidivism include educational programs, drug treatment programs, and cognitive behavioral therapy (Sherman, Farrington, Welsh, & MacKenzie, 2002). Sherman and his colleagues have regularly reported their findings to the U.S. Congress and there seems to be a renewed commitment to rehabilitation among criminal justice practitioners and policymakers.

Another more interesting trend in juvenile corrections is the move toward **habilitation** programs. Although habilitation is not a new idea (see Palmer, 1991), it has not been widely applied in the juvenile correctional setting (Dodson, n.d.). Habilitation starts with a very different premise than rehabilitation. Rehabilitation implies that offenders have lost the skills they once possessed and, therefore, they need to "relearn" the behavior or skill. Habilitation recognizes that offenders never had the skills or learned the behaviors they need to be successful in life. In the state of Iowa, for example, several juvenile correctional facilities have implemented two programs based on the idea of habilitation: *Inside Out* and *Criminal Addictive Thinking*. At least one study suggests that reoffending has been significantly reduced since the implementation of these two programs (Elias & Rice, n.d.).

We also know that there are programs that do not work to reduce recidivism. For example, we know that boot camps, shock incarceration, and counseling programs that fail to include offenders' individual risk factors for reoffending do not work (Sherman et al., 2002). It also is important to note that juvenile treatment programs based on confrontational methods like "Scared Straight" actually increased the odds that juveniles will reoffend (Klenowski, Bell, & Dodson, 2010). This is certainly not the outcome we want and these types of programs should be abandoned.

There is more positive news to report in juvenile justice—the public seems more willing to support alternatives to incarceration. A recent survey by the National Council on Crime and Delinquency (Hartney & Marchionna, 2009) shows the majority of adults believe that some crimes for which offenders are currently incarcerated do not require jail or prison time. The public also feels there are several reasons to support sending fewer offenders to jail and prison including costs, overcrowding and the dangers it poses for inmates and correctional personnel, and the fairness or proportionality of the punishment relative to the crime.

The preceding paragraphs point to some encouraging trends in juvenile corrections. However, juvenile correctional facilities are not without problems. It is important to note that the quality of juvenile correctional facilities in the United States varies greatly. Not all states embrace rehabilitation for juvenile offenders and many continue to use outdated "get tough" policies. There is some evidence that suggest that southern states tend to be tougher on juvenile offenders than other regions of the country (Pinkham, 2009; Stimson & Grossman, 2009). However, even within the southern states, we have seen a move toward rehabilitation for juvenile offenders (Campaign for Youth Justice, 2011).

One of the most serious problems facing juvenile prisons and jails is overcrowding. Overcrowded facilities create a host of problems including negative psychological effects (e.g. stress and depression), increased risk of inmate-on-inmate physical or sexual assault, an increased risk of inmate-on-staff assault, a rise in disciplinary infractions, and health-related issues (e.g. high blood pressure). These deficiencies also may open up correctional administrators to civil liability and there seems to be a consistent push by the courts to intervene on behalf of juvenile offenders (see, e.g. *Brown, Governor of California et al. v. Plata et al.*, 2010; *Farrell v. Cate*, 2004).

JUVENILES DOING ADULT TIME

People might be surprised to learn that most juveniles in the adult system have convictions for minor offenses. The perception that juvenile offenders are predominantly violent is the result of the perpetuation of three specific crime myths. First, media coverage of youth crime trends tends to focus on stories of gang violence and murder that ultimately distort the true nature of juvenile crimes. In fact, youth arrests for violent crime are rare and only account for 5% of all juveniles arrested annually (Uniform Crime Reports, 2011). Second, there is a public perception that juvenile crime is on the rise. In reality, juvenile crime is at its lowest and between 1999 and 2008 juvenile crime dropped 15.7% (Uniform Crime Reports, 2011). Third, many believe that juveniles commit the majority of crime committed in the United States. This is simply false. Juveniles commit 12% of violent crime and 18% of crime (Uniform Crime Reports, 2011). There are several serious problems with housing youth in adult correctional facilities and we will highlight some of them here.

RECIDIVISM AMONG JUVENILES CONFINED IN ADULT JAILS AND PRISONS

All states in the United States allow juveniles to be housed in adult jails and prisons. Robert Johnson has conducted extensive research on the subject and he believes this practice should end. He claims:

> The practice of transferring juveniles to the adult system fails young offenders and society at large. While in adult prisons, impressionable youth offenders are placed among hardened criminals who take them under their wings and groom them for a life of crime.
> **Centers for Disease Control and Prevention (2007, p. 1)**

Johnson's assertions seem to be on target when we consider that there is a substantial body of research that shows placing juveniles in adult correctional facilities increases the likelihood that juveniles will reoffend (Redding, 2010). According to both the U.S. Centers for Disease Control and Prevention (2007) and the Office of Juvenile Justice and Delinquency Prevention (see Redding, 2010), juveniles who serve time in adult correctional facilities are about 34% more likely to reoffend than juveniles who serve time in juvenile correctional facilities. Public opinion polls reveal that seven out of 10 respondents believe that housing juvenile offenders in adult correctional facilities makes them more likely to commit crime (Krisberg & Marchionna, 2007).

Although there is a push in some states to lock up juveniles in adult correctional facilities, at least one state is considering just the opposite. The Maine Department of Corrections has put forth a proposal (LR 373, An Act to Allow Young Adult Offenders to be Confined in Juvenile Correctional Facilities) that would change a state law banning young adults from being housed in juvenile facilities (Long, 2013). The law would allow young adults (18–25 years old) to be housed in juvenile facilities with juvenile offenders (11–21 years old). At first glance, some might oppose the legislation. However, according to Jody Breton, Associate Commissioner for the Maine Department of Corrections, the intent of the bill is to improve the rehabilitative services for young adult prisoners by placing them in facilities where more appropriate services are available. Breton also stated that he felt the programs available at the juvenile facilities would improve an inmate's chances of successful reentry (Long, 2013). The American Civil Liberties Union is backing the Department of Corrections and heralds this legislation as a step in the right direction for decreasing recidivism.

Several states have moved to reverse the trend of locking up juveniles in adult facilities. Table 18.1 presents the list of states that have placed limits on the number of youth placed in adult jails and prisons and their legislative changes. There seems to be a growing trend to eliminate or significantly reduce the number of juveniles in adult prisons. This move would suggest that state legislators and criminal justice policymakers are more amenable to rehabilitation than they have been in the last two decades during the height of "get tough" on crime policies.

SEXUAL VICTIMIZATION BEHIND BARS

Regrettably, researchers sometimes uncover abusive treatment of juvenile offenders by correctional personnel and other inmates. For example, a recently released report by the Bureau of Justice Statistics indicates that 9.5%

Table 18.1 States with Limits on Youth Incarceration in Adult Jails and Prisons

State	Legislative Changes
Arizona, Colorado, Connecticut, Delaware, Illinois, Indiana, Nevada, Utah, Virginia, and Washington	These 10 states changed transfer laws, which increase the odds that young offenders will remain in the juvenile justice system.
Connecticut, Illinois, and Mississippi	These three states expanded their juvenile court jurisdiction so that older youth who would have been automatically tried as adults are not prosecuted in adult criminal courts.
Colorado, Georgia, Texas, and Washington	These four states have changed their mandatory-minimum sentencing laws that consider the developmental differences between juveniles and adults.
Colorado, Texas, and Washington	Colorado and Texas states banned life-without-parole sentences. Washington eliminated the application of mandatory-minimum sentences for juveniles tried as adults.
Colorado, Maine, Virginia, and Pennsylvania	These four states passed laws limiting the use of incarceration of juveniles in adult jails and prisons.
Mississippi and Connecticut	Maine passed a law that requires youth under the age of 16 who receive adult sentences to be housed in juvenile facilities until they turn 18. Connecticut raised the age of juvenile jurisdiction to 18.

Campaign for Youth Justice, 2011.

of incarcerated youth at both publically and privately run correctional facilities report being sexually victimized in the past 12 months (Beck, Cantor, Hartge, & Smith, 2013). Approximately 8% report sexual victimization by staff and another 2.5% of sexual victimizations were committed by other inmates. In addition, 3.5% of incarcerated juveniles report that having sex or sexual contact with facility staff was the result of force or some other type of coercion, while 4.7% report that having sex or sexual contact with staff occurred without any force, threat, or explicit kind of coercion (Beck et al., 2013).

The results also indicate that about 8% of males and 3% of females report sexual activity with staff. Of the 1,390 juveniles who reported staff victimization, 89% were males who had sexual contact with female staff and 3% of males who reported sexual contact with both female and male staff. About one in five or 20.3% of youth victims reported suffering physical force or the threat of force, 12.3% were offered protection, and 21.5% were supplied alcohol or drugs in exchange for sexual contact (Beck et al., 2013). Black youth reported higher rates of sexual victimization by staff (9.6%) than white (6.4%) or Hispanic (6.4%) youth.

It is extremely difficult to keep children safe in adult jails. When youth are placed with adults in adult jails, they are at an increased risk of physical and sexual assault. Studies confirm that there are high rates of sexual violence against youth in adult correctional facilities. For instance, findings from two Bureau of Justice Statistics studies conducted in 2006 and 2007 indicate that 21% and 13%, respectively, of victims of substantiated inmate-on-inmate sexual violence in jails were youth under the age of 18 (Beck, Harrison, & Adams, 2007; Snyder & Sickmund, 2006). When we consider that only 1% of jail inmates are 18 years or younger, this seems like an alarmingly high percentage of victims. Beck et al. (2013) found that 4.7% of 16–17-year-olds housed in adult prisons and jails reported some form of sexual victimization. These numbers should concern us because we know that juveniles who report sexual abuse while incarcerated are more likely to suffer a host of other problems, not only during their incarceration, but throughout their lives.

SUICIDE

Youths have the highest suicide rates of all inmates in jail. We know that juveniles are 36 times more likely to commit suicide in an adult jail than in a juvenile detention center. Juveniles incarcerated in adult jails are 19 times more likely to commit suicide than non-incarcerated youth (Campaign for Youth Justice, 2011). Research also tells us that sexual victimization increases the likelihood of suicide (Turner, Finkelhor, Shattuck, & Hamby, 2012). Because the risk of victimization and suicide is lower in juvenile facilities this is yet another reason to keep juvenile offenders in the juvenile system.

SEPARATE IS BETTER: A UTILITARIAN APPROACH

According to utilitarian ethics, we judge the morality of an action by the consequences it produces. Actions that are moral produce good or positive consequences, while immoral actions produce bad or negative consequences. Utilitarians define a good action in terms of the happiness it yields. A morally right action will result in happiness (pleasure and the absence of pain). A morally wrong action will result in unhappiness (pain and suffering).

A utilitarian might argue that the actions of offenders, even if they are juveniles, produce a great deal of pain and suffering for their victims. There is little doubt that this is often true. Depending on the severity of the crime, victims report a wide range of negative effects. There may be emotional and psychological ramifications that leave victims feeling vulnerable, frightened, and powerless. Crime victims may suffer physical effects ranging from hospitalization for their injuries to stress-related disturbances such as trouble sleeping and loss of appetite. They may also suffer substantial monetary losses as a result of the need to pay for physical therapy and mental health services, repair or replace damaged property, or lost wages from an inability to work (Dodson, in press). In terms of calculating the morality of an action, crimes would obviously be viewed as immoral.

A utilitarian might also argue that the criminal justice system's response to juvenile offending produces a great deal of pain and suffering for the offender. Once a juvenile has been officially processed through the system, they are forever labeled a criminal. Even if a juvenile offender tries to turn his or her life around, many in the general public remain skeptical. The offender's motives will almost always be in question, and they rarely receive the benefit of the doubt. If they are sincerely remorseful for the harm they have done, that response is treated with suspicion, too. People often react with indignation and claim that offenders are not sorry, they are just sorry they got caught.

The question we must consider is whether we can strike an ethical balance between victims and offenders. Ultimately, utilitarians would ask what action produces the greatest good for the greatest number. Adjudicating juveniles as adults and the push to process juvenile offenders through adult criminal court would not produce the greatest good. We know one thing for sure—most juveniles will eventually return to our communities. The research on processing juveniles as adults indicates that recidivism rates are higher for these youths. This is not the outcome we would want or expect and it would seem counterproductive to continue to endorse a policy that is ineffective at best and detrimental to juveniles at worst. In addition, if the use of juvenile transfer increases the likelihood of offending, then it is not likely to be in the best interest of society, and it will only serve to undermine the safety and security of victims.

On utilitarian grounds, we can reject practices and policies that treat juvenile offenders as adults because they do not produce a morally just outcome for victims or offenders. It seems that juveniles and victims would be better served if juveniles were to be processed through the juvenile system. In doing so, we recognize that although there is a need for punishment, we are still leaving open the opportunity for rehabilitation.

When we consider other harms that are perpetrated against juveniles housed in adult correctional facilities, these do not stand up to utilitarian principles either. It is not in the best interest of a juvenile to be sexually victimized by staff or other inmates. Most of these juveniles will return to our communities embittered by their experiences in adult correctional facilities. They will have the additional burden of coping with their victimization as they try to make a successful reentry into the community. The likelihood that they will be successful is reduced and they will often end up reoffending. This situation does not create the greatest good for the greatest number. Housing juvenile offenders in adult prisons and jails and/or the elimination of the juvenile justice system would not produce a morally just outcome for the offenders or the community.

SEPARATE IS BETTER: APPLYING PEACEMAKING

There are three themes of peacemaking—connectedness, caring, and mindfulness (see Chapter 3). The idea of connectedness suggests that human beings are not isolated individuals, but each of us is integrally "connected" and bonded to other human beings and the environment. Connectedness suggests that one person's actions or behaviors affect many others. When someone commits a crime, they send a ripple effect through the community. The offender has injured a victim and the victim's family and friends experience harm as well. The offender's family and friends are affected as well. The police, courts, and corrections are impacted by an offender's action. Depending on the severity of the crime, one offender's actions can heighten the fear of victimization in the community.

How we choose to respond as criminal justice professionals sends out a ripple effect, too. As a police officer we can choose how to respond to an offender. Although we may not agree with the offender's actions, we can choose to respect that individual's worth as a human being. We must remember that we often are seeing offenders at the lowest point in their lives. They have violated the law and we may be tempted to judge them on this single event. The question we must ask ourselves is would we want to be judged by the worst thing we ever did? One bad decision is not the sum total of a person's value over a lifetime.

As citizens who are responsible for the criminal justice system, we should consider our motives for punishment. Are we motivated by a true desire to rehabilitate the offender and eventually welcome that person back into our community? Are we willing to help the offender acquire the skills he or she will need to be successful in the community? Or are we motivated to act retributively toward the offender to "teach them a lesson"? We must search our motives and realize that our response will impact not only the offender, but also our communities. Remember, what we do to one, we do to many.

Another central component of peacemaking is caring. Caring as it is used in peacemaking is best described as natural caring—similar to the care a mother has for her newborn child. The juvenile justice concept of *parens patriae*—"the state as parent" seems to apply here. A caring and loving parent would recognize their child's wrongdoing. They would likely punish the child for their wrongdoing, but the ultimate goal would be to reconcile with the child. Criminal justice professionals can choose policies that punish the offender while at the same time reintegrate and accept that person back into the community as a valued member. We can also choose to reject policies that harm offenders, and in turn the community. Retaining a juvenile justice system founded on the principle of *parens patriae* and expanding an ethic of care are preferable to the harm the adult criminal justice system undoubtedly creates.

Mindfulness also plays a central role in peacemaking. Mindfulness permits us to experience a more transcendent sense of awareness. It also allows us to become more fully aware of the "bigger picture" in terms of the needs of others and helps us to explore a broader range of possibilities when presented with a problem. In the criminal justice arena, mindfulness helps us fully consider the needs of offenders and to treat the whole person. In addition, mindfulness encourages us to move away from our own self-interest to a sense of compassion that includes others and their needs.

THE DEATH PENALTY AND LIFE WITHOUT PAROLE FOR JUVENILES

In 2012, there were 14,612 homicides in the United States and 651 juveniles were arrested for murder. Juveniles made up about 12% of the persons arrested for murder (Federal Bureau of Investigation, 2012). This is dramatically lower than the approximately 3,800 juveniles who were arrested for murder in 1993, the peak year for murders by juveniles (Snyder, 2005). Despite this decrease, however, we will probably see continued media attention on juveniles who kill.

In the past, some juvenile murderers were sentenced to death. More recently, increasing numbers of juvenile murderers have been sentenced to **life without parole (LWOP)**. Both the death penalty and LWOP for juveniles raise serious ethical issues. This chapter will discuss the ethics of both sentences.

■ Learn More on the Internet

For current information on the death penalty, go to the website of the Death Penalty Information Center: www.deathpenalty.org/. For reports on life without parole for juveniles, go to the Human Rights Watch website: www.hrw.org/. ■

A number of writers describe life without parole as equivalent to the death penalty: as the death penalty by another name (Feld, 2008), as "America's other death penalty" or as "death by incarceration" (Johnson & McGunigall-Smith, 2008), or a slow form of the death penalty or some similar nomenclature (Feld, 2008; Herivel & Wright, 2003). In other words, this sentence results in death just as capital punishment does, although the death takes years longer than an execution would.

In 2005, in *Roper v. Simmons*, the United States Supreme Court resolved the constitutional issue of the death penalty for juveniles by ruling that it is not constitutional (more about this case below). As a result, there are no juveniles on death row at present. Even though the Supreme Court so ruled, some disagree, including several Supreme Court justices who dissented from the ruling. Since some would argue that the United States should still have the option of sentencing juvenile murderers to death and since others call LWOP "America's other death penalty" (Johnson & McGunigall-Smith, 2008, p. 328), we think it is worthwhile to consider the ethics of both points of view.

The most recent estimate is that there are more than 2,000 persons serving LWOP sentences who were under 18 when they committed their crimes (Clark, 2013); the figure was 2,225 in 2005 (Human Rights Watch, 2010). Of the youths serving such sentences, 97% are male and 60% are black. Sixteen percent were 15 or younger at the time of their crimes (Human Rights Watch, 2010). The status of LWOP is in flux as states have been varied in their response to Supreme Court rulings on LWOP for juveniles.

SUPREME COURT DECISIONS ABOUT THE DEATH PENALTY AND LWOP FOR JUVENILES

As noted above, in *Roper* the Supreme Court ruled that the death penalty for juveniles was unconstitutional. The majority reasoned that juveniles are not fully mature and that there is a greater chance for reform for juvenile offenders than adult murderers.

The Supreme Court has issued two major rulings on life without parole for juveniles in recent years. In *Graham v. Florida* (2010) the Supreme Court ruled that juveniles cannot receive a life without parole sentence for a nonhomicide offense. The Court noted that at the time of the decision, there were 123 juveniles in prison for nonhomicide offenses, including 77 in Florida alone. So the *Graham* decision will at least prevent some juveniles from receiving this sentence. In *Miller v. Alabama* (2012), the U.S. Supreme Court ruled that mandatory life without parole sentences for juveniles were unconstitutional. In other words, a state cannot have a law that states that when a juvenile is found guilty of murder, the sentence is automatically life without parole. Instead "a judge or jury must have the opportunity to consider mitigating circumstances before imposing the harshest possible penalty for juveniles" (*Miller v. Alabama*, 2012). The decision was based on the reasoning in both the *Roper* and *Graham* decisions about the diminished culpability and increased capacity for change in juvenile offenders compared to adult offenders. Together, these two decisions should decrease the number of juveniles sentenced to life without parole. However, since the Court did not issue a complete ban on such sentences for juveniles, it is likely that some undetermined number of juveniles will continue to receive the sentence. In addition, some states have not interpreted the Supreme Court ruling in *Miller* to apply retroactively to juveniles already serving an LWOP sentence (Clark, 2013). Given this adjustment, a logical question concerns the ethics of sentencing juveniles to life without parole sentences.

ETHICAL ARGUMENTS ABOUT THE DEATH PENALTY AND LWOP FOR JUVENILES

Utilitarian ethics weighs the positive and negative consequences of choices (see Chapter 2). The principle of the greatest good for the greatest number dictates that whatever policy or course of action produces the most positive consequences determines the ethics of that policy or course of action. So a utilitarian analysis of the death penalty and LWOP entails a critical analysis of the positive and negative consequences of the policy and practice. Both the death penalty and LWOP share the positive consequence of perfect incapacitation in that a juvenile sentenced to either the death penalty or LWOP will not commit any more crimes on the street. Parenthetically, the juvenile might commit one or more crimes in prison, either while awaiting execution or serving an LWOP sentence. It may be worth noting that society, in general, does not seem overly concerned with the crimes prisoners commit against either fellow prisoners or even prison staff.

Another positive consequence is that both sentences provide a high degree of retribution for the severe crime of murder. The severity of the death penalty is evidenced by the Supreme Court saying that capital punishment is "different." One gauge of the degree of retribution of LWOP is that one pair of authors (Johnson & McGunigall-Smith, 2008) label LWOP as "America's Other Death Penalty: Sentence of Death by Incarceration" and another author (Feld, 2008) calls it a slower form of death.

A third positive consequence is that both generate high agreement rates in public opinion polls. For example, in a 2012 Gallup Poll 63% of Americans favored the death penalty for the crime of murder. In a 2010 Gallup Poll that asked respondents to choose between the death penalty and LWOP, 49% of Americans favored the death penalty and 46% of Americans chose LWOP as their preferred choice of penalty for murder (www.albany.edu/sourcebook). So significant proportions of Americans favor each penalty. On the other hand, in the past (prior to the Supreme Court abolishing capital punishment for juveniles) there was reduced support for the death penalty for juvenile murderers.

There are, however, a number of negative consequences. First, both sentences make no allowance for the eventual rehabilitation of the juvenile. Even the U.S. Supreme Court (*Miller v. Alabama*, 2012; *Roper v. Simmons*, 2005) has noted that juveniles have more possibility to reform than adults. An LWOP sentence sends the message that society has no hope for the sentenced juvenile.

Second, both the death penalty and LWOP sentences are costly. One estimate is that each death sentence can cost a state between $2 and $3 million. Given the current estimate of approximately $24,000 a year to house an offender (Pew Center), every 10 years of confinement costs a state about a quarter of $1 million to house one LWOP offender. Forty years amounts to about $1 million in incarceration costs. If a state chooses LWOP for a juvenile of 16, then 60 years of incarceration is possible, at a total cost of approximately $1.4 million.

Third, there is no clear evidence of any significant deterrent impact. Although there are mixed findings on the deterrent effect of the death penalty, one reading of the research is that there is insufficient evidence to claim a deterrent effect. Specifically, the National Research Council recently concluded that the research from the last 30 years on the deterrent effect of the death penalty does not allow a conclusion concerning the effect of the death penalty on homicide rates (National Research Council, 2012). Although there is no set of studies that specifically focuses on LWOP sentences, there is a record of research on three strikes and you're out sentencing (Kovandzic, Sloan, & Veiraitis, 2004). That research finds no clear deterrent impact. A recent issue of *Criminology & Public Policy* was devoted to the theme that imprisonment does not contribute as much to deterrence as do various police practices. The authors recommended reduced spending on imprisoning offenders and increased spending on various police tactics that appear to increase the certainty of apprehension and thereby increase deterrence.

Fourth, evidence of juvenile victimization in adult prisons suggests that some sentenced juveniles will experience victimization in prison. More specifically, there is some evidence that young prisoners in adult prisons are at greater risk of assault, including sexual assault (see Benekos & Merlo, 2008). Suicide risk is also higher for juveniles in adult prisons (Mumola, 2007).

Fifth, given the disproportionate impact of the death penalty and LWOP on minority offenders, both practices produce racial resentment and hostility. This appears to be true no matter how much of the disproportionate impact is due to police or court discrimination or to disproportionate minority involvement in criminal activity. The disproportionate impact is most likely related to both factors: system bias in processing and disproportionate involvement. The perception of minority members that the system is unfair, however, does not necessarily distinguish between the two sources of disparity.

Sixth, both sentences preclude the possibility that such an offender can change and make positive contributions to society. An ABC documentary entitled *Life After Death Row* showed that of 40 murderers released from death row, 20 married and fathered 20 kids. Many also got jobs and some even started their own businesses. Research on the *"Furman* murderers," who were released after the *Furman* decision rescinded their death sentences, shows that only one of 188 murderers released on parole committed a new murder and only 10.6% committed a new felony with an average of 5.3 years after release (Marquart & Sorensen, 1997). So both the death penalty and LWOP prevent offenders from the possibility of changing and being released back into society and making positive contributions such as starting a family or starting a business.

Finally, even the first alleged positive consequence of perfect incapacitation from capital punishment and LWOP is flawed. Research on criminal careers demonstrates that criminal activity peaks in the teens and twenties. At some point in their lives, criminals, like the rest of us, slow down. With age comes desistance from crime. This is a major Achilles heel of capital punishment, three strikes and you're out legislation, LWOP sentences, or any type of long-term sentencing. At some point in the prisoner's sentence, the probability is that he or she will not re-offend. The prisoner can be released safely with reduced likelihood of reoffending. Parole statistics for released murderers bear this out. Paroled murderers have much better records on parole than other types of parolees such as robbers. A major reason for this is that parole boards do not release murderers until they have served an appreciable number of years in prison. By that time, the prisoner has matured out or aged out of crime. Crime is typically a pursuit of the young. With age comes reduced physical abilities and reduced impulsiveness and perhaps a little more wisdom. Even the alleged positive consequence of perfect incapacitation is not really an uncontested positive outcome. Career criminal research demonstrates that criminals age out of crime. At some point, most offenders do not need to be in prison. If we let them out, they would not likely commit more crimes.

DEONTOLOGICAL ANALYSIS

A **deontologist** might argue that a serious crime such as murder deserves a corresponding severe punishment, that society has a duty to punish. The late Ernest van den Haag made this argument for capital punishment (see, for example, van den Haag (2003)). The logic for LWOP is the same.

Often proponents of punishment who make this claim, go the extra mile and give excruciating details of the horrifying pain that the murderer inflicted on his/her victim(s). Van den Haag (2003) recounts a case in which the two murderers tortured a young woman with unspeakable cruelty. Similarly, the Heritage Foundation (Stimson & Grossman, 2009) offers accounts of 16 juveniles who received LWOP sentences for unspeakable acts of violence and cruelty against their victims. Both van den Haag and the Heritage Foundation are making the same claim: horrendous acts of violence and cruelty are the worst harms individuals can inflict. Such horrendous harms deserve the most severe punishments, either the death penalty or LWOP. Since the Supreme Court has ruled out the death penalty for juveniles, society has a deontological duty to impose LWOP on such despicable murderers, despite their youthfulness. Reinforcing that point of view, the case in which the Supreme Court ruled that the death penalty is unconstitutional for juveniles involved a very gruesome murder, which also showed the juvenile murderer bragging that he would not be treated that severely due to his youthful status.

However, a deontologist might also make the claim that society has a duty to make allowance for the reduced culpability of juveniles whose brains/central nervous systems are not fully developed, who are more susceptible to peer pressure, and who are more reformable than adults. The Supreme Court made this exact same point in *Roper v. Simmons* in ruling that the death penalty is unconstitutional for juveniles and again in the Graham and Miller cases pertaining to LWOP for juveniles.

There is universal agreement that a child of three or five or seven lacks the requisite culpability to be sentenced to the death penalty or LWOP or even a lengthy prison term. There is agreement that a mature adult can be so sentenced. The debate is over persons in the middle range.

In other areas, society recognizes the immaturity of juveniles. Juveniles cannot sign contracts, marry, or enlist in the military. Society requires that a juvenile reach a certain age before he or she can do these things. It seems logical to argue that a juvenile who cannot vote or sign up for the military should also not be subject to a penalty that should be reserved for adults whom society considers fully culpable and fully responsible for their actions.

One critical point that punishment proponents such as van den Haag and the Heritage Foundation conveniently omit in their ostensibly compelling argument that horrific harm requires the most severe punishment is any consideration of the actual background of the offender. If a youth is born into a loving family and is raised by loving parents, sent to good schools, offered guidance, support, and love, then it would be legitimate to ignore the background of the youth when it comes time to sentence him for heinous murder.

Chances are, however, that the juvenile who commits that heinous murder did not have a storybook childhood with two loving parents, a nice home with a picket fence, one or two well-adjusted siblings for playmates, the best public or private school education, caring coaches, den mothers, pastors, and even a friendly neighborhood foot patrol officer to offer guidance along the way.

In *Death of Innocents*, for example, Sr. Helen Prejean (2005) offers the example of Jeremy Gross. He committed an almost textbook death penalty-deserving murder. In fact, his own defense attorney stated in court that if ever a crime was meant for the death penalty, Jeremy's was such a crime. He shot a storeowner in cold blood and did things that clearly fit the caption of "heinous." The defense attorney did not stop there. He spent 18 months investigating the childhood of Jeremy Gross. What he found was a horrifying record of abuse and neglect, including abuse such as his father slamming his mother's head against the refrigerator and Jeremy's removal out of the home and placement with child welfare services.

The ethical question that such an abusive and neglect-filled childhood raises is: Is it ethical to sentence an offender solely on the details of the murder OR does the criminal justice system have a duty to examine the background of the murderer and make allowances for factors such as childhood abuse, childhood neglect, mental conditions not rising to incompetence or insanity, poverty and/or other significant disadvantages? It is interesting that both van den Haag and the Heritage Foundation make no mention of any background factors in the lives of the murderers that they present as demonstrating the heinousness of murderers who deserve either capital punishment or LWOP. A challenge is in order: can a punishment proponent present a case of both a heinous murder and clear evidence that the murderer had a reasonably positive childhood with no evidence of mental or emotional disturbance or of other major trauma that contributed to the act of murder?

Capital homicide cases require a weighing of aggravating and mitigating factors. LWOP cases arguably should require similar considerations. But logic and experience raise the question: Is it likely that any murderer who commits an unspeakably cruel murder had an unflawed childhood or has no mental/emotional problems? Is it not very likely that such a murderer underwent abuse, neglect, mental/emotional disturbance, and/or other trauma that contributed to at least some degree to the genesis of the murder?

Still another deontological argument is that human beings deserve a sense of hope; that hope for the future is part of the dignity and worth of being a human being. Both the death penalty and LWOP deny any hope and therefore are violative of human dignity and worth. For example, the German Federal Constitutional Court ruled that "the principle of human dignity is compromised if the prisoner must abandon all hope of ever being released" (Appleton & Grover, 2007, p. 610).

In fairness, one study found a decline in mental health disorders after a period of time serving one's LWOP sentence. Leigey (2010) found that the "LWOP inmates...were active agents in creating purpose and finding meaning in their lives" (Leigey, 2010). However, Johnson and McGunigall-Smith (2008) offer a much more negative view of LWOP sentences: "A lifetime of boredom, doubt, and anxiety punctuated by piercing moments of insight into one's failings as a human being" (Johnson & McGunigall-Smith, 2008, p. 344).

RELIGIOUS ETHICS

Although not a philosophy of ethics, Christian doctrine also addresses the questions of capital punishment and LWOP for juveniles. Although the Catholic Church has not spoken out against LWOP for juveniles, it has spoken out against capital punishment. Specifically, the U.S. Catholic bishops issued a Statement on Capital Punishment in 1980 and Pope John Paul II issued his encyclical Evangelium Vitae in 1995, both of which opposed capital punishment (Pope John Paul II, 1995; U.S. Council of Catholic Bishops, 1980). Those pronouncements and their rationale provide insight into how the Church might address the related issue of LWOP for juveniles. More recently, the Catholic bishops have stated that "it is time for our nation to abandon the illusion that we can protect life by taking life" and that "ending the death penalty would be one important step away from a culture of death and toward building a culture of life" (U.S. Council of Catholic Bishops, 2005).

One salient factor in the bishops' statement is the prominence of forgiveness in Jesus' teaching, such as the clause in the "Our Father" prayer where the supplicant asks to be forgiven as he or she forgives others (Matthew 6:12). If forgiveness is a major theological principle that guides the believer's behavior, it would seem that forgiveness is incompatible with both the death penalty and LWOP. If believers practice and promote forgiveness, it would seem logical for Christians to support penal policies that allow for parole, for example, after an offender has served some time in prison, come to a realization of the evil and harm he or she has done, is remorseful and promises to try and do better. In the words of Jesus himself, "Go and sin no more" and "forgive seventy times seven" would seem to be more consistent with parole than with life without parole.

Another consideration is that since the Catholic hierarchy has renounced capital punishment, it also seems logical for the hierarchy to renounce LWOP because LWOP is in a sense, the equivalent of the death penalty. In the words of Barry Feld (2008), LWOP is simply "a slower form of death." In other words, a juvenile sentenced to LWOP is being sent to prison to die. He or she will not be executed but the actual result of his/her sentence is that the person in question goes to prison to die. It should be noted, of course, that not all Christian denominations oppose the death penalty. Some, such as the Southern Baptist Convention, endorse the death penalty (Bohm, 2012).

Research on LWOP prisoners shows that they experience this sentence as a death sentence. As one prisoner told a researcher: "my life is ruined for life; there is no redemption, and to some that is a fate worse than death" (Johnson & McGunigall-Smith, 2008, p. 344).

Persons who call for LWOP sentences do have legitimate concerns and credible reasons for their opinion. Some juveniles do commit unspeakable crimes. Lethal violence is abhorrent. And lethal violence is final; nothing can undo the violence. Nothing can bring back the victim.

Theologian George Boyd (1988) has argued that he opposes the death penalty because he does not want any murderer to think that he or she has compensated for their horrible crime by undergoing any execution. He does not want any murderer to think that his or her forthcoming execution will in any way compensate for the harm they did: "Murderers should never be allowed the comfort of the illusion that they can 'pay' for their crime" (Boyd, 1988, p. 163). This reasoning can be extended to LWOP. No sentence, capital punishment, LWOP, 40 years in prison, even torture if the Constitution allowed for it, can compensate for a murder. No punishment brings back the victim. The family of the victim is forever punished.

Given that capital punishment and even LWOP are imperfect attempts to right wrongs that cannot be completely righted, why not use punishments that although imperfect, result in fewer flaws? A prison term with parole eligibility allows for society to achieve punishment, retribution, incapacitation, deterrence, rehabilitation, and cost savings. A prison term is not perfect; no sentence is perfect. But a prison term with possibility of parole has fewer negative consequences than LWOP and greater potential for possible positive consequences.

Also, if an offender never does anything positive in prison, shows absolutely no signs of change, or becomes more dangerous to society, no parole board has to release him or her. Parole eligibility does not mean inevitable parole. A sentence to prison, but with parole eligibility, entails the possibility that some unknown number of juveniles will in fact serve a life without parole sentence. Still, LWOP sweeps too broadly; it makes no allowance for change.

Parole eligible sentences make an allowance for change and eventual release and restoration for some juvenile offenders.

CONCLUSION

Using utilitarianism, deontology, peacemaking, and religious ethics, it appears that numerous objections can be made to both capital punishment and life without parole sentences for juveniles. In contrast, a life with the possibility of parole sentence would allow for those juveniles who are so depraved or anti-social that they would be a pervasive threat to society to be confined for life. No parole board would have to release such an offender. Conversely, juveniles who come to understand and feel genuine remorse for the harm they have caused, and are motivated to become productive citizens, may at some point be released by those same Parole Boards. More generally, these ethical perspectives can be relied on to call for retaining a separate juvenile justice system that does not easily resort to transferring juveniles to adult courts and prisons.

It can be alluring to see the world in black and white. Good persons behave and bad persons commit crimes. A 15-year-old who kills is presumptively mature enough to be considered an adult "monster." The "black and white" picture is simply not the entire picture. A multitude of factors influence good, productive, and virtuous individuals. A multitude of factors can also lead to bad or even evil consequences. Even "monsters" have histories.

A *Frontline* documentary (*When Kids Get Life*) shows that Jacob Ind, who at age 16 killed his stepfather and mother, did not suddenly become a horrible murderer. Instead, there are years of reasons why he turned to patricide. The main reason was sexual abuse; Jacob's older brother testified to years of sexual abuse at the hands of their stepfather. A second critical reason was emotional abuse and neglect from his mother. According to a neighbor and friend, Jacob's mother and natural father had their second child, Jacob, as a last ditch step to save their marriage. When it did not save the marriage, Jacob's mother began to see Jacob as a reminder of her failed marriage. She even told him that she did not love him. So paternal sexual abuse and maternal emotional abuse and neglect are two clear factors that were prominent in Jacob's childhood. While even factors like these do not excuse what he did, it is clear that his murder of his stepfather and mother did not suddenly arise out of a vacuum.

The Supreme Court ruled that the death penalty is unconstitutional for juveniles. The Supreme Court has also limited but not eliminated LWOP for juveniles. More generally, states continue to transfer some juveniles to adult court. As a result, some juveniles are sentenced to adult prisons. In the end, whether through the courts, corrections or the community, the more we give up on our youth—even those who commit crimes—the more we give up on our collective future.

CASES CITED

Frontline Documentaries: Available at www.pbs.org/frontline
    The Killer at Thurston High
    When Kids Get Life

REFERENCES

Appleton, C., & Grover, B. (2007). The pros and cons of life without parole. *British Journal of Criminology, 47*, 597–615.

Bakken, N. W. (2007). *You do the crime, you do the time: A socio-legal history of the juvenile court and transfer waivers.* International Foundation for Protection Officers. Retrieved from www.ifpo.org/articlebank/Bakken_Juvenile_Justice.pdf.

Beck, A. J., Cantor, D., Hartge, J., & Smith, T. (2013). *Sexual victimization in juvenile facilities reported by youth, 2012. Bureau of Justice Statistics.* Washington: U.S. Department of Justice.

Beck, A. J., Harrison, P. M., & Adams, D. B. (2007). *Sexual violence reported by correctional authorities 2006.* Washington: U.S. Department of Justice Statistics.

Benekos, P. J., & Merlo, A. V. (2008). Juvenile justice: The legacy of punitive policy. *Youth Violence and Juvenile Justice, 6*, 28–46.

Blackstone, W. (1759). *Commentaries on the laws of England: Of public wrongs (book the fourth).* Retrieved from avalon.law.yale.edu/subject_menus/blackstone.asp.

Bohm, R. M. (2012). *Deathquest* (4th ed.). Boston: Elsevier (Anderson Publishing).

Boyd, G. N. (1988). Capital punishment: Deserved and wrong. *The Christian Century, 105*, 162–165.

Brown, Governor of California et al. v. Plata et al., No. 09–1233 (2010).

Butts, J. A. (2000). *Can we do without juvenile justice.* Urban Institute. Retrieved from www.urban.org/publications/1000232.html.

Campaign for Youth Justice. (2011). *State trends: Legislative victories from 205 to 2010 removing youth from the adult criminal justice system.* Retrieved from www.campaignforyouthjustice.org/documents/CFYJ_State_Trends_Report.pdf.

Cauffman, E., & Steinberg, L. (2012). Emerging findings from research on adolescent development and juvenile justice. *Victims & Offenders, 7*, 428–449.

Centers for Disease Control and Delinquency Prevention (2007). *Prosecuting youths as adults creates younger repeat offenders: Separate justice system is essential to reduce recidivism.* www.campaignforyouthjustice.org/documents/CDCFS_YouthTransfer_000.pdf.

Clarke, C. A. (2005). The baby and the bathwater: Adolescent offending and punitive juvenile justice reform. University of Kansas Law Review, *53* (1), 659–665.

Clark, M. (August 26, 2013). *How will states handle juveniles sentenced to life without parole?* USA Today. Available at www.usatoday.com/story/news/nation/2013/08/26/stateline-juvenile-sentences/2699467/.

DiIulio, J. J. (1995a). The coming of the superpredators. *The Weekly Standard, 1*(November 27), 23.

DiIulio, J. J. (1995b). Arresting ideas. *Policy Review, 74*, 12–16.

DiIulio, J. J. (1996). They're coming: Florida's youth crime bomb. *Impact, 1*, 25–27.

Dodson, K. D. (n.d.). Correctional officers' perceptions of offender treatment and rehabilitation in jail, in preparation.

Dodson, K. D. Victims and related services. In Lough, T., Myers, J.J. (Eds.), *Illinois's criminal justice system*. Durham: Carolina Academic Press, in press.

Elias, P., & Rice, J. (n.d.). *Scott County Jail programs research study*, unpublished.

Farrell v. Cate, No. RG 03079344 (2004).

Federal Bureau of Investigation (2013). *Crime in the United States*, 2012. Available at www.fbi.gov.

Feld, B. B. (2008). A slower form of death: Implications of *Roper v. Simmons* for juveniles sentenced to life without parole. *Notre Dame Journal of Law, Ethics & Public Policy, 22*(1), 9–65.

Feld, B. C. (1998). Abolish the juvenile court: Youthfulness, criminal responsibility ad sentencing policy. *Journal of Criminal Law & Criminology, 88*, 68–136.

Frontline. (2013). The reasons for treating juveniles differently. Retrieved from www.pbs.org/wgbh/pages/frontline/shows/juvenile/bench/different.html.

Graham v. Florida, 130 S.Ct. 2011 (2010).

Grisso, T., & Schwartz, R. G. (2000). *Youth on trial: A developmental perspective.* Chicago: The University of Chicago Press.

van den Haag, E. (2003). Justice, deterrence, and the death penalty. In J. R. Acker, R. M. Bohm, & C. S. Lanier (Eds.), *America's experiment with capital punishment* (pp. 233–249). Durham: Carolina Academic Press.

Hartney, C., & Marchionna, S. (2009). *Attitudes of US voters toward nonserious offenders and alternatives to incarceration.* Oakland: National Council on Crime and Delinquency.

Herivel, T., & Wright, P. (2003). *Prison nation: The warehousing of America's poor.* New York: Routledge.

Howell, J. C., Feld, B. C., & Mears, D. P. (2012). Young offenders and an effective justice system response. In R. Loeber, & D. P. Farrington (Eds.), *From juvenile delinquency to adult crime* (pp. 200–244). New York: Oxford University Press.

Human Rights Watch (2010). *Distribution of estimated 2,589 juvenile offenders serving juvenile life without parole.* Retrieved from www.hrw.org.

Jensen, E. L., & Metsger, L. K. (1994). Opportunity is in the eye of the beholder: The role of publicity in crime prevention. *Criminology, 40*, 96–104.

Johnson, R., & McGunigall-Smith, S. (2008). Life without parole, America's other death penalty: Notes on life under sentence of death by incarceration. *The Prison Journal, 88*, 328–346.

Klenowski, P. M., Bell, K. J., & Dodson, K. D. (2010). Evidence-based assessment of faith-based programs: Do faith-based programs 'work' to reduce recidivism? *Journal of Offender Rehabilitation, 50*(6), 367–383.

Kovandzic, T. V., Sloan, J. J., III, & Vieraitis, L. M. (2004). Striking out as crime reduction policy: The impact of 'three strikes' laws on crime rates in U.S. cities. *Justice Quarterly, 21*, 207–239.

Krisberg, B., & Marchionna, S. (2007). *Attitudes of U.S. voters toward youth crime and the juvenile system.* Oakland, CA: National Council on Crime and Delinquency.

Lee, D. S., & McCrary, J. (2005). *Crime, punishment, and myopia.* Working Paper 11491. Cambridge, MA: National Bureau of Economic Research.

Long, R. (January 4, 2013,). *State wants to lock up offenders in the 20s alongside juveniles.* BDN Maine Politics. Retrieved from bangordailynews.com/2013/01/04/politics/proposed-laws-would-allow-juvenile-detention-facilities-to-house-young-adults-change-harassment-complaint-protocol/.

Leigey, M. E. (2010). For the longest time: The adjustment of inmates to a sentence of life without parole. *The Prison Journal, 90*, 247–268.

Marquart, J. W., & Sorensen, J. R. (1997). A national study of the Furman-commuted inmates: Assessing the threat to society from capital offenders. In H. A. Bedau (Ed.), *The death penalty in America: Current controversies* (pp. 162–175). New York: Oxford University Press.

Miller v. Alabama, 132 S.Ct. 2455 (2012).

Mumola, C. J. (2007). Arrest-related deaths in the United States, 2003–2005. In *Bureau of justice statistics special report*. Washington: U.S. Department of Justice.

National Research Council (2012). Deterrence and the death penalty. Committee on deterrence and the death penalty. In Daniel S. Nagin, & John V. Pepper (Eds.), *Committee on law and Justice, division of behavioral and social sciences and education*. Washington: The National Academies Press.

Palmer, T. (1991). The habilitation/developmental perspective: Missing link in corrections. *Federal Probation, 55*, 55–66.

Pinkham, P. (2009). *State to argue tough juvenile sentencing in Jacksonville case*. Retrieved from jacksonville.com/news/metro/crime/2009-09-23/story/state_to_argue_tough_juvenile_sentencing_in_jacksonville_case.

Pope John Paul II (March 25, 1995). *Evangelium vitae*. Retrieved from www.vatican.va.

Prejean, H. (2005). *The death of Innocents: An eyewitness account of wrongful executions*, New York: Random House.

Redding, R. E. (2010). *Juvenile transfer: An effective deterrent to delinquency?* Washington: U.S. Department of Justice, NCJ 220595. Retrieved from www.ncjrs.gov/pdffilesl/ojjdp/220595.pdf.

Risler, E. A., Sweatman, T., & Nackerud, L. (1998). Evaluating the Georgia legislative waiver's effectiveness in deterring juvenile crime. *Research and Social Work Practice, 8*, 173–205.

Roper v. Simmons, 543 U.S. 551 (2005).

Scott, E. S., Reppucci, N. D., Antonishak, J., & DeGennaro, J. T. (2006). Public attitudes about the culpability and punishment of young offenders. *Behavioral Sciences and the Law, 24*, 815–832.

Sherman, L. W., Farrington, D. P., Welsh, B. C., & MacKenzie, D. L. (2002). *Evidence-based crime prevention*. New York: Routledge.

Singer, S. I., & McDowall, D. (1988). Criminalizing delinquency: The deterrent effects of the New York Juvenile Offender Law. *Law and Society Review, 22*(3), 521–535.

Snyder, H. N. (1998). Serious, violent and chronic juvenile offenders: An assessment of the extent of and trends in officially-recognized serious criminal behavior in a delinquent population. In R. Loeber, & D. P. Farrington (Eds.), *Serious and violent juvenile offenders: Risk factors and successful interventions* (pp. 428–444). Thousand Oaks: Sage.

Snyder, H. N., & Sickmund, M. (2000). *Challenging myths*. Washington: U.S. Department of Justice, Office of Juvenile Justice and Delinquency Prevention.

Snyder, H. N. (2005). *Juvenile arrests, 2003*. OJJDP Juvenile Justice Bulletin. Washington: U.S. Department of Justice, Office of Juvenile Justice and Delinquency Prevention.

Snyder, H. N., & Sickmund, M. (2006). *Juvenile offenders and victims: 2006 national report*. Washington: U.S. Department of Justice, Office of Justice Programs.

Steiner, B., & Wright, E. (2006). Assessing the relative effects of state direct file waiver laws on violent juvenile crime: Deterrence or irrelevance? *Criminal Law and Criminology, 75*, 1222–1245.

Stimson, C. D., & Grossman, A. M. (2009). *Adult time for adult crimes: Life without parole for juvenile killers and violent teens*. Washington: The Heritage Foundation.

Turner, H. A., Finkelhor, D., Shattuck, A., & Hamby, A. (2012). Recent victimization exposure and suicidal ideation in adolescents. *Archives of Pediatric and Adolescent Medicine, 166*(12), 149–1154.

Uniform Crime Reports (2011). *Crime in the Unites States, 2011*. Washington: U.S. Department of Justice, Federal Bureau of Investigation.

U.S. Council of Catholic Bishops (1980). *Statement on capital punishment*. Retrieved from www.usccb.org.

U.S. Council of Catholic Bishops (2005). *A culture of life and the penalty of death*. Retrieved from www.usccb.org.

Whitehead, J. T., Dodson, K. D., & Edwards, B. D. (2013). *Corrections: Exploring crime, punishment, and justice in America*. Boston: Elsevier (Anderson Publishing).

Wilson, J. Q. (1995). Crime and public policy. In J. Q. Wilson, & J. Petersilia (Eds.), *Crime* (pp. 487–507). San Francisco: ICS Press.

CHAPTER 19

Corporate Misconduct and Ethics

Bradley Edwards, Michael C. Braswell

KEY CONCEPTS

Dodd-Frank Act	symbolic politics	white-collar crime
Sarbanes-Oxley Act	STOCK Act	
subprime lending	whistleblowers	

There are good and bad corporations just like there are good and bad individuals. While no corporation or person is without flaws, some corporate cultures like Starbucks have a better reputation than others in providing healthcare benefits for its workers and their children. Other corporations like Enron deceived their employees and left many of them penniless. Our grandparents and great-grandparents focused on "making a decent living" while many in our generation focus on "living large." The virtues of their world were "waste not, want not." They saved until they could purchase what they needed or they did without. They were inclined to be independent and self-reliant and community-minded. In today's world with the help of corporate advertising, we are encouraged to consume, not conserve. We are told we should "have it our way"— right here and right now. We do not need to save for college. We can borrow the money. After all, it is for our education so it is okay to go into thousands of dollars worth of debt. We are also entitled to a house whether we can afford one or not. We are not here to serve others, but to be served. It is an 'all you can get as quick as you can get it' world—everybody for themselves. Self-esteem more than self-respect is what we are after. No matter how we feel or what problem we face, the ad on TV reassures us that there is a drug we can purchase that will solve our problem. Not only are we entitled to the good life, but if we just invest in this or that stock or financial scheme, we can retire rich and early. Our value is equated with how much money we make and how much we can spend on the latest fashion and technological gadget. We live in a world of "bling" where excess is a virtue and simplicity is a vice. In the world of credit cards and online shopping, the Internet with its tracking devices knows us better than we know ourselves. It is in this kind of world that some corporations thrive in taking advantage of our vanity and insecurities, a culture that buys and sells influence and avoids legal and ethical responsibility whenever possible for the sake of profit and power.

In July 2012, the pharmaceutical manufacturer GlaxoSmithKline was fined 3 billion dollars after pleading guilty to paying kickbacks to doctors for prescribing several drugs, failing to report safety concerns regarding a popular diabetes drug, promoting drugs for unapproved uses, and false price reporting (U.S. Department of Justice, 2012a). The GlaxoSmithKline settlement represents the largest fine to date involving a healthcare fraud and represents a clear case of a large corporation placing profits ahead of the public's welfare. Unfortunately, corporate wrongdoing occurs much more often than most Americans realize, expands far beyond the healthcare industry, and has effects that can outweigh traditional street crime in both economic and public safety aspects.

Edwin Sutherland is credited by most criminologists with developing the concept of **white-collar crime**. Sutherland defined white-collar crime as "a crime committed by a person of respectability and high social status in the course of his occupation" (Sutherland, 1949, p. 9). This definition encompasses a wide range of criminal activity by people of wealth and power. One of the most publicly recognizable forms of white-collar crimes is insider trading. Insider trading involves the buying or selling of a company stock with the use of privileged information. By utilizing information that is not publicly known, such as a pending profit report or a takeover bid by another company, incredible profits can be realized (Clarke, 1990). Sutherland argued that white-collar crime such as insider trading is not considered as serious by the public as street crime. Almost 20 years later, the President's Commission on Law Enforcement and Administration of Justice agreed with Sutherland, concluding that "the public tends to be indifferent to business crime or even to sympathize with the offenders who have been caught" (1967, p. 48). This indifference may finally be changing. Though still given less attention than conventional crimes, a wave of well publicized stock-market and other corporate scandals in recent years appears to have shifted public awareness of these issues. Americans now appear to view white-collar crimes more seriously than in the past (Holtfreter, Slyke, Bratton, & Gertz, 2008; Unnever, Benson, & Cullen, 2008).

Insider trading and related financial scandals have also contributed to Congress garnering its lowest rating in history by an increasingly skeptical public (Mendes & Wilke, 2013). It appears that until an investigative report by *60 Minutes*, few people realized that the laws and regulations related to insider trading did not apply to members of Congress. In other words, elected officials who drafted and voted on financial laws and regulations after being lobbied by a variety of "special interests" including Wall Street firms could buy and sell stocks related to those firms with relative impunity (Schieberl & Nickles, 2013).

The **STOCK** (Stop Trading on Congressional Knowledge) Act was passed in response to public outcry and activist watchdog groups to remedy such an egregious oversight, but when the furor died down and attention shifted to other crises, Congress quietly amended the law to limit public access to their stock-market transactions (Vardi, 2013). To use a colloquial expression: "It seems that the fox has put itself in charge of guarding the hen house." It seems that the laws and regulations Congress writes and enacts to regulate financial markets apply more to the general public than it does to them.

A subgroup of white-collar crimes—and the primary focus of this chapter—is criminal or otherwise unethical behavior committed within the corporate world. Corporations have tremendous influence on the everyday life of all Americans. Businesses of various sizes and types employ most Americans, determine what goods and services are available to the public, and ultimately are responsible for growing the national economy. Along with the incredible number of positive contributions that corporations can make, the business world also has a duty to act in an ethical and legal way. As Shichor (2012) points out, the business environment is based upon a certain level of trust. For example, many Americans put their retirement funds into a 401k, IRA, or other investment tool which buys stock in publicly traded companies. In doing so, they rely on the accuracy of the financial statements released by the companies as well as the integrity of fund managers who are paid to work in the best interests of their clients. Likewise, when one seeks medical attention, a healthcare professional is expected to use their knowledge of a patient's medical condition to work in the best interest of that patient. In each of these instances, the public places their trust in the hands of those who are expected to have professional knowledge and be free of self-serving practices. A violation of that trust by those in power creates unique ethical issues and deserves special attention.

As with white-collar crime in general, corporate crime has traditionally been underrepresented both by the media as well as in criminology research literature and academic program curriculums (Lynch, McGurrin, & Fenwick, 2004). This is unfortunate given that the societal costs associated with corporate crime are vast and substantial. While approximately 2.25% of Americans were a victim of a violent crime in 2011 (Truman & Planty, 2012), nearly every American is affected in some way by corporate crime. Aside from the obvious impact that corporate misconduct can have on its employees, additional harms to society include higher retail prices, increased insurance rates, higher interest rates, loss of investor money, and loss of charitable contributions (Fusaro & Miller, 2002). The effects are not limited to economic harm. The physical and related costs of corporate crime may even exceed the injuries and death caused by street crime (Cullen, Cavender, Maakestad, & Benson, 2006). The dangers of corporate misconduct are often hidden and can come in many forms including occupational dangers, dangers to consumers such as unsafe and defective products, unnecessary medical procedures, and environmental contamination (Spurgeon & Fagan, 1981).

Criminal penalties for corporate crimes are different than for any other type of crime in one critical way: corporations cannot be placed in prison. The most severe sanctions available for corporations are fines, the loss of their business license, and/or the reputational impact of a conviction. As will be shown, however, corporations are most often not formally charged for their misconduct. It is also important to note that not all of the actions outlined in this chapter are criminal in nature. Decades ago, Sutherland pointed out that businesses often were successful in influencing the passage of laws lenient toward corporate wrongdoing (Friedrichs, 2012). This concern still has merit since roughly $2 billion was contributed to the 2012 Presidential election from business interests (Porter, 2012). These donations, along with extensive lobbying efforts, are paid in an attempt to influence laws regarding matters such as governmental oversight, the production of hazardous waste, and accounting rules, etc. (Passas, 2005).

TYPES OF CORPORATE MISCONDUCT

Corporate misconduct can take many forms. These practices can range from price fixing, false advertising, marketing unsafe products, pollution, disregard of safety guidelines, to political payoffs (Clinard, 1983). An exhaustive examination of each type would be beyond the scope of this chapter. However, a few distinct forms of misconduct have been prevalent in the most recent waves of public scrutiny. These include false reporting of income and other accounting manipulations, unethical mortgage financing, healthcare fraud, student loan mismanagement, and excessive executive pay (see Box 19.1).

BOX 19.1 TYPES OF CORPORATE MISCONDUCT

Accounting Fraud	Student Loan Mismanagement
Mortgage Fraud	Excessive Executive Compensation
Healthcare Fraud	

Accounting Fraud

To place the accounting fraud prevalent in the early 2000s into some context, a basic understanding of the financial markets is necessary. Four times per year, each publicly traded company must release their quarterly earnings statement showing their profit or loss for that fiscal quarter. Increasingly, attention is focused on the performance of this statement compared to Wall Street's expectations to determine the strength or weakness of a company. A company that underperforms the expectations by just a few pennies per share is likely to lose millions of its net worth due to mutual fund and other investment brokers' selling of the company stock in search of more profitable investments (Berenson, 2004). Such actions can punish even those companies who are performing well. In fact, companies that consistently produce strong profits often face the most pressure to outperform their previous year's profits. Eventually profits will peak, level out, or even decline slightly from their higher rates of return. This is often viewed by investors as a weakness even when the performance is still quite strong.

With the immense pressure to over-perform in response to the expectations of Wall Street, it is easy to understand a company's temptation to use creative ways in order to meet their expected profit numbers. Creativity in the early 2000s came in the form of elaborate accounting frauds and/or inflation of revenue reports in an effort to artificially keep stock prices high. One common accounting trick involved long-term contracts. Under the accounting rules, some companies were allowed to count the full value of a long-term contract as revenue for the year in which the contract was signed (Berenson, 2004). For example, if a company signed a contract that would pay $50 million over a 10 year period, the full $50 million would be counted in the first year instead of being spread out over the course of the contract. This obviously inflates the short-term profits, but at the expense of long-term gains. The company makes money in each year of the long-term contract, but cannot legally report that revenue. Instead, the pressure is to continuously obtain new long-term contracts or other accounting gimmicks in order to maintain the expectations of the stock market. While some of the accounting tricks were approved by a Wall Street culture that at the time could not envision the scope of the problem, they were intentionally misleading investors. Many of the methods were illegal and other financial shenanigans that may have met the lowest technical bar of legality were clearly unethical.

Perhaps the most publicly criticized accounting scandal, and certainly one with great destructive effects to the economy, involved the Texas-based energy company, Enron. Enron's downfall was a combination of poor performance and very complex but misleading accounting practices that hid the massive debt that the company had incurred. For example, Enron created a series of "special purpose entities," which are essentially companies with no real employees or office space. These special purpose entities were used to hide much of the debt that Enron incurred from company losses and expenses, thus greatly exaggerating the worth of the company (Healy & Palepu, 2003). The Enron case, along with a number of other major corporations that faced criminal or civil litigation in the early 2000s for similar accounting gimmicks, had a great impact on the overall economy, the political and legal environment, and the public's perception of business ethics (Friedrichs, 2012). The general public as well as investors' reaction to these crimes was intense anger and fear. These companies had violated the very trust that is crucial to a market society and led to many unanswered questions. How systematic were these accounting scandals? Were any corporation's earnings reports accurate? The uncertainty created a panic in the stock market, harming millions of innocent Americans. The result was that citizens not only lost confidence in the trustworthiness of big corporations, but many lost everything—their retirement savings and their hope in the future.

Mortgage Fraud

While still recovering from the accounting fraud scandals of the early 2000s, the economy received another significant blow beginning around 2007. This economic meltdown was largely attributed to the unscrupulous banking practices known as **subprime lending**. Part of the problem was (and still is) a result of the very real problem of individual mortgage fraud. More than $10 billion in loans were obtained with fraudulent application data in 2010, and typically are viewed in terms of either fraud for property/housing or fraud for profit:

> Fraud for property/housing entails misrepresentations by the applicant for the purpose of purchasing a property for a primary residence. This scheme usually involves a single loan. Although applicants may embellish income and conceal debt, their intent is to repay the loan. Fraud for profit, however, often involves multiple loans and elaborate schemes perpetrated to gain illicit proceeds from property sales. Gross misrepresentations concerning appraisals and loan documents are common in fraud for profit schemes, and participants are frequently paid for their participation.

> **Federal Bureau of Investigation (2011, p. 17)**

While mortgage companies did not routinely encourage mortgage fraud, they did not take many, if any, steps to discourage it. In fact, much of the lending crisis was due to mismanagement and the lack of regulation within the mortgage industry. Before the housing bust, Americans had witnessed significant increases in their homes' values that had withstood the economic downturn in the early 2000s. In this environment, lenders would approve mortgage terms that included short-term, low-interest rates, but would then either automatically adjust to larger rates or require a lump sum payment in full at the end of a set number of years. To make matters worse, lenders would often make these loans to clients who they either knew or should have known could not continue to make the house payments after the adjustment. Loans were often made without income verification, making it much easier for a borrower to engage in mortgage fraud. This was not an immediate problem before the housing-bust era. Homeowners could simply refinance their loans before the adjustment occurred using the home equity that most homeowners and lenders assumed would have built up after taking out the original loan. However, after the housing prices corrected themselves from their record highs, homeowners found themselves owing more on their homes than the home was worth, thus making refinancing impossible. As a result, many homeowners lost their homes, had to declare personal bankruptcy, or simply moved away and quit making payments.

The housing bust in the late 2000s resulted in significant hardship for many financial companies such as Fannie Mae and Freddie Mac, both government-backed entities that guarantee mortgage loans. Following the subprime lending crisis, the federal government was forced to take over these companies to ensure continued operation. From 2008 to 2012 alone, this arrangement has cost the taxpayers over $187 billion (DeMarco, 2012). Other large investment banks and mortgage lenders such as Bear Sterns, Countrywide, and Lehman Brothers were either forced to go out of business or be bought out by other companies at steeply discounted prices. Despite the financial damage caused by subprime mortgages, the actions by the banks involved were often found not to be criminal. For example, the jury in a trial against senior management executives at Bear Sterns determined that the men had made poor judgments, but that doing so was not a criminal offense (Geis, 2012). Likewise, the government did not pursue criminal charges for the former executives of Countrywide and Goldman Sachs (Puzzanghera, 2012; Reckard, 2011).

Healthcare Fraud

The most common type of major fraud in the United States occurs within the healthcare system. In fact, 10 of the 14 largest financial settlements negotiated between the government and corporate offenders in 2012 involved the healthcare industry (Taxpayers Against Fraud, 2012). It is estimated that between 3% and 10% of all healthcare spending is lost due to some type of fraud (Payne, 2012). A portion of this fraud is due to dishonest individuals who, for example, will lie to the government in order to obtain public benefits such as Medicare or Medicaid disability. This certainly is illegal behavior, but is a relatively small percent of fraud cases. Approximately 80% of healthcare fraud is committed by healthcare professionals and corporations, and can come in a variety of forms (see Box 19.2). The effects of this fraud are profound. In fact, this level of loss would be enough to fund healthcare coverage to all uninsured Americans (Rosenbaum, Lopez, & Stifler, 2009).

BOX 19.2 COMMON TYPES OF HEALTHCARE PROVIDER FRAUD

1. Billing for services never rendered
2. Performing medically unnecessary services for profit
3. Misrepresenting noncovered treatments as medically necessary
4. Falsifying a patient's diagnosis to justify tests

5. Accepting kickbacks for patient referrals
6. Over-billing the insurance plan

Rosenbaum, S., Lopez, N., & Stifler, S. (2009). Health care fraud. The George Washington University Department of Health Policy, p. 14.

Pharmaceutical fraud is perhaps the most prevalent type of healthcare fraud. Some of the most common offenses committed by pharmaceutical companies in the last decade involve marketing drugs for unapproved uses, misrepresentation of safety data, and kickbacks to doctors to induce prescriptions (Kesselheim, Studdert, & Mello, 2010). Each of these offenses risks harming unsuspecting patients. Americans expect their physicians to prescribe medication based on what will best treat their ailment instead of which pharmaceutical company is paying the doctor to prescribe a particular drug. In the same sense, the public expects that all known risks will be disclosed and the medicine has been approved for treatment of their condition. The breach of this trust clearly undermines the integrity of the healthcare system and threatens public safety.

Large healthcare programs such as Medicare and Medicaid are a favorite target of healthcare fraud in the form of fraudulent billing. Leap (2011) describes many of the different types of billing fraud. In one common scheme, a doctor will make a knowingly false diagnosis, provide medically unnecessary treatments to the patient, and then receive payment from the insurance company. Another scam involves a doctor recruiting and compensating patients to undergo fraudulent and often painful medical procedures in order for the physician to receive the insurance payment. Insurance scams come in dozens of varieties and are prevalent in all sectors of the healthcare field, including nursing homes, home healthcare, and durable medical equipment markets (Leap, 2011).

Temptations for ethical misconduct are somewhat inherent in the very structure of healthcare in the United States. Healthcare is typically provided on either a fee-for-service or capitation basis. Problems can arise in both models. In a traditional fee-for-service model, the healthcare professionals are either reimbursed by an insurance company or paid out-of-pocket by the patient for "each" service provided. This model can be good for the patient, as it may ensure more comprehensive treatment. This compensation model can also lead to increased healthcare costs. The physician, either seeking additional profit or as a defense against increasing malpractice lawsuits on the basis of missed diagnoses, is often all too willing to overutilize medical testing that is often unnecessary (Berenson, 1998; Berlin, 2005).

Another option for compensating doctors involves a capitation model, which is common in managed care plans such as HMOs. In this model, members pay a fixed monthly premium that entitles them to receive health care services (Leap, 2011). These plans inherently control costs and improve efficiency, but often at the expense of quality healthcare. Since an insurance company's revenue is relatively fixed, the only way to make a profit is by reducing costs. Doctors who participate in these plans often face both subtle and overt pressure to limit tests, hospital admissions, and treatments (Fein, 1998). Both the fee-for-service and capitation models are not only legal, but very popular. However, each provides an incentive for healthcare providers and insurance companies to put profits ahead of prudent medical decisions regarding what is best for the patient. This may be a somewhat more subtle form of misconduct, but is no less inappropriate than other forms of fraud that have been deemed illegal.

Student Loan Mismanagement

Improving oneself through higher and advanced education is sacrosanct in our culture, a highly regarded and virtuous undertaking. Although such sentiments may be changing somewhat with ever-rising tuition costs and the challenges of a competitive job market, education continues to be viewed by most persons as an almost sacred right and duty in pursuit of the good life. Combine such notions with the rapid expansion of online colleges and for-profit schools, it seems easy enough to understand the formula for quick profits and exploitation at the expense of students. Mix one part of young 18-year-olds starting college or desperate mid-career professionals who have been laid off and are looking for a marketable vocation to support their families with one part aggressive and too often unscrupulous student loan companies—add a splash of colleges and universities that use student loans as a de facto recruiting device to increase enrollments—and you end up with a recipe for disaster. Unethical corporate choices are made for the purposes of quick and massive profits at the expense of long-term debt burdens incurred by students that in many cases will take a life time of work to repay if repayment is even possible. For-profit colleges spend millions of dollars each year to lobby against federal regulations. For example, they are particularly hostile to federal rules that tie a college's eligibility for student aid to graduates' incomes and ability to repay the student loans. They also lobby against a federal rule requiring no more than 90% of a university's revenue to come from sources other than federal student loans, a threshold that many for-profit colleges are in danger of crossing in the coming years (Lauerman, 2011). The students who take out the educational loans are not the only victims of the rise in online and for-profit universities. Educational student loans are almost exclusively provided by the federal government. Since for-profit universities spend considerably more money on non-educational spending such as marketing and executive compensation, the five largest for-profit schools alone costs the taxpayers over $3 billion annually (Sipley, 2011).

Excessive Executive Compensation

Modern American corporations are complex and the search for competent executives is very competitive. As a result, corporate executives are compensated at far higher levels than average employees. Executives have always received more compensation than average workers, which is understandable, but executive pay has emerged as a major social issue as the wage gap has significantly widened over the past three decades. In 1980, the average CEO earned 42 times more than the average American worker. By 2012, CEOs were earning 354 times more than the average worker (Liberto, 2013). As the overall economy has weakened in recent years, large increases in executive pay have become quite controversial. The public is particularly critical of the extraordinary compensations that the executives of poorly performing companies receive at the same time that investors in these companies lose their retirement funds, such as the approximately 100 Enron executives who received over $300 million in cash payments in the year before Enron collapsed (Barboza, 2002). Executives are sometimes even able to contractually isolate themselves from financial harm when the stock value decreases. For example, a chief executive in 2003 negotiated a clause ahead of a stock offering which would have paid him almost $1 million if the stock substantially lost value and stayed at a low level for more than 30 days (McGeehan, 2003).

A current trend is for corporations to use stocks and stock options as a form of compensation for executives. Stock options give the owner the right to buy a number of shares of the company stock at a predetermined price (usually current market price), any time in the future until a pre-set expiration date (Berenson, 2004). If the stock value increases from the initial date, the option owner makes a profit equal to the increase multiplied by the number of shares. If the stock declines in value during that time period, the option has no value. Compensation packages that include stocks and options do serve the purpose of inherently linking executive pay with the performance of the company (Faulkender & Senbet, 2010). However, evidence is very mixed as to whether executive compensation can be linked to increased performance (Devers, Cannella, Reilly, & Yoder, 2007; Friedrichs, 2009). Furthermore, measuring the performance of the company solely on stock prices is an inaccurate measure of a company's strength. Linking executive pay directly to the stock market is likely to increase the pressures and likelihood of misconduct in order to achieve Wall Street's expectations. It may also have the unintended consequence of further increasing the income gap between the average worker and executives, since the average worker is likely to feel the largest impact of any cost-cutting measures, including lay-offs, meant to increase profit margins and meet Wall Street's expectations.

Each year, thousands of companies merge with or are acquired by another company. Mergers and acquisitions allow companies to grow or compete more efficiently by consolidating their workforce. Consolidation often leads to the elimination of jobs at one or both of the companies. This can be a stressful time for employees, but executives are often able to isolate themselves from any financial loss resulting from a merger or acquisition through the use of "golden parachutes." The negotiations of these severance packages, often millions of dollars, are provided in compensation for an executive that either leaves the new company or takes a reduced role in the new entity (Hartzell, Ofek, & Yermack, 2004). At first glance, these severance packages might seem reasonable for outgoing executives. The executives are, after all, surrendering the pay and overall prestige associated with their former positions. However, these severance packages can come at a cost in terms of shareholder value. Simply put, the amount that is paid to an executive's severance package could have otherwise been used to pay a larger price for the acquired company and in turn to that company's shareholders.

The common thread among all types of extraordinary and excessive executive compensation is the possibility of alienating employees and shareholders. Recent legislation has, for the first time, given shareholders of a company a voice in executive compensation. The **Dodd-Frank Act** (2010) mandates that shareholders of publicly shared companies must be provided an advisory vote on executive pay. Interestingly, shareholders in the post Dodd-Frank era have generally supported executive compensation packages, but this support is influenced by how much executives are paid and the performance of the company. As would be expected, the votes most likely to disapprove of compensation packages were in companies with poor performance but high executive pay (Thomas, Palmiter, & Cotter, 2012). Although these votes are nonbinding, there is some reason to believe that they can make a difference in excessive pay. For example, Ertimur, Ferri, and Muslu (2011) studied activist shareholders who had organized "vote no" campaigns protesting excessive CEO pay in targeted companies before the Dodd-Frank Act was enacted. Those companies that were targeted by these campaigns responded by significantly reducing their CEO pay. It will take many more years to determine what effect, if any, impact these new mandated shareholder votes will have on excessive executive pay. At a minimum, it should improve transparency and give disgruntled shareholders an avenue to voice their concerns.

CAUSES FOR MISCONDUCT

The first step in attempting to combat corporate crime is to understand why these acts of misconduct take place. Much of the blame for corporate misconduct can be attributed to dishonest individuals within the corporations.

There are many reasons that a manager or executive might engage in unethical conduct. Individual dishonesty, greed, or even the thrill gained by engaging in unethical behavior might be partially to blame. Perhaps executives do not have adequate incentives to safeguard the company's finances due to guaranteed severance packages and other compensation. Finally, it is possible that CEOs and other managers tend to have an exaggerated sense of self-confidence and worth which, based off of past successes, may lead them to believe that they cannot fail (Hayward & Hambrick, 1997).

Whatever the individual-level motivations for corporate misconduct, these decisions do not occur in a vacuum; certain aspects of the business environment influence such choices. The marketplace in which the publicly traded companies and healthcare companies compete creates enormous temptations and opportunities to engage in fraudulent or otherwise unethical behaviors. Even so, these temptations do not exist to the same degree in every company or for every employee within a company. For example, employees at Enron were evaluated by a system that ranked the top and bottom 5% of each division. The top 5% were rewarded by extravagant trips, while the bottom 5% were disciplined (Knottnerus, Ulsperger, Cummins, & Osteen, 2006). Along with individual performance evaluations, Enron also encouraged good performance from its employees by rewards based on the company stock price (Eichenwald, 2002). Rewards based on arbitrary measures such as the stock price can obviously be problematic. Whatever the specific goals provided, the mere existence of these rewards could act to foster an environment in which unethical behavior is either readily accepted or quietly tolerated within a given company.

The pressure to meet organizational goals is arguably the most intense in the middle management positions. The sheer size of many modern organizations has increased reliance on committees and mid-level managers to make decisions, delegate responsibility, and relay information up the chain of command. In a comprehensive (but now dated) interview from middle-level managers, such pressure was found to be commonly cited as a reason for unethical behavior. One mid-manager described this problem by stating: "You start out of college with high ideals and due to pressures these ideals deteriorate during one's corporate experience. Middle management violates their ethics, mainly to get the job done" (Clinard, 1983, p. 96). The business environment is so competitive that it often takes up a devoted employee's entire life. The dedication required to be successful in business often requires constant travel, changes of residence, and few friendships outside the business sector (Punch, 1996). In this sense, corporate managers share many of the same difficulties that police officers experience in their private lives and can lead to the internal justification of unethical behavior.

ASSESSING BLAME

Mechanisms are in place to expose corporate misconduct. Federal oversight is provided in the form of groups such as the Financial Fraud Enforcement Task Force. This task force includes high ranking members of various branches of the federal government, including the Securities and Exchange Commission and the Federal Bureau of Investigation. In addition, a board of directors is typically in place to oversee the top-level management and make sure that all regulations are followed. Unfortunately, these control mechanisms are not always enough to prevent fraud and other misconduct. In order to address these discoveries, we will first focus on individual whistleblowers and then the influence of the media and how it broadcasts critical information to a mass audience.

WHISTLEBLOWERS

Most cases involving fraud rely on current or former employees with direct knowledge of the fraud, known as **whistleblowers**, initiating litigation against a particular corporation (U.S. Department of Justice, 2012b). Thus, it is very important to have mechanisms in place to enhance the ability for whistleblowers to come forward and report any known fraud. Employees who are aware of fraud or other criminal behavior are understandably hesitant about disclosing this information for fear of retaliation. The experience of being involved in a whistleblower suit against an employer can have a great personal toll, including pressures from his or her employer and the threatened loss of employment (Kesselheim et al., 2010). In response to these concerns, two laws have strengthened the protections for whistleblowers.

The **Sarbanes-Oxley Act** was passed in 2002 in an attempt to regain investor confidence by enhancing punishments for corporate executives, addressing the need for more accurate financial statements, and making reporting easier for those with inside knowledge (Recine, 2002). The Act had two primary functions relating to whistleblowers. First, the Act protects whistleblowers against retaliation by employers. Specifically, a company cannot "discharge, demote, suspend, threaten, harass, or in any other manner discriminate against an employee in the terms and conditions of employment because of any lawful act done by the employee" (18. U.S.C. §1514A). The Act also requires that employers create a more meaningful procedure for employees to disclose illegal activity than existed before. This requirement is meant to eliminate the ability of the management to mute any employee-initiated complaint that might arise. Though problems still exist with the new law (Brickey, 2003; Moberly, 2006, pp. 1107–1180), it appears to be a significant improvement over previous laws.

The Dodd-Frank Act, which passed in 2010, also contained provisions to encourage whistleblowers to come forth with information. Specifically, this law created a fund that allows for a whistleblower that has given original information to authorities to be awarded between 10 and 30% of any monetary sanction taken against a company as a result of an investigation (Meissner, 2010). Providing a financial incentive for whistleblowers to come forward with information is not a new concept. For example, the False Claims Act, which specifically targets fraud against the government, has for many years provided an incentive of up to 30% of any funds recovered (Kesselheim & Studdert, 2008). Under the Dodd-Frank Act, financial incentives are now available to whistleblowers in any company that is regulated by the Securities and Exchange Commission and the recovered funds total more than $1 million. Building on existing legislation, the Dodd-Frank Act also allows any whistleblower to remain anonymous even from the authorities, and any whistleblower who is discriminated against can sue for reinstatement at the same seniority level and for double back pay (Meissner, 2010). If these programs are well implemented, they may provide the best protection to date for whistleblowers and will hopefully provide the incentive to come forward with critical information.

THE ROLE OF MEDIA

On December 2, 2012, the television show *60 Minutes* ran a segment which focused on a hospital administration company called Health Management Associates (HMA). In this segment, the show interviewed various doctors who testified that HMA had set a quota of admitting 20% of all emergency room patients and 50% of all Medicare patients. The admission decision was allegedly made to increase profits regardless of the medical necessity of admission. After the show aired, the company became the target of a federal investigation, the hospital admissions (as well as profits) declined, and the CEO announced his retirement (Hornblower, Rey & Zill, 2013).

"The first trial is always in the court of public opinion" is a quote that came from the attorney for former HealthSouth CEO Richard Scrushy following Scrushy's acquittal in a $2.7 billion accounting fraud case (Farrell, 2006). In the months leading up to his trial, Scrushy's legal team successfully orchestrated an intense media and public relations campaign, including media interviews for programs such as *60 Minutes*, a personal website, and a 30 min religious television show airing in the city where his jury would be chosen (Brickey, 2008). The media can be a very important lens through which the public views current events, including criminal or unethical behavior. Media coverage serves to introduce these events to the public and then frame these events into a story line that the public can relate to (Cavender, 2004). At times, the media has served to promote a public agenda, encouraging a moral crusade against a specific type of wrongdoing such as corporate crime (Surette, 2011). As illustrated in the example above, the media can also be used as a public relations tool for corporations and their executives facing criminal sanctions. In either case, the prevalence of investigative reporting by media programs such as *60 Minutes* has emerged as a strong force for changing the landscape of public discourse for such issues.

Politicians also rely on the media for public relations purposes. Following a scandal, executives are subpoenaed to appear in front of Congress to participate in what might best be described as **symbolic politics** (Edelman, 1964). During these congressional hearings, "pomp and circumstance" are the order of the day. Executives are scorned for their actions and punitive sanctions are threatened. Politicians rely on the media coverage of these hearings to create a sense that Congress understands the problem and is taking action to prevent the wrongdoing (Cavender, Gray, & Miller, 2010). Though the messages relayed at these hearings might be largely symbolic, the media scrutiny can put pressure on prosecutors and judges that might not exist without increased public attention. In this way, the media is very important in assessing blameworthiness to corporate wrongdoers.

PROSECUTING CORPORATE CRIME

The prosecution and sentencing process in corporate crime cases has become increasingly aggressive in recent years. The most common punishment for corporate crime has been civil punishments, primarily consisting of fines and increased regulatory sanctions. However, the criminal justice system is also sometimes used against corporations and/or their executives. Corporate cases present many complex factors that complicate the decision of whom and how to prosecute.

Investigating and prosecuting corporate misconduct can often be incredibly difficult due to the complexity of the cases and the sophisticated cover-up techniques used by corporate wrongdoers. The scope of the case as well as jurisdictional issues largely determines whether it will be handled by a local or federal prosecutor. It is important to point out that not all corporate crime is committed by large multinational corporations involving thousands of victims and widespread effects to the economy. In fact, a large number of corporate criminal cases deal with small, locally based companies that engage in fraudulent behavior and are often prosecuted effectively by the local prosecutor (Benson & Cullen, 1998). However, prosecution can also involve some of the largest corporations in America, such as many of those mentioned throughout this chapter. These cases often cross jurisdictional boundaries or are otherwise simply too expensive or complex for a local prosecutor's office (see Box 19.3). For example, simply obtaining the required evidence could take up to 10 years in large cases expanding into foreign countries (Larence, 2009). For these reasons corporate cases are typically prosecuted at the federal level.

BOX 19.3 FORD PINTO CASE

The infamous Ford Pinto case in 1980 involved allegedly faulty placements of fuel tanks resulting in an increased risk of fire during rear-end collisions. After an accident in Indiana, a local prosecutor decided to charge Ford as an entity in a criminal trial. The reckless homicide case represented the first time in American history that a major corporation was criminally prosecuted for the death of a customer from allegedly using a defective product. The case was brought by a local prosecutor in Indiana, and faced a host of obstacles. First, Ford obtained a prestigious law firm to represent them in the criminal case and had far more financial resources than the $20,000 prosecution budget. This budget was first tested by numerous motions filed by Ford in an attempt to prevent the case from proceeding to trial. The prosecution won that fight, and was allowed to take the case to trial. However, Ford was able to obtain a change of venue. This added travel and lodging expenses to the already meager prosecution budget. The prosecution was outmanned at every stage of trial, from picking a jury to securing and interpreting the evidence, even what the jury would and would not hear in the trial. This financial advantage ultimately paid off, as Ford was acquitted. This underscores the complexity of corporate crime cases, as well as the difficulties often experienced by local prosecutors. For a very comprehensive overview of the trial, see Cullen et al. (2006).

A fundamental ethical dilemma for corporate crime involves whether society should prosecute a company as an entity or instead focus criminal sanctions on the individual offender. Using the utilitarian perspective, punishment could have a more deterrent effect on the corporation than an individual. However, punishing the corporation to the extent that would effectively produce a deterrent effect could cripple the finances of the company, thus causing significant harm to innocent people in the form of lost jobs or increased prices (Braithwaite, 1982). This dilemma was recently acknowledged by Attorney General Eric Holder in testimony to the Senate Judiciary Committee:

> I am concerned that the size of some of these institutions becomes so large that it does become difficult for us to prosecute them when we are hit with indications that if we do prosecute- if we do bring a criminal charge- it will have a negative impact on the national economy, perhaps even the world economy. I think that is a function of the fact that some of these institutions have become too large....The greatest effect is not to prosecute a corporation- although that is important- the greatest deterrent effect is to prosecute the individuals in the corporations that are responsible for the decisions.
>
> **Holder (2013)**

Conversely, another approach might also focus on holding executive decision makers "personally" responsible as a means of discouraging wrongdoers from hiding behind the corporate skirt of professional ignorance and memory lapses.

Criminal prosecutions of corporations are rare, but do sometimes occur. The most celebrated case in recent years was the 2002 conviction of Arthur

Andersen, which served as Enron's accounting firm. Arthur Andersen was charged with obstruction of justice in connection with the shredding of documents that would have assisted the government's investigation of Enron. Prosecutors charged the corporation as well as the head of the Enron division at Arthur Andersen, David Duncan. Duncan pleaded guilty, while Arthur Andersen was found guilty and received five years' probation and a $500,000 fine (Fowler & Flood, 2002; *United States v. Arthur Andersen, 2004*).

Arthur Andersen's prosecution and conviction sent a strong public message that the government can successfully prosecute wrongdoing. The conviction did not come without a cost, however. Aside from the cost associated with prosecuting the case, the conviction (which was eventually overturned by the Supreme Court) resulted in the closing of Arthur Andersen and the loss of 85,000 jobs worldwide. The expenses of prosecution as well as the loss of jobs by innocent employees represent significant "collateral costs" of prosecuting corporations (Oded, 2011). In an effort to reduce the collateral costs of a criminal prosecution, the use of deferred and non-prosecution agreements with the corporate entities involved in misconduct has increased over the past decade.

DEFERRED AND NON-PROSECUTION AGREEMENTS

Deferred prosecution agreements (DPA) can be viewed as a type of corporate probation. In these agreements, corporations are charged with a crime, but the prosecution is delayed and ultimately dismissed after a period of time if the corporation complies with certain requirements. Companies are most often required to comply with one or more of the following conditions: (1) institute internal compliance programs, (2) pay restitution to victims and/or fines, (3) cooperate with investigations, or (4) hire independent oversight monitors in lieu of a criminal trial (Larence, 2009). Non-prosecution agreements (NPA) are similar except for the lack of formal charges in return for the above concessions. In either case, the prosecution maintains the right to prosecute if the corporation fails to comply with the terms of the agreement (Wray & Hur, 2006). The use of deferred and non-prosecution agreements is often viewed as a win–win for both the government and the corporation. The agreements can be attractive for corporations, as the reputational costs of being indicted or convicted might well destroy the company in the eyes of the consumers. The government also prefers such agreements as a way to effectively prevent future wrongdoing while reducing the associated collateral costs, all at a minimal cost to the government.

The usage of deferred and non-prosecution agreements is not without its share of critics. For some, the agreements are too lenient, undermine the justice system, and are another way in which corporations can buy their way out of being prosecuted (Morgenson & Story, 2011). However, most criticism comes from legal scholars who are concerned with possible constitutional violations. Deferred and non-prosecution agreements give prosecutors extraordinary leverage against companies who want to avoid the stigma of prosecution at all costs. This has, on occasion, led to instances of prosecutorial misconduct. The requirement for companies to fully cooperate with government investigations is perhaps the most potent tool available for prosecutors preparing cases against individual wrongdoers within the company. Prosecutors in the past have used their power to coerce corporations to waive attorney-client privileges, turn over results of internal investigations that could implicate employees, or even force employees to self-incriminate themselves or face termination (Ball & Bolia, 2009; Gallagher, 2010). An important shift in the use of these agreements occurred in 2007, when a federal judge overturned the indictments of 13 employees of a large accounting firm that was under investigation for possible tax fraud. The prosecutor in this case used the leverage of a possible deferred prosecution to force a change in the company's longstanding policy of paying legal fees for employees in investigations. This was found to violate the defendant's Fifth Amendment right to effective assistance of counsel (*United States v. Stein*, 2007). The current guidelines from the Department of Justice instruct prosecutors not to consider a corporation's advancement of legal fees to employees or its willingness to waive attorney–client privilege when evaluating a corporation's level of cooperation (Gallagher, 2010). Many legislative bills have been proposed since the Stein decision in an attempt to further regulate the prosecution's power regarding deferred and non-prosecution agreements. To date, none of these bills have become law.

The criminal prosecution of corporate misbehavior almost exclusively targets the employees responsible for the wrongdoing. The Sarbanes-Oxley Act of 2002 has assisted prosecutors by (1) broadening the legal definitions of corporate crime to encompass more behavior and (2) substantially increasing the maximum punishments for corporate-related crimes (Lowell & Arnold, 2003). This legislation, together with the increased protections for whistleblowers and the information available through investigations of companies subjected to the NPAs and DPAs, has resulted in an onslaught of federal corporate prosecutions. From 2002 to 2008, the Department of Justice successfully convicted nearly 1,300 corporate fraud cases involving more than 200 CEOs and hundreds more persons with roles such as vice presidents and chief financial officer (Filip, 2008). Those convicted of corporate crimes face increasingly punitive sentences. Responding to public pressure and media attention, the sentences of some high-profile corporate executives are larger than at any point in history (Gustafson, 2007). Current federal sentencing guidelines now advise judges to sentence many of these economic crimes at the same levels as violent felons and even murderers. However, the recommended guidelines should be viewed with some caution since federal judges have been consistent in their reluctance to impose such extreme sentences (Bowman, 2008). Still, some of the highest profile offenders receive decades-long prison sentences. Corporate executives tend to plead guilty and become cooperating witnesses against other defendants (Brickey, 2006). This allows prosecutors to bring criminal sanctions against an even wider net of corporate employees who have engaged in wrongdoing. Executives that do insist on a trial do not tend to fare well, as the overwhelming majority of these cases result in convictions and receive increased sentences (Barker, Baxter, Frankel, & Raymond, 2008).

CORPORATE MISCONDUCT: WHAT'S NEXT?

Hopefully, the examples of wrongdoing in the past 20 years will encourage and promote more ethical and socially responsible conduct by corporations going forward. Likewise, it is hoped that the compliance measures both from within the organization and from law enforcement agencies will benefit from past incidents of misconduct in order to prevent similar scandals in the future. The Sarbanes-Oxley Act and the Frank-Dodd Act both serve as important steps in the regulation of corporate misconduct. In addition, the Affordable Care Act passed in 2010 contained provisions to decrease fraud in the healthcare sector, specifically imposing more stringent requirements for applicants who seek permission to bill Medicare (Iglehart, 2010). There are encouraging signs that regulators and law enforcement are starting to crack down on fraud. From 2009 to 2012, the Department of Justice recovered $13.3 billion in settlements and judgments of fraud cases, including record settlements related to healthcare and housing fraud (U.S. Department of Justice, 2012a). Since 2011, the government has also revoked the ability of over 14,000 providers and suppliers to bill Medicare (Kennedy, 2013). These numbers represent large increases from past years. However, if history is any indication (and it usually is), the future seems likely to repeat some of the mistakes of the past.

Policy regarding regulations of corporations as well as the culture of the corporate world seems to go in cycles (Berenson, 2004; Lowell & Arnold, 2003; Minkes, 2010). Immediately after a scandal, politicians create new regulations and punishments in order to show the public that corporate crime is being taken seriously. After the public frenzy regarding the seriousness of a particular corporate crime or scandal wears off, these rules are either relaxed or passively ignored.

There will inevitably be another economic "bubble" that will test both the constraint of corporate executives and the effectiveness of oversight and enforcement agencies as well as the various policies that were put into place in response to the last wave of corporate misconduct. As the old saying goes, "The most important virtue a politician can have is honesty. If he can fake that, he's got it made." The same can be said of corporate strategists and executives. Most corporations exist to provide goods and services in order to make money. Some go about their business with integrity while others act on the premise that "the end justifies any means" when it comes to increasing profits. Many corporations will not act more ethically than the law, enforcement agencies, and citizens require them to. For that to happen, citizens will have to remain vigilant and elect representatives that will consistently advocate and enact morally responsible laws and regulations governing corporate misconduct.

REFERENCES

Ball, D., & Bolia, D. (2009). Ending a decade of federal prosecutorial abuse in the corporate criminal charging decision. *Wyoming Law Review, 9*, 229–261.

Barboza, D. (June 18, 2002). *Officials got a windfall before Enron's collapse.* The New York Times.

Barker, E., Baxter, B., Frankel, A., & Raymond, N. (2008). Progress report: How the Justice Department's 440 highest profile corporate fraud cases turned out. *Federal Sentencing Reporter, 20*(3), 206–214.

Benson, M., & Cullen, F. (1998). *Combating corporate crime: Local prosecutors at work.* Boston: Northeastern University Press.

Berenson, A. (2004). *The number.* New York: Random House Trade Paperbacks.

Berenson, R. (1998). The doctor's dilemma revisited: Ethical physician decisions in a managed care environment. *Generations, 22*(2), 63–68.

Berlin, L. (2005). Errors of omission. *American Journal of Roentgenology, 185*, 1416–1421.

Bowman, F., III (2008). Sentencing high-loss corporate insider frauds post-Booker. *Federal Sentencing Reporter, 20*(3), 167–173.

Braithwaite, J. (1982). Challenging just deserts: Punishing white collar criminals. *Journal of Criminal Law and Criminology, 73*(2), 723–763.

Brickey, K. (2003). After the Sarbanes-Oxley Act: The future disclosure system: From Enron to Worldcom and beyond: Life and crime after Sarbanes-Oxley. *Washington University Law Quarterly, 81*, 357–401.

Brickey, K. (2006). In Enron's wake: Corporate executives on trial. *Journal of Criminal Law and Criminology, 96*(2), 397–433.

Brickey, K. (2008). From boardroom to courtroom: The media and the corporate governance scandals. *Journal of Corporation Law, 33*(3), 625–663.

Cavender, G. (2004). Media and crime policy: A reconsideration of David Garland's the culture of control. *Punishment & Society, 6*(3), 335–348.

Cavender, G., Gray, K., & Miller, K. (2010). Enron's perp walk: Status degradation ceremonies as narrative. *Crime, Media, Culture, 6*(3), 251–266.

Clarke, M. (1990). *Business crime: Its nature and control.* New York: St. Martin's Press.

Clinard, M. (1983). *Corporate ethics and crime: The role of middle management.* Beverly Hills: Sage.

Cullen, F., Cavender, G., Maakestad, W., & Benson, M. (2006). *Corporate crime under attack: The fight to criminalize business violence.* Cincinnati: Anderson.

DeMarco, E. (2012). *Report to Congress: 2012*. Washington: Federal Housing Finance Agency.

Devers, C., Cannella, A., Reilly, G., & Yoder, M. (2007). Executive compensation: A multidisciplinary review of recent developments. *Journal of Management, 33*, 1016–1072.

Dodd-Frank Wall Street Reform and Consumer Protection Act (2010). Public Law 111–203.

Edelman, M. (1964). *The symbolic uses of politics*. Urbana: University of Illinois Press.

Eichenwald, K. (March 1, 2002). *Enron's many strands: Executive compensation; Enron paid huge bonuses in '01; Experts see a motive for cheating*. The New York Times.

Ertimur, Y., Ferri, F., & Muslu, V. (2011). Shareholder activism and CEO pay. *The Review of Financial Studies, 24*(2), 535–592.

Farrell, G. (May 29, 2006). *Scrushy's lawyer says Lay strategy was wrong*. USA Today.

Faulkender, M., & Senbet, L. (2010). Executive compensation: An overview of research on corporate practices and proposed reforms. *Journal of Applied Corporate Finance, 22*, 107–118.

Federal Bureau of Investigation. (2011). *2010 Mortgage fraud report*. Directorate of Intelligence, Financial Crimes Intelligence Unit.

Fein, R. (1998). The HMO revolution. *Dissent, 45*(2), 29–36.

Filip, M. (2008). *Report to the President Corporate Fraud Task Force, 2008*, Washington, DC.

Fowler, T., & Flood, M. (October 16, 2002). *Andersen gets the maximum sentence*. Houston Chronicle.

Friedrichs, D. (2009). Exorbitant CEO compensation: Just reward or grand theft? *Crime, Law & Social Change, 5*, 45–72.

Friedrichs, D. (2012). Enron et al.: Paradigmatic white collar crime cases for the new century. In D. Shichor, L. Gaines, & A. Schoepfer (Eds.), *Reflecting on white collar and corporate crime: Discerning readings* (pp. 117–134). Long Grove: Waveland.

Fusaro, P., & Miller, R. (2002). *What went wrong at Enron: Everyone's guide to the largest bankruptcy in U.S. history*. Hoboken: Wiley.

Gallagher, J. (2010). Legislation is necessary for deferred prosecution of corporate crime. *Suffolk University Law Review, 43*, 447–473.

Geis, G. (2012). The Great American Meltdown of 2007 and onward. In D. Shichor, L. Gaines, & A. Schoepfer (Eds.), *Reflecting on white collar and corporate crime: Discerning readings* (pp. 175–195). Long Grove: Waveland.

Gustafson, J. (2007). Cracking down on White-Collar crime: An analysis of the recent trend of severe sentences for corporate officers. *Suffolk University Law Review, 40*, 685–701.

Hartzell, J., Ofek, E., & Yermack, D. (2004). What's in it for me? CEO's whose firms are acquired. *The Review of Financial Studies, 17*, 37–61.

Hayward, M., & Hambrick, D. (1997). Explaining the premiums paid for large acquisitions: Evidence of CEO hubris. *Administrative Science Quarterly, 42*(1), 103–127.

Healy, P., & Palepu, K. (2003). The fall of Enron. *Journal of Economic Perspectives, 17*(2), 3–26.

Holder, E. (2013). *Quote from: U.S. Congress*, Hearing of the Senate Judiciary Committee. Oversight of the U.S. Department of Justice. Date 03/06/2013. Retrieved from www.judiciary.senate.gov/resources/transcripts/.

Holtfreter, K., Slyke, S., Bratton, J., & Gertz, M. (2008). Public perceptions of white-collar crime and punishment. *Journal of Criminal Justice, 36*, 50–60.

Hornblower, S., Rey, M., & Zill, O. (December 2, 2012 & June 9, 2013). *Hospitals: The cost of admission. 60 Minutes*. CBS. Transcript.

Iglehart, J. (2010). The ACA's new weapons against health care fraud. *New England Journal of Medicine, 363*(4), 304–306.

Kennedy, K. (June 5, 2013). *Policing of medicare fraud explodes over two years,* USA Today. Retrieved from www.usatoday.com/story/news/politics/2013/06/05/medicare-revoking-providers-billing-fraud/2393561/.

Kesselheim, A., & Studdert, D. (2008). Whistleblower-initiated enforcement actions against health care fraud and abuse in the United States. *Annals of Internal Medicine, 149*, 342–349.

Kesselheim, A., Studdert, D., & Mello, M. (2010). Whistle-blowers' experience in fraud litigation against pharmaceutical companies. *The New England Journal of Medicine, 362,* 1832–1839.

Knottnerus, J. D., Ulsperger, J., Cummins, S., & Osteen, E. (2006). Exposing Enron: Media representations of ritualized deviance in corporate culture. *Crime, Media, Culture, 2*(2), 177–195.

Larence, E. (2009). *Preliminary observations of DOJ's use and oversight of deferred prosecution and non-prosecution agreements.* United States Government Accountability Office.

Lauerman, J. (2011). *For-profit colleges facing loss of taxpayer funds fighting aid limit,* Bloomberg. Retrieved from www.bloomberg.com/news/2011-01-12/for-profit-colleges-facing-taxpayer-funds-loss-fight-aid-limit.html.

Leap, T. (2011). *Phantom billing, fake prescriptions, and the high cost of medicine: Health care fraud and what to do about it.* New York: Cornell University Press.

Liberto, J. (April 15, 2013). *CEO's earn 354 times more than average worker,* CNN Money. Retrieved from money.cnn.com/2013/04/15/news/economy/ceo-pay-worker/index.html.

Lowell, A., & Arnold, K. (2003). Corporate crime after 2000: A new law enforcement challenge or déjà vu? *American Criminal Law Review, 40,* 219–240.

Lynch, M., McGurrin, D., & Fenwick, M. (2004). Disappearing act: The representation of corporate crime research in criminological literature. *Journal of Criminal Justice, 32,* 389–398.

McGeehan, P. (December 3, 2003). *Market place; for this chief, a loss would be a big gain.* The New York Times.

Meissner, S. (2010). *Law lets whistle-blowers get rich for doing the right thing,* Forbes. Retrieved from www.forbes.com/2010/07/27/finreg-dodd-frank-markets-financial-advisor-network-whistle-blower.html.

Mendes, E., & Wilke, J. (2013). *Americans' confidence in Congress falls to lowest on record,* Gallup. Retrieved from www.gallup.com/poll/163052/americans-confidence-congress-falls-lowest-record.aspx.

Minkes, J. (2010). Silent or invisible? Governments and corporate financial crimes. *Criminology and Public Policy, 9*(3), 467–473.

Moberly, R. (2006). *Sarbanes-Oxley's structural models to encourage corporate whistleblowers.* College of Law Faculty Publications. Paper 27.

Morgenson, G., & Story, L. (2011). *As Wall St. polices itself, prosecutors use softer approach.* The New York Times. Retrieved from www.nytimes.com/2011/07/08/business/in-shift-federal-prosecutors-are-lenient-as-companies-break-the-law.html?_r=0&pagewanted=print#.

Oded, S. (2011). Deferred prosecution agreements: Prosecutorial balance in times of economic meltdown. *Law Journal for Social Justice, 2,* 65–99.

Passas, N. (2005). Lawful but awful: Legal corporate crimes. *The Journal of Socio-Economics, 34,* 771–786.

Payne, B. (2012). *White collar crime: A text/reader.* Thousand Oaks: Sage.

Porter, E. (November 6, 2012). *Get what you pay for? Not always.* The New York Times.

Presidents Commission on Law Enforcement and Administration of Justice (1967). *The challenge of crime in a free society*. Washington: United States Government Printing Office.

Punch, M. (1996). *Dirty business: Exploring corporate misconduct*. Thousand Oaks: Sage.

Puzzanghera, J. (August 10, 2012). *Goldman Sachs won't face U.S. charges for mortgage securities*. Los Angeles Times.

Recine, J. (2002). Examination of the white collar crime penalty enhancements in the Sarbanes-Oxley Act. *American Criminal Law Review, 39*, 1535–1570.

Reckard, S. (February 18, 2011). *U.S. Drops criminal probe of former Countrywide chief Angelo Mozilo*. Los Angeles Times.

Rosenbaum, S., Lopez, N., & Stifler, S. (2009). *Health care fraud*. The George Washington University School of Public Health and Health Services, Department of Health Policy.

Sarbanes-Oxley Act of 2002. (2002). Public Law 107–204.

Schieberl, J., & Nickles, M. (2013). Congressional insider trading: Is it legal? *Journal of Business Case Studies, 9*(3), 221–226.

Shichor, D. (2012). Criminal and legal "looting" in corporations. In D. Shichor, L. Gaines, & A. Schoepfer (Eds.), *Reflecting on white collar and corporate crime: Discerning readings* (pp. 135–153). Long Grove: Waveland.

Sipley, J. (2011). For-profit education and federal funding: Bad outcomes for students and taxpayers. *Rutgers Law Review, 64*, 267–293.

Spurgeon, W. A., & Fagan, T. (1981). Criminal liability for life-endangering corporate conduct. *Journal of Criminal Law & Criminology, 72*(2), 400–433.

Surette, R. (2011). *Media, crime, and criminal justice: Images, realities, and policies* (4th ed.). Belmont, CA: Wadsworth Cengage Learning.

Sutherland, E. (1949). *White collar crime*. New York: Dryden Press.

Taxpayers Against Fraud (2012). *FY 2012 is record year for FCA recoveries*. Retrieved from taf.org/blog/fy-2012-record-year-fca-recoveries.

Thomas, R., Palmiter, A., & Cotter, J. (2012). Dodd-Frank's say on pay: Will it lead to a greater role for shareholders in corporate governance? *Cornell Law Review, 97*, 1213–1266.

Truman, J., & Planty, M. (2012). *Criminal victimization, 2011*. Bureau of Justice Statistics Bulletin. Washington: Department of Justice.

United States v. Arthur Andersen, 374 F. 3d 281 (2004).

United States v. Stein, 495 F. Supp. 2d 390 (2007).

Unnever, J., Benson, M., & Cullen, F. (2008). Public support for getting tough on corporate crime: Racial and political divides. *Journal of Research in Crime and Delinquency, 45*(2), 163–190.

U.S. Department of Justice (July 2, 2012a). *GlaxoSmithKline to plead guilty and pay $3 billion to resolve fraud allegations and failure to report safety data*. Office of Public Affairs. Retrieved from www.justice.gov/opa/pr/2012/July/12-civ-842.html.

U.S. Department of Justice (December 4, 2012b). *Justice Department recovers nearly $5 billion in False Claims Act cases in fiscal year 2012*. Office of Public Affairs. Retrieved from www.justice.gov/opa/pr/2012/December/12-ag-1439.html.

Vardi, N. (2013). *Did Obama and Congress use National Security Fears to gut the Stock Act?*. Retrieved on July 15, 2013 at forbes.com/sites/nathanvardi/2013/04/21/did-obama-and-congress-use-national-security-fears-to-gut-the-stock-act/.

Wray, C., & Hur, R. (2006). Corporate criminal prosecution in a post-Enron world: The Thompson memo in theory and practice. *American Criminal Law Review, 43*(3), 1095–1188.

CHAPTER 20

Ethics and Criminal Justice Research

Belinda R. McCarthy, Robin J. King, Michael Bush

All areas of life contain ethical dilemmas, and the field of research is no exception. A number of concerns related to the professional behavior of academic researchers have made newspaper headlines, stirred government inquiries, and ultimately raised questions about what is considered appropriate within the research process. Academic researchers have been accused of such acts as falsifying data to obtain additional research funding and fabricating or misrepresenting results in order to get their research published. Even celebrated researchers have been found to have fabricated some or all of the research upon which their scholarship is based (Bhattacharjee, 2013).

One of the most notorious cases in recent times involved Diederik Stapel, a psychologist whose research demonstrated that exposure to litter and graffiti makes people more likely to commit small crimes (*Los Angeles Times*, 2011). Motivated by a desire to continue to produce clear and consistent results that he believed would be more readily published, his efforts at deception were extensive and elaborate, and lasted for many years. His efforts compromised the scholarship of the graduate students he supervised as well as his own integrity.

The issue of research fabrication and misrepresentation in academic publications is an area that merits considerable concern. Published research has the potential to influence criminal justice policy and planning (Garrison, 2009) as well as practice. The strategy of developing guidelines for practice based on research findings, often referred to as "evidence-based practice," is increasingly utilized in the human services professions including corrections. Decisions related to community safety and offender supervision are being made based on research that has identified "a few core principles [that] stand out as proven risk reduction strategies" (National Crime Information Center, 2013, p. 3).

Issues of plagiarism and theft of data may also arise during the process of publishing research results. Sociology faculty once levied such vitriolic charges and counter-charges against their department colleagues that a dispute at Texas A&M University escalated to a degree that required investigation by the university, the National Science Foundation, and the American Sociological Association (*Chronicle of Higher Education*, 1999, p. A18).

One might think that scientific endeavors, with their objective and unbiased approach to the world, would create fewer dilemmas than other occupational activities. Although most researchers are not faced with the same kind of corrupting influences confronting street-level criminal justice officials, the pressures of "grantsmanship" and publication provide significant motivations for researchers to engage in unethical behaviors. The dilemmas of working with human participants in a political environment can be equally challenging. In addition, the goal of scientific purity and unbiased objectivity may be corrupting, because adherence to these perspectives may encourage researchers to put scientific objectives before their concern for the welfare of others; namely, those whom researchers will collect data from or about.

This chapter examines the nature of ethical dilemmas confronting the criminal justice researcher. To a large degree these problems are comparable to the difficulties faced by other social scientists. However, additional problems may arise as a result of the particular research focus on deviance and law-breaking.

ETHICAL CONSIDERATIONS INVOLVING WORK WITH HUMAN PARTICIPANTS

Researchers typically work with other individuals when conducting research. Most notable are the individuals from or about whom they will collect data. These individuals are often referred to as research "subjects." Considering that the study of ethics focuses on how individuals treat one another, one could argue whether it is ethical to apply such a label within the research process. Could referring to an individual as a research "subject" have any influence on how researchers treat those individuals within the process? Could the term "subject" influence how individuals engage with the researcher? Furthermore, could such a term influence an individual's responses? Accordingly, this chapter will utilize the term "participant" rather than "subject" when referring to individuals who provide information to researchers.

Cook (1976) lists the following ethical considerations regarding research with human participants:

1. Involving people in research without their knowledge or consent.
2. Coercing people to participate.
3. Withholding from the participant the true nature of the research.
4. Deceiving the research participant.
5. Leading the research participants to commit acts that diminish their self-respect.
6. Violating the right to self-determination: research on behavior control and character change.
7. Exposing the research participant to physical or mental stress.
8. Invading the privacy of the research participant.
9. Withholding benefits from participants in control groups.
10. Failing to treat research participants fairly and to show them consideration and respect (p. 202).

INVOLVING PEOPLE IN RESEARCH WITHOUT THEIR KNOWLEDGE OR CONSENT

Ideally for gaining accurate information, the best way to study human behavior is to observe people in a natural setting without their knowledge. Self-reported descriptions of behavior may be unreliable because people forget or are uncertain about their actions. Furthermore, most people might tell you that they would attempt to return a lost wallet, but a hidden camera focused on a wallet lying on the sidewalk might reveal very different behaviors. People who know they are being watched often act differently, especially when unethical, deviant, or criminal behaviors are involved. For these reasons, researchers may prefer to study deviance through direct observation, which involves listening as well as visual examination.

At times, the observer participates to some degree in the activities being studied. For example, Whyte's (1955) study of street-corner society involved just this form of participant observation, as Whyte resided with an Italian family in the community where he was conducting research. Likewise, Humphreys's (1970) examination of homosexual behavior in public restrooms, Short and Strodtbeck's (1965) study of delinquency in Chicago, and Cohen's (1980) observations of female prostitutes in New York all involved the observation of persons who did not consent to becoming research participants.

Research efforts about persons on the other side of the criminal justice process have also been undertaken without their knowledge or consent. Meltzer (1953) studied jury deliberations through the use of hidden microphones as part of a growing research interest regarding the judicial process. The significance of discretion in the criminal justice process and the hidden nature of most decision making provide support for arguments calling for greater use of such techniques. These efforts are generally favored when the desire is to understand how police, prosecutors, correctional personnel, jury members, or other persons involved in the process of criminal justice carry out their duties.

The ethical dilemma, however, is a complicated one: Is the value of the research such that persons should be turned into study "participants" without their permission? The conditions of the research are extremely important to this deliberation. If the behaviors being studied would have occurred without the researcher's intervention, the lack of consent seems less troubling. Such studies involve little personal cost to unknowing subjects. Unobtrusive research that involves only behaviors that occur in public view is also less questionable, because the invasion of personal privacy is not at issue.

What about experiments that create situations to which participants must react, such as those involving a "lost" wallet? Or a study of witness response to crimes that involve an actor or actress screaming and running from an apparent assailant down a crowded street? Observation might be the only method for determining how citizens would truly respond, but the personal cost of being studied could be considerable.

Not only may such research be troubling for the persons involved, but when sensitive activities that are normally considered private or confidential are the subject of study, additional problems can arise. Cook (1976) reports that Meltzer encountered such difficulties in his study of jury deliberations:

> Members of Congress reacted to the jury recording as a threat to fundamental institutions. When the news of the study came out, a congressional investigation resulted. Following the investigation legislation was passed establishing a fine of a thousand dollars and imprisonment for a year for whoever might attempt to record the proceedings of any jury in the United States while the jury is deliberating or voting (p. 205).

Although the response might be less severe, one could anticipate similar objections to the taping of discussions involving police personnel, attorneys, judges, correctional officials, and probation and parole authorities.

COERCING PEOPLE TO PARTICIPATE

You have probably received a questionnaire in the mail at some time that offered some small incentive for completing the form—perhaps a free pen or a dollar bill. Similarly, college students are often provided a grade incentive for participation in their instructor's research. Dillman et al. (2009) explains this process from the perspective of social exchange theory—that such incentives are designed to establish trust between researcher and participant. The researcher both demonstrates and encourages trust by providing the incentive before data collection. These practices are common, reflecting the assumption that people who are compensated for their efforts are more likely to participate in research projects than those who receive nothing.

When, though, does compensation become **coercion**? When is the researcher justified to compel participation? The issues here involve not only the nature and quantity of the incentives that can be ethically provided without creating an undue influence, but also the concern of having the freedom not to participate.

The person receiving the questionnaire in the mail is free to keep the compensation and toss away the form. Students may be similarly free not to participate in their instructor's research, but the instructor's power over the grading process might make students feel compelled to participate. Thus, the relationship between students and researcher as teacher can be particularly coercive.

One example of the coercive nature of this relationship can be seen when researchers, acting as teachers, *require* student participation in a research project as part of their course grade (Moreno, 1998). Again, there is a discernible difference in power that could eliminate students' capacity to refuse participation in the research project. This problem becomes especially critical when research participants are vulnerable to coercion. Although students might be considered a captive population, jail and prison inmates are clearly some of the most vulnerable research participants.

In the early 1990s, research on prisoners was allowed under federal regulations. In order to pass federal guidelines, research on prisoners had to take one of four forms: (1) studies of treatment or therapies that were implemented with the goal of helping prisoners; (2) low-risk research examining inmate behavior and inmate criminality; (3) studies of correctional institutions; and (4) research that examines inmates as a class or group (Moreno, 1998). The standards by which prisoner or prison research was determined to be ethical would depend on the degree to which the research would ultimately benefit individual prisoners or prisoners as a class or group.

The history of inmate involvement in research is not a very proud one. For example, prisoners have been used as "guinea pigs" by pharmaceutical companies that set up laboratories at correctional institutions. For minimal compensation, or the possibility that participation might assist in gaining parole, inmates have participated in a variety of medical research projects. In the United States, the first use of inmates for medical experiments took place at the Mississippi state prison in 1914, when researchers attempted to discover the relationship between diet and the disease pellagra. The governor of Mississippi promised pardons to persons volunteering for the experiment. Another experiment in New York was completed in which eight prisoners were inoculated with a venereal infection in order to test possible cures. In exchange for their voluntary participation, the subjects, in their own words, "got syphilis and a carton of cigarettes" (Geis, 1980, p. 226). Today, prisoners are forbidden to engage in such research efforts, but inmates are still frequently required to participate in efforts to evaluate the impact of correctional treatment, work, or education programs.

It might seem that the easiest way out of this dilemma is to simply rely on volunteers for research participants. However, volunteers are different from others simply by virtue of their **willingness to participate**; at a minimum, they are more highly motivated than non-volunteers. Also, relying on their participation might produce more positive outcomes than the intervention alone would merit. Ideally, the researcher aspires to obtain a group of participants who are representative of the actual persons to whom results of the study will be applied.

Freedom of choice is highly valued in our society, but how much freedom of choice should prisoners have? Before denying a participant the opportunity to refuse participation, it should be clear that the overall value of the research outweighs the harm of coercion. In this consideration, the nature of the participation must be carefully evaluated—coercion to participate in weekly group therapy is quite different from coercion to participate in eight weeks of paramilitary training. One must also assess whether coercion is the only or best means available to obtain research results. Confronting this dilemma requires a balancing of such research matters with a concern for individuals' rights.

WITHHOLDING FROM THE PARTICIPANT THE TRUE NATURE OF THE RESEARCH

Ethical codes of conduct require researchers to disclose the nature of their research to potential respondents prior to data collection. Such information is typically communicated within an **informed consent** document. The informed consent document explains the general purpose of the research inquiry, the perceived importance and usefulness of participation, and how the data will be both collected and used. However, even in the most benign circumstances, written notification may deter further action. Furthermore, full and complete disclosure has the added potential of influencing responses. Often more accurate assessments are achieved when the participant believes that one aspect of his or her behavior is the focus when the research interest is actually elsewhere.

Researchers are understandably reluctant to provide too much information in this regard, especially in the early stages of a project, when the need to develop trust and a willingness to cooperate are especially important. From a research perspective, fully disclosing the purpose of the research could severely limit findings of the study. For example, a participant's mindfulness of being observed can seriously alter his or her behaviors. Specifically, research participants are typically less willing and likely to admit to undesirable attitudes or behaviors if they know they are being studied (Singleton & Straits, 1988). This **social desirability effect** can produce error in the data collected from the research (DeVellis, 2003; Fowler, 2002). Ethically speaking, informed consent should precede involvement in the study, so that individuals are given a meaningful opportunity to decline further participation.

Balancing research interests and respect for human dignity requires that participants be informed about all aspects of the research that might reasonably influence their willingness to participate. Any risks that participants may expect to face should be fully discussed. Geis (1980) recommends that researchers remember the example of Walter Reed, who participated as a subject in his own experiments on yellow fever because he could ask no one to undergo anything that he himself was not willing to experience.

DECEIVING THE RESEARCH PARTICIPANT

A key ethical dilemma within social science research is the issue of deception (Warren & Karner, 2005). Perhaps the most flagrant example of deception in criminological research is provided by Humphreys' (1970) study, *Tearoom Trade*. Humphreys assumed the role of lookout in public restrooms so that strangers unaware of his research objective could engage in uninterrupted homosexual activity. After observing the individuals in the restroom, Humphreys copied down the automobile license tags of the individuals he observed and obtained their addresses from police. Later, he went to their homes, explaining that he was conducting a health survey. Humphreys then asked the respondents many personal questions that became part of his research on public homosexual conduct.

■ Learn More on the Internet

Go to web.missouri.edu/~bondesonw/Laud.html to read a brief description of Humphreys' study (1970), *Tearoom Trade*.   ■

The rationale for deception emphasizes the importance of research and the difficulties of obtaining accurate information through other means. Deception may be considered an affront to individual autonomy and self-respect or an occasionally legitimate means to be used in service of a higher value (Cook, 1976). All deceptive acts are not equal. There are differences between active lying and a conscious failure to provide all available information. The researcher must evaluate the nature of the research and weigh its value against the potential impact the deception may have on the integrity of participants.

The degree to which privacy is invaded and the sensitivity of the behaviors involved are important considerations. Moreover, the possibility of harming the research participant should be considered before attempting to deceive the participant. If the nature of the research is potentially harmful, the research participant should be able to fully assess whether he or she wishes to risk participating in the study. One alternative to deception is to provide only general information about the research project prior to the experiment and offer full disclosure after the research has been completed. Another technique relies on participants to role-play their behavior after the nature of the research project has been explained. There is mixed evidence, however, on the effectiveness of this technique (Cook, 1976). Contrary to deception, establishing trust with potential research participants may also increase both participation and the truthfulness of the information received.

■ Learn More on the Internet

Go to www.experiment-resources.com/deception-and-research.html and consider the following questions: What are the ethical concerns for the studies mentioned on the website? What could the researchers have done to alleviate these concerns?   ■

LEADING THE RESEARCH PARTICIPANTS TO COMMIT ACTS THAT DIMINISH THEIR SELF-RESPECT

Research participants are sometimes experimentally induced into states of extreme passivity or extreme aggression. Efforts provoking participants to lie, cheat, steal, and harm have proven very effective. Cook (1976) describes a study in which students were recruited to participate in a theft of records from a business firm. The inducements described included an opportunity to perform a patriotic service for a department of federal government. A substantial number of students were significantly encouraged to take part in the theft, although ultimately the burglary was never completed.

Research conducted by Haney, Banks, and Zimbardo (1973) involved the simulation of prison conditions, with 21 participants assuming the roles of prisoner or guard. After a very short time, the guards began behaving in an aggressive and physically threatening manner. Their use of power became self-aggrandizing and self-perpetuating. As a result, the prisoners quickly experienced a loss of personal identity, exhibiting flattened affect and dependency; eventually they were emotionally emasculated by the encounters.

Despite planning to observe the simulation for a two-week period, the extreme nature of the participants' responses to the guards encouraged termination of the project after only six days. The debriefing sessions that followed the research study yielded the following comments:

Guards

"They (the prisoners) seemed to lose touch with the reality of the experiment—they took me so seriously."

"... I didn't interfere with any of the guards' actions. Usually if what they were doing bothered me, I would walk out and take another duty."

"... looking back, I am impressed by how little I felt for them..."

"They (the prisoners) didn't see it as an experiment. It was real, and they were fighting to keep their identity. But we were always there to show them just who was boss."

"I was tired of seeing the prisoners in their rags and smelling the strong odors of their bodies that filled the cells. I watched them tear at each other, on orders given by us."

"... Acting authoritatively can be fun. Power can be a great pleasure."

"... During the inspection, I went to cell 2 to mess up a bed which the prisoner had made and he grabbed me, screaming that he had just made it, and he wasn't going to let me mess it up. He grabbed my throat, and although he was laughing, I was pretty scared. I lashed out with my stick and hit him in the chin (although not very hard), and when I freed myself I became angry."

Prisoners

"...The way we were made to degrade ourselves really brought us down, and that's why we all sat docile towards the end of the experiment."

"... I realize now (after it's over) that no matter how together I thought I was inside my head, my prison behavior was often less under my control than I realized. No matter how open, friendly and helpful I was with other prisoners I was still operating as an isolated, self-centered person, being rational rather than compassionate."

"... I began to feel I was losing my identity, that the person I call _____, the person who volunteered to get me into this prison (because it was a prison to me, it still is a prison to me, I don't regard it as an experiment or a simulation...) was distant from me, was remote until finally I wasn't that person; I was 416. I was really my number, and 416 was really going to have to decide what to do."

"I learned that people can easily forget that others are human."

In Milgram's (1974) research, participants showed "blind obedience" to a white-coated "researcher" who ordered them to provide what appeared to be electric shocks of increasing intensity to persons who failed to respond correctly to a series of questions. Although they were emotionally upset, the participants continued to follow their instructions as the "shocked" individuals screamed in agony. Follow-up research revealed that participants in Milgram's study experienced only minor and temporary disturbances (Ring, Wallston, & Corey, 1970). One might argue that some participants benefited from the project as a result of their greater self-awareness, but the fact that the educational experiences occurred without their initial understanding or consent raises ethical concerns.

To what degree should participants be asked to unknowingly engage in activities that may damage their self-esteem? Again, the researcher is required to engage in a balancing act, reconciling research objectives and the availability of alternative methods with a concern for the integrity of research participants. At a minimum, such research efforts should provide means to address any possible harm to those involved, including debriefings at the conclusion of the research and follow-up counseling as needed. See Box 20.1.

BOX 20.1 THE LUCIFER EFFECT

Philip Zimbardo is most commonly known for his role as researcher in the Stanford Prison Experiment. Zimbardo's more recent research interests focus on *The Lucifer Effect: Understanding How Good People Turn Evil*. How would you design a research project to study this particular topic?

Go to the following link to visit the homepage for Professor Philip G. Zimbardo: zimbardo.com/lucifer.

html. At the top of the link, click "Enter Here" to enter Dr Zimbardo's website. Next, click on the link to the right titled "Prison Experiment" to view a slideshow about the experiment. What are your thoughts about this study? What could the researchers have done differently to protect research participants?

VIOLATING THE RIGHT TO SELF-DETERMINATION: RESEARCH ON BEHAVIOR CONTROL AND CHARACTER CHANGE

The film *A Clockwork Orange* provides an excellent illustration of the dilemmas of behavior-modifying research and violating the **right to self-determination**. In the film, a thoroughly violent and irredeemable individual named Alex is subjected to therapy that requires him to observe violent acts on film while simultaneously ingesting chemicals that make him physically ill. After a while, the violent acts Alex has observed make him sick as well, and he is changed from a violent individual to one who avoids violence at all cost, including that which is required for his own self-defense. At the end of the film, the "powers that be" decide to reverse his treatment for political reasons.

Although there is little possibility of behavior modifications being used to exact such effect in the near future, the question remains: To what extent should experimental efforts be made to alter human behavior against the will of the participant? Remembering the vulnerability of the inmate to coercion (in the film, the character Alex participated in the violence control therapy only because he thought it would help him gain early release), it becomes clear that the greatest desire to use behavior control strategies will be evident in areas involving those persons most vulnerable to coercion—criminals and persons with problems of substance abuse. Although research on crime prevention and control generally has only the most laudable aims, it should be remembered that it is often well-intentioned actions that pose the greatest threat to individual freedoms.

EXPOSING THE RESEARCH PARTICIPANT TO PHYSICAL OR MENTAL STRESS

How would you evaluate the ethics of the following research project: an evaluation of a treatment program in which persons convicted of drunk driving are required to watch and listen to hours of films depicting gory automobile accidents, followed by horrifying emergency room visits and interviews with grieving relatives? Would it matter whether actions of the drunk drivers had contributed to similar accidents? When thinking about your answer, consider whether the viewers deserve the "punishment" of what they are forced to observe on film.

This not-so-hypothetical scenario raises a difficult issue: Is it acceptable for a research project to engage in activities that punish and perhaps harm participants? To test various outcomes, participants in different settings have been exposed to events provoking feelings of horror, shock, threatened sexual identity, personal failure, fear, and emotional shock (Cook, 1976). Some of the participants in Haney, Banks, and Zimbardo's study and Milgram's research were clearly stressed by their experiences. To what extent is it acceptable to engage in these practices for the objective of scientific inquiry?

In most situations, it is impossible to observe human reactions such as those described above in their natural settings, so researchers feel justified in creating experiments that produce these reactions. The extent of possible harm raises ethical dilemmas; however, theoretically there is no limit to what might be contrived for creating "researchable" reactions. Thus, balancing research objectives with a respect for human participants is a delicate undertaking, requiring researchers to scrutinize their objectives and the value of their proposed studies dispassionately.

INVADING THE PRIVACY OF THE RESEARCH PARTICIPANT AND MAINTAINING CONFIDENTIALITY

Privacy and confidentiality are related concerns. Ethical questions arise from research that invades an individual's **privacy** without his or her consent. Consider information about participants that has been obtained for reasons other than research (e.g., the development of a criminal history file); there are questions about the extent to which such data should be released to researchers. Some records are more sensitive than others in this regard, depending on how easily the offender's identity can be obtained, as well as the quantity and nature of the information recorded. Even when consent has been given and the information has been gathered expressly for research purposes, maintaining the confidentiality of responses may be a difficult matter when the responses contain information of a sensitive or illegal nature.

Respondents are most likely to participate in research projects when they are allowed to participate anonymously—that is, when it is impossible for the researcher to associate any particular data with the individual who provided that data (Dillman et al., 2009; Neuman, 2004). Anonymity is not always possible; therefore, researchers typically offer research participants the protection of confidentiality.

Confidentiality is especially important in the study of crime and deviance. Participants will generally not agree to provide information about criminal and deviant behaviors unless their responses are to remain confidential. This is sometimes a more difficult task than it appears. Sometimes it is important to be able to identify a research participant so that his or her responses can be linked to other sources of data that he or she has provided. For example, institutionalized delinquents might be asked in confidence about their involvement in drug use and other forms of misconduct during confinement. An important part of the research might involve gathering background information from the offender's institutional files to determine what types of offenders are most likely to be involved in institutional misconduct. To do this, the individual's confidential responses need to be identifiable; therefore, complete anonymity is unfeasible and confidentiality becomes increasingly important.

As long as only dispassionate researchers have access to this information, there may be no problems. Difficulties arise when third parties, especially criminal justice authorities, become interested in the research responses. Then the issue becomes one of protecting the data (and the offender) from officials who have the power to invoke the criminal justice process. However, the relationship between researcher and research participant is not privileged; researchers can be called upon to provide information to courts.

One response to this dilemma is to store identifying information in a remote place; some researchers have even recommended sending sensitive information out of the country. Lewis Yablonsky, a criminologist/practitioner, while testifying in defense of Gridley White (one of Yablonsky's main informants in his study about hippies), was asked by the judge nine times if he had witnessed Gridley smoking marijuana. Yablonsky refused to answer because of the rights guaranteed him in the Fifth Amendment of the U.S. Constitution. Although he was not legally sanctioned, he said the incident was humiliating and suggested that researchers should have guarantees of immunity (Wolfgang, 1982).

It is also important that researchers prepare their presentations of research findings in a manner that ensures that particular responses of individuals cannot be discerned. Presentation of only aggregate findings was especially important for Wolfgang (1982) when he reinterviewed persons in a birth cohort who were included in his earlier study of delinquency. His follow-up consisted of hour-long interviews with approximately 600 youths. The participants were asked many personal questions, including questions about their involvement in delinquency and crime. Four of his respondents admitted committing criminal homicide, and almost 75 admitted to forcible rape. Many other serious crimes were also described, for which none of the participants had been arrested.

At the time of the research, all of the respondents were orally assured that the results of the research would remain confidential, but Wolfgang raises a number of ethical questions regarding this practice. Should written consent forms have been provided to participants, detailing the nature of the research? Wolfgang concludes that such forms would have raised more questions than they answered. Could a court order impound the records? Could persons attempting to protect the data be prosecuted for their actions? Could the data be successfully concealed?

The general willingness to protect participants who admit to serious crimes also requires close ethical scrutiny. Wolfgang (1982) takes the traditional scientific stance on this issue, proposing that such information belongs to science. Since the information would not have been discovered without the research effort, its protection neither helps nor hinders police. The ethical judgment here requires a weighting of interests—the importance of scientific research balanced against society's interest in capturing a particular individual.

It should be noted that if researchers were to inform on their participants routinely, it is likely that all future research relying on self-reports could be jeopardized. The issue at hand is not simply that of the value of a particular study, but the value of all research utilizing personal disclosure. Researchers are generally advised not to undertake such research unless they feel comfortable about protecting their sources. This requires that all research involving the use of confidential information provide for controlled access to the data and protect the information from unauthorized searches, inadvertent access, and the compulsory legal process (Cook, 1976).

WITHHOLDING BENEFITS TO PARTICIPANTS IN CONTROL GROUPS

The necessity of excluding some potential beneficiaries from initial program participation arises whenever a classical experimental design is used to evaluate a program. This research design requires random assignment, or **randomization**, of participants to experimental and control groups. Research participants in the control group are excluded from the program or receive "standard" treatment rather than "experimental" treatment.

In a program evaluation, it is important that some participants receive the benefits of the program while others do not, to determine whether the outcomes observed are the direct result of the experimental intervention and not something else (e.g., participant enthusiasm or background characteristics). It is important for those who receive the program/treatment (the experimental group) and those who do not (the control group) to be as identical in the aggregate as possible, so that a clear assessment of program impact, untainted by variation in the characteristics of participants, can be obtained. The best way to ensure that experimental and control groups are identical is randomization, which requires that every participant have an equal chance to be assigned to either the experimental or control group.

In many ways, randomization may be more ethical than standard practices based on good intentions. Geis (1980) reports:

> For most of us, it would be unthinkable that a sample of armed robbers be divided into two groups on the basis of random assignment—one group to spend 10 years in prison, the second to receive a sentence of 2 years on probation. Nonetheless, at a federal judicial conference, after examining an elaborate presentence report concerning a bank robber, 17 judges said they would have imprisoned the man, while 10 indicated they favored probation. Those voting for imprisonment set sentences ranging from 6 months to 15 years (p. 221).

Although randomization is inherently fair, it often appears less so to the participants involved. Surveys of prisoners have indicated that need, merit, and "first come, first served" are more acceptable criteria than a method that the offenders equated with gambler's luck (Erez, 1986). Consider Morris's (1966) description of "the burglar's nightmare":

> If eighty burglars alike in all relevant particulars were assigned randomly to experimental and control groups, forty each, with

the experimental to be released six months or a year earlier than they ordinarily would be and the control released at their regularly appointed time, how would the burglar assigned to the control group respond? It is unfair, unjust, unethical, he could say, for me to be put into the control group. If people like me, he might complain, are being released early, I too, deserve the same treatment.

Cited in Erez (1986, p. 394)

Program personnel are also frequently unhappy with randomization because it fails to utilize their clinical skills in the selection of appropriate candidates for intervention. Extending this line of thought, consider the likely response of judges requested to sentence burglary offenders randomly to prison or probation. While this might be the best method of determining the effectiveness of these sanctions, the judicial response, and perhaps community response as well, would likely be less than enthusiastic. This is because it is assumed, often without any evidence, that standard practices are achieving some reasonable objectives, such as individualizing justice or preventing crime.

Randomization is acceptable under law, because its use is reasonably related to a governmental objective; that is, testing the effectiveness of a program intervention (Erez, 1986). Though randomization is important and appropriate from a methodological perspective, the participants who, by chance, end up in the control group are often denied treatment, or possibly services, that could be of the utmost importance to their lives. The Minneapolis Domestic Violence Experiment is a classic example of how those persons involved in the control group were denied potential law enforcement interventions that could have benefitted them. Box 20.2 is a description of the Sherman and Berk's (1984) study, which looked at various responses to domestic violence.

BOX 20.2 THE MINNEAPOLIS DOMESTIC VIOLENCE EXPERIMENT

Domestic violence was beginning to be recognized as a major public affairs and criminal justice problem. Victim advocates were demanding the automatic arrest of domestic violence offenders. However, there was no empirical research that showed that arresting domestic violence offenders deterred future acts of domestic violence. Thus, Sherman and Berk, sponsored by funding from the National Institute of Justice, designed a randomized experiment that looked at the effects of arrest on domestic violence.

Sherman and Berk enlisted the help of the Minneapolis Police Department. When on misdemeanor domestic

violence calls, the police were to respond to the call depending on the random call response they were assigned. There were three responses with which the police could respond to the misdemeanor domestic violence call: arrest; removal of batterer from the premises without an arrest; or counsel the batterer and leave the premises. While the initial findings of this research indicated that arresting domestic violence offenders reduced the incidence of future incidents, the methodology and ethics of this experiment have been heavily scrutinized. The victims of the misdemeanor domestic violence certainly did not

Continued...

> ### BOX 20.2 THE MINNEAPOLIS DOMESTIC VIOLENCE EXPERIMENT
> *Continued*
>
> consent to the randomized assignment of response to the situation. Thus, not only were potential benefits withheld from certain women, some victims could have been placed at greater risk as a result of the random treatment. While the benevolent intentions behind this research agenda were admirable, the implementation of the experiment and the variable being randomized
>
> (i.e., type of response to domestic violence) should have been further considered before implementation of the research.
>
> _____
>
> *Based on Sherman, L. W., & Berk, R. A. (1984). The specific deterrent effects of arrest for domestic assault.* American Sociological Review, *49(2), 261–272.*

Randomization does produce winners and losers. Of critical importance in weighing the consequences of randomization are the differences in treatment experienced by those in experimental and control groups. The Federal Judicial Center (1981) highlights six factors that are relevant:

1. *Significance of the interest affected.* Early release is of much greater consequence than a change of institutional diet.
2. *Extent of difference.* Six months' early release is of greater significance than one week's early release.
3. *Comparison of the disparity with standard treatment.* If both experimental and control group treatment are an improvement over standard treatment, then the discrepancy between the experimental and control group is of less concern.
4. *Whether disparity reflects differences in qualifications of participants.* If the disparity is reasonably related to some characteristic of the participants, the denial of benefits to the control group is less significant.
5. *Whether the experimental treatment is harmful or beneficial to participants compared with the treatment they would otherwise receive.* A program that assigns members of the experimental group to six weeks of "boot camp" may be more demanding of inmates than the standard treatment of six months' incarceration.
6. *Whether participation is mandatory or voluntary.* Voluntary participation mitigates the concern of denial of benefit, while coercion exacerbates the dilemma (pp. 31–40).

Similar to the management of other ethical dilemmas, a substantial effort is required to balance values of human decency and justice with the need for accurate information about intervention effectiveness. Problems arise not in the extreme cases of disparity but in more routine circumstances. Consider the following example: How do we judge a situation in which a foundation grant permits attorneys to be supplied for all cases being heard by a juvenile court in which attorneys have previously appeared only in rare instances?

A fundamental study hypothesis may be that the presence of an attorney tends to result in a more favorable disposition for the client. This idea may be tested by comparing dispositions prior to the beginning of the experiment with those ensuing subsequently, though it would be more satisfactory (from a research perspective) to supply attorneys to a sample of the cases and withhold them from the remainder, in order to calculate in a more experimentally uncontaminated manner the differences between the outcomes in the two situations.

The matter becomes more complex if the researchers should desire to determine what particular attorney role is the most efficacious in the juvenile court. They may suspect that an attorney who acts as a friend of the court, knowingly taking its viewpoint as *parens patriae*, and attempting to interpret the court's interest to his or her client, will produce more desirable results than one who doggedly challenges the courtroom procedure and the judge's interpretation of fact, picks at the probation report, raises constant objections, and fights for his or her client as he would in a criminal court. What results are "more desirable" (Geis, 1980, pp. 222–223)?

It could be contended that little is really known about how attorney roles influence dispositions and that, without the project, no one would have any kind of representation. Over the long term, all juveniles stand to benefit. On the other hand, it could be argued that it is wrong to deprive anyone of the best judgment of his or her attorney by requiring a particular legal approach. What if there are only enough funds to supply one-half of the juveniles with attorneys anyway? Is randomization more or less fair than trying to decide which cases "need" representation the most?

Randomization imposes a special ethical burden because it purposefully counters efforts to determine the best course of action with the element of chance. The practice is justifiable because the pursuit of knowledge is a desirable objective—as long as the overall benefits outweigh the risks. The balancing of risks and benefits is complicated by the fact that judgments are often made in a context of ambiguity, attempting to predict the benefits of an intervention that is being tested precisely because its impact is unknown.

The Federal Judicial Center (1981) recommends that program evaluations should be considered only when certain threshold conditions are met: (1) the status quo warrants substantial improvements or is of doubtful effectiveness; (2) there must be significant uncertainty about the value or effectiveness of the innovation; (3) information needed to clarify that uncertainty must be feasibly obtainable by the program experimentation but not readily obtainable by other means; and (4) the information sought must pertain directly to the decision whether to adopt the proposed innovation on a general, nonexperimental basis (p. 7).

Several conditions lessen the ethical burdens of evaluative research. Random assignment is especially acceptable when resources are scarce and demand for the benefit is high. Additionally, denying benefits to the control group is acceptable when members of the control group can participate in the program at a later date. Finally, discrepancies between the treatment of experimental and control groups are less noteworthy when the groups are geographically separated (Federal Judicial Center, 1981).

Experimental studies on the effectiveness of "hot spot policing" have been particularly well received because they utilized place-based randomization rather than person-based randomization (Weisburd, 2005). This place-based approach was developed "not because of ethical or practical concerns, but rather as a direct response to the theoretical innovations in criminology and criminal justice" (Weisburd, 2005, p. 223). Routine activities theory promoted a situational approach to crime prevention; the goal became reducing opportunities to commit crime in specific areas, as opposed to focusing on the individuals who might commit a crime. In these studies, benefits were not denied to the control group—preventive policing continued to be implemented in the control areas and "higher dosages" of preventive patrol were utilized in the intervention sites.

FAILING TO TREAT RESEARCH PARTICIPANTS FAIRLY AND TO SHOW THEM CONSIDERATION AND RESPECT

The basic tenets of professionalism require that researchers treat participants with courtesy and fulfill the variety of commitments they make to participants. For example, in an effort to obtain cooperation, participants are often promised a follow-up report on the findings of the research, although such reports may be forgotten once the study has been completed. Participants also are often led to believe that they will receive some personal benefit from the research. This may be one of the more difficult obligations to fulfill. For some, the opportunity to be heard and to share their experiences will provide some benefit. More important is the notion that researchers should treat the individuals from whom they collect data with respect.

Researchers need to treat their human participants with constant recognition of their integrity and their contributions to the research endeavor. This is especially important when participants are powerless and vulnerable. Although such treatment may be a time-consuming chore, it is the only ethical way to practice scientific research. It may also be the best way to acquire the information sought.

BALANCING SCIENTIFIC AND ETHICAL CONCERNS

This discussion has emphasized the importance of balancing concerns for research participants against the potential benefits of a research inquiry. Cook (1976) identifies the following potential benefits of a research project:

1. Advances in scientific theories that contribute to a general understanding of human behavior.
2. Advances in knowledge of practical value to society.
3. Gains for the research participant, such as increased understanding, satisfaction in making a contribution to science or to the solution of social problems, needed money or special privileges, knowledge of social science or of research methods, and so on (p. 235).

The potential costs to research participants can be considerable, and it is often difficult for the researcher to be objective in assessing such issues. For these reasons, many professional associations have established guidelines and procedures for ethical research conduct. Because little active monitoring occurs in social science research, the professional is honor-bound to follow these guidelines.

INSTITUTIONAL REVIEW BOARDS AND SETTING ETHICAL STANDARDS

How are the ethical standards being set within the criminal justice community, and how and to what degree are ethics being taught in criminology and criminal justice academic settings? To ensure that their faculty follow acceptable procedures (and to protect themselves from liability), universities have established Institutional Review Boards (IRBs) to scrutinize each research project that involves human participants. Specifically, a university's IRB reviews each submitted research project prior to implementation. The purpose of these reviews is to ensure the protection of human participants within the research design. IRBs are generally incapable of providing direct monitoring of research projects, so again the responsibility for ethical conduct falls on the researcher. IRBs serve a valuable function and often are the primary source for ethical guidance and standards for the criminal justice academic researcher (McSkimming, Sever, & King, 2000).

McSkimming, Sever, and King (2000) analyzed 11 research methods textbooks frequently used in criminal justice and criminology courses to determine the types of ethical issues that were covered and the extent to which they were addressed. The authors found that there was no collective format being utilized in the major criminal justice texts regarding ethics in criminal justice research methods. Furthermore, the significance and positive functions of institutional review boards were rarely mentioned. Of further concern was the noticeable absence of some important ethical topics related to the dissemination of information into the criminal justice audience, such as "plagiarism, fabrication of data, authorship rank, and ethical considerations in journal editing and grant-writing" (p. 58). It is imperative that graduate students, publishing professors, and other disseminators of information within the criminal justice discipline have some instruction or gauge with which to measure ethical standards.

■ Learn More on the Internet

Go to the following links from university websites to review the Institutional Review Board (IRB) process:

www.etsu.edu/irb/

www.iup.edu/page.aspx?id=6637

rgsrs.nku.edu/research/rgc/irb/irb.html

What similarities do you see within each of the IRB processes? Are there any differences between the various IRB processes?   ■

ETHICAL/POLITICAL CONSIDERATIONS

Applied social research—that is, research that examines the effectiveness of social policies and programs—carries with it additional ethical responsibilities. Such research influences the course of human events in a direct fashion—occupations, education, future opportunities, and deeply held values and beliefs often are affected by the outcomes. Researchers must be prepared to deal with a variety of pressures and demands as they undertake the practice and dissemination of research.

According to MacCoun (1998), some research topics are matters of eternal debate; examples include research about pornography (see Linz & Malamuth, 1993), gun control (see Nisbet, 2001), the death penalty (see Costanzo & White, 1994), and drug prohibition (see MacCoun, 1993; MacCoun & Reuter, 1997). In fact, on several occasions government officials have attempted to condemn or prohibit entire topics of research. One such effort attempted to discredit early studies reporting that some individuals diagnosed as alcoholics are able to engage in sustained drinking at less problematic levels (see Chiauzzi & Liljegren, 1993; Marlatt, Larimer, Baer, & Quigley, 1993). Other examples (as cited by MacCoun, 1998) include the cancellation of a National Institutes of Health-funded conference about genetic influences affecting violence (see Johnson, 1993), an effort to ban epidemiological research about gun violence by the Centers for Disease Control and Prevention (see Herbert, 1996, p. A15), and several attempts to prevent research about adolescent and adult sexual behavior (see Gardner & Wilcox, 1993; Miller, 1995). The private sector also engages in research censorship. Consider the actions of a pharmaceutical company that blocked publication of study results revealing the effectiveness of its drug and less expensive generic alternatives (see Dong, Hauck, Gambertoglio, Gee, & White, 1997; Rennie, 1997).

It is generally acknowledged that organizations asked to measure their own effectiveness often produce biased results. Crime statistics provide a notorious example of data used to show either an effective police department (falling crime figures) or a need for more resources (rising crime figures). Criminal justice researchers are often asked to study matters that are equally sensitive. For instance, a correctional treatment program found to be ineffective may lose its funding, or a study that reveals extensive use of plea bargaining may cost a prosecutor his or her election.

The truth can be complicated. A survey revealing the decline of drug use in the general population may prove troublesome for those lobbying for the establishment of more drug treatment facilities. The survey results may lead the public to believe the problem is diminishing while at the same time there is a substantial need for treatment facilities for indigent persons.

Such research has been known to produce unintended consequences. Consider the publication of selected results of a study on the effectiveness of correctional treatment programs (Martinson, 1974), which was used by many persons to justify limiting funds for education and treatment programs in correctional institutions. The research revealed that there was little evidence that correctional treatment programs were effective means of reducing recidivism (a finding that has been widely challenged). Rather than stimulating the development of more theoretically supported programs and rigorous evaluations of these efforts, the apparent product of the research was a decrease in the humaneness of conditions for confinement.

Research results can sometimes conflict with cherished beliefs. Studies of both preventive police patrol (Kelling, Page, Dieckman, & Brown, 1974) and detective investigations (Chaiken, Greenwood, & Petersilia, 1977) revealed that these practices were of little value to police; these practices were long assumed to be essential elements of effective law enforcement. Researchers can expect findings such as these to meet considerable resistance.

Researchers may be asked to utilize their skills and their aura of objectivity to provide an organization or agency with what it wants. When the group that pays the bills has a direct interest in the nature of the outcome, the pressures can be considerable. Wolfgang (1982) reports:

> I was once invited to do research by an organization whose views are almost completely antithetical to mine on the issue of gun control. Complete freedom and a considerable amount of money to explore

the relationship between gun control legislation and robbery were promised. I would not perform the research under those auspices. But the real clincher in the decision was that if the research produced conclusions opposite from that the organization wanted, the agency would not publish the results nor allow me to publish them. Perhaps their behavior, within their ideological framework, was not unethical. But within my framework, as a scientist who values freedom of publication as well as of scientific inquiry, I would have engaged in an unethical act of prostituting my integrity had I accepted those conditions (p. 395).

In-house researchers, who are employed by the organization for which the research is being conducted, face special problems in this regard, because they lack the freedom to pick and choose their research topic. These individuals must balance their concern for rigorous scientific inquiry with their need for continued employment.

Generally, the issues confronted are subtle and complex. Although researchers may be directly told to conceal or falsify results, more often they are subtly encouraged to design their research with an eye toward the desired results. The greatest barrier to such pressures is the development of a truly independent professional research unit within the organization. Such independence protects the researcher from political pressures and at the same time promotes the credibility of the research being conducted. Without this protection, the individual is left to his or her own devices and standards of ethical conduct.

THE PURITY OF SCIENTIFIC RESEARCH

The end of the twentieth century was fraught with assertions about the perceived legitimacy of science for determining truth (MacCoun, 1998). Keltner and Robinson (1996) offer the concept of *naïve realism* to explain the disjuncture between individuals' perceptions, and, perhaps, an elemental explanation for the erosion of scientific-based thinking. People often assume their own worldviews are objective, based on science or truth, while the views of others (and the reason why others do not agree with their perspective) are subjective, or based on personal ideology as opposed to some objective criteria. Unfortunately, individuals on both sides of such debates tend to function similarly in terms of their one-sided views.

Often, these discussions are centered on the issue of bias. In some instances, biased interpretations are justifiable (MacCoun, 1998). However, the claim that a social science researcher has produced biased results is often perceived by the researcher not only as a scornful criticism about his or her work, but also as a personal attack about his or her credibility, integrity, and honor. In fact, the very decision to study a particular topic can lead some consumers of research to assume the investigator is biased.

The idea of scientific inquiry is the pure, objective examination of the empirical world, untainted by personal prejudice. However, research is carried out by human beings, who typically have a variety of motivations for undertaking their research endeavors. Topics may be selected because of curiosity or from a perceived need to address a specific social problem; the availability of grants in a particular field may also encourage researchers' efforts. This is critical if one is working for a research organization dependent upon "soft" money. In addition, the need for university faculty members to publish and establish a name for themselves in a particular area may encourage them to seek "hot" topics for their research, or to identify an extremely narrow research focus in which they can become identified as experts.

Merton (1973) expressed four *norms of science* that are widely acknowledged by both scientists and nonscientists alike:

1. *Universalism*—scientific accomplishments must be judged by impersonal criteria; the personal attributes of the investigator are irrelevant.
2. *Communism* (as in communalism)—scientific information must be publicly shared.
3. *Disinterestedness*—cautions investigators to proceed objectively; researchers must be aware of and guard against personal biases and prejudices.
4. Finally, *organized skepticism*—new findings must be scrutinized rigorously through peer review, replication of experiments, and the testing of rival hypotheses.

There is some evidence that the nature of one's research findings influences the likelihood of publication (*Chronicle of Higher Education*, 1989d, p. A5). A curious author submitted almost identical articles to a number of journals. The manuscripts differed only in one respect—the nature of the conclusions. One version of the article showed the experiment had no effect; the other described a positive result. The experiment produced some interesting results—the article with positive outcomes was more likely to be accepted for publication than the other manuscript.

As reported by the *New York Times*, Diederik Stapel did not deny that his deceit was driven by ambition. But it was more complicated than that:

> He insisted that he loved social psychology but had been frustrated by the messiness of experimental data, which rarely led to clear conclusions. His lifelong obsession with elegance and order, he said, led him to concoct sexy results that journals found attractive. "It was a quest for aesthetics, for beauty—instead of the truth," he said. He

described his behavior as an addiction that drove him to carry out acts of increasingly daring fraud, like a junkie seeking a bigger and better high.

New York Times **(April 26, 2013)**

If research studies concluding that "the experiment didn't work" or that "differences between Groups A and B were insignificant" are indeed less likely to be published, then pressure to revise one's research focus or to rewrite one's hypotheses to match the results produced can be anticipated. These elements of the research process should function to remind us that actions justified in the name of scientific inquiry may be motivated by reasons far less "pure" than the objective they serve.

PUBLIC POLICY PRONOUNCEMENTS AND TEACHING CRIMINAL JUSTICE

When is a researcher speaking from the facts and when is he or she promoting personal ideology? If there were any fully conclusive and definitive studies in the social sciences, this question would not arise. However, research findings are always tentative, and statements describing them invariably require conditional language. On the other hand, researchers have values and beliefs like everyone else, and few of us want to employ the same conditional language required to discuss research when we state our views on matters of public policy and morality. Researchers thus have a special obligation to carefully evaluate their remarks and clearly distinguish between opinion and apparent empirical fact. This is not always an easy task, but it is the only way to safeguard the objectivity that is critically important to scientific inquiry.

Criminal justice researchers acting as teachers and mentors have a responsibility to students, due to the influence their position has concerning the lives of their students (ACJS, 2000). Specifically, a researcher's influence and authority, used inappropriately, has the potential to mislead and distort the perspectives of their students by disseminating information that was based merely on personal ideology rather than scientific findings.

ETHICAL CODES

In order to address ethical considerations related to the research process, associations of academic researchers develop and make known standards or **codes of ethics**. The Academy of Criminal Justice Sciences (ACJS) has advanced a standard for those persons researching and writing within the discipline of criminal justice. It does an excellent job of addressing the ethical standards of conducting social science research as well as the dissemination of information within the criminal justice discipline. The ACJS code provides criminologists with ethical standards concerning fair treatment; the use of students in research; objectivity and integrity in the conduct of research; confidentiality, disclosure, and respect for research populations; publication and authorship standards; and employment practices (ACJS, 2000). See Box 20.3.

BOX 20.3 MEMBERS OF THE ACADEMY OF CRIMINAL JUSTICE SCIENCES AS RESEARCHERS

Objectivity and Integrity in the Conduct of Criminal Justice Research.

1. Members of the Academy should adhere to the highest possible technical standards in their research.

2. Since individual members of the Academy vary in their research modes, skills, and experience, they should acknowledge the limitations that may affect the validity of their findings.

3. In presenting their work, members of the Academy are obliged to fully report their findings. They should not misrepresent the findings of their research or omit significant data. Any and all omitted data should be noted and the reason(s) for exclusion stated clearly as part of the methodology. Details of their theories, methods, and research designs that might bear upon interpretations of research findings should be reported.

4. Members of the Academy should fully report all sources of financial support and other sponsorship of the research.

5. Members of the Academy should not make any commitments to respondents, individuals, groups, or organizations unless there is full intention and ability to honor them.

6. Consistent with the spirit of full disclosure of method and analysis, members of the Academy, after they have completed their own analyses, should cooperate in efforts to make raw data and pertinent documentation available to other social scientists, at reasonable costs, except in cases where confidentiality, the client's rights to proprietary information and privacy, or the claims of a field worker to the privacy of personal notes necessarily would be violated. The timeliness of this cooperation is especially critical.

7. Members of the Academy should provide adequate information, documentation, and citations concerning scales and other measures used in their research.

8. Members of the Academy should not accept grants, contracts, or research assignments that appear likely to violate the principles enunciated in this Code, and should disassociate themselves from research when they discover a violation and are unable to correct it.

9. When financial support for a project has been accepted, members of the Academy should make every reasonable effort to complete the proposed work on schedule.

10. When a member of the Academy is involved in a project with others, including students, there should be mutually accepted explicit agreements at the outset with respect to division of work, compensation, access to data, rights of authorship, and other rights and responsibilities. These agreements should not be exploitative or arrived at through any form of coercion or intimidation. Such agreements may need to be modified as the project evolves and such modifications should be clearly stated among all participants. Students should normally be the principal author of any work that is derived directly from their thesis or dissertation.

11. Members of the Academy have the right to disseminate research findings, except those likely to cause harm to clients, collaborators, and participants; those which violate formal or implied promises of confidentiality; or those which are proprietary under a formal or informal agreement.

Disclosure and Respect of the Rights of Research Populations by Members of the Academy

12. Members of the Academy should not misuse their positions as professionals for fraudulent purposes

Continued...

BOX 20.3 MEMBERS OF THE ACADEMY OF CRIMINAL JUSTICE SCIENCES AS RESEARCHERS *Continued*

or as a pretext for gathering information for any individual, group, organization, or government.

13. Human subjects have the right to full disclosure of the purposes of the research as early as it is appropriate to the research process, and they have the right to an opportunity to have their questions answered about the purpose and usage of the research. Members should inform research participants about aspects of the research that might affect their willingness to participate, such as physical risks, discomfort, and/or unpleasant emotional experiences.

14. Subjects of research are entitled to rights of personal confidentiality unless they are waived.

15. Information about subjects obtained from records that are open to public scrutiny cannot be protected by guarantees of privacy or confidentiality.

16. The process of conducting criminal justice research must not expose respondents to more than minimal risk of personal harm, and members of the Academy should make every effort to ensure the safety and security of respondents and project staff. Informed consent should be obtained when the risks of research are greater than the risks of everyday life.

17. Members of the Academy should take culturally appropriate steps to secure informed consent and to avoid invasions of privacy. In addition, special actions will be necessary where the individuals studied are illiterate, under correctional supervision, are minors, have low social status, are under judicial supervision, have diminished capacity, are unfamiliar with social research, or otherwise occupy a position of unequal power with the researcher.

18. Members of the Academy should seek to anticipate potential threats to confidentiality. Techniques such as the removal of direct identifiers, the use of randomized

responses, and other statistical solutions to problems of privacy should be used where appropriate. Care should be taken to ensure secure storage, maintenance, and/or destruction of sensitive records.

19. Confidential information provided by research participants should be treated as such by members of the Academy, even when this information enjoys no legal protection or privilege and legal force is applied. The obligation to respect confidentiality also applies to members of research organizations (interviewers, coders, clerical staff, etc.) who have access to the information. It is the responsibility of administrators and chief investigators to instruct staff members on this point and to make every effort to insure that access to confidential information is restricted.

20. While generally adhering to the norm of acknowledging the contributions of all collaborators, members of the Academy should be sensitive to harm that may arise from disclosure and respect a collaborator's need for anonymity.

21. All research should meet the human subjects requirements imposed by educational institutions and funding sources. Study design and information-gathering techniques should conform to regulations protecting the rights of human subjects, regardless of funding.

22. Members of the Academy should comply with appropriate federal and institutional requirements pertaining to the conduct of their research. These requirements might include, but are not necessarily limited to, obtaining proper review and approval for research that involves human subjects and accommodating recommendations made by responsible committees concerning research subjects, materials, and procedures.

BOX 20.4 MEMBERS OF THE AMERICAN SOCIETY OF CRIMINOLOGY AS RESEARCHERS

The American Society of Criminology (ASC) is another professional association of academic researchers and practitioners who contribute to further understanding within the criminal justice discipline through

research. Although ASC does not have its own formal code of ethics, their website does refer interested persons to various codes of ethics, including the ACJS code. See www.asc41.com/ethicspg.html

■ **Learn More on the Internet**

View the complete Academy of Criminal Justice Sciences (ACJS) code of ethics at: www.acjs.org/pubs/167_671_2922.cfm. What are your general thoughts about the ACJS code of ethics?

Go to the American Society of Criminology (ASC) website: www.asc41.com/ethicspg.html. Click on some of the links to the left to view codes of ethics for various professional associations. What similarities do you see within each of the codes of ethics? Are there any differences between the various codes?   ■

CONCLUSION

It would be convenient to conclude that the best research is that which is conducted in an ethical fashion, but such a statement would skirt the dilemma. Conducting ethical scientific research in criminal justice and criminology can be a difficult task; it requires constant weighing and balancing of objectives and motivations. This is the exact nature of the problem: those actions required to meet the demands of scientific rigor sometimes run counter to ethical behavior. However, evaluating rather than avoiding ethical dilemmas does provide a learning experience, the benefits of which can be expected to spill over into all aspects of human endeavor. Thinking and doing in an ethical way requires practice, and conducting research provides considerable opportunities for the evolution of experience.

Discussion Questions

1. Discuss the importance of research in criminal justice. Are there any circumstances in which it is acceptable for a research project to involve activities that punish and perhaps harm participants? Where should the researcher draw the line? Can you think of any situations in which the ends justify the means? Support your answer.

2. What are some of the benefits gained by doing a research project? Do the benefits outweigh the costs to participants? Explain. What are some of the pressures that may be placed on researchers that could compromise the integrity of their research results?

3. Go to the following website to take an online tutorial for Human Participants Protection: phrp.nihtraining.com/users/login.php. You will be prompted to create a user account (at no charge) and will then be able to navigate through the tutorial and corresponding quiz to determine if you meet the requirements for conducting research with human participants.

4. Pick one of the following studies: the Stanford Prison Experiment, Tearoom Trade, Obedience to Authority, the Kansas City Preventive Patrol Experiment, or the Minneapolis Domestic Violence Experiment, and answer the following questions:

a. What are the ethical issues that need to be addressed to determine if the study could be regarded as ethical? Which ethical model (e.g., utilitarianism, deontology, or peacemaking) supports your answer? Explain.

b. Could the researcher(s) have used alternative methodological strategies to acquire the same information?

c. Do you think this study should have been done? Why or why not?

CASE STUDY 20–1: RESEARCH ISSUES

Imagine you are a professor, newly graduated from your doctoral program and recently hired in a tenure-track position as an assistant professor at the university of your choice. Your new position requires you to maintain an active scholarly agenda, meaning you must activate a research agenda to progress toward earning tenure.

You have always been interested in aspects related to policing. Perhaps this is because your father and brother are police officers, and you have more family members who have worked in other areas of the criminal justice system. Regardless, you decide to design a research study that will examine job satisfaction among police officers. Specifically, you are interested in individual-level and organizational-level variables that influence police officer satisfaction.

Individual-level variables may include age, race, gender, level of education, marital status, officer rank, and number of years as a police officer. Organizational-level variables might include the structure and mission of the police department, organizational policies, elements of shift work, amount of training received, and administrative support.

Think about the items discussed in the chapter when answer the following questions:

1. Are there any personal biases that may affect your research study? If so, how will you control for these concerns?

2. How will you collect data? What will you do if an administrator at your university suggests that you should pick a different topic? Why would some people not want to know about police officer satisfaction?

3. How will you provide/maintain confidentiality of the data? What will you do if the police chief wants a copy of your data?

4. What concerns must you address regarding the presentation of research results? What if university officials do not want the data published? What if the police chief or some of the officers do not want the data published?

REFERENCES

ACJS. (2000). *Academy of Criminal Justice Sciences: Code of ethics.*

Bhattacharjee, Y. (April 26, 2013). *The mind of a con man.* New York Times. www.nytimes.com/2013/04/28/magazine/diederik-stapels-audacious-academic-fraud.html?pagewanted=1&_r=0.

Chaiken, J., Greenwood, P., & Petersilia, J. (1977). The criminological investigation process: A summary report. *Policy Analysis, 3,* 187–217.

Chiauzzi, E. J., & Liljegren, S. (1993). Taboo topics in addiction treatment: An empirical review of clinical folklore. *Juvenile Substance Abuse Treatment, 10,* 303–316.

Chronicle of higher education. (June 14, 1989b). p. A44.

Chronicle of higher education. (August 2, 1989d).

Chronicle of higher education. (November 1999). 46.

Cohen, B. (1980). *Deviant street networks: Prostitutes in New York City*. Cambridge: Lexington Books.

Cook, S. W. (1976). Ethical issues in the conduct of research in social relations. In C. Sellitz, L. Rightsman, & S. Cook (Eds.), *Research methods in social relations* (3rd ed.). NY: Holt, Rinehart and Winston.

Costanzo, M., & White, L. T. (1994). An overview of the death penalty and capital trials: History, current status, legal proceedings, and cost. *Journal of Social Issues, 50*(2), 1–18.

DeVellis, R. F. (2003). *Scale development: Theory and applications* (2nd ed.). Thousand Oaks: Sage.

Dillman, D. A., Smyth, J. D., & Christian, L. M. (2009). *Internet, mail and mixed-mode surveys: The tailored design method* (3rd ed.). New Jersey: John Wiley & Sons.

Dong, B. J., Hauck, W. W., Gambertoglio, J. G., Gee, L., & White, J. R. (1997). Bioequivalence of generic and brand-name levothyroxine products in the treatment of hypothyroidism. *Journal of American Medical Association, 277*, 1205–1213.

Erez, E. (1986). Randomized experiments in correctional context: Legal, ethical and practical concerns. *Journal of Criminal Justice, 14*, 389–400.

Federal Judicial Center. (1981). *Experimentation in the law: Report of the Federal Judicial Center Advisory Committee on experimentation in the law*. Washington: Federal Judicial Center.

Fowler, F. J. (2002). *Survey research methods* (3rd ed.). Thousand Oaks: Sage.

Gardner, W., & Wilcox, B. L. (1993). Political intervention in scientific peer review: Research on adolescent sexual behavior. *American Psychology, 48*, 972–983.

Garrison, A.H. (2009). The influence of research on criminal justice policymaking. *Professional Issues in Criminal Justice, 4*(1), 9–21.

Geis, G. (1980). Ethical and legal issues in experiments with offender populations. In S. Talarico (Ed.), *Criminal justice research: Approaches, problems and policy*. Cincinnati: Anderson.

Haney, C., Banks, C., & Zimbardo, P. (1973). Interpersonal dynamics in a simulated prison. *International Journal of Criminology and Penology, 1*, 69–97.

Herbert, B. (July 5, 1996). *More N.R.A. mischief*. New York Times.

Humphreys, L. (1970). *Tearoom trade: Impersonal sex in public places*. Chicago: Aldine.

Johnson, D. (1993). The politics of violence research. *Psychological Science, 4*, 131–133.

Kahn, A. (November 5, 2011). *Dutch scientist accused of falsifying data*. Los Angeles Times. Retrieved at articles.latimes.com/2011/nov/05/science/la-sci-science-fraud-20111106.

Kelling, G. L., Page, T., Dieckman, D., & Brown, C. E. (1974). *The Kansas City preventive patrol experiment*. Washington: The Police Foundation.

Keltner, D., & Robinson, R. J. (1996). Extremism, power, and the imagined basis of social conflict. *Current Directions Psychological of Science, 5*, 101–105.

Linz, D., & Malamuth, N. M. (1993). *Pornography*. Newbury Park: Sage.

MacCoun, R. J. (1998). Biases in the interpretation and use of research results. *Annual Review of Psychology, 49*, 259–287.

MacCoun, R. J. (1993). Drugs and the law: A psychological analysis of drug prohibition. *Psychology Bulletin, 113*, 497–512.

MacCoun, R. J., & Reuter, P. (1997). Interpreting Dutch cannabis policy: Reasoning by analogy in the legalization debate. *Science, 278*, 47–52.

Marlatt, G. A., Larimer, M. E., Baer, J. S., & Quigley, L. A. (1993). Harm reduction for alcohol problems: Moving beyond the controlled drinking controversy. *Behavioral Therapy, 24*, 461–504.

Martinson, R. (1974). What works? – Questions and answers about prison reform. *Public Interest*, *35*, 25–54.

McSkimming, M. J., Seve, B., & King, R. S. (2000). The coverage of ethics in research methods textbooks. *Journal of Criminal Justice Education, 11*, 51–63.

Meltzer, B. A. (1953). A projected study of the jury as a working institution. *The Annals of the American Academy of Political and Social Science, 287*, 97–102.

Merton, R. K. (1973). *The sociology of science.* Chicago: University of Chicago Press.

Milgram, S. (1974). *Obedience to authority: An experimental view.* New York: Harper and Row.

Miller, P. V. (1995). They said it couldn't be done: The national health and social life survey. *Public Opinion Quarterly, 59*, 404–419.

Moreno, J. D. (1998). Convenient and captive populations. In J. P. Kahn, A. C. Mastroianni, & J. Sugarman (Eds.), *Beyond consent: Seeking justice in research.* New York: Oxford University Press.

Morris, N. (1966). Impediments to penal reform. *Chicago Law Review, 33*, 646–653.

National Crime Information Center (2013). Available at: www.fbi.gov/about-us/cjis/ncic.

Neuman, W. L. (2004). *Basics of social research: Qualitative and quantitative approaches.* Boston: Pearson Education.

Nisbet, L. (Ed.). (2001). *The gun control debate: You decide* (2nd ed.) Amherst: Prometheus Books.

Rennie, D. (1997). Thyroid storm. *Journal of American Medical Association, 277*, 1238–1242.

Ring, K., Wallston, K., & Corey, M. (1970). Mode of debriefing as a factor affecting subjective reaction to a Milgram type obedience experience: An ethical inquiry. *Representative Research in Social Psychology, 1*, 67–88.

Sherman, L. W., & Berk, R. A. (1984). The specific deterrent effects of arrest for domestic assault. *American Sociological Review, 49*, 261–272.

Short, J. F., Jr., & Strodtbeck, F. (1965). *Group processes and gang delinquency.* Chicago: University of Chicago Press.

Singleton, R. A., Jr., & Straits, B. C. (1988). *Approaches to social research* (3rd ed.). New York: Oxford University Press.

Warren, C. A., & Karner, T. X. (2005). *Discovering qualitative methods: Field research, interviews, and analysis.* Los Angeles: Roxbury.

Weisburd, D. (2005). Hot spots policing experiments and criminal justice research: Lessons from the field. *The Annals of the American Academy of Political and Social Science, 599*, 220–245.

Whyte, W. F. (1955). *Street corner society.* Chicago: University of Chicago Press.

Wolfgang, M. (1982). Ethics and research. In F. Elliston, & N. Bowie (Eds.), *Ethics, public policy and criminal justice.* Cambridge: Oelgeschlager, Gunn and Hain.

CHAPTER 21

Terrorism and Ethics

Bernard J. McCarthy

"But just as surely as we are a nation at war, we also are a nation of laws."

Attorney General Eric Holder (April 15, 2010)

INTRODUCTION

In the more than a decade since the September 11, 2001, terrorist attacks against the United States, a number of ethical issues associated with combating terrorism have come to the forefront of a national discussion on how to respond. In this essay, we will examine some of the more compelling issues that arose during the course of the last decade. Probably, the most important one has to do with the issue of balancing public safety, i.e., the protection of the American people, with a continuing respect for their civil liberties. Following the terrorist attacks in 2001, our society was faced with some difficult questions: how do we protect ourselves from terrorism? What tactics should we use? Will these tactics compromise our rights?

The terrorist attacks of September 11, 2001, took the nation by surprise and exposed our vulnerabilities. The **9/11 Commission Report** called September 11 a day of unprecedented shock and suffering in the history of the United States. On that day 19 young men from the Middle East hijacked four commercial airliners. They crashed those fuel-laden jets into the World Trade Center in New York City and the Pentagon in Arlington, Virginia, a suburb of Washington, DC, and the fourth jet crashed in a field in Shanksville, Pennsylvania, where presumably it was on its way to a target in Washington, DC. A total of 2,981 victims were killed that day, countless others injured, and property/economic damage was reported to be in the billions of dollars. More Americans died from these attacks than in the attack on Pearl Harbor. The 9/11 Commission observed "that the institutions charged with protecting our borders, civil aviation and national security did not understand how grave this threat could be and did not adjust their policies, plans and practices to deter or defeat it" (The 9/11 Commission Report: xvi).

It was apparent that the agencies responsible for protecting the United States had failed in their mission. The commission found that our political leaders did not understand or appreciate the grave threat terrorism posed and called into question whether existing agencies had the capability of protecting the nation. They concluded that the nation was unprepared for responding to this new form of terrorism we were confronting. The 9/11 Commission Report also declared that the major problem was a failure of "imagination" across federal agencies whose mission and task was to protect the United States.

In the aftermath of the September 11 attacks, the United States responded by taking several bold steps. First, the authorization of military force was approved by Congress and provided to the President for action. Second, the USA PATRIOT Act was passed into law. Third, Afghanistan, the country believed to be providing safe haven to al Qaeda, was attacked and the government in power at the time (the Taliban), who provided a safe haven to al Qaeda, was ousted. Fourth, a major government reorganization occurred with the creation of the U.S. Department of Homeland Security, where 22 federal agencies were brought together. This was the largest government reorganization since the end of World War II. Finally, all of this was followed with the invasion of Iraq over the suspicion that they possessed weapons of mass destruction that threatened the United States. In the immediate days following the September 11 attacks, many within the United States questioned the efficacy of the criminal justice system in preventing and fighting terrorism. Others suggested that new laws were needed to protect the safety and security of the country. Still others believed that the fight against terrorism required using methods that would be construed as illegal if used in the criminal justice system, such as expanded surveillance of citizens without court-approved warrants or the use of torture on terrorism suspects as an interrogation method to thwart an impending attack (e.g., a ticking time bomb situation in which a person has information about an impending deadly attack). A vigorous debate followed regarding whether terrorists might be shielded or protected by the cloak of civil liberties.

In the days and weeks following the attacks on the World Trade Center and the Pentagon, the USA PATRIOT Act was pushed through Congress and signed into law on October 26, 2001 (P.L. 107-56, 115 Stat. 272 (2001)). The act contained sunset provisions for some of the more controversial sections.

■ Learn More on the Internet

For highlights of the USA PATRIOT Act see: www.justice.gov/archive/ll/highlights.htm. ■

The USA PATRIOT Act was reauthorized on May 26, 2011, for a four-year period. The aim of the act was to enhance law enforcement abilities to investigate terror-related acts by easing restrictions on the use of intelligence gathering and removing legal obstacles that prevented the sharing of information by intelligence and law enforcement agencies. The PATRIOT Act also greatly expanded the federal government's ability to effectively investigate money laundering related to terrorism.

THE WAR STRATEGY TO COMBAT TERRORISM

Soon after the attacks, the George W. Bush Administration decided that the war designation for handling terrorism and terrorists should be used. A formal declaration of war by Congress was never made; rather, Congress passed an open-ended authorization to use military force against terrorists. This was approved in short order after the attacks on September 11, 2001. This authorization granted the President the authority to use all "necessary and appropriate force" against those whom he determined "planned, authorized, committed or aided" the September 11th attacks, or who harbored said persons or groups. This authorization is still in force today and is used to justify drone attacks overseas on al Qaeda-affiliated targets in Pakistan and Yemen. The seriousness of this action was underlined by the use of the war metaphor. However, what differentiated this war was who it was directed against; the organization we were engaged with was a nonstate actor as opposed to a nation state. It was apparent from the very beginning that this war was declared against an elusive enemy that was highly mobile. Instead of fighting against another nation we were fighting an organization that had spread across several countries. The September 11 conspirators were inspired, trained, and supported by a terrorist group (al Qaeda). The war term was used to mobilize public opinion in support of the action, but also to signal the seriousness of the issue. The use of the military was pushed into the forefront for combating terrorism and the military justice system was proposed for handling the arrest, interrogation, and confinement of suspected terrorists. What followed was an aggressive military campaign, followed by the creation of **military tribunals**, the use of secret prisons to hold terror suspects, the use of **renditions** (i.e., the handing over of terrorism suspects to foreign countries for interrogation purposes), and the adoption and application of harsh interrogation practices for suspected terrorists under the jurisdiction of the U.S. military. These practices and tribunals were created in the days and months after September 11 and were the result of presidential executive orders.

Within the United States these policies set off a debate over whether this was the right path to follow. One of the most critical ethical questions had to do with whether the constitutional protections of due process, privilege against self-incrimination, right to privacy, and freedom from cruel and unusual punishments should be diminished or compromised in the interests of fighting terrorism. In the debate that followed, the first and foremost question was whether the criminal justice system and the accompanying rule of law should play a role in the war against terrorism. Some have argued, because we faced such an extreme threat, that extralegal methods were required that involve the suspension or modification of certain civil liberties, such as due process.

THE USE OF THE MILITARY SYSTEM OF JUSTICE

This jurisdictional issue arose when, following the September 11, 2001, attacks on the United States, President Bush issued an executive/military order on November 13, 2001, that shifted the responsibility for handling suspected international terrorists who were not United States citizens to the Secretary of Defense. The Secretary was authorized to set up military tribunals or commissions to detain and adjudicate suspected terrorists associated with al Qaeda or other international terrorist groups (see Military Order of November 13, 2001, Detention, Treatment, and Trial of Certain Non-Citizens in the War Against Terrorism).

In his executive order, several reasons were put forward by President Bush to justify such drastic action. These included:

> Given the danger to the safety of the United States and the nature of international terrorism, and to the extent provided by and under this order,...that it is not practicable to apply in military commissions under this order the principles of law and the rules of evidence generally recognized in the trial of criminal cases in the United States district courts.

> Having fully considered the magnitude of the potential deaths, injuries, and property destruction that would result from potential acts of terrorism against the United States, and the probability that such acts will occur, I have determined that an extraordinary emergency exists for national defense purposes, that this emergency constitutes an

urgent and compelling government interest, and that issuance of this order is necessary to meet the emergency.

Military Order (November 13, 2001)

In addition, United States Attorney General Alberto Gonzales provided an opinion to the President that the terrorists, because of their actions targeting civilians, when captured would not qualify for prisoner of war status. They were declared to be unlawful enemy combatants. This in turn suggested that legal prohibitions against harsh interrogation methods would not apply (Gonzales, 2002). On February 7, 2002, the President accepted the recommendation of the Attorney General, over the objections of the Secretary of State, and declared that the Geneva Convention governing the use of torture did not apply to the treatment of prisoners who were members of the Taliban or al Qaeda. This decision set in motion a series of policies that had ethical implications and unforeseen consequences for the treatment of those prisoners.

In 2002, confinement facilities for suspected terrorists were set up overseas, including the one at **Guantánamo Bay**, Cuba. Suspects were brought to those facilities and subjected to conditions of confinement and interrogation processes that would have been considered illegal if conducted in jails or prisons in the United States. The government argued that since they were noncitizens and not in the territorial jurisdiction of the United States, constitutional protections such as habeas corpus, privilege against self-incrimination, and the prohibition against cruel and unusual punishments did not apply. This interpretation of the law was quickly challenged by a series of court cases by lawyers supporting the rule-of-law perspective.

THE MILITARY COMMISSIONS/TRIBUNALS

The use of military tribunals was quickly challenged in federal court. Legal advocates of rule of law charged that the suspects were being denied basic due process and their confinement violated the Geneva Convention, which prohibits cruel and/or inhumane treatment of prisoners under custody.

■ Learn More on the Internet

An excellent overview of the issues may be found at the Council on Foreign Relations website at www.cfr.org/terrorism-and-the-law/terror-military-tribunals/p7842.   ■

Eventually, the cases made their way to the United States Supreme Court. In 2006, the Supreme Court declared in *Hamdan v. Rumsfeld* that the military commissions as initially construed were flawed and violated due process. However, this case did not end the use of military commissions; they were instead revised to comply with the concerns expressed by the Supreme Court. In response to the *Hamdan* decision, Congress passed the **Military Commissions Act of 2006**, which addressed the due process deficiencies that the court had previously identified. Two key concerns were addressed. First, eligibility for the military courts was narrowly defined in that the act determined who could be transferred to the military system (i.e., alien unlawful enemy combatants; i.e., not U.S. citizens); and second, the act specified what due process procedures should be followed. Civil libertarians continued to argue that suspects were not being accorded basic rights and that the military judicial process was a violation of fundamental fairness. Of particular concern was the provision that the commissions could use evidence obtained through coercive or harsh interrogation methods that would otherwise be considered illegal as a violation of the Fifth Amendment privilege against self-incrimination.

In 2009, the act was revised and replaced with the **Military Commissions Act of 2009**. Under this act some of the major controversial issues were addressed, such as the exclusion of evidence collected or obtained through torture or cruel, inhuman, or degrading treatment. It also established procedures for the handling of sensitive classified information that might be presented during a case. The act also limited the jurisdiction of the tribunals to alien unlawful combatants. The law of war defines who may be treated as a lawful combatant and who is treated as a prisoner of war. Their treatment is guided by the Geneva Convention's protocols. An **unlawful combatant** is a person who is not considered a prisoner of war and, as a result, such person's treatment is not guided by the Geneva Convention. Under the revised act, U.S. citizens would not be tried in military courts.

A new approach to these issues arose when President Barack Obama took office in 2009. During his presidential campaign, the new President had made it clear that he intended to shut down both the use of military commissions and the use of the confinement facility in Cuba. On January 22, 2009, the President issued an executive order closing down the confinement facility in Guantánamo Bay (Executive Order 13492) that stated that the facility would be closed down within a year. Moreover, seven months later, a President-appointed task force on detention policy issued a report that recommended that the government reserve the right to use military commissions in special cases but suggested that the preferred option would be to use the federal criminal courts to administer justice.

Further, President Obama's administration announced a change in tactics in 2009 when the administration revealed its plans to prosecute five detainees in U.S. federal courts. This required that they be transferred from Guantánamo Bay to the United States to stand trial for criminal offenses related to the September 11 terrorist attacks. This change in policy provoked a strong response against this decision by President Obama's political opponents. His opposition mobilized their forces and was successful in having the U.S. Congress pass legislation that defunded such prosecution and prohibited any noncitizen held at Guantánamo Bay from being tried in U.S. courts. This left military tribunals as the only option available to bring these defendants to justice.

THE TORTURE MEMOS

Another controversial issue associated with counterterrorism was the adoption of harsh interrogation policies designed to elicit information from terrorism suspects regarding possible impending attacks against the United States. This was sometimes described as a "ticking time bomb scenario." The justification for the use of extreme measures was based on the "means justify the ends" argument.

Under this practice the Fifth Amendment privilege against self-incrimination was called into question. This amendment states that "No person….shall be compelled in any criminal case to be a witness against himself, nor be deprived of life, liberty, or property without due process of law." The U.S. Supreme Court ruling in *Miranda v. Arizona* (384 U.S. 436, 1966) made it quite clear that without a waiver of a person's right to counsel, incriminating evidence could not be introduced in a criminal proceeding in a U.S. courtroom. The question raised was whether authorities can ignore or waive the Fifth Amendment when a ticking time bomb situation exists, i.e., where there is an imminent threat of a terrorist attack and loss of life when a suspect is believed to have information that might prevent the attack or injury of civilians. Should torture be used to extract the information?

In 2009, following a Freedom of Information Act request from the American Civil Liberties Union, the U.S. Justice Department released a series of four memos prepared by the Office of Legal Counsel of the Attorney General's office. These memos, known as the **torture memos**, provided the legal framework and justification for the government's use of harsh interrogation procedures, such as **waterboarding** (in which water is poured over a cloth covering the face and breathing passages of an immobilized captive, causing the individual to experience the sensation of drowning) or sleep deprivation (involving keeping detainees awake for several days at a time while subjecting them to bright lights and loud noises). Under ordinary circumstances the use of these practices would violate domestic and international law.

John Yoo, an attorney and one of the advisors to Attorney General Gonzales, argued that the war against al Qaeda could not be waged within the context of the existing criminal law and that unique circumstances required that special methods needed to be employed (Yoo, 2005). As a counselor to the Attorney

General, Yoo believed the attacks of September 11 represented acts of war and that a military approach needed to be used. He also pointed out that al Qaeda was not to be considered a regular military force because they did not adhere to the rules and laws of war. Accordingly, he argued that the Geneva Convention and the protections regarding the handling of prisoners of war did not apply to members of the Taliban or al Qaeda. They were not to be treated as lawful combatants with the legal protections provided by the Geneva Convention regarding the treatment of prisoners of war. Instead, they would be defined as unlawful combatants and would not be afforded, nor did they deserve, prisoner of war status.

■ Learn More on the Internet

For more information, go to: berkeley.edu/news/media/releases/2005/01/05_johnyoo.shtml.   ■

In retrospect, the lawyers for the Justice Department did not fully understand or appreciate the forces they were about to unleash. Within a short period of time of opening detention and interrogation centers, serious abuses were found to be routinely used in the facilities, particularly in Abu Ghraib and Guantánamo Bay. The government quickly investigated the reports and blamed the degrading and dehumanizing practices on "bad apples" within the military.

If the justice department lawyers had taken the time to consult with their colleagues in the criminal law branch, they would have realized that the criminal justice system has had considerable experience with the misuse of power and authority and that this misuse can become endemic in a system that is based on coercion and hidden from view. History has taught us that in a democracy, rule of law, judicial oversight, and strict controls must be used to structure the application of law and use of discretion. The criminal justice system has had a long history of abuses that have taken place when individuals working in the system have been placed under pressure to get results. A cursory review of the literature on coerced confessions will reveal their unreliability and identify the wide range of problems that have occurred in the past.

HARSH INTERROGATION AND THE "TORTURE MEMOS"

One issue that has been raised with handling of detainees has to do with harsh interrogation practices. The Office of Legal Counsel in the Department of Justice issued an advisory opinion on the interrogation of al Qaeda operatives. A revised definition of torture was proposed:

Physical pain amounting to torture must be equivalent in intensity to the pain accompanying serious physical injury, such as organ failure, impairment of bodily function, or even death. For purely mental pain or suffering to amount to torture (under U.S. law), it must result in significant psychological harm of significant duration, e.g., lasting for months or even years.... We conclude that the statute, taken as a whole, makes plain that it prohibits only extreme acts.

Under this definition, interrogation methods that go beyond polite questioning but fall short of torture could include shouted questions, reduced sleep, stress positions (e.g., standing for long periods of time), and isolation from other prisoners. In an opinion provided to the Central Intelligence Agency, the following type of case was cited by the Counsel's office as justifying the use of extreme measures:

X is currently being held by the United States. The interrogation team is certain he has additional information that he refuses to divulge. Specifically, he is withholding information regarding terrorist networks in the United States or in Saudi Arabia and information regarding plans to conduct attacks within the United States or against our interests overseas. X has become accustomed to a certain level of treatment and displays no signs of willingness to discuss further information. At the same time, the Central Intelligence Agency is reporting that intelligence indicates that there is currently a level of "chatter" equal to that which preceded the September 11 attacks. In light of this information you believe X has and the high level of threat you believe now exists, you wish to move the interrogations into what you have described as "increased pressure phase."

The memo from the Attorney General then goes on to suggest the approval of a number techniques that could be considered as part of the increased pressure phase:

- Cramped confinement
- Dietary manipulation
- Facial slap/abdominal slap
- Nudity
- Sleep deprivation
- Stress positions
- Walling
- Waterboarding
- Water dousing

Under United States criminal law, any confession obtained through the use of these techniques would not be permitted if a police department or correctional agency employed these methods. In fact, the employees involved could and would be prosecuted for violations of the individual's civil rights, especially under section 1983 of the Civil Rights Act. In addition, there is also a question whether these practices violate the United Nations Convention Against Torture of 1994.

News about these legal opinions was leaked to the news media. Subsequently, the *New York Times, Washington Post,* and *Wall Street Journal* all carried stories regarding the torture memos. The *New York Times* set up a web page at: www.nytimes.com/ref/international/24MEMO-GUIDE.html.

ABU GHRAIB AND GUANTÁNAMO BAY

Along with the torture memos, conditions at confinement facilities operated by the United States overseas began to draw the attention of the public when widespread abuses were reported. The Eighth Amendment of the U.S. Constitution prohibits the infliction of cruel and unusual punishment, and this applies to prison conditions as well.

ABU GHRAIB

Under the authority of the Secretary of Defense, confinement facilities in overseas locations were established to handle prisoners that were being arrested and detained overseas. In 2004, reports started to appear that suggested that degrading confinement conditions, coupled with harsh interrogation methods, were being employed in a military prison holding detainees in Iraq. At about the same time, a military police officer filed a complaint that contained disturbing allegations regarding practices being employed in a confinement facility. Alarming photographs of inmates subjected to various forms of degradation started appearing on the Internet. The military police officer's allegations included sexual, physical, and psychological abuse of detainees.

A military commission was appointed to investigate the charges, known as the Taguba Report, and confirmed the allegations. The investigation found that in 2003 at the **Abu Ghraib Confinement Facility**, "numerous incidents of sadistic, blatant, and wanton criminal abuses were inflicted on several detainees." The report indicated that "systemic and illegal abuse of detainees was intentionally perpetrated by several members of the military police guard force" in Tier (section) 1-A of the Abu Ghraib Prison. The allegations of abuse were substantiated by detailed witness statements (ANNEX 26) and the discovery of digital photographic evidence that was both graphic and gruesome. See Box 21.1.

BOX 21.1 ABUSES IN ABU GHRAIB

1. Punching, slapping, and kicking detainees; jumping on their naked feet;
2. Videotaping and photographing naked male and female detainees;
3. Forcibly arranging detainees in various sexually explicit positions for photographing;
4. Forcing detainees to remove their clothing and keeping them naked for several days at a time;
5. Forcing naked male detainees to wear women's underwear;
6. Forcing groups of male detainees to masturbate themselves while being photographed and videotaped;
7. Arranging naked male detainees in a pile and then jumping on them;
8. Positioning a naked detainee on an MRE box, with a sandbag on his head, and attaching wires to his fingers, toes, and penis to simulate electric torture;
9. Writing "I am a Rapest" (sic) on the leg of a detainee alleged to have forcibly raped a 15-year old fellow detainee, and then photographing him naked;
10. Placing a dog chain or strap around a naked detainee's neck and having a female soldier pose for a picture;
11. A male MP guard having sex with a female detainee;
12. Using military working dogs (without muzzles) to intimidate and frighten detainees, in at least one case biting and severely injuring a detainee;
13. Taking photographs of dead Iraqi detainees (ANNEXES 25 and 26, p. 16).

Major General Taguba also determined that the testimony of several detainees was "…credible based on the clarity of their statements and supporting evidence provided by other witnesses" (ANNEX 26). The detainees described the following acts of abuse:

1. Breaking chemical lights and pouring the phosphoric liquid on detainees;
2. Threatening detainees with a charged 9 mm pistol;
3. Pouring cold water on naked detainees;
4. Beating detainees with a broom handle and a chair;
5. Threatening male detainees with rape;
6. Allowing a military police guard to stitch the wound of a detainee who was injured after being slammed against the wall in his cell;
7. Sodomizing a detainee with a chemical light and perhaps a broomstick.
8. Using military working dogs to frighten and intimidate detainees with threats of attack, in one instance actually biting a detainee (need cite here).

These actions reportedly took place because of a misguided intention by the military police officers, who were serving as correctional officers, to assist military intelligence officers by "softening up" the suspects before their interrogation. The subsequent investigation did not reveal or find any evidence that the soldiers were ordered by superiors to subject the inmates to degrading and dehumanizing practices. After an investigation, almost two dozen soldiers were removed from duty and 11 were formally charged with abusing the inmates.

At the same time this was happening, a television show was gaining a lot of notoriety in the United States. The show was *24*, and the leading character was

Agent Jack Bauer. Bauer was portrayed as a character whose philosophy was "to do what it takes to get an end result" and who frequently was called upon to use extralegal methods to interrogate subjects. With Agent Jack Bauer's use of harsh methods of interrogation in "ticking time bomb" situations, *24* popularized the message that extralegal methods would work in combating terrorists. Although academics and legal experts debated the merits of torture to obtain confessions, the impact of this show should not be underestimated. According to reports, the military was greatly concerned over the impact *24* was having on soldiers—so much so that, according to one report:

> U.S. Army Brigadier General Patrick Finnegan, the dean of the United States Military Academy at West Point, flew to Southern California to meet with the creative team behind "24." On behalf of the Army, he had come to voice their "concern that the show's central political premise—that the letter of American law must be sacrificed for the country's security—was having a toxic effect." In their view, the show promoted unethical and illegal behavior and had adversely affected the training and performance of real American soldiers. "I'd like them to stop," Finnegan said of the show's producers. "They should do a show where torture backfires." Tom Regan, csmonitor.com, "Does '24' encourage U.S. interrogators to 'torture' detainees?"
>
> **February 12, 2007**

At the confinement facility at Guantánamo Bay, some of the same complaints regarding the degrading treatment of inmates were also being aired. The *Washington Post* carried a story on December 21, 2004, that stated FBI agents' alleged abuse of detainees at Guantánamo Bay. In their story, the FBI reported a series of abuses occurring at the confinement facility over a two-year period. The FBI reported that extremely aggressive interrogation techniques were being used that far exceeded the "boundaries of standard FBI practice." The *New York Times* carried a story that the FBI was concerned that military interrogators "abused prisoners by beating them, grabbing their genitals and chaining them to the cold ground."

■ Learn More on the Internet

A complete listing of these memos was obtained by the American Civil Liberties Union and is available at www.aclu.org/torturefoia/released/052505/.   ■

Finally, allegations of harsh treatment were also made by the International Red Cross on their inspections of **Guantánamo** Bay. According to a *New York Times* article, the International Red Cross concluded following field visits and interviews that "the American military has intentionally used psychological and sometimes physical coercion 'tantamount to torture' on prisoners at Guantánamo Bay, Cuba" (Lewis, 2004).

What Has Been the End Result of Military Commissions and the Torture Memos?

First, the federal courts have consistently ruled against the denial of due process rights and have supported the need to adhere to the Geneva Convention on Torture. The courts have also pointed out the need for further legal protections for the detainees. The latest iteration of the Military Commissions Act of 2009 includes two major protections identified by the courts that needed to be addressed, including the right to *habeas corpus* (the right to challenge their prosecution in federal courts) and the prohibition against using information obtained through the use of extreme methods (i.e., torture).

Second, despite all of the publicity, as of 2013, only six captives had been convicted by the Military Commission process, and four of the six convictions involved plea deals (Congressional Research Service Report, 2013, p. 10). These include David Hicks, who pleaded guilty and was released for time served and deported to his home in Australia; Salim Hamdan, of Yemen, who served a 66-month sentence that ended in 2009; and Ali Hamza al Bahlul, also of Yemen, who was sentenced to life in prison ("By the Numbers," *Miami Herald*, July 29, 2010).

Third, the military has had to do some serious soul searching over the events occurring in the confinement facilities they operated. In 2005, the Detainee Treatment Act of 2005 was passed into law. This act prohibited the use of extreme interrogation procedures by mandating that only interrogation practices listed in the Army interrogation field manual be used, none of which included the use of torture. In addition, the U.S. Army in 2007 created the Army Center of Excellence for the Professional Military Ethic, located at West Point. This center is responsible for providing training to prevent the reoccurrence of abuses revealed at Abu Ghraib.

USING THE CRIMINAL JUSTICE SYSTEM TO HANDLE TERRORISTS

While a great deal of debate has taken place regarding the use of military tribunals, the reality is that most terrorists have been processed by the criminal justice system. According to both government and nongovernment reports, several hundred terrorists have been successfully prosecuted and processed by the federal criminal justice system.

The Justice Department reports: "Since September 11, 2001, the Department has charged 512 individuals with terrorism or terrorism-related crimes and convicted or obtained guilty pleas in 319 terrorism-related and anti-terrorism cases."

■ Learn More on the Internet

For more information, go to: www.justice.gov/cjs/docs/terrorism-bush-admin.html. ■

> ## BOX 21.2 CRIMINAL JUSTICE CASES OF CONVICTED TERRORISTS

- Richard Reid, a British citizen, was arrested in December 2001 for attempting to ignite a shoe bomb while on a flight from Paris to Miami carrying 184 passengers and 14 crew members. He was advised of his right to remain silent and to consult with an attorney within 5 min of being removed from the aircraft (and was read or reminded of these rights a total of four times within 48 h), pled guilty in October 2002, and is now serving a life sentence in federal prison.
- In 2003, Iyman Faris, a U.S. citizen from Pakistan, pled guilty to conspiracy and providing material support to al Qaeda for providing the terrorist organization with information about possible U.S. targets for attack. Among other things, he was tasked by al Qaeda operatives overseas to assess the Brooklyn Bridge in New York City as a possible post-9/11 target of destruction. After initially providing significant information and assistance to law enforcement personnel, he was sentenced to 20 years in prison.

- In 2002, the "Lackawanna Six" were charged with conspiring, providing, and attempting to provide material support to al Qaeda based upon their pre-9/11 travel to Afghanistan to train in the Al Farooq camp operated by al Qaeda. They pled guilty, agreed to cooperate, and were sentenced to terms ranging from 7 to 10 years in prison. There are many other examples of successful terrorism prosecutions, including Zacarias Moussaoui (convicted in 2006 in connection with the 9/11 attacks and sentenced to life in prison).
- Ahmed Omar Abu Ali (convicted in 2005 of conspiracy to assassinate the President and other charges and sentenced to life in prison) to Ahmed Ressam (convicted in 2001 for the Millennium plot to bomb the Los Angeles airport and sentenced to 22 years; this sentence was recently reversed as too lenient and he has been remanded for resentencing).

Criminal Justice as a Counterterrorism Tool, www.justice.gov/cjs.

The New York University Center on Law and Security publishes a *Terrorist Trial Report Card (2010)* a scorecard on terrorist prosecutions. They report that:

> Ten years after Al Qaeda's attack on the United States on September 11, 2001, the federal government's record on terrorism prosecutions is relatively easy to summarize: a heavy reliance on preventive law enforcement, an increasingly aggressive use of material support statutes, and a high conviction rate. Strikingly, during the first two years of Barack Obama's presidency, the annual number of prosecutions for jihadist-related terrorism doubled.

They go on to report that 431 of 578 cases have been resolved and 87% of these have resulted in a conviction (p. 7).

See Box 21.2 for information on some criminal cases of convicted terrorists.

THE QUESTION STILL PERSISTS: HOW SHOULD WE RESPOND TO TERRORISM?

Presently we have two options or systems of justice available for handling terrorists. The first is the traditional option that involves the criminal justice system. The suspected terrorist is treated as a criminal and is accorded the same rights as a citizen. Under the second option, the terrorist is viewed as a combatant (either lawful or unlawful) and tried in a military tribunal following procedures set forth by the Uniform Code of Military Justice and governed by the rules set forth by the Military Commissions Act of 2009.

See Title 18 Military Commissions Act at www.defense.gov/news/ commissionsacts.html

The Obama Administration has clearly stated that they prefer the criminal justice option, which is guided by the **rule of law**. However, as history has taught us, in a democracy there are checks and balances; and the Congress has not agreed with this choice and has refused to fund both the closures of Guantánamo Bay and the prosecution of noncitizen terrorism suspects in the United States federal court system. The debate continues, and if we look at the record we see how policy makers have struggled with this issue. How do we determine which system to use? A former United States Attorney General, who served under George W. Bush, answered the question this way:

> When asked how to distinguish whether to use a military tribunal system or criminal courts for terrorist suspects, Attorney General Ashcroft said: "It depends on the circumstances...Our priority should be a priority of preventing further terrorist attacks and to automatically allocate people from one system to another, without understanding what best achieves that priority, would in my judgment be less than optimal."
>
> **Stein, 2010**

More recently, the Obama Administration faced a similar question—what to do with terrorists? President Obama and his Attorney General, Eric Holder, have taken the view that either option should be available for use, but all things being equal, the terror suspects' cases should be handled in the federal criminal justice system. This has raised some controversy in political circles, especially by those who support the military option.

Some legislative leaders, such as Senator Lindsey Graham of South Carolina, have argued that the terrorists behind the September 11, 2001, attacks should not be tried in United States courts, but rather in military tribunals. To ensure that terrorists would be tried by the military, he co-sponsored a bill in Congress to deny federal funding to support civilian trials for the September 11 conspirators. This, in effect, would take the discretionary decision away from the executive branch of the government. In a press release, he argued:

> "I believe it is inappropriate to give the mastermind of the 9/11 attacks the same constitutional rights as an American citizen...It has never

been done in the history of warfare and now is not the time to start. Military commissions are the proper venue for the trial of KSM and the other 9/11 conspirators."

Senator Lindsey Graham, 2010

Graham was joined by Senators John McCain (R-Arizona), Joe Lieberman (IND-Connecticut), Jim Webb (D-Virginia), Jeff Sessions (R-Alabama), Blanche Lincoln (D-Arkansas), Orrin Hatch (R-Utah), Saxby Chambliss (R-Georgia), and John Barrasso (R-Wyoming).

■ Learn More on the Internet

For more on Senator Graham, go to: www.lgraham.senate.gov/public/. ■

In a later press release on the Christmas-day attack attempt by a suicide bomber, Senator Graham stated,

> "The whole process of criminalizing the war is misguided. There is a reason why we have never given unlawful enemy combatants legal counsel at the time of capture. The impact of that decision is that it makes our nation less safe. It was a mistake to read him Miranda rights after he was apprehended and to suggest otherwise is just political spin."

Senator Lindsey Graham, 2010 senate.gov/ public/index.cfm?FuseAction=PressRoom.

In another press release, Graham gave a glimpse into his reasoning for his stand regarding the use of the military tribunals for Guantánamo detainees in preventive detention: "Remember, these detainees are warriors, not common criminals. They should be treated as such, and the legal system we use to detain them must be built around that concept" (Senator Lindsey Graham, 2010).

In response, Attorney General Holder stated that "the proposal by some respected leaders in Congress to ban completely the use of civilian courts in prosecutions of terrorism-related activity obscures some basic facts and allows campaign slogans to overtake legal reality. The reality is this: Since 9/11, more than 400 individuals have been convicted of terrorism or terrorism-related offenses in civilian courts. Without civilian law enforcement and civilian courts, we would be denied the use of what has been our most effective weapon for disrupting, dismantling and defeating terror plots. It would hinder our ability to secure actionable intelligence and to enlist international cooperation in our fight against terrorism" (Holder, April 15, 2010). The posture of the present administration appears to look at each of the cases it handles on a given case's particular merits and then decide what process would be most appropriate.

However, as Congress has pointed out, the transfer of noncitizens for trial in the United States would not be funded.

THE OBAMA APPROACH

As one of his campaign promises, candidate Barack Obama promised that if he became president he would close down Guantánamo Bay. Following the election, he directed his Attorney General to appoint a Detention Policy Task Force whose mission was to develop options regarding policies for the apprehension, detention, and treatment of suspected terrorists. The commission grappled with the nature of terrorism where in some cases it is a clear violation of criminal law and in other cases it represents a violation of the laws of war. The task force concluded that all options needed to be on the table in order to respond to terrorism and that both federal courts and military commissions should be considered. The preference, however, was that when terrorists clearly violate criminal law they should be treated as criminals and prosecuted in federal courts. In cases where the violations are clearly defined as violations of the law of war, military commissions would be the preferred choice. To address concerns regarding due process protections, the Obama Administration has introduced five rule changes to military commissions that have expanded defendant rights (Kris, 2010).

The presumption favored by the Obama Administration is that suspected terrorist cases be prosecuted in a criminal court. The Attorney General's Task Force advises that each case deserves individual attention and should be assessed in terms of a variety of factors, including the nature of the offense, the identity of the victims, the location of the offense, and the context of the apprehension, as well as the way evidence was gathered.

CLOSING GUANTÁNAMO

After his election, President Obama issued executive order 13492 calling for a review of the detainees held at the Guantánamo Bay Naval Base, with the aim of phasing out and closing the detention facility. A multiagency task force, including lawyers from the Defense Department, reviewed the cases of the 240 detainees housed there and made the following recommendations:

- One hundred twenty-six detainees were approved for transfer. Of these, 44 detainees have been transferred to countries outside the United States.
- Forty-four detainees were recommended for prosecution in either a federal court or a military commission, and 36 of these detainees were still being investigated. The Attorney General has announced that the government will pursue prosecutions against six of these detainees in

federal court and will pursue prosecutions against six others in military commissions.

- Forty-eight detainees were determined to be too dangerous to transfer and their cases were determined to be not eligible for prosecution. They will remain in detention pursuant to the government's authority under the Authorization for Use of Military Force passed by Congress in response to the attacks of September 11, 2001. However, the detainees may challenge the legality of their detention in federal court and will periodically receive further review within the executive branch.

- Thirty detainees from Yemen were designated for "conditional" detention based on the current security environment in that country. They are not approved for repatriation to Yemen at this time, but they may be transferred to third countries, or repatriated to Yemen in the future if the current moratorium on transfers to Yemen is lifted and other security conditions are met (U.S. Department of Justice, n.d.).

Under Attorney General Eric Holder, the Justice Department examined both systems of justice (civilian and military) and identified the advantages and disadvantages of both systems of justice for handling suspected terrorists. Assistant Attorney General David Kris laid out their strategy during a speech given to the Brookings Institution in Washington, DC. Kris specified five general advantages for using each of the approaches (military tribunals or civilian federal courts). See Box 21.3.

In contrast, Assistant Attorney General Kris laid out the five options' main advantages of using federal courts rather than military commissions or law of war detention (see Box 21.4).

BOX 21.3 FIVE ADVANTAGES OF THE MILITARY APPROACH

1. **Proof Requirements**. In military commissions, the burden of proof is the same as in civilian court—beyond a reasonable doubt—but in noncapital cases only two-thirds of the jurors (rather than all of them) are needed for conviction. Under the law of war, if tested through a habeas corpus petition, the government need only persuade the judge by a preponderance of the evidence that the petitioner is part of al Qaeda or affiliated forces, though that is not always easy, as our track record in the Guantánamo cases has shown.

2. **Admissibility of Confessions**. In a military commission, unlike in federal court, Miranda warnings are not required to use the defendant's custodial statements against him. While the voluntariness test generally applies in the commissions as it does in federal court, there is an exception in the commissions for statements taken at the point of capture on or near a battlefield. For law-of-war detention, the test is reliability, which may in practical effect be pretty similar to a basic voluntariness requirement.

3. **Closing the Courtroom**. While both federal trials and commission proceedings are generally open proceedings, compared to federal court, there may be some increased ability to close the courtroom in a military commission, and certain military commission trials have implemented a 45-s delay of the broadcast of statements to permit classified

BOX 21.3 FIVE ADVANTAGES OF THE MILITARY APPROACH
Continued

information to be blocked before it is aired in certain cases. There certainly is a greater ability to close the courtroom in a habeas corpus proceeding, and—unlike both military commission and civilian trials—the petitioner is not required to be present, which can help in dealing with classified information.

4. **Admissibility of Hearsay**. The hearsay rules are somewhat more relaxed in military commissions than in federal prosecutions, and they are significantly more relaxed in habeas proceedings. This can be good for the government in some cases, particularly in protecting sensitive sources, but it can also help the defendant/petitioner in some cases. In the *Hamdan* case, for example, Hamdan used the hearsay rules more than the government did.

5. **Classified Evidence**. The rules governing protection of classified information are very similar in the two prosecution forums—indeed, the military commission rules were modeled on the federal court rules. But the rules may be somewhat better in military commissions because they codify some of the federal case law and adopt lessons learned from litigating classified information issues in federal court. I would say the classified information rules in habeas proceedings over law of war detention are both more flexible and less certain.

David Kris, U.S. Assistant Attorney General. Speech at the Brookings Institution. June 11, 2010.

BOX 21.4 FIVE ADVANTAGES OF THE FEDERAL COURTS APPROACH

1. **Certainty and Finality**. The rules governing civilian prosecutions are more certain and well established than those in the other two systems. This can speed the process, reduce litigation risk, promote cooperation and guilty pleas, and result in reliable long-term incapacitation. This is a very significant factor for now, but it will hopefully recede over time as we gain more experience in the commissions.

2. **Scope**. The civilian criminal justice system is much broader than the other two—it has far more crimes (covering everything from terrorism to tax evasion), and applies to everyone. Military commissions are not available for U.S. citizens—folks like Anwar Awlaki and Faisal Shahzad—and neither commissions nor law of war detention apply to terrorists not related to al Qaeda or the Taliban: groups like Hamas, Hizbollah, or the FARC are out of bounds, as are lone wolf terrorists who may be inspired by al Qaeda but are not part of it (like the two individuals I mentioned who allegedly tried to blow up buildings in Illinois and Texas last year).

3. **Incentives for Cooperation**. The criminal justice system has more reliable and more extensive mechanisms to encourage cooperation. While the military commissions have borrowed a plea and sentencing agreement mechanism from the courts-martial system which could be used for cooperation—Rule 705—this system has not yet been tested in military commissions and its effectiveness is as yet unclear. In law of war detention, interrogators can offer detainees improvements in their conditions of confinement, but there is no "sentence" over which to negotiate, and no judge to enforce an agreement. Detainees may have little incentive to provide information in those circumstances. On the other hand, in some circumstances law-of-war detainees may lawfully be held in conditions that many believe are helpful to effective interrogation.

4. **Sentencing**. In federal court, judges impose sentences based in large part on tough sentencing guidelines, while sentencing in the military commissions is basically done by the jury without any guidelines.

Continued...

BOX 21.4 FIVE ADVANTAGES OF THE FEDERAL COURTS APPROACH
Continued

What little experience we have with the commissions suggests that sentencing in that forum is less predictable—two of the three commission defendants convicted thus far (including Osama bin Laden's driver) received sentences of 5–6 years, with credit for time served, and were released within months of sentencing. Under the law of war, of course, there is no sentence; if their detention is lawful, detainees may be held until the end of the conflict. But the Supreme Court has warned that if the circumstances of the current conflict "are entirely unlike those of the conflicts that informed the development of the law of war," the authority to detain "may unravel." As circumstances change, or if active combat operations are concluded, it is not clear how long the detention authority will endure. It may also be worth noting that there may be some advantages to bringing a capital case in federal court rather than in a military commission, in light of the different rules. The military commissions, for example, may not permit a capital sentence to be imposed following a guilty plea, at least for now.

5. **International Cooperation.** Finally, the criminal justice system may help us obtain important cooperation from other countries. Unfortunately, some countries won't provide us with evidence we may need to hold suspected terrorists in law-of-war detention or prosecute them in military commissions. In some cases, they have agreed to extradite terrorist suspects to us only on the condition that they not be tried in military commissions. In such cases, use of federal courts may mean the difference between holding a terrorist and having him go free. This is not, of course, a plea to subject our counterterrorism efforts to some kind of global test of legitimacy; it is simply a hardheaded, pragmatic recognition that in some cases, where we need help from abroad, we will have to rely on law enforcement rather than military detention or prosecution.

David Kris, U.S. Assistant Attorney General. Speech at the Brookings Institution. June 11, 2010.

A CASE IN POINT: THE TIMES SQUARE BOMBER

The policies regarding the use of the criminal justice option were tested with a U.S. citizen when, on May 1, 2010, an attempted car bombing took place in Times Square, New York City. Following an intensive multiagency investigation involving a variety of local, state, and federal agencies, the suspect, Faisal Shahzad, was arrested on May 3, 2010, by law enforcement authorities at JFK Airport as he attempted to flee the country. He was detained and subjected to traditional interrogation practices. On June 21, 2010, he pleaded guilty to 10 federal charges leveled against him. He faced mandatory life sentences for at least two of the counts. According to the U.S. Department of Justice, Shahzad admitted to the following:

In December 2009, Shahzad received explosives training in Waziristan, Pakistan, from explosive trainers affiliated with Tehrik-e-Taliban, a militant extremist group based in Pakistan. On February 25, 2010, Shahzad received approximately $5,000 in cash in Massachusetts sent from a co-conspirator (CC-1) in Pakistan whom Shahzad understood worked for Tehrik-e-Taliban. Approximately six weeks later, on April 10, 2010, Shahzad received an additional $7,000 in cash in Ronkonkoma, NY, which was also sent at CC-1's direction.

On March 15, 2010, Shahzad purchased a semiautomatic 9 mm Kel-Tec rifle in Connecticut. This rifle was found, loaded, in Shahzad's car on the day of his arrest.

In April 2010, Shahzad contacted the seller of a Nissan Pathfinder after seeing an advertisement posted on a website. Thereafter, on April 24, 2010, Shahzad and the seller of the Pathfinder agreed to meet in a supermarket parking lot in Connecticut, where Shahzad paid the seller $1,300 for the Pathfinder. In April 2010, Shahzad also purchased components for the improvised explosive and incendiary devices that he loaded into the Pathfinder on May 1, 2010.

On May 1, 2010, Shahzad drove the Pathfinder, loaded with the improvised explosive and incendiary devices, to Manhattan and parked the Pathfinder in Times Square in the vicinity of 45th Street and Seventh Avenue. After parking the Pathfinder, Shahzad attempted to begin the detonation process of the improvised explosive and incendiary devices. Thereafter, Shahzad abandoned the Pathfinder and returned to his residence in Connecticut.

On May 3, 2010, Shahzad drove from Connecticut to JFK Airport as he attempted to flee to Dubai. He was arrested later that same day at JFK Airport. After his arrest, Shahzad admitted that he had recently received bomb-making training in Pakistan. He also admitted that he had brought the Pathfinder to Times Square and attempted to detonate it (U.S. Department of Justice, 2010).

CONCLUSION

The September 11 terrorist attacks shattered the American illusion that the United States was somehow immune from catastrophic terrorist attacks. On September 12, 2001, the nation woke up to the realization that our way of life was under attack. The most powerful nation on earth had its security violated by 19 terrorists sent from abroad. We immediately, as a nation, struggled to respond to the threat we faced. The initial response was to empower the Office of the President with extraordinary powers to pursue a war against terrorism. Initially, certain steps were taken to arrest, interrogate, and detain terrorists within the military justice system. The criminal justice system was deemed inappropriate at the time. Public safety needed to be a priority and civil liberties needed to be compromised. A lively debate ensued within our society about whether the war against terrorism required the United States to reconsider whether exceptions should be made concerning our civil liberties. Underlying this debate was the issue of "does the ends justify the means." In other words, if the end goal is to protect society, to what extent should extraordinary means be used to achieve this goal? All branches of government and the general public became involved in this debate. As a consequence, over the course of several years we have evolved a policy that reinforces the use of the "rule of law" in our society as we continue to deal with terrorists and acts of terrorism. As a guide, we should perhaps keep in mind a suggestion made by Benjamin Franklin: "Those who desire to give up freedom in order to gain security will not have, nor do they deserve, either one" (www.bartleby.com/100/245.html).

Discussion Questions

1. What ethical perspective do you believe should apply to the issue of responding to terrorism in our society? Should policies be guided by a utilitarianism or deontological perspective?

2. If the drug cartel problems Mexico is experiencing spill over to the United States and the "ticking time bomb" issue comes up with regard to criminals who might kidnap and threaten the lives of hostages, should the use of torture be considered as a way of persuading the suspects to "man up"?

3. Should suspects arrested for terrorism be given their Miranda rights prior to interrogation? What is one argument in favor and one against? Where do you stand and why?

4. Should the Eighth Amendment of the U.S. Constitution (prohibition against cruel and unusual punishments) apply to convicted terrorists? What is one argument in favor and one against? Where do you stand and why?

5. Philip Zimbardo has an excellent presentation on Abu Ghraib. In this presentation he describes a process he calls the "Lucifer effect." You can find it at: www.ted. com/talks/philip_zimbardo_on_the_psychology_of_evil.html.

Zimbardo argues that the external factors (i.e., the situation) cause people to become good or evil. At Abu Ghraib, the situation contributed to the transformation of the soldiers from good to evil. Do you agree or disagree with his assessment? Why or why not?

REFERENCES

By the Numbers (July 19, 2010). *The Miami Herald*, Retrieved on August 2, 2010, from www.miami-herald.com/2007/11/27/322461/by-the-numbers.html.

Congressional research service report (2013). p. 10.

Franklin, B. In J. Bartlett (Ed.), *Familiar quotations* (10th ed.). Retrieved on July 30, 2010, from www.bartleby.com/100/245.1.html.

Gonzales, A. (January 25, 2002). Decision re application of the Geneva convention on prisoners of war to the conflict with al Qaeda and the Taliban. *Memorandum for the President*. Retrieved on July 30, 2010, from www.gwu.edu/~nsarchiv/NSAEBB/NSAEBB127/02.01.25.pdf.

Hamdan v. Rumsfeld, 548 U.S. 557 (2006).

Holder, E. (Speaker). (2010). In R. Reilly (Ed.), *Holder's prepared remarks at the U.S. Constitution Project Awards Dinner*. Washington, DC: Main Justice. Retrieved on July 30, 2010, from www.mainjustice.com/2010/04/15/holders-prepared-remarks-at-the-u-s-constitution-project-awards-dinner/.

Kris, D. (2010). U.S. Assistant Attorney General. Speech at the Brookings Institution. June 11, 2010.

Lewis, N. A. (November 30, 2004). *Red cross finds detainee abuse in Guantanamo*. The New York Times. Retrieved on July 30, 2010, from www.nytimes.com/2004/11/30/politics/30gitmo.html.

Military Order of November 13, 2001, Detention, Treatment, and Trial of Certain Non-Citizens in the War Against Terrorism.

Miranda v Arizona, 384 U.S. 436 (1966).

Regan, T. (February 12, 2007). *Does '24' encourage U.S. interrogators to 'torture' detainees?* Retrieved on July 30, 2010, from csmonitor.com/2007/0212/p99s01-duts.html.

Senator Lindsey Graham (January 22, 2010). Press releases. *Graham reaffirms support for holding detainees in preventative detention*, Retrieved on February 2, 2010, from lgraham.senate.gov/public/index.cfm?FuseAction=PressRoom.PressReleases&ContentRecord_id=94b692e5-802a-23ad-4641-1a34b485c7dd&Region_id=&Issue_id.

Stein, S. (February 19, 2010). John Ashcroft: civilian trials for terrorists have 'use and utility'. *The Huffington Post*. Retrieved on July 30, 2010, from www.huffingtonpost.com/2010/02/19/john-ashcroft-civilian-tr_n_469022.html?.

The Center on Law and Security, & New York University School of Law (January 2010). *Terrorist trial report card*, Retrieved on August 2, 2010, from www.lawandsecurity.org/publications/TTRCFinalJan14.pdf.

U.S. Department of Justice. (n.d.) *Fact Check: Terrorism and Terrorism Related Prosecutions by the Bush Administration More than 300 after 9/11*. Retrieved on July 30, 2010, from www.justice.gov/cjs/docs/terrorism-bush-admin.html.

U.S. Department of Justice (June 21, 2010). Press release. *Faisal Shahzad pleads guilty in Manhattan federal court to 10 federal crimes arising from attempted car bombing in Times Square*.

U.S. Department of Justice (2010). *Final report Guantánamo review task force*. Washington: U.S. Government Printing Office.

Yoo, J. (January 4, 2005). *Commentary: Behind the 'torture memos.'* UC Berkley News. Retrieved on July 30, 2010, from berkeley.edu/news/media/releases/2005/01/05_johnyoo.shtml.

SECTION 6

Ethics and the Future

Where there is life, there is hope.

Latin proverb

When thinking about the future of our institutions of justice and other processes that are related to them, a number of questions come to mind. What philosophical model or models will guide us personally and professionally? How will we attempt to balance the rights of the individual with the needs of the larger community? How will these same models help define and redefine the roles of the courts, policing, and corrections? The heart and mind of our system of justice from which our policies and programs spring forth are composed of our personal and professional philosophical models. Will our collective heart and mind of justice use its long arms of the law to simply keep the peace, or will it begin to try to encourage and contribute to the peace? And how will all the interrelated aspects of this process be evaluated? How will we define success in the future?

It seems evident that, as we come to this last section of this book, there are many more questions than answers. Perhaps that is as it should be. As we look to our future, we may find the beginnings of the answers we seek through the asking of clear, accurate, meaningful questions about our personal sense of justice and how it is expressed through our formal justice process.

CHAPTER 22

Criminal Justice: An Ethic for the Future

Michael C. Braswell, Robert C. England

KEY CONCEPTS

mindfulness   order keeping   peacemaking

Now that we have come to the end of this volume, we would like to finish by once again considering its beginning. The first three chapters were concerned with developing a philosophical framework through which we could consider the ethical implications of a variety of criminal justice issues from personal, social, and criminal justice perspectives. Now that we have attempted to examine contemporary issues within this framework, we are challenged to look toward the future of criminal justice, a future that is found hidden in its present. How are we to find the eyes to see such a future—a vision that can empower us to contribute to its promise? Will our contributions as individuals and institutions be expressed in the context of a community of hope or a community of fear and cynicism? Will we protect and serve the status quo (focus on the criminal), or will we move ahead, riding the crest of a long shot—that the larger sense of justice is what will be accentuated and that the possibility of social peace can increasingly become a reality? Are we only to be engaged in colorful, crisis-minded rhetoric, or can we translate contemporary justice dilemmas into opportunities for encouraging more substantial policies and practical applications toward restitution and reconciliation?

If we choose to commit to seeking justice and peace in a community of hope, we will need to begin acting on an enlarged vision that includes an ethic for the future. Of course, to some, this sort of thinking may seem to be too romantic a notion when considered against the hard realities of today's justice problems. Still, it would appear that it's worth pursuing an attitude of hope that empowers us on a personal and systemic level and is anchored in something more than another blue-ribbon task force or budget increase. Whether in reference to offenders, victims, citizens, or criminal justice professionals, it seems to be in our best interests to recognize and encourage an attitude of personal empowerment, that perhaps we need to restore the balance of our interaction with our environment, that problems and solutions come from the inside out as well as from the outside in. Thich Nhat Hanh, (1987) writes:

> The problem is to see reality as it is. A pessimistic attitude can never create the calm. But, in fact, when we are angry, we ourselves are anger. When we are happy, we ourselves are happiness. When we have certain thoughts, we are those thoughts…. In a family, if there is one person who practices mindfulness, the entire family will be mindful…. And in one class, if one student lives in mindfulness, the entire class is influenced (pp. 40, 52, 64).

THE NEED FOR MINDFULNESS

If we are to develop an ethic for the future of criminal justice, we need to cultivate **mindfulness**, that is, to become more mindful and conscious of ethical truths concerning justice that are found in the present. For example, the utilitarian's priority for community good and the individual integrity of the deontologist become conscious of one another in the context of connectedness and, more important, are reconciled in an ongoing response of active care. At some point in our lives, we are inclined to become aware that no matter how strong our personal needs and interests, no one is an island. We need to be with other people in the community in order to survive and grow.

Whether we live in suburbia, the inner city, or rural America, we begin to realize that we are connected: parents to children, teachers to students, guards to prisoners, and offenders to victims. We like the ideas of "one for all and all for one" and "one nation under God with liberty and justice for all," and we are also connected to our environment. Drought, acid rain, forest fires, and oil spills all raise our consciousness of our interdependence with our physical environment as well.

The dynamic interaction between the community and the individual along a continuum of connectedness and care can be demonstrated in a specifically criminal justice context. We may still find it necessary to remove an offender from society. We may decide to place this person in prison "for the good of the community," yet, even in prison, we need to realize that offenders are entitled to certain rights of basic care and safety. In other words, we need to see that they are treated humanely on ethical and moral grounds, even if in some cases we may feel they are not deserving because of the crimes they have committed or that our correctional treatment efforts have little effect on their behavior.

Although the offender may be inside prison and we may be outside in the community, we are still connected in a number of ways. We are bound together from the past by the fear and suffering of the victim and the vicarious feelings and perceptions of our citizens. There are also the fear and suffering of the offender and the offender's family, who may also be victims. We are brought together in the present through the quality of life of the prison staff, who are also members of the community and are tied to the offenders they supervise and with whom they interact. The promise of the future connects us in the knowledge that, especially with current prison overcrowding problems, most offenders will eventually return to our communities. We might even consider the notion that the way we as a community allow prisoners to be treated in prison and in correctional programs may say much about how we see ourselves and expect to be treated. Becoming more mindful can allow us, as individuals and communities, to take greater care in seeing and responding more meaningfully to the connections that bind us together in relationships.

ORDER KEEPING AND PEACEMAKING

Hans Mattick (in Conrad, 1981) once said, "If I could sum up my entire education experience and reflection in a single sentence, it would be: 'Things are not what they seem'" (p. 14). Yet often, in our haste to find and keep order, we try to do just the opposite of what Mattick suggests: We try to eliminate the ambiguity and paradox from human behavior—we try to make things "be as they seem." If we limit our search for justice to crime and criminals, we are likely to miss the larger truth of Mattick's point. Our search for justice can instead become subverted to a search for order. It is even possible that the ambiguity that is an inevitable part of democracy's birthright can, over time, be replaced by the certainty and predictability of a totalitarian society.

Too much emphasis on **order keeping** encourages us to review problems or failures in the justice process as technological difficulties that can be corrected through sound engineering rather than fundamental problems of design. We imagine that if we can just do things more efficiently, crime and justice problems can eventually be solved, or at least reduced to an insignificant level. Unfortunately, an order-keeping focus may inhibit us from expanding our area of concern to include the impact of the interaction within the larger social arena, which addresses more specific crime and justice issues. It is worth remembering that if we have not asked the right questions, which include a variety of diverse perspectives, our solutions—no matter how efficiently implemented—are no solutions at all; rather, they simply add another layer to the confusion and difficulty that already exists and end up creating additional problems and suffering.

The importance of viewing criminal justice and related issues from a variety of perspectives is well illustrated by a Sufi writer: "What is fate?" Nasrudin was asked by a scholar. "An endless succession of intertwined events influencing each other," Nasrudin replied. "That is hardly a satisfactory answer. I believe in cause and effect." "Very well," said the Mulla, "look at that." He pointed to a procession passing in the street. "That man is being taken to be hanged. Is that because someone gave him a silver piece to buy the knife with which he committed murder, or because someone saw him do it, or because nobody stopped him?" (Meredith, 1984, p. 48).

Even though keeping the order is important, keeping the peace is more than that. Peacekeeping represents a larger vision with potentially profound implications for the individual and the community. Peacekeeping can in fact emerge into a practice of **peacemaking**. Such a practice requires that we encourage a greater sense of mindfulness that allows us to remain conscious that human behavior is not an either/or proposition but a continuum that includes and connects offenders, victims, and nonoffenders. Order keeping focuses on the "guilty few," whereas the mindfulness of peacekeeping and peacemaking remind us that "few may be guilty, but all are responsible" (Quinney, 1980).

Isaiah (32:17) states, "Justice will bring about peace, right will produce calm and security." Is that what is happening in our crime- and justice-conscious culture? Are our citizens experiencing a greater sense of peace, calm, and security? How can we, in a meaningful and balanced way, maintain that order yet keep and even contribute to the peacefulness, calm, and security in our communities? Such existential questions seem challenging at best and overwhelming at worst. It is easy enough to think and talk about peacemaking, but it's quite another thing to put it into mindful action. Hubert Van Zeller (in Castle, 1988) adds yet another twist when he writes, "Thinking about interior peace destroys interior peace. The patient who constantly feels his pulse is not getting better" (p. 180). Van Zeller would lead us to believe that if we are able to contribute to the peacefulness, calm, and security of our community, we must learn to be more peaceful, calm, and secure within ourselves. Can we offer calm if we are angry, security if we are fearful, or hope if we are cynical? It seems that if we are to contribute to a more just society, we must not simply think, talk, or write about peacekeeping and peacemaking but personally struggle to increasingly be peaceful. Quinney (unpublished paper) writes, "Rather than attempting to create a good society first, and then trying to make ourselves better human beings, we have to work on the two simultaneously…. Without peace within us and in our actions, there can be no peace in our results" (pp. 19, 23). Critics of peacemaking as a viable way to improve our justice process would point to its impracticality. Such an approach seems to have little in common with popular notions, such as "getting tough" on crime. Unfortunately, though such popular notions may get people elected to political office and make many of us feel better emotionally, their practical applications have done little to reduce crime or increase the calm and security of citizens. Although perhaps requiring an alternative mindset, peacemaking may not be as impractical as many critics suggest. Dass and Gorman (1985) offer an account by a police officer who struggled to see himself primarily as a peacekeeper and peacemaker:

> Now there are two theories about crime and how to deal with it. Anticrime guys say, "You have to think like a criminal." And some police learn that so well they get a kind of criminal mentality themselves.
>
> How I'm working with it is really pretty different. I see that man is essentially pure and innocent and of one good nature. That's who he is by birthright. And that's what I'm affirming in the course of a day on the job. In fact, that is my job. The "cop" part of it … well, they call us "cops," to me, my job is I'm a peace officer.
>
> So I work not only to prevent the crime but to eliminate its causes—its causes in fear and greed, not just the social causes everyone talks about.
>
> Even when it gets to conflict. I had arrested a very angry black man who singled me out for real animosity. When I had to take him to a paddy wagon, he spit in my face—that was something—and he went after me with a chair. We handcuffed him and put him in the truck. Well, on the way I just had to get past this picture of things, and again I affirmed to myself, "This guy and I are brothers." … When I got to the station, I was moved spontaneously to say, "Look, if I've done anything to offend you, I apologize." The paddy wagon driver looked at me as if I was totally nuts.
>
> The next day I had to take him from where he'd been housed overnight to criminal court. When I picked him up, I thought, "Well, if you trust this vision, you're not going to have to handcuff him." And I didn't. We got to a spot in the middle of the corridor, which was the place where he'd have jumped me if he had that intention, and he stopped suddenly. So did I. Then he said, "You know, I thought about what you said yesterday, and I want to apologize." I just feel deep appreciation.
>
> Turned out on his rap sheet he'd done a lot of time in Michigan and had trouble with guards in jail. I symbolized something. And I saw that turnaround, saw a kind of healing, I believe.
>
> So what really happens if you're going to explore whether or not this vision of nature really has power? Maybe people will say you're taking chances. But you're taking chances without any vision; your vision is your protection. Maybe they'll say you're sentimentalizing people. But it's not about people. It's about principle and truth. It's about how the universe is. Maybe they'll think it's idealistic; things could never be

this way. Well, for me, things are this way already; it's just up to us to know that more clearly.

I see that my work is to hold to an image of who we all truly are and to be guided by that. And I have been guided by that, to greater strength and security … within myself and on the street.

SOME SUGGESTIONS FOR CRIMINAL JUSTICE

If we are to look to the future of criminal justice with some measure of hope rather than a growing sense of cynicism, we must seek out fresh possibilities rather than defend traditional certainties. We need not be naïve to remain open to creative alternatives concerning justice, philosophy, policy, and programming. As Geis (1984) suggests, we need to "stand apart from the parade" to see old problems with a new perspective. Nettler (1982) exhorts us to spend more time and energy in asking the right questions before seeking answers. We need reflection before action. Lozoff puts our dilemma in perspective when he writes, "We all want to know the way, but very few of us are willing to study the maps" (1989, p. 3).

It seems more important than ever for us to look past our individual and agency interests into the larger community of which we are a part. The corporate body of this larger community includes both the best and the worst that we have to offer. The sinner and saint, offender and victim all share the consequences of our formal and informal responses to matters of crime and justice. The choice between prevention, intervention, or no response at all holds meaning for each part of our community as well as the whole. We have to keep trying to look at the problems of crime and justice with fresh eyes, through the eyes of overworked bureaucrats, prison guards, caseworkers, victims, and offenders. We need to look beyond the next career opportunity and try to see through the eyes of our children, and even their children, for we are responsible to them as well. The following suggestions are offered as observations to consider, as food for thought.

LAW AND JUSTICE

Can legal statutes or the justice system make up for our lack of community, for our feelings and experiences of fragmentation? Can morality or a responsible and caring community be legislated? The answer to both questions is, of course, no. However, the way we define laws and the way our justice system enforces them can enhance or diminish our opportunities for more peaceful and orderly communities. Conflict and ambiguity are an inevitable part of how social ills are connected to problems of crime and justice, but intervention (in the form of prevention efforts) must occur before as well as after crimes are committed. Adequate health care and opportunities for meaningful work are at least as important as simply improving the efficiency of the criminal justice process. As we consider how laws must be changed and our justice system needs to be improved, an expanded vision can allow us to create a space in which we can more honestly address differences between how we view the justice process ideally and how it often functions in reality. Myths—such as white-collar crime is nonviolent, the rich and poor are equal before the law, the punishment can fit the crime, and law makes people behave—can be examined and responded to in a more enlightened context of community.

There are also issues of law and justice that must be struggled with on a personal basis, in terms of our being both criminal justice professionals and members of families and social communities. For example, it seems that many people have come to believe that a legal act and a moral act are essentially the same thing. Politicians or corporate executives charged with crimes typically declare to the press and the public that they have done nothing illegal and, indeed, they may often be correct. But does that make it right? Can legal behavior be immoral and illegal behavior moral? Were Martin Luther King, Jr, and Mahatma Gandhi criminals or heroes? In a society in which success is measured primarily in terms of money and prestige, are we encouraged to do whatever is necessary within (and sometimes outside) the law to be successful (Braswell & LaFollette, 1988)? We are appalled when public figures are convicted of large-scale fraud, yet we may consider it acceptable to cheat on our income taxes or college exams. It seems as though we are saying, "It's all right to do something wrong as long as we don't get caught at it." Of course, in life or in criminal court, when we do get caught, our plea is for mercy. From minor greed to major fraud, when we are the victims, we are inclined to want retribution, yet when we are the offenders, we want mercy. This contrasting desire seems true in personal relationships as well as in a professional or criminal justice context. Can we truly have it both ways: mercy when we are the offender and retribution or revenge when we are the victim? Or do we need to accept responsibility and make a stand for one way or the other?

Policing

With more minorities and women entering police work, the opportunity exists for a greater openness in defining and redefining police roles and function. In addition, as issues surrounding the family, such as domestic violence and child abuse, are translated into law and criminal justice policies, the need for police officers to possess meaningful communication and interpersonal skills should become more apparent. It seems ironic that police officers are expected to intervene with families who are in crisis, whereas few, if any, helping services are available to many police when they experience family crisis situations. Shift work and a closed professional system are just two of the factors that can contribute to difficulties regarding family life. To make matters worse, in some instances, a stigma perceived as weakness is identified with officers who do seek professional help for family-related problems (Miller, Braswell, & White-head, 2010). Shernock (1990) observed that the more police believe they have to hide, the more they are likely to resist outside control. Shame or guilt tends to make the police more clannish, more committed to the code of silence, and harder to regulate.

Police agencies are also responsible for detaining offenders in jails until courts dispense with them. Current problems associated with prison overcrowding have also spilled over into jails, turning many of them into little more than institutions for extended incarceration. Most jails are operated by law enforce-ment agencies more inclined toward enforcement and order maintenance strategies than correctional intervention with offenders. And the offenders who end up in jail are typically from the underclass and represent the least affluent in the community because they often cannot afford bail. Suggestions for more creative options such as pretrial release, diversion programs, and speedier trials have long been a possibility, but they are often not utilized. Such an attitude of neglect has additional implications for one of the criminal justice system's most missed opportunities: its potential impact on first-time offenders who have their initial contact with the system at the jail. It seems ironic that the point in the justice process at which the first-time offender is usually the most open to intervention is also the place where the least resources are allocated.

Are police officers tough, unyielding crime fighters, or are they much more than that? Many police officers consider social services calls as "garbage calls," not worthy of their time and effort, yet the majority of their typical workday is spent dealing with human service situations. Paradoxically, the more mindful they are of the ethic of care, as translated through effective communication and interpersonal skills, the less likely they are to have to get tough with the people with whom they come in contact. Still, the image persists: "Dirty Harry" crime fighter or peacemaker? It is interesting to note that an informal survey given each semester to introductory criminal justice students consistently reveals that, all things (i.e., job responsibilities, pay, etc.) being equal, the overwhelm-ing majority of them would prefer to be identified as a police officer or deputy sheriff rather than as a public safety officer. How can we enlarge our vision of police work to include a primary emphasis on peacemaking as well as law enforcement? It is simply a matter of not only knowing how to shoot well but also knowing *when* to shoot—as well as being open to possible nonviolent alternatives. Given the litigious nature of today's world, such an orientation has pragmatic as well as peacemaking advantages. It is unfortunate that the nature and tradition of contemporary police work make the previous exam-ple of the police officer who saw himself as primarily a peace officer seem so unusual (Dass & Gorman, 1985). With so much research focused on police corruption and deviance, we might find it worthwhile to follow Maslow's (1954) example and turn our attention to what motivates well-adjusted, creative, and psychologically healthy police officers. Given the discretion and immediacy of response necessary for police officers in the community setting, there is perhaps no other criminal justice professional who is as connected to the community and who has as great an opportunity to contribute to the community's sense of care and well-being. There are a number of positive developments in policing, particularly in the area of community policing (Kappeler & Gaines, 2011).

Police officers are entrusted to provide security, peace, and fair and impartial treatment to all individuals with utmost regard for the law. The police should act as agents of morality to ensure that every person has the ability to live a law-abiding life as he or she chooses. However, sometimes police officers do not adhere to the same rule of law that they have been sworn to uphold. Police officers ostensibly take an oath of office to uphold these basic liberties of life and accept their duty to perform the acts in an ethical, moral, and lawful manner.

Corrections

Corrections directly addresses the "least of the community"—the two-time losers, the nuisance factor, the disenfranchised, and the violent. Along the continuum of connectedness, offenders appear to be the least useful to the community. They have demonstrated their disdain or inability to do their duty as citizens, to adequately contribute to the common good, or to provide meaningful care. As a result, the larger community often retributively feels that such people themselves are deserving of the least care. Ironically, although we want them to pay for crimes and be corrected, we are not particularly supportive of their feeling good about themselves. The paradox "be good, but don't feel good about it" can often put our correctional process at odds with itself. Is our priority to provide corrections or punishment? Is our emphasis to repair the connection and restore both offender and victim to our community or to disconnect and distance one or the other, or both, from community? Are we to be more interested in restitution and reconciliation whenever possible, or in retribution? Thomas Merton writes, "You cannot save the world with merely a system. You cannot have peace without charity" (Quinney, 1988, p. 71).

The effectiveness of correctional treatment is a worthy and important topic for debate between the pro- and anti-rehabilitation factions in criminal justice (Cullen & Gilbert, 2013; Whitehead & Lab, 2013), but is it the only (or even the most important) basis for funding and providing correctional treatment services for offenders? Are the moral and ethical grounds for treating offenders at least as important, if not more so, as the utilitarian demands for effectiveness? Perhaps we need to develop and articulate a treatment ethic that is restorative in nature and that more honestly addresses the community's (including its lowest-status members) sense of duty to itself. Such a turn of focus also allows us to pay closer attention to the art of correctional treatment rather than strictly to its scientific aspect—to the creation as well as the operation of correctional process. The restorative justice and peacemaking movements, through such nonprofit organizations as the Prison Fellowship (Van Ness & Strong, 1997) and Human Kindness Foundation (Bazemore & Schiff, 2001; Braswell, Fuller, & Lozoff, 2001; Fuller, 1998), offer correctional alternatives that encourage offenders to take responsibility for their actions and be restored to a sense of community in which personal and spiritual transformation can take place.

It is interesting that when we think of correctional treatment interventions we are inclined to think of them more as treatment systems or clinical approaches to be evaluated and less as existential processes to be experienced. Though this tendency may also be true of our psychotherapeutic colleagues, there are more among them that are sensitive to and grounded in a vital sense of the existential that makes the philosophy and science of theory come alive in the art and process of relationship (Rogers, 1980; Satir, 1973). It is worth noting the substantial and continually evolving research of Carkhuff (1987), which indicates that the further graduate students progress in clinical help professions, the more proficient they become in diagnostic, assessment, and evaluation skills but the less effective they seem to become in demonstrating meaningful and effective communication skills.

To put the "art of treatment" perspective into a more specifically correctional context, we can turn to the groundbreaking work of John Augustus and Alexander Maconochie. We can become so enamored of their innovative approaches that we can easily forget, or at least take for granted, the inner aspect of who they were that made their approaches come alive in experience. Dressler (1959) writes of John Augustus's interaction with offenders in a police court: "It is probable that some of them know him, for as he walks to the box two or three turn their blood-shot eyes toward him with eager glances.... In a moment he is with them, gently reproving the hardened ones, and cheering ... those in whom are visible signs of penitence" (p. 25). Dressler continues in commenting on Maconochie's restorative impact on an incorrigible and disturbed inmate: "He was out of touch with reality most of the time, unaware of what was going on about him, but when Maconochie, his wife, or their children, visited him, he returned to reality, recognized his callers. He showed affection for them to the day he died" (p. 67). It is true that evaluating treatment effectiveness is important, as are educating and training competent clinical professionals in diagnostic, assessment, and evaluation skills. However, the art of helping requires more than cognitive or affective sensitivity; it requires a synthesis of both these dimensions and more—emerging from within and lived out in experience with others. "A staff person who's calm and strong and happy is worth his or her weight in gold. People who are living examples of truthfulness, good humor, patience, and courage are going to change more lives—even if they're employed as janitors—than the counselors who can't get their own lives in order" (Lozoff & Braswell, 1989, p. 52).

Perhaps we can begin to rethink our attitude regarding corrections. Do we really want it to work or not? Is corrections to be little more than an opportunity for an incomplete community to express its feelings of retribution, or can it be more than that? Can we realize the possibility that corrections, even with its need for punishment, can also include restitution, rehabilitation, and restoration as means for the community to experience reconciliation? After speaking to a local Kiwanis group about juvenile crime and corrections in their community, one speaker was asked by one of the group members what they could do to help. His response: "Create recreation opportunities for the least of your community and for yourselves—join the local PTA."

JUSTICE AS A WAY RATHER THAN A DESTINATION

It is in our best interests to begin to see justice as an evolutionary way of service rather than as an efficiently engineered technological destination. We need an ethic for our future that will empower us to act on an enlarged vision of what justice is about—a vision that will include the community of which we are all a part, the best of us and the worst of us (and the best in each of us and the worst in each of us). We need a prophetic vision to energize the empowerment of such an ethic. The passion of prophetic vision resounds in the words of Amos (5:24) in the Bible and is repeated by Martin Luther King, Jr, in a striking address: "Let justice roll down like waters. And righteousness like a mighty stream." Quinney (1980) adds, "For the prophets, justice is like a mighty stream, not merely a category or mechanical process. In contrast, the moralists discuss, suggest, counsel; the prophets proclaim, demand, insist" (p. 25).

Justice as a way of service requires more than just the passionate zeal of the visionary; it also requires the mindfulness of quiet compassion. Creative and humane policies and plans are one thing, but making them work is something else. It is the compassionate professionals in public schools, courts, law enforcement, corrections, and other human service agencies that make the ethic of care come alive in the community. Such people are mindful of the suffering that crime and social injustice create for victims and offenders. Their mindfulness is born of their own suffering as well. Dietrich Bonhoeffer, himself incarcerated and finally executed in a Nazi prison camp, wrote (in Castle, 1988), "We must learn to respond to people less in the light of what they do or omit to do, and more in the light of what they suffer." Seeing a Ted Bundy or a Charles Manson through the eyes of compassion keeps us from closing ourselves off from the terrible suffering they have given and received. Their acts are not excused, nor is our irresponsibility in choosing not to commit our collective resources and energies toward preventing the creation of future Bundys or Mansons. Compassionate professionals realize it is not how much they do but rather how mindfully they do whatever they do. To put it another way, as Mother Teresa suggested, "It is not how much you do, but how much you do with love." From a compassionate way of service comes a sense of peace and well-being.

Success, happiness, and even justice are all preludes at best, and second-rate substitutes at worst, to what we really seek—peace. Only peace has the potential to remain calm and resolute even in the midst of suffering that connects each of us to the other in community. Peace comes from the inside out. It cannot be implemented organizationally from the top down. People at peace with themselves create peaceful organizations that can then become instruments for peacemaking in the larger community. To reiterate Dass and Gorman's (1985) cogent observation: "If we ourselves cannot know peace, be peaceful, how will our acts disarm hatred and violence?" (p. 165). And, to borrow once again from Isaiah (2:17): "How else will our justice system bring about peace, produce calm and security for our people?"

Discussion Questions

1. Can legal behavior be immoral and illegal behavior moral? Give your opinion on this statement and defend your answer with examples.
2. Braswell and England think an ethic for the future can improve the criminal justice system. Do you agree or disagree with their viewpoint? Why or why not?
3. Why is mindfulness important to one's personal and professional life? Can you think of any personal example?

REFERENCES

Amos 5:24.

Bazemore, G., & Schiff, M. (2001). *Restorative community justice: Repairing harm and transforming communities.* Cincinnati: Anderson.

Braswell, M. C., Fuller, J., & Lozoff, B. (2001). *Corrections, peacemaking and restorative justice.* Cincinnati: Anderson.

Braswell, M. C., & LaFollette, H. (1988). Seeking justice: The advantages and disadvantages of being educated. *American Journal of Criminal Justice* (Spring), 135–147.

Carkhuff, R. (1987). *The art of helping III.* Amherst: Human Resource Development Press.

Castle, T. (1988). *The new book of Christian quotations.* New York: Crossroad.

Conrad, J. (1981). *Justice and consequences.* Lexington: Lexington Books.

Cullen, F., & Gilbert, K. (2013). *Reaffirming rehabilitation* (2nd ed.). Boston: Elsevier (Anderson Publishing).

Dass, R., & Gorman, P. (1985). *How can I help?* New York: Alfred A. Knopf.

Dressler, D. (1959). *Practice and theory of probation and parole.* New York: Columbia University Press.

Fuller, J. R. (1998). *Criminal justice: A peacemaking perspective.* Boston: Allyn & Bacon.

Geis, G. (1984). Foreword. In H. Pepinsky, & P. Jesilow (Eds.), *Myths that cause crime.* Cabin John: Seven Locks Press.

Hanh, T. N. (1987). *Being peace.* Berkeley: Parallax Press.

Isaiah 32:17.

Kappeler, V. E., & Gaines, L. K. (2011). *Community policing: A contemporary perspective* (6th ed.). Boston: Elsevier (Anderson Publishing).

Lozoff, B. (1989). Editorial. *Human Kindness Foundation Newsletter, 3.*

Lozoff, B., & Braswell, M. (1989). *Inner corrections: Finding peace and peace making.* Cincinnati: Anderson.

Maslow, A. (1954). *Motivation and personality.* New York: Harper.

Meredith, N. (1984). The murder epidemic. *Science* (December), 48.

Miller, L., Braswell, M., & Whitehead, J. (2010). *Human relations and police work* (6th ed.). Prospect Heights, IL: Waveland.

Nettler, G. (1982). *Explaining criminals.* Cincinnati: Anderson.

Quinney, R. (1988). Crime, suffering, and service: Toward a criminology of peacemaking. *The Quest* (Winter), 71.

Quinney, R. *The way of peace: On crime, suffering, and service,* (November), 19–23, unpublished paper.

Quinney, R. (1980). *Providence: The reconstruction of social and moral order.* New York: Longman.

Rogers, C. (1980). *A way of being.* Boston: Houghton Mifflin.

Satir, V. (1973). *Peoplemaking.* Palo Alto: Science and Behavior Books.

Shernock, S. K. (1990). The effects of patrol officers' defensiveness toward the outside world on their ethical orientations. *Criminal Justice Ethics, 9,* 24–42.

Van Ness, D., & Strong, K. H. (1997). *Restoring justice.* Cincinnati: Anderson.

Whitehead, J., & Lab, S. (2013). *Juvenile justice* (7th ed.). Boston: Elsevier (Anderson Publishing).

Index

Note: Page numbers with "*f*" denote figures; "*t*" tables.

A

ABA. *See* American Bar Association
Absolute value, 19
Abu Ghraib Confinement Facility, 436–439, 437b
Abuse of power, 153, 157
Academic literature, 94–95
Academy of Criminal Justice Sciences (ACJS), 420–421, 421b–422b
Acceptable penal content, 235, 309–310
Accounting fraud, 377–378, 388–389
Accusatory, police interrogation, 78
ACJS. *See* Academy of Criminal Justice Sciences
Actions
  connectedness of, 30, 32
  criminal justice research and diminished self-respect from, 404–406, 406b
  duty and moral, 17
  happiness and right, 14
  karma and, 31
  morality of, 13–15, 357
  pain and suffering in wrong, 14
  police ethical dilemmas and right, 109
Active role, 142–143
Adams, Randall Dale, 155
Adult court, 351–352, 368
African Americans. *See* Race
Alternative dispute resolution, 261–262

American Bar Association (ABA), 134–135, 137–144, 153b. *See also* Model Rules of Professional Conduct
American Society of Criminology (ASC), 422
American values, 51–52
Andragogical approach, 96–97
Apologia, 63–64
Appeals to higher loyalties, 125–126
Arbitrariness, death penalty, 214–215
Aristotle, 14
Arrest, 102–103
Arthur Anderson, 388–389
ASC. *See* American Society of Criminology
"Atlanta Child Murders" case, 154–155
Attorney-client privilege, 139–141
Atypical information, 335
Authority, misuse of, 283–284
Awareness, 7, 9b, 29, 38, 264. *See also* Mindfulness

B

"Back-end net widening," 234
Background, 364–365
Beccaria, Cesare, 193–194, 340
Behavior
  analysis, 84–88
  codes of, 324, 334
  control, 406–407
  criminal or fraudulent, 138, 230
Bentham, Jeremy, 13–15, 171, 193–194

Bias, 152, 156–157, 212–213, 363
Blame, 385
Blue curtain, 104–105
Boomerang, 164–165
Bribery, 103
Brown v. Mississippi, 75–76
Brutality, 73–76
Buddhism, 32–33
Burglary, 300
Bush administration, 151–152, 430–431
Business, environment of, 384. *See also* Corporate misconduct and crime

C

Cabana, Donald, 215b–216b
Canons of Police Ethics, 93
Capital Jury Project, 213, 216–217
Capital punishment. *See* Death penalty
Caring and ethics of care, 34–37, 108, 140, 209
Categorical imperative, 17–20
Chain gangs, 304, 309–310
Choice, 54–56, 129b–130b
Christianity, 33, 37
Circumstances, crime, 5
Civil commitment, 243
Civil Rights of Institutionalized Persons Act of 1980 (CRIPA), 292
Client
  attorney privilege with, 139–141
  decision making of, 137–138

467

Client (*Continued*)
   lawyer relationship with, 134–144
   moral agents and, 134–137
   privatization and selection of,
     242–243, 314
   probation fees and payment ability
     of, 234, 242
   prosecutorial failings and public
     as, 159
Client-centered or friend role,
   136–137
A Clockwork Orange, 406
Codes of ethics, 422, 420–421,
   421b–422b
Coercion
   in criminal justice and
     criminal justice research,
     8, 9b, 400–402
   death penalty and, 8
   false confessions by, 87
   police interrogation and, 74
   in police occupation, 47
   power and, 385
   psychological, 76
   willingness to participate and, 402
Collective responsibility, 126–130
Communication, inaccurate,
   334–335
Community. *See* Parole, probation,
   and community corrections
   criminal justice future and
     hope-based, 453–454, 458
   in ethics, crime, and justice, 4
   law and justice in, 458–463
   mindfulness of connected,
     454–455, 461
   parole, probation and service to,
     228
   police relations with, 67
   public opinion and outreach
     programs of, 335–336
Community of Veterans Engaged in
   Restoration (COVER),
   264–265
Community oriented policing
   (COP), 64–65, 67
Compassion, 27–28, 37–38
Condemning the condemners
   technique, 124–125

Confessions. *See also* Police
   interrogation
   by brutality and torture, 73–75
   in criminal justice system, 73–74,
     87
   false, 86–88, 87b
   in police interrogation, 74–76, 89
   for prosecution in legal system,
     74–75
   psychological dimension to, 76
Confidentiality, 408–410. *See also*
   Attorney-client privilege
Confinement or incarceration,
   178–179, 352–354. *See also*
   Prison and correctional facilities
Conflict, 21–22, 135–136, 252
Conformity, 49–50
Connectedness
   of actions, 30, 32
   awareness of, 29
   definition and nature of, 28–29
   dysfunctional families and, 31
   Earth metaphors and, 29–30
   of human beings, 28–30, 32
   karma and, 30–31
   mindfulness of community,
     454–455, 461
   to natural world, 29
   as peacemaking theme, 28–33, 209
Consciousness, 335–336
Consent, 399–400, 402–403
Consequences, 13–14, 357, 412
Consequentialism, 11b, 13–14,
   19–20
Conservatism, 49–50
Constitution, 430
Contingencies, 63
Contraband trafficking, 282–283
Contract, 241, 314
Control, 64–69, 122, 290–292,
   406–407, 410–414, 411b–412b.
   See also Crime control; Prison
   control
COP. *See* Community oriented
   policing
Corporate misconduct and crime
   accounting fraud as, 377–378,
     388–389
   blame assessment, 385

business environment in, 384
causes for, 383–384
crime and justice myths of, 337
DPAs for, 389–391
through excessive executive
   compensation, 382–383
Ford Pinto case, 388b
government, public opinion, and,
   374–375
healthcare fraud as, 379–381,
   380b, 391
individual dishonesty and,
   383–384
in law and legal system, 385–391
media and, 386–387
from middle management, 384
mortgage fraud in, 378–379
personal interest and, 373–374
politics and, 387, 391–392
prosecuting, 387–391
student loan mismanagement,
   381–382
types of, 376–383, 376b
whistleblowers of, 385–386
white-collar crime and, 374–376
Corrections and correctional facilities. *See* Juvenile; Parole,
   probation, and community
   corrections; Prison and
   correctional facilities
Corruption, 103, 244–245, 284, 286,
   288–292, 343. *See also* Prison
   corruption; Prison staff
COVER. *See* Community of Veterans
   Engaged in Restoration
Crime. *See also* Corporate
   misconduct and crime; Ethics,
   crime, and justice
   circumstances and victims of, 5
   criminal sentencing and
     seriousness of, 183
   deceptive interrogation technique
     of normalizing, 81–82
   government controlling
     information on, 331–332
   government on severity of,
     331–332
   in local media, 326–328
   loyalty and minor, 104

media on juvenile, 326, 338–339
media worldview on, 127
myths about, 336–338
offenders and violent, 300–301
police as fighters of, 51–53, 61
police ethics and fighting, 50–53
police pressure and, 83
politics and juvenile, 338–339
politics and manipulating rates of, 332
politics and public fear of, 330–331
positivist theories of, 230
predicting, 180–182
strangers and violent, 339
war on, 120
white-collar, 374–376
Crime and justice myths
corporate misconduct and, 337
of crime control, 340–344
of criminals, 338–339
of drug control policy, 331–332, 336–337, 342
exercise concerning, 345b
FOAF in, 325
"get tough" measures and, 323, 341–342
internet on, 330b, 339b
law and law enforcement in, 324–325, 337–338
media influencing, 325–330, 335
in movies and television, 329
politics impacting, 325, 330–334
public opinion influencing, 325, 334–338
summary of, 344–345
whistleblowers and government spying in, 333–334, 333b
Crime control
corruption from, 344
crime and justice myths of, 340–344
in criminal justice, 340
death penalty in, 341
deterrence and, 340–341
ethical orientation and due process versus, 84
financial costs, 343
"get tough" measures and, 341–342

justice balanced against, 89
model, 84
police ethics, crime-fighting, and, 50–53
politics and research in, 341–344
rehabilitation in, 192
severity in, 341
for society, 340
"three strikes" laws in, 342–343
Criminal defense, 138, 141–142, 210–212, 212b
Criminal justice and criminal justice system
confessions in, 73–74, 87
for corporate crimes, 376
crime control in, 340
criminal justice research and teaching, 420
deception in, 19–20
deceptive interrogation techniques and, 84
deontology compared to utilitarianism in, 19–20
in ethics, crime, and justice, 4f, 5–7
ethics' exploration and coercion in, 8, 9b
ethics taught in, 94–95
government and failing, 330
in higher education, 11
legal limits in, 6
media on, 328
meditation and, 39
morality in, 12
peacemaking in, 33
police and education in, 53–54
prediction in, 180–182
prosecutorial misconduct ethics' problems in, 156–158, 156b, 158b
public opinion impacting policies of, 323–324, 335–337
rule of law in, 441
terrorism handled through, 439–443, 440b, 445b–446b, 446–447
use of force in, 11–12, 21
utilitarianism in, 16
victim's rights in, 174

Criminal justice future
community of hope and, 453–454, 458
corrections in, 461–463
justice in, 458–464
law and, 458–463
mindfulness in, 454–455
multiple perspectives needed in, 455–456
order keeping and peacemaking in, 455–458
policing in, 459–461
Criminal justice research, ethical dilemmas in. See also Randomization
actions that diminish self-respect in, 404–406, 406b
case study on, 424b
codes of ethics in, 422, 420–421, 421b–422b
coercion in, 400–402
confidentiality in, 408–410
deception in, 397–398, 403–404, 419–420
ethical and political considerations in, 416–418
ethical and scientific balance in, 415
evidence-based practice in, 397–398
fabricated evidence in, 397–398, 419–420
fairness towards participants in, 414
human participants and, 398–399
informed consent and knowledge in, 399–400, 402–403
institutional review boards and ethical standards in, 415–416
internet and, 403b–404b, 416b, 423
plagiarism and data theft in, 398
prison simulation, 404–406
privacy invaded in, 408–410
public policy and criminal justice instruction in, 420
randomization and control group benefit withholding in, 410–414, 411b–412b

Criminal justice research, ethical
dilemmas in (*Continued*)
    scientific research purity and,
        418–420
    self-determination right violated
        in, 406–407
    stress exposure in, 407
    summary of, 423–424
    willingness to participate and,
        402
Criminal or fraudulent behavior,
    138, 230
Criminal sentencing and punishment
    contemporary ethical concerns in,
        179–184
    crime's seriousness and, 183
    dessert in, 174–177
    determinate and indeterminate,
        178, 189–190
    deterrence as part of, 172–173,
        177
    discrimination in, 182–184, 184b
    disparities in, 176
    equity *versus* utilitarianism in,
        175–177
    ethical issues in, 171–172,
        179–184
    factors in, 182–183, 212–213
    Federal Guidelines for, 214
    honesty or truth in, 179–180
    incapacitation in, 173, 177
    incarceration in, 178–179
    legislature on, 178
    nature and function of, 171
    "paradox of retribution" in,
        175–176
    practice of, 177–179
    prediction as part of, 180–182
    punishment in, 171
    purpose of, 172–175
    restoration as part of, 174–175,
        177
    restorative justice and circles for,
        255b, 257–258
    summary of, 184–185
    treatment in, 173, 306–309
Criminals, 126–127, 230, 333–334,
    333b, 338–339. *See also specific
    topics*

Criminology, 422, 11, 33
CRIPA. *See* Civil Rights of Institution-
    alized Persons Act of 1980
Critical thinking and analytical skills,
    7–8, 9b
Culture, 48, 52. *See also* Police,
    policing, and police occupation;
    Society and social context
Cummings, Homer S., 164–165

D

Death penalty
    alternatives to, 219–221
    arbitrariness of, 214–215
    coercion and, 8
    in crime control, 341
    criminal defense mistakes and,
        210–212, 212b
    critical thinking and analytical
        skills on, 7–8
    deterrence through, 176, 205–207,
        362
    discrimination and racial bias in,
        212–213, 363
    ethical arguments on, 361–363
    financial costs of, 219, 362
    governor's prerogative case study,
        221b–222b
    for incapacitation, 207–209, 361,
        363
    on internet, 221b
    jurors in cases of, 216–217
    in juvenile justice, 359–363,
        366–368
    laws, legal system, and application
        of, 204, 210–212, 214–217,
        360–361, 368
    LWOP and, 219–220, 359–363
    as moral issue, 8
    murderers' paroled and, 220–221
    peacemaking perspective and,
        209–210
    philosophy on, 204
    privatization of, 313
    public opinion on, 362
    in punishment, 196
    rehabilitation missing from,
        362–363

religion and, 217–219, 366–368
    research, 206
    retribution through, 190, 361
    social interest in, 203
    statistics, 203
    summary of, 221–222
    time involved in, 207
    for utilitarians, 205
Death row, 215–216, 215b–216b
Deception and deceitfulness
    in criminal justice, 19–20
    in criminal justice research,
        397–398, 403–404, 419–420
    in police interrogation, 73–92
    privacy violated by, 20
    in prosecutorial misconduct, 157
    as prosecutors' ethical challenge,
        153
    psychological, 77
Deceptive interrogation techniques,
    78b
    crime normalization or
        minimization in, 81–82
    criminal justice view and, 84
    fabricated evidence in, 80–81
    identity misrepresentation in, 82
    interview compared to
        interrogation in, 78
    legal system on, 78–83
    Miranda warnings in, 80
    offense exaggeration as, 81
    promises used in, 82–83
    role playing in, 79
    utilitarianism justifying, 86
Decision making, 94, 106–107,
    137–138
Deferred and non-prosecution
    agreements (DPAs), 389–391
Denial
    of due process, 153, 157
    of injury, 123
    of responsibility, 121–123
    of victim, 124
Deontology and deontological ethics,
    16–19, 171
    attorney-client privilege in,
        139–140
    case study involving, 23b–24b
    on death penalty arbitrariness, 214

definition and nature of, 16
duty studied in, 16
on juvenile justice, 364–366
Kant on, 16–17
on parole and probation, 232–233
utilitarianism combined with, 22
utilitarianism compared to, 19–20
Deprivation. *See* Pain, deprivation, or suffering
Dessert, 174–177
Deterrence
Beccaria and Bentham on, 193–194, 340
crime control and, 340–341
in criminal punishment, 172–173, 177
through death penalty, 194–195, 205–207, 362
essential elements of, 194
general and specific, 172, 193
hedonistic calculus in, 193–194
juvenile transfers and, 351–352
LWOP and, 362
in probation, 229
problems with, 194, 205
in punishment, 193–195
research on, 206
Disagreement, 107
Discovery, 160
Discretion
definition and nature of, 97
ethical criteria in, 100
example cases involving, 97–98
in family dispute cases, 98–99
personal or professional relationships and, 99–100
in police ethical dilemma training, 97–100
in police ethical practice, 94
in police values, 62
in policing, 50–51, 62
prosecutors' ethical challenges and, 155, 161
in traffic violation cases, 98
Discretionary misconduct, 284–287, 284t
Discrimination, 182–184, 184b, 212–213, 309, 363
Diseases, communicable, 101

Dishonesty, 383–384
Disproportionate minority prison populations, 302–303
Dodd-Frank Act, 383, 385–386, 391
Donovan, Raymond, 154
DPAs. *See* Deferred and non-prosecution agreements
Drug
control policy, 42b, 120, 183, 331–332, 336–337, 342
courts, 263
offenders, 301
Due process, 84, 153, 157
Duke Lacrosse case, 152–153, 158, 162, 164
Duty, 16–17, 20–24, 100–101

E

Earth, metaphors of, 29–30
Economy and economics, 52. *See also* Financial costs
Education. *See specific topics*
Einstein, Albert, 7
Elected officials, 149
Electronic monitoring, 237
Embezzlement, 283
Enrichment, 102
Enron, 377–378, 388–389
Environment. *See specific topics*
Equal protection, 129b–130b
Equality, 18
Equity, 175–177
Ethical
behavior, 57
formalism, 108
framework analysis, 101, 107–109
orientation, 84
Ethical dilemmas, 195, 196–197. *See also* Criminal justice research, ethical dilemmas in; Police training, ethics and ethical dilemmas in
Ethics, crime, and justice
community in, 4
contexts for understanding, 4–7
criminal justice in, 4f, 5–7
ethics defined in, 3–4
personal in, 4–7, 4f

social in, 4f, 5–7
study approach to, 3
unknown in, 6–7
Ethics and ethical issues. *See also* Prison and ethics; *specific topics*
awareness of, 7, 9b
of care, 34–37, 108, 140, 209
criminal justice and coercion in, 8, 9b
criminal justice and teaching, 94–95
criminal justice research, political, and, 416–418
criminal justice research and science balanced with, 415
criminal justice research and standards of, 415–416
criminal sentencing and, 171–172, 179–184
critical thinking and analytical skills in, 7–8, 9b
of deceptive police interrogation, 83
discretion and criteria of, 100
ethics, crime, and justice defining, 3–4
evil and, 3–4
feminine approach to, 34–36
of intensive supervision, 236–240
justice within, 12
in juvenile death penalty and LWOP, 361–363
juvenile justice and religious, 366–368
law, morality, and, 118
lawyers, conflict of rules, and, 135–136
masculine approach to, 34–36
of nonviolence, 32
parole and probation dimensions in, 233
personal responsibility in, 8, 9b
of probation fees, 233–235
professional, 11
prosecutorial, 164–165
prosecutors' misconduct and, 144–145, 149–150
punishment and, 188, 195b
of rights, 140
terrorism and, 427–450

Ethics and ethical issues (*Continued*)
 universal in, 13
  wholesight development and
   exploring, 8–9, 9b
Evidence and evidence tampering,
 80–81, 143–145, 153b, 160,
 397–398, 419–420
Evil, 3–4
Executive compensation, excessive,
 382–383
Existential questions, 456–457, 462

F

Fabricated evidence, 80–81,
 397–398, 419–420
Fairness, 18, 76–83, 190, 266–267,
 410–411, 414
Faith-based programming, 307–309
False positives and negatives, 181
Family and families, 31, 98–99,
 255b, 256–257, 459–460
Favoritism, 156–157
Federal Judicial Center, 413
Feminine and femininity, 34–37
Field Training Officers (FTO), 49,
 58–59
Financial costs
 crime control, 343
 of death penalty, 219, 362
 of LWOP, 362
 in privatization, 240–242, 313
 of probation fees, 234–235,
  241–242
Finch, Atticus, 133
Flawed personal life, 158
FOAF. *See* Friend of a Friend
Fraud. *See specific types*
Free will, 76–83
Friend of a Friend (FOAF), 325
Friendship, 79, 289
Fringe benefits, 61–62
FTO. *See* Field Training Officers
Fundamental good, 14
Furman cases, 208–209

G

Gandhi, Mohandas, 28, 32–33, 41b
Gershman, Bennett, 163–164, 163b

"Get tough" measures, 323, 341–342,
 353
Gifts, 105–106
GlaxoSmithKline, 374
Golden Rule, 18
Gonzales, Alberto, 151–152
Good, 14–16, 20–22
Good will, 17
Government
 corporate misconduct, public
  opinion, and, 374–375
 crime and justice myths impacted
  by, 330–334
 crime information controlled by,
  331–332
 crime severity set by, 331–332
 criminal justice failing and, 330
 criminals defined by, 333–334,
  333b
 whistle blowing and spying on,
  333–334, 333b
Governors, 221b–222b
Graham, Sen. Lindsay, 441–442
Graham v. Florida, 360–361, 364
Gratuities, 105–106
Greatest good or happiness principle,
 14–16, 20–22, 361
Guantánamo Bay, 431, 438, 443–444
Guards, 405. *See also* Prison staff
Guilt, 88
Guru or godfather role, 136

H

Habitation, 352
Hamdan v. Rumsfeld, 431–432
Happiness, 14–15
A Hard Straight Look, 232
Harris, David Ray, 155
Hazing, 268–269
Health, psychological, 31–32
Healthcare and healthcare fraud,
 379–381, 380b, 391
Hedonistic
 calculus, 15, 193–194
 utilitarianism, 14
Heroic exceptionality, 116
Hinduism, 32–33
"Hired-gun role," 133–134

Home, 235
Honesty, 102–103, 179–180
Hope, 453–454, 458
Hot calls, 59
"Hot spot policing," 414
Human beings, 18–19, 28–30, 32,
 398–399
Hustling, 288
Hypothetical imperative, 11b, 17–18

I

Identity, 82, 235
Incapacitation, 173, 177, 190–191,
 207–209, 301–302, 361, 363
Incarceration. *See* Confinement or
 incarceration
Incompetence, 137
Indictments, 151, 154, 159, 162,
 164–165
Individual and individual behavior,
 48, 196, 383–384
Informed consent, 402
Injustice, 20–21, 31–32
Insider trading, 374
Institutional review boards, 415–416
Internal affairs unit, 282, 291
International relations, 273–274
Internet. *See specific topics*
Interrogation, 78, 434–436. *See
 also* Deceptive interrogation
 techniques; Police interrogation
Interview, 78
Intrinsic value, 18–19

J

Jails, 460. *See also* Prison and
 correctional facilities
Johnson, Robert, 354
"Judge shopping," 159
Judgment, 5
Jurisprudence literature, 135–136
Jurors, 216–217
Justice. *See also* Crime and justice
 myths; Ethics, crime, and
 justice; Juvenile justice; Military
 justice system; Peacemaking,
 justice, and ethics; Restorative
 justice

in community, 458–463
crime control balanced against, 89
in criminal justice future, 458–464
for democratic society, 89
duty and, 20–24
efficiency *versus*, 85
in ethics, 12
evolution of social, 27
in police values, 62
restorative justice compared to traditional, 252
theories of, 12
Juvenile
arbitration programs, 262–263, 366–368
corrections, 266, 352–356, 355t, 362–363, 368
superpredator, 338–339, 351
transfer, 351–352, 368
Juvenile justice
adult prisons and, 353–356, 355t, 368
background considered in, 364–365
confinement in, 352–354
criticism of, 350
death penalty and LWOP in, 359–368
deontological analysis of, 364–366
"get tough" policies in, 353
on internet, 352b, 360b
juvenile corrections in, 352–353
juvenile transfer in, 351–352, 368
legal system of, 350–351, 360–361, 368
myths concerning, 351, 353–354
peacemaking on, 358–359
public opinion on, 353
recidivism and, 353–355
rehabilitation in, 349–353, 362
summary of, 368–369
underlying philosophy of, 349
utilitarianism on, 357–358

K

Kant, Immanuel, 16–22, 171
Karma, 30–31
Kennedy, John F., 324

King, Jr., Martin Luther, 32–33, 41b
Kitchen, Ronald, 73
Knowledge, participant, 399–400

L

Latent content, 57–58
Law and legal system. *See also* Criminal justice
adult court in, 351–352, 368
brute force eliminated in, 75–76
on chain gangs, 309
in community, 458–463
confessions for prosecution in, 74–75
corporate misconduct in, 385–391
in crime and justice myths, 324–325, 337–338
criminal justice context and limits of, 6
in criminal justice future, 458–463
criminal justice system and rule of, 441
death penalty and application in, 204, 210–212, 214–217, 360–361, 368
on deceptive interrogation techniques, 78–83
drug courts in, 263
in educational restorative justice, 269–270
international, 263
on juvenile death penalty and LWOP, 360–361
of juvenile justice, 350–351, 360–361, 368
lawyers and conflicting ethics and rules of, 135–136
legal advocate in defense, 135–137
military tribunals or commissions challenged in, 431–433, 439
morality and, 6, 118–119, 336–337
in narcotics investigations, 120
police subculture on, 59–60, 62
prison corruption and intercession of, 292–296
on prison overcrowding, 177
prosecutorial failings and processes of, 159

prosecutors' governed by, 159
randomization under, 411
restorative justice in, 261–264
"three strikes," 182, 191, 342–343
on torture, 433–436, 439
unethical conduct and manipulation of, 120–121
unethical conduct but permissible by, 118–121
in war on crime, 120
whistle blowing, 385–386
Law enforcement. *See also* Police, policing, and police occupation
caring in, 36–37
in crime and justice myths, 324–325, 337–338
ethics training for, 95–96
masculine and feminine in, 36–37
police ethics and reform, control, and legitimacy of, 47–48
Lawyers. *See also* Attorney-client privilege; Legal advocates, lawyers as; Model Rules of Professional Conduct; Moral agents, lawyers as; Prosecution and prosecutor
child rape case study involving, 146b–147b
client relationship with, 134–144
in client-centered or friend role, 136–137
criminal defense and, 138, 141–142, 210–212, 212b
criminal or fraudulent behavior from, 138
decision making of, 137–138
ethics and rule conflicts for, 135–136
Finch as model for, 133
in guru or godfather role, 136
in "hired-gun role," 133–134
as legal advocates and moral agents, 133–148
Model Rules for, 137–144
on parole and probation privatization, 241–242
randomization and role of, 412–413

Learned-perspective values, 54–60, 55f
Lee, Harper, 133
Legal advocates, lawyers as, 133–148
in legal defense, 135–137
Model Rules, moral agents, and, 134–135
moral agents compared to, 133–136, 145
morality of, 134
prosecutors within, 144
Legislature, 178
Legitimacy, 64–69
Lex talionis, 189
Life without parole (LWOP)
death penalty and, 219–220, 359–363
deterrence of, 362
ethical arguments on, 361–363
financial costs of, 362
incapacitation through, 208–209, 361, 363
in juvenile justice, 359–368
public opinion on, 362
racial bias and, 363
rehabilitation missing from, 362–363
retribution through, 361
as severe punishment, 204–205
Loyalty, 61, 103–105, 125–126
LWOP. See Life without parole
Lying. See Deception

M

Malfeasance, 158b, 285
Manifest content, 57–58
Manipulation, 74–76, 120–121
Marola, Mario, 154
Martin, Trayvon, 150–151
Masculine and masculinity, 34–37
Masters, Jarvis, 209–210
Material accommodations, 289
Material practices, 291
Maximization, 81
Meaning and meaningfulness, 55–56
Media
collective responsibility impact of, 126–127

corporate misconduct and role of, 386–387
crime and justice myths influenced by, 325–330, 335
crime in local, 326–328
crime in worldview of, 127
on criminal justice, 328
on criminals, 126–127
on juvenile crime, 326, 338–339
late twentieth century growth of, 325–326
on police as crime fighters, 52–53
in police ethical dilemma training, 97
in prosecutors' ethical challenges, 149, 162
on race, 327–328
symbolic politics and, 387
on victims, 328–329
on white-collar crime, 375–376
Mediation, 261, 264
Medicare and Medicaid, 380
Meditation, 38–39, 39b
Mercy, 27–28
Middle management, 384
Middle-class values, 50
Militarism, 65–67
Military Commissions Act of 2006, 431–432
Military Commissions Act of 2009, 432
Military justice system
Guantánamo Bay in, 431, 438
military tribunals or commissions in, 431–433, 439
after 9/11, 430–431
terrorism and use of, 430–431, 440–443
unlawful combatant in, 432
Military tribunals or commissions
advantages of, 444b–445b
legal challenges to, 431–433, 439
Military Commissions Act of 2006 and 2009 in, 431–432
in military justice system, 431–433, 439
terrorism and, 429–430
Mill, John Stuart, 13–14

Miller v. Alabama, 360–362, 364
Mindfulness
awareness through, 38
of community connectedness, 454–455, 461
compassion through, 37–38
in criminal justice future, 454–455
through meditation, 38–39
of Mother Teresa, 37–38
need for, 454–455
as peacemaking theme, 37–39, 209
Minorities, 302–303
Miranda v. Arizona, 74–77
Miranda warnings, 78, 80
Mirroring, 79
Misconduct. See Corporate misconduct and crime; Discretionary misconduct; Police, policing, and police occupation; Prison corruption; Prosecutorial misconduct, ethical problems in
Misfeasance, 158b, 285
Mistakes, 210–212, 212b
Mistrust, 307
Model Rules of Professional Conduct from ABA, 134–135, 137–144
on attorney-client privilege, 139, 141
on ethical criminal defense, 141–142
ethics of care and rights in, 140
on evidence tampering, 143–144
incompetence or negligence and, 137
on lawyer and client relationship, 137–138
for lawyers, 137–144
on moral agents, 134–135, 141, 141b
on moral dialogues, 141, 141b
on perjury, 142–143
on zealous advocacy, 137, 140, 143–144
Moral
dialogues, 141, 141b
experiences, 63
reasoning, 34–35

Moral agents, lawyers as, 133–148
  clients and, 134–137
  legal advocates compared to,
    133–136, 145
  Model Rules and, 134–135, 141,
    141b
  moral dialogues of, 141, 141b
  principles for, 134b
  prosecutorial failings and, 159
Moral career, of police, 62–64, 63t
Morality and moral issues
  of actions, 13–15, 357
  awareness of, 7, 9b
  categorical imperative in, 17–18
  in criminal justice, 12
  death penalty within, 8
  duty and, 17
  fairness or equality in, 18
  law and, 6, 118–119, 336–337
  of legal advocates, 134
  openness to, 7
  order and, 117–118
  in police career, 62–64
  utilitarianism and actions', 13, 15,
    357
Mortgage fraud, 378–379
Mother Teresa, 37–38
Movies, 53, 227, 329
Murderers, 208–209, 220–221,
    364–365. See also Death penalty
Myths. See also Crime and justice myths
  behavior codes and values from,
    324, 334
  about crime, 336–338
  juvenile justice, 351, 353–354
  juvenile superpredator, 351
  nature of, 324–325
  outsiders impacted by, 324–325

N
Narcotics, 120
Nature and natural, 29, 35, 38–39
Negligence and neglect of duties,
    137, 153, 157–158, 158b
New Age movement, 27
Nifong, Michael B., 152–153, 158,
    162, 164
9/11, 427–428, 430–431

Noble cause, 50–51, 50f, 103
Nolle prosequi, 161
Nonfeasance, 158b, 285–286
Nonviolence, 32–33
Normative ethics, 12–13

O
Obama administration, 432–433,
    441–444
Occupational predisposition, 49. See
    also Police, policing, and police
    occupation
Offenders
  burglary, 300
  chain gangs and reaction of, 310
  drug, 301
  elderly, 311–312
  parole, probation, and concerns
    of, 240
  prison, ethics, and, 299–302
  restorative justice for victim and,
    255b, 257–259
  sex, 243
  society on prison, 299–300
  utilitarianism on juvenile,
    357–358
  violent crime, 300–301
Offense, exaggeration of, 81
Officers. See specific topics
Olson, Jeff, 333–334
Openness, 7
Opportunities, role of, 286–288
Order, 117–118, 280, 455–458
Organization, in police ethics, 56
Outsiders, 324–325
Overcrowding, 195–196, 353, 460

P
Pain, deprivation, or suffering,
    14–15, 304–305
"Pains of imprisonment," 280
"Paradox of retribution," 175–176
Parole, probation, and community
    corrections. See also Probation
    fees
  acceptable penal content or
    identifying labels in, 235

  armed officers in, 238b
  community service in, 228
  corruption in, 244–245
  deontological approach to,
    232–233
  deterrence and treatment in, 229
  effectiveness of, 231–235
  electronic monitoring in, 237
  ethics and dimensions of, 233
  fees' ethics, 233–235
  home visits, 235
  internet on, 245b
  mission of, 228–231
  movies and television on, 227
  for murderers, 208–209, 220–221
  offender concerns in, 240
  privatization of, 233, 240–243
  punishment and treatment balance
    in, 230–231
  punishment emphasis in, 228, 235
  restorative justice model in, 229,
    260
  sex offender, 243
  sexual harassment case study, 246b
  social debt in, 230–232
  statistics, 227, 231–232
  summary of, 245–246
  supervision in, 228–229,
    236–240, 243
  uniform in, 228–229
  volunteers used in, 244
  voting rights in, 231b
Passive role, 142–143
Patriarchy, 36
Peacemaking, justice, and ethics,
    27–44
Peacemaking and peacekeeping,
    171–172
  caring in, 34–37, 209
  case study, 42b
  in Christianity, 33
  compassion and mercy in, 27–28
  connectedness in, 28–33, 209
  in contemporary prisons, 33,
    209–210
  in criminal justice, 33
  in criminal justice future, 455–458
  death penalty and, 209–210

Peacemaking and peacekeeping
    (*Continued*)
  difficulty of, 40
  exercise, 41b–42b
  on internet, 39b, 43
  on juvenile justice, 358–359
  mindfulness in, 37–39, 209
  New Age movement in, 27
  order keeping compared to,
    456–457
  personal context for, 40, 41b
  for police, 457–458
  practice, 34b
  prison for, 33, 209–210
  in restorative justice, 251–252
  social debt in, 230
  summary of, 40–43
Perjury, 142–143
Personal
  gain, 156
  responsibility, 8, 9b, 254f,
    255–256
Personal context or relationships
  corporate misconduct and interest
    of, 373–374
  of death penalty mistakes, 212b
  discretion and, 99–100
  in ethics, crime, and justice, 4–7,
    4f
  for peacemaking, 40, 41b
  public opinion from
    overgeneralized, 334–335
Philosophy, 204, 349
Plagiarism, 398
Plato, 31–32
Plea bargaining, 160
Pleasure, 14–15
Police, policing, and police
    occupation. *See also* Unethical
    conduct or behavior; police
  case study, 67b–68b
  coercion in, 47
  community relations with, 67
  conservatism and conformity in,
    49–50
  crime and pressure on, 83
  as crime fighters, 51–53, 61
  criminal justice education for,
    53–54

in criminal justice future, 459–461
  culturalization, 54–60
  discretion in, 50–51, 62
  family crises and, 459–460
  hot calls in, 59
  jail overcrowding and, 460
  law and morality in, 118
  meaningfulness in, 55–56
  metamorphosis, 60
  militarism of, 65–67
  misconduct, 95, 64–65, 94–95, 113
  moral career of, 62–64, 63t
  morality and order in, 117–118
  movies on dirty, 53
  nature and purpose of, 114–115
  occupational predisposition for, 49
  occupational stages in, 56f
  peacemaking in, 457–458
  public trust in, 113–115
  randomization and "hot spot," 414
  restorative cautions in, 260
  restorative justice in, 259–261
  social service and, 460–461
  society on legitimacy of, 65
  subculture, 48, 58–60, 62
  use of force, 119
  war metaphor and, 65–67, 120
Police ethics and ethical practice,
    47–72. *See also* Police training,
    ethics and ethical dilemmas in;
    Unethical conduct or behavior;
    police
  academic literature on, 94–95
  conservatism and conformity in,
    49–50
  control, reform, and legitimacy in,
    64–69
  crime control and fighting in,
    50–53
  criminal justice and teaching,
    94–95
  discretion and decision making
    in, 94
  for law enforcement, 95–96
  law enforcement reform, control,
    and legitimacy in, 47–48
  militarization impacting, 66–67
  noble cause, efficiency, and
    utilitarianism in, 50–51

organization in shaping, 56
  overview of, 47
  police misconduct and, 64, 94–95
  police training in, 95
  social concern with, 114–115
  socialization model of, 54
  values, value systems, and, 48–62,
    56f
Police interrogation. *See also*
    Deceptive interrogation
    techniques
  as accusatory, 78
  behavior analysis reliability in,
    84–88
  coercion in, 74
  confessions in, 74–76, 89
  custodial, 78, 80
  deception in, 73–92
  efficiency *versus* justice in, 85
  ethics of deceptive, 83
  fairness, free will, and reliability
    in, 76–83
  on internet, 90b
  manipulation in, 75
  Miranda warnings in, 78, 80
  psychological, 74–76
  public trust and, 86
  Reid Technique in, 84–86
  slippery-slope argument applied
    to, 85–86
  summary of, 88–90
  techniques, 73–74, 76–83
  torture in, 73–75
Police socialization
  basic training and, 56–58
  choice, 54–56
  police ethics model of, 54
  police metamorphosis in, 60
  police subculture in, 58–60
  values-learned perspective
    through, 54–60
Police training, basic or academy
  ethical behavior impacted by, 57
  law and morality at, 118–119
  police ethics in and after, 95
  in police socialization, 56–58
  symbolic assailant in, 58
  values impacted by, 56–58
  war stories in, 57–58

Police training, ethics and ethical
dilemmas in, 93–112. *See also*
Discretion; Duty; Honesty;
Loyalty
andragogical approach to, 96–97
Canons of Police Ethics in, 93
case studies for, 96
decision making regarding
"small," 106–107
disagreement analysis in, 107
discretion in, 97–100
duty in, 100–101
ethical framework analysis for,
107–108
example of, 93–94
gratuities in, 105–106
grouping of, 107
honesty and, 102–103
on internet, 109b
loyalty in, 103–105
media in, 97
mid-career, 95
overview of, 94
public intoxication within,
108–109
right action in, 109
summary of, 109
for supervisors, 95
traditional pedagogy in, 96
variety of solutions for, 107
Police values
content of, 60–62
in culture and economy, 52
discretion in, 62
force in, 60–61
on fringe benefits, 61–62
justice in, 62
loyalty in, 61
in society, 52–54
time in, 61
Policy, departmental, 106, 290. *See
also specific topics*
Politics
corporate crime and, 387,
391–392
crime and justice myths influenced
by, 325, 330–334
crime control, research, and,
341–344

crime rate manipulation in, 332
criminal justice research, ethics,
and, 416–418
juvenile crime and, 338–339
media and symbolic, 387
prison control and environment
of, 292
in prosecutors' ethical challenges,
149, 162
public fear of crime and, 330–331
POP. *See* Problem oriented policing
Positivist theories, 230
Power, 149, 153, 385
Power accommodations, 289
PREA. *See* Prison Rape Elimination
Act
Predictions, 180–182
Predisposition perspective, 49–52,
54–55
Prejean, Sister Helen, 217–218, 365
Principle of least eligibility, 306
Prison and correctional facilities
composition, 301
conditions, 303–306
in criminal justice future, 461–463
criminal justice research
simulating, 404–406
juvenile, 266, 352–356, 355t,
362–363, 368
meditation in, 39
peacemaking in, 33, 209–210
punishment and overcrowding of,
195–196, 460
restorative justice in, 264–266
STDs in, 195–196
treatment in, 461–463
Prison and ethics. *See also* Offenders
case study, 316b–317b
chain gangs and, 309–310
disproportionate minority
representation in, 302–303
elderly offenders and, 311–312
incapacitation and, 301–302
internet on, 302b
introduction to, 299
offenders belonging in, 299–302
prison composition and, 301
prison conditions in, 303–306
privatization and, 313–315

safety, security, and, 310–311
statistics, 299–303
summary of, 315–316
treatment, rehabilitation, and
programming in, 306–309
victimization in, 310–311
women and, 312
Prison control
administrators in, 293
through material practices'
management, 291
policy in, 290
political environment in, 292
of prison corruption, 290–292
prison corruption and defects in,
288
through prison staff selection and
management, 291–294
proactive mechanisms for, 291
Prison corruption
case study involving, 294b–295b
contraband trafficking in,
282–283
defining, 281–282
discretionary misconduct in,
284–287, 284t
embezzlement as form of, 283
through friendship, reciprocity,
and default, 289
hustling in, 288
incentives for, 288–290
internal affairs unit for, 282
internet on, 279b, 293b
legal intercession in, 292–296
through material, power, and
status accommodations,
289–290
misused authority as, 283–284
opportunities' role in, 286–288
overview of, 277–279
"pains of imprisonment"
undermined by, 280
prison control defects and, 288
sexual misconduct as, 283–284
staff role in, 279–281, 287–288
theft in, 282
types and impact of, 280, 282–284
Prison Rape Elimination Act (PREA),
293

Prison staff
  corruption opportunities,
    280–281, 287–288
  juvenile sexual victimization by,
    355–356
  prison control through selecting
    and managing, 291–294
  in prison corruption, 279–281,
    287–288
  quality of, 279–280, 290
Privacy, 20, 408–410
Privatization
  client selection in, 242–243, 314
  contract oversight in, 241, 314
  of death penalty, 313
  efficiency and effectiveness in, 241,
    313, 315
  financial costs in, 240–242, 313
  of parole and probation, 233,
    240–243
  prison, ethics, and, 313–315
  profit motive in, 241–242, 314
  of punishment, 196
Probation. *See* Parole, probation, and
    community corrections
Probation fees
  "back-end net-widening" and, 234
  client payment ability of, 234, 242
  ethics of, 233–235
  financial costs of, 234–235,
    241–242
  program and service, 233
  for supervision, 233
Problem oriented policing (POP),
    64–65
Professional
  ethics, 11
  relationships, 99–100
Profit motive, 241–242, 314
Programming, 306–309
Promises, 82–83
Proportionality, 187–188, 190, 214
Prosecution and prosecutors
  confessions in legal system for,
    74–75
  of corporate crime, 387–391
  ethical misconduct, 144–145,
    149–150

evidence and evidence tampering
    for, 144–145, 153b, 160
  law governing, 159
  as legal advocates, 144
  prosecutors' ethical challenges and
    fired federal, 151–152
  Sarbanes-Oxley aiding, 390–391
Prosecutorial ethics, 164–165
Prosecutorial failings, unique, 159
  "judge shopping" and, 159
  law and, 159
  moral agents and, 159
  public as client and, 159
  zealousness and, 159
Prosecutorial misconduct, ethical
    problems in
  abuse of power as, 157
  bias and favoritism as, 156–157
  in criminal justice, 156–158, 156b,
    158b
  deceitfulness as, 157
  denial of due process in, 157
  DPAs and, 389–390
  flawed personal life and, 158
  Gershman on, 163–164, 163b
  internet on, 145b
  neglect of duties in, 157–158,
    158b
  overlapping, 158
  persistence of, 162–164
  personal gain pursuit as, 156
  winning and, 163
Prosecutors, ethical challenges of,
    149–170
  abuse of power in, 149, 153
  "Atlanta Child Murders" case and,
    154–155
  bias in, 152
  case study on, 166b–167b
  deceitfulness within, 153
  denial of due process in, 153
  discovery and, 160
  discretion in, 155, 161
  Donovan trial and, 154
  Duke Lacrosse case and, 152–153,
    158, 162, 164
  as elected officials, 149
  evidence in, 153b

federal prosecutors fired and,
    151–152
  indictments in, 151, 154, 159, 162,
    164–165
  internet on, 165b
  introduction to, 149
  neglect of duties within, 153
  nolle prosequi and, 161
  plea bargaining for, 160
  politics, public, and media in, 149,
    162
  prosecutorial ethics and *Boomerang*
    in, 164–165
  reasonable doubt and, 155–156
  summary of, 165–166
  "Thin Blue Line" case and,
    155–156
  "Trayvon Martin Homicide" case
    and, 150–151
  unreliable "snitches" and,
    161–162
Psychology and psychological
    context, 31–32, 74–77
Public and public opinion
  attorney-client privilege aned
    interest of, 140–141
  atypical information in, 335
  client and prosecutorial failings,
    159
  community outreach programs
    and, 335–336
  consciousness lacking in,
    335–336
  corporate misconduct,
    government, and, 374–375
  crime and justice myths influenced
    by, 325, 334–338
  criminal justice policies impacted
    by, 323–324, 335–337
  criminal justice research and
    policy of, 420
  on death penalty and LWOP, 362
  intoxication and police ethical
    dilemmas, 108–109
  on juvenile justice, 353
  personal experiences
    overgeneralized in, 334–335
  police and trust of, 113–115

Sexually transmitted diseases (STDs), 195–196
Slippery-slope argument, 85–86
"Snitches,", 161–162
Snowden, Edward, 333–334, 333b
Socialization. *See* Police socialization
Society and social context
  corporate crime prosecution and, 388
  crime control for, 340
  of death penalty, 203
  in ethics, crime, and justice, 4f, 5–7
  evolution of justice from, 27
  judgment in, 5
  justice in democratic, 89
  on law and morality, 337
  parole, probation, and debt of, 230–232
  patriarchal, 36
  police ethics and concern of, 114–115
  on police legitimacy, 65
  in police occupation, 52
  police values in, 52–54
  to policing, 460–461
  on prison offenders, 299–300
  punishment and individual balanced against, 196
  punishment practiced in, 195–196
  unethical behavior and situational, 121–126
  white-collar crime cost to, 375–376
Socioeconomic status, 182–183
Socrates, 13
Special populations, 196–197
Spying, 333–334, 333b
Staff. *See* Prison staff; *specific topics*
Stapel, Diederik, 397–398, 419–420
Statistics. See *specific topics*
Status accommodations, 289–290
STDs. *See* Sexually transmitted diseases
STOCK (Stop Trading on Congressional Knowledge) Act, 375
Strangers, 339
Stress, 407

Stride circles, 265–266
Student loan mismanagement, 381–382
Study. *See specific topics*
Subculture, police, 48, 58–60, 62
Subprime lending, 378
Suffering. *See* Pain, deprivation, or suffering
Suicide, 356
Superpredator. *See* Juvenile
Supervision and supervisors
  in community corrections, 228–229, 236–240, 243
  conditions of, 229
  intensive, 236–240
  offender concerns in, 240
  officer impact from, 238–239
  police training in ethical dilemmas for, 95
  probation fees, 233
  of sex offenders, 243
Supreme Court. *See* Law and legal system
Symbolic assailant, 58
Symbolic politics, 387
Sympathy, 79

T

Taoism, 35–36
Tearoom Trade, 403
Techniques of neutralization
  appeals to higher loyalties in, 125–126
  condemning the condemners in, 124–125
  denial of injury in, 123
  denial of responsibility, 121–123
  denial of victim within, 124
  in unethical behavior, 121–126
Television, 227, 329
Terrorism. *See also* Military justice system
  Abu Ghraib, torture, and, 436–439, 437b
  Constitution and, 430
  criminal justice system for handling, 439–443, 440b, 445b–446b, 446–447

  ethics and, 427–450
  Guantánamo Bay, torture, and, 438
  internet on, 429b, 431–432, 431b, 434b, 438b–439b, 442b
  military justice system and, 430–431, 440–443
  military tribunals, renditions, and, 429–430
  9/11, 427–428
  summary of, 447–448
  of Times Square bomber, 446–447
  torture memos and, 433–436
  unethical conduct and homegrown, 128b
  USA PATRIOT Act and, 428–429
  war strategy against, 429–430
"Testifying", 103
Theft, 398
"Thin Blue Line" case, 155–156
Thinking, unethical conduct and, 115–116
"Three strikes" laws, 182, 191, 342–343
Time. *See specific topics*
Times Square bomber, 446–447
To Kill a Mockingbird (Lee), 133
Torture
  Abu Ghraib, terrorism, and, 436–439, 437b
  confessions by, 73–75
  Guantánamo Bay, terrorism, and, 438
  harsh interrogation and, 434–436
  internet on memos of, 438b
  legal system on, 433–436, 439
  in police interrogation, 73–75
  terrorism and memos of, 433–436
  waterboarding, 433
Traditional pedagogy, 96
Traffic accidents and violations, 98, 104, 120–121
"Trayvon Martin Homicide" case, 150–151
Treatment
  correctional, 461–463
  in criminal punishment, 173, 306–309
  mistrust and, 307

police interrogation and trust of, 86

politics and crime fear of, 330–331

in prosecutors' ethical challenges, 149, 162

Punishment. *See also* Criminal sentencing and punishment; Death penalty; Life without parole

community corrections emphasis on, 228, 235

in criminal sentencing, 171

death penalty as, 196

defining, 187–188

deterrence as part of, 193–195

ethical dilemmas in, 195, 196–197

ethics and, 188, 195b

incapacitation in, 190–191

individual and social interest balanced in, 196

internet sources for, 197b

LWOP as severe, 204–205

parole and balancing treatment and, 230–231

prison overcrowding and, 195–196, 460

privatization of, 196

proportionality in, 187–188, 214

purposes of, 188–195

reflexive nature of, 188

rehabilitation in, 191–193

retribution in, 189–190

severity of, 192b, 194–195, 204–205, 364

social practice of, 195–196

of special populations, 196–197

summary of, 197–198

unintended consequences of, 195–196

R

Race, 182–183, 212–213, 302–303, 327–328, 363

Racketeer Influenced Corrupt Organization Act, 118

Randomization

consequences in, 412–413

in criminal justice research, 410–414, 411b–412b

fairness of, 410–411

Federal Justice Center on, 413

"hot spot policing" and, 414

under law, 411

lawyer's role and, 412–413

values balanced against, 412–413

Rape, 146b–147b, 293

Reasonable doubt, 155–156

Recidivism, 306–307, 353–355

Reciprocity, 289

Reconciliation, 254f, 255b, 256

Reform, 64–69

Rehabilitation

in crime control, 192

death penalty and LWOP missing, 362–363

habitation compared to, 352

impact of, 192–193

in juvenile justice, 349–353, 362

prison, ethics, and, 306–309

in punishment, 191–193

Reid Technique, 84–86

Reliability, 76–88

Religion, 217–219, 366–368

Renditions, 429–430

Reparation and reparative boards, 255–256, 255b, 258

Research. *See* Criminal justice research; *specific topics*

Responsibility, 8, 9b, 121–123, 126–130, 254f, 255–256

Restoration, 174–175, 177

Restorative cautions, 260

Restorative justice, 174–175, 178–179

conflict resolution and, 252

defining, 253–256, 254f

in education, 266–271

family group conferences and, 255b, 256–257

international relations and, 273–274

in legal system, 261–264

peacemaking in, 251–252

in policing, 259–261

in prison setting, 264–266

in probationary practices, 229, 260

program types, 255b, 256–259

real-world applications of, 259–274

reparation and reparative boards in, 255–256, 255b, 258

sentencing circles and, 255b, 257–258

sexual violations and, 272–273

summary of, 274

traditional justice compared to, 252

understanding, 252–253

victim-offender, 255b, 257–259

victims in, 265

in workplace, 271–272

Retribution, 175–176, 189–190, 361

Rights, ethics of, 140

Role playing, 79

Roper v. Simmons, 360–362, 364

Rule of law, 441

S

Safety and security, 310–311

Sarbanes-Oxley Act, 385, 390–391

Science and scientific issues. *See specific topics*

Self-conception or self-perception, 60, 116–118

Self-determination, right to, 406–407

Self-protection, 102

Self-respect, 404–406, 406b

Sentencing. *See* Criminal sentencing and punishment

Severity, 192b, 194–195, 204–205, 331–332, 341, 364

Sex, 182–183

Sex offenders, 243

Sexual harassment, violence, and violations

parole and probation case study involving, 246b

prison, ethics, and, 310

in prison corruption, 283–284

restorative justice and, 272–273

victimization and juvenile corrections, 355–356, 362–363

Williams, Wayne, 154–155
Willingness to participate, 402
Winning, 163
Workplace, 271–272
World and worldview
    connectedness to natural, 29

crime from media, 127
Gandhi on blunders of, 28
restorative justice and applications
    in real, 259–274
unethical conduct and simplistic,
    116–119, 121

Z

Zealous advocacy, 137, 140,
    143–144, 159
Zimmerman, George, 150–151

parole and balancing punishment and, 230–231
prison, ethics, and, 286
in probation, 229
recidivism and, 306
Trust. *See* Public and public opinion
"Truth in sentencing," 179–180
Turow, Scott, 220b

U

Unethical conduct or behavior, 113–114
Unethical conduct or behavior, police
through appeals to higher loyalties, 125–126
choice and equal protection exercise, 129b–130b
collective responsibility for, 126–130
condemning the condemners in, 124–125
in denial of injury, responsibility, or victim, 121–124
heroic exceptionality and, 116
on internet, 127b
law, narcotics investigations, and, 120
legal manipulation and, 120–121
legally permissible but, 118–121
path to, 115–118
self-perception and, 116–118
simplistic worldview impacting, 116–119, 121
socially situating, 121–126
techniques of neutralization in, 121–126
terrorism case study, 128b
thinking as start of, 115–116
use of force and, 119, 122–123
Universal ethics, 13
Universizability, 18
Unknown, 6–7
Unlawful combatant, 432
USA PATRIOT Act, 428–429, 429b
Use of force
brute, 75–76
control and, 122

in criminal justice, 11–12, 21
excessive, 21
police, 119
in police values, 60–61
unethical conduct and, 119, 122–123
Utilitarian
calculus, 15, 20–21
rationale, 175
Utilitarianism, 13–16, 171
actions' morality in, 13, 15, 357
attorney-client privilege in, 139–140
from Bentham and Mill, 13
case study involving, 23b–24b
on consequences, 13–14, 357
as consequentialist theory, 13, 19–20
in criminal justice system, 16
criminal punishment and equity *versus*, 175–177
death penalty in, 205
deceptive interrogation techniques justified by, 86
deontology combined with, 22
deontology compared to, 19–20
greatest good principle in, 14–16, 20–21, 361
happiness in, 14–15
hedonistic, 14
injustice in, 20–22
on juvenile justice and victims, 357–358
Kant on, 16–17
in police ethical dilemma training, 108
in police ethics, 50–51
recidivism measured in, 307

V

Values and value systems. *See also* Police values
American, 51–52
basic training impacting, 56–58
choice in, 54–56
conservative, 49–50
defined, 48

educational restorative justice, 267–269
learned-perspective, 54–60, 55f
middle-class, 50
myths for, 324, 334
occupational predisposition in, 49
in police ethics, 48–62, 56f
of police subculture, 58
predisposition perspective of, 49–52, 54–55
randomization balanced against, 412–413
terminal and instrumental, 48
van den Haag, Ernest, 204, 212
Victim-offender restorative justice, 255b, 257–259
Victims and victimization
of crimes, 5
criminal justice and rights of, 174
denial of, 124
juvenile corrections and sexual, 355–356, 362–363
media on, 328–329
prison, ethics, and, 310–311
in restorative justice, 265
utilitarianism on juvenile justice and, 357–358
Voluntariness, 76–77
Volunteers, in parole and probation, 244
Voting rights, 231b

W

War
on crime, 120
on drugs and drug control policy, 183, 336, 342
policing and metaphor of, 65–67, 120
stories, 57–58
terrorism and strategy of, 429–430
War stories, 58–59
Waterboarding, 433
Whistle blowing and whistleblowers, 103–105, 333–334, 333b, 385–386
White-collar crime, 374–376
Wholesight, 8–9, 9b